WASSERSTROM

Messianic Mystics

MOSHE IDEL

Messianic Mystics

Yale University Press New Haven & London

Published with assistance from The Lucius N. Littauer Foundation.

Designed by James J. Johnson and set in Adobe Garamond type by Keystone Typesetting, Inc., Orwigsburg, Pennsylvania.
Printed in the United States of America by Vail-Ballou Press, Binghamton, New York.

Library of Congress Cataloging-in-Publication Data

Idel, Moshe, 1947–
Messianic mystics / Moshe Idel.
p. cm.
Includes bibliographical references and index.
ISBN 0-300-06840-9 (hardcover : alk. paper)

1. Messiah—Judaism—History of doctrines. 2. Cabala—History.
I. Title.
BM615.I34 1998
296.3′36—dc21 98-13905

A catalogue record for this book is available from the British Library.

The paper in this book meets the guidelines for permanence and durability of the Committee on Production Guidelines for Book Longevity of the Council on Library Resources.

10 9 8 7 6 5 4 3 2 1

Contents

Preface

The present book has its origins in a series of articles dealing with the theosophical-theurgical and magical treatments of redemptive acts in Kabbalah, as well as in a still unpublished chapter of my Ph.D. dissertation (1976) regarding the messianism of Abraham Abulafia. In a public lecture in 1980 I proposed three major models for redemptive activities: the mystical, basically an ecstatic model; the theosophical-theurgical, as represented by the late-thirteenth-century Castilian Kabbalah; and, since the fifteenth century, the magical model.[1] Since that lecture, several studies dealing with a variety of messianic texts and concepts have been printed, for example, those found in *Sefer ha-Meshiv* or the magical traditions attributed to Shlomo Molkho.[2] In 1989, an invitation by Tirzah Yuval to deliver a series of popular lectures over Israeli Army Radio allowed me to put together some of the trends that emerged from those previous studies and to integrate a few new developments in scholarship concerning Kabbalistic messianism. The booklet that emerged from these lectures could not, however, allow a more complex and scholarly presentation of many of the issues treated therein.[3] An invitation to deliver the Nemer Lectures at the University of Southern California in the fall of 1991 afforded a further opportunity to expand on some of the ideas included in the broadcasts.

The present book offers an incomparably more elaborate articulation of some of the material that was discussed in 1989 and 1991. Moreover, the structure of this English-language edition is substantially different from the original Hebrew, some chapters having been merged into single, greater units and other new ones having been added. In the present format, it was possible to take better account of a wide range of recent studies. Especially important are the innovative treatments of the Zoharic, Lurianic, and Sabbatean messianisms in several studies by Yehuda Liebes, whose original approach to some of the main forms of Jewish mysticism and messianism constitutes a major departure from the common wisdom,[4] as well as the contributions to the study of apocalypticism and messianism by Bernard McGinn, Ronit Meroz, Havivah Pedaya, David Ruderman, Shalom Rosenberg, and Stephen Sharot. From my own point of view, the years between 1989 and the completion of the present version have contributed to what I believe is a better understanding of the significance of those elements in Kabbalah which strive for a much more stable vision of the universe and its processes. This was the result of two other projects that I was involved in: a study of the various views of nature in Kabbalah, funded by the Yeshayah Horowitz Foundation, and the publication of the writings of Abraham Abulafia, with the help of the Fund of Higher Education. On the other hand, the importance of the talismanic model and of the contribution of some aspects of astrology for understanding some forms of messianism became, for me, more conspicuous, and I have integrated it in a more expanded version in the following discussions.

Even in the present format, the expositions of messianism are still limited in scope, as I have decided to focus on the messianic dimension of Jewish mysticism and not on messianism in Judaism. This study is therefore intended to be neither a comprehensive nor an exhaustive survey of any of the phases of Jewish messianism that are dealt with here. Unlike the monographs dedicated to Jewish messianism, such as Julius Greenstone's *The Messiah Idea* ore Joseph Sarachek's *Doctrine of the Messiah* or A. Z. Aescoly's monumental collection of messianic documents, this book concentrates on a very small segment of the broader eschatological phenomena related to messianism. Efforts have been made, however, to point out the necessity to more fully integrate the messianic elements that are found in older traditions, as understood by modern biblical scholarship in the descriptions of the medieval messianisms, and to describe some phenomena against larger historical and cultural developments outside Jewish culture. As in my other studies, I have attempted here to adduce significantly new material from manuscripts in order to buttress my positions. Still, some major phenomena that could reasonably be seen as belonging to the present study, such as the messianic views of the Maharal of Prague,[5] the Frankist movement,[6] mid-nineteenth-century messianism in the circle of the students of the Gaon of Vilna,[7] or modern Lubavitch messianism, have been treated here only casually, because no new texts or insights concerning this literature could be offered. Unless a minimum of fresh contribution could be adduced, I preferred not to address issues that would consist in an exposition of the studies of other scholars. I have attempted to reduce to a bare minimum summaries of available scholarly literature on the subjects analyzed here in order to concentrate more on neglected texts, especially on those points that, in my opinion, have been marginalized or, I would like to believe, are relatively novel in scholarship.

Naturally, many of the discussions below are part of an oftentimes critical dialogue with the magisterial studies of the most important scholar of Jewish messianism, the late Gershom Scholem. His numerous contributions to this field have been crucial to the modern understanding of a wide range of messianic phenomena, as have various elaborations of his views that flowered in his school. No serious treatment can evade renewed reflection on them. The superb treatments of so many messianic themes in Scholem's extensive oeuvre, as well as their epochal influence on modern scholarship, nevertheless invited closer readings of the Kabbalistic sources that underlay Scholem's formulations, as well as reflections on the interpretive schemes he employed. More than any other scholar's contribution, Scholem's special interest in messianism and his vast knowledge, coupled with penetrating formulations, have illuminated the field with a strong light that often transfigured the earlier scholarly contours. Light has been brought to many of the subjects under Scholem's investigation, and this light has been spread in a long series of faithful repetitions, most of them popularizations, found in the articles on messianism by J. Dan and R. J. Zwi Werblowsky, which enhanced the glamour of the master's views. I shall refer to these extensions of Scholem's views in the notes.

The present book can be seen to supplement some of the discussions found in my earlier books. In *Kabbalah: New Perspectives* I treated only tangentially the phenomenology of messianism, though the historical aspects of this topic were hinted at in the last chapter. In my printed studies on Abraham Abulafia, his view of messianism did not receive the full treatment it deserved, and this is also the case regarding my treatment of Hasidism. Though I have resorted here to a methodology more fully expressed in *Hasidism: Between Ecstasy and Magic,* in that book the theory of models was not applied to messianism. To a great extent, the present study attempts to continue the approach to Jewish mysticism articulated methodologically in the earlier book.

The Hebrew edition of the present book, which provided approximately a quarter of the material for this English-language edition, has been translated into English by Iris Felix, for which I am very grateful. I have used her translation as a starting point for further revisions, elaborations, and changes. A significant part of the work on the longer version was done while I served as visiting professor in the Department of Religion at Princeton University, where a warm reception and a calm atmosphere contributed much to the completion of the manuscript. Part of the time necessary for writing and revising the first draft was spent at the Shalom Hartman Institute of Advanced Studies in Judaism in

Jerusalem, where I am a member. The easy resort to the rich resources of the Institute of Hebrew Manuscript and of the library of the late Gershom Scholem, both at the National and University Library in Jerusalem, facilitated the consultation of much of the material presented here. Many thanks are due to the staff of those institutions for their indefatigable assistance over the years.

David Ruderman has followed the emergence of the English version, offering important suggestions as to both form and content. Discussions with Moshe Greenberg, David Hartman, Moshe Lazar, Byron Sherwin, and Israel Ta-Shma helped sharpen some points in my treatment of a number of issues. Many of the topics addressed in the following pages have been discussed over the years, in one way or another, with my friend Yehuda Liebes of the Hebrew University, whose original views regarding Jewish messianism have contributed to a fresh understanding of this subject in many historical periods and Kabbalistic schools.

Le vrai realisme en histoire, c'est de savoir que la realité humaine est multiple.

—MARC BLOCH

The creations of the primitive mind are elusive. Its concepts seem ill defined, or rather, they defy limitations. Every relationship becomes a sharing of essentials. The part partakes of the whole, the name of the person, the shadow and effigy of the original. This "mystic participation" reduces the significance of distinctions while increasing that of every resemblance. It offends all our habits of thought. Consequently, the instrument of our thought, our language, is not well suited to describe primitive conceptions.

We want to isolate a single notion. But, whenever we make the attempt, we find ourselves holding one mesh of a widely flung net; and we seem condemned either to trace its ramifications into the remotest corners of ancient life or to cut the skein and pretend that the concept thus forcibly isolated corresponds with primitive thought.

HENRI FRANKFORT

La depersonalisation du Messie qui n'est resté personnel que dans la croyances populaires est une phenomene essentiel a l'histoire philosophique du judaisme.

VLADIMIR JANKELEVITCH

definitions

Introduction

The Sources of Messianic Consciousness

MESSIANISM may be approached from various vantage points. The sociological approach emphasizes the expressions of messianism that appear in the various strata of the population, particularly the masses,[1] while the psychological approach is ideal for analyzing the messianic consciousness of the masses and the extraordinary personality of a Messiah. Messianism may also be studied as part of a complex of religious concepts, with the aim of integrating them into a certain theology or placing them within the framework of the history of ideas. Yet it is also possible to investigate the relationship between messianic awareness and an individual's private mystical experience. An analysis of this nexus belongs more to the field of mysticism than to those of theology, history, psychology, or sociology.

It is difficult to define precisely the two concepts *messianism* and *mysticism*. Both terms refer to a wide variety of personal experiences, to diverse systems of belief and modes of activity. In my view, mystical experiences stem from an intimate connection, sometimes described as a direct contact with God,[2] strong though often indefinable, which is designated in some extreme cases as "mystical union" or *unio mystica*. This contact can then inspire the mystic to the practical implementation of these concepts on the communal or historical scene. On the other hand, I will designate by the term *messianism* those ideas, concepts, and figures which are related to present or future states of redemption. It is not my intention to suggest more elaborate definitions of either messianism and mysticism, but rather to concentrate on a description of the deep bonds that exist between certain forms of messianism and messianic personalities and certain kinds of mystical experiences.[3]

This assumption is not meant to restrict the importance of messianism to a certain type of mysticism; nor does it imply that mysticism is necessarily and inherently a messianic phenomenon. My main concern here is to focus on a number of related cases where the mystical experience is at the very heart of a messianic self-awareness.[4] I shall deal only with Messiahs and messianic figures who were also mystics, or with mystics who considered themselves to be Messiahs, or mystics who articulated clear opinions about the nature of the Messiah as involving mystical experiences of whatever sort. The medieval and more modern Jewish mystical literatures have something new to contribute to the genre of apocalyptic literature as expressed in earlier Jewish texts. The ancient apocalyptic literature emphasized revelation concerning eschatological events (and sometimes eschatological figures) granted to nonmessianic figures. These revelations were attributed to biblical personages as spurious authors of apocalyptic treatises, while the identity and personality of the real authors escape scrutiny. In principle, these anonymous authors might have cultivated messianic aspirations and expectations. Their anonymity, however, prevents any solid scholarly speculation. In the medieval and later mystical literature, the messianic messages are revealed to messianic figures. The recipient of the message is deeply and personally concerned with the content of this message, and eventually he and his role are even its subject.

On what grounds can we assume there indeed exists a connection between mysticism and messianism? The more pervasive view, at least insofar as Jewish mysticism is concerned, is that the two attitudes are exclusive. Werblowsky, in a symptomatic statement, has superbly expressed the direction inspired by Scholem:

> Mysticism is not necessarily messianic. On the contrary, it can be argued that mysticism, because of its contemplative immersion in the absolute, the eternal and the unchanging, the "everlasting now," operates in a climate very different from that of messianism. It is sufficient, in that connection, to study of lack of messianic tension in Maimonides' theory of devequt, in Bahya's doctrine of abandonment to and love of God, or in the teachings of the earlier kabbalists. Messianism presupposes a certain relationship to the time process, that is, to history as a goal-directed sequence of changes ending in a social, political, moral, or even cosmic, fulfillment.[5]

Given this way of formulating the two stands, is it possible to demonstrate an integral and meaningful connection between various private, inner phenomena, even when experienced by quite different Messiahs? In my opinion, such a position is problematic. By and large, the description of the mystical immersion in the unchangeable may be appropriate for a few types of mystical phenomena but does not represent mysticism as a whole. To take just an evident example from Christianity, mystics such as Meister Eckhart would perhaps suit some of Werblowsky's formulations, but most of the others would assume that the object of their contemplation is not necessarily the unchangeable but rather the Christ, who suffers and reveals himself. In fact, what I shall call *via passionis*—the route of Teresa de Avila or Juan de la Cruz—does not fit Werblowsky's description of mysticism. Even more incongruous would be the description of the aim of the mystical quest in the case of the early Kabbalists, with their emphasis on the *deus revelatus* and *determinatus,* the dynamic system of the ten *sefirot* as the ultimate goal of contemplation and the realm for mystical and theurgical actions. Likewise, Abraham Abulafia's extreme mysticism is strongly related to the last and lowest of the ten separate intellects, the Agent Intellect. In other words, Werblowsky's phenomenology of mysticism as dealing with the absolute is, ironically enough for someone who is both a student and a practitioner of Eastern mysticism, strongly biased by a certain Western, rather limited vision of mysticism.

Historically speaking, however, early Kabbalah (if we include in this term all the thirteenth-century phenomena described as Kabbalistic, as Scholem does) displays some examples of union with the ultimate divine which were systematically ignored by Scholem and his school. A correlate of some of the above remarks on the phenomenology of mysticism is that if the mystical goal is defined as uniting not only with the absolute and unchangeable but also with the revealed and changeable, the mystic, as part of an *imitatio dei,* may be incited to act in the temporal and changing world. It appears to me that the essence of some forms of messianic self-awareness, and even of messianic activities, have their origin in inner experiences which are close to or even identical with what is generally called a mystical experience. In other words, I assume that the emergence of a messianic consciousness can often be tied to special, inner spiritual occurrences, which can provide a person with an awareness of his own special importance that will sometimes express itself in a overtly messianic mission. This assumption, which seems quite simple at first glance, has yet to receive detailed consideration within the context of the study of Jewish messianism.

Most modern scholarship of Jewish messianism has preferred to concern itself more with the public, communal, or historical—in short, outward—manifestations of the Jewish messianic phenomenon than with its inner sources. This approach assumed that the overt facets of Jewish messianism indeed revealed its true character.[6] In contrast to the emphasis upon inner experiences typical of the study of Christian mysticism, whose scholars were apt to ascribe special meaning to those private sensations that are considered to be the precursors of redemption, some of the contemporary scholars of Jewish messianism have depicted their subject essentially as a public affair.[7]

Another view has been proposed by Yehuda Liebes and myself. Through examining different forms of thirteenth-century Kabbalah, the Zoharic corpus, and the ecstatic Kabbalah, we have both come to the conclusion that intense mystical life does not preclude redemptive or even messianic efforts.[8] By emphasizing the spiritual aspects of some phenomena, it is not my intention to deny the messianic nature of certain public events. The question that concerns me, however, is what type of self-awareness, what spiritual experiences, might have induced someone to break away from the norm, to deviate from accepted social modes, in the expectation of a dramatic shift in history. It is precisely the emphasis on the active and public nature of Jewish messianism that demands a more profound explanation than is necessary in cases where messianic self-awareness does not translate itself into overt, dramatic forms. The greater the outward efforts to convince others of the messianic mission of a certain person and to move them to appropriate activity, the greater our need to understand the sources of the spiritual powers necessary to spur this type of effort.

A scholarly attempt to point to the mystical experiences that contribute to or even form a messianic awareness is laden with difficulties that at times may be impossible to overcome. The subject under examination is the most recondite aspect of human consciousness. The inner turmoil from which a messianic awareness springs is not usually something a person shares with others or commits to paper. The processes of raising or sublimating the awareness of one's being an extraordinary personality, as well as the call of duty to alter the norm, are often wrapped in ambiguity. So nebulous are these topics that a precise study of the religious consciousness is all but impossible. However, the obscurity and the intimacy of such experiences, and their opaqueness to more analytic approaches, should not deter scholars if the understanding of the complex messianic experiences, rather than the external events, concerns them. Scholarship in humanities in general, and in the realm of mysticism in particular, should not be seen as a matter of arguments in a court. It is not a judicial truth that is at stake here but an effort to penetrate zones of human consciousness that have been neglected. No regular forensic procedures are available. The attempts to unravel the processes taking place there involve a great amount of speculation in order to extrapolate from the scant literary evidence what happened in the consciousness of an aspirant to messianic status.

In most cases, the emergence of a messianic self-awareness is presented as a private theophany. The mere fact of a divine revelation becomes the basis for the legitimacy of a messianic claim or messianic activity. Yet the spiritual anguish that preceded the final crystallization of the revelatory experience is only seldom disclosed. What materials, then, are pertinent to a discussion of the mystical nature of the experiences that may have contributed to the creation of a messianic awareness? Generally speaking, the material we possess is disjointed and fragmentary, more often than not nebulous and unclear. These materials can be found in the autobiographical texts of the Messiahs themselves, in the accounts of their believers, or the testimonials of their contemporaries. Sometimes there is cause to carefully analyze texts written in the third person, given over by the Messiah himself as a tool for learning about the experiential level that is quintessentially messianic. Obviously, this type of analysis is complex and delicate. The recurrence of messianic concepts in a text does not necessarily imply a special messianic awareness on the part of the author. Since these concepts are central to the Jewish tradition, there is need of additional evidence before we can credit traditional messianic formulations as a true insight into the writer's psychological baggage.

Even the use of biographical and autobiographical materials for the purpose of reconstructing the nature of messianic awareness is not at all simple. The extraordinary events that are usually linked to the birth and to the life story of the Messiah can sometimes be a repetition of well-known motifs of popular folklore pertaining originally to other heroes.[9] The use of a certain cliché, however, does not automatically mean a lack of messianic awareness. One could borrow the existing and normative nomenclature if one had actually possessed some sort of messianic awareness. One can imagine that in some cultures the proper way to declare one's messianic status would be to invoke clichés—or, to use a less pejorative term, set expressions and epithets—that are traditionally associated with the Messiah. In the staking of such a claim, originality may not be an asset. For it is not a pedestrian claim to be a Messiah, nor is it usual for others to attribute extraordinary occurrences to someone who seems quite ordinary. This all goes to show that even when we do possess materials that can shed light on the relationship of internal and external events, they can be fragmentary, untrustworthy, or outright impenetrable.

In light of these difficulties the problem remains: is it really worthwhile to expend the tremendous effort needed to decipher this kind of material? Perhaps it is more reasonable to do as most scholars of Jewish messianism have done: stick to a overt, historical description of messianism that may be simpler, more founded, and, in the final analysis, even more meaningful. After all, it is quite plausible to doubt the legitimacy of attaching great importance to minor textual inferences that touch upon the innermost thoughts and feelings of a specific person, when the ramifications of those inner realities exist as external and objective facts that can be more easily reckoned with. It seems to me that this question must be dealt with before we can invest our energies in complex arguments.

One possible solution to this problem derives from the meaning of messianic activity per se. For even in the discussion of historical events, historians cannot always overcome the danger of anachronistic analysis. The value system or belief system of the scholar is ever-present in the analysis and evaluation of distant and often hazy events. Objective standards only rarely, if ever, govern the choice of the "relevant" aspects of a such a subject. It is very likely that ideological motivations, be they conscious or subconscious, guide the selection of the facts used in the research of the histories of various Messiahs. Arranging and interpreting the facts according to preconceived notions can result in the misrepresentation of the original intentions of the messianic protagonists. An understanding of the original intention of the factors involved in a certain historical event can contribute greatly towards illuminate the meaning of the events as they occurred at the time, not as they may appear today to a modern scholar. The two perceptions are by no means similar. Even in situations where the original intention and the overt activity are not consistent with each other, it well may be that uncovering the original intention is bound to shed light on the desired goal of the activity. Then the activity could be explained on its own terms, in a way that modern scholars could not be privy to if left to their own devices.

Having drawn attention to the existence of the possibility of mystical experience as a source of messianic awareness, we can now ask what other sources may contribute to the appearance of that awareness. Historical crisis is one. The psychological pressure people are exposed to in times of mass murder, pogroms, expulsions, or even prolonged religious oppression is a recurring reason given for the appearances of Messiahs and for other manifestations of messianism. I will call this model the traumatic-historic interpretation, and it is very close to the deprivation explanations of apocalypticism. This is the explanation that has been most widely accepted in the academic establishment of Jewish studies, by and large in order to explain the instances of acute messianism that surged throughout the Jewish world after the expulsion from Spain. According to some of these scholars, the expulsion was perceived as a crisis of such tremendous force that it alone would serve as the basis for the messianic outbursts of the following generations.

The main problem with this interpretive model is that the mystics among these Messiahs downplayed or even ignored completely any historical crisis when presenting their messianic claims. If there were a connection between the crisis and the messianic future a Messiah purports to usher in, there is no reason he should hesitate to affirm it. Hence when such a connection is not explicitly expressed, there is great need for caution before we can come to this conclusion. For it is very possible that we are projecting a scholarly hypothesis or an expectation based on modern circumstances and perceptions onto the consciousness of a person who, despite his own historical context of objective crisis, was not inspired to an eschatological awareness by it at all. The notion that what modern scholars choose to describe as a crisis was felt or viewed as such by people living in that time is a preconceived notion that needs corroboration from contemporary sources. Such a position is even more difficult to maintain when the Messiah did not himself personally experience the trauma, but scholars are assuming that the fraught atmosphere breathed by others was the inspiration for his messianic self-awareness.

Now it could very well be that a background of crisis can encourage the transition of an inner process of messianic awareness to an outright and public display of messianism. It would then follow that at all times there exist "Messiahs unto themselves," and that only under special conditions does messianic self-awareness come to the surface and translate itself into public acts of overt messianism. As I will show, we can detect in different historical periods examples of figures that indeed possessed a strong messianic awareness but, because of the historical circumstances, their overt attempts to create a messianic movement were abortive.

Yet even when the traumatic-historic interpretation is applicable, there remains the issue of private mystical experience that creates, encourages, and often accompanies the messianic awareness and activities of a certain individual. Even then there are revelations whose essence, details, and language all play a decisive role in understanding the messianic phenomenon. If the traumatic-historic model does not always help us to understand the private experiences of the Messiah in question, sometimes an analysis of these inner experiences would. An attempt to investigate this aspect of messianism can prove helpful even in a case where the traumatic-historic construct is appropriate.

Let me, however, adduce two other explanatory models that compete with the traumatic-historical one. There is a recent tendency among scholars of mystical apocalypse to minimize the use of the traumatic-historic model. In a trend that has yet to find its way into the scholarship of Jewish messianism, these scholars assert that the apocalyptic phenomenon is always more than just a reaction to basic changes in the existing order.[10] Or, as Bernard McGinn has articulated it, in cases of apocalyptic behavior the feeling of an immediate crisis can be considered more an opportunity or framework than a motivational force. Moreover, he indicates that it is better to define the apocalyptic man as one who is actively seeking a crisis than as one who simply reacts to a crisis when it occurs.[11]

Likewise, the findings of Robert E. Lerner, who suggests the significance of a "deep structure" that informs many of the apocalyptic prophecies in the Middle Ages, attribute to preexisting small prophecies an important role in apocalyptic literature, even when an obvious crisis is precipitating their circulation.[12] In general, from the reading of eschatological literature the feeling is that the great persistence of preexisting material is evident in many cases when the claim is that the author is addressing a present or imminent crisis. The recurrence of the older material in Christian contexts, like the Joachimian traditions or the prophecy of Tripoli, should invite scholars of Jewish eschatology to be more sensitive to the relative continuity of the apocalyptic material, and to attenuate the emphasis laid upon their innovations based upon too strong an historicistic attitude to messianism.

There is another historical model of explanation that may more successfully illuminate the essence of the awakening of a messianic awareness. Instead of positing catastrophe and the despair that follows as the main causes of eschatological ideas and events, it is possible to stress, at least in certain cases, the kindling of hope as a prelude to a messianic awareness. Thus the appearance of Jewish apocalyptic behavior in the seventh and eighth centuries might be explained as the result of great waves of hope that spread in the wake the Arab victories over the Christians. As we shall later see, certain messianic phenomena which occurred during the last part of the thirteenth century can also be neatly explained as heightened messianic expectation due to the Mongol conquests throughout Eastern Europe and the Middle East. This may explain the messianism of Abraham Abulafia. Similarly, it would seem that the fall of the Christians in the East and the conquest of Constantinople by the Turks were more likely to inspire messianic expectations than was the expulsion from Spain. In any event, it is clear that important manifestations of messianic phenomena happened among the Jews of Spain prior to the actual expulsion. Finally, it seems that the terrible trauma of the Holocaust did not stimulate messianic phenomena at all, while in fact this type of activity has emerged after the establishment of the state of Israel, often termed "the beginning of our redemption," and especially after the Israeli victory in the Six Day War of June 1967. These examples underline the importance of hope, unconnected to crisis, as a contributing factor to the emergence of a messianic self-awareness.

Another factor that can encourage the cultivation of messianic phenomena is what can be called the existential view. The concept of messianism accords special meaning to history in general and to the life of the Messiah in particular. As Frank Kermode would say, the Messiah, as all people do, attempts to understand, "and to make sense of their span they need fictive concords, with origins and ends, such as give meaning to lives and to poems."[13] This interpretive model grants meaning to messianism through a certain perception of reality which is not necessarily tied to historical events or crises. It is essentially part of the ongoing human search for meaning, for purpose, for security, whose validity as explanations transcends the tides of history. As such, it may often be detached from meaningful contact with the external facts or may freely manipulate them.

The existential explanation may clarify some of the attempts made by exceptional personalities to locate themselves within wider, more meaningful contexts than daily life provides. It can offer an insight into the bold will of human beings to know and understand the meaning of their lives and to make sense of the chaos and disorder of events. Seen in this light, most of the course of Jewish history is a series of crises, starting with the destruction of the two temples and continuing through later crises in the Diaspora, with each Messiah predicting the final date of the exile's end. From this perspective the Messiah, as apocalyptic thinker, resembles certain types of historians, or historiosophers, who construct intricate systems in order to explain the forces that move history, as part of a deep yearning for understanding. Messiahs are similarly preoccupied with a search for the mystical dimension of history. They seek the clue to what Frank Manuel has described as euchronia, the good times.

If this understanding or explanation endows with special meaning the moment of history in which the Messiah lives, then it follows that extraordinary spiritual experiences which occur at that time find their meaning as well. These experiences, which Manuel calls eupsychia, the good spiritual event, may fall within the scheme that explains the euchronia. Inner extraordinary experiences can be understood as part of the uniqueness of time, and a mystic can interpret his special type of experiences as part of a feeling that his life is a time of great destiny. Unlike the views of such scholars as Scholem and Jacob Taubes that would relegate the appearance of the spiritual messianisms to the crises of the external redemption, I would say that many examples of inner messianism, which consists of eupsychical experiences, are not a reaction to the despair concerning the euchronia but, on the contrary, triggered the construction of euchronical pictures.

Accordingly, the search for the meaning and purpose of existence and the translation of eschatological terms for the existential purpose bear a certain relation to the appearance of the paranormal experiences themselves. The emphasis on the mystical nature of messianic phenomena brings Jewish messianism closer to Christian messianism. But only in rare cases is it possible to convincingly identify Christian influence on Jewish messianism. In most instances, the Jewish conceptions of spiritual messianism derive from either a mystical understanding of messianism or a messianic understanding of mysticism. This form of understanding is not exclusively bound up with the Christian spiritual conception but, as we shall see, is more often related to the absorption of Greek philosophical ideas in their medieval versions. I contend that these new conceptual systems, whose origins are to be found outside of Judaism, contributed decisively to the spiritual interpretation of Jewish messianism and the appearance of a new model of messianism. This proposal should be seen from the perspective of the more dominant view, which maintains, according to one of its more exaggerated formulations, that "for a thousand years, during the whole of the Middle Ages, messianic thought and creative theological thought existed as separate entities without any integral or close points of contact between them."[14]

The two main forms of Greek philosophy relevant to our discussion are the Aristotelian and the Neoplatonic. Both systems of thought contributed new psychological concepts to Jewish philosophy and sometimes to Jewish mysticism, and enabled more complex description of spiritual processes. Concomitantly there arose the ideal of intellectual and mystical activity as the apex of human perfection.[15]

Alongside the Halakhic system, which promised religious perfection, now stood inner processes, such as perfect intellection or mystical union, promising the eternity of the soul. Certain Jewish texts since the Middle Ages have equated the attainment of intellectual or mystical perfection with the achievement of individual redemption or a messianic state. The collision of certain forms of Greek thought and Jewish eschatological concepts—and to a certain extent Christian and Moslem ones—such as exile, redemption, Eden, other world, and Messiah, gave rise to new interpretations of these eschatological terms as inner processes that do not necessarily require overt expression. As for the contribution of Greek philosophy to Jewish messianic ideas, we can posit a radical shift in the scene of the messianic drama. As presented in the apocalyptic literature and popular doctrine of "the end of days," it will not be an external war that will usher in the messianic age but rather an internal war: the victory of mind over imagination or of soul over body is now a prerequisite for an individual's redemption, forming the basis for a messianic self-awareness. The eschatological combat, which takes place in the ancient and early medieval Jewish apocalyptic literature on the historical and sometimes cosmic planes, is here transposed onto various other planes: the spiritual, the demonic, or the divine. This vision of some moments in Jewish mysticism is very similar to Bernard McGinn's recent description of the double background of Christian mysticism. According to him, the "apocalypses and the philosophical-religious tradition begun by Plato were major components of the background of Christian mysticism, and not just because of some historical accident. They were ways of making God accessible to a world in which the divine was no longer present in its traditional forms, and as such they made Christianity and Christian mysticism possible."[16]

However, unlike Christian thought, which absorbed Greek elements at a very early stage of its formation and thereby displays more internalized forms of spirituality, Jewish mysticism has only lately resorted to the Platonic and Aristotelian psychological ways of thought.[17] Christian mysticism as a whole is indebted to the Greek elements, and only for some of its phases is it dependent on Jewish apocalypses. In the case of Jewish mysticism, the earlier phases related to apocalyptic thought, the Heikhalot literature, did not have recourse to Greek psychological concepts, while the later phases are more indebted to Greek thought and relatively less influenced by apocalyptic thought and images. From the inspection of some of the versions of medieval Jewish messianism it is possible to inscribe them in the more comprehensive scheme of the encounter between the Jewish and Greek forms of thought delineated in H. A. Wolfson's analyses of medieval philosophy.

The various Kabbalistic forms of messianism, just as the more popular forms, are to be treated here not only theologically, namely by emphasizing the more abstract tenets involved in a certain messianic paradigm, but also as a certain type central to the medieval *imaginaire*. The religious imaginary, in particular the medieval one, which was the subject of extensive research in the last generation, especially in France,[18] may provide some tools to understand the very rich imaginative production of the messianic visions. What are kinds of miracle are related to the Messiah? How is this extraordinary being to be classified within the realm of the miraculous? What are the various interactions between the ancient messianic imagery and the medieval one? What is the meaning of the recurrent royal imagery related to the Messiah in a medieval setting? How is the Messiah conceived of as a powerful king related to the *rois thaumaturges* of France and England? How were crown, unction, and oil interpreted symbolically? These and other similar questions are to be addressed especially by the scholars of Jewish mysticism, in itself another mode of discourse replete with exotic *imaginaire*.[19] The vague figures of the Messiah, a classical deus ex machina who will solve all the insoluble problems, or the messianic prophets and messengers like David ha-Reuveni or Nathan of Gaza, who invented imaginary kingdoms ruled by allegedly Jewish kings (in the case of the former) and would have their Messiah go to the river of Sambatyon and marry the daughter of Moses (as Nathan prophesied), should be understood not only alongside theological and traditional forms of conceptualization, but as standing at the borderline of quasi-history and pure work of human imagination, or as examples of how imagination is able to shape history. Finally, the rather colorful figure of the Jewish Antichrist, the notorious Armilus, is the center for projecting a rich variety of negative images.

The vagueness of all the themes related to messianism helps to explain their being circulated in so many different religious circles over the centuries. The room left for the imagination was large enough to allow everyone to project his utopian or dramatic expectations into the traditional terms available in almost canonic texts. These figments of imagination enveloped traditional terms, and sometimes even real figures or events, in order to produce a rich gamut of perceptions of messianism. The absence of more detailed discussions in the biblical and rabbinic literature concerning the Messiah, in comparison to the voluminous analyses of the details of prayer or other commandments, facilitated the efflorescence of the more popular-apocalyptic elaborations. Messianism may be seen in the Middle Ages as essentially an open book, which invites the reader to fill in a great amount of details and events that are no more than hinted at in the founding documents of the earlier bodies of literatures.

Moreover, in most cases the relations between the Messiah and his audience, and even his self-image, are dictated by images projected by each of the actors onto the other. The image the Messiah himself would like to project is influential mainly because of the preconceptions of the audience, which may be nourished by traditions quite different from those that form the spiritual history of the elitist Messiah. The pyramid of the messianic phenomena, which brings together the active aspirant to the title of Messiah on the top, the few messengers, apostles, and prophets in the middle, and the much larger audience at the base presupposes a variety of mutual misreadings and misprisions of the nature and intentions of each of the three components by the two other. The often distorted mirroring in the imagination of the nature of the other components was indispensable for the very existence of this pyramid, which combined disparate factors having different expectations and agendas.

I propose to be aware of the sociological aspects of the messianic constellation of ideas, but also to be cognizant that, though the Messiahs were at the top of the pyramid, their concern was nevertheless to redeem the more ordinary people. Thus, the pyramidic structure does not prevent a commitment on the part of the Messiah and his apostles to a wider audiences than a small group, though the concepts that guided them would differ from that of the candidates for redemption. The messianic elites were, by definition, conjunctive elites who flowered on the social level more in periods when, to use a term from modern economics, the "aggregate demand" was greater.

Though such a sociological reading is correct in most of the messianic movements I am acquainted with, in the popular forms of messianism the pyramid seems to be much more flat since the elaborate ideology is less important and the distance between the top and the base is smaller. The more sophisticated the messianic ideology, and more esoteric the doctrine involved in the experience of the Messiah, the greater the distance between the top and the base.

This latter case often involves more comprehensive schemes explaining the nature of the universe, of history, or of the religion within which the messianic elements are embedded. In other words, the Messiahs who were mystics produced movements that consisted in pyramids that are higher than those generated when the Messiah was less learned, because between the base and the top new elements had been integrated. The conceptual frameworks, such as philosophy or magic, have informed the Kabbalistic and Hasidic models that shaped their concept of messianism, which was only rarely shared by the multitude.

Another distinction that should be kept in mind is between the Messiah as a person and the message of the Messiah. The term *mashiyaḥ* originally described the anointment of a person as king or priest and was never assumed in ancient Judaism to denote a single person. In all the orthodox forms of Judaism, the messianic function has ever remained unpersonalized. This means that though there were names for the Messiah, such as Menaḥem "the consoler," and a few personal traits were ascribed to him, the precise identity of the person who is or will be the Messiah has not been specified. In other words, in Judaism, with the exception of Sabbateanism, the messianic function is incomparably more important than the personality who will fulfill it. By contrast, Christianity, which started as a messianic movement gravitating around the personality of a specific Messiah, tends to subsume function to persona. This is why, at least at its beginning, Christianity was an acute messianic phenomenon. If, however, the messianic function comes to overshadow the messianic persona, then the possibility of several persona who may fulfill that function will emerge. The transpersonal vision of the messianic function was central in some mystical schools, which were most concerned with the function as part of a general economy of their elaborated system, producing what I shall called the messianic model. This emphasis on the function rather than the idiosyncracies of individuals is more striking in modern Jewish philosophies, where the assumption of multiple Messiahs has been advanced in order to fulfill the various messianic functions.

In these systemic modes of thought, the message becomes more important than the persona, as the function is conceived in terms of its ultimate purpose. Consequently, the stronger the persona, the more peripheral the message becomes. This seems to be exemplified in early Christianity and in seventeenth-century Sabbateanism, while the proposition that a potent function makes the message central seems to fit Buddhism and some of the Kabbalistic schools, especially the ecstatic Kabbalah. The messianic function is shaped by systemic elements formulated before the emergence of the persona that presumes to embody the function and to play a messianic role. Though there can be no doubt that the aspirant will adapt himself as much as he can to the prescribed ingredients of the function, the differences between the expectation and its realization will remain significant, even if during the development of a certain movement the function and the message are redefined to fit the actual messianic persona. An emphasis on the uniqueness of the persona that assumes the function of Messiah is part of the ultimate personalization of a previously transpersonal function. These personalizations, because of their emphasis on the enigmatic persona, involve much more an attitude of faith rather than of hope, action, or understanding, which are more congruent when the functional aspects of messianism are emphasized.

The combination of imaginary elements, realia (or what some scholars would call history) and traditions, so characteristic of medieval thought, is especially pertinent in the case of messianic themes and images. By definition the messianic phenomena we will be dealing with are complex and represent synthetic approaches which should be analyzed from various angles.

Again, this open mode of expression is also to be understood in the context of the prior observations to the effect that messianic thought may well be part of an attempt to find direction and meaning in the chaos of the events, and of the spiritual quest of some unusual individuals. This seems to be even more crucial in cases where the Messiahs were also mystics. In addition to envisioning the messianic and mystical hermeneutical grids as interpreting and intersecting each other in different manners, we should inspect them as representing the coalescence of different types of religious imaginary: magical, theosophical-theurgical, political, or astrological.

Alternative Proposals

Before proposing other approaches for understanding the relationship between Jewish mysticism and messianism, let me clarify that by both mysticism and messianism I refer to a variety of experiences and self-conceptions of the Messiahs themselves and much less to their followers' perceptions of their role. Even in analyses of mystical writings composed by Kabbalistic and Hasidic masters who did not claim for themselves a distinct messianic role, the major issue will nevertheless be to highlight the mystical persona, the role, and the imaginary themes concerning the Messiahs themselves, not their reflection and refraction in more popular circles. The methods for studying mass movements which are not necessarily those most suitable for probing the inner states of consciousness or eschatological symbolism of the messianic figures. Thus, turning to materials relevant for the construction of the Messiah images or of a Messiah's self-perception, my concern will be to emphasize the differences between the various models rather than the continuity of one messianic "idea."

The resort to the term *messianism* often creates ambiguities that obscure a proper understanding of the topic. Thus messianism stands both for the general belief in someone's messianic role and for someone's belief in his own messianic role. Though the subject of these two beliefs is the same, phenomenologically we are speaking about different religious orientations. While the belief of a group in the imminent or remote advent of a Messiah is best understood by means of academic tools appropriate for the analysis of mass movements, the belief of someone in his own messianic role requires the application of psychological tools.

On the other hand, messianism may sometimes stand for a more abstract idea. Messianism may also comprise strong personal and group experiences which differ dramatically from the more intellectual attitude necessary in order to subscribe to the abstract idea. While the latter may benefit from an approach based upon the method of the history of ideas, the former may be better served by resorting to tools developed for the study of mysticism, where the role of experience is more central.

The historical and phenomenological proposals that I will present differ from the more prevalent historicistic approach to the relationship between messianism and mysticism on several main points. Though I accept the possible affinities between historical events and eidetic structures that emerge in some historical contexts, I see a much weaker correlation between the two than do proponents of historicism. Consequently, messianism should be explored from a variety of angles, not least of which is the characteriological approach, namely paying more attention to the characters of the various Messiahs as crisis personalities. This more variegated methodology is not less historical, as the main purpose is to study historical phenomena. By severely narrowing the range of methods applied to the study of such a complex phenomenon as messianism, a scholar is prone to simplify the phenomenon under scrutiny. Indeed, one of the most obvious common denominators of the messianic figures and concepts under discussion here is that they were complicated characters operating within intricate conceptual systems.

A common feature of most of the mystical Messiahs covered in this book is that they were itinerants. This is the case with Abraham Abulafia, Shelomo Molkho, William Postel, Ḥayyim Vital, Sabbatai Tzevi, Moshe Ḥayyim Luzzatto, and perhaps Asher Lemlein. I see in this propensity for peregrination a characteriological dimension which may be relevant to the unusual role these individuals played on the public scene. The heterogenous nature of a society, including the small Jewish ones, is therefore part of my conception of the development of Jewish mysticism and of the emergence of messianic ideas.

Moreover, instead of assuming that one basic conceptual response was shared by a community of disparate Kabbalists or Hasidic masters, I find it much more plausible that there exists a variety of contemporary responses to a specific historical event, which are determined not only by the event itself but also by the spiritual physiognomy of the mystic and the intellectual paradigms that were at his disposition.

The sharp historical demarcations between messianic and Kabbalistic thought which has been advocated by scholars for some phases of earlier Kabbalah is, in my opinion, hardly tenable. Messianism was a more integral part of Kabbalistic thought—and in some cases of Kabbalistic experience—than one might think on the basis of prevalent scholarship. An important starting point for the study of many medieval forms of messianism has to be the mystical experiences of the future Messiah, which probably triggered his later public manifestations. Consequently, the study of messianism has to take in account much more the mystical, namely psychological, elements as the formative factor of the messianic phenomena, which are of interest mainly because of their impact on the public arena. Kabbalistic messianism should be understood as a topic worthy of detailed inspection even if the public arena is not affected by it at all and it remains the patrimony of a single person. Even in such a case, when the historical influence of a certain type of mystical messianism cannot be pinpointed, a messianic mystical paradigm is nonetheless entitled to an academic, mainly phenomenological analysis.

In my opinion, many forms of messianism and mysticism share a certain intensification of the religious life, which separate these phenomena from the more ordinary religious attitude. This intensification is evident in many types of Jewish mysticism which were informed by activist approaches to religious life and strove for more extreme religious goals by means of mystical techniques. In other words, there are good reasons to look for similar experiential wavelengths between some forms of elite messianism and redemptive mystical states of consciousness. This is not only a matter of a proliferation of prophetic figures in the context of a "messianic" event, or the emergence of a messianic figure, which should not automatically be described as mystical, as I assume that it would be better not to describe every revelation as mysticism. However, my perusal of texts has convinced me that less articulated forms of experiences which should be labeled as mystical occur more often in ambiances permeated by messianic hopes and expectations.

In the following pages, a discussion within a text will be considered messianic when the term *Messiah* or a cluster of strong terms relating to redemption explicitly occur. Presuppositions as to what is genuine messianism should not guide us, otherwise we are in the danger of determining the results of our analysis from the very beginning, regardless of the findings in the field. We must be much more attuned to what the sources claim in explicit terms to be messianic and not decide in advance what is authentic and what not. This observation implies that a much greater variety of ideas should be understood as messianic.

In many modern scholarly discussions of events that span more than two millennia, the phrase *messianic idea* is quite a recurrent locution. Though the great variety of literatures under inspection would invite an assumption that many sorts of messianic ideas would compete, the phrase *messianic idea* looms too prominently in the titles of many books and articles. This is the case in Joseph Klausner's book,[20] in Scholem's *The Messianic Idea in Judaism,* and in the collection of studies on messianism printed on the occasion of Scholem's eightieth birthday.[21] Three leading articles on messianism composed in Hebrew contain the same phrase in their title: Tishby's "The Messianic Idea and Messianic Trends at the Beginning of Hasidism," Mendel Pierkacz's "The Messianic Idea in the Beginning of Hasidism through the Prism of Homiletic and Ethical Writings," and D. Schwartz's "The Neutralization of the Messianic Idea."[22]

It is not, however, the mere recourse to the phrase that is problematic, but rather the conception that it expresses: that there is one major messianic idea which runs continuously throughout Jewish history, a view I call monochromatic diachronism.[23] More recently, the messianic material of late antiquity has been described in a more variegated manner by several scholars, most notably Morton Smith,[24] John J. Collins,[25] Shemariahu Talmon, David Flusser, and Jacob Neusner.[26]. This has also been the basic assumption for my discussion of medieval Kabbalistic messianism.[27]

I propose to call this approach *synchronic polychromatism.* Unlike the views of those scholars dealing with forms of messianism in late antiquity and types of Messiahs, synchronic polychromatism emphasizes the multiplicity of messianic concepts and events while attempting a typology that will not only take in consideration diversity in one limited period of time but also organize the much larger spectrum of literatures and events into more unified categories, or models. We may discern three major models for understanding messianism in Jewish mysticism: the theosophical-theurgical, the ecstatic, and the magical.[28] Synchronic polychromatism, as well as the diachronic one, should be organized into more unified diachronic conceptual schemes. Some of them are quite early, other emerged in the Middle Ages, under the influence of the encounter with the Greek forms of speculative thought. Indeed, the major methodological assumption informing many of the discussions below is that the literatures, events, and the experiences expressing and concerning Jewish messianism should be understood as displaying a great variety of ideas, concepts, modes, and models. The multidimensional nature of most of the messianic ideas is quite evident, and it should be remembered that traditional concepts, found in the canonical writings, historical circumstances, personal aspirations, and apologetic and polemic stands conspired together to produce the wide spectrum of messianic views which cannot be easily reduced to transformations, metamorphoses, or neutralization of one basic "messianic idea." I believe that the implicit assumption that one such monolithic idea was in existence and that it is possible to describe it over many centuries, while reducing all its disparate versions to the status of neutralizations and liquidations, is hardly plausible and quite suspect within a nonorthodox mode of discourse, as the academic one is supposed to be.[29]

In studying Kabbalistic and Hasidic messianisms, it is necessary to pay attention to the inner experiences (personal psychology) as a way to understand the external events (historical acts), and vice versa. The strong methodological assumption of Scholem's historical-critical school as to the irrelevance of psychology for the study of mysticism and messianism seems to be too dogmatic an approach, which reduces the variety of experiences and events to an analysis that is methodologically too narrow.[30] Indeed, it was Scholem himself who took exception to this rejection of psychology and suggested a certain psychological diagnosis in order to better understand the personality and acts of Sabbatai Tzevi.[31] But in addition to the "subjective," characteriological aspects of messianism, there are also other, "objective" components that should be taken more into consideration. Scholem's vision of the crisis of tradition—understood as implicit in the very process of actualizing the messianic hope—should be complemented by another viewpoint. Scholars should allow a greater role for ritual in understanding some messianic events, which should sometimes be understood as attempts to attain a moment in history that will allow a perfect performance of the ritual.

In attempting not to prefer one form of messianism over another within the domain of Jewish mystical conceptualizations we should nevertheless be aware that a stronger distinction between the ideals and the means to attain them should be introduced much more than has been done in the existing scholarship. Thus a mystic may find a certain version of the messianic idea "plausible" and may suggest fantastic means to implement it; or vice versa, he may resort to what could be considered more realistic means, such as the recurring attempts of various messianic figures to meet and speak with the pope, in order to achieve a rather utopian messianic ideal. Activism, for example, should not be seen as separated from the type of ideal it attempts to enact. More pragmatic minds, like Maimonides, were suspicious of messianic activism, while a more deranged personality like Sabbatai Tzevi was much more inclined to act on the historical scene. If we remember that Messiahs were judged by their contemporaries by the outcome of their enterprises, the more confident and activist a Messiah was, the greater his evident failure. A comparison of Tzevi and his contemporary, Menasseh ben Yisrael, by Harold Fisch, put in evidence how the dialogue between the messianic thinker and actor ben Yisrael differs from the self-centered personality of Tzevi, as well as the different outcomes of their activities.[32]

From this viewpoint, the more spiritual and introverted a Messiah was or, to put it differently, the greater his concern with changing the inner rather than the external reality for himself or other human beings, the greater the possibility that he will have been felt to have achieved his goal. Unlike Buber, who preferred the hidden, preparatory, and suffering messianic figures,[33] Scholem was much more attracted to the manifest and activist—in a word, the apocalyptic ones. It would be wise, however, to suspend any preliminary preference. From a scholarly perspective, there is no special need to prefer the apocalyptic over the spiritual eschatology, or Christian over Jewish forms of messianism. Indeed, some of the distinctions I have mentioned are approximations which rarely exist in pure form and often show up in combination. For example, the typology that strongly distinguishes the allegedly external Jewish messianism from the Christian, described by Scholem as more eminently an inward kind of salvation, seems to me to be not only biased by a certain type of spiritual predisposition, but also too neat, simplistic, and often misleading from the historical point of view. Indeed, if the earlier Christian views which became, under the influence of St. Augustine, the classical Christian stand were less concerned with apocalyptic elements, at the turn of the millennium Christian thought in Europe became more and more inclined toward apocalypticism, which remained active in the Christian eschatology up to the end of the seventeenth century. It was Augustine, incidentally, who was instrumental in the introduction of a more external form of eschatology,[34] similar to that which may be found in the Jewish sources, namely the so-called prophecy of Elijah,[35] which speaks of the six thousand years of the existence of the world, whose history in medieval Christian eschatology was rich and lasting.[36]

The course of Jewish eschatology, however, runs another path. Judaism, being more concerned with external apocalypse in late antiquity and the early Middle Ages, gradually demonstrated strong proclivities toward the inward path and away from the apocalyptic since the eleventh century. It is precisely in the thirteenth century, when the apocalyptic trend of eschatology presented by Joachim of Fiore erupted in Christianity, that the more psychological versions of messianism in Judaism flowered. Thus, we may better have recourse to two different histories of messianic concepts, which not only differ from the phenomenological point of view—a present experience or a future Messiah (in Judaism) versus one who has already come (in Christianity)—but also allow for alternating rhythms of ascent and decline of the individual and apocalyptic forms of eschatology in the two religions. Though there are some moments of synchronization between the two rhythms, like the common accent upon apocalypticism in the sixteenth and seventeenth centuries, by and large each had its own separate course. Therefore, the differences between the two religions concerning forms of salvation is in what type of redemption had the upper hand in a given period, much more than which phenomenological structure predominated in Judaism or Christianity in general. Indeed, the impression one gets from the scholarly literature on Christian eschatology is that its elitist literature indulged more in apocalyptic themes than did the Jewish one. In any case, one of the main points in the following discussions is the similarity between Jewish mystical messianic views and Christian ones, as well as the possible mutual historical influences.

Scholem and his followers do distinguish sharply between apocalyptic messianism, understood as consisting in activistic approaches, and other forms of "diluted" messianism found either in Jewish mystical sources (and viewed as neutralizations) or in modern Jewish liberalism. I would propose, however, to distinguish between the preponderance of the apocalyptic mode of writing in the East, namely in Israel, Babylonia, or Yemen, and the more spiritual approach preponderant in Europe.[37] To be sure, this distinction is no more than an approximation, especially insofar as some of the former eschatological writings arrived to Europe and were accepted and quoted positively. The thrust of most of the creativity in Europe, however, is definitively in the direction of non-apocalyptic forms of messianism. I would say that in Europe the apocalyptic mode as accepted by the elite is often viewed by these figures as exoteric, while the more allegorical and symbolic versions of messianism stand for the esoteric layers of their thought and experiences. Scholem's distinction somewhat resembles Kaufmann's fascinating suggestion concerning the Eastern reaction to national and religious suppression by means of military revolt, which according to his view is characteristic of the Jews until the seventh century C.E., and the emergence of the "messianic movement which consists, in its entirety, of faith and fantasy."[38] Elaborating upon Kaufmann's distinction, we may indeed conceive the late biblical and rabbinic views of apocalyptic messianism as nourished by more general attitudes to the concrete, either in the emphasis on the more immediate link to the land of Israel, as pointed out already by Kaufmann,[39] or in the plain sense of the canonic texts, as is evident in those forms of literature. On the other hand, many of the European forms of Jewish speculative literature have adopted a variety of metaphorical readings of the text, either allegorical or symbolic, as well as metaphorical understandings of the land of Israel, which are reminiscent of and sometimes directly related to spiritual conceptualizations of messianism.[40] This remark holds also for those forms of literature in the East since the sixteenth century that were written under the influence of the European speculative literature. Thus, in lieu of a system that views apocalyptic messianism as the main, "authentic" form from which other messianisms then diverge, one may consider a viewpoint that places the different forms of messianic concepts on equal footing, attributing their variety to the different cultural centers that generated them.

Scholem concludes that messianism was not only rather uniform in its apocalyptic thrust but also homogeneously influential in the Jewish nation when it exploded onto the public arena. His conception of a unified eschatological ideology that has spread across three continents and two millennia, seems to me doubtful.[41] I am much more inclined to look for the importance of specific regions or centers of messianic activities and speculations, even cities where these forms of utopia were most prominent. This approach will give more space to authors who were active in great urban centers such as Rome and Venice. Just as I have suggested concerning the sociological implication of the messianic pyramid,[42] we shall also be aware of a heterogenous geographical distribution of the various messianic ideas.

On the other hand, it is essential to pay attention to specific moments in time, or sacral times, in order to better understand an eschatological event. I shall attempt to highlight the recurrence of the New Year festival in several cases in the history of Jewish mysticism, as well as the importance of the decades in Abulafia's messianism. A special concern in this regard arises from analyses of the sacral royalty by the myth-and-ritual school, which despite the criticism and revisions of some of its main claims over the last decades, made vital contributions.[43] The scholars belonging to the different branches of this school dealt, each in his own way, with the unique relation between a special individual, such as the king, and God. The adoption of the king by God, Sonship, the king's anointment, his becoming a channel between God and the nation, or the nexus between ritual and myth—detailed analysis of all these themes may help to open new historical and phenomenological vistas for scholars of Jewish mysticism.[44]

At the same time, it should be emphasized that prominent exponents of the myth-and-ritual approach, such as S. H. Hooke and Sigmund Mowinckel, had discovered in the pattern of sacral royalty the origin of apocalypticism.[45] This is particularly important for a study of so central a topic as messianism, which should be described against its sources as well as the historical and cultural backgrounds of its particular manifestations. Linkages between kingship, adoption, apocalypticism, and messianism were pointed out in, among other places, Mowinckel's monumental *He That Cometh,* Aage Bentzen's *King and Messiah,* and Geo Widengren's series of studies entitled *King and Saviour.* But while those scholars were naturally concerned primarily with ancient literature, one of the main foci in this book will be to pick up the threads suggested by those scholars, though my concerns have much to do with the mystical and not only the mythical aspects of messianism.

The present attempt to explore the much earlier forms of religiosity for what they can tell us about the earliest Israelite apocalyptic and messianic phenomena seems to be met by some more recent contributions, including the discovery of the relevance of the Mesopotamian background for the book of Daniel and the Enochic literature.[46] As we shall see in chapters 2 and 6, the the redemptive nature of the angel Metatron, who was sometimes described as related to Enoch, is paramount for some developments in Jewish mysticism and messianism. Some modern scholars' claims as to the Mesopotamian background of Enoch and his translation on high is quintessential for understanding the profound impact of the descriptions of this figure on Jewish mysticism, and perhaps also on Christian messianology. Interestingly enough, the turn of a medievalist like Norman Cohn to look for the roots of the millenarian phenomena he had described in his earlier books may represent a more open-minded and realistic scholarly approach to studying some concepts in the Middle Ages than a purely historicistic one.[47]

Indeed, more and more adequate antecedents to some later phenomena are being found as the apocalyptic material is researched in greater detail. The possible relevance of the Mesopotamian literature for significant segments of Jewish esotericism is being discussed more frequently and is beginning to assemble a rather loose framework for further treatment of the subject.[48] Though dealing with ancient material, most of the scholars belonging to the so-called patternist schools made efforts to elucidate the background of the biblical sacral royalty. In at least one case, however, the writings of Geo Widengren, an effort has been made to trace the vestiges of the pattern long after the cessation of the Israelite monarchy. Should his sometimes speculative proposals be accepted, the continuity between the Mesopotamian pattern and early medieval phenomena could become much more plausible.[49] Yet even in the present state of the art, when many scholars think the links between medieval views and ancient myths and rituals are improbable, in the case of the medieval messianism we may nevertheless point out plausible literary links, in addition to the biblical material, that may reduce the gaps between the earlier and the later material. The Jewish apocryphal and apocalyptic literatures may mediate ancient views to the medieval redeemers by preserving elements of royal sacrality in the context of the Messiah figures.

To understand the affinity between the myth-and-ritual schools and the treatment of messianic issues, we must pay attention to those elements that apparently survived in the messianic constellation of ideas and bear a certain similarity to the view of the ancient king as described by these schools. In a talmudic text the Messiah is called by the name of Tetragrammaton, in a Midrash he is called by the divine name 'Adonai, My Lord,[50] while elsewhere he is designated 'El.[51] On the other hand, God is widely described in Judaism as the Redeemer, *go'el*, a term also sometimes applied to an angel or a human redeemer. These common appellations, as well as the different views on the preexistence of the Messiah, may point to a much more substantial link between the divine and the messianic personae. Moreover, I propose to take toward some literatures a panoramic approach, a view that presupposes that the mystical Messiahs had access to several of the models of messianism that had emerged in Jewish literature and could select among them, appropriating what seemed to them to be the most features. Consequently, the later the era in which a Messiah or messianic thinker lived, the broader his panorama become. The primary example to be addressed in this book is the most influential Messiah, Sabbatai Tzevi.

This panoramic approach, which has been applied already in other cases,[52] should be complemented by what I call a global approach. The panoramic one risks turning into a simplistic inventory of the models that may have inspired a particular Messiah. There is a danger that such an approach may deal more with possibilities than with processes. The global approach may, however, allow us to inspect the developments of each of these models, point out the different processes that connected them, and account for the ascent and decline of the models in different historical circumstances. Or, from another point of view, the emergence in the late biblical books and the apocalyptic literature, in Philo of Alexandria, in Christianity, and in Gnosticism of a mesocosmos, an intermediary realm of beings between the divinity and humans, opens the door for inserting a transcendent depersonalized Messiah within the quasi-divine company, a fact that will have a deep impact on the nature of the later concepts of the Messiah. The gap created by the attenuation of the direct involvement of God in history, and His initiative to reveal Himself, was filled with surrogates that gradually substituted more and more the divine acts and created different forms of interaction based on a threefold structure of the religious universe, rather than a twofold one, as in most of the biblical writings.

In some biblical traditions the intervention of angels, these once impersonal messengers of the divine have become personalized; previously anonymous angels have received not only proper names but also different functions, sometimes related to those names. Thus a whole mesocosmic bureaucracy has emerged, involving in some cases a preexistent, transcendent Messiah. We may speak about a systemic development, similar to the emergence of modern bureaucracy, which develops because of an built-in logic of expansion and differentiation of functions. The concept of *mashiyaḥ* itself is to be seen as part of a differentiation process that attributed the formerly divine role of savior to one of God's officers. En passant, this systemic development of angelology and angelophany should not be seen as independent and divorced from cultural, historical, and political circumstances. Only a combination of unrelated factors could account for the later exploitation of the potential spiritual contribution of the concept of the Messiah as an extension of the divine activity by a more personalized angelic entity. Subsequently, in Kabbalah and Hasidism, it even led to ascribing messianic attributes to a variety of human beings, or fragmentization of the personalization of the redemptive function. This proposition differs from the well-known description of G. van der Leeuw, who in chapter 12 of *Religion in Essence and Manifestation* offered a quite different description which assumes that the function of the personalized savior emerged out of a more structured perception of salvific understandings of more natural factors or powers.

Or, to mention another main question that haunted Jewish messianism, the emergence of Christianity, a messianic religion drawing upon Jewish sources and attempting to reinterpret some of the messianic claims cherished by the Jews, problematized some of the earlier Jewish concepts, which were marginalized in order to make a clearer distinction between Judaism and Christianity. If early Christian views of the Messiah reflect Jewish stands, their separate developments should be treated together, as different options inherent in earlier sources but actualized in various, often antagonistic religious ambiances. Likewise Islam, though less permeated by messianic views than Christianity is, should be taken into account, particularly as relates to the spiritualization of eschatology in Sufism, as is the case with Al-Ghazzali, for example. It seems, however, that a greater influence of Islam on Jewish mysticism is visible through mediating Greek views in matters of psychology, which inspired some of the important mystical phenomena that also absorbed eschatological and messianic elements. Thus, the two other monotheistic religions could serve not only as cultural backgrounds for Jewish thinking or provide topics that were opposed by Jewish messianism, but also sometimes inspired eschatological modalities for Jewish thinkers.

Such global attempts require the inspection of huge amounts of material written over a vast period of time. One should consider the ancient plausible sources, biblical and prebiblical, as formative for some of the mystical concepts of messianism, as I shall attempt to show was the case in Abulafia's mystical messianism.[53] An acquaintance not only with Judaism but also with Babylonian religion, Greek thought, Christianity, and Ottoman civilization is essential for discerning the trajectories and the forms of the various constellations of messianic ideas. Moreover, the material must be digested and conceptualized in a manner that will allow the insertion of Jewish messianism into more comprehensive developments in the respective locations. Global shifts from corporate identities as the major factors in the various versions of the redemptive drama, to the soul or the intellect of the individual as the arena of the redemptive processes, and then the return of the corporate identity in some cases such as in Hasidism, are examples of the interface between the various cultural systems that are so characteristic of the history of Jewish thought. In fact, it is possible to speak of several different narratives that may organize the history of the various models, and of narratives that will deal with the tensions, interactions, or synthesis between them. In other words, the fragmentation of the alleged messianic idea into different and basic forms of messianic concepts may have a dramatic effect not only on the phenomenology of the messianic idea but also on the way its history has to be written. In lieu of a single master narrative, one should prefer several lines of narratives which may converge, intersect, and diverge.

In elite literatures, moreover, messianism is always to be understood as part of broader conceptual systems. What the method based upon the theory of models suggests is that we should gradually build up more comprehensive syntaxes of the various forms of Jewish mystical literatures, which will be able to describe the concatenations between the major categories of religious concepts, messianism among them.[54] A certain type of mystical literature may prefer individual redemption and describe it expressly as messianism, together with political activity and propaganda, while other types may deal with magical activity as necessary for the advent of the Messiah and apocalyptic propensities, without engaging political acts or searching for personal redemption. In the former, the mystical experience as a direct contact with God, what is called *unio mystica,* would be crucial, while in the latter it may be absent. A third mystical model, the theosophical-theurgical, would be much more sensitive to the importance of the performance of the classical Jewish ritual than the individual mystical experience or the magical formulae. Therefore mystical experiences, myths, magic, theology, rituals, and philosophies of different types all become associated with messianic concepts and define them in various ways. Messianic ideas become part of complex syntaxes which modify and enrich them as part of cultural encounters between Jews and alien forms of knowledge. Therefore I shall engage significant discussions of the ingredients of expressions used by mystical Messiahs to be described in this book. They, unlike the more popular apocalyptic writers, offer much more complex schemes, because by their more learned makeup they come in contact with different forms of culture and conceptual systems.

Messianism and Myth

Gershom Scholem's sensitively described the way the apocalyptics expressed their view: "[M]otifs of current history, which refer to contemporary conditions and needs, are closely intertwined with those of an apocalyptic, eschatological nature, in which not only the experience of the present exercises an influence, but often enough ancient mythical images are filled with utopian content."[55] He is correct, if only we exclude the mystical Messiahs or the messianic mystics. By "the experience of the present" Scholem means the historical experience shared by the whole nation and expressed by the Kabbalists in a more symbolic manner, by resorting also to the ancient apocalyptic terminology. My approach lays a much stronger emphasis, on the one hand, on the mystical experiences, understood as having strong teleological aspects of searching for meaning for the individual and the nation and, on the other hand, on what can be described loosely as theological aspects, represented by the theory of models that informed the mystics. Experiences were shaped by models, and models have been enriched by their intersections with individual experiences.

The "mythical images" Scholem referred to deal with apocalyptic issues, and there is no doubt that they have been filled with new contents. The nature of those contents, however, is not always related to the utopian elements, as implied by Scholem, but sometimes has to do with ritualistic performances. Indeed, while Scholem tilts the balance of the creativity of some of the Kabbalists by assuming that they instilled a utopian meaning in the old mythical images, I propose to entertain the possibility that those images have been filled with messages that concern the old ritualistic performances. Myth, in the way I shall use the term, is a conservative rather than a subversive category. I accept the view of Paul Ricoeur, who suggested the following definition: "Myth will here be taken to mean what the history of religion now finds in it: not a false explanation by means of images and fables, but a traditional narration which relates to events that happened at the beginning of time and which has the purpose of providing grounds for the ritual actions of men of today and, in a general manner, establishing all the forms of action and thought by which man understands himself in the world."[56]

The messianic elements that fit this concept of myth have to do more with the restorative aspects of messianic ideas, which strive to recover lost time, as Claude Levi-Strauss proposed to define myth.[57] However, to the extent that messianic elements become more utopian, the mythical elements, as defined by these two scholars, recede to the margin. Unlike Buber, I assume that the utopian future is more a matter of aspiration and expectation than of repetition and ritual, as the mythical mode may be defined.[58] Indeed, I propose to see the integration between myth and messianism as belonging to what Edmund Leach has described as the "icon of orthodoxy," while some of the samples of the affinities between mysticism and messianism will be understood in terms of what Leach referred as the "icon of subversion."[59] This subversive propensity is responsible for a great many innovations in religious life, opened to the Messiahs by divine revelation. As Scholem insightfully pointed out, "There seems to be an intrinsic connection between active messianism and the courage for religious innovation. Messianic movements would often produce individuals with sufficient charismatic authority to challenge the established authority of rabbinic Judaism."[60] One of the main concerns of this book will be to explicate some of the innovations found in the writings of messianic mystics, restricting the analysis, however, to their contributions to the messianic constellation of ideas.

My basic methodological assumption is that more in-depth, or what Clifford Geertz called "thick," descriptions of specific messianic phenomena should be offered before attempting to generalize about the "messianic idea." To quote Geertz more precisely, "the essential task of theory building here is not to codify abstract regularities, but to make thick description possible, not to generalize across cases but to generalize within them."[61] For the topic at hand, this means paying much more attention to single figures and models, in an attempt to accentuate their particular conceptual structure, integrating whenever possible the affinities between the persona, the experience, and the eschatological message.

Modern Scholarship on Messianism

Messianism has always been a controversial topic. It has created tensions within the existing social and cultural structures, provoked interreligious controversies, and defined and redefined the ideals of a certain religious group by projecting them into the future. Societies and groups in search for stability were not prone to encourage extensive explorations into explosive concepts, and that was especially the case with Jewish scholarship in the nineteenth century, which was much more concerned with matters related to Jewish Kabbalah than with those bearing on Jewish messianism. Even some of the pioneers in the study of Kabbalistic literature—Meier H. Landauer, Adolph Jellinek, Adolphe Frank, and, in a rather different manner, R. Elijah Benamozegh[62]—did not display a sympathetic attitude toward messianism. Consequently one of their main subjects, Abraham Abulafia's Kabbalah, was perceived in more favorable terms than his claim to messianism, which Jellinek branded an *enthusiasmus*. It seems that they conceived the two spiritual phenomena as separate issues which, despite some areas of overlap, were not essentially related to each other. Jellinek, who had published a large amount of Midrashic and Kabbalistic material from manuscripts, only rarely referred to apocalyptic or messianic texts or issues in his more general discussions.

Some of their contemporaries, like Heinrich Graetz and Moritz Steinschneider, did assume a certain correlation between Kabbalah and messianism, but their attitude to both mysticism and messianism was negative. At least Graetz saw what he conceived to be the deleterious forms of messianism, in contrast to the more rationalistic and positive ones, as the culmination of Kabbalah. This basic attitude obtains in the twentieth-century scholar Louis Ginsburg's quite impressive project, *Legends of the Jews,* where, as Gershom Scholem has remarked,[63] the apocalyptic elements have been marginalized from the otherwise comprehensive exposition of the rabbinic imagination as displayed in legends.

Since the beginning of the twentieth century, it is possible to discern three major ways of understanding the affinities between messianism and mysticism. Some scholars hold that there is no important messianic element in Jewish mysticism. This is the case in the writings of Hillel Zeitlin, Martin Buber, S. A. Horodetzky, and Abraham Y. Heschel. In the studies of two prominent contemporary scholars of Kabbalah, Alexander Altmann and Georges Vajda, the messianic elements are only very rarely discussed; in general these scholars have been concerned more with the speculative aspects of Kabbalah.

Other scholars, however, assume that there is no need to refer to mystical thought in order to understand messianism. Scholars who devoted lengthy analyses to Jewish messianism did not address systematically the question of an essential link between the two phenomena, and they proceeded to describe messianism as a separate realm. In the writings of A. Posznanski, Joseph Sarachek, Yehezkel Kaufman, Aaron Zeev Aescoly, Yehudah Even Shmuel, and Abba Hillel Silver, the messianic elements, aspirations, or activities were analyzed without resorting to dense treatments of their mystical backgrounds.

It is Gershom Scholem and his school who have closely examined the relationship between Jewish mysticism and messianism, establishing significant connections between the two phenomena after the expulsion of the Jews from Spain. Following Scholem's lead, important scholars such as Isaiah Tishby, Rivkah Schatz-Uffenheimer, Joseph Dan, R. J. Zwi Werblowsky, and Rachel Elior—and, much more independently and creatively, Yehuda Liebes—have elaborated upon this messianic-Kabbalistic link in a long series of studies. Though already at the beginning of the twentieth century a more positive attitude toward both messianism and Kabbalah had appeared in Julius H. Greenstone's unfortunately neglected monograph *The Messiah Idea,* Scholem's school has revolutionized modern research into messianism and mysticism and their mutual affinities. This argument became the dominant attitude in the generation of scholars who established themselves in the 1950s in the leading center of Jewish studies, the

Hebrew University in Jerusalem, and has radiated therefrom into many studies written elsewhere. No doubt this view represents an Israeli phenomenon of that period of transition which included the establishment of the state of Israel. The concept of messianism attracted scholars who participated actively in the historic changes of their own time to explore changes in the past. This is true not only in the case of Scholem's school but also insofar as the second line of viewing messianism is concerned.

But before proceeding with a more detailed exposition of the views of Scholem's school, I would like to mention a factor that has had a strong impact on medieval and some of the modern discussions of messianism: Christianity. Given the fact that most of the messianic and Kabbalistic material was committed to writing in medieval and premodern Europe, whose population was overwhelmingly Christian, the Jewish mystical treatments of messianism and the Christian views of redemption should be compared in order to better understand the religious background of the Jewish discussions.

Jewish and Christian Messianisms

As part of the early twentieth-century attempts to define Judaism, several scholars undertook a comparison of Judaism and Christianity. Messianism was seen as an issue over which the two religions drastically diverged. Leo Baeck, Martin Buber, and Gershom Scholem all attempted to separate Jewish and Christian messianic ideas, also the tendency is also evident in Joseph Klausner's *The Messianic Idea in Israel.* Baeck made this comparison as part of his effort to define the essence of Judaism. He envisioned the approach of the kingdom of God on Earth as a distinct trait of Jewish messianism, while ascribing an escapist attitude to Christianity. Augustine's *civitas dei* is symbolic, according to Baeck, of the Christian religion, while the worldly kingdom has been explicitly opposed (at least by Martin Luther) as a Jewish doctrine. Even the more activist approaches in Christianity, like missionary work, were understood by Baeck as vestiges of Jewish views, though primarily directed toward the salvation of the soul.[64]

On the other hand, Martin Buber embraced a more spiritualistic version of messianism, emphasizing the daily redemptive experience over the importance of an ultimate national redemption. Buber was uneasy with the very existence of apocalyptic elements in Judaism, which he thought to be of alien extraction. He favored a messianism of continuity that is more concerned with the preparation for redemption than its achievement; his preference was conspicuously for everyday salvation rather than apocalypse. Buber was more concerned with the "suffering" aspect of the messianic figure than with his hypostatic existence or his public status. Buber's messianic ideal, while deeply informed by mysticism (especially by Hasidic mysticism), attempted to divorce messianism from apocalypticism. Buber came much closer to some of the Christian views of messianism and redemption than did Baeck and Scholem.[65]

Scholem proposed a view that seems almost diametrically opposite to Buber's. He repeatedly emphasized the radical divergences between the Jewish and Christian forms of messianism, and conceived of the apocalyptic component as quintessential to Jewish messianism, relegating the more spiritual versions of messianism to a secondary or derivative status. He said that messianism is "based on the assumption that redemption either transforms or destroys history and is therefore an event bound up with the future."[66] In fact Scholem attributed to Christianity an unqualified emphasis on inwardness that he considered to be uncharacteristic of Jewish messianism. Scholem's stand is much closer to Baeck's, though they differ radically insofar as the apocalyptic element is concerned. He was much more concerned, however, with the spirituality produced by an apocalyptic rupture in history than Baeck was. In his attempt to differentiate Jewish eschatology from the Christian one, Scholem went too far by overemphasizing the national and historical elements, above all apocalypticism, in the constellation of ideas that constitutes Jewish messianism, at the expense of the spiritual ones, while reducing Christian views of redemption to solely one stand, the spiritual one. In fact, both Judaism and Christianity have shown a great variety of responses to this vital issue, and the comparisons between the two must be made in a much more complex and sensitive manner. We may learn from the comparison between some Jewish and Christian forms of messianism not only about the differences and tensions between them but also about common denominators, which stem from ancient Jewish views that were accepted by Christianity and eventually marginalized in subsequent Jewish texts, though they recur in Ashkenazi Hasidism and Kabbalah.

Scholem's Phenomenology of Messianism

Gershom Scholem resorted to the term *apocalyptic* not in its precise original meaning, namely as a term related to revelation, but more as one pointing to an imminent historical and cosmic upheaval connected to the time of the end, the eschaton. Scholem's apocalypticism is similar to the terms *millenarianism* and *chiliasm* in the scholarly discussions of some Western eschatologies. The most explicit and helpful description of the relationship between apocalypticism and messianism in Scholem's thought is contained in his statement that apocalypticism is a "form necessarily created by acute messianism."[67] The acceptance of this assertion will facilitate the distinction I wish to draw in the following discussions between some forms of messianism, which may not be apocalyptic, and others, which are. Let us address, however, the surfacing of the modern scholarly fascination with apocalypticism in Judaism.

With the appearance of the extensive and far-reaching research of Gershom Scholem and his school, messianism became one of the main topics under investigation in order to better understand both the history of the Jews and the development of Jewish mysticism. This preoccupation of such scholars as Ben Zion Dinur, Yitzḥak Baer, Aaron Z. Aescoly, Joseph Klausner, Yehezkel Kaufman, and Yehudah Even Shmuel with messianism as a crucial issue in Jewish mysticism is related, in my opinion, not only to their findings of new material in manuscripts but also to their Zionist ideology and nationalistic enthusiasm. I do not intend by this observation to minimize the importance of the remarkable scholarly contribution of Scholem's school, but rather to locate it within its historical background and describe one of the main impulses that shaped the choice of its subject matter and the kind of treatment it received. My present concern is not the role and nature of messianism in the general economy of Judaism but the relations between messianism and scholarship of Jewish mysticism.

Despite his immense contribution to the study of Jewish mysticism, Scholem was interested mostly in one specific form of Jewish messianism: the apocalyptic. He asserted, for example, that "Jewish Messianism in its origins and by its nature—this cannot be sufficiently emphasized—is a theory of catastrophe. This theory stresses the revolutionary, cataclysmic element in the transition from every historical present to the Messianic future. . . . The elements of the catastrophic and the vision of the doom are present in peculiar fashion in the Messianic vision."[68] He stated that to the extent that messianism entered "as a vital force in the messianism of the mystics, it is permeated by apocalypse and it also reaches . . . utopian conclusions which undermine the rule of the Halakhah . . . in the days of redemption."[69] Fascinated by the antinomian potentialities inherent in this extreme form of mysticism, he regarded the more mystical and less radical interpretations of messianism as forms of "neutralizations" of this phenomenon, even as its "liquidation."[70] Though he never expressly denied the messianic beliefs of any of the Jewish philosophers or mystics, Scholem nevertheless saw the more individualistic forms of Jewish eschatology as very significantly deviating from the vital version of apocalyptic messianism. He was more attracted by the dramatic, revolutionary, and public manifestations of messianism than by its private, inner, or spiritual aspects.[71] Indeed, as Harold Bloom has aptly noted, Scholem had "an obsession with the imagery of catastrophe."[72]

Phenomenologically speaking, Scholem defined messianism in a way that excluded the more private and mystical "interpretations" or "neutralizations" of the popular, apocalyptic understanding of the term. According to him, Jewish messianism is drastically different from the Christian emphasis on the redemption of the soul, the later being "not considered by either Rabbinism or Kabbalism as having anything to do with Messianism."[73] Thus, by pointing out the apocalyptic components to the entire range of messianic phenomena after their neglect by some earlier scholars, Scholem actually identified and even fused the two concepts. His project was explicitly intended to counter the marginalization of apocalypticism in Jewish scholarship during the previous century, which preferred less dramatic versions of Judaism. This less apocalyptic reading of messianism in still evident in the way Joseph Sarachek has treated the doctrine of the Messiah. Sarachek emphasizes the philosophical literature and relegates the Kabbalistic literature to the periphery, totally ignoring Messiahs like Abraham Abulafia and Shlomo Molkho or major discussions on the Messiah in the the Zohar. Among the representatives of the mystical version of messianism, one can find in Sarachek's books thinkers who are much closer to philosophy, such as Yehudah ha-Levi, Abraham bar Ḥiyya, or Yitzḥaq Abravanel.

On the other hand, Gershom Scholem's attempt to offer a much more dramatic and mythical version of the messianic idea in Judaism took him too far. Scholem overemphasized the centrality of one of the extant versions of messianism as the only authentic one, dispensing with other versions as derivative phenomena. His efforts to escape the essentialistic approach of some of his predecessors in defining Judaism provoked the establishment of another strong form of essentialism, which gravitates around what Scholem would call the "radical" elements implicit in the apocalyptic idea. What concerns me here is his emphasis upon the "oneness" of the messianic idea. Scholem wrote, for example, that "the first principle that characterizes messianism in Israel, and the history of the messianic idea and the history of the messianic movements, is continuity. Indeed, this is a continuity that implies dialectics, but a living dialectics, which testifies as to the intense vitality that was quite alive in the heart of the nation and was expressed in various and different ways that the messianic idea has undertaken during more than a millennium and a half. The first roots of this dialectical continuity are found in the Bible."[74] A similar stand had already been expressed by him much earlier, when he stated, "If I have demonstrated something [at all], in my writings, I have shown that ancient apocalypse has accepted some forms and replaced them, but it is one under its metamorphoses after the destruction of the second Temple, and one it is in its first metamorphoses beforehand."[75] Indeed, the "messianic idea" is qualified by the assumption that it took different forms, which are nevertheless dialectically bound to the one messianic idea. It is the singular rather than the plural, however, that attracts my attention. This resort to an alleged singularity is backed by Scholem's view of its continuity, which precluded the existence of fundamentally significant and different models of messianism. This is why I prefer to describe Scholem's view as diachronic monochromatism, an approach that stresses a type of messianism whose most important characteristics consist in an emphasis upon the national, historical, and geographical elements of redemption through the centuries. Thus Scholem defines messianism in one of his more elaborate discussions of the topic: "Messianism is based upon the assumption that redemption generates a transformation of history or destroys it, and it is therefore an event bound to the future. Religious redemption, which turns to the individual, is an experience that may happen here and now. It is devoid of messianic contexts, messianic redemption as it has been conceived in Judaism as the result of a long development which underwent different stages; it is a collective phenomenon, the liberation of the nation from the exile and the restoration of its freedom and the constitution of a vision of a just society."[76] As we shall see, the scholars' resort to the formula of "the messianic idea" is often coupled with the assumption that diverse eschatological ideas different from the messianic idea emerged as the result of processes of neutralization.

In the following pages I shall inspect precisely those mystical paradigms that remained beyond the scope of Scholem's rather monolithic phenomenology, namely those "religious" redemptions which he excluded from the realm of messianism. Scholem's stark distinction between religious and messianic types of redemption is crucial for his understanding of messianism. But does individual redemption truly have no link to messianism? I think otherwise. Not that Scholem was unaware of the existence of much of the material I shall analyze; he was certainly acquainted with most of it. However, he would regard many of these discussions as less "authentic" than the public drama evolving in the more apocalyptic descriptions. It is perhaps one of the most interesting paradoxes of the modern study of mysticism that the most magisterial description of messianism has been inclined to accept the rather popular understanding of the eschaton in strongly apocalyptic terms, as the dominant form of messianism, while the mystical models have been shunted aside. By assuming throughout this book that there are significantly different paradigms of Kabbalistic messianism, I am attempting to avoid the preference of one form of messianism over the others. I shall try to explain the inner logic of each Kabbalistic and Hasidic model or paradigm, irrespective of its historical importance or influence. In lieu of the essentialistic view of Scholem, gravitating around the central role of the apocalyptic, and the historicistic views of some scholars, who allow for what I see as too great a role to historical events, I prefer a theory of models and modes that may solve some of the problems created by the dominant essentialistic or historicistic approaches.

My assumption will be that each of the models—the ecstatic, the magical, the astrological, the descent-model, and the theosophical-theurgical—is both a production of human fiction or part of the Jewish *imaginaire,* when envisioned from the point of view of a modern scholar, and quite realistic and effective from the point of view of the Messiahs themselves and their followers. This reality and efficacy are related to the mimetic nature of traditional societies, a fact that is conspicuous even in the case of the most innovative among the Jewish mystics.

On the other hand, I suggest that we should distinguish between two main modes that differentiate some of the models from one another. Some models may be grouped around the ideal of perfection and follow what may be called *via perfectionis.* This is the case in the more naturalistic approaches, as found in ecstatic Kabbalah, as represented in passages from Abraham Abulafia and Yitzḥaq of Acre; in theosophical-theurgical Kabbalah, as represented in a passage from R. Moses de Leon; and in talismanic forms of Kabbalah and, finally, some forms of Hasidism. This mode is informed by the assumption that the Messiah gained a certain type of experience ro knowledge that, when imparted to others, will enable them to imitate the messianic figure and be redeemed. The redeemer elevates others toward the mode of existence he has already achieved. Some of the forms of this mode are inspired by views accepting a perfectibility of nature and human character, related in some cases to Greek forms of thought. On the other hand, there are models which may be described as following the *via passionis,* which is taken here to mean that the messianic figure is suffering in order to atone for others and so save them. Though better known from Christianity, this is a much more ancient view found, for example, in rituals connected to the royal sacral ideologies, where the king and gods had to undergo a certain experience understood as death, and in the concept of the suffering servant in Isaiah. The talmudic expressions of the eschatological importance of suffering had been studied by A. Agus in *The Binding of Isaac,* and it had repercussions in the katabatic models that are represented in the Zohar, R. Yitzḥaq of Acre, R. Joseph Al-Ashqar, R. Shlomo Molkho, R. Yitzḥaq Luria, Sabbatai Tzevi, and emphasized in Buber's descriptions of Hasidism and even in Emmanuel Levinas's concept of substitution. This mode expresses the idea that the Messiah is able either to relieve the suffering of others vicariously, by his own suffering, or to battle apocalyptic wars with the powers of evil, or to descend into the realm of evil in order to release the souls of those captive there. It is evil, in other words imperfection, rather than perfection that is primarily addressed by the redeemer's activity according to this path. Redemption means therefore the evacuation of evil from the world by its concentration on the vicarious redeemer. It is the act of substitution, rather than that of distribution, that is characteristic of this mode—the descent of the redeemer rather than his elevation on high.

My resort to the theory of models and modes is part of a more comprehensive attempt to distinguish between main forms of Kabbalistic concerns which found their expressions in recurrent terminologies and structures of thought. In addition to paying attention to the very occurrence of the term *mashiyah*, I assume that we may find some basic recurrences of specific meanings of this term, which allows the theory of the existence of different models. I take these models to be not necessarily the precise replica of the same type in different contexts, but structures of thought whose basic elements predated the discussions of the term *mashiyah* and which recurrently informed this term with valences stemming from originally nonmessianic forms of thought.[77]

Though some readers acquainted with the influential oeuvre of Gershom Scholem and persuaded by its magisterial formulations may wonder whether some of the texts to be dealt with in the following chapters could represent messianic motifs at all—despite the explicit mention of messianic sets of imagery in these passages and even of the term *mashiyah* itself—I am confident that, methodologically, we should start with exploring what I conceive to be the pertinent material and present it phenomenologically, independent from what is considered in some scholarly circles as "real" messianism. By doing so, a much less dogmatic approach will avoid marginalizing those views and concepts that do not fit the "messianic idea" as preconceived by some scholars.

Scholem's Historiography of Messianism

Scholem's detailed historiography of messianism contains significant departures from the common wisdom of the nineteenth-century descriptions of Jewish history. Indeed, Scholem was well aware of the novelty of the modern scholarship in this field; as he once put it, rather ironically, "The very historical research of the topic of messianism is new. Today, we are all wise, we all understand [this topic], we all read Zion, we all read books on messianic movements."[78] I assume that Scholem was not only referring to his readers but actually intended to say that we all *write* books on messianic movements. Indeed, a historiography emphasizing messianic movements and having a predilection for the messianic over the religious has abruptly emerged in the last two generations.

Scholem's own descriptions of the relationship between messianism and Jewish mysticism assume the existence of three distinct stages.[79] During the first phase, roughly between 1180 and 1492, Kabbalah was indifferent towards messianism. If messianism means speculations as to the nature of the eschaton, strong apocalyptic aspirations, and beliefs that the end is around the corner, the early Kabbalists turned their backs to such preoccupations, preferring to focus their attention upon the processes related to creation by emanation, the nature of theosophy, and salvation that was sought by the contemplative return to the beginning rather than by attempts to hasten the end. Sometimes Scholem would even say that this move was an antimessianic mode of thinking.[80]

After and because of the forced expulsions of the Jews from Spain and Portugal, messianism gradually became part of the core of Kabbalistic thought. There are three major forms of mystical messianism in this second phase. The first arose between the expulsion in 1492 and the emergence of the Lurianic Kabbalah around 1570. In this phase, according to the different and not easily consistent statements, either Kabbalah was still divorced from messianic thought or Kabbalists were deeply involved in messianic propaganda. In some cases these two types of thought were combined, but no original form emerged from that combination. The second major form appeared between 1570 and the birth of Sabbateanism around 1660. In this period messianic concerns became part and parcel of the Lurianic version of Kabbalah.[81] This somehow deterministic vision of the history of Kabbalah, within which messianism played an important role, is evident in some of Scholem's discussions: "The spread of Lurianic Kabbalism with its doctrine of Tikkun . . . could not lead but to an explosive manifestation of all the forces to which it owed its rise and its success."[82]

In other words, Lurianic Kabbalah was portrayed as having become imbued with eschatological issues, though the advent of the Messiah himself was recognized to be marginal for the Lurianic corpus. Rather, this messianism is only implicit, embodied in the Kabbalistic concept of reparation, restoration, or *tiqqun*,[83] and it is not paralleled, according to Scholem, by anything similar in the previous versions of Kabbalah. By and large, Kabbalistic messianism is based on the assumption that the cumulative efforts of the whole Jewish nation to amend or repair the primordial metaphysical catastrophe, the breaking of the vessels and its deleterious repercussions, by the performance of the commandments according to their Kabbalistic intentions, are paramount for the advent of the redemption.

The final segment of the second stage is marked by the dominance of the Sabbatean and Frankist movements, acute forms of messianism fueled by the Lurianic version, which was disseminated to the masses during the third and fourth decades of the seventeenth century. During this period, messianism was not only a Kabbalistic and relatively esoteric form of mystical ideology or lore, but also a mass movement that at the center of Jewish life all over the Jewish world.

In the third stage, Hasidic mysticism, messianism was neutralized as the result of the fears of the pernicious consequences of the messianic outburst in Sabbateanism and Frankism. Instead, according to Scholem's view, a new form of eschatology emerged, the individual redemption, which did not exist in Judaism before the middle of the eighteenth century.[84] Its reform was to exchange the Lurianic *tiqqun,* the reparation of divinity, which Scholem saw as fraught with a tremendous messianic cargo, for the concept of *devequt,* adherence to or union with God, which was thought to have been free of any messianic connotation.[85]

Consequently, in Scholem's oeuvre there are three phases of relations between these two major forms of experiences in Jewish mysticism: indifference, synthesis, and neutralization. Each phase, according to Scholem's historiography, is well defined chronologically.In the second and third phases the particular relations between messianism and mysticism were conditioned by specific historical events, and it is reasonable to speak of them as reactions that shaped, according to Scholem, the nature of the different attitudes of the Jewish thinkers to messianism. In other words, to the extent messianism penetrated Jewish mysticism, it was part of a need to respond to the challenges imposed by history, but not essentially the result of the inner development of either Kabbalah or messianism. The interaction between messianism and Kabbalah involves, according to Scholem's historiography, a shift from an individualistic religious mentality toward a nationalistic one which includes the apocalyptic elements as part of the debate regarding the fate of the Jewish nation within history.

It is this move towards recapturing the importance of the apocalyptic eschaton for the Kabbalists that reintroduces, according to Scholem, the more collective aspects of messianism in the general economy of Kabbalah. Viewed from such a perspective, Hasidism became a deviation from the line espoused by postmedieval Jewish mysticism, since apocalyptic messianism had earlier played a vital role in the shaping the course of Jewish history.[86] Interested as he was in history, in the question of the Jewish self-definition by comparison to Christianity, and in apocalypticism per se, Scholem conceived of the messianic elements as predominantly a collective phenomenon. Indeed, this is the case when he addressed the messianic movements, though the very resort to this term, especially as it appears in the title of Aescoly's book *The Messianic Movements in Israel,* is often problematic. On the other hand, the collective aspects of some important manifestations of messianism in Judaism should not be neglected or marginalized. The following proposal is therefore intended to address decisive moments of inner experiences that may precede the emergence of these collective manifestations.

Pre-Kabbalistic Jewish Forms of Messianism

THE treatment of messianic concepts and figures in Kabbalah and Hasidism conspicuously depends on earlier concepts of messianism, which evolved from the biblical, rabbinic, and Jewish philosophical literatures. Therefore, a brief survey of those concepts of messianism that inspired and nourished some Jewish mystical medieval and premodern developments is in order.[1]

Biblical Models of Messianic Figures

Three models of messianic phenomena may be distinguished in the biblical literature:[2] (1) the Messiah as a person who maintains order—a king, priest, or (rarely) prophet—and who functions in the present; (2) the Messiah as an eschatological figure who will come in the future and typically is an Israelite King;[3] (3) apocalyptic "messianism," which does not resort to the use of the term *mashiyaḥ* and which can be called "diffuse-redemption hope."[4]

According to several biblical discussions dating from the pre-exilic period, the term *mashiyaḥ* is related to the special status of the Israelite king or to that of a priest, who were anointed in order to assume office. Thus, expressions like *kohen mashiyaḥ* refer to someone who fulfills, in the immediate present, the role of a priest.[5] Likewise, the king is referred to as "the anointed of YHWH," *meshiyaḥ YHWH,*[6] because the rite of anointment was prerequisite to the living king's fulfilling the royal role.[7] Anointment promoted a person to the sacral sphere of superhuman being, protected by God, and any harm to him would be perceived as a kind of *blesse majesté*. The very act of unction conferred, according to some interpretations, magical powers upon the new king.[8]

The cultic background of the institution of king has been the subject of many scholarly discussions and controversies.[9] There does appear to be a general acknowledgment, however, that there was an ideology of biblical kingship, dealing with central figures, especially that of the anointed king, and that the cultic role of the oriental king was primarily to maintain the given social and cosmic order:[10] "The king is thus the representative of the gods on earth, the steward of sovereignty, and he is the channel through which blessing and happiness and fertility flow from the gods to men."[11] According to some scholars, the anointed king as portrayed in Psalms 2 and 89 and the books of Samuel and Kings not only was a political ruler, a chieftain elected by the people, but also acquired semidivine status by the acts of election, filial adoption, and enthronement that were preceded by the act of anointment. He was seen as responsible for the blessing necessary to ensure the regular course of the natural processes as well as the well-being of his people. He served, as S. Mowinckel has noted, as a channel of the divine blessing onto the lower world: "The king receives the promises of blessing and the power of blessing which are to benefit the whole congregation."[12] This mythical-magical role was later attenuated in some parts of the Bible.

The ancient Near Eastern and Mesopotamian sources describe a type of king who was a conservative figure par excellence, because his cultic role was to ensure the preservation or the continuation of the structured present into the immediate future. The mythical aspect of this function is paramount, while a historical orientation, dealing with the redemption of the king's nation in a future time, plays at most a marginal role. The king is described by some scholars as a part of cosmic processes and also as an active participant in these processes. This ritual function of the king is part of a more comprehensive mythical vision of the world, which may be considered intrinsically alien to eschatology (S. B. Frost) or even utterly anti-eschatological, though it has become, as Mowinckel has asserted, the very matrix of later eschatology.[13]

There are striking similarities between some descriptions of the medieval Messiah and the more magical-mythical understanding of the king in the ancient period as expressed in some biblical texts. In certain cases, such as the view that the king is a channel for transmitting power to others, scholars' findings are astonishingly close to the mystical and mythical conceptions of the ideal type of Messiah in later Jewish texts.

In other biblical sources this cosmic-ritualistic role has been substantially reduced in favor of a more political one. After the Babylonian exile, however, the term *mashiyaḥ*, which had previously stood for the anointed king who played the conservative role, gradually starts a rather different career. It no longer stands for the present king who secures the political and natural order as it is, but for the future king, the one who will restore the splendor of the old days to its pristine state, or to an ideal, utopian condition. But insofar as the biblical view of the future king is concerned, he is destined nevertheless to play his part in history. As Aage Bentzen, summarizing Mowinckel's view, put it: "He comes *in* history, called by the God of history, *not* at the end of history and of time, between the aeons."[14]

The move from the ritual-performing and present-ruling king, sometimes referred to as the anointed, *mashiyaḥ,* to a political savior who will come in history, has made yet one more move, "from experience to hope";[15] that is, it has been eschatologized.[16] Thus, though coming in future historical time, the king-Messiah does not destroy history but rather restores an old regime. Here the conservative and restorative drives are cooperating.

The *mashiyaḥ* is often viewed in ancient Jewish sources as the apocalyptic redeemer. While the two models of kingship are explicitly connected to the term Messiah, the third, eschatological model, which assumes the advent of a figure who will not only transcend history but also destroy it, was not so linked to that term in the Bible. This means that the major role of the apocalyptic Messiah figure has been conceived now to be instrumental in radically transcending present history, viewed as a negative state of affairs, by obliterating it. The fallen order, or the present historical one, is to be undone by the advent of this figure. Hence, it is not a continuation of the mythical order that the Messiah seeks, but rather a rupture, or a more radical innovation or re-creation This Messiah does not rely on ritual as the main avenue of activity but rather takes political action, wages war against the enemies of God, who are also the enemies of his people. This is an apocalypse, which is at the same time a much more utopian eschatology than the second one. The emergence of an apocalyptic mode of hope has been explained by S. B. Frost and Martin Buber as the synthesis between an amythical eschatology and a ritualistic myth. As Frost observed, "eschatology only took on its mythological dress in the time of the Exile."[17]

The fateful concept of the suffering servant played an important role in the apocalyptic tradition in exile.[18] This duality of a political role in the future (according to the two last models) versus a much more priest-like one in the present, as in the first model, of restoring the degraded present order versus sparking a national renewal, has remained part of the significance of the term *mashiyaḥ.* The two phases of the evolution of the term remained embedded in the biblical literature that has become part of the canonic heritage of Judaism. Further developments of the messianic complex of ideas put a stronger emphasis upon the hope, the future-oriented aspect of the Messiah or of the messianic figures, rather than on the original present-oriented aspect.

Common to those three models is the national function of the Messiah, who plays these various roles not in privacy but as the representative of the community, the figure responsible for its well-being either in the present or in some remote future. In some instances, the Messiah has been conceived also as the representative of the divine into this world.[19] The very fact that the phrase *meshiyaḥ YHWH* recurs in the sources show that a special connection between him and God. This nexus could sometimes be stronger and richer, as it later became in Christian theology, in the ecstatic Kabbalah and Sabbateanism, or, less evidently, in some other cases in Jewish sources, though such a view is found also in the rabbinic literature, where the Messiah is described as one of the three entities designated by the Tetragrammaton.[20]

The special powers with which he is invested, however, and the cosmic roles he plays demonstrate that being the Messiah is not only a matter of a person's deliberate choice but also of his special nature. In the apocalyptic literature, both in the late biblical books, such as Daniel, and in some intertestamental writings, the messianic figure, though not the term *mashiyaḥ*, is connected with the concept of the Son of Man, and the metaphysical or transcendental aspects of this personality has become more evident.[21] In this phase, he is much more a supernatural figure, living in a supernal world and just waiting to enter into history. His preexistence, and not only his election, assumes a divine nature. After the eschatologization of the figure of the Messiah, a remythologization took place in the later biblical sources, in Jewish apocalypses, and in Christianity. The supernatural entered the discourse, not in a ritualistic enactment that will preserve the order, but in a strong figure whose extraordinary powers will shatter it.[22] Nevertheless, as S. Talmon reminds us, the general picture in the different phases of the biblical literature is that "the spiritual dimension of Jewish messianism continued to manifest itself in historical realism and societal factuality."[23]

Yehezkel Kaufmann, in his monumental *Golah ve-Neikhar,* proposed to sharply differentiate between biblical eschatology, which is focused upon the redemption of the Jewish nation, and soteriology, by which he means the redemption of gods, prevalent in the ancient Middle Eastern mythologies.[24] This emphatic categorization puts in high relief the turn away from the biblical eschatology, visible in the rabbinic and some Kabbalistic versions of redemption, which incorporate both eschatological and soteriological dimensions. The later developments in Jewish eschatology accentuate the soteriological elements, which in some mystical systems became quite dominant. It should be emphasized that though many eschatological discussions focus upon the figure of the

Messiah, in the Bible there are numerous "diffuse" views of redemption, which are concerned more with the state of things to be attained than with the persona of the Messiah.[25]

Jon Levenson has described two different tendencies, relevant to our discussion, which are found in the biblical corpus: the royal ideology and the Sinaitic one.[26] The former is concerned with divine intervention in history, while the latter emphasizes the effect of the performance of the divine commandments. Charles Mopsik has elaborated on this distinction, whereby Sinaitic ideology would represent the substratum for the further development of the theurgical Kabbalah, while royal ideology would be more consonant with the medieval ecstatic Kabbalah. Indeed, the apotheotic impulse, similar to the theory of kingship in Mesopotamia, where the king was thought to have been adopted by God, is central to the development of Jewish mysticism, especially in the Heikhalot literature, ecstatic Kabbalah, Sabbateanism, and Hasidism, whereas the theophanic mode, reminiscent of the Egyptian view of the king as God, is more operative in the theosophical-theurgical Kabbalah.[27]

The Messiah in Rabbinic Literature

The more articulated discussions regarding the Messiah and the messianic era appear quite late, in the Amoraic period. Earlier, in the Qumran literature[28] and the Mishnaic tracts, the extant material is scant and the status of the Messiah and messianism precarious. Though sometimes—in the Mishnaic literature—the idea of a salvific figure who will produce the eschaton is found, it is only marginally addressed by the bulk of this literature. Interestingly enough, immediately after the destruction of the Temple, and in a period when the revolt of Bar Kokhbah still was quite fresh in memory, the canonical Jewish literature did not devote notable descriptions and analyses to the nature of the redeemer and to the course of events that will restore the ancient glory of Israel. As several scholars have already pointed out, the apocalyptic vision of the redeemer was quite in the shadow in the writings of the earliest rabbinic circles.[29] Jacob Neusner has sensitively described their attitude: that the Messiah is a figure who is "neither to be neglected nor to be exploited."[30] In a period of a deep restructuring of Jewish life after the destruction of the Temple, as the mishnaic period was, the cultivation of an restorative, utopian, or revolutionary ideology, which would project the focus of religious activity into the future, could evidently disturb the constructive efforts of the elite to offer an alternative to the ritualistic version of the second Commonwealth cult, with the temple at the center. The concerns were much more with the present, and with the future as an organic extension of the present, to be shaped by the regulations of Halakhah. At the same time, the distinct messianic nature of emerging Christianity, which could hardly escape the attention of the Jewish authors, might have inhibited an elaboration of eschatological issues in those areas of Jewish speculation where Christianity became influential.

We should keep in mind, however, that the talmudic-midrashic literature is only rarely interested in discussing in detail metaphysical or theological issues. It is reticent to elaborate the nature and structure of the divine retinue, of hypostatical entities and preexisting beings. The scantiness of the material related to the transhistorical Messiah is typical of the more this-worldly attitude of this genre of literature, which is mainly concerned with fleshing out a legal system. In any case, the importance of repentance for the coming of the Messiah is a lasting contribution to the messianic constellation of ideas.[31]

In the post-mishnaic Jewish bodies of literature, there are three major types of writings wherein the messianic ideas play a notable role: the talmudic-midrashic literature, the Heikhalot literature, and popular apocalyptic literature. Roughly speaking, these three literary corpora were composed in the same period, between the third and the eighth centuries. Again, it seems that the geographical areas of composition and the influences upon these kinds of literature overlap: Jews in the Orient residing in Palestine, Babylonia, and in the Byzantine empire. In the talmudic treatises, apocalyptic messianic ideas received much greater prominence than in the earlier corpora. The reasons for this resurgence in describing the Messiah and his functions are various. The talmudic literature allows more space to legendary material, thereby ensuring a more extensive treatment of the Messiah. The myths related to him are much more salient for masters indulging in the Midrash than for those who more inclined to legalistic topics, as in the tannaitic literature.[32] As far as the Babylonian Talmud is concerned, the inhibitions related to discussing messianic issues that may resemble Christian theology were only rarely relevant. Writing in Babylonia, its authors were less conversant with Christian thought and less aware of the possible dangers of Christian proselytizing activity.

Talmudic thought is complex and variegated, consisting of sometimes quite divergent ideas and views, as we see with respect to the Messiah. Though a talmudic master would only rarely deny the existence and the future advent of the Messiah, the centrality of this figure for the eschatological events nevertheless differs from one trend of talmudic thought to another. There is a certain proclivity to attribute the beginning of the messianic era to the moral behavior of the generation. Extreme pictures of the human depravation that will precede the advent of the Messiah—or, on the contrary, the merits that characterize humanity in that generation—are attempts to attenuate the unexpected coming of the redeemer and to portray it as an event unrelated to religious activity. In this literature it is religious behavior that determines the advent, not the unknown, "irrational" divine decree, as in some of the rabbinic sources. The reference to the merits or sins of the Jews as a condition for the advent or deferral of the messianic era is intended to align the messianic outbursts with a more predictable behavior, which at the same time reinforces the importance of the ritual as the most sublime form of behavior.[33]

This move away from an emphasis on the unknown grounded in the divine will toward a more ordered structure of reality offered opportunities to mold the vague Jewish eschatological ideas into new models. Apocalyptic messianism, dealing primarily with the destruction of a fallen order, gave way to forms of religiosity which strive more toward instruction about a stable, or at least perfectible, order. Some of the mystical messianisms we shall inspect therefore shift the focus away from the future and toward the present. It seems that these alignments reduced the dramatical role of the messianic persona, sometimes ascribing a greater role to the common effort of the whole generation. Thus, in lieu of the divine will and the unpredictable arrival of the great warrior, both acting oftentimes violently, the new forms of messianism adopted more detailed manners of behavior that would produce more predictable results.

Nevertheless, the most evident characteristics of the talmudic concepts of the Messiah are still apocalyptical. The talmudic and the few popular apocalyptic treatments of the Messiah have some important features in common: the Messiah is a national figure, namely a descendant of an elite Jewish line, that of King David, and his main purpose is to save the children of Israel. He is not supposed to save all the nations or to restore the world to a state of pristine harmony, or to help the divine presence, the *shekhinah,* to return to her former state. In this literature the redemption of the Jews alone is the main purpose of the eschaton; there is very little that resembles the universalistic attitude of the Christian savior, the Muslim Mahdi, or the Buddhist Bodhisattva. The Messiah was commonly understood in those texts to be a flesh-and-blood person, mainly a warrior and a king, though in some cases also a scholar. The recurrence of the phrase *ha-melekh ha-mashiyaḥ* testifies to this more mundane conception of this figure. He does not embody the revenge of the Jews on the other nations (*goyim*), though he is instrumental in this expected event. In principle, the dominant concept of the Messiah in these literatures was not simply the personification of an aspiration of a certain group of people, though such an aspiration is closely connected to the Messiah's activity. Though his personality was not worked out in detail, the emphasis on his activities still reflects the political aspirations of the biblical sources. Though a more modern approach to these texts may read (correctly, in some instances) this figure and its roles as both embodying and symbolizing aspirations of different layers of Jews, a symbolic attitude is not evident in these texts.

The Messiah was conceived in some rabbinic sources as part of the course of human history, more exactly, he is related to the end of this form of history, though his existence, or sometimes also his preexistence, transcends mundane reality. He exists in that supernal realm where all the cherished values of the people of Israel are located: the Temple, the altar, the divine chariot, the souls of the righteous.[34] The preexistence of the Messiah seems to convey the idea that his person represents a dimension of hyperreality which surpasses the temporary vicissitudes of history. The basic framework of reference for the understanding of the role and nature of the Messiah is history, and not some systematic type of metaphysics, ontology, or psychology. The early medieval Jewish writers were not interested in the psychology of the Messiah as an individual.[35] He was perceived as giving expression to the vicissitudes of the nation without, however, becoming the personalization of those sufferings, even when he was described as the suffering servant. He participates in but does not personify the fate of the nation, as the king in the rituals of the Near Eastern religions did. An absent king, he is nevertheless often described as suffering, though not atoning for the sins of the children of Israel. In lieu of the annual akitu rite, which was performed in ancient Mesopotamia in the presence of the king and with his visible participation as a major actor, the rabbinic New Year ritual was still interested in a king and his coronation, but it is now God that takes the main role in the liturgical literature of post-biblical Judaism. The king-Messiah, the older actor in the New Year rite, remained a viable figure, but he was separated from the actual ritual, though he is described as restoring the Temple service in the eschaton. In other words, if the myth-and-ritual understanding of sacral royalty is correct in regards to the ancient Israelite kings, in the rabbinic literature the myth of the Messiah has been separated from the ritual that accompanied him in the New Year festival.

In most of the rabbinic sources, the Messiah, like the ancient kings, is described as active on the public plane: he does not restrict his activity to the redemption of a single person or of a small congregation or sect, but is destined to save all the righteous of the nation as a whole. Since he is not a personal savior, as a rule, ordinary people play no significant role in the eschatological drama of the talmudic-midrashic literature—one reason for the absence of the particular traits of this figure. The antimessianic figure Armilus, the Jewish counterpart of the Antichrist[36] is depicted in much more vivid colors, and sometimes extensive descriptions of his origins, countenance, and personality arise in the popular apocalyptic treatises.

In the popular apocalyptic literature, collected and edited in Even Shmuel's *Midreshei Ge'ullah,* the Messiah is understood to be far more crucial to the redemption drama, and the eschatological events are depicted in much more apocalyptic colors. The events preceding redemption, the so-called signs of the Messiah, *'otot ha-mashiyaḥ,* preoccupy the anonymous writers of the apocalyptic texts much more than they did their predecessors, the authors of the earlier talmudic-midrashic and Heikhalot texts. The impact of the apocalyptic literature is obvious in a range of books, including those having Halakhic orientations, such as *Maḥzor Vitri.* In general, the later literature seems to be open to a much wider spectrum of questions.

A recurrent figure in the apocalyptic literature, whose eschatological role has not drawn due attention from scholars, is the archangel Metatron. Though some of its feature reflect earlier traditions, its emergence in Jewish angelology as the prince of the divine countenance was a momentous development that was destined to influence some interesting themes in later messianism. Meanwhile it should be mentioned that in several apocalyptic treatises, like *Sefer Zerubbavel, Nistarot deR. Shime'on bar Yoḥai,* and the *Prayer of R. Shime'on bar Yoḥai,* Metatron is the angelic mentor of the apocalyptic figures in search of the date of the Messiah's advent. The richness of the traditions related to Metatron—he is variously portrayed as possessing qualities similar to God's and at the same time as suffering punishment by pulses of fire—should be seen as part of a constellation of traditions which were appropriated by the different messianic paths in Kabbalah, for different purposes.

Apparently reflecting views found also in the ancient apocalyptic writings and in rabbinic and Heikhalot literature, the role of Metatron in the late apocalyptic literature, as well as in some later Jewish mystical works, is paramountly apocalyptic: he is not only the revealer of secrets in general but is the revealer of the time of the end. This eschatological function of Metatron remained important in some medieval constellations of messianic ideas. Metatron was integrated into the emerging mesocosmos, which was populated by intermediary agents, messengers, angels, and sefirotic powers that become more and more visible with the centuries that passed since the destruction of the first Temple. This ontologization of the Messiah, by its being projected on high, means also a significant process of dehistorization and depersonalization. Metatron's personalization within the angelic world was still not sufficient to create a full-fledged persona, and the Messiah, who was sometimes identified with the archangel, in fact lost some of his personal features in this process.

The utopian elements of the end of the days are reminiscent, as has been pointed out by Raphael Patai, of the role of the king as magician in the various ancient oriental cultures. Accepting the approach of the myth-and-ritual school,

Patai has drawn several significant parallels between the ancient visions of the king, who is the source of fertility and opulence, and the situation in the messianic days.[37] The messianic ideas that are patent in the ancient and early medieval texts have been studied incomparably more than subsequent developments.[38] The main reasons for this concentration are a profound concern with the ideas circulating during the formative period of Christianity and the great emphasis upon the rabbinic literature as the framework for later developments in Judaism. In the case of Judaism, however, in matters of theological thinking this overemphasis is quite problematic. Whereas Christian theology was shaped to a great extent in late antiquity, and thus the different ancient Christologies have been quite formative for the later developments, in Judaism the important formulations regarding theology were ushered in only during the high Middle Ages. In fact, most of the models, in addition to the apocalyptic one, were articulated before the end of the thirteenth century. Thus, the bulk of the different understandings of messianism still awaits fuller description and more subtle analysis. Throughout the different genres of rabbinic literature, Mishnah, Talmud, and Midrash, it is difficult to find conceptually consistent systems of thought on the topic of messianism. They vary between an emphasis on the apocalyptic and a more spiritual understanding of this phenomenon.[39]

Messianism in Heikhalot Literature and Ḥasidei Ashkenaz

In the two primary stages of Jewish mysticism preserved in Hebrew, within the Heikhalot literature and the writings of the Ḥasidei Ashkenaz, mystical experiences were not given to messianic interpretation. My concern, however, is not whether there are messianic discussions in a mystical literature, but whether the messianic discussions are significantly related to the mystical theories and praxis. From this point of view, neither of these two schools of mysticism have produced even one famous messianic personality who played an active role on the stage of history. Despite a certain amount of interest in eschatology that can be detected within the Heikhalot literary corpus, only seldom was the mystical voyage into the supernal worlds employed in order to attain knowledge of the end of days. It is difficult to find a significant messianic interpretation for actual ascent to the heavens or for the mystical experiences undergone there by "the contemplators of the chariot." Such apotheoses are presumably indicative of personal redemption than components of a messianic drive. In any case, precise messianic terminology does not occur in these contexts.[40] Two Messiahs do appear in *Heikhalot Rabbati,* where R. Ishmael ascends in the divine chariot in order to inquire about the eschatological plans of God.[41] If, however, direct contributions to the constellation of messianic ideas cannot be detected in this literature, its general atmosphere contributed to the formation of concepts that become part of later Jewish messianism. I refer to the rich angelological speculations that populate this literature: angels and other divine figures form a mesocosmos, acting in two different manners.

On the one hand the mesocosmos represents the divine in its relationship to man; that is, angelophany serves theophany. On the other hand, as the transformation of Enoch into Metatron demonstrates, it is the locus for human ascent and the place the transformed mystic reaches—the place of apotheosis. The emergence of a median world, mythic in some of its characteristics, facilitated the commerce between man and God as it reformulated many of the earlier divine interventions in human affairs into angelic missions. The divine intervention in history was now attributed to the Messiah as part of a theophanic mode, or myth, but it also allowed the mystic who ascends on high either to identify with the Messiah, as we shall see in the case of Abulafia and the way Sabbatai Tzevi was described, or at least to converse with the Messiah after a mystic's successful ascent on high, as in the case of the Besht. Therefore, the extension of the divine nature to a mesocosmic transcendent entity having redeeming powers could, and did, serve both apotheotic and theophanic purposes. A certain type of angelology emerged which is of great importance both for some forms of Jewish mysticism and messianism and for some forms of ancient Christology.

As Shlomo Pines has pointed out, already in the second century a special theory about the nature of angels has been formulated in a Jewish group. According to this view, angels are beings that emanate from God, but they are not separated from Him when sent to perform a mission. These angels were conceived of as an extension of God, which retreat within the divine source after accomplishing their mission. The assumption of the existence of a continuum between God and some of the angels is paramount not only for a better understanding of ancient Jewish angelology, but also for the more adequate apprehension of Kabbalistic theories of emanation as an inner divine process. The relation between Metatron and God should be understood against the background of this conception.[42] Thus, Metatron as the angel of the divine countenance is organically related to this divine limb and as such serves the theophanic function of the divine face in the Bible.[43] This theory, as described by Justin Martyr, differs from the type of speculation common in the Heikhalot literature and testifies to the complexities and diversities of the earlier Jewish theologies and angelologies.

Aside from this apocalyptic literature, the Jewish mystical literature that is closest to some of the elements of the Heikhalot literature is the voluminous works composed in the late twelfth and early thirteenth centuries in the Rhineland. In this vast corpus, penned by the so-called Ḥasidei Ashkenaz or the pious of the German territories, the messianic elements are peripheral issues. Though formulated by a group of writers deeply concerned with personal eschatology and ascetic ways of life more strict than the prescriptions of Halakhah, the role of the Messiah was not put into relief. The Hasidic sect sought personal achievement of a beatific vision in the next world rather than an immediate national salvation in this one.[44] One of the most important statements related to messianism is in this passage from *Sefer Ḥasidim:*

> If you see one making prophecies about the Messiah, you should know that he deals deeds of witchcraft and deeds related to demons or with the deeds related to the divine name. And because they [the deeds] bothered the angels, they tell him about the Messiah, so that he will be disclosed[45] in public, that he has bothered the angels and at the end he will be shamed and despised by the world because he bothered the angels or the demons, which come to teach him the calculations and the secrets to his shame and to the shame of those who believe in him, for no one knows anything about the coming of the Messiah.[46]

The opposition to calculations and other occult means to learn about the advent of the Messiah is quite explicit and well taken by scholars. What I am interested in here is not so much the Hasidic attitude to messianism but the testimony it adduced concerning the prophecies about the coming of the Messiah. This piece of evidence, together with a testimony dealing with a prophet that emerged in the Slavonic territories as well as a similar event in France,[47] points to a popular messianic efflorescence. Although known by the Ashkenazi elite, they did not give expression to any form of acceptance of these prophecies. I am more concerned, however, with what we can learn from the above passage about magic and messianism. What was made public by the prophets are messianic calculations; the accusation concerning magic is speculation by the Ashkenazi masters, who would like to restrict the apocalyptic elements by relegating them to the domain of forbidden lore. Thus, though I do not doubt the existence of the apocalyptic rumors and events, and I recognize the possibility that magic was involved in messianic calculations, I am inclined to minimize the importance of the above quotation for the emergence of a significant link between magic and messianism. Though this linkage is clearly made by the author of *Sefer Ḥasidim,* it is far from certain that it reflects an actual practice. I would like to stress a point already made explicit by Scholem,[48] that both these genres of mystical literature crystalized, each of its own accord, about two centuries after some of the most bitterly tragic episodes in Jewish history. The Heikhalot literature developed after the destruction of the second Temple and the doomed Bar-Kokhbah rebellion, whereas the writing down of the esoteric teachings of the Ḥasidei Ashkenaz was preceded by the massacre of whole Jewish communities in the year 1096 in Germany, even the slaughter of the family of the most important writer of this group, R. Eleazar of Worms.[49] Nevertheless, these Jewish mystics, unlike some of their contemporaries who were much less mystically oriented, were not inclined to messianic interpretations of those events, and in their works discussions of messianism are quite moderate. Under pressure to convert or die, Jews understood the alternative of martyrdom in terms of precipitating the apocalyptic eschaton by the very acts of self-sacrifice, which were imagined to be able to hasten the divine wrath upon the Christians.[50]

An anonymous treatise dedicated to the enumeration of the seventy names of the archangel Metatron, *'Ain Shemot shel Metatron* or *Sefer ha-Ḥesheq*, combines what seems to me to be much earlier mythologoumena with some theories characteristic of Ḥasidei Ashkenaz. Though in the extant versions of the book messianic motifs are rare, these scanty remarks are nevertheless reflect much older ideas. Moreover, this small magical treatise was known, apparently in another version, by an important messianic mystic, Abraham Abulafia. The discussions of Metatron in this treatise include numerous references to the archangel's function as high priest—for example at paragraphs 1, 6, 55, 56, 59, 67, and 73, and more implicitly in paragraph 58. Also the references to messianic issues in paragraphs 6, 7, and 52 seem to show a greater concern with messianism than one typically finds in this period. I am most concerned, however, with a discussion that occurs in paragraph 59:

> YHWH WHYH, in gematria *Ben*, because he was a man, who is Enoch ben Yared. Yaho'el, in gematria *be-Yam* [by the sea], because it is written [Exodus 14:2] "before it [Nikheḥo] shall you encamp by the sea," and from Nikheḥo emerges [by anagram] Hanokh, because he revealed himself by the sea. And in gematria *ba-kol*, because he bears the entire world, and he is relying on the finger on God. And the Tetragrammaton is hinted at two times twenty-six and also the gematria of *'Eliyahu* [is 52], also Yaho'el also *Ke-Lev* [namely, like a heart], because it is the heart of the world, and all the [divine] names are hinted at, because it is appointed over the Torah, and the Torah commences with Bet and ends with Lamed . . . and it is the prince of the world, and in gematria it is *'Ana'*, because it is the high priest, and when the high priest was pronouncing *'Ana'*, he was first calling to the Prince of the Face, and this is the meaning of *'Ana'* and only then pray to the supreme Name.[51]

Metatron, the main subject of this passage, is referred to by the angelic theophoric name Yaho'el, a theme that will reverberate in Abraham Abulafia's mystical messianology. The salvific nature of this angel is hinted at by its revelation by the sea, the most salvific moment in the whole Pentateuch. There can be no doubt that Metatron-Yaho'el reflects the divine intervention under the guise of an angel that bears the divine name. This passage reflects the two main tendencies I have hinted at: apotheotic, as represented by the transformation of a man into an angel, and theophanic, as suggested by the redemptive revelation by the sea.

Indeed, the proposal to detect in the main angelic manifestation a redemptive role is obvious from another Ashkenazi text as well, dealing with the redemption from Egypt. Commenting on Exodus 12:42, "It is a night of watchfulness to YHWH, for bringing them out from the land of Egypt," an anonymous Ashkenazi author writes that the verb *le-hotziy'am* 'for bringing them out' "is numerically equivalent to *ve-zeh hayah Yaho'el mal'akh,* because the Holy One, blessed be He, has sent Yaho'el, the prince of the face, to bring them out, as it is said [ibidem, 23:21], 'and the angel of his Face had rescued them.' "[52] We may conclude that the biblical verses dealing with the redemption from Egypt, and involving the intervention of angels, had been thought of as typologically redemptive, as pointing to the future redemption, as we learn from fragmented discussions in Ashkenazi writers, especially R. 'Efrayyim ben Shimshon. The Ashkenazi literature should be seen as an intermediary corpus that preserved fragmented traditions concerning the ancient angel Yaho'el as instrumental in redemption of the people of Israel. Such traditions diverge dramatically from the view perpetuated in the regular version of the *Passover 'Aggadah,* which conspicuously opposed the redemptive role attributed to angels and messengers in the redemptive processes related to the Exodus from Egypt.

Neoplatonism in an Eschatological Garb

While the earlier forms of messianism in Judaism may be described as consonant with the primal, pre-axial forms of religiosity, in the Middle Ages some Jewish elitist groups became acquainted with views emanating from early Greek philosophers, especially Plato and Aristotle and their later interpreters. These approaches, which emphasize the individual and spiritual attitude toward intellectual and religious life, are part of what Karl Jaspers and others have designated "axial values," namely, attitudes emphasizing the more individual and mental experiences.[53] In the Jewish literatures under investigation here messianism went through one more phase—from the collective as the center of redemption to the individual. Among the ancient Greek philosophies, the Platonism and Neoplatonism nearest to the religious approaches to existence. The various concepts concerning the alienation of the soul, which descended into the exile of this material world, the soul's return to the source, or topics concerning contemplation and theurgy were more easier acceptable in the Muslim, Jewish, and Christian intellectual milieus. Beginning in the tenth century, the impact of Arabic Neoplatonism on Jewish thinkers became more and more visible, and in the eleventh century Shlomo ibn Gabirol, better known in the West as Avicebron, offered what is perhaps the most important Neoplatonic treatise composed in Europe. Ibn Gabirol apparently resorted to rather mild terms in order to describe the liberation of the soul from its captivity within the realm of corporeality; in the Latin translation of his mostly lost *Fons Vitae* he assumes that "science [or wisdom] and deed liberate the soul," a view that was often quoted in Hebrew translations, using a variety of Hebrew verbs for 'liberant': *ga'al, padah, paraq*.[54] These verbs have nothing to do with a national redemption or deliverance in a given time. Similar views can be found in the work of a twelfth-century thinker in Barcelona, R. Abraham bar Ḥiyya.[55] This conception of redemption as the combined effect of knowledge (or wisdom) and deeds had an influence on two thirteenth-century Kabbalists, R. Yitzḥaq ibn Latif[56] and his acquaintance R. Todros ben Joseph ha-Levi Abulafia, who adduces it already as the opinion of "few Kabbalists" who assume that the soul will "return to her source," apparently the third sefirah, Binah, by dint of "the deeds and wisdom."[57]

Not until the second part of the thirteenth century was a more obvious messianic vocabulary adopted in the context of Neoplatonic discourse. Resorting to a Plotinian passage which reached him through the mediation of the so-called *Theology of Aristotle*,[58] R. Yeda'yah of Beziers wrote in his *Commentary on the Talmudic 'Aggadot* that the study of the Torah is best achieved by someone who is ready to die for the sake of this study: "the intention is that he should kill all his desires. And likewise it is said that 'the Son of David will not come until the souls will be exhausted from the Body.' This means that no one can attain the perfection, designated by the name 'Shlomo ben David,' which is derived from Shalem [namely Perfect], before he exhausts all the forces of his body, [preventing] them from following his animal inclinations, and desist from dealing with his senses."[59] One of the classical appellations of the Messiah, "the son of David," is therefore understood as pointing not to a future redeemer, a scion of David, but to the actualization of an ideal behavior in the here and now.[60] Perfection on the personal, spiritual, and (implicitly) noetic level is the main attainment envisaged by resorting to the messianic title.

Later on, at the end of the fifteenth century in Florence, a much earlier pseudo-Empedoclean text strongly inclined to Neoplatonism has been interpolated by Yoḥanan Alemanno by introducing again the *Yevamot* dictum. The original text describes the more pure and spiritual existence of the soul in the "world of the intellect," where it functions in a more unified manner. Again, according to the pseudo-Empedoclean source, the world of the soul, in comparison to that of the intellect, is like a body. In this context we find the following glossa: "And I say . . . that this agrees with the view of those who keep the Torah, who say that 'The Son of David will not come until the souls will be exhausted from the Body.'[61] Their intention is to say that not until all the souls emanating from the Universal Soul, called Body in comparison with the Agent Intellect—which encompasses her in an intellectual manner—are exhausted will the souls [stemming] from the source of the Intellect, not from the Body, be emanated. Then the days of the Messiah will come."[62] This concept of the supernal Body is somehow part of the original text that has been glossed by Alemanno; on one occasion it stands for the relation between the individual and the universal soul.[63] It is probable that it is Alemanno who has transferred this type of relationship to that between the universal soul and universal intellect. In any case, Alemanno's assumption is that the spiritual emanation of the souls, characteristic of the ordinary situation, will be exchanged for another kind of generation of the souls, stemming from a higher source, that of the Universal Intellect. This spiritual state constitutes the days of the Messiah. This reading of the messianic days may be interpreted in historical terms as a defined period in the development of the cosmic order or as part of a certain form of existence, in a manner similar to that of R. Yeda'yah of Beziers. In any case, the two examples adduced above show that it is the spiritual rather than the national or political redemption that is addressed in this form of discourse. In a way reminiscent of the Neoplatonic contribution to the concepts of individual redemption in Sufism,[64] Neoplatonic sources informed these cases with a more individualistic interpretation of redemptive terminology.

On Maimonides's Messianism

A much more influential exposition of concepts of the Messiah than the Neoplatonic one is to be found in Maimonides' *Code of the Law,* which gives a more political and intellectual portrait of the messianic days.[65] Though dealing mainly with national salvation, the intellectual, contemplative ideal was nevertheless perceived by Maimonides to be the ultimate target of redemption. Attenuating the apocalyptic elements in the earlier Jewish sources, Maimonides moves closer to the Platonic ideal king—both a prophet and a philosopher—as portrayed in the Arabic versions of Plato.[66] Understood in terms derived from Aristotelian epistemology, the achievement of perfect intellection was presented as the *eudaemonia,* and the national independence was described as instrumental in allowing continuous immersion in contemplation. While in the Aristotelian understanding of messianism the intellect was the main organ of perfection, which was actualized by subduing the influence of the imaginative power, in the case of Neoplatonism and in some forms of Kabbalah[67] it is the separation of the spiritual from the corporeal, the *psychomachia,* that is envisaged as the most important salvific operation. The spiritualistic approach is much more evident in the extreme formulations of medieval Jewish Aristotelian philosophy, as in the cases of R. Moses ibn Tibbon and R. Levi ben Abraham, both late thirteenth-century Provençal figures, who said of the arrival of the age of forty: "then the intellect will manifest and the days of the Messiah will commence."[68] Maimonides' eschatology had a strong impact on many developments of Jewish messianic thought, including figures active in sixteenth-century Safed such as R. Ya'aqov Berav, and it remained a challenge for Sabbatean thinkers such as Abraham Michael Cardoso.

Some Medieval Jewish Messianisms: Encounters between Jewish and Greek Concepts

The two forms of soteriology discussed above, the Neoplatonic and Aristotelian one, constitute a bold departure from the earlier versions of Jewish eschatology, which were much more concerned with national rather than personal redemption. The earlier Jewish traditions are based on the assumption that the Messiah is either the extension of the divine into this world or the instrument of the will of God; thus the divine voluntaristic picture dominates the Jewish forms of discourse. It is the divine knowledge of the end, unfathomed by man, that is presupposed. Whether restorative, in the sense of recovering a religiously constituted order, or the eruption into history of a novel form of existence, the emphasis manifest in the pre-philosophical interpretations of the persona of the Messiah presupposes an active power, whose impact will surpass both the historical and the natural order.

With the absorption of philosophical explanations in some Jewish elitist circles, it is the concept of a more stable nature that emerged and contributed to very substantial qualifications of the earlier traditions about the nature of the Messiah and his age. Newly imported ideas encouraged the acceptance of solidified forms of order, which are evident in the different realms of existence: divine, natural and psychological; this became part of the speculative elitist literatures and had a dramatic impact, as seen above in the case of the philosophers. Even if the nature of man is initially imperfect in a given moment, according to the Greek view the potential for perfection was nevertheless found within nature, be it divine, natural, or psychological. This emphasis on potential perfection predominated in the Jewish speculative sources, mostly in the philosophical ones but also in some of the mystical ones.

The emphasis on various ideas of constancy in nature, which was accepted by some elite Jewish groups from Greek and hellenistic forms of thought, having been mediated by Arabic speculative literatures created new spaces of discourse within Jewish eschatology. Naḥmanides accurately formulated the stand of rabbinic thought when he claimed, in the context of the controversy over Maimonides' emphasis on nature, that "one who believes in the Torah may not believe in the existence of nature at all."[69] Now, the question was much less what is the hidden will of God, when will the national restoration take place, or how will the most important place of worship, the Temple, be rebuilt, but more the elaboration upon the spiritual aspirations of an elite. To a certain extent, this return to stability in some philosophical sources and (under their influence) among a few of the Kabbalists is congenial to the early rabbinic attitude toward messianism. Therefore, the order of the Torah was perceived by the early rabbis as offering the ideal way of life, which may in principle be superseded by an even more perfect performance of ritual and study in the messianic era. The emphasis on the perfection of the will of God as manifested in the revealed Scriptures could provide, and sometimes in the Middle Ages indeed provided, a certain stability similar to that inspired by the acceptance of the Greek forms of thought.

The philosophical and some of the mystical versions of medieval Jewish messianism reflect different encounters and syntheses between, on the one hand, the Jewish mild eschatology of some parts of the Bible and of the earlier rabbis, the apocalyptic fervor of some of the later rabbinic figures in the talmudic period, as well as more popular attitudes, and, on the other hand, the variety of Greek concepts of perfection. Thus, some Kabbalistic circles adopted more constant types of nature, sometimes identifying them with God and resorting to the numerical value of the consonants of the Hebrew words for God and nature, *'Elohim* and *teva'*, opening a long line of argument that would produce in Spinoza and some of his predecessors a more naturalistic and political form of messianism.[70] Therefore, the new ideas of nature, either when dealing with external reality or when describing the inner constitution of man, determine not only these respective planes of being but also a variety of religious topics that were part of those systems which turned out to be more "naturalistic"—among them messianism. In the confrontation between the will of God and the new ideas of nature, messianism underwent a dramatic change in the Middle Ages. Conjoined as it was to various concepts of nature that should be managed as part of the messianic events, messianism traveled from a strongly voluntaristic stream of phenomena to a variety of understandings that presuppose processes that strive to perfect the given state of things.

Early Kabbalah and Christian Medieval Eschatology

The two main forms of Kabbalah which emerged in medieval Europe, the theosophical-theurgical and the ecstatic, flourished in the same time and place as the most important form of Christian medieval eschatological literature, the Joachimite one.[71] Scholars have already suggested the possible impact of Joachim's thought and that of his followers' on Jewish mysticism, including eschatological issues. Gershom Scholem pointed out the possibility that the Kabbalistic *Sefer ha-Temunah* describes a theory of various cosmic eons and the corresponding changes in the canons, which is similar to Joachim's views.[72] However, Scholem's assertions that *Sefer ha-Temunah* was composed in early thirteenth-century Gerona or, according to his later proposal, late thirteenth-century Provence[73] are, in my opinion, conjectures; a better suggestion would locate the book in mid-fourteenth-century Byzantium.[74] Thus, *Sefer ha-Temunah,* influenced as it was by earlier Kabbalistic literature composed in Spain and elsewhere, was not composed in the areas affected by the Joachimist spiritualists.

A more detailed and specific proposal was put forward by Yitzhak Baer, who suggested the influence of the Joachimist literature on the later layer of the Zoharic literature, though the eschatological aspects of this influence are not so important.[75] Some of Baer's suggestions have already been challenged,[76] and there is indeed room for doubts insofar as other parts of the alleged influence are concerned. Furthermore, R. Abraham Abulafia's ecstatic Kabbalah, formulated for the first time in Catalonia and Castile, was elaborated much more in Italy, particularly Rome and Sicily, in the 1280s, a period that witnessed a great flourishing of Joachimism.[77] Yet despite the vicinity of time and space, it is difficult to pinpoint significant affinities between the two systems of thought. Thus, on the ground of existing studies, Joachimite eschatology had only marginal impact, if any, on the Kabbalistic forms of eschatology.[78] This tentative description may change with the discovery of new texts, but for the time being I see the emergence of the major models of Jewish mystical messianism in the thirteenth century as unrelated to direct influences of Joachimism.

On the Place of Apocalyptic Elements in Messianic Discussions

In the light of these observations, the apocalyptic elements in pre-Kabbalistic Jewish texts should be understood not as a constant and monolithic idea but as a model returning to Judaism and pulsating within it with varying intensity. These elements are marginal in, or even absent from, the ideology of the "present" royal Messiah of the Bible, more intense in the post-exilic prophetic literature, where they often moved to the center, less evident in early rabbinic literature but again gradually strengthening in the later rabbinic writings; they were again marginalized in many of the speculative corpora of elitist writings in the Middle Ages.[79] The fluctuating intensity of apocalyptic messianism corresponds, in some obvious cases, to the social setting of the groups that generated each kind of literature. In my opinion, the more elitist a certain group of thinkers is, the less perceptible the preponderance of these apocalyptic ingredients.[80]

A last point before embarking on the analysis of the main literary corpora is the underlying assumption that most of the existing modes of perceiving messianism were not only due to various circumstances that were, in some instances, decisive for their emergence. Though the nexus between cultural, historical, economic, and political circumstances and the creation and formulation of a certain model is quite plausible in principle, and therefore should be analyzed as an issue in itself, this historicistic approach should not become the center, and certainly not the single, approach to studying messianic and other spiritual phenomena.

Those modes, or models, survived the specific circumstances that coincided with and perhaps even influenced them; often they remained available, sometimes even vital and influential for many generations after their emergence. A more phenomenological inquiry, focusing on the conceptual structure informing these models, is quintessential for elucidating their subsequent significance of these models. Thus, over the centuries a gradual accumulation of messianic models, as well as the mystical ones to be identified and described in the following chapters, should be presupposed as a major and fundamental historical fact which confronted later thinkers and Messiahs more than the earlier ones. The panoramic approach to messianic themes and models, which has been proposed elsewhere as necessary for a better understanding of Hasidism[81] and the various attitudes toward language in Jewish mysticism,[82] is a *sine qua non* which should be adopted for the sake of a more nuanced scholarly attitude toward the sources. Messianisms, like many other topics in culture, are rarely the result of linear developments, and I propose to delineate a variety of currents and cross-currents for understanding the array of processes that constitutes the messianic constellation of ideas.

Abraham Abulafia: Ecstatic Kabbalah and Spiritual Messianism

The most prominent example of a profound synthesis of Kabbalah and messianism is embodied in the writings, experience, and life of Abraham Abulafia. Abulafia was the first Kabbalist to have seen himself explicitly, and apparently also publicly, as a Messiah. He is also the first Kabbalist whose messianic calling arose in exactly the same year as he commenced his Kabbalistic studies. He combined the mystical path in the forms of *via perfectionis* with a strong quest for apotheotic experiences, and regarded both apotheosis and theophany as having strong eschatological and messianic valences.

Abraham ben Shmuel Abulafia was born in Saragossa, in the province of Aragon, in the year 1240. While he was still an infant, his family relocated to Tudela. In 1260, two years after the death of his father, he left Spain for Acre, in the Galilee, in order to find the mythical Sambation River.[1] These were the very years of the Mongolian invasion of Syria and the land of Israel, a matter that was well known throughout Europe. It is quite possible that Abulafia thought, as did many others of his generation, that the Mongols were themselves the "hidden ones," *ha-genuzim,* the ten lost tribes of Israel reputed by legend to be dwelling beyond the Sambation River.[2] But Abulafia never journeyed past the town of Acre; nearby wars and the awareness, which could be more easily reached in the East, that the Mongols were not one of the lost tribes, apparently convinced him to abandon his quest. Instead he went back to Europe. While in Greece he married; thence he went to Italy, where he studied philosophy, specifically Maimonides' *Guide of the Perplexed,* in Capua, near Rome. Afterwards he arrived in Catalonia, where he was living around the year 1270.

This was the year in which he claims that he received a revelation in which he was commanded to go and seek an audience with the pope.[3] The revelation took place in Barcelona, where, in the same year when he claims to have begun to study the different commentaries on *Sefer Yetzirah,* apparently within a group of Kabbalists. These studies proved fateful for the development of Kabbalah as a whole and, specifically, for Abulafia's spiritual metamorphosis. He went on to develop a new conception of Kabbalah that he called variously "Prophetic Kabbalah" and "Kabbalah of the Names." The first title expresses the ultimate purpose of his Kabbalah, that is, to guide the initiate to an ecstatic experience which was sometimes described in the Middle Ages as prophecy; the second arises from the fact that the letters of the names of God play a major role in the technique that should lead the initiate to the ecstatic experience.

Abulafia's spiritual life can be sharply divided into pre-Kabbalistic and Kabbalistic phases. He was captivated by the mystical lore he had learned and, though never renouncing his philosophical views from the earlier period, he understood the whole range of Jewish thought and practice in the light of the ecstatic Kabbalah. An important question is whether the 1270 revelation was the result of Abulafia's resorting to certain techniques for reaching a mystical experience, or whether this revelation was a matter of divine grace. If the later explanation is preferred, then the messianic message not only precedes his involvement in mysticism and mystical techniques, but may also demonstrate Abulafia's concerted attempt to renew this form of experience. If the former possibility is ever proven by new documents, the messianic message will be seen as a single central aspect of ecstatic Kabbalah, though less, or even much less, its trigger. As I shall suggest later, it seems to me wiser to prefer the latter explanation.

Between the years 1280 and 1291 Abulafia was active almost exclusively on the island of Sicily, in Palermo and much more often Messina. In this most stable and creative period of his life, he produced the bulk of the literary legacy now in our possession. During these years he developed a following of students, among them R. Aḥituv of Palermo, one of the most learned men of Sicily. Abulafia's success in establishing a school devoted to the study of his Kabbalah and the survival of many of his writings are indeed causes for amazement. For during this period, some prominent Sicilian Jews had questioned Abulafia's messianic pretensions and turned to one of the giants of the Halakhah, as well as the spiritual leader of Spanish Jewry, R. Shlomo ben Abraham ibn Adret (known by the acronym Rashba), to decide the question: could Abulafia be the Messiah or a prophet as he claimed to be? The original version of the question and Rashba's responses are not extant, but from slightly later documentation we can reconstruct the course of the argument between the two figures. This dispute proved to be one of the first major polemics concerning Kabbalistic messianism during the Middle Ages.

The Rashba flatly denied Abulafia's claim to be the Messiah. He expressed this in a letter, now lost, which was sent to Palermo and shown to Abulafia's students. The students were taken aback by the sharp tone of the letter and presumed that it could not have been written by the Rashba. They showed it to Abulafia, who confirmed its authenticity. He sent a reply to a colleague of the Rashba's in Barcelona, R. Yehudah Salmon, who had been a student of Abulafia's in the early 1270s. In this epistle, entitled *Ve-Zot li-Yhudah,* written relatively late in his literary career, Abulafia develops an interesting rebuttal of certain Kabbalistic views embraced by some theosophical Kabbalists; this could well be the first heated controversy between the Kabbalists belonging to different schools. A prevalent belief of Kabbalists in Castile and Catalonia was that the essence of the divine realm was composed of ten *sefirot,* or divine powers. Abulafia describes the theosophical doctrines that are based on this view of the divine world as worse than the Christian doctrine of the Trinity. The Christians, he says, at least only believe in three divine hypostases, while those Kabbalists hold by ten.[4] This attack is without doubt a reaction to the stinging tone of the letter from the Rashba, who was himself a theosophical Kabbalist. Apparently, the Rashba answered Abulafia's attack in another missive to the Sicilians, but the argument stops there owing to the paucity of documentation. Another probable factor is that Abulafia died somewhere around 1291, and the Rashba, who outlived him by some fifteen or twenty years, was able to claim that he won the argument because he succeeded "in closing the doors before Abulafia." Still, we can conclude from the Rashba's own words that Abulafia was very influential in Sicily. This dispute, it must be emphasized, was between two Kabbalists and was, at least partially, concerned with the preference of one Kabbalistic system over another. Yet the central issue of the argument, as well as its starting point, was Abulafia's claim to be the Messiah and to prophesy.

This controversy had significant repercussions for the subsequent development of the Kabbalah in Spain, because in effect the ecstatic or prophetic Kabbalah of Abulafia was banned as a result of the firm opposition of the Rashba. Indeed, the Rashba apparently dealt with both the theoretical side of the problem, namely Abulafia's messianic pretensions, and with the practical repercussions of Abulafia's activities, expressly admitting that Abulafia almost managed to lead astray the Jews of Sicily. During that period, Sicily was a seat of wide-ranging Jewish cultural activity, mostly in the domain of philosophy. Abulafia's ability to attract students and win the admiration of some elite figures shows that he certainly possessed great intellectual capabilities.

Prophecy and Messianism

Unlike most of the eschatological Jewish literature of the early Middle Ages, some of Abulafia's writings belong to what has been described as prophetic eschatology. In his writings, and I assume in his spiritual life as well, prophecy and messianism were two branches that grew from the same trunk,[5] more precisely from the vision he had in Barcelona in 1270. It was in this very period that he started his Kabbalistic studies and ultimately went on to develop his own system. In a commentary on one of his prophetic compositions, *Sefer ha-'Edut* (Book of Testimony), he relates: "In the ninth year [nine years before composing this testimony] I was aroused by God to go to the great city of Rome, as I was commanded in Barcelona in the year of thirty."[6] This command resounds with strong messianic portent, since the journey to Rome was established, according to Naḥmanides, as a prerequisite of the coming of the Messiah. In a famous disputation held in Barcelona, Naḥmanides took the position that as a result of a directive from God, the Messiah will come before the pope and proclaim himself as such:

> For here it is not stated that he had arrived,[7] only that he was born on the day of the destruction [of the Temple]; for was it on the day that Moses was born that he immediately went to redeem Israel? He arrived only a number of days later, under the command of the Holy One Blessed Be He, and [then] said to Pharaoh: "Let my people go that they may serve Me."[8] So, too, when the end of time will have arrived the Messiah will go to the pope under the command of God and say: "Let my people go that they may serve Me," and until that time we will not say regarding him that he has arrived for he is not [yet] the Messiah.[9]

Naḥmanides clearly distinguishes between the one who was born and in the future will be the Messiah, and the Messiah's actual revelation due to the fulfillment of his mission, which would make him the actual Messiah.[10] This idea is also expressed by Abulafia when he says: "And he said that the Messiah will arrive immediately, for he is already born."[11] We may conclude that Abulafia also conceived of two stages in the career of the Messiah: his birth, when he apparently has been destined to be a Messiah, and his arrival. His birth makes him the Messiah *in potentia* and his arrival makes him the actual Messiah. The advent of the Messiah, formulated by Naḥmanides as part of a religious dispute with the Christians and by Abulafia as part of his self-perception as a messianic figure, is expressed in Hebrew by the verb *ba'*. This arrival at the end of time should also be understood as connected to the Messiah's appearing in the presence of the pope. This decisive act recalls not only Moses' coming into the presence of

Pharaoh but also the advent of the redemptive figure of Shiloh, described in Genesis 49:10 by the verb *ba'*, and of course the designation of Jesus as the Lord Who Cometh.[12]

According to some Jewish (including midrashic) sources, the Messiah is waiting, among the poor, in Rome.[13] Thus, it seems that Naḥmanides had good reason to use in his description of the coming of the Messiah the same verb in connection to the Messiah's coming to Rome. In fact, this is a typological approach that sees the future Messiah in terms of earlier similar events.[14] Unlike the confrontation between Moses and Pharaoh, however, Abulafia's perception of his mission to the pope is not so much as a power struggle or demonstration of superior magic as it is a spiritual contest between Kabbalah and Christianity—perhaps even the coronation of the Jewish Messiah by the Christian pope. If the Messiah was perceived as the king of the Jews, the possible implication of such a meeting would be that the pope would anoint him as he did other kings.

The proximity of prophecy and messianism in Abulafia's writings is not accidental. It underlines the strong bond between them and provides a rationale for the continued complimentary coexistence of these two conceptual entities. In a few places Abulafia even mentions prophecy and messianism in one breath. For example, he writes, "When I arrived at [the knowledge of] the Names, by my loosening of the bonds of the seals,[15] the Lord of All[16] appeared to me and revealed to me his secret and informed me of the end of the exile and of the time of the beginning of redemption. He compelled me to prophesy."[17]

The initial stage of preoccupation, expressed by the phrase "When I arrived at [the knowledge of] the Names" (that is, by his Kabbalistic practices), enabled Abulafia to free himself of the bonds of the material world; only thereafter was he graced with a revelation. Within this revelation lies the mystical experience Abulafia termed *prophecy*. It was only then that God revealed "to him the secret of the end of the exile and the time."

In other words, specific mystical techniques have facilitated a spiritual development which involves both a sharp mystical awareness, described here as the liberation of the conscience from the burden of corporeality, and an ensuing revelation that is fraught with messianic overtones. The text is based on a gematria that was crucial for Abulafia: *ha-kol*, according to the way I decode Abulafia's text, stands for five thousand and fifty, which corresponds to 1290, the year when Abulafia thought that the redemption, *ha-ge'ullah,* would come. The word *ha-ge'ullah* is numerically equivalent to fifty, another hint at the same year. The implication of the text is quite eschatological, as a precise time for the beginning of the redemption is mentioned. The apocalyptic themes, however, have been ignored. To believe Abulafia, the mystical technique and the loosing of the knots have preceded the revelation, which has an eschatological meaning.

Thus, in this period of his activity, mysticism is not seen as derived from the messianic awareness, but rather the messianic message is the culmination of a mystical path and achievement. This is also the picture one gets from the earlier writings of this Kabbalist: in the first books the messianic elements are absent, and only some years later do the messianic elements become more conspicuous, yet never do they become essential to Abulafia's Kabbalah.

The absence of the eschatological elements in some of Abulafia's writings does not invalidate the view that redemptive experiences are the culmination of the Kabbalistic way of life. Thus, prophecy (or ecstasy) and messianism should be seen as a more particular aspect of broader mystical phenomena in Abulafia's life and thought. For him prophecy stands for the more mystical spiritual processes—instances of *unio mystica,* epistemic or ontic—which are indeed conceived of as spiritually salvific, as well as for the reception of more precise revelations which are closer to eschatological prophecy. From this point of view, Abulafia is following tendencies found in Muslim illuministic philosophical forms of thought.

This type of relationship between messianism and ecstatic Kabbalah is not, however, the only plausible way to formulate the question. Indeed, the above proposal follows Abulafia's explicit stand, but the story might nevertheless have been more complex. Abulafia's visit to the Middle East in search of the Sambation can be seen as part of a messianic enterprise related to the ten lost tribes. Thus, long before entering the field of Kabbalistic studies, he at least flirted with messianism. I assume that though his first Kabbalistic studies may indeed have been divorced from messianic hopes, his success may have encouraged a return of his earlier aspirations. The rejection of the eschatological speculations in his earlier writings, with the exception of the revelation he reported in 1280 as having taken place in 1270, might have been part of his disillusion when learning that the Mongols are not the ten lost tribes.

In the early 1260s, while studying Maimonides' works, Abulafia could have been acquainted with the idea that the return of prophecy will precede the coming of the Messiah; given the Kabbalistic techniques to achieve prophecy, he could easily see this development as conductive to a messianic consciousness. In other words, the earlier messianic adventure might have created in him a form of consciousness that resurged in a much more sophisticated manner later, in the form of the mystico-messianic version. Such an explanation does not subordinate the mystical to the messianic but nevertheless presupposes that Abulafia's insistence on referring to his mystical experiences in terms of prophecy may have something to do with the prophecy-messianism nexus. Prophecy and messianism also appear together in a later work of Abulafia's, where the sequel between the mystical phase and the eschatological one fits this suggestion. Thus he writes:

> the prophet is necessarily called *mashiyaḥ*[18] because he is anointed with the supernal oil that is called "the oil of anointing" . . . with which he utilizes the Names. Actually the *mashiyaḥ* must possess two qualities: one, that he first be anointed by God with wondrous prophecy[19] and, two, that he continue to be consecrated by God and people who will hail him as their great king of all times and he will rule from sea to sea.[20] And this is all due to the great intensity of his clinging[21] to the divine intellect and his reception of the power in a strong manner as it was the matter of Moses, Joshua, David, and Solomon. And the issue of *mashiyaḥ* will be known by everyone, and this is the reason why there is no more need to announce here its issue, because he is destined to reveal himself shortly in our days.[22]

Here again there are two phases in the messianic enterprise. The first one consists of the prophet being called by the title *mashiyaḥ*. This stage is actually an expression of the identical nature of the mystical phenomenon and the messianic phenomenon. It is only after this anointment by God "with wondrous prophecy," namely after reaching a mystical experience, that the prophet is able to enter the second stage of being accepted by "people who will hail him as their great king of all times." Indeed, this resort to the image of the king is frequent in Abulafia's writings and is reminiscent of the royal ideology. We read, for example, in *Sefer Mafteaḥ ha-Tokheḥot:* "And Divine virtues are added to him until he speaks with the holy spirit, whether in his writing or with his mouth; on this issue it is said that this is in truth the king of kings of flesh and blood, as is said among people about a unique king of kings, that he alone and those like him have passed the boundary of humanity and cleaved in their lifetime to their God, and even more so when their natural and contingent matter dies."[23]

There can be no doubt that this statement treats of an apotheotic transformation which involves also a messianic perception of the king. The king appears to be none other than the *mashiyaḥ*. This spiritual phenomenon possesses—and this is what Abulafia intended to emphasize—mystical meaning, and the messianic attainment is due to the great intensity of his clinging to the divine intellect and his being imbued with the power possessed by Moses and other prophets. The comparison with Moses in the above passage resounds with messianic significance since Moses was often portrayed in the Midrash as the first savior and the Messiah as the last. Although mentioning the power of the Messiah, however, Abulafia is not particularly concerned with Moses' miraculous deeds, even less so with the apocalyptic Messiah's miraculous and violent ones. Strength still remains as a trait ascribed to the Messiah, though the violence characteristic of most of the apocalyptic dramas is drastically marginalized. Abulafia's view of the Messiah reflects his vision of God more as an intellect than as a will, while the concepts of the apocalyptic Messiah are structured within a theology where the power and will of God are one of the major forms of theophany. As we shall see, the concept of Agent Intellect, which plays a central role in Abulafia's messianism, is not devoid of the concept of power, but it is an impersonal or depersonalized form of power that does not depend on will. Abulafia sees spiritual messianism as preceding the more external one.

Mashiyaḥ as a Spiritual Experience

There is, however, more than a two-stage process (divine anointment and popular acclaim as king) in the making of a Messiah. Abulafia also terms the components of the process by the name *mashiyaḥ*. Thus, he writes in another of his works:

> the term *mashiyaḥ* is equivocal, [designating] three [different] matters; in truth, first and foremost the Agent Intellect is called the *mashiyaḥ* . . . and the man who will forcibly bring us out of exile from under the rule of the nations due to his contact[24] with the Agent Intellect—he will [also] be called *mashiyaḥ*. And the material human hylic intellect is called *mashiyaḥ*, and is the Redeemer and has influence over the soul and over all elevated spiritual powers. It can save the soul from the rule of the material kings and their people and their powers, the lowly bodily desires. It is a commandment and an obligation to reveal this matter to every wise man of the wise ones of Israel in order that he may be saved because there are many things that oppose the opinions of the multitude of the rabbis, and even more differ from the views of the *vulgus*.[25]

This passage is of paramount importance for Abulafia's conceptualization of the *mashiyaḥ*. The main assertion is that *mashiyaḥ* denotes three different entities. The first is a transcendent entity, while the two other are found in the human world. It is this approach, reminiscent of the Maimonidean hermeneutics of the biblical text, which imposed some philosophical meanings on some sensitive biblical terms in order to discard their anthropomorphical ones. Abulafia, while adopting this strategy, is less inclined when dealing with *mashiyaḥ* to abandon the more popular significance of the term, although it is implicitly marginalized. Though pretending to be the *mashiyaḥ* himself, he interprets this concept to cover an impersonal transcendent entity as well.

The first meaning of *mashiyaḥ* is Agent Intellect. This term translates the Greek *nous poetikos,* used for the first time in book 3 of Aristotle's *De Anima,* in a context that has long been under dispute. The first explanation, accepted by medieval Latin scholastics, argued that the *intellectus agens,* the Latin translation of *nous poetikos,* is an inner human capacity, found in the soul, which activates the intellectual processes. According to the version of Aristotelian philosophical psychology dominant in many circles of Muslim-Jewish thinkers in Middle Ages, the Agent Intellect, denoted by the terms *'aql al-fa'al* or *sekhel ha-po'el,* is a cosmic, not an internal human, power, oftentimes the last in a series of ten intellects which were emanated by the divine intellect; the Agent Intellect causes all the changes in nature and all the processes related to human intellect.[26] The medieval ideal of human intellectual perfection was conceived by some philosophers as the actualization of the potential of the intellect, be it material or human. This actualization of any human act of intellectual cognition is attained, according to Neoaristotelian epistemology, by the influence of or illumination exerted by the Agent Intellect, for if it were not so this lower intellect would disappear.

The Agent Intellect may therefore imagined as a savior of what some trends of medieval philosophy saw as the most important part in man, and as such it is prone to be conceived of as a Messiah, although it is not a person but rather an objective-spiritual impersonal power. Abulafia apparently offers a synthesis of the philosophical concept, which has some redemptive qualities vis-à-vis the human intellect, and the apocalyptic view of the preexisting Messiah found in the supernal world and waiting to appear in due time. In both cases the Messiah as a transcendent entity exists prior to its actual eschatological performance, and though sometimes strongly related to it, he also has cosmological contexts. In the former case the Messiah is incessantly active, while in the latter the salvific approach is impeded by the apocalyptic date. In the two cases, however, there is a vital affinity between the nature of God and the nature of His representative. God as the divine warrior produced, according to B. Halpern's thesis, the king-warrior, who is the clue to the emergence of the apocalyptic perception of the Messiah-warrior. Thus, Abulafia is much less concerned with the martial aspects of redemption, or the concept of the Messiah as a suffering servant, and his thought belongs to the *via perfectionis.*

Union or contact with the Agent Intellect should be thought of, in my opinion, as a full-fledged mystical experience, despite the fact that this cosmic intellect is the lowest of the ten separate intellects. As we shall see, the expressions used to convey the conjunction with the *intellectus agens* are quite extreme, and they invite a reading of these descriptions as pointing to *unio mystica.* It is much more important, it seems to me, to pay attention to the quality of the experience as it transpires in the Kabbalistic texts than to the object of union, be it God or the Agent Intellect.

On the other hand, the philosophical vision of God in medieval Jewish Neoaristotelianism is related to the concept of the Agent Intellect, which reproduces the intellectual nature of the divine, and it in turn was identified with the Messiah as an intellectual entity. Neoaristotelian concepts were of the utmost importance for the ecstatic Kabbalistic view of the Messiah. Aristotelian philosophy, which apparently does not initially display an explicit interest in issues of human redemption, generated, together with the (sometimes eschatological) archangel Metatron a certain form of soteriology.[27] The myth of the preexisting salvific personality, as formulated in apocalyptic sources, is attenuated here by the transformation of the redemptive process, achieved by the act of cleaving, into an intellectual event. While the apocalyptic Messiah was conceived of as a rather static entity which will enter history at a preestablished time and become an active force, the Agent Intellect is ever active and by definition omnipresent. It incessantly pours the intellectual forms upon the lower world, and as such its activity is quite atemporal. The messianic interpretation of the Agent Intellect involves a transpersonal and thus depersonalized function, which is always present and active, whose message is strongly connected to the nature of the entity that fulfills the function. A separated and ever-acting intellect is emanating forms, or acts of intellection, and they are, ultimately, the factors that constitute the quintessence of this model of messianism: to perfect all the existing intellects. The peculiar character of the specific human persona who will be instrumental in conveying the message in human terms is much less important. In a domain dominated by the spirit, here the intellectual activity of both the human and the separate intellect, preestablished dates lose the crucial role they ordinarily play in eschatological messianism.

Identifying the Agent Intellect with a supernal Messiah provides a clue to understanding the significance of the revelatory experiences, at least insofar as the so-called prophetic books of Abulafia are concerned. For this Kabbalist, the Agent Intellect is the source of all intellectual acts in man, as well as the main source of revelation. Thus, the information imparted by this intellect, and correct information in general, is presupposed to be either of a salvific nature, closer to the philosophical view of redemption as an inner spiritual change, or of an apocalyptic nature, dealing with dates and historical events. It is this ontological transpersonal Messiah qua source of knowledge that, according to ecstatic Kabbalah, the mystic is unified with and informed by.

But as pivotal as knowledge is in the works under discussion and in medieval philosophical theories, we should not forget the aspect of power that is involved in this concept. Indeed, some philosophers and mystics emphasized the noetic aspect of the Agent Intellect. This is not, however, an intellect involved only in the human acts of cognition but explicitly a cosmic power responsible, according to some versions, not only for the actualization of the human intellect but also for every shift of forms in this lower world. In a deep sense, the medieval discussions of the Agent Intellect as articulated after Abu Nasr Al-Farabi betray it to be a ruler of the sublunar world. Any significant change is related to it, and it may be understood as a version of *deus revelatus,* with the assumption that the highest intellect, identified with God, is not concerned with processes taking place in the mundane world. As the cosmocrator, the Agent Intellect is related to power, though this power is seen as totally impersonal. However, the impersonal tone of the philosophical descriptions of the Agent Intellect were modified by some of the mystics' experiences of the cosmocrator; this is especially the case in ecstatic Kabbalah, in the cases of Abraham Abulafia and R. Yitzḥaq of Acre. This aspect of power facilitated the identification of the Aristotelian *nous poetikos,* which had purely noetic functions in the system of the Starygite, with some of the Jewish concepts of savior. In other words, the personal and violent power of the Messiah of the apocalypticians was adopted, and thus domesticated, by the elevation of the Messiah to the rank of a cosmic and therefore more constant form of power. Roughly speaking, the more popular groups remained interested in the personalized power, which was connected to political and miraculous actions of the king-savior, while the elites conceptualized messianism in terms or regularity and omnipresence. From this point of view, the Messiah's descent from the line of David remained crucial in apocalyptic messianism, while the more elitist version could not but use a more emanational explanation for the emergence of the transcendent redeemer.

In this context, let me discuss briefly a gematria proposed by Abulafia in *Ḥayyei ha-'Olam ha-Ba',* where he equates "David ben Yishai Mashiyaḥ" to "Mashiyaḥ ben David, Na'ar."[28] The phrases are numerically equivalent, as their letters amount to 742. That David is the son of Yishai and thus related to the Messiah is a commonplace, indeed a core idea in Jewish messianism. What is significant here is the introduction of the noun *na'ar,* which means literally a youth or a servant. Neither meaning, however, makes sense in this context. In my opinion, *na'ar* here stands for the archangel Metatron, who is sometimes designated by this term in the literature of late antiquity; it should be understood as pointing to the office of a minister. Metatron, was identified by several authors in the Middle Ages, but most eminently by Abulafia, with the Agent Intellect. Indeed, there is a certain phenomenological correlation between the two concepts, albeit they stem from radically different intellectual backgrounds. Imagined as the angelic power into which Enoch has been translated, Metatron is an eschatological figure, because he serves as the redemptive level for human existence. On the other hand, Metatron was described in many early sources as the ruler of the world and the scribe that keeps account of the deeds of men, again a role that has eschatological implications. Therefore, the eschatological potential of Metatron is hinted at already in the ancient Jewish texts dealing with this angel.

The salvific nature of the Agent Intellect is also implied in its role in actualizing the potential human intellect. According to some epistemological theories in the Middle Ages, the Agent Intellect is the telos of human intellectual activity and the peak of human intellection as the union with this entity. From this point of view, the philosophical interpretations of messianism were more teleological, in the individual sense, than theological. In some cases we may assume that the philosophers were not only theoreticians, scholastic analysts of ancient philosophical texts or their harmony with the religious authoritative texts, but also individuals in search for self-realization, and the conceptual framework they discussed so carefully also meant for them a way of spiritual deliverance. In the last quotation we witness once again an identification between the Messiah, here called ben David, and the ontological entity that served as a noetic salvific power, exactly as in the passage from *Sefer ha-Melitz*.[29] However, in addition to the noetic function of the union, namely the knowledge acquired through contact with the cosmic intellect, there are instances in both Muslim and Jewish philosophy, and certainly in Abraham Abulafia, of descriptions of ontic identification that were deemed to produce a more substantial transformation of the human intellect.

The third meaning of the term *mashiyaḥ* is "material human intellect," namely the intellect after it has undergone a process of actualization. This intellectual human capacity is the Messiah of the human soul because it saves the soul from its bodily powers. Phrases like "the corporeal kings," "and their peoples and their powers," all express, allegorically, the material side of man. This hylic Messiah will save the "people of Israel" from the "historical" kings; or, understood metaphorically, the human intellect within each man will save his soul from the rule of the kings—the material element in man, his desires, and his imagination. Mastering them is considered by Abulafia to be part of a redemptive phenomenon as well. This more "ordinary" vision of the Messiah as a hylic intellect assumes in fact that the Messiah is not only a transcendent transpersonal power available to everyone, in the form of the Agent Intellect, but also an intellectual power inherent in each person. In other words, everyone possesses the Messiah, at least *in potentia;* the Messiah is a dimension of man qua man. The philosophical interpretation of messianism in terms of intellection, though found in the writings of a few other medieval thinkers, was never elaborated in such detail as Abulafia did. Indeed, he was aware of the novelty of his proposal and the divergences between such an intellectualistic interpretation and the more common concepts of the Messiah found among the rabbis or held by popular Jewish circles. The tension between these views is evident in the closing sentence of the above passage, and it reverberates from time to time in other discussions. Nevertheless, Abulafia presents his exposition of such an unpopular view as an imperative, designed to help the illuminati to redeem themselves. By disseminating such an intellectual understanding of the concept he means to help others to save themselves, an event that apparently has nothing to do with their expectation of the advent of a savior as a human form.

Another passage from Abulafia elaborates on the messianic potentiality found in every human hylic intellect. After mentioning the "influx of Satan," which is none other than the "likeness of Satan," and then God and "His Messiah," the ecstatic Kabbalist writes:

> you already know that body is an animal, and the soul is a light, and the intellect is an influx. And man, by dint of his flesh and blood, is like an animal, and [his] soul like the light of the sphere, which governs over the flesh and the body, and the intellect like the influx that governs the sphere by its light, because the sphere is a body and its soul is a living light, which conceptualizes by its intellect . . . and likewise man is threefold, his body from this lower world, and his soul from the world of the sphere, and his intellect from the intellectual world . . . and the intellectual world is an intellect, and the [world of the] sphere is intelligizing, and the lower world is the intelligibilia, and man is compound of the three of them, in the moment of his departure [from this world] he inherits them all, because at the beginning he is intelligizing, at the middle he is intelligibilia, and at the end he is an intellect. The intention of his creation was that he will become an intellect, an [act of] intelligizing and intelligibilia.[30]

This text builds a parallelism between God, the influx, and intellect, on the one hand, and the Messiah, the soul or the light and the spheres, and finally the animal, corresponding to the body or Satan, on the other. All these elements are found in man, whose creation means an integration of them. The Messiah is therefore dormant in every person, and this capacity should be actualized. The above texts conspicuously seek to disseminate a spiritual model of messianism in which the object of redemption is the human soul or, according to its first formulation, the human intellect, and not necessarily the nation or even a certain group of people. This spiritual messianism is an integral part of Abulafia's Kabbalah. The spiritual forms of messianism are expressed by the first and third meanings of the term *mashiyaḥ*, which consist of intellectual processes that occur within the human soul and not necessarily on the stage of history.

Let me examine closely the range of concepts that are subsumed under the heading of *mashiyaḥ*. Two deal exclusively with internal messianism—that is, with psychological or noetic phenomena—treating either relations between the Active Intellect and the human intellect or those between the actualization of the human intellect and the soul. The term *mashiyaḥ* refers in these instances to a process that has no external, objective, or immediate historical implications. This is a definitive example of individual salvation being expressly described by the term *mashiyaḥ*.

As we have seen, Abulafia calls the term *mashiyaḥ* equivocal, because the three entities it refers to—the Agent Intellect, the material intellect, and the persona of the Messiah—differ from each other. It is possible, however, to envision them also as part of an ontic continuum, with the Agent Intellect on the top, the material intellect as the materialization of the Agent Intellect—following perhaps Averroistic psychology—and the persona as the external expression of the noetic processes between the two spiritual entities. Indeed, this concept of a continuum is important because it may allow a more unified reading of Abulafia's messianism, which will encompass the spiritual and individual, and the material and national, within a more comprehensive scheme. In the following example Abulafia discusses a continuum that starts with God and ends in man:

> Intellect is a term [applied] to the entity which rules over everything, i.e. the first cause of all; and it is called the form of the intellect. The [term] intellect is also [applied] to the entity separated from matter, which is emanated from the first cause; by the means of this emanation the first entity rules over the moving heavens. However He, may He be exalted, is the simple intellect. The [term] intellect is the name of the first cause which is close and acts upon whatever exists beneath the heavens, and this is the Active Intellect which causes [the emergence of] the intellect in the human soul. Therefore there are three stages, all three being but one essence: God, His emanation which is separated [from matter], and the emanation of this emanation, which is attached to the soul and the soul is attached to it in a very tenacious way, though the two [i.e. the soul and the emanation of God's emanation] are but one essence.[31]

In fact, the resort to the term *mashiyaḥ* is very similar structurally to the manner in which the term *intellect* is portrayed here. This intellectual continuum, whose importance in Abulafia's mysticism is immense, absorbs the messianic figure into a much more stable system and emphasizes the significance of perfectibility of the natural order, rather than the need to transcend the present order in a definitive manner, as the apocalyptic thinkers would assume. Indeed, in several treatises Abulafia identified the Agent Intellect, whose affinity to the transcendent Messiah is paramount, with the Torah, a fact that carries a conservative implication of the supernal Messiah.

One of the problems that haunts any messianic event is the discrepancy between the various functions of the Messiah as imagined by a given society and the persona of the aspirant. In some cases, the emphasis is laid on the persona and its idiosyncratic life. In the case of the theories described in this chapter, however, the persona of the Messiah is much less important than his function as a disseminator of salvific knowledge. In fact, though the transpersonal Agent Intellect in conceived of as embodying itself in the individual hylic intellect, according to the theory of Averroes, this initial personalization is followed by a depersonalization as part of the mental evolution of the person who is to become the Messiah. His acquiring more advanced forms of intellection means an imitation of the separate intellect, a removal of the importance of anything corporeal and emotional, in fact anything idiosyncratic. The evolving intellect gradually becomes disincarnated in order to be able to reach the unitive experience, loosing its *principium individuationis* in order to be able to become the savior of others. Abulafia describes the messianic experience, which is tantamount to and sometimes even precedes the supreme ecstatic one, in his most important handbook on a technique to reach an experience of the next world, namely a strong experience while alive: "And it will appear to him as if his entire body, from head to foot, has been anointed with the oil of anointing, and he was 'the anointed of the Lord' [*mashiyaḥ YHWH*] and His emissary, and he will be called 'the angel of the Lord' [*mal'akh ha-'elohim*]; his name will be similar to that of his Master, which is Shadday, who is called Metatron, the prince [namely the angel] of the [divine] Face."[32] Note the messianic tone, which accompanies the transformation into an angel, especially on the basis of the messianic background of the identification of Enoch with the Son of Man already in the Ethiopic Book of Enoch 9:17–19, 71, and, on the other hand, the process of anointment described in the *Slavonic Book of Enoch:*

> And the Lord Said to Michael, "Go, and extract Enoch from [his] earthly clothing. And anoint him with my delightful oil, and put him into the clothes of my glory. And so Michael did, just as the Lord had said to him. He anointed me and he clothed me. And the appearance of that oil is greater than the greatest light, and its ointment is like sweet dew, and its fragrance myrrh; and it is like the rays of the glittering sun. And I looked at myself, and I had become like one of the glorious ones, and there was no observable difference.[33]

Abulafia's description of the ecstatic mystic's transformation into an angel of God and his feeling of the anointment as a bodily experience is indeed reminiscent of the *Slavonic Enoch.* In both cases Enoch is involved, either implicitly or explicitly. The experience of anointment precedes that of becoming an emissary prophet, just as in the ancient Jewish ritual the anointment preceded the act of enthronement; and as we have seen, the anointment as prophet precedes the transformation of the Messiah from an individual into a national Messiah and king. To put it differently, the mystical experience, which is tantamount to individual redemption, precedes that of receiving the prophetic-political-messianic mission. Mysticism may transform someone into a prophet, and this achievement is preceding the royal installation which will take someone to more public forms of activity. The concreteness of Abulafia's description, which speaks not only about the reception of some secrets or a new understanding of the law but also about personal corporeal feelings, is indubitably related to an ecstatic experience.

The messianic experience as described above invites a reflection on the affinity between time and space in the context of the history of the messianic ideas.[34] The closer to the eschaton the messianic experience is in time, the more concrete it tends to be; by inserting the Messiah into the model of an ecstatic Kabbalah, Abulafia not only introduces the ancient theme of anointment, which is part of a ritual, but also that of the feeling of an anointment that has to do with the descent of divine influx into the mystic. Likewise, as in the case of Polish Hasidism, by modeling the Messiah on an eighteenth-century tzaddiq, one Hasidic author imported the ecstatic element that also affects the body, in a manner similar to Abulafia's mention of the feeling of anointment during the experience he conceived of as messianic.[35] This mention is paramount: it shows that an accomplished mystic not only imagined himself by resorting to messianic terminology, but also claimed to have experienced something that was part of the ancient royal ideology as part of a mystical experience that can be induced and repeated by means of a mystical technique. This feeling allows an interpretation of the mystical-messianic moment as one of an experiential plenitude. By depersonalizing the apocalyptic Messiah and investing the mystic with a feeling of anointment, metaphoric or concrete, this form of messianism renounced the rendezvous destined to take place only in the expected dates of the apocalyptic mode. It is a messianism that is more concerned, as Vladimir Jankelevitch put it, with a matter of today than of tomorrow.

In his commentary on his own prophetic book *Sefer ha-Ḥayyim,* Abulafia reports (in the third person) a revelation he had. This passage is one of the very few in which a medieval figure defines himself as a Messiah:

> And He said that the *mashiyaḥ* will arrive immanently, for he is already born. And he continued to discourse on the entire subject, and said "I am that individual." And by [means of] the "seven luminous windows" he indicated the secret of the seven names, and that who runs is [tantamount to] the order and the permutator. It is He who speaks to Raziel and informs him that he is the seventh of the prophets. At that time he was commanded to go to Rome and do all that he did, and it is clear that this secret has been revealed to him. And he said that during the fortieth year this matter returned to him and he was shown the image of a "son of a king," anointed for kingship, and he is the one well known. His secret is the form of BQM, the form of ShDY, the Name of Sufficient Power, and his secret name, in the 'AL-BM [method],[36] is YSSh YSSh . . . For forty years Israel was in gloom; light and darkness, day and night, two, four, the retribution of the limbs, Raziel ben Shmuel is familiar with the blessing and the curse, is acquainted[37] with the bastard "son of the menstruating woman," [namely] he is acquainted with Jesus, [and] Mohammed, the Measure of the Moon

> in the Frontier of the Sun. Upon them he will build and quarter, in the triangle and from his words you will comprehend wonders, and the honey he gives to taste is the "wisdom of the Names."[38]

This passage points up a vital affinity between mystical biography and messianic activity. The most important year in Abulafia's literary career and messianic activities was 1280, when he journeyed to the pope and wrote such major works as *Sefer Ḥayyei ha-'Olam ha-Ba'* and *Sefer Sitrei Torah,* as well as prophetic treatises. Abulafia was in his fortieth year, which according to some Jewish traditions is when a person reaches the height of his intellectual capabilities. Indeed, I assume that the phrase *ben ha-Melekh,* "son of a king," stands for the human intellect, often referred to by Abulafia as a son, while the king is the Agent Intellect. We learn from a passage in ecstatic Kabbalah that God told the Kabbalist, using a variety of biblical verses, " 'Thou art my son, this day I have begotten you' and also 'See now that I, even I am he,' and the secret [of these verses] is the union of the power—i.e. the supernal divine power, called the sphere of prophecy—with the human power, and it is also said: 'I I.' "[39] The resort to the verse from Psalm 2:7 at the beginning of the quotation is typical of scholarly discussions of the adoption theme in the ancient sacral royalty ideology. But whereas the ancient king was understood to be the corporeal offspring of a divine power, Abulafia and his school emphasized the intellectual affinity between the higher and the lower entities. It is a spiritual birth, or second birth, that is reflected here, allegorically portraying the emergence of the human intellect *in actu* and its mystical union with the supernal intellect, an event that not only is eschatological, in the psychological sense, but also implies a form of intellectual theosis. It does not seem coincidental that precisely in the fortieth year of his life Abulafia embarked on these extraordinarily intensive activities. Here we can feel how a certain period of life can be considered from an intellectual as well as a mystical standpoint as a time of critical development and the beginning of vigorous messianic activity. From this perspective, Abulafia's biography can be seen as a model of the integration of an intense and extraordinary mystical life and an adventurous messianic activity.[40]

It is, therefore, quite plausible that in the writings of the founder of ecstatic Kabbalah a messianic process is understood to occur in the realm of psychological as well as external events. Abulafia refers to himself as the Messiah by using his proper name in gematria: Raziel = 248 = Abraham. His confession that "I am that individual" comes in the context of the discussion that the Messiah has already been born. Moreover, he mentions the vision of the "son of a king," who is none other than himself. On the basis of Abulafia's use of the traditional term *ben David* to point to the Messiah, there is no doubt that the "son of a king" is the son of David. In other words, Abulafia experienced a vision which included an image of himself as the anointed one. Abulafia is at the same time a prophet of his own messianic status and the Messiah himself. His explicit confession, already at the beginning of the 1280s, that he is the Messiah coincides with his attempt to see the pope and contributes one more proof that the messianic nature of Abulafia's activity in Rome was a result of a prior revelation.

To be sure, Abulafia was by no means the first to invent this transfer of Neoaristotelian philosophy to a messianic understanding of inner processes. He was preceded somewhat by Maimonides himself,[41] but even more clearly by R. Abraham Maimuni, Maimonides' son, who presented a messianic explanation for psychological processes. He also denoted the bodily desires by terms that have messianic overtones such as *Leviathan* and *Satan.* He discussed the Agent Intellect as the entity that can actualize the human intellect and described this procedure in eschatological terms.[42] Moreover, in a late medieval anonymous work entitled *Midrash 'Aggadah* we find a homily on the verse " 'Poor and riding upon an ass'[43] to the effect that the soul is situated above the material or the meaning of this verse is that the soul can subjugate the body." This is an example of the concept of the Messiah understood in terms of internal rather than external processes, the relations of body and soul.[44] From this perspective, this is a conspicuous documentation of the enterprise of awarding messianic interpretation to Aristotelian-epistemological concepts during the Middle Ages. In other words, the reception of the Greek intellectualistic concepts by some Jewish thinkers had sometimes taken idiosyncratic forms, reflecting the structure of Jewish thought that invited a more eschatological understanding of the noetic processes.

Abulafia, however, represents an innovation in comparison to the texts of the *Midrash 'Aggadah* and R. Abraham Maimon. This Kabbalist was not just someone who granted philosophical explanations to Jewish eschatological terms, or a commentator on classical texts who had eschatological leanings, but was someone who proclaimed himself a Messiah as well. Ostensibly, we are not dealing solely with commentary and homiletics on Jewish messianic topics with the aid of philosophical concepts. Since Abulafia considered himself to be the Messiah, these spiritual and allegorical explanations of messianic concepts are directed toward Abulafia himself, namely to the nature of his inner life. They are descriptions of what is happening to him as he tries in practice to actualize both his messianic self-awareness and his messianic mission. From this standpoint, Abulafia moved philosophy as a hermeneutical tool, adopted already by others before him to explain concepts without personal implications—at least any that we can detect from their writings—to a more central position. Philosophy supplied terms for the inner processes of a man who saw himself as a Messiah. These processes can lead someone to a prophetic experience which only they can facilitate one to become a Messiah.

To be sure, Abulafia was not the first Messiah to appear in the Middle Ages. Earlier claimants may even have had a greater influence upon the historical scene than he had. But he is apparently the first Messiah who explicitly told us about his private mystical experiences. This is a phenomenological innovation: a person who conceives himself to be a mystic is also offering himself as a Messiah, or a pretender to the title of Messiah is also a mystic who established his own school. The two aspects should not, however, be seen as mechanically coexisting in one personality, but rather interacting and overlapping experiences. In this context, one should emphasize the relative neglect of magical elements in Abulafia's treatment of a variety of messianic themes. The affinity established between messianism and mysticism weakened, in Abulafia's case, the more traditional affinities between messianism and the magical powers of the Messiah. His general assumption is that magic, in principle, is possible but nevertheless not to be recommended as a desirable form of activity. However, even in the case of the activity of the Messiah he attempts to ignore these traits found in popular apocalyptic messianism. In Abulafia's thought the Messiah should disseminate a certain type of lore—the ecstatic Kabbalah that provides a salvific knowledge which will help others to redeem themselves. It is the noetic act of informing and the rhetoric necessary for persuading, rather than exercising force, that is the thrust of his endeavor.

By this synthesis between messianism and prophecy—the latter standing commonly in his writings for a certain type of ecstasy—Abulafia constructed a new model of understanding messianism in Jewish mysticism. Though this model does not subscribe to most of the apocalyptic elements common in other messianic models, I see no reason not to approach it as an independent and significant messianic model, to pay due attention to its phenomenological structure as well as to its historical influence. In any case, the neglect of the possible contribution of this messianic model to the more variegated developments of Jewish messianism or its description as belonging to "spiritual deviations"[45] may bring about an academic—and somewhat dogmatic—view of what Jewish messianism was, by reducing it to a monochromatic way of thought.

Abulafia's discussions of the Messiah and his Kabbalistic thought in general differ conspicuously from most of the thirteenth-century Kabbalah by its non-protological nature. By this term, derived from a word coined by Jon Levenson, I mean that the ecstatic Kabbalist was not particularly concerned with matters of the beginning, namely theories of the emanation of the ten *sefirot*, emanation in general, or creation. While Provençal and Catalan Kabbalists, as well as some Castilian ones, paid special attention to these issues, Abulafia was much more concerned with present spiritual attainments which, when achieved, might be conceived of as matters of the end, as spiritually eschatological. Psychology and techniques to attain the supreme spiritual experiences, more than ontological speculations or sacred history dealing with the *Urzeit* and *Endzeit,* dominate his numerous writings.

Noetic Eschatology

Abulafia was not the first Jewish figure in the thirteenth century to emphasize the present intellectual attainment as the major religious experience. A Provençal philosopher and translator named R. Moses ben Shmuel ibn Tibbon, who apparently was not known to Abulafia, shows how earlier mythologoumena influenced some philosophers and produced a synthesis very close to that of Abulafia's. In his *Commentary on the Song of Songs* R. Moses writes:

> As long as the material intellect was *in potentia* and did not attain the kingdom of God and was anointed with the holy unction, it was called Solomon alone. Then he is neither king nor the "son of David," as it was said that " 'the son of David' will not come until all the souls of the body are exhausted," neither the king of Jerusalem . . . and the beloved [in the Song of Songs] is the Causa Prima, and the first agent or His emissary and His angel, "whose name is like the name of its Master," which is identical to the Agent Intellect, and is Metatron, and it was counted at the end as the "lesser YHWH," because of the name of its Master, because it has been said that "my name is within it."[46]

The philosopher resorted to speculation typical of the *Hebrew Enoch* in order to point out the similarity between the Agent Intellect and the First Cause, which correspond, respectively, to Metatron and God. This is not, however, solely an ontological description of medieval Neoaristotelianism by means of Heikhalot literature. Prior to this discussion R. Moses mentions the potential human intellect that should be actualized, and the implication is that man's intellect should conjoin with the Agent Intellect, a union that is described in eschatological terms as the arrival of "ben David." Implicitly, Metatron too has been eschatologized, as the archangel is equivalent here to the messianic ben David. To what extent such a passage is a matter of an exegetical move or may betray some intellectualistic-eschatological experiences of the author is a matter of debate. It has to do with how to understand some forms of Jewish philosophies, and I cannot embark here the question of the possible salvific valences of noetic experiences. But the above passage is sufficient to locate this noetic aspect of Abulafia's eschatology closer to the followers of Maimonides than to the theosophical-theurgical Kabbalists.

Despite the fact that Abulafia passed on and did not bring the redemption, there is no doubt that his conception of a spiritual messianism thrived and remained influential in the generations to follow. There is quite a list of extant discussions that seem to be influenced by the writings and theories of Abulafia. One of the reasons is that his views approximated the philosophical thinking of his day as typified by R. Moses. The other was the fact that his idiosyncratic life did not become the most characteristic aspect of the eschatological scheme he proposed. I will present only one aspect, from an anonymous work dating from the middle of the fifteenth century and apparently composed in Italy.[47] Following the views of Abulafia, we hear an interesting exposition of messianic concepts through internal modes and philosophical constructs:

> The great salvation that is the true salvation and the perfect redemption which after it will never again be an exile will transpire through the agency of two angels.[48] One is called Elijah and the other the son of David. "Elijah" is an allusion to the intellectual power whereas "son of David" alludes to the prophetic power. The son of David will not come until all the souls of the body are exhausted.[49] This passage states that the power of prophecy, which is allegorically rendered as the son of David, will not indwell unless all the bodily powers and all the instincts be terminated, in other words be subjugated and acquiescent to the powers of intellect and prophecy.[50]

We can see how a classical Jewish apocalyptic conception which argues for the coming of Elijah before that of the Messiah, the son of David, is given to a philosophical-mystical explanation. Elijah is transformed into a term for the intellect or the power of the intellect that has been actualized. This process of actualization is the prerequisite for the arrival of the son of David, who becomes a metaphor for the prophetic faculty in man. This text exhibits the same type of perception that has as its reference philosophy or psychological-philosophical processes, as a prepositional stage for the actual prophetic phenomenon, all to explain the essence of the Messiah, the son of David. Obviously ben David is not conceived of here to be an historical personality but rather simply a stage in the mystical development of a certain person. When the redemption is finally reached, all of material forces, "all the bodily powers," will be subjugated to the spiritual ones, just as the Messiah-king will behave in history in relation to the foes of God. This is the applied meaning of spiritual messianism: there is to be no substantial change in historical reality, sociological structure, or geographical location of the nation; there is to be an alteration solely in the relationship of the spiritual world to the material world. As long as the spiritual world can rule over the physical or corporeal, then we have the special indicator of the time of the Messiah. Even though it is possible to have the involvement of a historical personality, he is not mentioned and he is not a necessary component of this process. It follows that this specific "messianic idea," the redemption of the individual, allows for different types of redemption for different people. Redemption depends ultimately on the spiritual perfection of the individual, who alone is responsible for his personal salvific attainment.

This point should be stressed because a dominant theory in modern scholarship denies categorically that Judaism contained a conception of individual salvation or personal messianism before the middle of the eighteenth century. Scholem, for example, asserts that "the question of private or individual redemption is a totally modern dilemma, and does not exist in Jewish tradition before 1750."[51] It is obvious, then, that Abulafia's view marks a radical departure from popular eschatological notions. Here the historical stage is abandoned, at least in two out of three definitions of the term *mashiyaḥ*, which are presented as philosophical processes.[52] These discussions invite a revision of Scholem's view of messianism, which is inclined to restrict this phenomenon to its apocalyptic forms.[53] A similar propensity is evident in the view of religion as presented in the works of Joachim Wach, who emphasized the role of salvation in the general economy of religion. According to Wach, "The presence of a savior is a mark that distinguishes religious from philosophical doctrines of salvation. Philosophical doctrines teach that human beings are saved by their own efforts: religious doctrines proclaim the principle of salvation by another."[54] This strong distinction between the philosophical and the religious ignores some medieval forms of syntheses between the two forms of spirituality, which attempted to internalize the traditional savior understood as an external factor and to interpret the objective sources of knowledge as the savior, what Wach would call the "other." I suspect that Wach's reduction of the other to a human or a human-divine figure constitutes a bias stemming from his particular religious background. His emphasis on *Grenzsituationen,* those human experiences that reflect the finitude and nothingness of the individual and the necessity of a redemption coming from outside, more precisely as grace, is quite relevant.[55] They reflect the search for salvation as generated by a feeling of finitude, want, or crisis, in a way reminiscent of some of Scholem's formulations.[56] No one would deny that *Grenzsituationen* may inspire salvific or messianic aspirations. It would be advisable, however, not to reduce the whole range of messianic models to a total, apocalyptic restructuring of a distorted nature or a terrible history. More positive drives may also be at work in models that are inspired by much more activistic, dynamic approaches fertilized by forms of thought like Aristotelian noetics.

Natural Redemption

Thus far we dealt with the issue of inner, spiritual redemption in the writings of Abraham Abulafia. One would expect this emphasis on the mystical moment to lead to two antithetical processes. First, an individual who undergoes an extraordinary inner experience is likely to withdraw from taking an active part in community affairs and devote his efforts to his personal redemption. Second, someone who had experienced mystical union with God and received revelations, or prophecy, might envision himself as being capable of effecting catastrophic, historical changes. However, neither of these two possibilities fits the case of Abraham Abulafia. He did in fact play an active role on the historical scene and did not become a recluse; and the changes in the course of history he sought to effect were not at all catastrophic. Abulafia saw historical redemption as a natural process. In his view, the messianic event occurs without the need of any extraordinary intervention from supernatural powers—without breaking the framework of nature.

The first of three explanations Abulafia offers for this process is astrological. In a few of his writings Abulafia repeats an expression that is typical of him alone; the term 'renewal', *ḥiddush,* in order to describe the re-appearance of a government in Israel. In this context, Abulafia uses the term *memshalah.*[57] Abulafia's understanding of the concept of renewal is similar to many traditional Jewish understandings of this term: renewal of the month, for example, depends upon the ongoing renewal of the moon, a natural process of constant return to a previously existing condition. Hence the redemption of the government of Israel is a return to a certain situation, just as over the course of time constellations return to previous positions in the sky. From this perspective, Abulafia holds a highly special view of redemption. It would appear that he is not advocating a process in which history reaches its end and then enters a new, irreversible phase of messianic existence from which there is no return to a state of diaspora. Instead he is describing a spiral in which the Jewish people can regain their lost statehood. All this is part of what he conceives to be a natural process that can be compared to the procession of the stars every several thousand years.[58] This theory of Abulafia's recalls Nietzsche's opinion concerning the recurrence of events (though not in a regular cyclical pattern) an infinite number of times, for eternity.

The second model of the natural interpretation of redemption is Aristotelian. This explanation is based upon the assumption that all potentialities will at some point in time reach their actualizations. The idea is that since time is eternal, it is illogical to suppose that a potential reality will not at some point be actualized. Therefore the notion of Jewish statehood, which is actually an idea that has already proved feasible, must again come to fruition.[59] The notion of necessary actualization is not unique to Abulafia. Ideas of this type circulated among Jews and Arabs during the Middle Ages through pseudo-epigraphic writings attributed to Aristotle.[60] Even so, it seems that Abulafia places a stronger emphasis upon this notion than can be found in other compositions, including pseudo-Aristotelian works, and in the appropriation of R. Yitzḥaq ibn Latif, apparently because of his conviction that the actualization of this particular potentiality was to happen in his time, the very decade in which he was writing.

The third interpretive model is concerned with the progressive nature of man. Abulafia's insight into history, dealing the rise and fall of nations, apparently convinced him that the Jewish people could rise again. In his youth, the 1250s and 1260s, the land of Israel was the focal point of a gigantic struggle between the superpowers of the Middle Ages: the Mongols and the Mameluks, in addition to the Crusaders. In an unstable situation such as this it would be fitting to suppose that the Jews could also be integrated in an historical process that would allow them a foothold or even a victory by exploitation of a certain constellation of events. This background of bitter struggle seems to be pertinent to the rise of messianic expectations during times of great international crisis. Abulafia was not the only one to recognize the inherent messianism of this particular historical situation. This is the same background for the thoughts of R. Yehudah ha-Levi when he pondered the success of the Crusaders in capturing the land of Israel. This perspective also relates to the modern Zionist ideal, which flourished and gained strength while another great power, Britain, to occupied Israel. These international struggles seemed to foster among the Jewish people underlying expectations of political and military activism. As long as the international situation remained stable, the Jews had very little chance of regaining political power.

The contemplation of human nature, in the ways in which nations rise and fall, is strong in Abulafia's writings. In *Sefer ha-Melammed,* for example, he states: "Even what will happen in the future, such as the coming of the Messiah and the kingdom of Israel, are not impossibilities or to be denied logically, because thus we see every day with the nations of the world. Sometimes these have dominion over those (and vice versa), and this is not a matter that nature can deny but rather human nature decrees that it be so."[61]

Abulafia's theory of human nature had a certain historical influence. At the end of the thirteenth century a Jewish intellectual, R. Joseph Caspi of Provence, raised the possibility of the reestablishment of the Jewish state on the basis of his contemplation of the rise and fall of nations throughout history. It is likely that through Caspi this idea later appeared in a composition of Spinoza's, as has been suggested by Shlomo Pines.[62] Spinoza suggested that a Jewish state might be founded under particular political conditions. An historical affinity between Abulafia and Caspi is likely, for the latter was indeed aware of another work of Abulafia's as well.[63] This could explain how Spinoza came to know this concept.

These three interpretations, the astrological-repetitive, the Aristotelian-probabilistic, and the ecstatic-spiritualistic, possess a common denominator.

Unlike the popular outlooks, as presented in Jewish eschatological works produced during the talmudic period and in the early Middle Ages, Abulafia does not advocate a disruption of nature as a necessary condition for messianic redemption, but rather calls for the fruition of its hidden potentials. This development indicates a rise of a certain special train of thought that is more characteristic of the second elite among the Jews in the Middle Ages than of popular thought that tended to link redemption to a total disruption in history and in nature.

Abulafia's views of inner redemption and outer nature are quite similar. In both, what is referred to is the actualization of something that is already in potentia. Redemption of the soul or of the intellect does not disrupt the spiritual development of a person but rather brings that endeavor to its final perfection. It is an ongoing process of evolution, much like explanations of objective nature. The changes that occur in both the inner and outer natures can be understood as processes that do not require a disruption of their respective frameworks.

New Year, Anointment, Messianism

Abulafia composed books in a variety of literary genres. A *Commentary on the Pentateuch,* works on the secrets included in Maimonides' *Guide of the Perplexed* and on *Sefer Yetzirah;* mystical handbooks which deal with the required techniques to reach ecstatic experiences; and "prophetic books" which record the revelations he experienced. All but one of the prophetic books have beenlost, but the commentaries he wrote on them are extant. Most of these prophetic books and commentaries were written around 1280, the year when Abulafia planned to meet the pope. Indeed, the more interesting messianic expressions used by Abulafia occur precisely in those dense and concise booklets. Let me focus on just one passage, found in the commentary on *Sefer ha-'Edut,* a book originally composed in Rome in 1280, where he records, two years later, what he heard from the supernal realm:

> He said that he was in Rome at that time, and they told him what was to be done and what was to be said in his name, and that he tell everyone that "God is king, and shall stir up the nations," and the retribution[!] of those who rule instead of Him. And He informed him that he was king and he changed [himself] from day to day, and his degree was above that of all degrees, for in truth he was deserving of such. But he returned and again made him take an oath when he was staying in Rome on the river Tiber. . . . And the meaning of his saying: "Rise and lift up the head of my anointed one"—refers to the life of the souls. "And on the New Year" and "in the temple"—it is the power of the souls. And he says: "Anoint him as a king"—rejoice in him like a king with the power of all the names. "For I have anointed him as a king over Israel"—over the communities of Israel, that is the commandments. And his

> saying: "and his name I have called Shadday, like My Name"—whose secret is Shadday like My Name, and understand all the intention. Likewise his saying, "He is I and I am He," and it cannot be revealed more explicitly than this. But the secret of the "corporeal name" is the "Messiah of God." Also "Moses will rejoice," which he has made known to us, and which is the five urges, and I called the corporeal name as well . . . now Raziel started to contemplate the essence of the Messiah and he found it and recognized it and its power and designated it David, the son of David, whose secret is Yimelokh."[64]

Between quotation marks I have put those phrases I believe are from the original but now lost prophetic book upon which Abulafia is commenting. Abulafia received a series of commands dealing with the installation and anointment of the Messiah in the Temple on the Jewish New Year. This presumably happened in Barcelona, the very city where, some few years earlier, Naḥmanides formulated his view on the Messiah's revelation in Rome. The anointment as king is connected here explicitly with the New Year.

Indeed, Abulafia insisted on meeting the pope on the eve of the New Year, and shortly after mentioning it he wrote the above passage.[65] Thus, the revelation about the installation of Abulafia as the king-Messiah and the attempt to meet the pope coincide. The anointment at the time of the New Year recalls an ancient Near Eastern ritual that had also been adopted, according to some scholars, by the ancient Israelites, when the king was installed.[66] The king referred to here is quite explicitly a messianic figure. Thus, we may learn something more about the self-perception of Abulafia from the revelation he received on the very day he went to see the pope. The proximity of planned events suggests that his visit to Rome may even have entailed not only a scholastic discussion about the nature of Judaism qua mysticism but also an attempt to be recognized and even be crowned the king-Messiah by the pope himself. If this conjecture is correct, may we assume that "the temple" (*miqdash*)is none other than St. Peter, where he intended to meet the pope on the eve of the New Year.

This hypothesis may illuminate the significance of Abulafia's use of the topos of the Messiah's coming to Rome in order to become an actual Messiah. It is also pertinent to point out the possible impact of the influential apocalyptic book *Sefer Zerubbavel* on the emergence of the role of Rome as the locus of the messianic advent. The book contains an important episode concerning the revelation of the Messiah and of Metatron to Zerubbavel ben She'altiel in Rome. In this revelation the Messiah appeared to the pseudepigraphic writer as a despised and wounded man, and then he transformed himself into an appearance "like a youth [*na'ar*] in the perfection of his beauty and pleasing, a young man the like of whom there is none."[67] In Abulafia's text the term *na'ar* describes both the Messiah ben David and Metatron. If Abulafia was acquainted with *Sefer*

Zerubbavel, it might have made encouraged him to expect a messianic revelation in Rome. If this conjecture is correct, the passage from *Sefer ha-Ḥayyim,* a book which was composed in 1280, apparently in Rome, allows the possibility that Rome may have constituted not only the place of a confrontation between the Messiah and the pope, but also the place of an eschatological revelation for both Abulafia and the author of *Sefer Zerubbavel.*

This eschatological scenario has been interpreted by Abulafia himself as dealing not only with an historical event but also with another one, accessible by means of allegory. Anointment is related to the spiritualization of the religious life, the "life of the souls" (*ḥayyei ha-nefashot*). This spiritual view is reflected in the title of one of Abulafia's commentaries on the secrets of Maimonides' *Guide: Ḥayyei ha-Nefesh* intended to redeem readers by divulging the secrets of the *Guide,* which were treated as the secrets of the Torah.[68] In fact, this redemption is formulated in extreme mystical phrases which presuppose a mystical union between the mystic-Messiah and God: "He is I and I am He."[69] The messianic mission is conceived on a double plane: the spiritual one, consisting of an anointment by God which is tantamount to a strong mystical experience, and the corporeal, consisting of designation as king of the communities of Israel. Yet even the term *yisra'el* should not be understood here in its plain sense alone. In several discussions in Abulafia's writings it stands for the numerical value 541—for the Agent Intellect, *sekhel ha-po'el*—and this gematria is quite important in the passage under discussion. In other words, an external event that Abulafia hoped will take place—his coronation, actual or allegorical—may be seen as more consonant with popular forms of eschatology, and in some cases even with the apocalyptic mode.[70]

Nevertheless, the spiritual interpretations of these aspirations have been inserted, consciously or not, into the very formulation of external messianism, both by allegory and by numerology. In other words, Abulafia's discourse involves two different registers: one apocalyptical, apparently the result of an earlier revelation, the other allegorical. While the former is much more dynamic, using more verbs and describing a drama evolving in a certain time and place, the spiritual allegoresis is more static, marked by a greater resort to nouns. While the first register is more temporally bound, the second appears to describe atemporal experiences. The corporeal, external events that are described by the "original" revelation serve as a text that, like the biblical stories, should be allegorized in order to point to inner, spiritual experiences. Even so, the spiritual interpretation, inspired by an axiology that prefers what Frank and Fritzie Manuel called the eupsychia to the euchronia, did not displace the allegorical, at least not explicitly. In fact, the more archaic axis, based upon sacred geography and time as well as hypostatic entities, was at least rhetorically preserved.

Metatron: Yaho'el, hu' ha-Go'el, Ben, Enoch

According to some scholars, already in pre-Christian forms of Judaism it is possible to detect a hypostatic angelic power which was granted the name of God and sometimes plays an eschatological role. This is true insofar as the Son of Man some of the early angelic conceptions of Jesus are concerned. In earlier Jewish texts the angel Metatron was conceived of as having a redeeming function. Some of these views are related to the redemptive role of God's leading angel, who possessed the divine name, in Exodus 23:20–21, or the expression "the redemptive angel," *ha-mal'akh ha-go'el,* in Genesis 48:16 or Isaiah 63:9. It stands to reason that these powers are nothing but angelophanies that represent the divine intervention in history. It is the divine name that is sometimes described as present within these angelic manifestations, which are devoid of proper names. The later Jewish eschatologies resorted to the redemptive role of these angelic powers in order to build up their own vision of the end. From this point of view, an important aspect of medieval eschatology—Kabbalistic, philosophical, and that of Hasidei Ashkenaz—should be better understood as different interpretations of ancient mythologoumena.

In my opinion, Abulafia must have been acquainted with some of the literary formulations of this development. He not only quoted some of the extant texts related to it but also claimed to have encountered some of those angelic powers as part of his own mystical experiences. In his greatest commentary on the *Guide of the Perplexed, Sitrei Torah,* we read:[71]

> The thing that is actualizing our intellect from its potentiality is an intellect which is called in our language by many names, and it is the prince of the world, and Metatron, the angel of the [divine] Face . . . and its name is Shadday, like the name of its master, and its cognomen is Metatron . . . and it is wise, [and] speaking,[72] the universal spirit, which has been called by the philosophers the Agent Intellect . . . and the divine Spirit, and Shekhinah, and the faithful Spirit, and the kingdom of Heaven[73] . . . and in our language the intellect has been designated by the [terms] *mal'akh* and *keruv,* and in some places it will be called 'Elohim, as we have said concerning the fact that its name is like that of its master, and behold the sages have called it Enoch and said that "Enoch Is Metatron" . . . and the first name out of the seventy names of Metatron is Yaho'el whose secret is Ben . . . and its name is 'Eliyahu[74] and it is also the explicit name Yod Yod Vav,[75] which is the double name . . . and behold, it also "is the Redeemer" (*hu ha-go'el*) and it is "in the whole" (*ba-kol*) of "your heart," (*libbekha*) and it is the ruler of the world.[76]

In this passage Abulafia draws upon a still unparalleled version of a *Commentary on the Seventy Names of Metatron,* which he attributes here to R. Eleazar of Worms. The correctness of this attribution has been questioned,[77] but certainly the text was written by an Ashkenazi figure who preceded Abulafia by at least decades. There are several differences between the manuscripts that preserved this early thirteenth-century text and its quotation by Abulafia, but I shall analyze in the version found in *Sefer Sitrei Torah,* where the explicit claim of the author is that he adduces a verbatim quotation, not a paraphrase.

Abulafia's version of the Ashkenazi text links by gematria several concepts Ben = 'Eliyahu = Yaho'el = hu' ha-Go'el = ba-kol = libbekha = Yod Yod Vav = YHWH + YHWH = 52. There can be no doubt that gematria was as essential for creating this equation as the eventual conceptual relations between its members. What is conspicuously absent in the Ashkenazi discussion is any intellectual-hypostatic status of Metatron, characteristic of Abulafia's writings. The arch-angel is described in stock traditional and mythical forms of late ancient and early medieval Judaism. The name Yaho'el is known from the ancient Jewish apocryphal literature, the Apocalypse of Abraham.[78] This angel was superseded by Metatron, and some of the former's attributes have been transferred to the latter.[79] Moreover, very ancient material related to Yaho'el survived for more than a millennium and surfaced in Ashkenazi literature.[80] Is this also the case for the relation between Yaho'el and the concept of redeemer? Only a tentative answer can be offered. It is not certain how relevant Abulafia's version is. Moreover, it might be claimed that relations between the disparate elements put together by the Ashkenazi author by the artificial means of gematria may not reflect any earlier correlation. Nevertheless, the linkage between the terms should be addressed as Abulafia has formulated it.[81]

Though the phrase *hu' ha-go'el* is not found in the Ashkenazi manuscripts of *Sefer ha-Ḥesheq,* the whole context of the sentence adduced by Abulafia describes Yaho'el as present in some critical moments in the history of the Jews, such as the Exodus: he was the messenger that saved the Jews at the Red Sea.[82] Thus, Yaho'el is identified with the anonymous angel that led the people of Israel into the desert, as the nexus between its theophoric name and the biblical view of the presence of the name of God within that angel demonstrates.[83] The assumption that Metatron's name is like that of his master reflects in fact a similar statement related to Yaho'el.[84] The angel of the divine presence, by dint of the dwelling of the divine name in it, is a redemptive entity by definition, and I see the occurrence of the gematria more as a technical issue which reflects a logic of the role attributed to Yaho'el. The Ashkenazi text assumes that Metatron, via Yaho'el, is related to the idea of sonship, *ben;* it is strongly connected to the divine name, either in the theophoric name of the angel Yaho'el or because of the significance of the much less clear formula *yod yod vav,* or because fifty-two is twice the numerical value of the Tetragrammaton. Several scholars have drawn attention to the affinities between certain ancient views regarding Jesus and Yaho'el.[85] The eschatological aspect of this constellation of hints, however, is crucial for our discussion here. Metatron is portrayed, according to Abulafia's quotation, which I accept as reliably preserving an earlier tradition, as the Redeemer.

The occurrence of the Redeemer in Abulafia's quotation is, I believe, part of the original vision of the Ashkenazi text and its source. This conclusion is corroborated by the eschatological implication of the figure of Elijah, as well as by the possibility of the occurrence of the phrase *yeshu'a sar ha-panim,* "Yeshua, Prince of the Face," which has been identified by Yehuda Liebes as a reference to Jesus Christ.[86] Liebes's proposal, originally based on the Ashkenazi text which does not contain the phrase *hu' ha-go'el,* is therefore corroborated by Abulafia's version. In my opinion, both Abulafia's passage and the Ashkenazi one reflect a more complete version, which combined the two phrases. If this conjecture is correct, than an early text treating Metatron as identical to Yaho'el, Yeshu'a Sar ha-Panim, Ben, Go'el, and the high priest was in existence before the extant versions but underwent at least two forms of censorship, which produced the two versions. How early such a text was is difficult to calculate. Whether this text reflects a pre-Christian Jewish concept of the angelic son who possesses or constitutes the divine name is also hard to ascertain. If late, the Christian, or Jewish-Christian, nature of such a Hebrew text cannot be doubted.

For the term *ben,* the justification proposed by the Ashkenazi manuscripts is not only a matter of numerical equivalence but is also related to the term *ben 'adam,* "man" or more literally "son of man," much as Metatron is the translation of Enoch, who was a man.[87] In fact, this justification is sufficient in the type of associative reasoning characteristic of the Ashkenazi texts based on gematria. This description, however, deserves a second look. The *ben* in the expression *ben 'adam* may be a reminder of the human extraction of Metatron qua Enoch, namely of his status before the translation. But this explanation, offered explicitly by the text, may reflect an earlier and different understanding of the nature of the Son. It may stand for an earlier perception of an ontological hypostasis possessing messianic overtones, named the Son of Man, known in ancient Jewish and Christian apocalypticism,[88] which reflects in the later sources the achievement of Enoch when he becomes Metatron. In the *Hebrew Enoch* (Chap. XLVIII, C, 7) God describes His relationship with the translated Enoch as that of a father. Such an assumption is corroborated by the view already found in the Ethiopian Enoch 71:5, where the patriarch describes a heavenly entity called Son of Man, which is also the eschatological judge of the world, an attribute found also in the Ashkenazi text.[89] I am inclined to see the sonship as reflecting the hypostatic Metatron rather than the righteous Enoch. If this view is correct, than the Ashkenazi material preserves a much earlier tradition on Enoch's ascent and translation. Already in 4 Ezra 7:27–30 God refers to the

Messiah as His son.[90] This sonship is interpreted by Abulafia is several discussions as dealing with the transformation of the mystic by means of the actualization of the intellect, produced by the illumination of Metatron, the Agent Intellect. While Enoch has become an angel by the elevation of his body, for Abulafia someone becomes a son in his spirit.[91] Different as these forms of sonship are, the Ashkenazi passage and Abulafia's numerous discussions expressed these sonships in the context of the same earlier figures, 'Eliyahu and Enoch, and earlier traditions.

It is difficult to prove to what extent Abulafia is drawing upon earlier stands. He belongs to what I call the innovative impulse of Kabbalah, an approach that allows the Kabbalist much greater room for creativity than earlier. Nevertheless, provided that he explicitly relies on an Ashkenazi text whose formulation is not matched by the available manuscripts, it may be assumed that he could get access to views that are less conspicuous in the extant versions of the passage Abulafia quoted, or to additional material that could inspire him to emphasize the sonship motif.

We may assume, for example, that the importance of sonship was found even in philosophical texts in relation to Metatron, as we learn from a passage written by Abulafia's younger contemporary, R. Levi ben Abraham, a Provençal philosopher:

> "Tell me what is His name" [Proverbs 30:4] because granted that His essence is incomprehensible [to anyone] but to Him, it is written [His] name in lieu of Himself. "What is the name of His son" [ibid.] hints at the separate intellect [namely Agent Intellect] that acts in accordance to His commandment, and it is Metatron, "whose name is the name of his Master" [BT, *Sanhedrin,* fol. 38b], and he [Metatron] also has difficulties in comprehending His true essence [*'amitato*] and in figuring out His essence [*letzayyer mahuto*] . . . the [separate] intellects are called His son, because of their proximity to Him and the fact that He created them without any intermediary.[92]

It seems that Abulafia shares with the Provencal philosopher as much as he does with the Ashkenazi author: the identification of Metatron with the Son of God, in a context explicitly mentioning the divine name. H. A. Wolfson has claimed that "in the history of philosophy an immediate creation of God has been sometimes called a son of God. Thus Philo describes the intelligible world, which was an immediate creation of God and created by Him from eternity."[93] If Wolfson is correct, then we may speak about a line of thought, independent of the christological sonship, that could have affected Abulafia's understanding of the Agent Intellect as the Son of God and as Metatron.

Metatron as the Son is also mentioned elsewhere in the work of Abulafia's school,[94] and, as Ch. Wirszubski has shown, Abulafian passages on Metatron and the Son were translated into Latin and become influential in Christian Kabbalah.[95] Indeed, the history (yet to be written) of the reception of the Metatronic constellations of ideas in Judaism would probably enable us to understand the significant impact of the various avatars of the figure of Enoch. The "Enoch movement," to use J. J. Collins's term,[96] did not completely disappear in late antiquity. By the mediation of the Enochic themes—which survived in Hebrew in the Heikhalot literature, in the succinct talmudic discussions concerning Metatron, the targumic discussions of the Son of Man as Messiah[97] and in fragmented mythologoumena transmitted into the Middle Ages, as the apocalyptic literature where Metatron reveals eschatological secrets and literature related to the seventy names of Metatron, or via the astrological and magical literatures,[98] or perhaps even additional material was available to some Kabbalists and conceived as later fabrications[99]—the apotheotic impulse become more and more accentuated. It was backed in the thirteenth century by the individualistic tendencies that were related to Greek philosophy and reverberated in Christian Kabbalah when combined with christological speculation. Enoch and Metatron were still invoked as part of the apotheotic ideal, and numerous passages in eighteenth-century Hasidism deal with the extraordinary mystical achievement of Enoch the shoemaker. In fact, owing to the influence of Kabbalah, both eighteenth- and nineteenth-century Hasidism and nineteenth-century Mormonism have adopted Enochic elements and represent, to a certain extent, an echo of the Enochic movement.[100]

The redemptive role of Metatron is attested long before the Ashkenazi texts. The insertion of the figure of the Redeemer required some mathematical legerdemain, as the anonymous author had to add the pronoun *hu'* in order to link numerically the idea of the redeemer, *ha-go'el,* to the series. Thus, it is quite reasonable to assume that the Ashkenazi writer attempted to offer a numerical justification for an idea already in existence, which presumably linked Metatron, Sonship, the divine name, and a redemptive figure. In the context of the dictum that "Enoch is Metatron," as in the Ashkenazi text as well as Abulafia (in the lines immediately following the above passage), and even more against the background of the ascent in the Hebrew Enoch with its description of Enoch's enthronement as the angel Metatron,[101] we are faced with another Jewish version of the royal ideology. Sonship, leadership, enthronement, the granting of a divine name, and the eschatological role—all these together when related to the same human being are reminiscent of important aspects of the Mesopotamian pattern. If we add the motif of anointment mentioned in the Slavonic Book of Enoch and its possible reverberation in a certain form in Abraham Abulafia's book *Ḥayyei ha-'Olam ha-Ba',* we may speak about a constellation of themes, described by some scholars (especially G. Widengren) as characteristic of the sacral royalty ideology.[102]

The constellation of ideas described above in the context of Yaho'el is, however, more than a continuation of speculations on themes that stem from hoary antiquity. In my opinion, in Abulafia's writings there is ample evidence to claim an experiential encounter with Yaho'el. In the most important apocalyptic writing extant, *Sefer ha-'Ot,* Abulafia reports a lengthy vision dealing with apocalyptic wars and asks God for an explanation of the meaning of his vision:

> My Lord, tell me the solutions[103] of the wars I have seen in a vision.[104] And he showed me an old man, with white hair, seated upon the throne of judgment . . . and He told me: Go and ask that man who sits on the mountain of judgment and he will tell you and announce to you what are those wars and what is their end, because he is out of your nation. And I have ascended to the mountain of judgment and come close to the elder man and I fell on my face towards the earth before his legs, and he placed his two hands upon me and he stood me upon my legs before him and said to me: "My son, blessed is your coming, peace, peace unto you" . . . "And my name [is] Yaho'el, that I have agreed[105] to speak with you now several years and this is the reason your name will be Ro'u'y'el[106] the visionary, the son of Meqor'el[107] . . . and the name of the fifth [*ḥamiyshiy*] king is Meshiyḥy,[108] and he will be a king after the end of the time of the four kingdoms."[109]

There can be no doubt that the fifth king is the Messiah. The fourth is the elder man, who was described as belonging to the nation of Abulafia. On the other hand, the elder man presented himself as Yaho'el. I take the two hints as pointing to 'Eliyahu, who is a permutation of Yaho'el. Indeed, 'Eliyahu, the fourth, precedes the Messiah, the fifth. If we accept the statement attributed to Yaho'el at its face value, this angel had already been revealing himself to Abulafia for years. Moreover, he addresses the mystic as a son, an issue that is reminiscent of the adoption theory in Abulafia's thought, as well as the occurrence of the term *ben.* The discussion in *Sefer ha-'Ot* between Abulafia, whose personal name is Abraham, and Yaho'el, recalls the sole other conversation of this angel with a human being, that found in the Apocalypse of Abraham, where again it is Abraham who is his partner in a revelatory dialogue.[110] Is this similarity a matter of coincidence? May we assume that Abulafia or his medieval sources had access to the ancient apocalypse, just as some Jewish authors between the eleventh and thirteenth centuries had access to ancient Jewish writings unknown in the rabbinic writings beforehand?[111]

Indeed, Abulafia's experience should be understood on two levels. First are the figurative visions, in which external events are interpreted eschatologically—in the present case pointing to the final battles between three kings, which are followed by the advent of Yaho'el-'Eliyahu and then the Messiah himself. On a second level, Abulafia would interpret both his vision and its eschatological interpretation allegorically, as dealing with internal spiritual processes, or processes taking place between the human intellect and the Agent Intellect. The eschatological scenario turns into a spiritual biography that addresses psychological events, which are much less restricted to a special time and space. In fact, the "external" drama described above should be understood in purely Docetistic terms, in keeping with Maimonides' assumption of the nature of the prophetic vision. Abulafia would never claim to have seen the visions he describes with his carnal eyes. In this inner process, the imaginary drama is then interpreted on two additional levels, the eschatological and the spiritual. The second opens the way for a more democratic distribution of spiritual achievements, as we learn from another important text which involves the idea of sonship:

> Therefore, it is possible for a person who enjoys the radiance of the Shekhinah in this world to be without food for forty days and forty nights, like Moses and 'Eliyahu.[112] And the secret of the names of both of them is known to you, and he combines one with the other: first Moses, and then 'Eliyahu, and their combination emerges as a divine name, and it is in its secret [meaning] the "name of the son," and he is the "son of God," and its secret meaning is *ba-neshamah.* And the invisible letters of MoSheH are Me-'Ayin, which declares that "I am from God" [or "from the Name," *'aniy me-ha-shem*] . . . 'Eliyahu is 'Elohiy and it is said "for he is mine"[113] . . . and the gematria of 'Eliyahu is Ben and see that his secret is "Son of Man" [*ben 'adam*].[114]

Abulafia invokes here the two most extreme instances of ascetic practice and mystical experience in the Bible. At the same time, however, he assumes that they are "possible for a person who enjoys the radiance of the Shekhinah in this world," which I read as assuming that most people, if not everyone, are in principle able to attain such an experience. Moreover, the ecstatic Kabbalist offers an anagrammatic reading of the names of Moses and Elijah, as Mosheh 'Eliyahu point to *shem ha-'elohiy*—the divine name—and, according to another permutation and a gematria, to *ben ha-shem,* namely, the "son of the name" or the "son of God," and *shem ha-ben,* the "name of the son". The mystical experience is therefore apotheotic, transforming the mystic into the son of God, as he is nourished now by the radiance of the Shekhinah, in the mythical parlance of the Midrash, or intelligizes the Agent Intellect according to the Neoaristotelian nomenclature. The inner experience indeed takes place within the soul, *ba-neshamah.* Again, the divine name, 'Eliyahu, and the son occur together, as part of the constellation of ideas found in the Ashkenazi passage analyzed above. *Sefer Ḥayyei ha-'Olam ha-Ba',* from which the last quotation was taken, was written shortly after *Sefer Sitrei Torah,* where Abulafia quoted from the *Commentary on Seventy Names of Metatron,* perhaps even within a year. Therefore, there can be no doubt that the speculations in *Ḥayyei ha-'Olam ha-Ba'* too were influenced by the Ashkenazi treatise, as corroborated by the resort to one of the seventy names of Metatron, Yefeifiyah, the "Prince of the Torah," in the very same context as the above passage.

In this context, influenced as it is by the Ashkenazi numerical speculations, the phrase *ben 'adam,* "Son of Man," occurs, dealing not with the human situation but with the affinities between the extraordinary individuals, Moses and Elijah, and God or His Name. However, Abulafia's discussions in *Ḥayyei ha-'Olam ha-Ba'* should be understood as prescriptive, pointing to the importance of a mystical way of life, and thegist of this book is to offer a detailed technique for achieving the mystical in this world, an experience that was described in explicit messianic terms.

Another instance of the reverberation of the Ashkenazi text in Abulafia's mysticism occurs in his *Sefer ha-Ḥesheq,* where he confesses that he would keep secret but nevertheless disclose only some very general principles of Kabbalah, unless certain circumstances obtained:

> What is compelling me is a divine [*'elohiy*] issue, and some of his secret has been revealed [in the expression] "Enoch, son of Yared"[115] who came in the form of an intellectual preacher[116] and spoke within us[117] and brought consolation upon our heart, and we have been consoled—we would remain silent, just as our ancient masters, blessed be their memory. And it is known that 'Eliyahu, whose name is Yaho'el, will not reveal himself to the wicked, but to the righteous one alone . . . who is the 'counters of His name' [*ḥoshevei shemo*] too. And likewise Enoch, son of Yared, will not reveal himself but to men of truth, those who hate greed, those who are wise men, and acquainted with this divine lore alone, and do not believe anything else. And know that 'Eliyahu and Enoch will come together at one time,[118] having one advice altogether, and they are the harbingers in truth . . . and they will disclose sciences which are very alien today to the wise men of Israel, who are acquainted with the lore of the Talmud.[119]

Thus again Abulafia confesses that he received a revelation from Enoch ben Yared, who is none other than Metatron. It is this revelation that convinced him to disclose Kabbalistic secrets which have conspicuous eschatological overtones, as mention of the advent of 'Eliyahu and Enoch demonstrates. It is therefore his Kabbalah, the "divine lore" he refers to, which ensures the reception of a revelation and then the disclosure of secrets. In *Sefer ha-'Ot* the throne of judgment is connected with the two divine attributes by which the world is governed. Metatron himself is at times depicted as possessing contradictory characteristics, as we find in a short passage by R. Reuven Tzarfati, a Kabbalist influenced by Abulafia: "The Agent Intellect, which is Metatron, the Prince of the Presence, has two impulses, that is, two angels—one appointed over mercy, and one over judgment—

and this refers to the angels 'Azriel and 'Azah."[120] This dialectical understanding is evidently connected with the perception of Enoch as having both good and bad qualities, and it is found already in a Midrash.[121]

Another issue that is found both in one of the versions of the Ashkenazi *Commentary on the Seventy Names of Metatron* and in Abulafia is the continuum between the hypostatical entity and the human mystic. In the *Commentary,* as preserved in the extant manuscripts, there is a play on the same five consonants in the names Yaho'el, 'Eliyahu, ve-'Elohaiy. The relation between the three words generated by the permutation of letters is described in these manuscripts as follows: "to whomever 'Eliyahu is revealing himself, it is from the power of Yaho'el and ve-'Elohaiy."[122] Therefore, 'Eliyahu is an angelic powerwhich reveals itself by dint of the higher angelic power, Yaho'el, and, to my mind, God,[123] referred to here by the term ve-'Elohaiy; namely, 'Eliyahu reveals himself by the power of both 'Yaho'el and "my God." This type of linguistic reference presupposes a certain type of connectedness between the three entities hinted at by the same linguistic material. Whether these three versions of the five consonants indeed reflect more specific and stable ontological levels, for example a possible identity between Yaho'el and divine glory, is still a matter of investigation.[124]

Abulafia, or his Ashkenazi version, did not retain all three permutations but mentions only 'Eliyahu and Yaho'el. Nevertheless, I assume that the concept of a certain type of continuity between the three elements was retained, in another form, in a passage that immediately follows the quotation, where the ecstatic Kabbalist alludes to another form of ontological continuity. Abulafia assumes that divinity is a pure intellect, while Metatron is the Agent Intellect and man a potential intellect. In my opinion, this intellectual continuum is related to the words Abulafia adduced as part of the quotation from the Ashkenazi treatise, where he refers to the words *ba-kol,* "in everything," and *libbekha,* "your heart." These words points to a form of immanence, linguistic in origin but understood by Abulafia as more intellectualistic and ontological at the same time. Abulafia emphasizes that an angel is an influx and a messenger.[125] Indeed, an immanentist propensity is also evident in another interpretation of the sentence "Enoch is Metatron," found in another commentary of Abulafia's on the *Guide of the Perplexed,* entitled *Sefer Ḥayyei ha-Nefesh,* where he interprets the divine name Shadday, related to Enoch-Metatron, as an entity expanding throughout reality.[126] To put these topics in more general terms: the occurrence of the term *go'el* as an attribute of Metatron and Abulafia's interpretation of it in a transcendent-ontological manner point to the median function of the hypostatic redeemer, on the one hand, and to the omnipresence of the radiation of the transcendental Messiah, on the other. Thus, a vertical approach to legitimizing messianism has been created: someone may become the Messiah not because he is of Davidic descent, nor because his soul is a transmigration of the soul of the Messiah—both horizontal explanations—but because he is able to plug in the omnipresent and incessantly active supernal intellectual structure by means of acts of intellection and ecstasy.

In another short discussion of the theme of Yaho'el a different form of relationship is established. in *Sefer Ner 'Elohim,* a treatise written by a follower of Abulafia's, the anonymous Kabbalist interprets the verse "from my flesh I shall see God"[127] as follows: "Mibesar-Y 'Eḥezeh 'Elohah, whose secret is Libby[128] and know and unify the Y with 'Eloha and you shall find 'Eliyahu and Yaho'el and it [amounts to] Ben."[129] Here the assumption is that God, 'Eloha, is numerically identical to "my heart," and together with Y, they point to Yaho'el and 'Eliyahu. In other words, both angelic powers are described as part of a revelatory experience—*'eḥezeh,* "I shall see"—which unites visionarily the heart with God. In Abulafia, the eschatological valences of Enoch, the protagonist of the ancient Jewish Enochic literature, itself influenced by Mesopotamian themes, have been recaptured by the mediation of a variety of motifs spread over the Jewish sources. Unlike the pseudepigraphic genre of the earlier apocalyptic literature, however, Abulafia was ready to resort to the "I am" formula, and even resorted (see appendix 1) to the form *ego,* though in a veiled manner. And in another passage quoted above, he or someone from his group resorted to the formula "I, I," in order to point to the relation between the human and the divine.

The possible impact of the Ashkenazi material, which likely preserved much older material, on the Spanish Kabbalist may open an additional vista onto the circulation of messianic ideas. Unlike the dominant view that the Spanish thinkers were more messianically oriented, in the case of one of the most prominent among them there is good reason to suppose at least a certain sort of influence coming from Ashkenazi circles. The above quotation is, insofar as Abulafia is concerned, part of a much deeper appropriation of Ashkenazi intense use of gematria, and this type of calculation played an important role in Abulafia's writings. It should also be mentioned that another messianic issue, the computation of texts from Daniel in a manner reminiscent of that of the Ashkenazi author R. 'Efrayyim ben Shimshon, can be detected in Abulafia's writings.[130]

Mashiyaḥ and Kohen

The ecstatic Kabbalist adopted the view, quite rare in the Jewish Middle Ages, that the Messiah is also Kohen, a priest.[131] In his *Mafteaḥ ha-Shemot,* a commentary on Exodus, Abulafia interprets the verse " 'Until the Kohen will stand for [the sake of] *'urim* and *tummim*' [Ezra 2:63]: and the secret I possess is that I am a Kohen from the side of my wife, and I am a Levi from the side of my mother, and Israel from the side of my father, blessed be his memory, and despite the fact that the primary order has been changed, in accordance with the thought of the intellect there is no change, for whoever knows the secret of "Melchizedek, the king of Shalem, brought bread and wine, and he is priest to the High God' [Genesis 14:18]."[132] This rare autobiographical description is quite uncharacteristic of Abulafia's writings. It is obvious that he is striving to find a connection to a form of priesthood, and by invoking the pedigree of his wife he offers a very weak argument indeed, as he himself understood. In Judaism, the wife's lineage does not confer any status on her husband. Thus, we learn about an unusual theory as to the combined nature of the Messiah as Israel, Levi, and Kohen at the same time. It is also conspicuous, however, that the main concern of the Kabbalist is to show that someone, like Melchizedek, who predated the Aharonite tribe by centuries, may nevertheless be a priest because, as I understand his position, he is connected to God the Most High. Therefore his type of worship and the nature of his God may confer on him the title of Kohen more than his extraction does. Moreover, Melchizedek was a marginal figure in Jewish religion, though he was more prominent in Christianity, where his name has been connected to the Christ and to the function of high priest.[133] Elsewhere, Abulafia offers another picture of the relations between the three religious classes in Israel: "The more noble man in his species is Israel, . . . and the most noble of Israel is Levi, and the most of Levi is the priest, and the most noble of the priest is the Messiah, who is the high priest, who is the greatest among his brethren, and knows the [divine] name and blesses the people of Israel by dint of the Explicit Name in the Temple and by its cognomen in the country,[134] according to the *qabbalah*[135]."[136]

One of the central functions of the high priest, the ritual of pronunciation of the Tetragrammaton, has been transferred here to the Messiah.[137] Indeed, the shift from the high priest to the Messiah is not so difficult to understand, as there was a ritual of anointment in the case of the priests, and the expression *ha-kohen ha-mashiyaḥ* is found in the Bible.[138] However, while in the biblical context it pointed solely to the present, officiating priest without implying any salvific role (this is also the way the function is portrayed in the rabbinic literature), for Abulafia the term *mashiyaḥ* stands for the Savior figure. The above passage from *Sefer Mafteaḥ ha-Shemot* should then be understood to say that the priest who will stand until *'urim* and *tummim*—which in Abulafia's writings and some earlier sources mean the divine names (Leviticus 4:3)[139]—is none other than the Messiah, who will be present when the Temple is rebuilt and the technique of linguistic divination reestablished.

Moreover, elsewhere Abulafia claims that he possesses a Kabbalistic tradition that God will reveal to the Messiah a divine name, previously unknown, just as

He did in the past to Moses in the case of the famous *'eheyeh 'asher 'eheyeh* ("I Am That I Am"), which Abulafia describes as surfacing in contexts related to redemption.[140] Abulafia does not disclose the precise nature of this name, and hints at the formula 'AHWY. Against this background we may better understand the significance of the word *shemi*, "my name," which is part of the redefinition of the "knowledge of the Messiah and the wisdom of the Redeemer": The divine Name, whatever its precise new formulation may be, is to be seen as part of the messianic gnosis. Though dealing either with a ritual of the past, the high priest's pronunciation of the Name in the Temple, or a future ritual—the same as that performed by the Messiah—Abulafia means something much more actual. On the same page where he describes the Messiah as a high priest he also divulges the technical details concerning the pronunciation of the divine names.[141] In several instances, he characterizes his own Kabbalah as having the status of the Kohen in relation to sefirotic Kabbalah, described by him as corresponding to the lower category of Levi.[142] Therefore, Abulafia not only assumes that he is in the possession of the unknown divine name, formally the prerogative of the Messiah, but he also claims to possess the precise way of reciting divine names.

Moreover, in the same book where he offers the technique for pronouncing the divine name, he claimes that the mystical experience induced by it is messianic, and he describes the feeling of anointment that accompanies it. On the basis of this antecedent, it seems that Sabbatai Tzevi's declaration, dated around 1648, that "I am the Messiah" in the context of the pronunciation of the divine name[143] should be better understood as following a pattern formulated in the writings of Abraham Abulafia. We have approached the question of the sacerdotal nature of the Messiah in Abulafia, from a specific angle, important historically because of the plausible reverberations in Sabbatai Tzevi.

However, there are additional reasons for identifying the Messiah with the high priest. In a twelfth-century Byzantine Jewish source, *Midrash Leqaḥ Tov* by R. Tuviah ben Eliezer, the Messiah ben Joseph is described as building the temple and offering sacrifices, a function that is characteristic of the priests.[144] Moreover, Metatron was connected in some apocalyptic sources, as well as in Abulafia's writings, with the Messiah and has been described in a rabbinic source and in the Hebrew Book of Enoch as a high priest in the supernal Temple; thus a possible identification between the three is possible.[145] The sacerdotal aspect of the Messiah is in fact his functioning as an ecstatic Kabbalist who attempts to reach a mystical experience. Unlike the other Kabbalists, who related the messianic experiences of the Messiah to the nomian way of behavior, Abulafia was resorting to an anomian one, namely the pronunciation of the divine name as a mystical technique. One should not, in my view, understand this Kabbalist's resort to the image of the high priest as an attempt to associate himself with the more popular form of apocalyptic messianism, which was indeed very much concerned with the rebuilding of the Temple by the Messiah. For Abulafia, the high priest was none other than an ecstatic Kabbalist, and a Kabbalist may become a high priest, as we learn from the end of one of his epistles: "Whoever wants to come to the Temple and enter the Holy of Holies should hallow himself with the holiness of the high priest, study and teach, keep and perform [the commandments?] until he becomes perfect in his moral and intellectual capacities, and then he may isolate himself[146] in order to receive the prophetic influx from the 'mouth of the Almighty.' "[147] *Beit ha-miqdash* and even the Holy of Holies are not conceived in the biblical and rabbinic traditions as being accessible to "whoever wants," a phrase that betrays a tendency to popularize one of the most exclusive places in the history of religion, which was done by means of its allegorization. Just as the high priest is the ecstatic Kabbalist, so is his experience identical to ecstasy, for which he must prepare himself carefully. Abulafia reinterpreted the nature of the high priest, and of the Temple, in order to open the gate for a more comprehensive mystical experience which he identified as messianic and redemptive.[148]

Abulafia's Life as Messianic Timetable

Messianism can be understood as part of someone's attempt to make sense of his life. This is certainly true in the case of Abulafia. In fact, we may use his biographical time frame to better understand his messianic activities. Abulafia was born in 1240 C.E., which corresponds to the Jewish year 5000. Abulafia himself describes that millennial year as the time of the beginning of prophecy. In 1260, apparently owing to the influence of the Mongolian invasion of Syria and the land of Israel, he departed on a journey to Israel in search of the Sambation River. In 1270 he received his first revelation in Barcelona. In 1280 he tried to arrange an audience with the pope, and his expected date of the final redemption was 1290. In fact, every complete decade can be seen as a time of special potential, and it seems that the rhythm of the round decade encouraged the messianic expression in Abulafia.

This emphasis on round decades may, after all, be meaningless. Are there additional facts which foster the messianic view of Abulafia's activity? As already mentioned, one of the signs of the Messiah according to Naḥmanides', and according to Abulafia's own revelation, is the journey to the pope, which recalls Moses' going before Pharaoh. This is a paradigmatic event which we will return to when dealing with Shlomo Molkho and Nathan of Gaza.

Abulafia's journey to Rome in 1280 is the first recorded sojourn of a Messiah with the explicit intention to meet the pope. It seems that Abulafia was trying to fulfill the divine revelation that he had received a decade previously in Barcelona. In order to get to Rome in time, Abulafia left Greece late in 1278 or early in 1279, and arrived in Capua in in 1279, where he attempted to gather a small group of students. In the summer of 1280 he arrived in Rome and attempted to meet the pope. The pope, for his part, was unwilling to speak to him, and left Rome to relax in a small castle in Soriano de Cimini. In his commentary on *Sefer ha-'Edut,* Abulafia testifies that he then received a message from the pope, that if he dared come to meet him in Soriano he would immediately be burned at the stake. In spite of this warning Abulafia nevertheless decided to go to Soriano de Cimini, north of Rome and arrived there, as he indicates, on the eve of the Jewish New Year 5041. As soon as he arrived there he was informed that the pope was dead. This episode sounds like a folktale, but the chronicles of the Vatican, as well as the extant historical documents concerning the death of Pope Nicholas III, support Abulafia's account. In all the Latin texts the word used to describe Nicholas's death is *subito,* which confirms Abulafia's description of it in Hebrew, *peta'*. In fact, the Christian chroniclers report that the pope died without confession, for his attendants did not have time to arrange for a priest to come to him. Abulafia was then, according to his own testimony, arrested, not to be burned at the stake but to be held in custody in Rome by a small sect of Franciscan monks known as the Minorites; he was set free two weeks later, apparently without explanation. He then left the Italian peninsula for Sicily, where he spent the last decade of his life, from 1280 to 1291.

The question remains, What did Abulafia want from the pope? or To what purpose did he seek this audience? To our great dismay, all that remains of any statement of Abulafia's intentions is a single sentence, which reads that he intended to speak with the pope about "Judaism in general." There are two opinions concerning the meaning of this sentence. One holds that Abulafia returned to the words of Naḥmanides, who stipulates that the Messiah journey to the pope to request his people's release from bondage, and sees this as simply a political plea: like Moses in the front of Pharaoh, the demand would be, "Let my people go." This explanation is also held, *mutatis mutandis,* by some historians, most eminently Gershom Scholem.[149] The other opinion, embraced by M. Landauer, A. Jellinek, H. Graetz, and others, holds that Abulafia was hoping to convert the pope to Judaism.[150] This extraordinary view is also found in different accounts of Abulafia's life. Yet it seems that neither of these interpretations fit Abulafia's own words. An important clue to understanding the purpose of Abulafia's attempt to win a papal audience is found in the correct interpretation of the term *yahadut,* "Judaism," to which throughout his works Abulafia gives special meaning. Abulafia derives the word from the name Yehudah, which is in turn from the Hebrew root for confession, *hodah.* Therefore a Jew is someone who admits to a specific issue, namely, he is dedicated to the divine names. Indeed, a real Jew is an ecstatic Kabbalist. As we have seen in the passage from *Sefer ha-'Edut,* even the Messiah is understood as a corporeal name, and he is anointed by the powers of the divine names. In Abulafia's system the special or specific issue that one admits to is, quite expectably, the power of the divine names, which stands at the center of the Kabbalistic thought that he developed. If this is indeed the original interpretation of *yahadut,*[151] then perhaps his abortive attempt at gaining an audience with the pope should be viewed as his attempt to converse with him about the "authentic" essence of Judaism. This does not mean that Abulafia felt it necessary to convert the pope to Judaism, as some scholars have claimed, but rather to aid him in understanding Abulafia's special status as a representative of this pure Judaism, or the Kabbalah which focuses on the use of the sacred names of God, as the means to attain prophecy and messianism.

This single dangerous attempt of Abulafia to go before the pope did not deter him from further messianic preoccupations. He interpreted the death of the pope in two ways. On the one hand Abulafia emphasized his own readiness to give his life for the love of God's commandment. In other words, he proclaimed his adherence to the challenge at all cost. On the other hand, Abulafia understood the death of the pope as a divine intervention or even as a testimony to his mission, for he writes of the event as a sign of God's having saved him from the hand of his enemy. Even after his release from the custody of the Minorites, he did not halt his messianic activities: he tried to proclaim his Kabbalistic message to Jews and Christians alike, an absolutely exceptional event in the Middle Ages. During the thirteenth century it was not customary behavior on the part of Kabbalists to spread their teachings among Jews, no less among Christians.[152] Abulafia, however, out of a feeling of messianic urgency, viewed himself as called to both a propaganda mission and an attempt to disclose Kabbalah in more exoteric terms. In a poem composed in the same year as his journey to Rome, he wrote: "You should vivify the multitude by the means of the name Yah, and be as a lion who skips in every city and open place."[153]

As we shall see in the next chapter, Abulafia explicitly connects the divine name Yah to the Messiah.[154] Thus, the attempt to speak with the pope is not solely an attempt to disseminate Kabbalah but is also an act that has redemptive overtones. Actually, Abulafia persisted in engaging in messianic activities in Sicily, where he founded a small school of Kabbalah.[155] This is not the place to discuss the influence of Abulafia's views on messianism; Aescoly has pointed out the possible resonances in *Sefer ha-Peliy'ah,* in the writings of Shlomo Molkho, and even the attribution of a crucial Sabbatean vision to Abraham Abulafia.[156] Though I am not convinced that all Aescoly's points can be proven philologically,[157] his highlighting of Abulafia's importance for the development of the messianic thought is still relevant for other reasons, as I shall attempt to show later.[158]

Altogether the profound messianic character of thirteenth-century Kabbalah betrays an extraordinary affinity between mysticism, messianism, and the biography of the messianic aspirant.[159] Seen from this perspective, the history of the relationship between messianism and Kabbalah must take into serious consideration the frequently repeated commonplace that messianism and Kabbalah were organically integrated only after the expulsion from Spain.[160] It is to be hoped that after learning about the synthesis offered by Abulafia and some of his followers, scholars who critically address these issues will entertain a more historical and less dogmatic approach to the development of the relations between messianism and Kabbalah, as well as a more adequate phenomenology of these religious phenomena.[161]

Concepts of Messiah in the Thirteenth and Fourteenth Centuries: Theosophical Forms of Kabbalah

Messianism in Early Kabbalah

THE main stream of the classical Kabbalah, the theosophical-theurgical trend, did not arise after any historical crisis in Jewish life. It is not characterized, at least not at its inception, by a distinct interest in messianism. This form of Kabbalah started its historical career in a period of spiritual renascence in the intellectual environments of the Kabbalists. Indeed, Kabbalah in general, including the ecstatic Kabbalah dealt with in the previous chapter, should be seen as part of the intellectual revival of Western Europe in the twelfth and thirteenth centuries which affected Christians and Jews alike.[1] In both the Provencal and Catalan stages of Kabbalah, the two first European manifestations of this lore, apocalyptic messianism as understood in the previous types of Jewish literature was treated in a peripheral manner. Gershom Scholem sees the marginality of the concern with messianism in this period as related to a deeper interest of those early Kabbalists with the processes of cosmogony and cosmology, with the emergence of the *arche,* while a state of redemption could be attained by the mystic's causing his soul to return to its source, in a Neoplatonic type of individual salvation.[2] Thus, a certain neutralization of eschatology, apocalyptic or not, has been presumed to have emerged. It has been explained by Scholem as the result of the accentuation of the doctrines concerned with the soul's attempt to ascend to the source.

If, however, there is a correlation between the deemphasis of the eschaton and a deeper interest in the primordial processes, then the Kabbalistic interpretations of *Ma'aseh Bereshit,* the "account of Creation," are to be understood also as an attempt to counteract the Aristotelian interpretation of this account as offered by Maimonides and his followers by resorting to more Neoplatonically oriented types of thought.[3] It could be said, for example, that R. Ezra of Gerona's juxtaposition of the first chapter of Genesis and the cosmogonic Psalm 104, as part of his *Commentary on Song of Songs,* is reminiscent of the similar literary, though not conceptual, enterprise of his contemporary R. Shmuel ibn Tibbon, an ardent follower of Maimonides' esoteric views on Creation.[4] Therefore, we may assume that some of the major Kabbalistic literatures composed before the middle of the thirteenth century do not reflect any special concern with acute messianism beyond what can be found in nonmystical Jewish sources.

This general statement notwithstanding, some concerns with theurgy, eschatology, and messianism can nevertheless be discerned in the writings of the very first Provençal and Catalan Kabbalists, as proposed in a detailed analysis by Ḥavivah Pedaya.[5] Central in this context is R. Azriel of Gerona's view of the Messiah as a divine power, *koaḥ 'elohi,* which rules over the seven opposites and apparently is identical with the third sefirah. This position recalls an ancient Jewish-Christian stand which conceived Jesus to be a power that presides over seven angels.[6]

The 1260s, however, mark a bold change with regard to this topic in the writings of some Catalan and Castilian Kabbalists. The subject of messianism surfaces more powerfully in the non-Kabbalistic works of R. Moses ben Naḥman, better known as Naḥmanides, R. Yitzḥaq ben Ya'aqov ha-Kohen, R. Abraham Abulafia, and especially in the *Zohar,* where messianism is successfully integrated within the overall framework of Kabbalistic ideas. Naḥmanides, one of the most influential figures among Spanish Jewry, dedicated a whole book to the problem of redemption, which includes also precise eschatological computations.[7] His view of the messianic eon as a return to the Adamic state, which might have been influenced by the negative attitude of Christianity toward the will of man as the reason for the Fall,[8] has been quite influential among theosophical Kabbalists.[9] It seems, however, that in his Kabbalistic system, at least as exposed by his disciples in the next two generations, messianism is no more than a marginal issue.

It is very difficult to discern a critical or traumatic event that immediately preceded this new turn in the Kabbalah, and yet it does not seem likely to me that the distinctive originality or the special penchant of one of these Kabbalists, R. Yitzḥaq ha-Kohen, can be the sole explanation for the sudden infiltration of messianic elements.[10] During one generation, several Kabbalists resorted to a variety of forms of messianism: Abraham Abulafia, who started his Kabbalistic career in Catalonia; R. Yitzḥaq, and the author of the *Zohar* in Castile. The fact that different Kabbalists of this one generation all embraced discussions of messianism seems to point to the existence of an unifying factor that simultaneously stimulated these otherwise different forms of mystical thought. To my mind, the widespread and quite terrifying rumors concerning the Mongolian invasion of Eastern Europe, Syria, and the land of Israel that abounded in the 1250s and 1260s, merely a few years before the composition of the messianic works of these Kabbalists, can be seen as just such a factor. Unlike the turmoil and panic provoked by this invasion among the Christians, however, for some Jews in Western Europe this "news" provoked strong hopes for an immediate redemption.[11] This can be a possible model of interpretation for an interest in messianism that did not originate from a feeling of traumatic crisis but, on the contrary, might have started with a definite feeling of hope in a more positive development of events for the Jews. Since the messianic thought of early Kabbalists spreads over many topics and is derived from diverse and sometimes even conflicting thought patterns, it is plausible to posit an historical event which was interpreted in various ways by different Kabbalists. In the course of our discussion I will expand on the differences between various messianic concepts that are characteristic of the different Kabbalistic schools. I presuppose the general impact of the positive perception of an historical event and its reverberations in the imagination of the contemporaries, causing the acceleration and intensification of messianic thought in some Kabbalists. I would refrain, however, from proposing too direct a link between the nature of the event and the variety of forms which the content of the Kabbalistic eschatological imagery took.

Messianism and Theosophic Kabbalah in Thirteenth-Century Castile

Alongside the mystical and theurgical models of messianism, there existed in the second half of the thirteenth century another model that I will term *traumatic messianism.* This type of messianism possesses a sharp apocalyptic character and is depicted in the works of a Castilian Kabbalist who wrote at mid-century, R. Yitzḥaq ben Jacob ha-Kohen. His messianic composition, as J. Dan has pointed out, is replete with discussions of the the struggle between good and evil.[12] Yet neither the mystical conception, positing the need for intellectual development toward attainment of the messianic state, or the theurgical mode, advocating the use of ritual activity in order to restore the divine perfection, are significant in R. Yitzḥaq's work. His model seems to be greatly influenced by popular Jewish eschatology, which emphasized the historical struggle and not inner human perfection or divine harmony. From this standpoint, we are dealing with a form of Kabbalistic messianism that is independent of the other models and seems to have only slightly influenced them.

The most influential of these phenomena are the messianic conceptions of the zoharic literature, the corpus considered to be the most important Kabbalistic canon.[13] The Kabbalah of the *Zohar,* as is the case with the majority of the Spanish Kabbalah, is founded on theological concepts that are radically different from Abulafia's. Whereas Abulafia largely followed Maimonides in his emphasis on the absolute unity and intellectual nature of God, most of the Spanish Kabbalists, including the view of the *Zohar,* imagined God as a composite of forces and dynamic processes which are in a constant state of fluctuation and activity, dependent upon the fulfillment of the divine commandments, the *mitzvot.*[14] The focus of this sort of Kabbalah is directed toward the restitution of these divine forces, the sefirot, to their original, harmonious state. Abulafia takes the anthropocentric view that the quintessence of messianism is the actualization of the intellectual potential, an internal human phenomenon that epitomizes human perfection. On the other hand, the *Zohar* and its type of Kabbalah emphasized a theocentric view in which the need for divine harmony is the ultimate goal of human endeavor, to be achieved by means of the regular Jewish ritual.[15]

R. Moses de Leon, one of the leading Kabbalists at the end of the thirteenth century and the main participant in the writing and editing of the *Zohar,*[16] was a proponent of theocentrism. In his *Sefer Maskkiyyot ha-Kesef,* a commentary on the daily liturgy, he wrote the following concerning the pronunciation of the liturgical piece *'Emmet ve-Yatziv*:

> You should know that all the sublime issues and the profound secrets are found in *'Emmet ve-Yatziv,* and the secret of His divinity and the issue of the secret of the redemption that is followed by prayer,[17] so that the Sensitive Light and the Intellective Light will be one . . . according to the secret of the exile [*galut*] and the redemptions [*ge'ullot*] in *'Emmet ve-Yatziv* . . . he should do what is good in his eyes[18] in order to connect redemption to prayer and cause the union of the Sensitive Light with the Intellective Light, without any separation between them, so that everything[19] will be[come] one.[20]

This passage is representative of a whole range of texts which assume that man can and ought to perfect divinity by performing ritual, a central aspect of the main trend of Kabbalah. This mode of thought can be described as part of *via perfectionis.* Though different from the ecstatic Kabbalah, which also belongs to that mode, they share an emphasis on perfection and the meeting with the divine as part of the redemptive processes.

There are several sources of the images used in this text. Exploiting a talmudic statement, Moses de Leon resorts to two crucial terms: redemption and prayer. They correspond to two pieces of daily liturgy, which were supposed to be recited consecutively and without interruption between them. In the Kabbalistic jargon, however, the two titles became symbols for hypostatic entities or divine powers. Prayer stands, according to Moses de Leon, for the divine manifestation of Malkhut, the last sefirah, while redemption is a symbol for the ninth sefirah, Yesod. On the other hand, the two kinds of light, the sensitive and the intellective, are just another instance of hypostatical reading of earlier sources. The two terms occur already in the twelfth-century *Sefer Kuzari* (I, ¶109); they were adopted by the Geronese Kabbalists,[21] but their interpretation as pointing to these two divine powers is found in the earlier books of R. Moses de Leon.[22] The two sefirot should be united by means of the theurgical performance of the commandments, in our case the precise pronunciation of the prayer according to the ritualistic prescription, which does not allow any speech between these two sections of the daily liturgy. The achievement of the union between the divine powers is depicted by the Kabbalist in strong erotic imagery.[23] The sexual union between the two powers means that redemption enters prayer, namely that the feminine manifestation, prayer, is redeemed by the male, symbolized by redemption, when the two become united. The fact that the two terms are related to these particular sefirot can be interpreted as pointing to the special dynamics involved in the act of redemption: the prayer, coming from below, reaches the feminine manifestation and prepares her for the act of union with the higher divine masculine power, which will bestow upon her his influx. To a great extent, the redemption of the last divine manifestation is tantamount to the redemption of the divine system in general, achieved by means of human activity, namely prayer. Redemption becomes, therefore, not only a process taking place in the remote future but a symbol for an already existing and active entity which is involved in whatever happens here below.

This type of Kabbalistic redemption is less dramatic and more modest than the advent of the Messiah at the end of time, when everything will undergo a total transformation. Its meaning is the improvement of the plight of the world by the descent of the influx to the mundane level. As we have seen in the case of the ecstatic Kabbalah Abraham Abulafia, the very fact that the messianic drama becomes part of a much more comprehensive process has a logic of its own which may overshadow the logic of the apocalyptic events. The eschatological elements in Jewish messianism became, in the case of the theosophical-theurgical Kabbalah, fraught with erotic images, with hypostatic forms of thought, and with inner-divine processes taking place between these hypostases.

Prayer, to a great extent, represents the human activity which ascends on high, meeting there the divine potency of redemption and interacting with it. Two active entities, both divine, are found in an ongoing and dynamic process. Yet the hypostatization of the two entities creates a certain mechanization of the processes: though this mechanization is attenuated by the erotic images, the personalistic approach is not dominant. The Messiah, even when he is introduced in such contexts, is not a genuinely free agent but becomes a symbol for and representative of a divine manifestation. The ostensibly ritualistic context of the discussion points to the daily nature of the encounter between the two sefirot. A Kabbalist, in our case a theurgical-theosophical one, is supposed to envision his performance of the commandments while remaining aware of their impact on the higher world.

Despite these remarks about mechanization, the daily liturgy, when redescribed eschatologically, may revitalize messianism and itself become much more activist. The already present potency of redemption, which is to be united with the hypostasis of the prayer of the entire community, invites another psychological mood or a different religious mode of experience than the more routine prayer. The Messiah, a preexisting person according to a view found in rabbinic literature, is to be met only by the very few who are able to ascend to heaven and discuss with him the plight of the people of Israel. The Kabbalistic rendering of the messianic potencies as approachable during the performance of the ritual opens another type of religious experience, which is to be compared to the Christian sacrament, where Christ is envisioned as present and sometimes even active during the ceremonial ritual.

Notwithstanding this awareness of the impact of prayer, it would be very unlikely to detect acute messianic aspirations in the Hebrew writings of Moses de Leon. There are, however, some Aramaic formulations of his views on that topic. In the earlier layer of the *Zohar,* the so-called *Midrash ha-Ne'elam,* we read: "When will the Redeemer come? When Israel will pray a prayer and will join redemption and prayer, and Israel are in the land of Israel [the Holy Land].[24] But when they do not cause the union between redemption and prayer, then One[25] is not united to the Other, and She [Shekhinah, the last sefirah] is going in exile."[26] Composed in Spain, when the prospects of the people of Israel to go back to the land of Israel were dismal, this statement reflects the attraction of messianic motifs into a discussion whose focus is not acutely eschatological. The eschatological mindset, present in Judaism as a cultural code, was activated associatively when the term *ge'ullah,* "redemption," occurred; in lieu of understanding it as an appellation to a certain part of the daily prayer, it has been conceived as pointing to the act of redemption itself. This understanding in turn attracts the use of its complementary term, *galut,* "exile," which clarifies and strengthens, by way of antithesis, the literal meaning of *ge'ullah.* Also the use of the plural form, *ge'ullot,*[27] in the first quotation above indicates that indeed the redemptive significance of this term is intended, as the plural cannot refer to a piece of liturgy.

Why a certain set of images was activated and valorized more in a certain period or by a certain school, in comparison to a relative indifference or neglect toward its contents in another period or school, is a matter of both the particular mindset of the Kabbalist and the general ambiance. The latter may have been more open to messianic motifs because of the eschatological effervescence caused by historical events. The Kabbalist, even when he belonged to what I have proposed to call the innovative or creative stage of Kabbalah,[28] as de Leon certainly did, was still immersed in the hermeneutical grids already in an authoritative position. Like any other human being, he not only was born in history but also was caught in a web of traditions. He had to take into account the rabbinic starting points, in our case the requirement not to pausse between the two prayers. Moreover, the hypostatical reading of the Kabbalah was formative for the hermeneutical enterprise of de Leon all over his writings. The messianic connotations were therefore only the third factor in shaping the discussion from de Leon.[29] In fact, the other elements were much more substantial and influential. The discussion was introduced by way of word association: Ge'ullah changed its meaning from a title of a part of the prayer dealing with the request for redemption to the concept of redemption. In other words, the fascination with the intellectual worlds of theosophy and theurgy, whose elaborate structures were established by the intensive creative activity of the religious imagination of the innovative Kabbalists, attracted the already existent messianic motifs into their nets and changed them; the messianic motifs in turn, to a certain degree, changed the theosophical-theurgical thought, which was thereby fraught with a greater experiential cargo. In my opinion, this description, which is focused here around texts of the thirteenth century,[30] is also valid in the sixteenth-century Lurianic brand of Kabbalah. In both cases, the restorative impact of the theurgical acts is the core of a religious paradigm or model;[31] in both cases some messianic elements serve as an additional hermeneutical grid. However, in de Leon's writings, as well as in the book of the *Zohar*, symbolism is more alluded to than explicitly invoked. Later on explicit symbolism, which turned to more technical forms of expression, became prevalent. The role of the persona of the Messiah became less important than that of the theurgical Kabbalist, who acts in order to open the way for his advent.

In line with these changes in theology are the variations in the outlook on messianic phenomena as presented in Abulafia's works, which conceptually contrast with the book of the *Zohar*. The *Zohar* presents messianism as the fruits of the human attempt to restore divine perfection, a state that was disturbed by the sins of Adam and Eve and humankind. When the original harmony of the divine pleroma will be restored, perfection will reign in the divine world and automatically that harmony will express itself in the human sphere as well, meaning that the world has reached the state of the end of days. Accordingly, the messianism presented in the *Zohar* is best defined as theocentric or—in Yehezkel Kaufmann's terminology—soteriological, for it concentrates first and foremost on the redemption of the divine itself from its relatively imperfect state of being in the present; only then, indirectly, will the Jewish people and ultimately the entire universe be redeemed. This stands in contradistinction to the messianic theory of Abulafia and to his self-awareness: there the order of redemption is concerned first with the perfection of the individual as a precondition for the redemption of the nation and possibly of mankind. From this perspective we can see two completely different intellectual structures that flourished simultaneously in two distinct Jewish cultural centers.

Most layers of the zoharic literature advocate the centrality of theurgical activity, meaning the fulfillment of the divine commandments with the intention of inducing a greater divine state of perfection. The bulk of the zoharic corpus does not exhibit a consciousness of acute messianism, one that is apt to burst forth in the immediate future, as is the case in Abulafia, but rather it presents a comprehensive and sometimes quite detailed messianic theory. Modern scholarship has yet to explore the messianic underpinning of the main body of the zoharic literature, and with the crucial exception of Liebes's brilliant exposition of the messianic basis of the *'Iddrot*, the prevalent assumption in scholarly circles is that messianism is not so salient in the *Zohar*. A perusal of this book, however, shows that there are hundreds of short treatments of eschatological, apocalyptic, and messianic topics. Yet in certain later parts of the *Zohar*, including the *'Iddrot* and the even later compositions of the *Tiqqunei Zohar*, we do find an even greater emphasis on the messianic elements as well as a heightening of the significance of messianic conceptions. According to Liebes, the messianic figure R. Shimeon bar Yoḥai was imagined as maintaining the world by his theurgical activity.[32] This is evident in terms of theurgical conceptions and several computations of the date of redemption, expressing a vivid messianic consciousness, although still falling short in comparison with the acute messianism in the writings of Abulafia at this very time.

The three models—Abulafia's mystical-ecstatic, the *Zohar*'s mythical-theurgical, and R. Yitzḥaq ben Jacob ha-Kohen's mythical-apocalyptic or traumatic—all bear witness not only to the substantial integration of messianism within a variety of forms of Kabbalistic literature but also to a dramatic diversification of the very concept of Kabbalah. In the earlier stages of the Kabbalah, during the first half of the thirteenth century, and also in specific types that developed in the second half of the thirteenth century in Castile, the messianic element is no more noticeable than in any other sort of normative Jewish literature. The strengthening of the messianic elements in other forms of writing is, in my opinion, related to the ideological conceptions that characterize only certain types of Kabbalistic systems, like Abulafia's and the *Zohar*'s. These systems represent a new phase in the development of the Kabbalah, one that can be described as the transition from a conservative Kabbalah which was handed down faithfully for generations, from traditions possessed by earlier Kabbalists, to a creative and innovative Kabbalah which experimented, through different hermeneutical systems and by virtue of the mystical experiences of these Kabbalists, opening new vistas of expression while elaborating on old ideas and occasionally developing new ones.[33] In this light, the permeation of the messianic idea is but a part of a larger complex of ideological reconceptualization that occurred in the Spanish and Italian Kabbalah. It is even possible to maintain that at the end of the thirteenth century the principle Kabbalistic developments are closely related to a variety of messianic ideas. Again, though positing the systemic development of a much more flexible understanding of the role of the Kabbalist in transmitting and transforming Kabbalah, I propose not to disregard the possible impact of the effervescence created by the rumors concerning the Mongols' invasion.

Moreover, in the 1290s there appeared another interesting messianic phenomenon which may not actually be related to Kabbalah in the strict sense of the word. In the early years of the decade there was a boy in the Castilian city of Avila someone who was thought to be illiterate but who nevertheless started to write down angelic revelations. These revelations contained a strong messianic element.[34] It is difficult to confirm whether the boy from Avila was influenced by the intense Kabbalistic and messianic activity noticeable in Castile at this time, yet from the manner in which this phenomenon is described, and implicitly opposed, by R. Solomon ibn Adret, it appears that this was the case. Just as with Abulafia, the boy revealed secrets of the basic document in the commentary upon it that was dictated to him by the angel, and from this vantage point at least we can see some similarity to the other indubitable Kabbalistic phenomena discussed above.[35]

Messiah: Symbol and Hypostasis

In the theosophical-theurgical stream of Kabbalah, a major mode of expression and of comprehending tradition was symbolism; almost the whole range of linguistic material in Hebrew was understood by the theosophical Kabbalists as pointing to a variety of hidden entities, primarily divine but also demonic. In fact, the symbolic interpretations are only rarely stable, and various Kabbalists have their own symbolic grids. Though we may detect some recurrent patterns, it would be a mistake to approach the huge Kabbalistic literature with the assumption that it is informed by one basic symbolic pattern. This is also the case with the concept of the Messiah, which is treated by different Kabbalists as pointing to various sefirot. Here I shall attempt to explore succinctly two main patterns: the meaning of the connection between the Messiah and the last sefirah, on the one hand, and of the Messiah and the first divine manifestation, on the other. In a later chapter I shall attempt to describe the momentous history of the symbolism of the Messiah as pointing to Binah, the third sefirah. It is quite easy, however, to find additional examples of sefirotic valences for this term. Quite recurrent is the view of two Messiahs as pointing to the sefirot of Netzaḥ and Hod,[36] or, even more influential, the many instances where the Messiah is related to the ninth sefirah, Yesod.[37] In most cases, the different symbolic values charge the meaning of the Messiah with different valences. In any event, the various sefirotic powers referred to as the Messiah had an impact on the concept of the Messiah when connected to each of these divine powers, contributing to a diversity of conceptualizations of this term even in the theosophical Kabbalah.

Messiah and Malkhut

The view of the tenth and last sefirah, as the attribute of kingdom, as the feminine manifestation of the divine presence (Shekhinah), is one of the more common attempts in theosophical Kabbalah to make sense of the traditional identification of the Messiah as the future king. This is conspicuous in the *Zohar* as well as in a book of R. Moses de Leon, *Sheqel ha-Qodesh*.[38] De Leon elaborated on the symbol of the king-Messiah as denoting the power ruling over the world, known as the sefirah of Malkhut.[39] This last term can be translated as "kingdom," and it is only natural that a connection emerged between the last sefirah and the concept of the Messiah as king. The major point de Leon makes at the beginning of the relatively intricate discussion is the very idea of anointment. He resorts to the recurring understanding of the oil as a symbol for the divine emanation within the sefirotic realm, in order to draw a parallel between the lower and higher worlds. Just as the last sefirah receives its influx from the higher sefirot and by dint of this descending power is able to rule over the lower, extradivine world, so too the king is to be anointed in order to be able to assume the task of kingship, namely to rule over his subjects. While in the biblical description, however, the oil is poured on the king by a human—a prophet or a priest—the Kabbalistic approach sees the king as receiving this special consecration from the higher, divine powers. Thus, the affinity between the king and the divinity becomes much more conspicuous in the Kabbalistic version than in the biblical one, and therefore more reminiscent of the ancient sacral royalty. Moreover, the biblical ritual of anointment is conceived by de Leon in terms of *imitatio dei;* the act of anointment is seen as a transference of power, which actually confers an extraordinary nature upon the recipient of the anointment.

Just as the last sefirah, which is the supernal Messiah, collects the influx (the oil) from the higher sefirot, so too the human Messiah is anointed by higher powers. Thus a continuum was created, stemming from the highest sefirot and descending to the lowest sefirah, which is the supernal Messiah, and thence to the human Messiah. This lower Messiah stands at the lowest extremity of the divine present in the mundane world, and thus he is both the representative of God on Earth and the individual who epitomizes the mystical attachment of a human being to God, not only in cognitive terms, as was the case in Abulafia's system, but in much more "concrete" forms which apparently affect more the Messiah's body than his intellect.

Beyond the parallelism between the acts of anointment, however, there was a special affinity between the supernal kingdom, designated in many Jewish as well as Christian texts as the "kingdom of heaven," envisioned by de Leon as tantamount to the last divine manifestation, and the flesh-and-blood king. King David is portrayed as longing for union, or communion, with the feminine divine power, called Malkhut David, "the kingdom of David." David searched for the "mystery of communion," *sod ha-hidabbequt.*[40] Only such a king, one who is a mystic but is also anointed by the horn of oil, will be able to establish a lineage of descendants maintaining the role of king,[41] a view expressed in an identical context in the *Zohar* (vol. 1, fol. 260b). According to this interpretation, the act of anointment should be supplemented by an act of mystical devotion to the sefirah of Malkhut, a search for an immediate contact with Her in order to safeguard the continuation of the royal line. This adherence to the supernal king-Messiah is decisive for having a lasting lineage of anointed kings on earth, a Jewish version for the medieval concept of *rex qui nunquam moritur.*

What may be the reason for this cleaving to the "supernal David"[42] as the last divine power? Unfortunately, Moses de Leon is not clear on this point. But we may extrapolate from his view of theurgical operation—namely the "constitution of the Shekhinah"[43] mentioned in this very context—and the act of adherence that they are intended to ensure the emergence and maintenance of a continuum between the higher and lower worlds, with the human king as the lower pole, a recipient of the higher emanation from the divine manifestation also called king. Such a reading would assume a return to the view of the king as portrayed by the scholars of the myth-and-ritual schools. The concept of king, like that of the last sefirah, involves two major processes: both the lower body and the divine power designated as king-Messiah are anointed with oil and cling to the source of the influx described as the holy unction. The symbolic relation and the narrowing of the gap between them by mystical devotion are therefore two different though overlapping moments of the beginning of the career of the king-Messiah.[44]

Here, however, we are more concerned with the transformation of the political role of the king, whose royal function is achieved by acts of anointment and coronation[45] into a mystical ritual conceived of as ensuring the descent of divine power, which means that the holy oil may be seen as a third understanding of the oil: it stands for the power descending from the higher to the lower world. Thus again the anointed king in de Leon's passage stands not so much for the future savior in an apocalyptic era but for the *perfectus* who is the operator of the descent of the sustenance of the whole world. I would count this view as part of *via perfectionis,* as in this Kabbalist's earlier discussion regarding prayer. In other words, the metaphysics built up by the theosophical-theurgical Kabbalah in the context of understanding the "authentic," mystical nature of the king presupposes a function for the king that is similar to the ancient Near Eastern royal ideology and, according to some scholars, to the ancient Israelite kings. Those biblical scholars hold that de Leon considers the human king not as being the son of God, in the manner the Egyptian religion, but as having been adopted by gods, as in the Babylonian religion.[46] Yet while the ancient kings and the biblical psalms—Psalm 2, for example—speak more about adoption of the king by God, the Kabbalists emphasize the human mystical initiative leading to adherence of the mystical king-Messiah to the supernal Messiah, or to use Edmund Leach's terminology, they belong more to the "icon of orthodoxy" than to the "icon of subversion." The hypostatic status of the king-Messiah as a last divine power is, however, more reminiscent of the ancient Egyptian vision of the king as an embodiment of a divine power. In different ways, these concepts of the king-Messiah both as a human person and as a divine manifestation have attenuated the apocalyptic model in favor of a much more organic and continuous vision of the structure of the world, which starts with the highest divine power producing the "oil" and goes down to the human king who becomes the Messiah by being anointed with the divine power which descends upon him.

The king-Messiah in de Leon's view re-creates, by performance of the ritual and his mystical devotion, the cosmic continuum, without breaking the historical processes as the apocalyptic Messiah is expected to do. On the contrary, he ensures not only the vertical but also the horizontal dynastic continuity. The role of adherence here is quite intriguing. It is only after the theurgical operation of constituting the Shekhinah has been accomplished that devotional adherence is mentioned. It seems that the human king prepares the higher king so that He may transmit His energy to the lower world, and the act of transmission is ensured by the adherence to the theurgically prepared entity.[47] This seems to be a crucial model in de Leon, as we learn from another passage in his *Sheqel ha-Qodesh:* "the quintessence of the commandments and of good deeds that a person performs in this world is to constitute [*le-konen*][48] his soul and to arrange[49] the great and good things on high, [so as] to draw down upon himself the influx of the light of the supernal emanation."[50] Indeed, the ontic continuum between the two worlds, which are conceived of as mirroring each other, is also found elsewhere in the same book of de Leon's.[51] In the larger context of the last quotation, the influx is symbolized by the recurring image of the oil.[52] Thus, the task of the king-Messiah is to be understood as not different, at least phenomenologically speaking, from that of a magical Kabbalist: both are supposed to bring down the power necessary for the welfare of the world. Indeed we may assume a sequence of three major mystical operations: two of them designated by the verb *le-konen,* "to constitute," one conveying the psychological preparation of the human soul, which will stand for the lower pole of the process, the other being the preparation (constitution) of the last divine power, the Shekhinah, which will be the supernal pole. The Shekhinah is the source of the power to be drawn down by means of the third process, mentioned in the last quotation but also hinted at in the first by the adherence that will ensure the dynastic continuity of the lower king.

While Moses de Leon's discussion of the Messiah points, at least formally, to the glorious past—though it may be understood as a paradigmatic way of acting—the last quotation should be understood to mean that what the Messiah has done in hoary antiquity for the whole nation could and should be done by the Kabbalist in the present day for his own benefit. As in the case of the identification of the redemption, *ge'ullah,* with the ninth sefirah,[53] the view of the supernal king-Messiah as identical with the last divine power should also be understood as part of an attenuation of the apocalyptic elements in Jewish eschatology, since the ever-existence of both redemption and Messiah as formative powers for the processes that shape the lower world does not depend upon a particular time in history. The hypostatization of some details of the classical "messianic" (namely, ontological) understanding of the unctional Jewish terminology, such as oil and crown, inherently attenuates the unexpected aspects of some of the earlier forms of messianic thought by integrating them in a more comprehensive system. This systematization of the earlier Jewish myths is a well-known phenomenon which is evident from the very beginning of Kabbalah.[54]

To better understand the move toward a metaphysics that creates a continuum which allows a much more natural explanation of the processes in the world, a comparison of the above discussion to a passage in the *Zohar* may be helpful. In a strongly apocalyptic passage the Messiah is described as entering a pillar of fire, where he will be hidden for twelve months after the great apocalyptic battles. This pillar, very similar to an *axis mundi,* brings him to the firmament, and there he receives the strength (*tuqppa'*)[55] and the crown of kingship (*'ateret malkhut*),[56] and afterwards the nations will also recognize him as the

Messiah.[57] Here too the act of coronation is obvious: the Messiah, apparently the Messiah ben Joseph who implicitly has been killed, is ascending in order to be revived and then return as a crowned king. The zoharic passage introduces another form of continuum between the two worlds, the pillar of fire. But the concept of the pillar climbed by the presumably dead Messiah, his having been hidden there, and his return to public activity are less concerned with the structure of the universe or the manner of reconstructing the ontic continuum by a mystical activity. They portray a more dramatic and thus less explainable move that seems to be much more mythical and much closer to the apocalyptic Midrashim rather than reflecting de Leon's views on the same topic. Indeed, the diversity of the messianic concepts in the zoharic literature attributed to Moses de Leon is much greater than the concepts developed in the writings of this Kabbalist, an issue—among many others—that problematizes the simple attribution of the main zoharic corpus to de Leon. The attention of the *Zohar* to the suffering Messiah, a recurrent issue in the midrashic and apocalyptic literature, seems to be marginal in the Hebrew writings of de Leon.

From this point of view, the position of the ecstatic Kabbalah is quite different from the zoharic mythology of the persona of the Messiah. In the writings of Abulafia, the passion of the Messiah had been radically mitigated. The views of the Messiah as a power on high in theosophical Kabbalah are reminiscent of the ecstatic Kabbalistic visions of Metatron, analyzed in the preceding chapter. Though historically different, the two structures share the common denominator of identifying the lowest level of their emanational system with the ruler of the world and the Messiah. I believe that a synthesis between the two trends is found in the work of a fourteenth-century Italian Kabbalist, R. Reuven Tzarfati. In his commentary on a classic of Kabbalah, the anonymous *Sefer Ma'arekhet ha-'Elohut,* he expatiates on its identification of the last sefirah and Metatron, writing that

> when the prince [Metatron] ascends from below on high to receive the influx, he is called Metatron, by six letters, because this name is attributed to it because of his safeguarding, because the safeguarding of the geni and the species is attributed to the abovementioned prince. However, when it descends from on high the prince comprises ten [sefirot] and the letter *yod* is added to its name and it is called Mitatron, by seven letters . . . and it is called Angel, because the lower world is ruled by it [Malkhut] and this is why it is also called Messenger. And it is called Ge'ullah because it redeems us [*go'el 'otannu*] from exile.[58]

This passage is symptomatic of a very long development. The last sefirah, which is the main topic of the whole quotation, is described by the commented text by a long series of symbols, the relevant ones for our discussion being

Metatron, *mal'akh ha-go'el, mal'akh,* and *shaliyaḥ.* The major assumption is that Metatron, the ruler over this world, is also maintaining it by means of the divine influx he brings down. Therefore, the redeeming angel is also the maintaining one. The description of the maintenance is interesting because it resorts to philosophical terminology, species and genus; the best interpretation is that this Kabbalist refers here, as he has done explicitly in some other cases, to the concept of Agent Intellect, whose influx was conceived of as creating the forms in the lower world. Unlike the philosophical concept, however, here Metatron is described not only as mediating the influx but also as changing itself by its ascent and descent, which not only mediate the divine power but also transmit it, referring thus to a much more mythical universe of discourse. As the last statement in the quotation shows, the ordinary maintenance function is combined with a future redemptive one, as issue that will be illustrated in a different manner by the thought of R. Shlomo Molkho (chapter 5).

Another instance when theosophical-theurgical Kabbalah was combined with the concept of the descent of the divine power and redemption is in the writings of the sixteenth-century Tunisian Kabbalist R. Joseph al-Ashqar. In his *Tzafnat Pa'aneaḥ* al-Ashqar notes that the keeping of the two Sabbaths consecutively, an issue envisioned already in the Talmud as bringing about the redemption, will repair the separation between the divine powers on high; and then, "when the unification of the two [days of] Sabbath is perfected on high . . . and when things return to their [primordial] existence, then the influx will be enhanced and from that influx an emanation, [consisting of, or symbolized by] the 'dew of blessing,' will come to the world and because of the descent of the influx the Redeemer will come in order to publicize the unity."[59] The return of all things to their source is a view reiterated in Kabbalistic literature in the context of the reintegration of the entire cosmos, including the lower sefirot, to its source within one of the higher sefirot.[60] The active, theurgical operation of unifying two divine powers, both designated as Sabbath, re-creates the lost unity which enables the descent of the power here below, an event presented as tantamount to redemption. The term employed by al-Ashqar for causing the descent is a rather strong form, *horadah,* which recurs in many texts related to magical talismanics and, as we shall see below, also in Moses Ḥayyim Luzzatto and, more explicitly, in Hasidism in the context of messianic activity.

Messiah and Keter

According to R. Yitzḥaq of Acre, prophecy is attained by the presence or radiance of angelic and divine powers, which descends upon different personalities from the various parts of the divine hierarchy. The lowest rank would be the prophecy stemming from the brilliance of an angel; a higher rank is that of the person who would be indwelled by the light of Metatron, which is often conceived of as the highest of the angelic powers. Higher still is the presence of the power of the last sefirah within the human soul, even higher is the reception of the brilliance of the sixth sefirah, Tiferet, which is described as having generated Moses' prophecy. The highest form of prophecy, however, is attributed to the Messiah, the son of David, who will receive, according to this Kabbalist, "the radiance of the light of the Crown [Keter, the first sefirah], will emanate the brilliance of his light from Keter and it dwells in his soul, and by it he will perform awesome and great things in all the lands."[61]

While for Moses de Leon the human Messiah is related to the last sefirah, conceived of as the supernal Messiah and as such inferior to Moses, who is a symbol of and connected to the sixth sefirah, Tiferet, R. Yitzḥaq of Acre and other Kabbalists—Abraham Abulafia, for example[62]—would see in the arrival of the Messiah a moment which transcends the rank of the most sublime prophecy and even the mystical cognition attained by Moses, being outstanding examples of *via perfectionis.* This high evaluation of the intuitive knowledge attainable in the messianic era is quite exceptional in Kabbalah, where the maximum attainment was commonly restricted to the intuition of the eighth sefirah.[63] This quotation raises the interesting question of the relation between the attainment and the human initiative (if any) toward it. This issue cannot be easily solved, and it is possible to assume, following the path of Abulafia's Kabbalah, that the Messiah will be someone who will take the initiative and become a mystic, possibly higher even than Moses. Indeed in one of Abulafia's texts we learn about the possibility of cleaving to the sefirah of Keter and drawing therefrom the blessing,[64] a model accepted in principle also by R. Yitzḥaq.[65] In general, R. Yitzḥaq's mystical path is more spontaneous and less calculated than that of the more technically oriented Abulafia, and this is the reason for my hesitation in introducing in his case the possibility of an hypothetical technique which would make someone the Messiah. Nevertheless, in at least one instance we learn from this Kabbalist that a mystical union with Metatron can be achieved by cleaving to him,[66] while elsewhere he mentions, in the name of a certain R. Nathan—in my opinion a student of Abulafia[67]—the possibility of cleaving to the divine intellect and becoming thereby a divine man capable of creating worlds.[68] Thus, it is still plausible that this Kabbalist will regard messianism not so much as a gift but as a mystical attainment initiated by man. In any case, the great mystical attainment is coupled with extraordinary magical powers. This conjugation of mysticism and magic is part of a wider model, the mystical-magical one, which was shared by many Kabbalists and Hasidic masters. Here it is envisaged as the achievement of the Messiah to undergo the highest mystical experience and to possess miraculous powers.[69]

Another explicit instance of the identification of the Messiah with the first sefirah is found in an anonymous note in the margin of Abraham Abulafia's *Ḥayyei ha-'Olam ha-Ba'* near the succinct identification of the Messiah with a Kohen. In the remark it is said that the sefirah of Yesod "is called Israel, and it is the place of corporeality; and Tiferet is called Levite, and it is the place of spirituality; and Keter 'Eliyon is called the priest, and it is the place of the intellect, and it is the priest. Therefore, it was said to the high priest Joshua, "Behold, I bring my servant Tzemaḥ,"[70] meaning that by means of the supernal Messiah he will bring the lower Messiah."[71] This resort to the concept of a double Messiah puts this anonymous commentator among those who preferred the *via perfectionis,* as the higher Messiah represents s transcendent, nonsuffering savior who ensures the advent of the lower one. The conciseness of the remark does not allow a more detailed understanding of the theory beyond the above gradation. In any case, the messianic rank corresponds on the human level to the intellect, which in the Abulafian context of the gloss is conceived of as the highest human quality, and on the ontological level to Keter. The arrival of the human or lower Messiah is construed in the context of the action of the supernal Messiah.

Whatever the meaning of the relations between the two forms of Messiah, it is clear that the intellectual quality of the supernal one would dominate over the activities of the lower, a view consonant with an Abulafian vision of the intellect and intellection as having messianic connotations. In these two last cases the political role of the Messiah is quite marginal in comparison to the role he plays in the symbolistic system that informed the views of de Leon, who combined the human Messiah with the divine power that rules over the lower world.[72] In R. Yitzḥaq of Acre, what is more important is the ultimate attainment of prophecy. It is the spiritual rather than the political function that is highlighted in the last quotations. The centrality of the search for contact with the ultimate source of being is reflected in the high status of the Messiah even in comparison to that of Moses, according to R. Yitzḥaq of Acre. The affinities between the Messiah and the first sefirah is reminiscent of one of the main appellations of Sabbatai Tzevi in the writings of Nathan of Gaza: the Messiah was designated by his prophet as "the power of Keter 'Elyon," because the consonants of the Hebrew phrase *koaḥ keter 'elyon* are numerically equal (814) to the name of the famous Messiah Shabbatai Tzevi.[73] Nathan (and perhaps Sabbatai Tzevi himself) borrowed the very rare phrase *koaḥ keter 'elyon* from *Sefer ha-Peliy'ah,* which had borrowed it from an earlier source.[74] Is this equivalence, then, only a matter of a mathematical computation, an incidental mind game, or does it also reflect the influence of an earlier conceptualization of the Messiah? On the basis of a comparison of the relevant sources, it is clear that the latter solution is much more plausible.

The Messiah's *Descensus ad Inferos*

As we have seen, messianic activity was understood by some Kabbalists to be connect to a search for contact between the human aspirant to the messianic role and the supernal spiritual world, sometimes conceived in terms of an hypostatical Messiah. This model belongs to *via perfectionis* and may be described as anabatic, namely one that assumes that only by the ascent on high it is possible to rescue people in the mundane world. This anabatic model had a great impact on Kabbalah, as I have attempted to show elsewhere.[75]

However, there is also in Kabbalah a katabatic model, which assumes that it is possible to rescue souls by the descent of the Kabbalist, and later on the Hasidic master, to hell or the demonic realm. This is a paramount example of *via passionis.* But before turning to this version of the model, I would like to mention two other Kabbalistic versions of *via passionis.* Both share the assumption that the Messiah has a strong contact with evil, even before the descent into the realm of evil or the beginning of the eschatological drama. One of them contends that the Messiah was born out of evil, the other that the Messiah must have some relation to evil in order to prevail. According to a passage written by R. Joseph of Hamadan, a late thirteenth-century Kabbalist active in Castile, the Messiah is the offspring of the intercourse between God and the collective spirits of evil, described both as the divine concubine and as Metatron. This is part of the divine strategy, in fact a divine deceit, to save the people of Israel by means of the Messiah who, coming from the demonic realm, is not opposed by evil forces when undertaking the redemptive activity. This is a very interesting case where the Messiah is described as the son of God. Whether the demonic mother is an attempt to counteract the Christian view of the birth from a virgin is a matter of conjecture. The second version is represented by texts of Safedian Kabbalists such as R. Moses Cordovero and R. Moses Galante, who claim that some form of *qelippah* (evil power) must be found in the Messiah, and a Hasidic text, which describes incest as necessary for the birth of the Messiah.[76]

The more classical form of the katabatic model is of ancient origin and, in Jewish mystical literature, is already visible in the *Zohar* in the context of the descent of the *tzaddiqim* or righteous; it was developed much further in the sixteenth-century Kabbalah, particularly in Safed.[77] The explicit tie between the katabatic model and messianism, and not only redemption in general, is thought by modern scholars to emerge in Nathan of Gaza's interpretation of

Sabbatai Tzevi's conversion to Islam as the immersion in the realm of the shells in order to explode the domain of evil.[78]

Again, however, it seems that the relatively early Kabbalah may provide an explicit antecedent, which may have something to do with the much more famous descent of Christ into hell in order to save the souls of sinners.[79] An anonymous manuscript, whose author I have identified as R. Yitzḥaq of Acre, reads as follows: "The Messiah will take out Koraḥ and his party and some of the wicked of Israel from hell, and he will revive many of the people of Israel."[80] Similar though this view is to the Christian messianic katabasis, there are some elements that distinguish it from the Christian counterpart. R. Yitzḥaq's passage speaks about a very limited sort of redemption, which unlike Christ's mission does not include all the sinners, not even all the Jewish sinners, but only some of them. Conspicuously, the Kabbalist speaks about a future deed, while in Christianity this is part of the past. This case of katabasis is interesting not only for its being the earliest known antecedent of the concept of a messianic act, attributed later by Nathan of Gaza to Sabbatai Tzevi in his capacity as the Messiah, but also because it is found in the writings of the same Kabbalist who presented the first, anabatic messianic version of the mystico-magical model. Therefore, R. Yitzḥaq of Acre, like the later Hasidic masters, attributed two dramatically different modes of activity to the same ideal religious figure.[81]

By identifying the Messiah with the lowest ring of their emanational system, both philosophers and Kabbalists elevated the concept related to the human redeemer to a spiritual and divine level. They put a strong accent on his status as an extension and thus on the theophanic representation of the divine. In this way the question of suffering, changing, and acting in a certain historical moment becomes more problematic than in the case of the human apocalyptic Messiah. Most of these intellectuals adopted *via perfectionis* rather than *via passionis,* a choice that betrays the intrusion of the Greek scheme into Jewish thought. Nevertheless, attempts to identify the Messiah with Metatron as an angel, in addition to the Agent Intellect, allowed a Kabbalist such as R. Yitzḥaq of Acre to appropriate the issue of suffering and of the descent to hell without much ado. In his writings, as in the Christian treatments of Jesus' divinity and suffering, the two moments are to be found, problematic as their coexistence in one system may be.

Another biblical figure who has been understood in explicit redemptive terms was Samson, whom R. Joseph al-Ashqar describes thus:

> He certainly was a perfect righteous [man], and whatever he did was done for the benefit of Israel. The Shekhinah, which is the daughter of Abraham our patriarch, was subdued under the powers of impurity, as it is written "for at that time the

> Philistines had dominion over Israel" [Judges 14:4], and he wanted all the [demonic] powers and opposite [powers] to be subdued under his hand, and this is why he wanted to enter unto them by means of cunning, to take a wife from them, in order to be supported by them, so that they would agree with him and would be subdued under his hand. This is certainly a secret known only to God.[82]

The sexual involvement of Samson with Delilah, an affair that the Bible treats in quite negative terms, is described here in a positive light. Samson is depicted, surprisingly enough, as a "perfect righteous"; his love for the alien woman, who is identified with Lilith, the mother of the demons,[83] was actually part of a cunning act, as he attempted to penetrate the stronghold of the enemy, seen in Kabbalistic terms as the demonic powers which should be destroyed in order to deliver the people of Israel and, on the more spiritual level, to release the divine power, the Shekhinah. In fact, Samson's death is presented as a self-sacrifice for the sake of the redemption of the people of Israel, and he is depicted in terms taken from Deutero-Isaiah as the suffering servant: it was Samson who suffered in order to atone for the sins of Israel.[84] In a manner reminiscent of Nathan of Gaza's portrayal Sabbatai Tzevi's conversion as a cunning act, Joseph al-Ashqar (or his sources) is ready to present biblical stories in a way that differs from the rabbinic taxonomy, by means of a Kabbalistic structure of thought that would turn the manifest acts into a cover for attaining deeper purposes. As when the Sabbatean prophet explains conversion as an attempt to confront the powers of evil by means of transgressive acts, Samson does not descend to the sinners, as the Messiah of R. Yitzḥaq of Acre does, but to sin as an indispensable means of redemption.[85]

To better understand the positive presentation of the role of Samson in *Sefer Tzafnat Pa'aneaḥ,* it should be compared to the rather negative picture emerging from a Kabbalistic book written in the middle of the sixteenth century, the anonymous *Sefer Galia' Raza'*. This book, which is conceptually close to the literature of *Sefer ha-Meshiv,* whose messianic ideas will be dealt with in the next chapter, sees no benefit from Samson's labors and suffering, all of them being in vain. He was none other than a reincarnation of Samael, the head of the demonic powers. Nevertheless the anonymous Kabbalist is ready to "allow" him to transmigrate into the persona of Seraiah, the general of the army of the Messiah ben Ephraim.[86] Implicitly, this Seraiah seems destined to have the same fate of the Messiah he is serving, namely to die during the apocalyptic wars he is destined to wage.[87] In any case, the messianic role of Samson has been reiterated in Sabbatean literature, where this protagonist has been described, apparently as a result of a misinterpretation of a Midrash, as the Messiah.[88]

Apocalypse and the *Zohar*

From the literary point of view, the *Zohar* is mostly a midrashic commentary on some parts of the Bible undertaken, presumably, by a group of Spanish Jewish Kabbalists.[89] The resort to a certain literary genre often means not only following a literary convention, exploiting an authoritative manner of writing; as is the case with the *Zohar,* it is not only a matter of pseudo-epigraphy. The views propagated by some forms of writings must be accepted when someone adopts that particular literary genre. Though I would like not to presuppose too strong a connection between form and content, it seems to me that some affinities between the two elements must nevertheless be taken into consideration. So, for example, Abraham Abulafia's writings, which do not subscribe to the midrashic and talmudic types of discourse, are indeed less influenced by the rabbinic forms of mythologies. His views and methods stem from the *Guide* and some other sources, such as Heikhalot literature, *Sefer Yetzirah* and commentaries on it, Ḥasidei Ashkenaz, and Naḥmanides. His "constellated" theology, namely an articulated vision of the nature of God as an intellectual entity, which presides over the most important processes here below, did not allow a more open approach to the interpreted sources, as the midrashic "dis-astered" approach does.[90]

Abulafia's conception of the Messiah is much closer to the philosophical than to the midrashic worldview. But insofar as the zoharic attitude toward the text is concerned, the situation is quite different. Though informed by complex theosophies, in many cases the theological concerns themselves are less important and less evident, whereas the interpreted text is understood *more midrashico,* presupposing multiple levels of meaning, some of them drawing heavily upon the midrashic and apocalyptic sources themselves, others reflecting a midrashic mode of writing and thinking. In the case of the overall approach to messianism, the bulk of the zoharic literature is much more open to the mythological elements found in the Jewish rabbinic traditions.[91]

The passage selected here for discussion is far from the only case of a mythological-apocalyptic expression of messianism in the *Zohar.* Another example consists in a lengthy and quite flowery description of the Messiah in the Garden of Eden, in a special palace named the "Nest of the Bird," which is part of the most apocalyptic elaboration on the persona of the Messiah in the entire zoharic corpus.[92] However, the following passage may reflect not only a sort of medieval apocalypse but also something that concerns me more in the context of the description of the imagination of Jewish eschatology: the transformation of an historical quasi-event, or perhaps a rumor, into an apocalyptic picture.

It is the great merit of A. Jellinek, the scholar who correctly severed the link forcefully proposed by his precursor, M. Landauer, between Abraham Abulafia and the author of the *Zohar* to reestablish the link in a much more solid though restricted manner. In 1853, two years after writing his famous refutation of Abulafia's alleged authorship of the *Zohar* and establishing, in a rather meticulous and brilliant way, the deep affinities between Moses de Leon's writings and the concepts and style of the *Zohar*,[93] Jellinek composed a short observation entitled "Ein Historisches Datum in Buche Sohar?"[94] This short article has not attracted due attention from the modern scholars of the *Zohar*. It is important not only for its own claim but also because it has been contributed by the very scholar who had earlier denied Abulafia's authorship of the *Zohar*.

Even Jellinek, however, was ready to concede that, at least in principle, in Avila it was possible to find some writings of Abulafia's that could be used by someone to contribute to the zoharic literature.[95] He referred to the following passage:

> Some of these things were fulfilled at that time [of Balaam] while some others later on, and others are left for the time of the king-Messiah . . . We have learned that the Holy One, Blessed be He, will rebuild Jerusalem and will reveal one fixed star that shoots as sparks seventy mobile stars, and with seventy sparks that are illumined from this star [found] at the center of the firmament, and from it another seventy stars will draw [their light] and will illumine and shine brightly for seventy days.[96] And on the sixth day [Friday] on the twenty-fifth day of the sixth month the star[97] will appear and will be gathered to the seventh day [the Sabbath]. And after seventy days, it will be covered up and will be seen no more. On the first day it will be visible in the city of Rome, and on that day three high walls of the city of Rome will fall, and the great palace there will collapse[98] and the ruler of that city will die. In that time the star will expand and become visible over the world, and then mighty wars will arise in all four quarters of the world, and faith there is going to be absent between them.[99]

Pope Nicholas III died on August 22, 1280, which fells on twenty-fifth day of Elul, the sixth month counting from Nissan.[100] As Jellinek has pointed out, this date agrees with what is reported in the *Zohar* regarding the demise of the ruler of Rome. The congruency between the predicted date for the death of the Roman ruler according to the *Zohar* and the death of Nicholas III is uncanny. Moreover, the similarity between the eschatological tone struck by the *Zohar* and the messianic tone of Abulafia's incident is highly suggestive. Is Jellinek correct in calling his note "Ein Historisches Datum in Buche Sohar"? If his supposition is correct, we have a postquem date for the composition of some of the last sections of the *Zohar* as not earlier than the end of 1280.[101] It is possible that not only the death of Nicholas but also other information about Abulafia's planned meeting with the pope at a certain time could have influenced this section of the *Zohar*. It should be mentioned that a trace of another Abulafia, R. Todros ben Joseph ha-Levi Abulafia, has been discerned by Liebes in the *Zohar.*[102] If Jellinek's proposal and the present analysis are corroborated by further studies, then we may witness the transformation of an event that in itself had no apocalyptic nature into an apocalypse. Abraham Abulafia's attempt to discuss with the pope issues of Kabbalah, and the latter's unexpected death, could have provoked a reaction among Kabbalists in Castile, who might have been personally acquainted with Abulafia and perhaps also aware of his plans years in advance.[103]

Moreover, it may well be that Abulafia's later claim, found in a book composed between the years 1285 amd 1288 and intended to be sent to "Sefarad" (apparently Castile), to the effect that he had killed the pope by means of the divine name might also have had an impact the author of the *Zohar.*[104] There is a possible connection between a detail in the zoharic treatment of the apocalyptic destruction of the wall of Rome and its leader and a theory found in Abulafia's Kabbalah. According to the above text, the first day out of the seventy days conceived as the period of the salvation drama is the sixth, namely Friday, the day of the death of the ruler in Rome. In a text Abulafia wrote in Rome in 1280 it is said that "the name Yah[105] . . . is part of the entire Name of God. It is half of this Name, and it is at the beginning of the Name, and it is [also] its end. Now although half of the Name is as the whole Name, behold, this half of the name signifies the mystery of the king Messiah, which is the seventh day, and rules over the "body of the Satan," whose name is Tammuz according to the verse "the women weeping for Tammuz" [Ezekiel 8:14]. This was a form of idolatry, worshipped by women of ancient times."[106]

Just before this quotation, Abulafia hinted at the half of the Name that alluded to "he who created the 'six.'" This "six" should be understood, on the basis of a parallel to this discussion, as referring to Jesus. In his *Commentary on Exodus* Abulafia wrote that the sixth and the seventh days correspond to Jesus and the Jewish Messiah, respectively. Elsewhere, in a writing composed in his circle, the same correspondence occurs.[107] Thus, we may safely conclude that just before the encounter with the pope, Abulafia entertained the following type of relationship between the king-Messiah, who corresponds to the seventh day, and Tammuz or Jesus or, according to other sources in Abulafia, the dying Messiah ben Joseph,[108] who corresponds to the sixth day. As he put it in his peculiar way of numerical equivalences, *yom ha-shishiy,* the sixth day, is tantamount to *yeshu ha-natzriy,* namely Jesus the Nazarete, as the value of the Hebrew consonants of each of these phrases is 671. On the other hand, *yom ha-shevi'iy,* the seventh day, is tantamount to the consonants of the phrase *melekh ha-mashiyaḥ,* whose numerical value is 453. This is also the numerical value of the word *tammuz* and the phrase *guf ha-satan,* the body of Satan. Thus, a link was established between the Messiah and its opposite, which means, in Abulafia's style, a significant relationship between the two.[109]

While various discussions concerning the Messiah in the context of the number seven are known in Kabbalah,[110] I am not aware of any other discussions stemming from non-Abulafian writings where the numbers six and seven are related to a Christian and a messianic figure, and to the two days of the week. The death of Jesus on Friday, the sixth day according to Jewish calendar, was indeed quite known; however, the juxtaposition of the sixth and seventh days as pointing to Jesus and the Messiah is, insofar as I know, novel with Abulafia. Does the death of the ruler of Rome on the sixth day, which does not correspond to the historical date of the death of Jesus in the spring, point to Abulafia's description of the relation between the Messiah and the pope as the representative of Christianity and Jesus? If the above description of the apocalyptic reading of a rumor about Abulafia's attempt to meet the pope is correct, we have a fine example of how precarious it would be to build the understanding of messianic ideas and treatments solely against the external vicissitudes of the Jews. As in the case of the rumors of a Mongol invasion, a certain "victory" over the Christians by the coming "lost tribes" or the death of the pope while Abulafia sought an encounter with him had reverberated in the imagination of some Kabbalists and was integrated into apocalyptic and eschatological portrayals of days of the end. In other words, what may be described by some forms of historical writings as marginal, minor, or epiphenomenic cause may be seen in some cases as causal waves.[111] Rumors, misunderstandings, fantastic aspirations all changed the minds of gifted figures, some of whom were able to translate them into more traditional views and integrate them into more systematic discourses, which sometimes may have had an impact on wider audiences. Changes in the forms of conceptualization, which might sometimes have a substantial impact on the course of history, could nevertheless start from secondary or even seemingly negligible factors. The relative isolation of the Jews from the geographical landscape and the social environment created a sort of *imaginaire* that attempted to describe other places and times, but also produced states of mind that allow a much easier credulity concerning the imminent changes in history, which were conceived of, often as a result of wishful thinking, as able to ameliorate their plight. Changes, sometimes expressed in eschatological terms, were more welcome by Jews than by the more sedentary sectors of the autochthon, in many cases Christian, population.

Continuities

The thirteenth century was a crucial period for the integration of messianism and Kabbalah. Later Kabbalistic views, developed from the fourteenth century right up to the Kabbalah of Safed, are founded on the compositions written during the last third of the thirteenth century. These same works became cornerstones of later Kabbalistic thought in general. Therefore, the different manners of integration of messianism in the classical Kabbalistic texts, like the *Zohar* and Abulafia's writings, should prevent a conception of the Kabbalah as a theory that has ever been essentially divorced from the fermenting element of messianism. We have shown that various models of messianism were intrinsically bound to the burgeoning Kabbalah during the formative period of the thirteenth century.[112] In the subsequent phases of the evolution of this mystical lore—in the fourteenth century and the first half of the fifteenth century—messianic elements do not extend much beyond a review of those elements found in the works previously discussed, with some new nuances added to the models analyzed above. The terrible ordeals of the mid-fourteenth century—the Black Death and the accusations of Christians that the Jews were somehow responsible for the pestilence—did not generate messianic responses among the Jews, just as the Christian reactions to this disaster were meager from the innovative eschatological point of view.[113] These were most painful events, which apparently not only were ignored by all the Kabbalists but did not attract the attention of Jewish eschatology in general.

Unmistakable concerns with messianic issues are evident also in two of the most important Kabbalistic writings of the fourteenth and fifteenth centuries: *Sefer ha-Temunah, Sefer ha-Peliy'ah,* and *Sefer ha-Qanah,* composed in the Byzantine empire in the fourteenth century,[114] and *Sefer ha-Meshiv,* composed in Spain around 1470. There can be no doubt that at least the latter book represents not merely the concern of a Kabbalist with messianic issues but a whole system which is conspicuously messianic and exposed explicitly in an unusually lengthy text. Therefore, the assumption that Kabbalists were indifferent toward messianism in the period that may be described as the first stage of Scholem's historiography, namely between the end of the twelfth and late fifteenth centuries, requires substantial modifications, not only insofar as the most recondite parts of the zoharic literatures are concerned.

Messianism and Kabbalah, 1470–1540

Sefer ha-Meshiv: Messianism, Apocalypse, and Magic

Two models of Kabbalistic messianism had crystallized during the thirteenth century: the theosophical-theurgical and the ecstatic. A third model, the talismanic one, was not yet so articulated, appearing in only one discussion in R. Moses de Leon's *Sheqel ha-Qodesh.* The fourteenth century did not contribute much toward a new vision of messianism. Except for some calculations regarding the date of the eschaton that appear in *Tiqqunei Zohar* Kabbalistic literature in this period is relatively scanty on the subject of messianism.[1] The Black Plague, which ravaged the Christian and Jewish populations of Europe in the middle of the fourteenth century, left no explicit trace on Jewish messianic thought. This is but one of the examples from which we can deduce that not every historical trauma will necessarily precipitate an outburst of messianism among the Jews, even when they are subject to enormous pressures from the surrounding populace.

Another significant event of the fourteenth century, the pogroms of 1391, drastically changed the situation of the Jews in Catalonia and Castile. To a certain extent, these events mitigated the influence of the prevalent messianic conceptions in Spain. In the theurgical model—and in the ecstatic one that was not influential in Spain—time does not play an essential role, for each model requires a slow and steady pace for either the proper development of the individual's intellect or for the restitution of the Godhead to its former state of perfection. But in the very tense situation that started to develop after 1391, any messianic theory that assumes a slow development, whether in the personal, national, or divine sphere, could not seriously speak to the hearts of the Spanish

Jews, who were under strong religious pressures. In the hundred years following 1391 they gradually developed messianic expectations and types of redemptive activities that were sometimes essentially different from either the theurgical project, which sought the restoration of God's powers to a more harmonious state as a way to the redemption, or from the ecstatic model, in which the major messianic activity occurred on the intellectual level and in personal ecstasy as a prophetic experience.

This new model of messianic activity, which emerged in the fifteenth century, may be termed the *magico-Kabbalistic model* or, as it is more popularly referred to, *practical Kabbalah*.[2] Here, for the first time, the Kabbalists argue that the advent of the Messiah is not to be accomplished through the fulfillment of biblical commandments or by the perfection of the human intellect, but rather by magical procedures enacted by a group of Kabbalists which will disrupt the continuum of history and cause radical change in the natural order. This theory of messianism sought to alleviate the heavy pressure felt by the Jews of Spain. This instant construct found its strongest expression in works that were composed approximately two decades before the expulsion from Spain. From 1470 to the end of the century, a huge corpus of Kabbalistic literature was composed by a particular school of Kabbalists, apparently in Castile. Many of these texts are still extant in several manuscripts. The principal work is known under the titles *Sefer ha-Meshiv* or *Sefer ha-Mal'akh ha-Meshiv*, which mean, respectively, *Book of the Responding [Entity]* or *Book of the Responding Angel*.[3]

The titles of these compositions reveal the nature of this new type of Kabbalistic literature, which is important for an understanding of a new model of messianism. According to the internal testimony of the texts, they were not composed by a Kabbalist or a group of Kabbalists, but were dictated by God Himself, who was believed to have narrated, or dictated, the texts in the first person or through holy angels who reveal lofty truths to the Kabbalist. This is the meaning of the term *ha-meshiv*, which stands, in some parts of the corpus, also for the angel who responds to the questions of the Kabbalist. From this perspective, these are compositions that express a conception of a direct revelation in which the Kabbalist plays the role of a mere transmitter, either as a scribe or as a channel, but not of a conscious creative and innovative writer.

This kind of Kabbalistic literature is apocalyptic in a double sense: not only is revelation of secrets the crucial issue in this corpus, but also the more dramatic events related to the eschaton are more evident in the treatises constituting these works than in other types of Kabbalistic literature. Indubitably, we are dealing with a body of mystical literature of a strong and special eschatological kind. Within its framework we find messianic views that had far-reaching repercussions in the sixteenth-century Kabbalah. The revelations extant in the corpus that remained in the manuscripts are not limited to messianic issues. A long series of topics is addressed by the divine powers during nocturnal revelations achieved by means of oneiric techniques; the most striking trait of the book is the proposal of magical techniques to compel God, the angels, and the demonic powers to come down and serve the needs of the human being. Thus, though central, the messianic element is but one of many topics that the Kabbalistic magicians were concerned with. Given the strong belief in the possibility of opening a direct channel to the supernal powers by means of techniques, mostly magical ones, the mystical element in this literature—defined as a direct contact with the divine—is instrumental in facilitating the reception of the messianic messages. From this standpoint, my main thesis, that there exists an integral bond between Kabbalistic mysticism and messianism, is fully validated by the contents of the compositions that constitute this brand of Kabbalistic literature.[4]

What are the main Kabbalistic theories of these compositions and how do they contribute to the messianic model under discussion? Apart from the revelatory element, which is quite dominant, there are other fundamental characteristics, such as the rise in the importance of demonology in the general scheme of Kabbalistic thought. Some of the works in this corpus generated a strange type of Jewish demonology, including names of demons that were hitherto unknown in Jewish magical literature. The repercussions of such a conception will have to be examined in terms of messianism, as the revelation of secrets is traditionally thought to be licit in the period which immediately precedes the advent of the Messiah.

This Kabbalistic literature involves a strong demonization of Christianity as well.[5] Though not totally novel, this trait is unparalleled in its potency in comparison to earlier Kabbalistic literature. Strong demonization is a process that can be well understood against the contemporary historical background and as a counterattack on the Christian formulation of the Synagogue of Israel as the Church of Satan. Here the notorious Christian cliché asserting that the Synagogue itself is the congregation of Satan, which had already a long history, has been inverted. This is a point that we will return to in the context of messianism.

A third feature characteristic of this literature is a strong effort to demonize philosophy and medieval science.[6] Just as in the case of Christianity, so philosophy and science are depicted throughout these texts as satanic revelations. From this perspective, they exhibit a view that presents authentic Judaism, according to its Kabbalistic interpretation, as a sublime revelation that does not come into contact with its general surroundings in a significant manner, nor is it affected by prior cultural progress. This general demonization demands what is essentially a fundamental reformation of the spiritual structure of contemporary Judaism and of the prevalent types of science. For instance, the argument in this literature that the Jewish people are still in exile solely because they studied and continue to study philosophy is but one illustration of the desire to purify and purge Judaism of all foreign influences. This Kabbalist, who offers instead an "unadulterated" Judaism and science, understands theoretical Kabbalah as "genuine" science, which is to be coupled with practical Kabbalah viewed as technology. Such were the conditions of the creation of this magnum opus of magical Kabbalah, which attempts a novel reinterpretation of no less than all of Jewish and scientific culture.

The new revelation of secrets is part of the messianic process. So, for example, the Deity reveals the following eschatological imperative to the Kabbalists in order to conquer the demonic powers: "You should recite onto them the 'terrible hand' when they [the two demonic archangels] are bound . . . and you and R. Joseph together should beswear and compel those [demonic] angels using this formula in order to bring the redemption because the year of redemption has already arrived previously. Despite the fact that there were sages of Israel who knew how to bind them, the time of redemption did not arrive until now."[7] Dealing with the powers of evil, which constitutes a great danger in the eyes of Kabbalists from this group and which, according the famous legends dealing with R. Joseph della Reina, has materialized, this attitude is part of the redemptive *via passionis.* Since the time for the redemption has arrived, it is permitted and, according to this corpus of writings, even necessary to disclose all of the lost secrets of Judaism. These secrets, dealing with a wide range of topics—astronomy, mathematics, medicine, and such theological issues as the Garden of Eden—were lost during the long exile, but they have now been revealed from above or forced to descend, or communicated in the first person by God.

As far as the subject of messianism is concerned, the line of reasoning that we described above is continued: God reveals the technique needed to succeed in the struggle against Christianity and the new secrets of the true science, but he also reveals the way in which the power of Christianity can be shattered in order to be able to bring the redemption. From this perspective messianism was not perceived as personal initiative, a need of the Kabbalists as part of their enterprise to free themselves of the yoke of history; rather the formulations of *Sefer ha-Meshiv* concur that this is a divine imperative coming from above. These revelations include specific orders meant to inspire messianic activity.[8] Many of the revelations found in *Sefer ha-Meshiv* are in fact descriptions of a variety of magical incantations necessary for the destruction of the demonic realm. Mysticism here is viewed as a means of attaining and eventually transmitting magical information. Heavenly revelation is now the channel for the descent of supernal magic, the main tool for the annihilation of the powers of evil as well as the bringing of the redemption. Since magic is the basic means of abolishing evil, I will call this messianic model the magico-Kabbalistic one. At the heart of this model lies the conviction that the time of the Messiah is fixed and imminent, the only impediment to the final advent being the presence of the forces of evil. The annihilation of evil by means of incantations is described numerous times throughout this body of literature.[9]

One of the prominent members of this school of thought was the notorious magician and Kabbalist R. Joseph della Reina.[10] Kabbalistic as well as more popular stories relate that this band of Kabbalists, apparently including the anonymous writer himself and della Reina, were visited by a heavenly revelation commanding them to cause the two princes of evil, Ammon of No and Samael, to descend and be tied, subdued, and have their wings clipped, which meant the Kabbalists were destroying the powers of evil. This neutralization of the powers of evil by destroying their princes or, according to a certain version, converting them to Judaism is tantamount to the destruction of Christianity, considered to be a product of evil. Thus, the redemption will be made possible. According to some of these texts, Christianity will have to undergo a total revolution which involves its abolishment only in order to be transformed into an army, namely into some sort of defending body of the now-victorious Judaism. In the apocalyptic Armageddon, Samael's contemporary embodiment will have to change its spots, forfeit its position as prosecutor and become its enemy's defender, a revolutionary turn of events. This is the inverse of the Christian view that when the redemption does come in the Second Advent, all the Jews will convert to Christianity. The Kabbalist who authored the *Sefer ha-Meshiv* and his followers in the sixteenth century envisioned the exact opposite scenario. Here we have a hitherto nondominant emphasis on the apocalyptic side of Kabbalistic messianism, a side that was not emphasized by Abulafia or the *Zohar* and only partially by Abulafia's earlier contemporary R. Yitzḥaq ben Jacob ha-Cohen.[11] Those thirteenth-century Kabbalistic circles were not so heavily influenced by the popular apocalyptic literature of the seventh and eighth centuries. But now, in the last third of the fifteenth century in some circles of Kabbalists, the apocalyptic element became much more prominent: Armageddon was supposed to include blood baths, the participation of superhuman evil beings—although not so monstrous as their prototype found in the original apocalyptic literature—a novel idea introduced by this circle into Kabbalah. From this perspective, there is a deepening of the use of demonology in discussion of the apocalyptic battles. Besides the magical techniques, which include oneiric devices, incantations, and medical recipes, in this huge corpus there is an attempt to describe the entire span of history. These Kabbalists attempted to describe the whole chain of evil powers and incarnations engaged in perpetual conflict with the Jewish people, only to be resolved by their religious metamorphoses in the end, believed by these Kabbalists to be witnessed in their time. This is an example of a comprehensive messianic historiosophy unlike the Kabbalistic systems discussed earlier. During the sixteenth century this view was embellished in the book called *Galia' Raza'*. Despite the fact that the wars themselves are depicted as involving hordes of demonic powers, for these Kabbalists the conflict was real and was due to occur in an historical context.

This messianic theory was not to be realized through inner intellectual or divine perfection explicitly described as gradual processes, but by a group effort to work together toward a national goal, bound to bring about the divine redemption as well as to attempt to bring to a halt an insufferable historical situation. This is the perception of people who see themselves as acting on the stage of history and not exclusively on some inner level. It is appropriate to emphasize the group nature of these activities. The most popular stories found in this literature, concerning magical practices and R. Joseph della Reina, depict the rites as the product of a group of Kabbalists and not as the outcome of one man's activities, for all have to join forces in order to vanquish evil. There is a wide gap between this magical model and the one developed by Abulafia, in which the individual who has reached his own perfection can then act alone on behalf of the whole nation. The roots of the concept of group effort can be traced back to the *Zohar,* which stipulates that theurgic activity was accomplished by a group as opposed to individuals acting alone.

Della Reina's attempt to secure the redemption by magical means, only twenty years or so before the expulsion from Spain, of course failed. Later on the two "events" were inextricably bound in the minds of some Kabbalists, who connected the unorthodox method of magic to hasten the redemption and the ensuing expulsion. The strong messianism of *Sefer ha-Meshiv* drew mixed reactions from later Kabbalists in Safed, who condemned the use of magic for religious or messianic ends.[12] Accordingly we find after the expulsion that the messianic theories of *Sefer ha-Meshiv* are continued by a small group of Kabbalists, whereas the great majority of the Kabbalists who had been compelled to leave the Iberian peninsula have rejected this magical model, whether by ignoring it in their writings, as in the case of the famous Kabbalists R. Yehudah Ḥayyat and R. Meir ibn Gabbay, or by explicitly stating their reservations. *Sefer ha-Meshiv* is one of the largest Kabbalistic compilations ever written, possessing tremendous scope and expressing a radical position on messianism and magic. It would be logical to expect that after the expulsion, Kabbalistic-messianic thought and activity would be no less represented than already demonstrated by the apocalyptical concerns of the author or the group of Kabbalists related to *Sefer ha-Meshiv.* Yet the empirical evidence shows that this vast literary phenomenon remains unduplicated after the expulsion. Therefore, the only realistic way to describe the subsequent development of messianism in Kabbalistic literature is to presuppose a certain tendency to moderate the eschatological elements, in comparison with those found before the expulsion.

The school of *Sefer ha-Meshiv* spawned two more major works, anonymous as well: a voluminous commentary on the Book of Psalms called *Sefer Kaf ha-Qetoret,* whose author composed, at the beginning of the sixteenth century, some less messianically oriented Kabbalistic writings; and, in the mid-sixteenth century, the book entitled *Galia' Raza'.*[13] These two works continue to develop the mystical and revelatory concepts of *Sefer ha-Meshiv,* as well as some of its messianic concerns. Nevertheless, they lack the burning and acute messianic tone prevalent in the stories of the attempts to bring the Messiah attributed to Joseph della Reina, active before the expulsion from Spain. Both works continue along the lines of *Sefer ha-Meshiv,* but in a more conservative manner. One of the Kabbalistic writings by the author of *Sefer Kaf ha-Qetoret* provides this example of the moderation of activistic messianism: "what is the benefit of arousing yourself concerning the topic of redemption? . . . Do not say that any objection is able to stop redemption to come. But you should believe that it will come immediately, when the great redeemer, the mighty and awesome one, who is 'El 'Elohim YHWH [will decide]."[14] The vision of God as the supreme redeemer, whose redemptive work cannot be stopped in any manner, seems to mitigate the effervescent dedication to bringing about the messianic era in *Sefer ha-Meshiv* itself. The predestination implied in this passage demonstrates that the approach of the anonymous Kabbalist does not allow too great a role for the activistic approach of an individual or even a group.

In contrast to these two works, the overwhelming majority of exiled Spanish Kabbalists do not mention *Sefer ha-Meshiv* explicitly and allow for little discussion of messianic phenomena. There is only one exception to this rule, R. Abraham ben Eliezer ha-Levi, one of the most interesting Kabbalists among the Spanish exiles. His works are both a continuation of and a departure from the messianism expressed prior to the expulsion.

R. Abraham ben Eliezer ha-Levi: Expecting the Imminent Apocalypse

One of the most colorful Kabbalists who flourished during the period after the expulsion was R. Abraham ben Eliezer ha-Levi. Through the numerous studies of Gershom Scholem, many of Abraham ha-Levi's works were rescued from oblivion, allowing his views to be seriously studied, though the majority of his compositions still remained in manuscript.[15] His eschatological stands especially attracted the attention of Scholem in his more general descriptions of the prevailing mood in the generation of the expulsion from Spain, as we learn from one of his statements: "The sharply etched and impressive figure of Abraham ben Eliezer ha-Levi in Jerusalem, an untired agitator and interpreter of events 'pregnant' with redemption, is typical of a generation of Kabbalists in which the apocalyptic abyss yawned."[16]

The description of this Kabbalist as "typical" is rather emblematic, since it conveys Scholem's totalizing vision of that generation. It is rather difficult, however, to substantiate the claim that the whole generation presents an apocalyptic *Weltbild,* and I wonder if this was indeed the case. Let us therefore inspect the background of this Kabbalist and his writings. I will concentrate solely on the messianic aspect of his thought. Abraham ha-Levi's concern with eschatology started already in Spain before the expulsion of the Jews. He states that he utilized an oneiric technique in order to ascertain the precise date of redemption. This technique is remarkably similar to the magical techniques employed for the composition of *Sefer ha-Meshiv* and *Sefer ha-Mal'akh ha-Meshiv,*[17] yet the similarities in his books and those of the circle of the magical Kabbalists before the expulsion do not stop here. For instance, these authors show an avid interest in the special type of demonology discussed above. Abraham ha-Levi describes the nature of Ammon of No, one of the princes of the realm of evil, a demon who was hardly discussed before *Sefer ha-Meshiv* and who there suddenly took on a more central role in Kabbalistic demonology.[18] From his range of interests, conceptual details,[19] and techniques, as well as the resort to the coming of the Lost Tribes found in ha-Levi and in the Kabbalah of the author of *Sefer Kaf ha-Qetoret* it is clear that ha-Levi, in one way or another, was close to the authors or the school of *Sefer ha-Meshiv* and that there is even a historical connection.[20] In any event, he is the first writer who preserved for posterity the earliest version of the story of R. Joseph della Reina, a literary product describing the fateful event that made the school of *Sefer ha-Meshiv* so notorious.

However, R. Abraham ha-Levi's acute messianism was not only a direct, though more moderate, continuation of the quite extreme magical messianism dominant in *Sefer ha-Meshiv.* He responded to messianic tensions that he felt by introducing special prayers and vigils in Jerusalem to alleviate the expected birth pangs of the Messiah, who was to arrive in the Jewish year 5300, which corresponds to 1540 C.E..[21] From this perspective there is a dramatic change in attitude toward messianism: magical messianism is no longer on the main agenda of Kabbalists. Rather, messianic activities are to be seen as readaptations of recognized traditional patterns. Special vigils, *mishmarot,* consisting of prayers recited by individuals who linger after regular prayers, were said in the regular quorum. These types of prayers are especially meant to ease the sufferings necessary for the advent of the Messiah, whose time is already pre-set by divine decree. The radical nature of the activities advocated by the magical model of messianism was replaced by more traditional methods and accepted modes of religious activities, which were now co-opted for messianic ends. R. Abraham ha-Levi also was preoccupied with circulating his messianic message through his writings concerning the secret of the redemption, and it seems likely that these epistles were influential.

Nevertheless, he was aware of the possible negative outcome of an unrestrained dissemination of his messianic visions. Despite his propagandistic zeal, he was quite cautious about sending his messianic writings to Italy, the stronghold of Christian Kabbalah. In one of his epistles he writes to his Italian Jewish corespondent:

> In my opinion there is a danger in sending to you this commentary, since it is said that our brethren, the sons of Esau, study Hebrew and these matters are ancient, and whoever will write anything there, it may, God forbid, fall in their hands. And despite the fact that those who study are faithful to us, nevertheless it is reasonable and compelling to conceal these matters from them, and there is also a severe ban concerning it. In any case, I have refrained from sending to you these treatises constituting the *Epistle of the Secret of the Redemption,*[22] and you, my masters, those who conceal the wisdom and "the secret of the Lord is to the fearers of God" [cf. Psalm 25:14], the participants in the covenant, will contemplate it, but this will not be accessible to every gentile.[23]

A committed propagandist for the imminence of the Messiah, R. Abraham ha-Levi nevertheless took precautions: even this most ardent disseminator of messianic computations betrays a more moderate attitude. Ha-Levi was aware of religious developments in the Christian camp in the forms of the Christian Kabbalah, and he attributed, for example, an eschatological significance to Martin Luther's reform. Whether he was aware also of the apocalyptic stands of the Christian reformer it is not clear, but ha-Levi's resort to the emergence of a figure like Luther as a signpost of the messianic era is quite remarkable.[24] It is doubtful that he knew of the use of Kabbalah by Christians in an apocalyptic context, as may have been the case with his contemporary, Egidio da Viterbo, but his refusal to send his apocalyptic writings to Italy is quite interesting.

Expulsion and Messianism

The influence of the contents of R. Abraham ben Eliezer ha-Levi's epistles can also be attributed to the previous messianic activities of R. Asher Lemlein (see below) and not entirely to the readiness and willingness of the Spanish expellees to accept messianic tidings. The vast majority of the exiles did not develop any Kabbalistic-messianic ideas in all the voluminous Kabbalistic literature that was produced around the time of the expulsion. A perusal of the works of contemporary Kabbalists such as R. Yehudah Ḥayyat in Italy, R. Meir ibn Gabbay in Turkey, R. Yehudah Ḥallewah in the land of Israel, or R. Joseph Al-Ashqar and R. Abraham Adrutiel, both active in North Africa, as well as other Kabbalists, shows that activistic messianism is practically absent in their thought. In comparison to the staggering amount of material produced by these and many other Kabbalists, ha-Levi's messianic literary output is but a small drop in a big ocean.[25]

Consequently, when focusing upon ha-Levi's messianic epistles, as historians of culture we are not dealing with mainstream thought or with a post-expulsion Spanish Kabbalistic movement, or even with a separate stream of thought at all, but rather with the activities of one man alone or perhaps a small group of people, whose activities were not integrated into the literature that was to comprise the classics of the later Kabbalah. The classical Kabbalistic works—the compositions of R. Meir ibn Gabbay or R. Yehudah Ḥayyat, which constitute the two influential summaries of the Spanish schools—completely ignore the Kabbalah of *Sefer ha-Meshiv,* and ibn Gabbay, writing after the death of ha-Levi, ignored the latter's works. This neglect demonstrates that there was a conscious effort to neutralize any significant forms of acute messianism, and there are only marginal attempts to adapt it to the historical reality, despite the expulsion. It would seem that the Kabbalists were more committed to rebuilding their shattered communities and to stabilizing daily Jewish life in their new-found refuges, whether they be in the diaspora or the land of Israel, and they expressed themselves accordingly in their writings. Acute messianism could only have succeeded in upstaging the establishment of society and undermining the religious institutions and religious norms needed to establish the as yet unsettled communities and their hosts.

The special character of the classical Kabbalistic works composed after the expulsion underlines clearly the thrust of the Kabbalah to align to itself with the general efforts to rebuild Jewish life. These works, like the ethical Kabbalistic literature written in the following two generations in Safed, possess strong conservative elements. They constitute a systematic review of all the Kabbalistic materials extant prior to the expulsion, now re-evaluated and synthesized to fit into wider frameworks. The drive to preserve of the old as well as to impose order on the Spanish literary tradition (with the sole exception of *Sefer ha-Meshiv*) expresses the desire to rebuild the Jewish world and not to encourage fermenting elements. This characterization is valid for the writings of Meir ibn Gabbay and Joseph Al-Ashqar, as well as Abraham Adrutiel, the author of the *'Avnei Zikharon* (Cornerstones of Remembrance). This author, writing in North Africa, preserves the Kabbalistic traditions he learned while still in Spain. This is the fundamental character of the book, and it is therefore reasonable that messianism, in any acute form, did not have a real place within such a worldview.

The Case of R. Yehudah Ḥayyat

The sad fate of R. Yehudah Ḥayyat is relatively well documented. In the preface to his *Minḥat Yehudah,* the single Kabbalistic treatise he composed, he tooks pains to report his tragic wanderings, including terrible experiences during his departure from the Iberian peninsula and while in North Africa. Nevertheless, there are many crucial details we do not know, and they may affect our understanding of the formation of his thought. We do not know where he studied Kabbalah, who his main master was, or what his Kabbalistic views were before the expulsion. His commentary on *Sefer Ma'arekhet ha-'Elohut,* entitled *Sefer Minḥat Yehudah,* is our main source for his Kabbalah, but it was composed in Italy. There are, however, some indications as to his avatars and the basis of his Kabbalistic thought before the expulsion. From his preface we learn that he was a Spaniard, though we do not know from what part of Spain he came. It seems that he was a respected figure there, since he presents himself as such and the reaction to his plight by the Sephardi people in Italy implies, at least according to Ḥayyat's version, that he was already well known in Spain.[26] From the fact that he left the Iberian peninsula from Lisbon, we may assume that he was a Castilian Jew, and not a Catalan one, since he preferred the western trajectory to the eastern one.

Sometime during the winter of 1492/93 he left Lisbon, together with his family and some two hundred persons. After wandering for four months, having been refused entry at several ports because the expellees carried plague, the boat was finally permited to make anchor in Malaga, where they were robbed by Basques. Christian authorities—or according to another version, the priests—and famine convinced about a hundred of the expellees to convert. Some of the others, including Ḥayyat's wife, died of hunger and disease. Having been detained two months in Malaga, the remainder of the expellees were at last allowed to leave. Ḥayyat arrived in Fez, in North Africa, where a Spanish Moslem acquaintance of the Kabbalist initiated a libel suit. Apparently Ḥayyat organized a festival on the occasion of the defeat of the Muslims, which included some form of denigration of Islam. He was rescued by the Jews, to whom he gave two hundred books in return for the ransom. In the autumn of 1493, under totally inhuman conditions, he left for Naples, where he witnessed the French invasion in 1494 and then left for Venice, where he was very well received by the "nobles," other Spanish refugees.

Sometime in the middle of the decade Ḥayyat went to Mantua, where he met another famous expellee, R. Joseph Yavetz, a conservative thinker and the author of several theological and exegetical treatises.[27] Under persuasion from other "nobles and wise men" and from Yavetz, Ḥayyat wrote a commentary on *Sefer Ma'arekhet ha-'Elohut,* because "their soul desired to contemplate the delight of the Lord and visit his palace,"[28] and he composed his commentary in order not to "prevent them from learning." Another reason for his composition is his own high evaluation of the book he was asked to comment on. *Sefer Ma'arekhet ha-'Elohut,* according to Ḥayyat, opened the gate to Kabbalistic issues that were not disclosed by other books of Kabbalah. Ḥayyat also mentions the fact that another Kabbalist, whose name he did not know,[29] had already commented on this book in an inappropriate manner. He indicates that this misbegotten commentary was widespread in the province of Mantua.[30]

None of these factors—the request of the Jews of Mantua, the intrinsic value of the book, and his critique of the already existing commentary—is related directly to the experience of the expulsion or to any messianic expectations whatsoever. Interestingly enough, the Kabbalist who has probably suffered more than any other from the vicissitudes of the expulsion does not cite this event as one of the rationales for his Kabbalistic activity.

Ḥayyat had started to study Kabbalah while still in Spain. He mentions that he collected fragments of the *Zohar* from various places and was able to put together most of the literature connected to the *Zohar.*[31] He was confident, as he expressly put it, that his devotion to the book, and to Kabbalah in general, had saved him throughout the ordeal of the expulsion. Indeed, he adduced the details of his own travails in order to demonstrate the apotropaic function of the *Zohar,* not as a personal story worth telling in itself. The most detailed and evocative description of the vicissitudes of a Kabbalist during the expulsion was deemed worthwhile only because it would evince the sanctity of the *Zohar.* It is incumbent upon scholars to read Ḥayyat's personal story in this context, namely as an illustration of the nature of the *Zohar,* a book widespread in Spain but only little known in Italy. History, to the extent that it is mentioned, is introduced in order to prove the uniqueness of the mystical book, not vice versa. If I correctly guess the intention of Ḥayyat, it has something to do with the assumption that the holiness of the Kabbalah can prevail even in the case of the terrible ordeals he had undergone.

Some parts of the *Zohar*—Ḥayyat quotes mainly from *Tiqqunei Zohar*—are indeed the major source for the views and quotations which permeate the commentary.[32] The *Zohar* is described in Ḥayyat's introduction as practically unknown by the earlier Kabbalists, even by some important ones,[33] a situation that is explained by the theory, found in one of the later layers of the *Zohar* explicitly quoted by this Kabbalist, that the book will be revealed during the last generation, namely the generation of the Messiah. Ḥayyat indicates that this is his generation. Moreover, he continues to argue, by the study of the *Zohar* the Messiah will come. Prima facie, this is a confession of the eschatological role of the study of the *Zohar,* a point that may strengthen the views of those scholars who emphasize the importance of the Messianic change in Kabbalah as the result of the expulsion. Such a reading is, however, at least an exaggeration. Ḥayyat collected the various parts of the book while in Spain, therefore before the expulsion. Whether these messianic hopes nourished his activity before the expulsion cannot be established on the basis of our knowledge today. But if indeed messianism played a significant role in his Kabbalistic activity, he never related it to his experience of the expulsion. Moreover, the argument concerning the eschatological effect of the study is certainly not an innovation of Ḥayyat's but the rehearsal of a view he quotes from *Tiqqunei Zohar.*

It seems, however, that Ḥayyat did not even have the distinction of initiating the actualization of the zoharic view concerning the generation of the expulsion. Though he wrote his book earlier than has been assumed,[34] already in the circle of *Sefer ha-Meshiv* the relation between the study of the *Zohar* and redemption was adapted from earlier sources.[35] In any case, Ḥayyat did not plunge into the project of bringing the Messiah by printing the *Zohar* or by disseminating it. After all, he chose to comment on the nonmessianic book *Ma'arekhet ha-'Elohut.* His two sentences concerning the eschatological role of the *Zohar* remained without any impact on the bulk of his single masterpiece, *Sefer Minḥat Yehudah.* I wonder whether it is possible to adduce any evidence as to the affinity between one statement in the introduction and the tens of folios of his Kabbalistic writing. Indeed, the opinion that Ḥayyat's Kabbalistic thought includes some novel elements somehow related to his terrible personal experiences needs to be proven by scholars who would like to make such a connection not by merely stating it as a self-evident fact but by pointing to specific shifts in the details of his thought. In any case, the burden of proof lays on those who argue that one sentence, repeating an already known view, may indicate that the ethos of a book was changed.[36] In my opinion, the strong emphasis on the importance of the *Zohar* aimed to establish the supremacy of the Spanish Kabbalah in an Italian environment that cultivated much more philosophical approaches to this lore and, indirectly, to establish the emigre author as an authoritative Kabbalist. A much less salient purpose, if it is any at all, is to proclaim the coming of the days of the end.

Non-Kabbalistic Messianisms

In contrast to the scant discussions of messianism in Kabbalistic literature after the expulsion, R. Yitzḥaq Abarvanel, a leading figure in the generation of the expulsion, demonstrates in his works a clear, comprehensive, and well-developed exposition of messianic ideas. He wrote his important monographs on messianic topics, the most elaborate treatments of messianism ever written by a Jewish author, in Monopoli from 1496 to 1498 and later in Venice. His assumption was that redemption would start in 1503. Though his lengthy discussions on messianism resort to a variety of Jewish sources, Kabbalah played a marginal role in the economy of his discourse.[37] This allows us to compare the intense post-expulsion treatment of messianism by an individual who was not a Kabbalist, yet nevertheless tried to elaborate a historical program and propound an explanation of the essence of messianism, to the classical and Kabbalistic texts of the same period which failed to treat of messianism comprehensively and systematically. Moreover, Yitzḥaq Abarvanel's son, Yehudah, better known as Leone Ebreo, one of the leading Jewish thinkers of the period, paid no heed to the notion of messianism, in spite of the fact that he viewed the Kabbalah as one of the key sciences for understanding both philosophy and Judaism. As much as the father delves into the significance of the messianic idea, the son steadfastly avoids discussion of these fermenting elements, perhaps because of his attempt to speak to the Jewish world of the Renaissance.

Recently, Isaiah Tishby discovered, published, and meticulously analyzed an important document preserved in the Cairo Genizah that was written by a non-Kabbalist and deals with a variety of apocalyptic predictions, descriptions, and messianic computations composed as the result of divine revelations. This document, which provides a picture of an apocalyptic mood penned by someone who refrains from using Kabbalistic terminology, further demonstrates the relative apathy of Kabbalistic thought to the messianic idea in the generation of the expulsion.[38] The author was a Portuguese expellee, probably a man of learning with a background in astronomy and astrology, who makes numerous calculations as to the arrival of the end of time and expresses the feeling that he indeed is living in the period of the redemption. Despite his acute messianism, he does not integrate any Kabbalistic ideas into his reports on the progress of the messianic process, much like Yitzḥaq Abarvanel, who also desisted from the substantial use of Kabbalistic notions in his messianic discussions. Thus, though acutely messianic, the document printed by Tishby can serve as an additional foil to the moderacy of its Kabbalistic contemporaries in matters of eschatology.

In other words, there is no special reason to relate intense messianism with Kabbalistic figures, and in fact the two most outspoken authors on this topic among the expellees were not Kabbalists at all. Moreover, the most comprehensive and systematic theory of Jewish messianism, explicated in the late sixteenth and early seventeenth centuries by R. Yehudah Loew of Prague, is only marginally affected by Kabbalah, a fact that may reflect the relative indifference of the more messianically oriented thinkers to the basic principles of Kabbalah. In the case of R. Yehudah Loew, there is no claim that his views were either a reaction to the expulsion or were triggered by any other specific historical trauma. The two explicit messianic systems produced by either a Sephardi or an Ashkenazi major figure did not resort to Kabbalah as a formative sort of thought that may help understanding messianic constellations of ideas. On the other hand, the most important body of Kabbalistic literature to which scholars attributed messianic thought, Lurianic Kabbalah, does not have recourse to significant explicit messianic elements, an issue that problematizes the paramount importance of messianism in that type of literature.

R. Asher Lemlein Reutlingen

The first messianic figure to make his appearance after the expulsion was not of Sephardic extraction at all but an Ashkenazi Jew active in northern Italy. If the crisis thesis were true, we would have expected that the Spanish exiles themselves would have been inundated with messianic candidates attempting to exploit the expulsion for their own messianic ends, yet this was not the case. Abraham ha-Levi was the only one to attribute messianic significance to a great variety of historical events, such as the wars at the beginning of the sixteenth century between Turks and Christians or Ethiopian tribes, although he himself never claimed to be a Messiah.

A somewhat clearer messianic claim during the generation after the expulsion, in the first decade of the sixteenth century, is found in the writings of and the documentation about R. Asher Lemlein.[39] This Kabbalist was active in northern Italy and does not refer even once to the expulsion in any of his works. His brand of messianism reflects the influence of Italian Kabbalistic trends imbibed through his own upbringing. The writings of Abraham Abulafia are the backbone of the Italian Kabbalistic tradition, and Abulafia's book *Ḥayyei ha-'Olam ha-Ba'* is mentioned at least twice by Lemlein with great esteem.[40] Ironically, we are dealing with an Ashkenazi Kabbalist who exhibited extremely virulent anti-Sephardic tendencies and who had been in a sharp dispute with Sephardi Kabbalists.[41]. Furthermore, Lemlein did not deem it important to set aside a place in any of his works for the *Zohar*, the most important of the Spanish Kabbalistic works[42]. His main sources of Kabbalistic learning are, on the one hand, the works of Abulafia and, on the other, Ashkenazi traditions and the Heikhalot literature. We may then expect a certain impact of the type of nexus between messianism and mysticism that has been exposed in Abulafia's writings.[43] The acute expression of messianic thought within Kabbalistic works does not appear particularly in Sephardic compositions but rather, in this case, in the visions of an Ashkenazi Kabbalist, Asher Lemlein.

The messianic excitement surrounding Lemlein occurred first and foremost in northern Italy, an area populated primarily by Ashkenazi Jews. It did not seem to affect, as far as can be ascertained, the Spanish exiles who relocated in Italy. It appears that messianic agitation did not arise in the main centers of Sephardic populations. We have virtually no information concerning the aftermath of messianic movements in North Africa and very little of those that flourished in the Ottoman empire, the main population centers of the Spanish exiles.

Like his predecessor Abraham Abulafia, R. Asher Lemlein does not hold to a Kabbalistic system that relies on ten sefirot but rather embraces a Kabbalah that concerns itself with contemplating and explicating letter combinations and concentrating on obtaining heavenly revelations. Lemlein does not develop a theory of demonology characteristic of the Spanish Kabbalah prior to the expulsion, mainly elaborated in the literature of the circle of *Sefer ha-Meshiv*; likewise, certain magical elements found in Lemlein's writings are very different in character from those found in *Sefer ha-Meshiv* and hence do not reflect that book's influence. These magical-Kabbalistic elements point instead to Lemlein's grounding in the Italian Renaissance, where a general preoccupation with the occult sciences was exhibited. Consequently, we can establish a sort of control group. Lemlein's messianism is of the ecstatic version and not of the magical kind, though he was well acquainted with magical writings and mentions them. From this vantage point, he continues the traditions of the Italian Kabbalah and not of the Spanish, even though the two trends possess some common factors. In the case of Lemlein we can detect a common magical element, yet in terms of content these elements stand far apart. Lemlein does not quote any of the Spanish Kabbalistic works; all his sources are either northern Italian or German.

The Ashkenazi character of Lemlein's thought and messianism is demonstrated by his depictions of his personal revelations. He reports the hypostasis of a woman who speaks to him, named Tefillah, meaning "prayer." Tefillah acquires the mythical proportions of a woman who appears to Lemlein for the dual purpose of revealing secrets and castigating all those whose imperfect prayers are causing her damage, including Kabbalists, mostly Spanish. There can be no doubt that we are dealing here for the first time with the intensification of an Ashkenazi view, one which conferred supreme importance on the recitation of the correct version of the liturgy, as a full-blown personification of Tefillah.[44]

These revelations, received by Lemlein through the voice of a woman, apparently took place apparently in Safed and Jerusalem. In terms of external history, it is difficult to say whether we are dealing with solid facts or with mystical reality; Lemlein could have mystically perceived his revelations as occurring in Safed and Jerusalem. If it can be proven that Lemlein physically journeyed to the land of Israel, then we can consider him a forerunner of the messianic excitement that was to overtake an area populated by Spanish exiles. If this were the case, it would be possible to link the messianic fervor of the Ashkenazi Messiah to the later messianic activity of R. Abraham ha-Levi and perhaps even Shlomo Molkho. Unlike other Kabbalists who were engaged in Messianic activities, whether predecessors or contemporaries, Lemlein belongs to the Ashkenazi Jewish community. In the later course of Jewish mysticism, the Ashkenazi figure becomes more and more evident. Sabbatai Ṣevi and Nathan of Gaza, Jacob Frank and Yitzḥaq Aiziq Yehudah Safrin of Komarno, represent a certain change in the distribution of the messianic elements between the Sephardi and the Ashkenazi communities. The more activistic components of messianism were adopted later in history by Ashkenazi figures.[45]

It must be stressed that the documentation available on the messianism of Lemlein is scarce, most of it is late, and sometimes stemming from hostile sources. We do know that his career spanned approximately the first decade of the sixteenth century, just a few years before the main messianic activities of ha-Levi in Jerusalem. In view of the proximity of events, we seem to have a sound basis for undermining the theory that a strong reassessment of messianic consciousness developed primarily on account of the expulsion from Spain. It seems that the Ashkenazi precedent constitutes a meaningful component of this consciousness, granting that the paucity of historical materials limits the debate concerning the extent of this influence. In any event, if the 1520s and 1530s, unlike the years immediately following the expulsion, are marked by messianism, it is logical to suppose that at least there was a certain merger of pre-expulsion Spanish messianism and Ashkenazi messianism, which has no visible links to the act of expulsion from Spain.

Messianism and Christianity

Obviously, as David Ruderman and I have separately pointed out, the possibility of outside influences on Jewish messianism should also be taken into account, most notably the Christian messianic tensions that were exhibited during the Italian Renaissance, even though these concepts only rarely share common ground. Northern Italy was the location of many messianic phenomena in Christian circles during the later decades of the fifteenth century, for the most part connected to internal church strife. These events most likely had an influence on the Jews as well. There is clear evidence of Jews, such as R. Yoḥanan Alemanno, copying almost verbatim types of astrological predictions of the end made by Christians. The sources Alemanno copied and the details of those Christian astrological predictions naturally did not have any connection to the expulsion whatsoever.[46]

Beyond calculations of the end based on a neutral astronomical discourse open to different religious interpretations, some substantial influences may be detected with respect to theological issues. In *Sefer ha-Meshiv*, one of the most anti-Christian documents in Judaism, we may detect one of the most outstanding influences of Christology in any extant Jewish document. According to one passage, two Messiahs, sons of Ephraim and Joseph, have been born as the result of the mythical intercourse between the divine attributes, symbolized by Jacob and Esau, who were incorporated into the ninth sefirah, Yesod, and the last sefirah, Malkhut. This form of intercourse was rather oral than genital, which means that the efflux of the male organ into the mouth of the Shekhinah was presented as

> the mystery of a virgin, "neither had any man known her" . . . There is an actual virgin, made of fire, and she is sexually receptive [namely, has a receptive vessel], and this likeness was created for Israel, as a wife and as a virgin. . . . At the end of the redemption the mystery of the Messiah will come forth for Israel. Until that time, she will remain a virgin and then the supernal spirit will enter her mouth and a spirit of consuming fire will come forth at her opening and will emerge from that sanctuary, for there it will reside, shut away. At that time, when the spirit emerges, it will take the form of fire. This is the mystery of the constellation of Virgo. Therefore, it is the constellation of Israel, and this is the esoteric meaning of the verse: "Rise, the virgin of Israel!" . . . that is the secret interpretation of the verse, "A virgin, neither has any man known her" until the Lord's anointed one will come.[47]

In my opinion, this is a version of the immaculate conception of the virgin Shekhinah, impregnated by the influx descending from the two higher sefirot into her higher opening, the mouth, and as a result she will give birth to the two Messiahs. The nexus between virginity and the birth of the Messiah seems to be significant evidence for a Kabbalistic interpretation of a central Christological tenet. This unusual concern with the birth of the Messiahs seems totally unrelated to any specific historical event, and there are good reasons to assume that the above passage was composed before the expulsion from Spain. Another important Christian tenet, the divinity of the Messiah, is also well represented in the writings of this Kabbalistic circle. For example, we read that "the mystery of My Messiah is the mystery of My divinity."[48] Further support for the view that Jewish messianic expectations are not directly related to the expulsion from Spain may be found in the apocalyptic mood of Savonarola's sermons. Savonarola's expectations for an imminent end of the world started already in 1484, a year fraught with eschatological, mostly astrological, significance for several authors in this period. It is precisely in 1492, however, that Savonarola reported a revelation in the following terms: "In 1492 . . . I saw a hand in heaven with a sword on which was written: 'The sword of God will come upon the earth swiftly and soon.' Above the hand was written 'The judgments of the Lord are true and just' [Nehemiah 9:13]. . . . Then a great voice from the three faces thundered out over the whole world: 'Hear, all you who dwell on earth, thus says the Lord. I the Lord am speaking in my holy zeal. Behold the days are coming and my sword will be unsheathed against you.' "[49]

This apocalypse demonstrates that, from the vantage point of eschatology, the reduction of 1492 to the expulsion would be too limited a vista. Indeed, this passage from Savonarola, in its fullest context, demonstrates that apocalypticism is not always nurtured by external catastrophes. It is quite plausible that the eschatological effervescence of the Christian milieux contributed to the development of similar phenomena among the Jews.[50] Such a link may be the figure of Shlomo Molkho.

R. Shlomo Molkho

The greater part of the Kabbalistic literature composed by Spanish Kabbalists after the expulsion from Spain and Portugal was not based on heavenly revelations. From this perspective post-expulsion Kabbalistic literature can be considered a summary of Kabbalistic traditions that were widespread on the Iberian peninsula before the expulsion. Yet indubitably, immediately following the expulsion there was a distinct rise in the importance of revelation as a component of Kabbalistic literature,[51] owing in part to the activities of the school of *Sefer ha-Meshiv*. This is evident in the works of ha-Levi and Lemlein, as well as in certain other post-expulsion compositions. The most well-known example of this phenomenon is the Maggid or angel who revealed itself to R. Joseph Karo. These revelations are not directly connected to messianism, as is amply illustrated by Karo's voluminous writings.[52] Nevertheless, in some cases there does exist a correlation between the rise of revelation as a creative force and the new esteem accorded it in both Kabbalah and messianism.

This correlation is best exemplified by the person and thought of R. Shlomo Molkho, an ex-converso who reverted to Judaism and subsequently played a decisive messianic role during the 1520s and the beginning of the 1530s.[53] Molkho was viewed by his contemporaries, as well as by some authors in following generations, as an outstanding messianic personality, despite the relative paucity of explicit treatment of messianism in his writings.[54] His compositions are replete with details pertaining to revelations and are occasionally studded with calculations of the date of the end, sometimes including clearly messianic allusions. His main messianic activity and chief contribution to Jewish messianism was to promulgate a messianic message to the public through *derashot* or homilies.[55]

Who actually was R. Shlomo Molkho? Originally he was called Diogo Pires and was a young scribe at the court of the Portuguese king, where he encountered David ha-Reuveni, another colorful character with messianic tendencies. Ha-Reuveni arrived at the king of Portugal's court on an unclear mission of his own, and it would seem that his presence there aroused in the Molkho the desire to approach Judaism and ultimately to embrace it through the act of circumcision. This was done to the chagrin of ha-Reuveni himself, who feared the reaction of the king, which came swiftly. Molkho, however, managed to escape to the Ottoman Empire. The first Jewish period in Molkho's life probably took place in Salonika, most likely in the company of a group of Kabbalists who were connected to the works of the author of *Sefer ha-Meshiv*.[56] Although we cannot be certain, it is plausible that Molkho had access to such Kabbalistic works as *Sefer Kaf ha-Qetoret* and *Sefer Qe'arat ha-Kesef* and the sources of the much-later *Galia' Raza'*, all of which are messianic-visionary works composed in the Ottoman Empire in the environments where Molkho began his life as a practicing Jew. Within this same environment, Molkho encountered R. Joseph Taytatsak, whose precise relationship to Kabbalah is as yet unclear, since we cannot ascertain whether he was a Kabbalist in the full sense of the word, who produced a kind of revelatory writing similar to that found in the *Sefer ha-Meshiv* literature.[57] During this period R. Joseph Karo was active in Salonika, and he too was a personality associated with angelic revelations.

Molkho tells of a series of revelations that apparently started in Portugal, before his circumcision, and seemingly continued for the rest of his career. From this point the connection between mystical revelation and messianism is abundantly clear. It is also conspicuous that Molkho possessed great Kabbalistic knowledge, as we can see from an unedited manuscript where some of his Kabbalistic and messianic traditions are preserved. This is especially impressive considering that he immersed himself in the study of Kabbalah only for a short period, from the time he returned to Judaism until his death at the stake in 1532. Where exactly Molkho acquired his broad knowledge of Kabbalah is not clear, and it could be that he started studying when still a Marrano in Portugal. This possibility, however, does not seem entirely logical. A more credible supposition is that he delved deeply into this body of knowledge while living in the Ottoman Empire, in the company of Kabbalists connected to *Sefer ha-Meshiv*.[58] Whatever the case may be, his knowledge of Judaism and Kabbalah astonished his contemporaries. One Kabbalist wrote, after Molkho's death, "I have found stated in a true text and also there is written how the pious Molkho—blessed be his memory—there is no one that will deny that he suddenly was imbued with the spirit of this wisdom, the Kabbalah. It was not known from whence it came to him, just that his heart was opened by heaven, as a door of a great hall."[59]

This passage summarizes ideas that seem to repeat themselves. Even such an important and learned Kabbalist as R. Shlomo Alkabetz is said to have been amazed by the extent of Molkho's knowledge.[60] The source of the genius and innovation displayed in Molkho's writings remains a mystery. Another testimony to the astonishment caused by Molkho's erudition is found in a document written by a Kabbalist of the late sixteenth century, R. Abraham Yagel, who says of Molkho, "He was unlearned, and presented homilies to the public consisting of ancient matters, Kabbalistic secrets . . . and he wrote down some of these matters, as a testimony for posterity to his wisdom that he acquired in [the span of] '. . . what an eye has never seen'—the blinking of an eye [Isaiah 64:3]. In conclusion, these are matters that man does not know how to evaluate or from whence they come, because they are at the burning center of the universe."[61]

These words echo the great esteem in which Shlomo Molkho was still held in northern Italy during the seventeenth century, when the enigma of Molkho's personality and martyrdom continued to haunt Kabbalists. Both here and in a more explicit comparison elsewhere, Yagel does not ignore the resemblance between the Molkho and Joan of Arc, for both were visionaries and both were burned at the stake. Surprisingly enough, Molkho's public and messianic career was mainly in Italy, for a converso who had reverted to Judaism could only have found safe refuge within the Ottoman Empire. Nevertheless, Molkho decided to leave the welcoming empire and enter into the innermost sanctum of western Christianity, Rome. There can be no doubt as to the daring nature of this act, which entailed an imminent danger of life and death.

Why Molkho decided to journey to Rome and seek an audience with Pope Clement VII is not clear. It could be that he was influenced by Abraham Abulafia's attempt to see Pope Nicholas III. Molkho's Jewish education took place mainly in the Ottoman Empire, in modern-day Greece, where Abulafia's Kabbalah was rather widespread, so we can assume that Abulafia's act was one of the sources of inspiration for Molkho's journey to the pope. To what extent this journey was connected to his messianism remains, nevertheless, unclear. In any event, according to the testimony of his Jewish contemporaries, Molkho arrived at the court of Pope Clement as a proud Jew and did not attempt to hide his Jewishness. He spoke to the pope in superlatives about the Jewish faith, and this is confirmed by the pope himself in the church annals. What did Molkho hope to accomplish at this meeting? There does not seem to be any easy answer to this question. Between Molkho and the pope there clearly was a special chemistry, for after Molkho's trial by the Inquisition and his sentencing to be executed, Clement saved Molkho's life by having him impersonate someone else. Clement apparently responded to specific occult talents that he attributed to Molkho, among them the ability to predict the future. Molkho left Rome with written permission from the pope to print his homilies, on the condition that they not contradict the Christian faith. Molkho then traveled to northern Italy and gave a new set of public sermons, in which there were clear messianic allusions. He stayed mainly in Venice and Mantua.[62] He then decided to approach another powerful leader, King Charles V of Spain. When Molkho arrived at Ratisbon with David ha-Reuveni to see the king, he was arrested and shortly thereafter burned at the stake.

Molkho's messianic self-perception is absolutely clear. In one of his surviving poems he displays a strong messianic awareness, perhaps assuming that he is the Messiah, son of Joseph. Here is a corrected fragment of the single messianic poem penned by Molkho:

> With words concealed I shall reveal to men
> Choice words Like spices.
> From Mount Carmel You were sent by God
> [To be] The man [who] brings tidings [And take] Revenge upon the nations
> Nations shall war Warriors be crushed
> Foreigners shall be vanquished And to us peace
> He arose from the north To seek daughter and son
> Esau who is Edom The young Shlomo
> Will consecrate His polished sword
> In aid of his nation To redeem from nights
> Nations shall fear And gifts bestow
> Full with indignities Due to Salvation.[63]
> Israel shall rejoice Nations shall expire
> Then repaid Manifold
> Heavenly Mercy may be Upon the city of Jerusalem
> The scales are set For Judgement in Yemen.[64]

Molkho presents himself as he who will gird his sword and actively participate in the Armageddon struggle against Christianity, hinted at by the name Edom, and even against Islam, probably alluded to here by Yemen. It may be that the poem reflects a more historical strategy. It is likely that David ha-Reuveni's diplomatic manipulations within the Christian world and Molkho's proclaimed mission to the Ottoman Empire hint at a wider political conspiracy against these two superpowers. Thus, Molkho is but another example of someone who possessed a strong messianic self-awareness and who would like to participate in eschatological activities. We can now try to probe the true nature of those activities. One possible explanation concerns Molkho's obvious quest for danger. Molkho appeared to court a martyr's death, whether consciously or subconsciously. It is also possible that this shows a Christian influence on Molkho's thoughts, for he may have been attempting to reenact the death of Jesus. There is no doubt that Molkho was influenced by Christianity, as is evident in other instances.[65] It would seem that a psychological explanation is our only option for understanding how a man in Molkho's position could leave the safety of the Ottoman Empire for the place of greatest possible danger, Rome, and, upon his improbable rescue by the pope, place himself at the mercy of another powerful Christian leader. In this light Molkho appears to be a prime example of *via passionis* in Jewish messianism.

Another way of understanding Molkho's messianic activities could be connected to the influence of *Sefer ha-Meshiv*. We possess a legend assigned to Shlomo Molkho in which he performs the specific magical acts of Joseph della Reina. Molkho, like della Reina, was supposed to bring down the forces of evil, vanquish them, and pave the way for redemption. The attribution of the story to Molkho, after the expulsion from Spain, is due to the influence of a pre-expulsion legend on the historic Molkho. Moreover, Molkho was aware of the worldview of *Sefer ha-Meshiv* and could have tried to reenact the desperate attempt to bring the redemption by magical means; in that case we could give credence to this late legend as reflectiing an actual event. A legend about Molkho relates that he attempted by magical means to cause a church building to collapse. According to this account, he tried to destroy the Christian regime by ritual processions of circumscription accompanied by chants of the divine names. It would seem that the popular version and Molkho's statements are all connected to his actual audience with the pope.[66] There is good reason to assume that this is also the source of Nathan of Gaza's similar enterprise, to be dealt with below in detail. Nathan also made the journey to Rome and behaved in a similar fashion, a fact that demonstrates that the magical messianism of the *Sefer ha-Meshiv* school echoed, at least in the legend about Molkho, and continued to inspire this type of messianic behavior. There is, however, another clear connection between Molkho and the school of *Sefer ha-Meshiv:* the fundamental belief in the disclosure of Kabbalistic secrets by means of celestial revelation. Molkho insists in a number of texts that his innovative exegetical commentaries came to him by revelation. The basic thrust of *Sefer ha-Meshiv* and its later literature is to give "new" meaning to the Bible. The following passage from Molkho exemplifies his resort to supernatural agents in order to understand the hidden sense of the biblical texts, which has some relevance also for matters of eschatology:

> When God will bring me to pay to the land of Edom [cf. Ezekiel 25:14, but pointing here to Christianity], I shall compile a composition, edited from all my visions which I have seen, with a fine interpretation . . . and in those days the people of Israel

> will believe in me, without any doubt, [and] nothing will be strange and extravagant . . . and I would like to announce to you that since the day I left Portugal I have seen visions in dreams, because there I have been shown all the future things which will happen to me, and all the things to happen in my lifetime. Sometimes in these days I see the celestial academy[67] of sages, and the books are open before them and they study the Torah and they discuss [issues concerning Torah], and they comment upon verses and statements of our sages, blessed be their memory; and from their discussions I hear and learn something. And since I did not learn [Hebrew], neither was [I] accustomed to the holy language and I did not comprehend all their discussions. But from what I was taught there in that holy academy, I answer people who ask for interpretations of verses and statements, which are seen as difficult to understand for the sages of [our] generation. And whoever wishes may ask me whatever he wants, to comment on recondite verses and statements, [for] with the help of God, I am confident that I may answer everyone who asks me in a satisfactory manner sublime things which are sufficient for any intelligent person, which are not [written] in books, [but] which I was instructed from heaven.[68] But I had never learned lore from the mouth of a mortal master or colleague. And whatever anyone will ask me, I am allowed to answer, regarding the twenty four [books of the Jewish biblical canon], except the Book of Daniel.[69]

This is a seminal passage for the proper understanding of the spiritual portrait of Molkho. He explicitly attributes the messages he received to supernatural powers, including his interpretive capacities. There is an aspect of dissimilarity that emerges from this generally homogeneous picture. *Sefer ha-Meshiv* extensively utilizes the technique of dream responsa, whereas Molkho only mentions this technique once, in a fragment attributed to him. The calculations of the end that abound in Molkho's writings are by and large similar to those found in *Sefer ha-Meshiv, Sefer Kaf ha-Qetoret,* and the writings of R. Abraham ha-Levi, the ultimate date being 5300, or 1540 C.E.. Molkho cites other, earlier dates as preliminary stages of the redemptive process: 1530 and, as mentioned in the poem above, 1535.[70] Moreover, the very beginning of the above passage Molkho assumes that God will make him an instrument of his wrath against Edom, and this direct confession corroborates our analysis of the legend that attributes to this figure an attempt at destroying Christianity by means of magic. Moreover, Molkho's promise to commit to writing his visions, together with their interpretation, is reminiscent of Abulafia's commentaries on his own prophetic books. In both cases a messianic figure is prophet, visionary, and interpreter of his own visions. However, while Abulafia was much more audacious, explicating passages of Daniel related to the end in 1290, Molkho avowedly refused to do so, for reasons he does not specify. The question is whether there is an historical linkage between Abulafia's messianic Kabbalah and Molkho's. Molkho never quoted Abulafia, but he could be acquainted with Abulafia's thought either from his studies of *Sefer ha-Peliy'ah,* which incorporated large sections from Abulafia's writings verbatim, or from the possible studies of the ecstatic Kabbalah in the Ottoman Empire, where Abulafia's writings circulated in manuscript.

A short passage from a work in Molkho's circle deals with the Messiah as a constant presence accompanying human history. He was reported to have said, following early Kabbalistic traditions from Naḥmanides' school:

> Abel is Moses, who is Abel, because all the deliverances are done by him, because his soul will transmigrate into the Messiah, and this is why he [Moses] has been buried abroad. "What is the gain of man from all his labor that he labors under the sun," if the redemption does not come? And he [Solomon] answered: "One generation goeth, another generation cometh," namely it is a necessity that the Messiah will come, because he is the power of Satan [and] Serpent, and he removed the impurity of the Serpent from the world, and this is the reason that he goes, because in the very moment and time that Israel will repent, they will immediately be redeemed . . . this is why in each and every generation there was a person [stemming] from [the children of] Israel, worthy and prepared to become the Messiah, and fulfill what has been written . . . "because a generation goeth and another generation cometh, and the earth abideth forever" because it cannot subsist without the Messiah, because of the impurity of the Serpent . . . because the impurity of the Serpent spills over all the spheres and comes from the power of the seventh, lower sphere, which is that of the Moon.[71]

In this rich passage, the Messiah is conceived of as the antidote to the impure influx descending from above. In fact, he must return in every generation in order to ensure the preservation of the world, to maintain the cosmos against the centrifugal force of chaos. Therefore, the redemptive role of the Messiah is not only a matter of a certain final act or series of acts performed during the eschaton, but is an ongoing activity performed throughout common history. Though the redemptive role of the Messiah in the eschaton is mentioned explicitly in the above passage, as the potential for immediate redemption that depends only on the repentance of Israel shows, in the interim he sustains the world by continuously combating the descending impurity of the demonic Serpent. In more general terms it may be suggested that the present order, deleterious as it may be for the Jews, still must be maintained and a further deterioration prevented by the deeds of the Messiah. To formulate Molkho's view in terms stemming from Naḥmanides' thought, the advent of the Messiah will correspond to the manifest miracles, while his daily redemptive activity may be more cosmic in nature, corresponding to Naḥmanides' hidden miracles.

The hermeneutical move of the above passage is an attempt to correlate the coming and going of the generations, understood already from the very beginning of Kabbalah as pointing to the transmigration of souls, and the earth as abiding, mentioned in the same verse, Ecclesiastes 1:4. This exegetical achievement is related by Molkho to the "generations"; their coming and their going are for the sake of maintaining the earth, namely the cosmos. The Messiah is therefore, insofar as this aspect of his activity is concerned, a conservative power par excellence, while the renovation or revolution that will put an end to the transmigration of the soul of the Messiah means his revelation, which will apparently put an end to the influence of the Serpent. To compare the Messiah of this text to the other concepts in theosophical-theurgical Kabbalah, we may say that it is the horizontal aspect of this figure that enables him to act here below, rather than his devotion to the divinity. The reincarnation of the ancient soul is the basic mode of validation of his special powers. The continuum in time between the primordial source and later messianic figures is created by presupposing a transmission of an originally divine soul from one body to another, rather than the adherence of this soul to the higher powers through an act of mystical ascent, whose direction is vertical. This type of thought opens to way to a much more historical approach. Though dealing with present mythical battles between good and evil, the Messiah is destined to cause the continuation of the course of history and only in the final moment break it. As the maintainer of the historical order, he is called to act in the present by assuming the role of a warrior. Here the function of the Messiah is much more important than his human specific personalizations. The maintenance function is in any case performed by a variety of persona who may be connected to each other by means of the concept of transmigration or reincarnation, but Molkho is much less concerned with this issue.

Shlomo Molkho can be considered a late echo of pre-expulsion Spanish magical-mystical and mythical forms of messianism. Except for Jesus, he was the most influential Jewish Messiah to date. His intensive activities in the public domain, his connection to the pope, and his mobility, traveling from the Ottoman Empire to Rome and through northern Italy, caused much commotion in the Jewish world. Some of the spiritual preparation for the messianic awareness of the populace must be credited to the prior activities of R. Asher Lemlein. Molkho's influence was multifaceted. On the one hand, Molkho's willingness to give his life for the sake of his religion (at the stake he refused to recant and return to Christianity) was viewed as a heroic example. This deeply affected a personality of the caliber of R. Joseph Karo, who dreamed of being able to do as Molkho did, to sacrifice his life for the sake of God at the stake.[72] Yet on the other hand, in the East, or more specifically in the land of Israel, Molkho's activities were not always viewed in a positive light. In the writings of R. Moses Cordovero and R. Ḥayyim Vital, Molkho's magical activities were equated with that behavior of della Reina, all of them viewed as acts to be scorned.[73] Thus, simultaneous with the favorable reaction to Molkho's ultimate self-sacrifice, objections were raised to the magical methods he allegedly employed. In northern Italy and the central European communities, only the positive aspects of Molkho's activities were remembered. Strangely enough, his writings and thoughts were preserved and came to influence many generations precisely in the Ashkenazi territories. Once again we are struck by the ironic fact that the regions that were susceptible to messianic excitement and support were those that were not dominated, culturally or numerically, by the Spanish exiles.

We can conclude from the case of Molkho, as we did from that of Lemlein, that the Sephardi expellees were not easily caught up in messianic fervor, whereas spiritual sensibilities concerning messianism were demonstrated among the Ashkenazi communities of central Europe and northern Italy.

Scholem's View of the Expulsion and Kabbalistic Messianism

When dealing with the second phase of the development of Kabbalah in the accepted historiography of Kabbalah, Gershom Scholem envisaged the whole range of Jewish religious literature of this period as completely imbued with messianic fervor. "For the span of one generation, during the forty years after the expulsion from Spain," Scholem wrote, "we find a deep Messianic excitement as intense as before the eruption of the Sabbatian movement, and this thing is understandable as an immediate reaction to the expulsion from Spain. . . . It is easy to understand that the entire religious literature of the first generation after the expulsion from Spain is replete with this issue, being in its entirety an actual hope for a close redemption."[74]

Moreover, the assumption that a deep fertilization of Kabbalah by messianism during the second phase of the relationship between the two approaches, as envisioned by Scholem,[75] does not correspond to the facts. The choice of some of the writings of R. Abraham ha-Levi as representative of his generation is, in my opinion, rather questionable. Rather, ha-Levi represents what may be called the peripheral extreme left wing, by the dint of some of his writings that are indeed replete with strong messianic, sometimes even apocalyptic, themes and aspirations. Similar views are found, as Scholem pointed out, in the anonymous *Sefer Kaf ha-Qetoret,* written immediately after the expulsion.[76] None of them, however, seem to have reached the influence exercised by the messianic propaganda of a much less known figure like Asher Lemlein, whose impact has been described in terms that exceed whatever we know about the impact of the two Sephardi messianic Kabbalistic thinkers, ha-Levi and the author of *Kaf ha-Qetoret.* Writing in a region dominated by Ashkenazi culture, his influence was portrayed at the end of sixteenth century as follows: "He was prophesying and said that the time of the end has arrived and he warned the people to repent. And in the land of Ashkenaz and Italy and the other lands of Edom[77] they believed in his words and they decreed fasts and did great [acts of] repentance, and this issue has been revealed between the nations, and when some few simpletons have seen that after the repentance [redemption] did not come, they left [the nation] and converted."[78]

This passage approximates what may be designated as a modest messianic movement. In breadth it comprised several countries; in depth it displayed a profound commitment to the message, which includes external acts of repentance that complement the spiritual investment in the belief in the messianic message; when disappointed, this belief generated acts of conversion. In any case, nothing of the breadth of the diffusion of Lemlein's influence is known in the context of the Sephardi diaspora.

And yet the overwhelming majority of the Kabbalists among the expellees did not belong to the apocalyptic tendency. They were rather conservative thinkers, like R. Meir ibn Gabbay, R. Yehudah Ḥayyat, R. Joseph Al-Ashqar, R. Yehudah Ḥallewah, R. Joseph ibn Tzayyaḥ, R. Abraham Adrutiel, R. David ibn Zimra, and R. Joseph Karo. Their writings, which constitute the vast majority and most influential portion of the Kabbalistic literary activity in the generations following the expulsion, do not betray any special preoccupation with messianism; and by their influence they seem to have been much more representative than the eccentric though colorful R. Abraham ben Eliezer ha-Levi. This idea of a homogenous nature of an entire religious literature belongs to the realm of academic myths, even if we shall inspect the Kabbalistic literature alone, a fortiori the entire range of post-expulsion Sephardi literature. I would say that the floruit of the Sephardi religious literature after the expulsion was accomplished primarily along lines of thought and by resort to literary genres that are conservative and intended to build up the new centers following, as much as possible, the models of the communities in Spain.[79] Some forms of literature marginal in Spain, such as historiography, may indeed reflect certain forms of messianic impulses, although, as has been suggested by Y. H. Yerushalmi, their main approach was much more concerned with explaining the changing future than with accounting for the traumatic past[80]; or, to follow the suggestion of Robert Bonfil, some parts of Jewish historiography in the sixteenth century betray the impact of the Italian cultural background.[81] In principle, it seems that the much more pronounced messianism of the Ashkenazi Kabbalist Asher Lemlein, when compared to the relatively marginal status of messianism in the voluminous writings of the Sephardi Kabbalists of the early sixteenth century, calls into question Gershon Cohen's distinction between the attitudes toward this topic in the two Jewish communities.[82]

· CHAPTER FIVE ·

From Italy to Safed and Back, 1540–1640

THE sixteenth century witnessed a surge of interest in both mysticism and messianism in European culture. Michel de Certeau has proposed to see this century as the invasion of the mystics, an assessment that is appropriate not only for the Christian spirituality de Certeau addresses but also for Jewish spirituality.[1] The intense creativity of Christian mysticism, so evident at mid-century, invites a comparison to contemporaneous phenomena in Judaism. This comparison may offer another angle for inspecting some aspects of the efflorescence of Kabbalistic creativity in the last two thirds of the sixteenth century; in lieu of the "traumatic" explanation it looks to a dynamics of osmosis between the mysticisms flourishing in the two religions at the same time. The temporal parallelism is even more striking since the two religions substantially coexisted in at least one large region, Italy. Though some common factors may explain, at least in part, the concomitant flowering of these two different forms of mysticism, in my opinion the meaning of this synchronism escapes an ordinary historical explanation. Nevertheless, let me address the possible historical connections between them.

We may quite rightly evoke the contribution of the Jewish Kabbalah to the European intellectual culture in this period, on the one hand, and the return of some conversos to Judaism and their possible influence on Jewish mysticism—for example, Shlomo Molkho or R. Ya'aqov Ḥayyim Tzemaḥ—on the other. In the seventeenth century, this is also the case with one of the most important exponents of Sabbateanism, Abraham Michael Cardoso. A more open dialogue between the two religions is also evident in this period in the impetus that the phenomena of Christian Kabbalah and Hebraism would demonstrate. The circulation of ideas in the sixteenth century between the Jewish and Christian intellectual milieux had attained dimensions unknown in the Middle Ages. In some modern studies, the impact of Judaism is not only recognized but sometimes even exaggerated. This seems to be the case with some of the assessments of Dame Frances A. Yates, who eagerly attributed a profound influence of Kabbalah even in instances that would demand more caution. Nevertheless, despite this caveat, there is no reason to underestimate the influence of this type of Jewish lore on the European scene.

As regards messianism, an outstanding example of this influence is Aegidius Viterbus, a cardinal of the Augustinian order who was deeply interested in Kabbalah. Viterbus was one of the most productive Christian Kabbalists, but also an author who played a role in sixteenth-century mystical and apocalyptic Christian spirituality. His bridging of Christian mysticism, Jewish and Christian Kabbalah, the study of Hebrew, Renaissance culture, and ecclesiastic authority points up the intersection between the various spiritual vectors of the early sixteenth century. Especially interesting is Viterbus' identification of Christ, seen as the Messiah, with the Kabbalistic vision of the Shekhinah and his contacts with a figure connected to messianic aspirations, David ha-Reuveni.[2] Even more salient to the point I would like to make here is an aspect of the activities and beliefs of William Postel. In addition to his fine knowledge of Kabbalah—he was one of the few Christian Kabbalists who composed Kabbalistic works in Hebrew—Postel believed that Johanna, a virgin of Veronese extraction active in Venice (where Postel met her), was both an embodiment of the Shekhinah and the new Eve expiating the sin of the first Eve, just as Christ redeemed Adam. Postel claimed that Johanna would be visited by Christ, and he resorts to explicit Kabbalistic concepts concerning the androgenic nature of the Messiah as both male and female, reflecting the two lower sefirot, Tiferet and Malkhut. According to some of Postel's statements, Johanna exposed to him the secrets of the *Zohar*, despite the fact that she did not know Hebrew or Latin. Here a mystical Christology, expressing an intense eschatological aspiration, has been strongly influenced by Kabbalistic thought and sometimes even formulated in Hebrew. Prophetic elements played a central role both in Postel's self-perception and in his perception of Johanna. As a prophet, he identified himself not only with Elijah, a forerunner of the Messiah, but also with the lower Messiah, apparently with the sefirah of Malkhut.[3]

Despite the plausible impact of Kabbalistic symbolism and eschatology on Postel and Viterbus, we should also be aware of the simultaneous influence of Joachimite millenarian trends on them, as well as the more diffuse surge of concern with the Golden Age in the Renaissance. Outstanding as these examples may be, however, it is difficult to believe that they might have more than marginally affected the efflorescence of mystical literatures in the two religions. Since the renascence of late-thirteenth-century Castile, Kabbalah was never so creative and influential as it was in the sixteenth century. This flowering is attested by the great number of active and original Kabbalists and of books on Kabbalah that were composed then, by the wider circulation of Kabbalistic ideas among both Jewish and Christian elites, in print and in manuscript, and by the more massive infiltration of Kabbalistic ideas in larger audiences. The eagerness of the few Christian intellectuals to study Kabbalah made a strong impression—sometimes positive, sometimes negative—on the Jewish Kabbalists themselves. This new religious wave was a result of several factors: the greater openness toward occult literature, evident in the Renaissance period in general, which brought Kabbalistic lore to the attention of some intellectual groups in the Christian entourage; the dispersion of Spanish Kabbalists, who represent the most important center of Kabbalah, over the countries of the Mediterranean Sea; and the new availability of Kabbalistic books in print.

But these quantitative agents in the dissemination of Kabbalah are only part of a more complex picture, which includes a creative impetus nourished by a variety of causes. One of them has been already discussed: the Spanish Kabbalists wanted to have their heritage, conceived as the innermost sense of Judaism, preserved and respected, a factor that would help establish them in the new centers of Jewish culture they had created in the Mediterranean.[4] In the middle of the sixteenth century, however, this conservative drive was already in decline; the second generation of Spanish Kabbalists, as well as the Italian and Ashkenazi Kabbalists, become more and more involved with this mystical lore in ways different from their predecessors, one of them being a much greater interaction with other forms of thought than they had had the opportunity to experience in Spain. The different interactions between the variety of Kabbalistic traditions that encountered each other in Italy, the Ottoman Empire, Jerusalem, and Safed provoked reactions, syntheses of various Kabbalistic traditions, broader syntheses of Kabbalah in general, as well as mutual enrichments. This new situation, which in a few cases served as a melting pot, was one of the major catalysts for the outburst of creativity that characterizes the mid-sixteenth century. The darker side of Jewish life in the sixteenth century notwithstanding—the heavy repercussions of the expulsion of the Jews from Spain, Portugal, and Sicily, the creation of the ghetto in Italy, the intense use of Kabbalah by some Christian thinkers as a means of conversion,[5] and the dramatic decline of Jerusalem as a cultural and economic center in the middle of the century—it seems that a spirit of cultural renascence overcame the gloomy atmosphere that is commonly assumed to have dominated this period.[6]

There are good reasons to assume that in such a creative ambiance, quite substantially inclined toward mysticism, messianic ideas would also be given their share of attention. As we shall see, there was an intensification of discussions of eschatological issues among Jews, in the form of messianic calculations and eschatological types of exegesis. This activity was most pronounced in Italy, a place haunted by millenarian thought since the end of the fifteenth century, but also appeared in the Protestant areas, such as Germany and England, where the apocalyptic elements were burgeoning during the sixteenth century.[7]

The establishment of a new center of Kabbalah in the Galilee, in the town of Safed in the mid-sixteenth century, might be thought of as unrelated to the mystique of other spiritual authors that lived in this century. Yet it does have something to do with traditions concerning that particular locale, since Galilee was already identified in the *Zohar* as the place where the Messiah will arrive first. Thus, tradition predates the trauma of the expulsions of Spanish and Sicilian Jewry.[8] The intensification of the religious life in the immediate vicinity of the place where the *Zohar* allegedly was composed—by a mystical communion with the spirit of the author of the *Zohar*—together with a tradition about the coming of the Messiah in the Galilee should be taken in consideration as more concrete testimonies for the emergence of messianic expectations among the Kabbalists in Safed, fond as they were with zoharic thought. Moreover, some of the important Kabbalists staying at least for a while in this town were presumably aware of the Christian Kabbalah, as is evident from the writings of Moses Cordovero, Mordekhai Dato, and Ḥayyim Vital.

Kabbalah and Messianism in the Early Sixteenth Century

In the previous chapters we have dealt with the messianic activities of several Kabbalists, most notably Abraham Abulafia, Asher Lemlein, Abraham ben Eliezer ha-Levi, and Shlomo Molkho. Their impact was especially profound in Italy, an issue to which we shall soon return. There is no doubt that their messianic awareness, whether concerning the advent of the end or their own messianic roles, possessed rather clear lines. With this assumption in mind, we have to attempt to delineate the precise relationship between their messianic awareness and their preoccupation with Kabbalah.

Two contradictory positions have been argued concerning this relationship, both of them found in Scholem's writings. One position maintains that there is no relationship between historical messianic roles and the Kabbalistic leanings of the Messiahs or the revealers of secrets. The other considers such a split in personality inconceivable when dealing with Kabbalistic awareness, just as there is no absolute separation between a person's messianic awareness and mystical beliefs, on the one hand, and the speculative-mystical system that he was educated in and adheres to, on the other.[9] It seems that too sharp a distinction between mystical and messianic awareness is problematic, for it ignores the need to analyze these personalities in as psychologically integrative a manner as possible. Therefore, it is my opinion that there exists a profound connection between messianism and mystical revelation and that the problematical nature of this bond is to be stressed, for we are dealing with two sides of the same coin. In other words, in lieu of compartmentalizing the various facets of one's spiritual life, I would assume that in the case of most Kabbalists more integral structures conjoining messianism and mysticism are more plausibly.

In the light of the significant development of mystical literature in the sixteenth century, and of the affinity between mysticism and messianism in general, the growth of interest in messianism should be seen as part of a systemic development rather than as solely motivated by historical traumas. It would be wise, however, not to reduce all the messianic concepts and themes to the expansion of Kabbalah alone.

Messianic Calculations

There do exist types of messianic activity other than the propagandistic models of Asher Lemlein, Abraham ha-Levi, and Shlomo Molkho. For instance, many people delved into intricate calculations of the end, a preoccupation that indubitably indicates their own messianic awareness. In the years following the death of Molkho, the phenomenon of calculating the end was accelerated in Italy. As David Tamar has shown, the last half of the sixteenth century was replete with Italian Kabbalists who were deeply engaged in calculations of this sort. Essentially, the year of redemption was set as 1575, based on a numerical exegesis of the verse "The staff shall not depart from Yehudah, nor the scepter from between his feet, until Shiloh come" (Genesis 49:10). The numerical equivalence of the consonants of Shiloh is 335, a figure that points to the Jewish year 5335, which corresponds to the common year 1575.[10] Clear testimony of this calculation is found in a manuscript that R. Mordekhai Dato, a renowned Italian Kabbalist of the second half of the century, mentions in his book *Migdal David,* as does the unknown author of another work of the same period, *Sefer 'Avodat ha-Qodesh.*[11] Both works are Kabbalistic and contain calculations of the end that are very close to the time of their writing, yet it is virtually impossible to determine if either author possessed a messianic self-awareness.

Therefore this instance does not seem relevant to the overall topic of mystical revelation and messianic self-awareness. Here we can describe the phenomenon of engaging in messianic calculations as a kind of building of a "sense-making paradigm"[12] rather than a radical eruption of messianism. This is also the case for other calculators of the precise date of the end. One of the most prominent personalities of Italy in the sixteenth century, a philosopher who himself was in terrible conflict with Shlomo Molkho, actively practiced figuring the date of the end. I am referring to R. Jacob Mantino, a famous court physician and contemporary of Molkho, whom Molkho accused of having plotted against him.[13] Mantino translated into Latin many compositions of Averroes and he is taken to be a model of Italian rationalistic thought. Nevertheless, one of his extant manuscripts that I identified is replete with calculations of the end.[14]

Obviously, this does not demonstrate a messianic self-awareness, nor an acute belief in the immanent advent of the Messiah, but rather a type of intellectual activity that attempts to discover the recondite secrets of history. This is the case, in my opinion, with another set of calculations worthy of a more detailed discussion. In an anonymous manuscript we read about the Hebrew date 5358, which corresponds to 1598 C.E., as the year of the coming of the Messiah, because this figure derives from the numerical value of the Hebrew word *mashiyaḥ*, 358:

> The great purpose of the advent of the king Messiah and of the world to come [was not disclosed, as it is said], "The heart did not disclose to the mouth," neither to the vulgus or to all of the elite but to the few who merit this [i.e. the knowledge of the secret]. It is forbidden to the recipient of this secret to disclose it even to the elite, except to a friend exceptionally close to him. And in the year of Messiah, namely in the year whose secret is 358 of the sixth millennium, which is the year Shanah, then the Messiah will arrive. [However,] in an occult manner he has already arrived during the several cycles of the worlds which have already passed before the present one in which we are, since at the time when he has already arrived [in the past], then he will come again also this time. And it was said that 'and then he will come' means that the Messiah will come in the future at the same time he comes in our time, namely in our world.[15]

This pessimistic vision of the present era demonstrates that the macrochronic cycle is often permeated by a negative vision of the world. This particular school of theosophical Kabbalah maintains the crucial influence of the peculiar type of cycle under whose aegis they lived without denying the messianic aspirations and including calculations of the advent of the Messiah. Thus we read in a gloss found in R. Joseph ben Shalom Ashkenazi's *Commentary on Sefer Yetzirah,* "Each and every sefirah [of the seven lower sefirot] is working for six millennia, and [then] the work turns to one of them for a millennium. Then the work turns to the following sefirah. And just as in the six millennia that we are in today in the year 5190 [*ha-qetz.*] from the time of creation, the sefirah of Gevurah is working, and this is the reason for the epidemics and wars and exiles."[16] The great mystery revealed here concerns the advent of the Messiah at exactly the same time in every cosmic cycle; just as he came in the prior cycle in the year 358, he will appear in our cycle and so also in future cycles. Therefore, the real secret is not solely the computation of the precise date of the arrival of the Messiah but also the fact that this date is the archetype of all the messianic dates past and future.

Before considering the conceptual implications of this passage, let us elaborate on some philological details. First, the term translated as "cycles" is *gilgul;* its primary meaning is "rotation," but it was adopted by many Kabbalists as the primary term for metempsychosis.[17] In this particular context, however, where it is employed together with the word "worlds," I assume that its rendering as "cycle" does justice to the general intention of the text. Second, the coming of the Messiah is indicated in this passage by the verb *ba',* whose plain meaning is indeed "to come." But in some Kabbalistic texts this verb is used to hint at the soul that undergoes a process of metempsychosis, and at least in one instance this soul is the soul of the Messiah.[18]

Therefore, though the plain meaning of the text deals with the recurring coming of the Messiah at the same date in each cosmic cycle, a more careful reading may reveal an additional aspect of the subject: the Messiah who returns from time to time is preserving his existence in the interregnum by metempsychosis. What is interesting about this particular date is not the fact that *mashiyaḥ* is numerically equivalent to 358 but the general conception of history exhibited in the text. This Kabbalist posits that the Messiah will arrive in the year 5358 and in all the other years of 5358 of the cosmic cycles. So, once in every seven thousand years the messianic advent is to be repeated, mutatis mutandis, in each and every cosmic cycle. Thus a linear view of history is combined with a cyclical theory of time. The linear view posits a straight historical line, with developmental progress until history reaches the end point of the redemption. The circular theory of time presents each end of a cycle as but the beginning of the next one.[19]

These cases prove that not all endeavors of calculating the end originate in an integral connection to acute messianism or even the messianic self-awareness of the author. There are numerous examples of this type of messianic phenomenon in as yet unpublished manuscripts for the most part penned by Italian Jews. As already mentioned, Lemlein and Molkho, and even ha-Levi and David ha-Reuveni to some extent, all focused their propagandistic-messianic activities toward Italian Jewry. There is good reason, then, to view Italy as a main center of involvement in messianic issues, without significant or constant connection to the Spanish expulsion. There can be no doubt that the extensive messianic writings of R. Yitzḥaq Abravanel, composed in Italy, are a direct reaction to the trauma of the expulsion. Yet the subsequent interest in messianism in Italy during the sixteenth century is, in my opinion, largely divorced from the expulsion. This is not to say that the expulsion is never referred to in these later compositions, but it is too simplistic to attribute all the messianic calculations, as well as all the messianic activities that transpired in Italy, to that catastrophe.[20]

Eschatological Hermeneutics

In contrast to calculations of the end, another venue of messianic expression lies somewhere on the border between a feeling of acute messianism and a literary exegetical activity; this is the eschatological exegesis of the biblical canon.[21] There can be no doubt that this is quite an ancient endeavor, for the revealing of the secrets of the Bible, inherent in the floruit of Kabbalistic literature in the second half of the sixteenth century, becomes more acceptable if one believes that one is living in the age of redemption. To an extent this applies to the type of hermeneutical device employed by the Qumran community, a Second Temple–period sect in the Judean desert.[22] Eschatological hermeneutics retained validity during the Middle Ages among messianically self-aware personalities who were anxious to find authoritative backing in the canonical literature for their mystical revelations. For example, in an anonymous *Commentary on the Pentateuch* by an Ashkenazi author, the advent of the Messiah and Elijah is described as preceding the solution of all the quandaries and the revelation of the secrets of the Torah.[23] This is clearly shown also by the example of Abraham Abulafia, who composed an as yet unpublished commentary on the Torah entitled *Sefer ha-Mafteḥot.* In his introduction Abulafia explicitly notes the preparatory syndrome we described above; since he is living in the age of redemption, he is permitted to reveal secrets.[24] Likewise, his commentary on Maimonides' *Guide of the Perplexed,* named *Sitrei Torah,* is envisioned in such an eschatological perspective: "These secrets will be revealed during the advent of the Messianic era, by the prophets who will arise [then] and by the Messiah himself, because through them all of Israel and those who are drawn to them will be strengthened."[25] This phenomenon is even more conspicuous in *Sefer ha-Meshiv,* which is largely an esoteric commentary on the Pentateuch. There it is explicitly stated that the secrets can be revealed on account of the immanent advent of the end.

During the sixteenth century, the this trend is recognizable in the works of the school of *Sefer ha-Meshiv,* where the effort was made to complete the eschatological commentary started therein by extending it to all the books of the Bible. Belonging to this century is a lengthy anonymous commentary on the book of Psalms, *Sefer Kaf ha-Qetoret,* whose author did not stop at the biblical canon; in addition to his commentaries on the Song of Songs and Ecclesiastes, called *Qe'arat ha-Kesef,* he commented on talmudic passages as well as *piyyutim,* the liturgical poems that are recited on the High Holy Days.[26] Eschatological hermeneutics are products of messianic consciousness, despite the fact that we cannot always prove the connection between the personal and the historical circumstances and the content of the commentary. It is possible for someone to write an eschatological commentary like *Sefer Kaf ha-Qetoret* and at the same time for it to be difficult for the reader to ascertain whether or not the author is trying to convey a message of acute messianism. In contrast to the impression one gets from the scant scholarly literature concerning *Sefer Kaf ha-Qetoret,* I am not of the opinion that messianism is the solely dominant theme of this work.[27]

To a certain extent, this also holds true for Molkho. His printed homilies extensively dealt with eschatological interpretations of the Bible, yet when confronted by his adherents he admitted to refraining from commenting on certain verses, particularly the more sensitive ones from an eschatological perspective, such as some of those found in the book of Daniel.[28] It is conceivable that Molkho's avoidance of commentary on certain loaded canonic texts is bound up with his general tendency to refrain from outright discussions of messianic dates. Because of the Christian environment in which he functioned, Molkho avoided commenting on texts of a radical eschatological nature, presenting instead a more moderate eschatology based on less provocative texts. It is very likely that the papal warning to Molkho to refrain from publishing blatantly anti-Christian material in his sermons was taken to heart. From this vantage point we can view messianism as influencing the course of Jewish hermeneutics. Eschatological hermeneutics expresses a need to bridge the gap between a strong, or even a moderate, messianic awareness and the hidden truth of the biblical canon. This can be accomplished by hermeneutical techniques practiced within Jewish tradition, as demonstrated above by the use of gematria to compute the dates corresponding to the words Shiloh and Messiah.

Kabbalah and Messianism in Safed

The most important Jewish center during the middle years of the sixteenth century was located in the land of Israel, which in the middle of the century underwent dramatic developments in spiritual life when many already existing types of Kabbalah converged in Safed. In the first part of that century, interesting developments within the Kabbalah occurred in Jerusalem, where Kabbalists such as R. Yehudah Albotini, R. Joseph ibn Tzayyaḥ, and the more famous R. Abraham ben Eliezer ha-Levi were active.[29] It could be argued that the Kabbalistic literature then composed in Jerusalem was representative for the extensive creativity of the Jews of the land of Israel in the period immediately following the expulsion. Within the framework of this extensive Kabbalistic literature, which amounts to several thousands of manuscript folios, messianic themes are scarce, to be found only in some of the writings of Abraham ha-Levi.

The Kabbalistic center in Jerusalem started to wane around the end of the first half of the sixteenth century, when there was a shift to the Galilean city of Safed, where many active and influential Kabbalists resided. Some brotherhoods of Kabbalists, the majority of whom were Spanish expellees or their descendants, gradually consolidated there in the 1540s, and soon Safed become a place where, as Scholem put it, "all the arteries of Jewish spiritual life converged."[30] By the middle of the century these Kabbalists formed cohesive and influential groups that produced a voluminous literature that was to be extremely influential in throughout the Jewish diaspora. In the primary stage of the Safedian Kabbalah, in the mystical brotherhoods that had such members as R. Moses Cordovero, R. Joseph Karo, and R. Shlomo ha-Levi Alqabetz, messianism played a peripheral role. Obviously, each of these personalities took a different attitude toward the subject. Karo hardly deals with messianism at all,[31] while Cordovero and Alqabetz relate to it much more as calculations of the expected end and treat general eschatological issues such as questions about the cosmic cycles and the precise nature of the current cycle, the theory of Shemittah and Yovel, accurate prediction of the date of the end, and so forth.[32] In light of what we know today, it is hard to imagine that in the middle of the sixteenth century there existed a clear and acute messianic self-awareness within this main Kabbalistic school of Safed.

The huge literary corpus penned in this circle, which consists of outstanding Kabbalistic works such as Cordovero's and those of his students, only refers to messianism peripherally. The Kabbalistic pietistic literature, like R. Elijah de Vidas's *Sefer Reshit Ḥokhmah* and R. Eliezer Azikri's *Sefer Ḥaredim,* as well as Cordovero's own moralistic works, hardly exhibits an interest in messianism.[33] This literature had a lasting impact on most of the forms of Jewish spirituality in the following generations. This type of literary approach primarily focused on structuring the mystical life of the individual through Kabbalistic understandings of the meaning of ritual, the establishment of what were perhaps new customs and tiqqunim, with the intent of influencing daily behavior.[34] It attempted to form and idealize the mystical life and to spread these ideals all over the Jewish world. Such a tendency did not allow, in my opinion, significant room for acute forms of messianism. Since this was the most influential literature in the last third of the sixteenth century and during the seventeenth century, the messianic idea was not inculcated in the minds and hearts of the greater portion of the Jewish populace. Cordovero and his school's basic goal was to structure life in terms of mystical and religious meaning, without presenting a doctrine of acute or systematic eschatology.[35] They sought to secure stability, to celebrate the mystical life as part of the traditional Jewish way of life, rather than to create messianic tensions. The floruit of Kabbalah in this period should be seen as part of the process of the consolidation of Jewish life in new centers.

In any case, we had better not exaggerate the importance of the messianic element for the formation of the Safedian center of Kabbalah. What seems to be puzzling for such an emphatic understanding of the formative role of the messianic expectations would be that R. Ḥayyim Vital left Safed and, later on, the land of Israel in order to spend the last decades of his life in a less "sacred" place like Syria, while Cordovero's, R. Gedaliyah, preferred exile in Italy. I find these emigrations quite incompatible with the theory of acute eschatological aspirations that the advent of the Messiah is imminent, which are attributed to the Safedian Kabbalists.

On Individual Messianism in Safed

Sixteenth-century Safed was a city of spiritual encounters for Jews from all over the world. Spanish Kabbalists who themselves had experienced the expulsion and those born subsequently were among the members of R. Moses ben Jacob Cordovero's *ḥavurah* or brotherhood. It was mostly they who imbued some circles in Safed with its special mystical atmosphere. There were Kabbalists from other countries as well: R. Ḥayyim Vital from Calabria; R. Lapidot Ashkenazi, a less famous figure in the scholarly literature though quite venerated by his Safedian contemporaries Cordovero and Vital,[36] from Germany or Poland; R. Yehudah Ḥallewah from North Africa.[37] Even the Jewish community in Yemen contributed a visitor to Safed, testifying to the unique spiritual atmosphere in the town.[38] The convergence of Jews of different origins displaying diverse religious and mystical interests was one of the main precipitators of the great spiritual revival and enthusiasm that characterized Safed from the 1540s to the early 1570s. The school of Cordoverian Kabbalah, through its dissemination of an ethical literature and treatises on rules of behavior called *hanhagot,* managed to present the Kabbalah in a systematic fashion, making it available to all segments of the population.[39]

At the same time as this impressive achievement, there was another dramatic development in Safedian Kabbalah, led by R. Yitzḥaq ben Shlomo Luria Ashkenazi. Luria, better known by the acronym ha-ARI, which stands for "the divine R. Yitzḥaq," was born in Jerusalem, of Ashkenazi-Polish descent,[40] and was apparently raised in Egypt, whence he had immigrated to Safed in the year 1570. Within a very short time after the death of Moses Cordovero, his mentor in matters of Kabbalah, Luria succeeded in establishing a restricted circle of students, among whom were former students of Cordovero now loyal to Luria's teachings.

Luria developed a comprehensive Kabbalistic system that apparently captivated the minds and hearts of many of the Safed Kabbalists, while he himself strictly insisted on the esoteric nature of this lore.[41] Lurianic Kabbalah, as it became known later, possessed meaningful theoretical departures from the work of Cordovero and other contemporary Kabbalists, despite many clear contiguities with the tradition. Luria and his Kabbalah are important to our current study of messianism for two reasons: there were many rumors and legends that link Luria himself to a messianic role, and his Kabbalistic theoretical doctrines include some messianic elements.

These two components must be given separate consideration. The first, personal component is bound up not only with Luria but more conspicuously with his student, R. Ḥayyim Vital. The significance of this component is tied to specific mystical phenomena experienced by these two individuals. It is difficult to assess the meaning attributed to these experiences for the Jewish people as a whole, since most of the visions and traditions were sequestered within the boundaries of the brotherhood and were never to be divulged to outsiders. In contrast, the theoretical doctrines of the Lurianic Kabbalah were destined, despite Luria's explicit interdiction not to divulge his Kabbalah, to leave the confines of his mystical brotherhood and be developed by various scholars. It is well known that Luria claimed to have received revelations from Elijah. In fact, he attributed his Kabbalah to mystical and revelational events. A divine, or at least angelic, source was the basis upon which he revealed the secrets of the Kabbalah, not a human tradition stemming from reason.[42] Here we find a clearly mystical foundation for Luria's Kabbalistic activities. We might cautiously suppose a link between Luria's messianic self-awareness and these revelations, at the very least to posit that these secrets were being revealed to him on account of the impending arrival of the end. This phenomenon has been previously noted in our discussion of Abraham Abulafia, as well as in the school of *Sefer ha-Meshiv.*

We do not possess direct or explicit testimony from Luria himself concerning his understanding of the messianic role. His students, however, most notably R. Ḥayyim Vital, do sometimes present him as bearing the image of the Messiah, son of Joseph. Luria's entire career in Safed lasted less than two years, just a few years short of 1575, the date of the expected redemption as predicted by some Jewish authors of Italy and the Byzantine empire. The tradition of Luria's students presumed that had Luria lived and revealed additional secrets, he could ultimately have revealed himself as the true Messiah.[43] Luria passed away just after he took his first steps in Safed, and subsequently his messianic role remains bound with essentially Kabbalistic activities such as the revealing of recondite secrets.[44]

This is not, however, the case with his most preeminent student, R. Ḥayyim ben Joseph Vital Calabrese. Vital's literary legacy includes plenty of evidence penned by himself as well as by others as to his status and role, attesting beyond doubt to his possession of a clear messianic self-awareness. This awareness expresses itself in various forms. In his dreams he refers to himself as the "King of Israel" in the context of building the Third Temple. This dream is related to traditions concerning the doctrine of *gilgul* or metempsychosis. In one of his dreams he tells of an audience with the Roman Caesar (qeisar romi), to be discussed below.

Vital kept a dream diary, a special genre of mystical literature, called *Sefer ha-Ḥezyonot* (Book of Visions). There he relates his ideas about himself and his role, as well as pertinent dreams of others concerning especially his messianic aspirations.[45] *Sefer ha-Ḥezyonot* is an extraordinary book, not only special within Kabbalistic literature but also radical for this type of personal mystical account written by someone who lived in Safed. It is very different from R. Joseph Karo's book of mystical revelations, *Sefer Maggid Mesharim,* as it is from the diary of R. Eleazar Azikri, a student of Cordovero's who was indubitably known to Vital.[46] The central focus of Vital's dreams and visions is messianism, and an aroused messianic self-awareness that does not appear in other mystical diaries of Safed permeates *Sefer ha-Ḥezyonot.* From this perspective we may consider Vital to have possessed a messianic self-awareness that was not typical of the rest of his circle. Neither Karo or Azikri testifies to a clear self-perception of a messianic nature. We may conclude that while visions can lead to messianic awareness, they can also stay within a framework of mystical experience and not assume messianic dimensions.[47]

Time and again, in many of his works, Vital depicts himself as the reincarnation of various biblical and rabbinic personalities, most often the famous Rabbi Aqiva. The comparative investigation of several such texts conveys a consciousness on Vital's part of his role in correcting the wrongdoings or sins of these historical personalities of whom he is an avatar or gilgul. From this vantage point Vital's assertion of kinship to the soul of Rabbi Aqiva can be viewed as a clear claim of messianism.[48] According to several indications in *Sefer ha-Gilgulim* and *Sefer ha-Ḥezyonot,* the wide-ranging Kabbalistic activities of Vital had a corrective, reparative dimension.[49] Therefore, both Kabbalistic and messianic activities are considered to have corrective powers. Consequently, Vital envisioned himself, by virtue of his exclusive study of the Kabbalah, as someone who rectified the "iniquitous" soul of Maimonides, who had immersed himself in the study of philosophy.[50] This concept of corrective activity infuses all of Vital's many occupations with a special dimension.

The theory of gilgul is not only relevant to the individual fate of the soul of Ḥayyim Vital. Gilgul had been presented before as a technique that enabled one to cast a wide net of significance over history, mostly biblical history, thereby allowing a Kabbalist to personally relate to ancient as well as near-contemporary personalities. This view can be considered a clear type of personal historiosophy, expanding on relatively latent doctrines in pre-expulsion Spanish Kabbalah. In Safed we do not find any dramatically novel ideas concerning gilgul, but it is possible to detect a special emphasis on the personal meaning of that theory in those authors who wrote on the topic. Gilgul assumes a major position in the thought of not only those who attempted to formulate general historiosophical theories but also those who saw their own souls as taking part in a historical process and who were bound, more than others, to correct their previous sins. In other words, without negating the historiosophical aspects of the metempsychosis theory, I propose to see in it an important way to find out someone's status in the world. In some cases I would argue that this recurrent discussion of personalized cases of metempsychosis has something to do with the renewed concern with the individual that is characteristic of the Renaissance.[51]

Another important idea referred to repeatedly by Vital is the already existing notion that in every generation the Messiah reappears. Obviously, in his generation that person was believed by Luria's small group to be Luria himself. After the untimely death of the master in 1572, this messianic awareness was taken on by Vital. Here we see the strong connection between mysticism, by virtue of a visionary system, and messianic self-awareness acquired by means of these visions. The idea that the Messiah's soul transmigrates and lives in gilgul, namely that he is continuously reincarnated since the destruction of the Second Temple, is by no means an innovation. It is alluded to in the disputation of Naḥmanides in Barcelona, as Scholem has proposed, and it was also part, as pointed out by Liebes, of the vision of the Lurianic group as the reincarnation of the group of R. Shimeon bar Yoḥai.[52] This idea can probably be traced even further back. It seems that the Kabbalists of Safed developed an idea that had been known since the beginning of the Kabbalah in Catalonia.

Vital's messianic self-awareness is best expressed in another dream he reports. In it he sees himself arriving in Rome, only to be arrested by the officials of the Roman Caesar and brought before him.[53] Caesar commands all other persons to clear the hall. "We were left by ourselves," Vital relates. "I said to him: 'On what grounds do you want to kill me? All of you are lost in your religions like blind men. For there is no truth but the Torah of Moses, and with it alone can exist no other truth.' He replied: 'I already know all this and so I sent for you. I know that you are the wisest and most skilled of men in the wisdom of truth. I, most knowledgeable, want you to reveal to me some of the secrets of the Torah, for I already recognized the Names of your blessed Lord in Truth.' "[54] This dream dealing with a messianically self-aware Vital and a Roman Caesar, whom

I see as symbolically referring to the pope, is clearly reminiscent of Abraham Abulafia's failed attempt and Shlomo Molkho's somewhat more successful try at gaining a papal audience. There can be no doubt that Ḥayyim Vital was familiar with both these real-life adventures. We can also glean from this dream-story the positive nature of the attempt to influence Caesar, or the pope, by revealing to him the Names of God, for Vital continues: "Then I revealed to him a bit of this wisdom." Vital concedes that he did try to meet the demand and thereby have the pope recognize the true religion. In my opinion, Vital's messianic self-awareness had to be played out against the background of similar meetings, fantastic as well as realistic; for an audience with the pope had evolved to be an integral component of the messianic drama. Besides, the bare fact that Vital revealed that he was even willing to share Kabbalistic secrets with the pope warrants our attention, for the teachings of Luria were expressly limited to the few Jewish elite and barred from wider intellectual circles.

Thus there remains something puzzling about Vital's dream-declaration, even though he admits only to revealing "a bit of this wisdom." It does appear that Vital tried to understand and present some of his messianic awareness in concrete historical terms. Vital labored in Damascus toward arousing at least segments of the Jewish, as well as possibly the Moslem, public to repent, because the redemption was near. Most of this activity took place outside Safed, in the city of Damascus, where Vital lived out his later years. Many times in *Sefer ha-Ḥezyonot* Vital emphasized his attempts to encourage public repentance, although he was ridiculed and opposed by the rabbi of the Sephardi community, R. Jacob Abulafia (apparently of no relation to Abraham Abulafia). There can be no question as to the integral relationship between arousing the people to repentance and being conscious of the impending redemption. This consciousness is made clear if we analyze some of the dreams in which Luria himself encouraged Vital to persist in these extroverted activities. It seems that when Vital desisted, his revelations from Luria became less and less frequent. In one of his dreams Vital reports that Luria said, "Since you have left [him] also he [Luria] has left you. Because you know what your master, as well as others, have told you, that the entire world depends on you, and you have not come into the world except for arousing them to repentance, and you [alone] are responsible for the redemption."[55]

We are presented here with a clear messianic self-awareness that includes Luria as the revealer of secrets responsible to prepare Vital, as king of the Jewish nation, for the coming redemption. Ironically, this is happening in Damascus and not in Safed. Vital's dreams are suffused with apocalyptic messianism. In his diary there are descriptions of battles reminiscent of much earlier Jewish messianic literature, but they are integrated in descriptions that characterize exclusively the individual-messianic aspects which contrast the theoretical perceptions of messianism that we will discuss later, where the apocalyptic aspect does not fulfill a major role. In any case, the testimonies revealing the messianic consciousness remained sealed in Vital's diaries, which were hardly known outside his family. To believe him, his success in convincing the people of his city to repent was scant. Even more unsuccessful was his dissemination of Kabbalah, which was restricted to a post-mortem revelation of Luria to his disciples, only ten people in the whole world, seven of them in Damascus. In any case, I do not know about any seven Lurianic Kabbalists in the city in Vital's lifetime.

It is plausible to assume that the influence of individual-messianic enthusiasm in Safed was tied to the stream of people, ideas, and Kabbalistic materials that flowed there from Italy, the main center of apocalyptic calculations in the mid-sixteenth century. We can assume, moreover, as David Tamar has done, that we can understand at least part of the messianism of Safed on the basis of the influence of calculations of the time of the end prevalent in Italy.[56] The paramount importance of eschatology among the Italian Kabbalists, both Jewish and Christians, may help us explicate one of the quandaries of the development of sixteenth-century Jewish culture. Italy was the place where different forms of Jewish esoteric lore had arrived and coexisted before the emergence of the Safedian Kabbalah. Nevertheless, the Italian kabbalists did not produced any major book in the sixteenth century. Unlike the strong Spanish stronghold of Jewish culture in the fifteenth century, the Polish center at the end of the sixteenth century, and the Safedian one at the middle of the sixteenth century, Italian Jews were not among the most creative ones during this period. One of the reasons for this slight contribution, despite the relative affluent situation of the Jews during the first half of the century, may be related to the continuous messianic effervescence among Italian Jews. The cultural instability that accompanies any emphasis on the advent of the end means that classical and voluminous writings will be rare. On the other hand, in places where eschatology was less dramatic than in the Italian peninsula, like Poland and Safed, a process of consolidation of the religious groups may enable the emergence of much more comprehensive and influential writings. On the basis of this assumption, we can now turn to the analysis of the theoretical aspects of Lurianic Kabbalah.

Lurianic Kabbalah and Messianism

Already in the 1570s messianic hopes and beliefs were connected to two historical personalities living in Safed. R. Isaac Luria and his loyal student R. Ḥayyim Vital, were renowned not only as mystics but even more so as the creator and formulator, respectively, of a wide-ranging Kabbalistic system known as Lurianic Kabbalah. Lurianic Kabbalah has reached us largely through the lens of Vital, Luria's main scribe and the man responsible for the actual work of redaction. Vital may have even contributed to the articulation of Luria's ideas by his influence on his master.[57]

NB

There can be no doubt that Lurianic Kabbalah is one of the most complex intellectual systems ever produced by a Jewish author—indeed, as Gershom Scholem has correctly asserted, by any human mind.[58] It deals with all levels of theogonic and cosmogonic processes, beginning with primary divine processes and ending with the redemption, penetrated throughout by a wide-ranging interpretation covering all aspects of Jewish life. The framework of our present discussion will entail only those points in Luria's system that are relevant to messianism. The emphasis on the messianic elements within Lurianic Kabbalah is characteristic of Isaiah Tishby's description,[59] and so too of Scholem's in the chapter on Luria in his *Major Trends.* In a later essay Scholem states: "This latter Kabbalah, as it developed in classical forms in Safed in Palestine in the sixteenth century, was in its whole design electric with Messianism and pressing for its release; it was impelling a Messianic outburst."[60] It seems to me, however, that this exaggerates the spiritual messianic component. I do not deny the existence of messianic elements in this form of Kabbalah but argue that their share in the general economy of this mystical lore—a question that is indeed an interpretive one—is somewhat more modest. In any case, there were other forms of understanding of the role of Kabbalah in the Lurianic texts. We read, for example:

> It seems that the disclosure of this lore nowadays, in these bad generations, is to safeguard us by its means . . . because in those [earlier] generations, the majority was [constituted by] men of deeds and piety, and even scanty [parts of Kabbalah] were able to save them from all the opponents [*meqatregim*]. But now, as we are remote from the supernal source, just as yeast at the bottom of a barrel, who will safeguard us if not our reading this wondrous and profound lore? Especially as our Rabbi [Luria] said: "The secrets have become exoteric [knowledge], because in this generation prostitution and delation and slander and hate in the heart rule and the *qelippah* [evil powers] has become widespread to such an extent that persons are ashamed to behave in a pious manner; God shall safeguard us and forgive our sins.[61]

This apotropaic conception of Lurianism, which does not stress the future eschatological events but much more the present, normative, and conservative function of Kabbalah, has to be understood as a basic component of the self-perception of Lurianism. In fact, the comparison of this text to a similar one by Luria's teacher, R. Moses Cordovero, will show how much the student has marginalized the eschatological element. Cordovero claims that the *Zohar* was composed in hoary antiquity but its slow disclosure started much later, two hundred years before him; the whole text has been revealed only in the immediately preceding generations, while the end of the exile is approaching "because of the descent of the Shekhinah to the lowest point, in order to be the sustaining power for Her."[62] While for Cordovero the *Zohar* resurges as part of the eschatological process, in order to counteract the decline of the divine presence by helping the Shekhinah in the critical moment of redemption, for Luria Kabbalah is much more a matter of assisting human beings to survive the hardness of their times, which were aggravated by human misconduct in his lifetime. The mention of the misconduct in the above passage is of outmost importance, not because Luria's contemporaries were morally worse than the Jews in other generations, but this mention betrays the sense of both Luria's and Vital's mission to amend the way of religious behavior, a tendency conspicuous in Vital's more personal writings, such as *Sefer ha-Ḥezyonot.* Unlike the more common theme of the revelations of the secrets by the Messiah as a positive act, in Luria this revelation implies not a development but rather a retreat. The surfacing of secrets of Kabbalah is an indicator of the low point of the present generation, or, according to a famous legend, Luria himself did because he revealed Kabbalistic secrets. Kabbalah is therefore conceived of as part of involvement with the deteriorated situation and again is an example of *via passionis.*

Much modern scholarship has molded the complex phenomenon of Lurianism so that it seems to rotate around the messianic center of gravitation. We must, however, allow a more intricate understanding, perhaps a multifocal one which will take in consideration crucial religious nuclei; only such a view will do justice to the Lurianic literature. For example, the more conservative attitude toward time and history in Lurianism has been formulated by Liebes, who emphasized ritualistic and cyclical religious behavior "as expressed in *Sha'ar ha-Kavvanot,* where it is maintained that the [Lurianic] myth is not completed in the course of history but once in a year. More than the continuous historical development is described, it is the periodical myth that is dealt with, similar to Tammuz's or Adonis's death each year, in the pagan religions. The acute Messianic element emerged in Luria's Kabbalah only in its final stages."[63]

If Liebes is correct—and I am strongly inclined to believe he is—then the role of messianism in the spiritual configuration of Lurianism will be substantially reduced to one specific stage in the development of the system. Lurianic Kabbalah presupposes that the process of creation was bound up with a divine crisis, termed "the breaking of the vessels." This crisis caused the divine sparks to fall within the "world of the making" or the "world of the *qelippot*" or demonic shells. The role of the Kabbalist is to free or raise these divine sparks from the shells and cause their return to their original position and thus introduce perfection within that realm of the deity called *'adam qadmon.* One of the focal Kabbalistic activities, called *tiqqun* or reparation, aspires to return the divine situation to its original perfect state, and this reparation has without doubt messianic connotations. This view is somehow adumbrated in an old midrash, *Genesis Rabba'* 12:6, where the diminished stature of Adam will be given back to man in the time of the Messiah, though no theurgical activity on the part of man is involved. It is precisely this moment, however, that becomes central in theosophical-theurgical Kabbalah. Let me cite one example stemming from Lurianic Kabbalah:

> Concerning the study of Torah . . . all his intention must be to link his soul and bind her to her supernal source by means of the Torah. And his intention must be to achieve thereby the restoration of the supernal anthropos,[64] which is the ultimate intention of the creation of man and the goal of the commandment to study Torah. . . . As when studying Torah someone must intend to link his soul and to unite her and make her cleave to her source above . . . and he must intend thereby to perfect the supernal tree [of sefirot] and the supernal holy anthropos, so He is repaired by the repair of their souls and by their integration[65] and return in Him.[66]

The perfection of the souls is therefore a condition for the reparation of the divine world, and so it must precede it. Moreover, the main aim of this reparation is not the soul of man but the reconstruction of the supernal man destroyed by the primordial catastrophe. Elsewhere in the Lurianic corpus, in an interesting interpretation of another midrashic stand[67] as to the origin of all the souls of the *tzaddiqim,* the righteous persons, in the various limbs of the body of Adam, we learn that "when each and every tzaddiq is born into this world, he is a particular limb of the limbs of Adam. And when he [the tzaddiq] is perfected and repaired, also the first Adam himself is perfected and repaired, [restoring] what has been diminished and defective in the beginning."[68] The complete reconstruction of the supernal Adam, of the divine anthropos, is therefore an eschatological and cosmic project which involves automatically a preceding personal redemption. Thus this perfect anthropos is a reversion to the state of the primordial man. This redemption, which will naturally take plenty of time because what is involved is not only the theurgical operations of the few Kabbalists, or the tzaddiqim in the latter quotation, but the purification of all the souls, according to the former passage, which stem from the higher structure and return there. This vision implies not only the theurgical activity of some few Kabbalists but also the cooperation of all the souls, at least all the souls of the Jews. This accumulative perfection will take place not in this world but in the transcendental one, meaning that the main beneficiary of redemption is the upper rather than the lower world. In other words, the community or nation is to be seen much more as an instrument for, rather than agent or purpose of, redemption.

From different angles we can see this view as the contiguous development of the Kabbalistic doctrine of theurgy as presented in the *Zohar* and its school[69] and in other Kabbalistic works from the very beginning of Kabbalah.[70] Within Lurianic Kabbalah the major corrective activities were performed by the Kabbalists, according to a recent analysis of Lurianism, and the Jewish people as a whole do not play a significant role in the actual theurgical activities, such as preparing oneself (by fasting and special vigils) or by performing special Kabbalistic meditations meant to draw together the powers in the divine world.[71] The pioneer agent exercising theurgic activity, which sometimes carried messianic overtones, was always to be a small circle of Kabbalists. This is an intentional attempt to imitate the framework of the original historical circle of Luria, led by R. Ḥayyim Vital, and later of Vital's own circle. With this conception in mind, coupled with the fact that the doctrines of Lurianism are highly complex, it does not seem plausible that Lurianic Kabbalah could have been employed by the masses toward corrective theurgical purposes. It is more likely that within the context of Lurianic messianism the people were encouraged to repent and mend their ways, to study Torah rather than becoming full-fledged Kabbalists devoted to attaining the messianic goal. According to Luria's theory, and that of the Kabbalists of his school living in the land of Israel, the Kabbalists were obligated to free the divine sparks, causing the destruction from within of the *qelippot,* the demonic shells or the nations of the world as a stage in the messianic process.[72] This view regards the world outside the land of Israel as void of meaning, a place that must be conquered by holiness. This is an ideological conception that places the land of Israel at the center of its agenda.

On the other hand, Lurianic Kabbalists who did not reside in the land of Israel expanded this corrective theory into a broader approach. They saw worldwide residence as an opportunity to raise the local sparks from all places, but moreover to purify the countries of the diaspora, thus extending the borders of the holiness that is connected to the land of Israel.[73] R. Naphtali Bakharakh of Frankfurt, in the middle of the seventeenth century, describes as the mission of the Jews to make "the outer air of the lands of the nations . . . pure like the purity of the land of Israel, which forever retains her holiness even when she stands in her desolation".[74] His words attest to messianic activity being constructive, rather than destructive, of the lands outside of Israel through corrective activity meant to spread holiness in the abodes of impurity. This is an interesting example of how a Kabbalistic doctrine formulated in the land of Israel was later transformed to accommodate a mystical path that could give Kabbalistic meaning to a life outside of the land of Israel. We can discern in this inversion a fascinating dialectic granting justification to the Kabbalistic life outside of Israel. In the theoretical texts of Lurianic Kabbalah, composed mostly by R. Ḥayyim Vital, the status of the Messiah is not an outstanding issue.

We would expect, in a Kabbalistic system considered by modern scholars to deal extensively with messianism, a well-developed theology concerning the Messiah. It seems, however, that the classic roles of the Messiah were divided between the Messiah himself, who will appear after the completion or near-completion of the tiqqun, and other messianic figures that pave the way for the advent by revealing messianic secrets. These auxiliary messianic figures, including the mystical brotherhood, function as a sort of laboratory of revelation and development of Kabbalistic doctrines appropriate for the era just prior to the messianic advent. The very publication of these secrets is one of the activities that brings the redemption closer. According to some texts, Kabbalistic knowledge, limited during the period prior to the advent to the brotherhoods alone, will be widely known throughout the nation only after the tiqqun is complete and the Messiah appears. In this scenario, the nation loses much of the messianic role attributed to it by the academic literature concerning Lurianism. The main focus of the messianic doctrine within Lurianic Kabbalah is not to promote the sociopolitical aspects of the redemption, but rather to develop its spiritual aspects by promulgating the Kabbalah as the perfect type of knowledge.

The Messiah himself is depicted as a personality possessing the holy spirit and having experienced revelations from Elijah, without any doubt a mystical figure. Therefore he is able to raise or reveal the new Kabbalistic doctrine, including messianic secrets. As already noted, the activity of the Messiah contributes, together with the activities of the brotherhood, to the appearance of the redemption. The description of the Messiah includes an account of his death or martyrdom and subsequent rebirth.[75] Other figures can also participate in the messianic drama by specific mystical analogs of the ritualized death of the Messiah. This can be accomplished through prayer accompanied by Kabbalistic meditations, mainly in the prayers of Nephilat ʿAppayyim and the recitation of the Shemaʿ, or by prostrating oneself on the graves of known pious men. Consequently, there are venues for people who are not supposed to be the Messiah to go through similar processes, such as mystical death and rebirth, which accompany the events leading up to the Messiah's advent.[76]

Thus, even Luria's assumption of the messianic role does not transform his Kabbalah into a full-fledged messianic doctrine but rather turns it into a pre-eschatological system.[77] The initial dissociation of the Kabbalistic doctrine from the messianic implications related to Luria in particular allowed a continuation of this type of Kabbalah even after his death.[78] From this point of view we may compare the Lurianic Kabbalah to that of Abraham Abulafia, who also built up a Kabbalistic system that was interested in the messianic themes. Abulafia also considered himself a Messiah, though of a peculiar type, a spiritual Messiah. Nevertheless, he formulated his ecstatic Kabbalah in a manner that is practically independent of his personality and fate, this being one of the reasons for its lasting influence even after it was fiercely attacked by R. Shlomo ibn Adret during Abulafia's life and after his death. Neither Lurianism nor ecstatic Kabbalah, unlike Sabbateanism, is a messianocentric system of thought, namely a system that cannot survive the collapse of the messianic elements in its structure of thought.

The Circulation of Lurianic Messianism

The Lurianic system appears in a great many Kabbalistic works which were in the possession of a mere handful of Kabbalists toward the end of the sixteenth century and well into the seventeenth century. This was not due to the vicissitudes of history but rather the premeditated and explicit policy of both Luria and Vital to zealously guard the doctrines being redacted by Vital to be circulated only within closed groups. Until the end of Vital's life, his writings were secreted in his home, and only select persons were given access to them. This is an important point in terms of assessing the possible results of the appearance of the Lurianic Kabbalah on the Jewish cultural scene. The theory promoted by several modern scholars posits that the 1630s and 1640s heralded a new phase of widespread promulgation of the Lurianic doctrines to the public at large. "As Lurianic ideas were mediated to the masses by the popular preachers and moralists of the sixteenth and seventeenth centuries," writes Scholem, "the more dramatic and spectacular aspects of the mystery inevitably tended to become increasingly emphasized. In the popular mind, the history of the world was essentially the drama of God seeking to perfect His true image and 'configuration' and of man seeking to promote this aim by means of good works. An explicit statement to this effect will be sought in vain in kabbalistic literature, yet it is clearly the view that underlies the whole Lurianic system."[79]

Scholem introduces here agents of diffusion of Lurianism, preachers and moralists. If such is the case, then it would be possible to maintain that the messianic consciousness congenial to the framework of Lurianic Kabbalah also infiltrated wider audiences. Therefore, scholars have held that Lurianism was a propagandistic vehicle employed to disseminate certain messianic doctrines beyond the restricted circles of Kabbalists, and also a means of preparing a mass consciousness to accept the special Kabbalistic formulation of messianism.[80] Scholem, however, explicitly recognizes that the clear statements about the messianic structure of the religious acts "will be sought in vain in kabbalistic literature." Therefore, the system is imbued with underground messianic valences, which had been explicated by the "popular preachers and moralists," and we are invited to believe that in popular circles there were much more extreme formulations than those found in the original Lurianic works.

This set of assumptions is fraught with difficulties. All scholars agree that during the initial stages of Lurianism, from the end of the sixteenth century through the first quarter of the seventeenth, it is hard to establish a significant circulation of Lurianic works among wider audiences. This is not to say that writings did not leave the land of Israel, for it is certain that in small circles mostly situated in the north of Italy it was possible to acquire certain Lurianic writings as early as the 1580s. The majority of the literature available in Europe was spread by a Kabbalist named R. Israel Saruq in a special version of Lurianic Kabbalah that shows relatively little interest in most of the messianic elements of Vital's version. In this light it is untenable to connect the circulation of Lurianic Kabbalah to the circulation of the messianic idea: these are two distinct elements that are not necessarily bound up with one another.[81]

In the few Lurianic compositions to be published up until the middle of the seventeenth century, the messianic elements remained peripheral, with one major exception, R. Naphtali Bakharakh's *'Emeq ha-Melekh*. Other authors to write under the influence of Lurianic Kabbalah, including R. Abraham Cohen Herrera and R. Joseph Shlomo Del Medigo (better known by his acronym, YaSHaR of Candia), almost totally neutralized the messianic elements in their works. These two authors were deeply interested in philosophy, which caused them to reject the eschatological elements that are characteristic of much of the Lurianic corpus and therefore also to obfuscate the messianic aspects. Consequently, we should sharply distinguish between the modest circulation of Lurianic writings, at least according to the version of Saruq, and messianic propaganda. In fact, modern scholars have been inclined to see the emergence of Lurianic myth as a response to a collective crisis and trauma created by the expulsion from Spain and Portugal, an answer to the quandaries of the generations of Jews who looked into the vicissitudes of history, especially the ongoing exile, without being able to understand it. Luria, according to this view, was able to offer a theoretical formulation and solution to a more general problem. If this were true, then the repercussions of the dissemination of Luria's doctrines among the masses could be more easily grasped. The masses, would some scholars assert, were already prepared to absorb a message that gave expression to their spiritual needs on a more systematic level and in a more spiritual formulation.[82] In my opinion, just as scholars have not sufficiently recognized the different phenomenological structure of Saruq's Lurianism and its relevance for the topic of an alleged dissemination of messianism, so too the masses have become homogenized and reified around a traumatic experience that happened a century before. "The masses" is an easy answer, a myth created by believers in a type of history that does not distinguish between Ashkenazi and Sefardi communities, between those who were able to accommodate themselves to new conditions after the expulsion and those who were not.

Another difficulty involved in the spread of Lurianic messianism is the improbability that such a highly complex doctrine, which remains obtuse even for scholars today and defies detailed understanding, was able to be absorbed within the intelligentsia, especially considering the scarcity of Lurianic manuscripts. There are several testimonies of complaints by Lurianic Kabbalists that the most important Lurianic writings are not available to them; if and when they do finally arrive, the Kabbalists admit that they find it difficult to decipher them. Consequently, notwithstanding such exceptions as *Sefer 'Emeq ha-Melekh,* a complete Lurianic work did not circulate widely even among Kabbalists, including Lurianic groups. Surprisingly, even in the most important centers of Lurianism, Israel and Syria, Lurianic Kabbalists found it difficult to acquire Lurianic treatises. They tell of the great hardships necessary to procure these rare and sequestered documents. R. Shmuel Vital, the son of R. Ḥayyim Vital, was the authority who zealously kept watch over the Lurianic corpus. We can surmise that only through him personally could one obtain several of the more important texts of the Lurianic Kabbalah. Moreover, in the more disseminated form of Lurianism, that exposed by R. Yisrael Saruq, the messianic elements seem to be less evident than they are in the classical formulations of Luria's thought by his other students, including Vital.[83] In light of this information, there seems to be no substantial evidence of a significant circulation of the Lurianic corpus in the sixteenth and early seventeenth centuries. The spread of Lurianism reached notable proportions only much later, during the post-Sabbatian period, after this messianic movement subsided during the eighteenth century.[84]

Obviously, the figure of Luria himself had deep influence from the late sixteenth through the eighteenth centuries. Yet it is mainly his legendary persona, not his actual writings, that left deep traces. Legend portrays the man as possessing occult powers and extraordinary abilities, a mystic who is also able to correct and cleanse the souls of others. The legendary aspects of the figure of Luria were certainly widespread, yet his complicated doctrines did not enjoy the same audience and influence, for they were limited to very small circles of adherents.

Another important influence of Lurianism was the infiltration and acceptance of customs, termed *hanhagot* or *taqqanot,* established by Luria and his school. These are the songs composed by Luria that are sung on the Sabbath eve and at Sabbath day meals. Despite the fact that Luria describes these customs as based on specific Kabbalistic concepts, their spread does not imply the same for the theory that underlies them. Most people who adopted these rituals were not conscious then, as adherents are not conscious today, of their Kabbalistic origin. What conclusion can we reach as to the difference in the circulation of the various elements of Lurianism? The difference seems to be a function of the varied interests of the wider public. The vast majority of the Jewish people were interested in being shown a way of life and detailed rituals and were not capable of delving into the intricacies of its basic principles. Even the fundamental teaching of tiqqun could not have been absorbed. The wider Jewish community was more interested in the ritual and the legendary sides than the ideological side of Lurianism. It could hardly have been impressed with the implicit eschatological elements of Lurianism, which today are given special emphasis in the academic literature.

"Drawing Down" and Messianism

One of the most concentrated discussions of messianism in Lurianic Kabbalah is found in the writing of an ex-Marrano living in Jerusalem. The great Kabbalist R. Ya'aqov Ḥayyim Tzemaḥ, writing in the mid-sixteenth century, complained about the neglect of the study of Kabbalah. He claimed that as a result

> the sons do not draw down and hasten the Messiah, and it is said in *Sefer Qehilat Ya'aqov,* namely "our generation nowadays is the last generation, and the wisdom of the truth [Kabbalah] has to reveal itself, so that the Messiah will come and so it is written in *R[ay'a] M[eheimna]* fol. 124b, and in the *Tiqqunim* fol. 18b,[85] that because of the virtue of the *Zohar* the King Messiah will come." And in the book *Rannu Le-Ya'aqov,*[86] in the discussion on Naḥmanides it is written[87] . . . "In the footsteps of the Messiah,[88] as in our generation, the lights began to spread and turn to be as in the beginning, as they were at the time of the creation of the world, in a proper structure, and they began to be mended slightly." Behold how the discussions of the Rabbi [Luria], Blessed be his memory, demonstrate that he disclosed all the [secrets of] the configurations and the tiqqunim, and by the means of them people can understand and comprehend some [passages of] the *Zohar,* and to bring it [the *Zohar*] closer [to our understanding]. But, since there is no one who will pay attention to make an effort and prepare for the academies which will study this lore, and everyone draws his bread from the Halakhah, because of the supply [*haspaqah,* money donated for study of the Law], the majority of the students of this lore [Kabbalah] are poor, and they cannot afford to study Kabbalah, since no rich man will pay attention to it.[89]

The verb translated above as "draw down" is *moshekh,* the same term used by R. Moses de Leon in *Sheqel ha-Qodesh* in discussing the Messiah.[90] Tzemaḥ insists that drawing down is the result of Kabbalistic study, and apparently also Kabbalistic practice, offering thereby a more talismanic vision of this lore. This view of Tzemaḥ's as to the way of attaining the redemption differs drastically from classical Lurianic Kabbalah, where the assumption is that the Kabbalistic activity is primarily directed toward tiqqun, the mending of the supernal world, the advent of the Messiah being only an indirect result. This is the single case of talismanic expression referring to the Messiah that I have been able to find in the vast corpus of Lurianic literature, and I wonder whether the talismanic model, influential in Cordovero's Kabbalah, is not the source of Tzemaḥ's view.[91] Yet if the messianic interpretation of the talismanic thought is rather scant before the end of seventeenth century, it becomes much more evident in the writings of R. Moshe Ḥayyim Luzzatto and in Hasidism, as we shall see in the next two chapters.

Scholem's Exilic Interpretation of the Tzimtzum

Another link between messianism and Lurianic Kabbalah appears in the eschatological interpretation of the Kabbalistic concepts that were presented as innovations of the sixteenth-century Kabbalists, for they implicitly reflect the plight and hopes of Spanish Jewry after the expulsion. Thus we learn from Scholem's description of the mystical significance of *tzimtzum,* or withdrawal, that it represents "a profound inward Galut [exile], not the Galut of one of the creatures but of God Himself, who limited Himself and thereby made place for the universe. This is the Lurianic concept of limitation or concentration, *tzimtzum,* which supplanted the simpler idea of creation held by the Spanish Kabbalists."[92]

The idea that the act of *tzimtzum* represents a divine exile into Himself is a fascinating speculative interpretation of the Lurianic myth and one of Scholem's more dramatic contributions to modern Jewish historiosophy. But in spite of his persuasive tone, it seems that Scholem himself was at least sometimes aware of the highly speculative nature of his proposal. In one of his earlier and more cautious formulations, we read about the same topic as follows: "One is tempted to interpret this withdrawal of God into his own being in terms of exile, of banishing himself from his totality into profound seclusion. *Regarded this way,* the idea of tsimtsum is the deepest symbol of exile that could be thought of."[93] As Scholem duly acknowledged in his earlier expositions of the emergence of this view, it was not corroborated by the Lurianic texts themselves and it remains therefore in the domain of scholarly theological speculation. In one of his later formulations he even points out, openly and correctly, that "[t]he Kabbalists did not explicitly say that the act of *Ṣimṣum* was a divine type and prefiguration of the exile, though the analogy seems obvious."[94] Therefore, Scholem's view of the nexus between history and what he considers to be the new concept of withdrawal had emerged, in my opinion, no so much from an exposition of explicit statements of Kabbalists, or even from disclosing the inner logic of one of the Lurianic texts, but from modern interpretive presuppositions concerning the paramount importance of the idea of exile in Lurianic Kabbalah and its specific historical connections.

In the case of the other key Lurianic concept, the breaking of the vessels, *shevirat ha-kelim,* Scholem again refers to the Galut: "This 'breaking' introduces a dramatic aspect into the process of Creation, and it can explain the Galut. . . . In other words, all being is in Galut."[95]

Again, the national myth of the exile surfaces in contexts that never explicitly mention it, and it is again part of the theological enterprise of the interpretive scholar, who attempts to extract the religious significance from a text or conceptual construct that does not easily lend itself to such a strong interpretation. In any case, I consider these attempts of Scholem quite legitimate and creative, provided that they do not become hard "facts" but remain hypothetical, explanatory proposals. The question is, however, why so many scholars, including those who deal with Kabbalistic topics, have treated those speculations as describing historical fact. It is by their uncritical acceptance of legitimate speculations as if they were facts that Scholem's followers have done damage to scholarship.[96]

This pervasive "exilic" interpretation of the Lurianic myth is even more conspicuous in another of Scholem's statement: "All that befalls in the world is only an expression of this primal and fundamental Galut,"[97] or, to cite another sentence, "In all the expanse of creation there is imperfection, flaw, Galut."[98] Such a "Galutic" or exilic interpretation of the thought of Luria, a Kabbalist who was born in Jerusalem and died in Safed, needs much more than the inspired statements of a prestigious scholar to transform a fascinating intuition into a more scholarly argument. It has been, so it seems, the conviction of a great scholar and the weight of his undisputed authority that have persuaded many others to accept this inspired reading of such a complex theosophical system in terms of exile and redemption.[99] Thus, in addition to Scholem's view that the historical symbols articulated, or at least helped in articulating, the significance of historical experiences of the nation, he and his students also assume that those particular symbols comprise the accurate interpretation of Luria's intricate system, a fact that does not emerge from the Kabbalistic texts themselves.[100] By a historically oriented symbolic deciphering of the theosophical symbolism of the Lurianic Kabbalah, modern academic interpreters have too strongly projected myths of exile and redemption into Kabbalistic metaphysics and ritual. In so doing they have helped some scholars to claim an impact of a disastrous history on the mystical systems of the Safedian Kabbalists.[101]

Progress and Redemption

Another scholarly assumption related to a crucial development in medieval Kabbalah is the understanding of the naturalness of the eschatological processes, as compared with the more supernaturalistic attitude toward this issue in apocalyptism. Scholem proposed to see this change as taking place after the expulsion from Spain, since only then were the Lurianic Kabbalah and messianism "dovetailed into a genuine organic whole."[102] In the thirteenth-century *Zohar,* Scholem argues, redemption was not "the product of inward progress in the historical world, but as a supernatural miracle involving the gradual illumination of the world by the light of the Messiah."[103]

The emphasis upon the progress taking place in the historical world seems to me quite emblematic of Scholem's attitude toward messianism.[104] The significant rupture is between the older, apocalyptic-Kabbalistic world, as represented by the Talmud and the *Zohar,* with its emphasis on the miraculous, and the Lurianic Kabbalah, which is understood to have adopted a more immanentistic description of history, which allows the Kabbalist to integrate his activity within this evolutionary framework. This assumption implies a Kabbalistic historiosophy that is new, and locates the moment of the Kabbalist as immediately close to the eschatological drama. In my opinion, this naturalistic turn is part of the medieval framework, and it may be found in Abulafia's discussion of redemption as the eschatological actualization of potentialities.

Scholem's proposal to see in Luria's thought a paradigmatic shift from an utter supernaturalness to a more progressive historical vision seems problematic for several reasons. According to him, the background of Luria's Kabbalah is the introversion of a crisis, which though remote in time still haunted some of Luria's colleagues and perhaps Luria himself. The vision of "inward progress" that emerged against this background seems to me not very plausible, and in any case it was not explained in Scholem's writings. A Lurianic progressive history would involve attempts on Luria's part, or on the part of Luria's students, to situate historical events within a more comprehensive scheme. Progress is relative, and the sense of evolution demands the building up of a broader plan of redemption. Yet if this were so, then the absence from the Lurianic corpus of the expulsion from Spain, but also of any contemporaneous or significant event that took place in the Middle Ages, is quite conspicuous. I am not acquainted with salient attempts to suggest such a scheme.

Furthermore, the concept of progress seems to me to be irrelevant, if not impossible, in the framework of Lurianic Kabbalah for two reasons. First, Luria did not imagine himself as the peak of a gradual development within the domain of disclosure of Kabbalistic secrets. His major claim was that he was the recipient of a revelation from above, described as the revelation of Elijah, which is apparently not related to the Kabbalists of previous generations. As Vital put it, as representative of Luria's thought, Naḥmanides in the thirteenth century was the last reliable Kabbalist. Therefore, no gradual development in the domain of Kabbalah is to be expected in the historiosophy of Luria and his school. If this is the case, a corollary to this abruptness is the inability of the earlier Kabbalists, and even more conspicuously the non-Kabbalists, to contribute to the inward progress by resorting to Kabbalah. If Lurianism is the key to redemption, it cannot be the key to a redemption that is both progressive and imminent. It is either imminent but not progressive, or progressive—starting with the disclosure of Luria's theurgy—but not imminent. Second, as seen above in the quotation from R. Ya'aqov Ḥayyim Tzemaḥ, a leading Lurianic Kabbalist expressed the view that his lifetime, and apparently also Luria's, did not constitute moments of imminent redemption but, on the contrary, comprised periods described as "the bottom of the barrel,"[105] moments of exceeding regression. Indeed, the entire passage that contains this phrase describes a drastic decline rather than an improvement from the religious point of view.[106] In principle, the attribution of an inward progress to a form of religion that is conceived of as emphasizing the importance of the common enterprise of whole communities cannot easily arrive at the conclusion that the time of redemption is gradually coming closer without describing the stages of this development, be they imaginary or "real." This remark is not intended to negate the existence of expressions of graduate extraction of the sparks from the shells as part of the redemptive project, but it implies very slow processes which could start only with the revelation of the Lurianic Kabbalah as the key to redemptive activity.[107]

Finally, Ḥayyim Vital's description of eschatological events in which he himself was involved is much closer to apocalyptic than to progressive types of redemption. In keeping with the talmudic view, he calls for repentance, and he has dreams that include dramatic elements that do not betray any form of progression. Indeed, I do not propose to learn necessarily from the individualistic conception of someone as redeemer, to his systemic understanding of this issue, but anyone claiming a progressive approach as characteristic of this form of Kabbalah should found it in either systemic or personal testimonies of a messianic figure.

· CHAPTER SIX ·

Sabbateanism and Mysticism

"One's own experience depends on one's own name."
—FRANZ ROSENZWEIG

Remarks on the Sabbatean Movement

None of the mystical figures mentioned in previous chapters has created a significant messianic movement. Interesting as the phenomenology of their mystico-messianic experiences may be, the popular acceptance of their messianic ideas and claims was limited. We will concentrate now on the most important messianic phenomenon in premodern Judaism, both in terms of the role Jewish mysticism played in Jewish history and in terms of the resurgence of Jewish popular eschatology: the Sabbatean movement.[1] I would like to highlight issues that have remained at the periphery of the available scholarly treatments of Sabbateanism. The brief exposition of this major phenomenon which I offer here should not be understood as implying a marginal role for it on the historical scene. A popular belief in the Messiah, as well as other sociological issues—for example, the role and the expectations of the Marranos who returned to Judaism,[2] the impact of the massacres of 1648–49 in Poland,[3] or the result of the shared ideas about enthusiasm in Christian contemporary circles as well as a broad range of Christian millenarian concepts,[4] or the more vague though still interesting argument of the crisis of the seventeenth century[5]—were heavily responsible for the widespread belief in Sabbatai Tzevi's messianic claims which permeated many social strata of the Jewish people throughout many different countries.

The details of the proliferation of the belief in Tzevi's messianism have been described at great length by Gershom Scholem. His classic study *Sabbatai Ṣevi* is an exemplary work of epochal significance for Jewish pre-modern history, as well as a major contribution to the general understanding of the phenomenology of messianism. The main reason offered by Scholem for the proliferation of

Sabbateanism, the allegedly prior dissemination of Lurianic messianism, seems to be problematic in view of recent studies.[6] In my opinion, it is quite fitting to call Sabbateanism a movement, unlike the other messianic phenomena we have discussed. The historical and sociological factors at work from the time of Abraham Abulafia to that of Isaac Luria did not allow for the crystallization of full-fledged movements of the magnitude that we are confronted with here. Certainly, there were instances of dissemination of messianic ideas, but we have insufficient proof to argue for the full-scale development of ideological movements followed by significant sectors of the Jewish population, even in one country alone. Here lies the vast difference between Sabbateanism and the various mystical messianic phenomenon that had existed since the appearance of the Kabbalah. The very fact of the transformation of Sabbatai's self-perception as the Messiah and Nathan's belief and prophecy into a comprehensive movement requires both sociological and historical study. It cannot be posited that the diffusion of mystical complex theories within certain cloistered circles may sufficiently explain a mass movement.

As other scholars have already pointed out, the study of mass movements must be conducted with sociological tools. This type of research has yet to be undertaken, and to my mind it will yield a better grasp of the appearance of Sabbateanism as a widespread movement, in addition to the accepted explanation of the specific role of Lurianic Kabbalah.[7] The conversos, it should be emphasized, made a great contribution to the acceptance of the messianic message of Sabbateanism. The presence of significant numbers of former conversos in many centers of Jewish population paved the way for a positive response to Sabbatean nihilistic and antinomian doctrines.[8] These doctrines struck a deep chord within those religiously tormented people, sometimes unsatisfied or in many cases also more strongly uneasy with the painful process of acceptance of rabbinic Judaism. In the attempt to offer a total and complex explanation of Sabbateanism, the relative weight assigned to the different factors that contributed to its emergence is still subject to debate. For now, we must adopt a more open attitude toward understanding this phenomenon, without adhering to a single major interpretation, that focused around the impact of Lurianic teachings and Lurianic messianism.[9]

The common denominator between Sabbateanism and the other messianic phenomena discussed above, which is also the main topic of our specific interest in this study, is the centrality of the mystical experience to the essence of a certain form of messianism. The two main protagonists of this movement, Sabbatai Tzevi and Nathan of Gaza, not only were important messianic figures but also strove for mystical experiences. Scholem expressed this conjunction well in the subtitle of his work on Tzevi: the "mystical Messiah." From my perspective,

Tzevi should be examined not so much as part of the Lurianic Kabbalah but more as following other, much earlier forms of Kabbalah, where discussions regarding the Messiah could inspire—indeed, did inspire—the young Kabbalist. I will attempt to explicate the plausible relations between the mystical aspects of Tzevi's messianism and earlier Kabbalistic views.

Sabbatai Tzevi, Ecstatic Kabbalah, and Mystical Techniques

Sabbatai Tzevi was born in Smyrna in 1626. Early in his studies he moved on from the classic rabbinic texts to Kabbalah, concentrating on the *Zohar* and the *Qanah,* an anonymous, two-volume Byzantine composition of the late fourteenth century.[10] The fact that Sabbatai Tzevi did not study Lurianic Kabbalah and even opposed some of its doctrine at certain stages of his life shows that this form of Jewish mysticism was not a main source of his messianic self-awareness.[11] Lurianic ideas were employed by other figures, most notably Nathan of Gaza, in order to explain the messianic role of Sabbatai Tzevi, but this influence is not evident in Sabbatai's own few writings.

It is possible, however, to find various elements of Sabbatai's mysticism in the works he studied; *Zohar, Sefer ha-Qanah,* and *Sefer ha-Peliy'ah,* the latter two being included within the general title of *ha-Qanah*—common in extant manuscripts. It is likely that Sabbatai became familiar with some elements of Abraham Abulafia's ecstatic Kabbalah through the *Peliy'ah.* A whole book of Abulafia's, his *Sefer Gan Na'ul,* was copied verbatim in *Sefer ha-Peliy'ah,* as well as a lengthy passage from Abulafia's *Sefer Ḥayyei ha-Nefesh.*[12] From my perusal of the *Qanah* I am convinced that additional material belonging to Abulafia or his school, and apparently lost, have been either integrated in the book verbatim or at least strongly influenced it.[13] Considering the fact that Abulafia's Kabbalah focuses on techniques for meditating on holy names and that he also saw himself as the Messiah, his writings may constitute a crucial precedent for the first "strange deed" of Sabbatai Tzevi—the pronunciation of the Tetragrammaton. Scholem's explanation of this act, the first of the strange deeds to be explicitly mentioned in early sources dealing with Tzevi as messianic, seems problematic. Scholem maintains that no real messianic overtone should be read into this testimony, which he deems unreliable, and he advances an explanation based on the view that Tzevi confused this world and the next,[14] a claim that can hardly be proven philologically. On the ground of the existence of a relatively clear connection between the Messiah and the divine name in Abulafia's writings, I suggest that at least some glimpses of ideas stemming from ecstatic Kabbalah, already known by Tzevi, served as an inspiring paradigm. Indeed, a lengthy discussion in Abulafia's *Sefer Ḥayyei ha-Nefesh* about the nature of prophecy, the combinations of the letters of the various divine names and their pronunciation as a way to be in contact with God is quoted verbatim in *Sefer ha-Peliy'ah.*[15] Abulafia's Kabbalah was very well known in Byzantium, where he taught it to some students; it remained extant there in dozens of manuscripts, and through the Byzantine composition of *Sefer ha-Peliy'ah* it could have reached Sabbatai Tzevi's attention, since he was born and educated in the same environment.

If this proposal is correct, we should envision the spiritual and messianic development of the young Tzevi in terms substantially different Scholem's. As we shall see, there is good reason to believe that the paramount formative impact of Tzevi's later encounter with Nathan, which is a dominant working hypothesis in Scholem's historiography of the Sabbatean movement, was exaggerated. If we accept the evidence concerning the young Tzevi as pronouncing the divine name and proclaiming himself Messiah in public in 1648 or 1649, his later career should be understood as the culmination of a remarkable beginning long before his encounter with Nathan. Tzevi's public discussions, early in his career, of his vision of the Godhead (in *Ma'aseh Merkavah*) and divine names[16] may deal not with two separate topics but with a combination (*harkavah*) of the letters of the divine names in the manner espoused by Abulafia several times in his writings, including in *Sefer Gan Na'ul,* which was copied in *Sefer ha-Peliy'ah.*[17] Traces of possible Abulafian influence are found, by the mediation of Cordovero's *Pardes Rimmonim,* in a crucial Sabbatean document written by a certain R. Abraham Peretz, a disciple of Nathan of Gaza, who warns against some unidentified sages, apparently opponents to Tzevi, who were accused of not knowing either

> the pronunciation of the letters according to their roots (*ke-shorsham*) or the way they should be read, because they exchange the *shin* for a *sin* or *samekh* or *tzadei,* or *'aleph* for *he or 'ayin* or vice versa, or *kaf* for *qof,* or *ḥet* for *kaf,* or *bet* for *vav* or vice-versa, and this is the reason their prayer is not answered. And this is the reason they have been prevented from the knowledge of the [magical] use of names, either because of the aspect of the pronunciation of the letters according to their appropriate roots and places, in the five sources of the mouth, or in the moment of a certain combination of the [letters of the] Tetragrammaton is revolving (*mitgalgel bah*)[18] . . . and from what pericope this name emerges and by what color are the[se] letters colored, in accordance to the [corresponding divine] name.[19]

The Cordoverian nomenclature is obvious in the use of the term *beḥinah,* or aspect, and in the resort to the links between the divine names and the corresponding colors. Nevertheless, the Kabbalistic sources that informed Cordovero's view of letters, names, and colors[20] do not speak about the combinations of the letters of the Tetragrammaton, an issue copied by Cordovero from Abulafia's *'Or ha-Sekhel.*[21] Moreover, the pronunciation of these combined letters, which depends upon the various permutations of the vowels,[22] though not of the letters of the Tetragrammaton as it is commonly written, and is crucial for Abulafia's Kabbalah, is absent from the writings of the group of Kabbalists dealing with colors and letters, where visualization of these letters, in the order they are found in the canonic Jewish texts, is accentuated.[23] Thus, at least part of the above passage plausibly refers to a combination of the letters of the divine name, as exposed by Abulafia, which reached the Sabbatean author via Cordovero.

We may presume, however, that some experiences in Sabbatai's life may be connected with his acquaintance with ecstatic Kabbalah from one his main sources, *Sefer ha-Peliy'ah.* Already in his youth, at the age of fifteen, he had experienced revelations, some of them of a sexual nature; these revelations revisited him throughout his life and were central to his messianic self-awareness. It would be simplistic to reduce these experiences to a mere cultivation of ecstatic practices filtered through the intermediary sources he studied. But for the time being, I see no better alternative. In other words, there are good reasons to believe, on the basis of the historical data and phenomenological comparisons, that some of the earliest deeds of Tzevi, as well as his more general inclination to ecstatic phenomena, were influenced by the ecstatic Kabbalah as represented in one of the major Kabbalistic books studied by the future Messiah.

The impact of *Sefer ha-Peliy'ah* is, in my opinion, even greater than what I have suggested, but in order to approach the other major area of its influence on Tzevi let me start with a short survey of the linkage between the Messiah and the third sefirah, Binah, which will allow us access to the sphere of messianic consciousness of this figure.

Messiah, Binah, Saturn

There are three main approaches to the character of Sabbatai Tzevi in modern scholarship. The most widespread one, formulated by Scholem, who emphasizes the insanity of the messianic figure, diagnoses Sabbatai's mental malady as a manic-depressive neurosis and allowing him a relatively secondary role in the emergence and organization of the Sabbatean movement. For Scholem, Nathan was the dynamo behind the growth of the whole Sabbatean ideology and organization; Without Nathan, Sabbatai would remain a marginal figure. As pointed out above, however, the main factor for the success of Sabbateanism was, for Scholem, not only the genius of the prophet but also the preparation of the ground by the prior dissemination of Lurianic Kabbalah, with which Nathan was well acquainted.[24]

Another approach was suggested by Isaiah Tishby, who proposed to restructure the balance struck by Scholem in favor of allowing a greater role to the

Messiah himself in the practical organization of the movement. The prophet was sometimes regarded as more immersed in visionary states of mind which, by their nature, could not contribute to a stable organizational role. In line with Scholem, however, he also attributes to Lurianism the major role for the proliferation of this sort of messianism.[25]

Yehuda Liebes has paid more attention to the inner life of this Messiah. He portrays Sabbatai as a mystic who cultivated, as he explicitly claimed, a personal relationship with "his God" as an organizing aspect of his spiritual and sometimes his external behavior.[26] I will delineate yet another approach, more consonant with Tishby's and Liebes's but nevertheless presupposing a crucial role for the interaction between personality and speculative stands. In order to better understand the paradigm that could contribute to the messianic self-awareness of Tzevi let me describe some pivotal moments in the history of Messiah symbolism in Kabbalah from the thirteenth century to the time of the young Tzevi. Thus I hope to show how a certain type of symbolism in classical kabbalistic books belonging to a particular school could be reflected in the inner life of a mystic who became a Messiah. I hope thereby not only to clarify one detail of Tzevi's knowledge of Kabbalah or even to show the source of his messianic consciousness, but also to suggest that Sabbatean literature, like all the later forms of mystical literature, should be investigated on the basis of a panoramic view of Jewish mysticism for a better understanding of both the sources and the processes that generated later forms of Jewish mysticism.

In some of the writings of late-thirteenth-century Castilian Kabbalists, the terms *binah,* "understanding," or *teshuvah,* "return" or "repentance," are names for the third sefirah and are related to various forms of redemption. The origins of this view, however, may well antedate this period. The third sefirah figures prominently in the theosophy of the early-thirteenth-century master R. Isaac Sagi-Nahor and his school, where it is often named Teshuvah. Therefore, we may assume that both the *Zohar* and Joseph Gikatilla's later Kabbalistic writings have approached the depiction of this sefirah in redemptive terms much more than the earlier Kabbalists, though they did not invent this type of symbolism. In the *Zohar,* for example, the fifty gates of Binah mentioned in the Talmud, often related to the third sefirah, are described as opened by God at the time of the exodus from Egypt "in order to take out the people of Israel . . . as will He do also in the days of the Messiah."[27] In a manner quite similar to Gikatilla's, the *Zohar* would say that this sefirah will be the source of Israel's redemption.[28]

The Castilian Kabbalists' understanding of the redemptive role of the third sefirah reverberates, most significantly, in the writings of a Kabbalist of Ashkenazi extraction. R. Joseph ben Shalom ha-'Arokh Ashkenazi, a prolific Kabbalist of late thirteenth and early fourteenth centuries, offered one of the most influential descriptions of the explicit connection between the Messiah and the third sefirah.[29] But before discussing R. Joseph's contribution, it is important to address the repercussion of this view in some less famous writings in his entourage. One of them is by a Spanish Kabbalist, R. David ben Yehudah he-Ḥasid, whose Kabbalah is haunted by the ideas presented by Joseph Ashkenazi. In *Sefer Mar'ot ha-Tzove'ot* R. David writes:

> The king Messiah is the secret of Binah; and when the time of the redemption of Israel arrives, the Holy One, Blessed be He, who is K[eter] 'E[liyon], will cause him to smell all those fine smells and perfumes from the mounts of Afarsemon, and all the wells and springs and rivulets and rivers of K[eter] 'E[liyon], all are drawing forth and going out of that depth [Keter, the first sefirah] toward the Yesh [Ḥokhmah, the second sefirah] and from the Yesh toward that attribute called Mashiyaḥ as it is written, "and the spirit of 'Elohim is hovering over the face of the water," [Genesis 1:2] this is the spirit of Mashiyaḥ. And you shall understand it very carefully and be silent to God. Then, the Binah which is Mashiaḥ is judging the poor in a right manner, namely Knesset Yisrael, because she is arousing stern judgment and justice onto the nations of the world.[30]

The mythology of redemption is construed here in terms of the emanative drama in the higher divine realm, that of the three sefirot. The first sefirah arouses the third by means of smells and perfumes, symbols of the divine influx. Then, by this arousal, a power that apparently derives from the higher realms, the third sefirah distributes its influx to the last sefirah, symbolized by the Assembly of Israel, while keeping that influx from the demonic powers, symbolized by the nations. This description is characteristic of a series of symbolic readings of the meaning of redemption; it is not an extraordinary moment, a rupture with the past, or an upheaval. Here redemption is conceived of as the distribution of the divine forces from the first to the last sefirah. The Messiah is an agent that is active in differentiating the distribution of influx. The apocalyptic judgment which takes place in history is presupposed: it is neither negated nor explicated. What is important for this Kabbalist is the understanding of the supernal, divine processes rather than events taking place in "lower" history.

In R. David's Hebrew translation of a Zoharic passage, it is said that "the secret of the name 'Adam is: *'alef* on high, *mem* [is] Messiah, whose *mem* is closed."[31] This version should be understood not only against the original Aramaic Zoharic text (vol. 1, fol. 34b), which seems to be quite deficient in the versions that reached us,[32] but also in the context of the larger Kabbalistic views known at the end of the thirteenth century. The secret of the name 'Adam apparently points to a well-known acronym: 'Adam, David, Mashiyaḥ.[33] This acronym apparently means that Adam's soul has been reincarnated in the body of David, who will return as the Messiah. This nexus between Adam, the primordial ideal man, King David, representing the middle point of history, and the Messiah, betokening the end of history, is quite telling from the point of view of a Kabbalistic historiosophy. The letters in the acronym—*'alef, dalet, mem*—appear in alphabetical order, thus supporting the historical sequence of the personages they represent.

The Messiah, therefore, will possess the soul that first inhabited Adam and then David. This metempsychosis is corroborated by some thirteenth-century discussions, starting with the book of *Bahir*, concerning the transmigration of the soul of the Messiah. Thus David's soul represents a phenomenon reminiscent of the medieval view described by the phrase *rex qui nunquam moritur*, "the king who never dies.[34] This view, as I. Friedlaender pointed out, recalls the Shi'ite doctrine of the successive incarnations of the Prophet.[35] However, the question that should concern us here is whether there is also an ontological explication, within the sefirotic realm, for the above interpretation of the consonants of name 'Adam as pointing to three human figures. In other words, do the three consonants of 'Adam also correspond to divine powers, or sefirot? King David is widely identified in Kabbalah, particularly the *Zohar*, as a symbol for the last sefirah, Malkhut, or the kingdom; and Adam is seen as a higher sefirah. The question, then, is whether the Messiah himself is identified in some of those discussions on the symbolic reading of 'Adam with a specific sefirah. In the above quotation from *Sefer Mar'ot ha-Tzove'ot* it is quite plausible that Mashiyaḥ is to be identified with the sefirah of Binah.

A contemporary of these Kabbalists, who was perhaps acquainted with some of their thought, has expressed a similar idea. R. Isaac of Acre mentions that "the face of the soul of Moses hints at T[iferet], and that of Joshua at the 'A[tarah], that is a seat for T[iferet] . . . the soul of Messiah, our Righteous, hints at the [entity that] T[iferet] is a seat for, namely B[inah], as it is well-known from the verse 'And the spirit of God dwelled upon him, the spirit of Ḥokhmah and Binah' [Isaiah 11:2]."[36] It is conspicuous that this Kabbalist sees the third sefirah as connected to the soul of the Messiah. Unlike in the text of R. Isaac's discussed in chapter 3, where the Messiah was viewed as the recipient of the light from Keter, here this figure is connected only to the third sefirah. This obvious discrepancy between the two texts supports my view that R. Isaac was a rather eclectic Kabbalist who drew ideas from a variety of Kabbalistic sources without attempting to offer a systematic and coherent symbolism.

Does R. Isaac's flexible approach to the Messiah, to his symbols and functions, reflect a vital interest in this topic, or should we assume that the Kabbalist reproduced disparate theories because messianism was not one of the more pressing topics in his worldview? One possible answer is that we have here random statements, which together do not constitute a coherent system; therefore each of them reduces the weightiness of the other. Yet these statements share one crucial characteristic: the soul of the Messiah soul is described as higher than the soul of Moses. In this, R. Isaac shares the view of other Kabbalists, from Abulafia to Sabbatai Tzevi. Apparently, what is important for R. Isaac is to hint at a "web of relationship" in general, beyond the details which may possess only a secondary role and may differ from one another.[37]

Classifying the Messiah or his soul as higher than Moses, though already found in Midrash, stands for an urge to envision a higher form of spirituality than embodied in the plain sense of the Bible. The more secretive attitude of the Kabbalists toward the canonic writings, a development increasingly visible through the late Middle Ages in Jewish sources, needed an additional hero for anchoring the arcanization of Scripture. The concept of the Messiah as the revealer of "higher" secrets allowed a more flexible development of the generation of secrets in Kabbalistic literature, especially in the innovative forms of Kabbalahrepresented by many of the Kabbalists mentioned above. The resort to Isaiah 11:2 demonstrates that R. Isaac and, as we shall see, R. Joseph ben Shalom Ashkenazi strove to portray the Messiah as more mystical rather than as the great redemptive warrior. His soul is identical to the Binah, the divine attribute of understanding.

The fourteenth-century classic of Kabbalah, the anonymous *Sefer ha-Temunah,* also envisions a link between the third sefirah and the Messiah, apparently under the impact of the views surveyed above: " 'The Son of David will not come until the souls be exhausted from the Body' and then the supernal and lower redemptions will be united to the supernal light . . . because everything will return to the first redeemer, who has safely redeemed everything, and 'that who has been sold, will be redeemed and he will be free at the Jubilee' [Leviticus 25:28], which are the days of the Supernal Messiah."[38]

From the context, as well from some parallels found in the writings of R. Joseph Gikatilla dealing with terms pointing to redemption,[39] it stands to reason that the first redeemer, who is identical to the Supernal Messiah, refers again to the third sefirah, which points to the redemption of both the higher entities (the last seven sefirot) and the lower, mundane world. Redemption here stands not for national or individual salvation but for a cosmic process involving both the corporeal and the spiritual components of reality. This is a deterministic process, deeply influenced by astrology, which resorts to eschatological concepts in order to make these points in more traditional terms. Thus we find in the emphasis on the redemptive nature of the third sefirah, designated as redeemer and upper Messiah, a clear tendency to depict the process of the return to the source, a restoration of the primordial, a circular form of what I propose to call a cosmic macrochronos, and not a rectilinear vision of history which ends or culminates in the messianic era.

The most historically important formulation of the views from the circle of R. Joseph Ashkenazi and R. David ben Yehudah he-Ḥasid is found in the late-fourteenth or early-fifteenth-century *Sefer ha-Peliy'ah.* Composed in the Byzantine Empire, this vast compilation of various Kabbalistic sources includes a passage from R. Joseph Ashkenazi's *Commentary on Sefer Yetzirah,* which has been quoted quite faithfully by R. Abraham Peretz, a disciple of Nathan of Gaza, as follows:

> These are the words of Metatron to the holy Qanah[40] called *Sefer ha-Peliy'ah,* who is a wondrous man and it is found in our hands in a manuscript, and his words had been copied by Rabad in his *Commentary on Sefer Yetzirah* . . . And these are the words of Metatron to the holy Qanah, and these are his [Qanah's] words: "He has appointed the letter Bet over life and bound a crown to it and formed [the planet] by it; Sabbatai in the world, and Sunday[41] in the year [i.e., in the dimension of time], and the right eye in the person, namely that He elevated the letter Bet so that it is the head on 'the power of the Keter 'Eliyon.' And he put in it the power of Ḥokhmah and formed in it the planet Sabbatai, which is beneath the [divine name] 'ABGYTTz,[42] and the latter gave wisdom to Sabbatai. He said: 'Our master, tell us why Sabbatai is the planet of destruction, and it is nevertheless informed by the wisdom of [the name] 'ABGYTTz.' He told him: 'Despite the fact that Sabbatai is the power of destruction, by [dint of] the Shemittot, it possesses the power of Ḥokhmah, and the reason it is appointed over destruction is that it is not concerned with any corporeal issues, and this is the reason why it destroys them and does not mind them nor their adornments, but is concerned with the separate intelligences that are the sefirot [and the comprehensions of the heptades] and the comprehension of God, blessed be He . . . and it is appointed over the Jews, and this is the reason they are in trouble in this world. . . . And because it is appointed over the weight, it designates darkness and over everything that is black and over the black bile [namely melancholy] . . . and the planet Sabbatai is appointed over them and because it is appointed over the perpetuation [of things], when it will arrive to the ascent, it will not decline forever as it is said that 'the spirit of God dwells upon him, the spirit of Ḥokhmah and of Binah' [Isaiah 11:2]. See and understand that this is the secret of *meshiyaḥ* YHWH. . . . See and understand that the planet Sabbatai has the crown of Binah, and higher than this is Ḥokhmah."[43]

This passage is part of a much larger text, which may be the most detailed discussion of Saturn in the Jewish tradition and indubitably had a deep influence on a variety of Kabbalists. It is representative of the school of Kabbalists discussed above because, among other reasons, the Messiah was understood as connected to the third sefirah, as we learn from the occurrence of the name Binah. Mention of the cosmic cycles, the Shemittot, and of the heptade, which are related to the third sefirah, is also pertinent. But what is especially significant in this text is the recurrence of the name of the planet Sabbatai, which corresponds to the Latin deity and planet Saturn. The ambiguity of the attributes attributed to this planet reflects much older traditions, psychological, mythical, and astrological,[44] beyond the scope of this inquiry. In numerous astrological texts, the planet has been ascribed with both the quality of presiding over wisdom, understood by some authors and artists since the Renaissance as being the source of genius, and the celestial power responsible for the passive, destructive, and melancholic characters.

The name of the planet connected to the "secret of *meshiyaḥ* YHWH" is, in Hebrew, identical with the proper name of Sabbatai Tzevi. This coincidence may be much more than an accident. Sabbatai Tzevi studied this book and might have been influenced by this passage. In any case, his prophet used it explicitly in order to prove his messianism. I am inclined to attribute to this quotation, which has left other traces in the Sabbatean literature,[45] a much greater role than that of a belated and retrospective prooftext. Just as Tzevi's reading Abulafian quotations in *Sefer ha-Peliy'ah* prompted him to pronounce the divine name, so he conceived of himself as the Messiah at least in part because of the aforecited passage, where the planet Saturn, alias Sabbatai, was described as the secret of the Messiah. If this hypothesis is correct, then the late-thirteenth-century Kabbalah from the circle of R. Joseph Ashkenazi has contributed more to Tzevi's self-consciousness as the Messiah than any extant text belonging to Lurianic Kabbalah could possibly do.[46]

Indeed, an explicit discussion of the ascent of Tzevi to the sefirah of Binah is quite evident in the Yemenite apocalypse, stemming from a rather early period of the Sabbatean movement. In a passage already analyzed by Scholem, the Messiah is described as ascending from "one degree to another, [all] the degrees of the seven sefirot from Gedullah to Malkhut . . . after two years he ascends to the degree that his mother is there."[47] Scholem has correctly interpreted this text as pointing to the third sefirah, which is commonly symbolized by the Mother, and he even proposes, on the basis of this passage, to presuppose a mystical event in the spiritual life of Tzevi in 1650, and again he has correctly intuited that the meaning of this attainment would be the understanding of the secret of the Divinity.[48] What Scholem did not specify was the nature of that secret. On the basis of the above quotations, as well as others below, I suggest that this secret was not only understood by reaching the third sefirah. This sefirah may indeed be the very secret of the Divinity, namely the most intimate secret of Sabbatean theology as proposed by Tzevi himself.[49] In any case, elsewhere in the same epistle, the nest of the bird, the mystical place of the Messiah, is none other than the third sefirah.[50]

The Saturn clue can help clarify an important passage in one of Nathan of Gaza's famous epistles. Nathan mentions that believers' faith in Sabbatai Tzevi will ensure the reception of " 'the inheritance of the Lord,'[51] which is the mystery of the Jubilee Year that will become manifest at this time, and the 'rest,' which is the mystery of the manifestation of 'Attiqa' Qaddisha', within the configuration of Ze'ir 'Anppin, in the year 1670."[52] Two different topics are explicated in this passage. In 1670 a high revelation was to take place, when the highest divine hypostasis, 'Attiqa' Qaddisha', would illuminate the lower configuration within the intradivine structure. This view is found both in Zoharic theosophy and in Lurianic Kabbalah, and is somtimes connected with the glory of redemption.[53] Those who merit it would then gain rest, *menuḥah*. This redemptive significance is alluded to by the term *sod*, "mystery." However, an earlier phase of the salvific drama was already emerging "at this time," which is referred by the "mystery of the Jubilee." I assume that this mystery or secret designates a lower form of deliverance already present in 1665. But what is the theosophical significance of this present mystery of the Jubilee? It is abundantly clear from Kabbalistic symbolism and on the basis of the above discussions that the Jubilee is a symbol of the third sefirah. This symbolism points to the present presiding power, namely the sefirah of Binah.

This distinction between the two phases was overlooked by Scholem, who nevertheless quite correctly pointed out the salvific meaning of Binah in this context. He did not, however, pay attention to its possible implications, leaving the reader with the feeling that it is one global redemptive event that is mentioned here.[54] Moreover, in one of the later sentences of the same epistle, describing the future events during the next seven years, Nathan wrote explicitly that the miracles mentioned in the *Zohar* will take place until "the year of the next Shemittah. And in the seventh [year] ben David will come[55] and in the seventh year is Sabbath, which is the king Sabbatai[56], and at that time the above-mentioned rabbi [Sabbatai Tzevi] will come from the river of Sambatyon together with his spouse, the daughter of Moses, our master."[57]

The emphasis on the seventh is obvious; it is quite reminiscent of the mystery of the cosmic Jubilee and, at the same time, of the passage in *Sefer ha-Peliy'ah* where Saturn-Sabbatai was described as connected to the secret of Shemittot. Yet even more explicit is the allusion in the last quotation of King Sabbatai. The reign of this king should not, in my opinion, be confused with that of Tzevi himself. Immediately after mentioning King Sabbatai, Nathan introduces the

"Rabbi," namely Tzevi, thus preventing a possible intermixture of the two. In other words, from this quotation we can see that the importance of the reign of Saturn, the seventh planet, in the redemptive drama was utilized beyond the direct quotations from the thirteenth- and fourteenth-century passages that served as sources of inspiration. My assumption is that Tzevi, when studying *Sefer ha-Peliy'ah* in his youth, was attracted by the aforecited passage, and he might have been influenced by the nexus between Sabbatai-Saturn as a planet and its connection to the Messiah. His vision was passed on to Nathan, who integrates in one discussion both the man and the planet which possess the same name.

Historically speaking, this chain of events is quite plausible. We have here an interesting example of how the specific contents of Kabbalistic books may inspire some kinds of personalities; flights of imagination, a bold synthesis between disparate forms of thought—in our case Kabbalistic theosophy and astrology—may become the starting point for wide-reaching personal developments. Indeed, on the basis of the above texts it is plausible to propose another clue to the inner spiritual life of Tzevi. Scholem has suggested that a mental illness may explain Tzevi's emotional ups and downs: manic depression.[58] It is not my aim to dispute the accuracy of this modern diagnosis of a patient who died centuries ago, nor to address the crucial question whether in the seventeenth century this illness was common. It suffices for now to note that, influenced by his affinity to Binah as Saturn, the Messiah interiorized the peculiar emotional characteristic of those connected to that planet: melancholy.

We know about historical figures such as Marsilio Ficino and Girolamo Cardano, among many others, whose mood was substantially affected by their belief that they were born under Saturn.[59] This clue may help explain some aspects of Tzevi's behavior. The main impact of the possible nexus between Sabbatai and Saturn is relevant for the inner development of the young Tzevi; later on, he drew attention the attention of his intimate disciples to the discussions of that planet in Kabbalistic writings. One should not expect too great a role of this nexus for the messianic consciousness, after his messianic claim was established by means of other arguments, especially Nathan's Lurianic ones. Nevertheless, one contemporary of Tzevi's, who dedicated a poem to him, wrote as follows: "Come together like brethren—all the planets, in order to praise. . . . To Thou, the supernal Sabbatai, the head of the seven—greatness and dominion is appropriate. This is why God put Thou broad knowledge—Thy name was called by his name in the day of circumcision."[60] I understand these verses as dealing with Sabbatai the Messiah as the first among the seven planets, namely Saturn, which is also described as the reason the infant Tzevi was given the name Sabbatai at circumcision.

This text describing the reception of Sabbatai by someone living in Italy should not be thought to demonstrate the development of Tzevi's self-consciousness, but it does show that a connection between the high status of the planet Sabbatai and the Messiah Sabbatai could not escape his followers. In other words, the young Tzevi, who studied the Kabbalistic literature in the region where he was born, was shaped by a statement that linked his name to the homonymous planet and to the Messiah. If this is correct, we witness a classic situation in which personality interacts with ways of thought, in this case an astrological model, and which could influence not only an abstract messianic claim but also other aspects of a person's inner life.

The relation between the Messiah and the third sefirah does not point to an unknown reality on high, hidden from the eyes of the mystic and unattainable but by means of contemplating the linguistic symbol *mashiyaḥ* as the single channel for intuiting the higher divine reality. The way the Kabbalists belonging to the school of R. Joseph ben Shalom Ashkenazi use language betrays rather transparent discussions, which describe a precise symbolism that maps a way to the higher reality. The mystic, as least insofar as the Sabbatean authors are involved, is claiming that it is possible to reach the rank of the third sefirah. Therefore, the more precise type of symbolism concerning the messianic figure not only reveals something about the supernal powers, but it charts the way for an experiential encounter with them. It is the precision rather than their vagueness of the symbols dealt with above that determines their reception by and influence on later readers. This precision may also have something to do with the fact that in the passage above, the third sefirah is not only an entity that is represented in the world below by a symbol, but also a place to which the Messiah will have to ascend, as his mother has allegedly already done. It is therefore part of a map intended not only to point out the existence of a distant realm but also to encourage the belief that the eschaton will emerge when the Messiah, a mystical pioneer, performs the great rite of ascent. The symbols are capable of conveying more articulated contents, a quality which accounts for the persistence of Kabbalistic contents centuries after they have been formulated. The first substantial discussions concerning the Messiah and the third sefirah, stemming from the end of the thirteenth century, remained active over centuries and instilled a feeling that they were ancient prophecies of a mid-seventeenth-century figure. Symbols as used by some Kabbalistic schools were powerful vehicles, because their semiotic strategy included a symbolic efficacy that differs from Scholem's and Tishby's theory of Kabbalistic symbolism, which emphasizes the obscurity of the sefirot.

Before addressing a crucial issue in the Sabbatean vision of the nature of the Messiah, let me ponder the significance of the previous attempts to identify trends of pre-Lurianic Kabbalah as plausible sources for Tzevi's messianic self-perception and practices. The influence in Spain of ecstatic Kabbalah, as well as Kabbalah from the circle of R. Joseph ben Shalom Ashkenazi, was marginal. Their blend in this late-fourteenth-century compilation reflects forms of spirituality that include elements that do not fit the more nomian propensity of Spanish Kabbalistic schools. I assume that the Byzantine scene, less dominated by great halakhic figures, allowed the floruit of motifs that could not blossom in the more centralized Iberian peninsula. The fact that the anonymous compiler brought them together created an encounter of relatively anomian forms of Kabbalah, which together with the Spanish zoharic literature served as the starting point of Tzevi's studies. My impression is that alongside the implicit antinomianism of *Tiqqunei Zohar*, the anomianism of these two schools should be taken in consideration in order to offer a more balanced picture of the forces that shaped the Tzevi's consciousness.

The Divine Nature of the Messiah in Sabbateanism

A recurring theme in Sabbatai Tzevi's works, as well as in the works of others concerning him, is the innovative content of his revelations. They focused on God, or more specifically what is termed the mystery of the Godhead, *sod ha-'elohut*. This doctrine is the heart of Tzevi's mystical teaching. Its details are not entirely known, but the studies of Yehuda Liebes have shown that Tzevi's revelations evinced an intimate affinity between himself and his personal, and "true", God. So we are confronted with a clearly mystical bond between a man who is destined to be a Messiah and his God. The phrases "his own God" and "my own God" recur throughout Sabbatai Tzevi's letters.[61] This emphasis indicates a larger movement toward a much more personalistic understanding of religion, already starting in the sixteenth century but best exemplified by this formulation of Tzevi's. In one of Nathan of Gaza's epistles, he pointedly emphasizes the necessary relationship between possession of the knowledge of God and messianic awareness. Nathan posits that the ultimate difference between the Messiah and everyone else is that the former receives a special doctrine of the Godhead: "that he [namely the Messiah] [intellectually] reaches the understanding of the greatness of God, for this is the quintessence of the Messiah. And if he does not do so then he is not the Messiah. Even if he displays all the signs and wonders in the world, God forbid that one should believe in him, for he is a prophet to idolatry."[62]

Nathan, apparently following Tzevi's lead, viewed the Sabbatean messianic doctrine as focusing on the ability to perceive God, as opposed to what he would consider superficial phenomena belonging to the apocalyptic tradition, which has been concerned mainly with signs and wonders. These beliefs were seen as more typical of popular conceptions of messianism, and apparently were not fully shared by Nathan or Tzevi, who on this point are much closer to Maimonides' and Abulafia's stands.[63] Sabbatean messianism was essentially elitist and only rarely sought compromise with popular eschatological and messianic notions which emphasized supernatural events provoked by God's arbitrary intervention. On the contrary, Nathan argues that it is iniquitous for one to believe in a Messiah on the strength of his wonder-working abilities. "Due to our numerous sins," Nathan writes, "the majority of the community of Israel remains far from the truth. Not being familiar with the secret lore, they pridefully and mockingly say, 'What have we seen to make us believe in the Messiah?' "[64]

Nathan of Gaza admits that the Jewish people are not well versed in the Kabbalah and therefore seek a more simplistic form of messianism. In some more apocalyptic writings he satisfies this longing by providing a more popular version of messianism.[65] In Nathan's first statement quoted above, Sabbatai appears as a Messiah quite different from the classical apocalyptic one. It is as this type of Messiah that Nathan, it is asserted, rejected rumors of the imminent coming of the lost tribes.[66] Nathan did, however, resorted to revelation as a means of receiving messages. He most probably attempted to achieve this state by the aid of mystical techniques known in Jewish mystical sources. Consequently, they did not come to him suddenly but only after concentrated effort. He explicitly states that certain matters that came to him from "elevated and holy souls" were "revealed to me by way of the power of [meditative] concentration and [formulas of] unifications [*hitbodedut* and *yiḥudim*]."[67]

In other words, Nathan practiced abstinence and mystical techniques in order to achieve revelations from higher beings—*hitbodedut,* separation from worldly pleasures and social intercourse—through the *yiḥudim,* that is, by the agency of intellectual methods of meditation upon predesignated divine names. Sometimes he would receive revelations from a holy angel.[68] Nathan practiced a kind of mysticism that was more focused on messianic issues than was that of his predecessors, since he was able to harness his mystical experience for the purpose of receiving pertinent information concerning the status of the Messiah and his advent. Nathan explicitly states that higher beings communicated to him some secrets of Scripture and the Messiah, as well as permission to reveal these secrets. Like many of his Jewish predecessors, he offered, if not a full-fledged commentary on Scripture as a literary genre, an eschatological understanding of the Bible.

There is no doubt that the mystical propensity and intellectual capacities of Nathan of Gaza were responsible—as Scholem has already pointed out—for his authority as well as his self-confidence concerning the messianic mission of Sabbatai Tzevi. Nevertheless, we must keep in mind that the enterprise of interpreting the essence of Sabbatai Tzevi was primarily analyzed by Scholem in terms of Lurianic Kabbalah. The Messiah's conversion to Islam was explained as the descent to the depths of the shells, the *qelippot,* in order to free the fallen divine sparks, *nitzotzot,* as part of the messianic mission. Nathan was also a Lurianic Kabbalist. He studied the Lurianic doctrines in Jerusalem, yet he gradually liberated himself from many Lurianic practices and even historiosophical conceptions. His belief in the imminence of the final revelation of the Messiah allowed him to abolish much of Lurianic customs and practices, such as the intentions of prayer, *kavvanot ha-tefillah,* or an important aspect of the practice of *tiqqun ḥatzot,* on the grounds that these practices were now obsolete.[69] Nevertheless, Nathan resorted to the Lurianic view of the descent to the *qelippot* in order to accommodate the vicissitudes of the messianic persona to a messianic function that neither he nor Tzevi had emphasized. Therefore, despite the wide scope of the Sabbatean phenomenon, we should consider ita movement for religious reform rather than a movement for political changes.[70]

What seems to be better known from the Sabbatean vision of the Messiah is not so much its ecstatic, intellectual, and revelatory moments but the divine nature attributed to the persona of Sabbatai Tzevi. This issue is central for the theology and soteriology of the ideologue of the movement, Nathan of Gaza. As we have seen, the king-Messiah has been connected with the presence of the divine power on low, while the theosophical-theurgical Kabbalah identified the Messiah with a divine power, a sefirah. Also in the ecstatic Kabbalah, the view of the Agent Intellect as Messiah represents the hypostatic attitude found in the concept of the preexistence of the Messiah; moreover, the extreme transformation of the human into a divine intellect opened the way for a much stronger link between God and the Messiah. These bridgings of the gaps between the human figure and the divine power culminated in the deification of Sabbatai Tzevi's persona. A typical example is from the epistle of Nathan already quoted earlier:

> We must announce the greatness of the Messiah as it is understood from the writings of Ari [Isaac Luria], blessed be his memory, without the principles handed down to me. This is related to what he revealed about the secret of Adam before the sin, as he was greater than the greatness of Metatron, because he included the three worlds, B[eri'ah], Y[etzirah], 'A[siyah], as they were into him before the descent of the ten sefirot as the result of his transgression. But Metatron includes three worlds after their descent . . . as it is said in the book of *Heikhalot:* "Enoch is Metatron,[71] whose flesh has been transformed into torches of fire," and he was integrated [*nikhlal*][72] in the place of Eden and into those configurations, which are the vessels. And when the light of life is revealing within the vessels . . . he [Metatron] is founded by all the five configurations and thereby the lower matter is purified, achieving a sublime state as

> it becomes the body and the cloth to this wondrous light, and this is why it has been said that "My name is within him,"[73] because in the moment when the light of life is revealing, divinity is onto him, as we say that all the vessels of the world of Emanation are total divinity, because the "light of life" has been clothed in them. Look well into these words and let your spirit be not astonished, because this view indeed needs must emerge from the words of Ari.[74]

Adam before the Fall is described here as a *macroanthropos,* who includes into his constitution all the four worlds: the world of emanation, identical with the divine essence, and three extradivine worlds. The latter are inherited by Metatron, who is none other than the human Enoch, who was able to prepare his body in such a way as to become the substrate for the divine light that is revealed there. While Adam possessed this status a priori, Enoch attained it a posteriori. Metatron to a certain extent is regaining the lost status of Adam, a view found in a long series of mystical texts in Judaism.[75] This attainment is seen as a deification, because the light of life is infusing divinity into the purified body. Moreover, the additional assumption that allows this deification is the ascent of Enoch into Eden, or even to a higher rank, into the divine configurations. That is, an ascent and integration into the divine infrastructure of the messianic figure is complemented by the descent of the divine light onto this structure.

Nathan apparently was well aware of the radicalness of the view he was espousing. That is why he emphasizes that he is drawing the correct conclusions from Luria's thought, and he does not rely on "principles" received from unnamed sources, human or divine.[76] As Scholem has correctly pointed out, Nathan's discussion relies on a Lurianic text found in *Liqqutei Torah.*[77] However, Luria's view deals only with the hypostatic status of Metatron as compared to the initial status of Adam; it says nothing about the elevation of Metatron and his becoming divine, though such a move could have easily been made on the basis of earlier Kabbalistic literature, such as the writings of R. Isaac of Acre, who speaks about the "emanated Metatron."[78] Thus, the apotheotic moment, so important in the ecstatic Kabbalah insofar as the intellect or (according to other versions) the soul is concerned, is much less relevant for the theosophical Kabbalah as embraced by Luria in the above discussion.[79] Moreover, the Heikhalot passage about Metatron is not adduced by Luria in this context. Thus, though Scholem is definitely correct as to the identity of one of the sources of the above Sabbatean text, namely the Lurianic one, the clue to it, which consists in a mystical interpretation that allows a deification of Enoch qua Metatron, should not be drawn so simply from Luria's text hinted at by Scholem.

Already in Abraham Abulafia's writings, however, there are messianic implications of attaining the status of Metatron as part of a mystical experience;

and it is only in the case of Abulafia's *Sefer Ḥayyei ha-'Olam ha-Ba'* that an expressly messianic interpretation occurs.[80] Though I have inspected many texts in order to trace the possible sources of Nathan, for the time being the Abulafian source seems to be the sole significant parallel to Nathan's messianic reading of the ancient text from the Heikhalot and of Luria's passage.[81]

Another unmistakable indication of the Abulafian influence on this matter in Sabbateanism may be adduced from a Sabbatean apocalypse written in Yemen in the first years after the proclamation of Tzevi as Messiah. The anonymous Kabbalist wrote in the context of the redemption of Israel that "Israel is a special entity in the [lower] world [*segullah gedolah*] just as the Agent Intellect is on high, and *yisra'el* is numerically identical to *sekhel ha-po'el,* and to ShTzM HNKhL[82] that will be in their ascent, and [then] the illuminati will brighten [Daniel 12:3], namely the Righteous, like the splendor of the celestial firmament, which is the palace of Metatron, which is the Agent Intellect."[83] This quotation is based on a gematria that equates the terms *yisra'el* and *sekhel ha-po'el,* the numerical values of whose consonants is 541. This gematria is quite characteristic of Abulafia, who mentions the equation of *yisra'el* to *sekhel ha-po'el* many times in his writings.[84] Moreover, the mention of Metatron here is also reminiscent of the ecstatic Kabbalist's vision of the Agent Intellect as identical to this angel (see chapter 2). The eschatological context of the discussion also recalls Abulafia's mode of understanding the redemptive role of both the Agent Intellect and Metatron. At least this apocalypse is based on forms of Kabbalah which, as Scholem has already pointed out, were not fraught with Lurianic concepts.[85] Moreover, it is in Abulafia that the expression "supernal Adam" as an appellation for the Agent Intellect is found, which is identified in other places in his writings with Metatron or with the Messiah.[86]

The aforecited text from the epistle of Nathan serves him as the starting point for an even more radical conclusion, namely that had Adam not sinned, he would be in constant contact with the divine light and thus he would be "complete divinity" *'elohut gamur,* a a conclusion that is described as necessary for anyone who believes in Kabbalah.[87] This is a radical description but nevertheless not so remote from some descriptions of the highest achievements of mystics found in ecstatic Kabbalah. For example, one of Abulafia's descriptions mention that "divine virtues are added to him until he speaks with the holy spirit, whether in his writing or with his mouth . . . and those like him have passed the boundary of humanity, and cleaved during their lifetime to their God."[88]

Likewise, an anonymous Kabbalist close to Abulafia wrote several times in his *Sha'arei Tzedeq* that the mystic can transcend the limits of humanity and enter the realm of divinity.[89] In similar terms, Sabbatai Tzevi is quoted by his prophet as having said that belief in the Messiah actually expands the realm of the divine since God is not found outside the Messiah, the latter doing everything by the dint of God, who is present in him.[90] It is on this point that there emerges a stark contrast between Abulafia's way of thought and Nathan's—and perhaps also Tzevi's. My impression is that in Sabbateanism, including the scanty remnants of the writings of Tzevi himself, the emphasis is not only on the special nature of the soul of the Messiah but sometimes, as in the aforecited text, on the whole personality of Tzevi. It is not only, or perhaps even not primarily, Tzevi's soul that was understood as undergoing a dramatic transformation and becoming divine but more conspicuously his body. On this issue Abulafia would disagree in principle. The divine is often understood in his Kabbalah as immanent in the world but not identical to anything material. Transformation of the body may be identified already in earlier forms of Jewish mysticism, especially Heikhalot literature, as part of an angelization process, but Abulafia reinterpreted—in fact misconstrued—this earlier topic in strong spiritualistic or intellectualistic terms.[91]

Having built up the possibility that a man may become a complete divine being, Nathan now turns to the personality of his Messiah. He argues that unlike the mystical attainment of the Messiah, which is defined in terms of becoming a *merkavah,* a chariot of the divinity, Jesus's claim to incarnation is built upon another argument, which turned out to be the reason for Jesus's failure and ultimately the reason for the deception of the Jewish people. He proved to be a false Messiah because the standard for measurement of this claim was his ability to perform signs and wonders. Herein lies the fault, for the people believed primarily in this magical aspect of his messianism. According to Sabbatai Tzevi, the recognition of a personal divinity, which is conceived by him as being in direct conflict with the Lurianic image of the mechanistic, complex, and impersonal God, is quintessential.[92] When the strong bond between the Messiah and his God is created, the process of the deification of the Messiah begins. This process is the last stage in mystical development of the Messiah, not a starting point for messianic phenomena, as in Christianity. Thus Nathan of Gaza writes concerning Jesus, allowing us to infer about the manner in which he viewed Sabbatai Tzevi. According to Nathan, the mistake of Jesus[93] was that he called himself God at the beginning, whereas the true Messiah does so "after he perfects the lower world," and becomes the chariot to the Light of Life. "Then he is given the divine name, and then he will include the chariot of the three [upper] worlds."[94]

Actually, Nathan of Gaza alters the popular Jewish attitude toward Jesus. According to the Sabbatean prophet, the theological problem was not that Jesus was deified, as many Jewish thinkers would argue, for that is just the rank that the Messiah should attain. The cardinal failure was in Jesus' presenting himself as a wonder worker.[95] It may then be inferred that the process of deification of the Messiah will take place only after he has perfected the lower world. This transformation into the chariot of the Light of Life invests the Messiah with a new type of existence, which allows him to be called divine. By being absorbed into the divine structure, apparently after following a certain mystical path, one is able to be deified and so become a Messiah. The Lurianic concept of tiqqun as a reparation of the divine configurations is absent here; instead we are told that Messiah will repair the lower world before he becomes the chariot for the divine light.[96] In other words, the lower reparation is to be followed by a spiritual perfection, which will culminate in an apotheosis that will deify the mystic, who becomes the Messiah. The ultimate mystical attainment is conceived here as quintessential for the messianic enterprise. For this point of view, these forms of Sabbatean theories should be aligned with the earlier apotheotic impulses found in the ecstatic Kabbalah and, in more general terms, in the apotheotic impulse in Judaism that becomes evident in the postbiblical apocryphal literature, especially the Heikhalot literature.

Elsewhere, however, we learn about a different connection between messianism and mysticism. In another text of Nathan of Gaza it is said that "the soul of the king Messiah cleaves to the tree of life, [and] he is the master of all the treasures of the Father,[97] and he performs restorations in all aspects [of divine powers] and [all levels of] existence . . . by virtue of his adherence to the tree of life everything he does is a restoration."[98] This cleaving is the precondition for both the theurgical operations and the wonder workings alluded to by the mention of "[all the levels of] existence." Thereby the Messiah enters into another sphere of life, since all his operations will become, by virtue of his adherence, sublime acts of reparation of the divine powers. Though the messianic moment is quintessential for the above passage and characteristic of an intellectual ambiance saturated by acute messianism, the basic model that informs this text is nevertheless quite traditional and is fairly well articulated from the very beginning of Kabbalah, later becoming accentuated in Hasidism.[99]

The above text allows an interesting reflection on Buber's distinction between the occidental man, who strives to master the world, and the Jew, who intends to perfect it. Indeed, the Messiah is described as the master of the treasures of the father. However, this is just the starting point for his activity toward perfection. World as mastered is not world as perfected, and perhaps the possibility of mastering it is part of its imperfection. The Messiah, already conceived of as the great mystic, adheres to an unredeemed supernal world, not to an absolute and unchanging one. In fact, Nathan's vision of mysticism and of the theurgical operation that perfects the divine world represents a long history of Jewish perceptions of the divine *salvator salvandus* which, old as it was, suggests a connection between motor man and sensory man, to return to two of Buber's terms, in order to operate in a meaningful manner as a mystic.

Apparently related to the application of this persistent model is a peculiar atmosphere of intense belief in the imminent redemption which was fostered by the novel emphasis on broadening the range of activities that will have theurgical effects. The classical nomian acts prescribed by halakhah are now not the exclusive vehicles of the theurgical activities, as in the theosophical-theurgical Kabbalah; rather, every activity as such is informed by a peculiar redemptive power. This theory has something to do with an attempt to justify the "strange deeds" of the Messiah, but it may also be related to the extraordinary status of someone's soul when in a state of communion with a divine power, symbolized here as the tree of life.[100] Comparing this last view of Nathan of Gaza to that adduced above in the context of Jesus, we are confronted with a significant difference, if not an obvious contradiction. Here the cleaving to God confers extraordinary powers, theurgical and magical, upon the Messiah. The way these powers are presented presupposes the superiority of the theurgical over the magical ones, a view that is corroborated by another opinion of Nathan's, who would see the belief in the Messiah's doing wonders as an inferior conception characteristic of the vulgus. However, the quotation dealing with Jesus presupposes a different taxonomy: it is only after the completion of the perfection of the lower world that the higher worlds are mentioned. There an ascendant path is delineated, the last quotation implies a descending one, which combines mysticism, the cleaving, with the reception of extraordinary powers, a view characteristic of the mystico-magical model.

The occurrence of the two types of explanations about the acts of the Messiah is to be understood against the background of more than one model. This shows the complexity of the questions emerging from the encounter between the Kabbalah, or any other form of speculation, and acute messianism. The need to account for dramatic changes along mystical lines can hardly offer consistent types of discourse. No less important, however, is the fact that the divergences result from the encounter between the acute messianism of the prophet of Gaza and more than one type of Kabbalistic literature. More precisely, the disclosure of the influence of different Kabbalistic models and messianic forms of activism and hermeneutics is a bad prescription for someone who is concerned with conceptual coherence in a certain type of literature.

Emphasis on the ideal of *devequt,* which could be derived from a more ecstatic form of Kabbalah, andon the importance of theurgy, stemming from the theosophical-theurgical Kabbalah, can hardly produce a coherent system of thought. This is true in the case not only of Nathan but also of many of the later Kabbalists and Hasidic masters, as we shall see in the next chapter. They were exposed to diverging types of Kabbalah and attempted to absorb them, thus digesting a variety of available models. Before leaving the anabatic discourse, it would be interesting to adduce what is probably a somewhat later Sabbatean source, where to Tzevi himself is attributed the following statement addressed to his followers: "Do not err concerning me, God forbid, as angels did in the case of Adam when they wanted to praise him by saying 'Holy.' "[101] This warning shows how deep the awareness of the similarity between Tzevi and the glory of the pristine Adam had been among some Sabbateans.

Sabbateanism and Christianity

It is in this discussion of the divine status of the Messiah that Nathan puts forward the claim that, provided that Adam is actually the Messiah and the reparation of his sin will bring about a state even higher than he had at the beginning,[102] faith in the Messiah should stem from his divine nature, not his magical powers, which would be idolatry.[103] This conspicuous struggle with what he portrays as Christian messianism is quite fascinating. In the two forms of soteriology, Adam indeed plays an important role, as it is his primordial sin, not the loss of the national state, that is the starting point for the salvific effort. This is one of the foci of the Abulafian project, though Abulafia's views are to be understood much more allegorically than the latter Kabbalists' approach to Adam.[104] When the emphasis moved from the national toward the personal, messianism underwent an intriguing metamorphosis: it is not the mission of the present king, but that of the mystic, to reenact the lost perfection. Equating Adam with the Messiah is quite relevant, since the individual redemption rather than national salvation comes to the fore.[105] The individual's recuperation of the lost *imago dei,* a theory reminiscent of the Christian concept of *privatio,* informs this type of messianism. Despite the sharp critique of the Christian view of messianism, the Sabbatean prophet is quite close to some positions on the subject in Christianity. Unlike some views that take Adam to be the antitypos of the Christ, in other instances in Christian theology, particularly the thought of the ancient Judeo-Christian sect, Pauline theology, and Christian orthodoxy, the perfection of Adam as an anticipator of the Christ is evident.[106]

It is quite difficult to avoid the question as to the Christian sources of this affinity in a text where Jesus is explicitly mentioned. As Scholem has already pointed out, there is a series of topics in Sabbateanism which invite a fruitful comparison to Christianity. Scholem concluded that, unlike the phenomenological affinities, no solid historical links are known and probable.[107] I am not sure, however, that this purely phenomenological solution is the most plausible one. In mid-seventeenth-century Jerusalem, in a book written by none other than the former master of Nathan, the famous R. Jacob Ḥayyim Tzemaḥ, a person of converso origins who returned to Judaism, echoes of Christian Kabbalah are still visible. In fact, the more exalted vision of Adam as a prototype of Jesus characteristic of the Orthodox church could have reached the Sabbatean theologians. So, for example, when dealing with another christological topic, an important Sabbatean ideologue, Abraham Michael Cardozo, correctly distinguished between Catholic and Orthodox views.[108] In the light of Yehuda Liebes's theory that emphasizes the special mystical relationship between Sabbatai and his God, an explanation for his conversion to Islam—the most infamous of his strange deeds—has been proposed. It seems that Sabbatai Tzevi himself perceived his Islamic conversion as following the dictates of a personal revelation, not external pressure.[109] Apparently, he was ordered to embrace the Islamic faith as a punishment for the fact that the Jewish people do not understand the true doctrine of the Godhead. This shows us how revelation was consciously perceived by Tzevi as the cause for an external act, one that was thought to contain messianic portent.

The later understanding of Sabbatai Tzevi's conversion to Islam had a certain resemblance to an act committed by his prophet, Nathan of Gaza. Nathan made a journey to Rome and apparently performed a magical rite by the Vatican—together with a companion—consisting of circumambulating Saint Peter's while reciting *Kavvanot* and *Yiḥudim.*[110] Here we see a Messiah and his prophet operating in different modalities within the context of the two rivals religions, Islam and Christianity. Nathan of Gaza was indubitably influenced by the precedents of the two other messianic figures who also went to meet the pope, Abraham Abulafia and Shlomo Molkho, whose acts were most probably known to the Sabbateans.

Already in a passage printed in Tzevi's lifetime, Tzevi was described as the son of God. We read in John Evelyn's testimony about the Messiah's address to the people of Israel: "The Onely, and First-borne Son of God, Sabatai Sevi, the Messiah and Saviour of Israel, to all the people of Israel."[111] Tzevi's self-proclamation as *l'unico figliolo, e primogenito d'dio* has conspicuous christological overtones, and I see no way to explain it phenomenologically. It must be seen as an important case of direct influence of christology on Tzevi himself.

R. Moshe Ḥayyim Luzzatto (Ramḥal)

The great influence of Sabbateanism caused, especially in Europe, a rise in revelational phenomena. Whereas mysticism had previously led to messianic awareness, after Sabbateanism messianism sometimes became a decisive force in the rise of mystical, mostly revelatory, phenomena, often related to the apparition of a *maggid* or spiritual angelic mentor.[112]

One of the most important examples of this rise of the mystical, ecstatic, and visionary elementsis R. Moshe Ḥayyim Luzzatto, known by his acronym, Ramḥal.[113] Luzzatto is a model of integration of the mystical and the messianic modes of thought and experience. As Isaiah Tishby has shown, there are strong affinities between the messianic thought of Luzzatto and Sabbateanism.[114] It is also clear that a large portion of Luzzatto's compositions are products of the revelations he received from his heavenly mentor, a maggid, the Prince of the Divine Face—whose name alternates between Shem'u'el and Metatron. As a result of these maggidic revelations, Luzzatto composed an entire series of zoharic works imitative in their language and style.[115] These writings also display an idiosyncratic elaboration of the messianic element contained within the *Zohar,* most notably the *Tiqqunei Zohar.* From this vantage, it is conspicuous that heavenly revelation permits and intensifies the resurgence in the messianic elements already present in the classical Kabbalistic composition of the thirteenth century alongside Sabbatean messianic elements contained in the spiritual ambiance of Luzzatto. Luzzatto's writings, however, are crucial from another perspective. While Lurianic Kabbalah, and to a certain extent Sabbateanism, did not stress the notion of *devequt* or communion, or the experience of *unio mystica* with God, Luzzatto's writings underline the importance of a variety of unitive experiences. It is reasonable to infer a certain shift from the more predominant Lurianic and Sabbatean doctrines, which focused on the notion of tiqqun, which allegedly marks the advent of the messianic era. In contrast, devequt is an individual spiritual value, and consequently Luzzatto's thought integrates the mythical-messianic elements and the spiritual conception of the religious life. It is most likely, as Tishby has already pointed out, that Luzzatto contributed to the formation of the next important stream in Jewish mystical thought, Hasidism.[116]

The task here is to address a special connection between redemption in Luzzatto, who conceived himself a messianic figure, and one of the models that has informed Jewish mysticism since the Middle Ages, the talismanic one. The awareness of this model on the part of Luzzatto, as well as of Hasidism, will help us understand the spiritual phenomena related to messianism and the historical filiation of ideas. In his Kabbalistic composition *Da'at Tevunot,* Luzzatto describes the nexus between the fulfilling of the commandments here below, understood as an act of repair or tiqqun, and the descent of the divine influx upon the "preparation" done by the righteous. This is a gradual process, which will culminate in complete redemption: "What is needed now is to repair the deficiencies . . . and this is being done until the time of the redemption, because this is the final intention of the exiles, to cause repairs of whatever has been broken . . . and when this issue will be completed, then we shall be redeemed by a complete redemption."[117]

Performing the commandments is seen as the best means to restore the initial perfection of reality, destroyed by Adam's sin. By their performance the initial purity will ensure the maximum presence of God on earth, even transcending the Adamic form of perfection.[118] Thus, the tiqqun in the "nature of the lower world"[119] is envisioned as operating not on the intradivine structure, though such a view recurs many times in other discussions of Luzzatto's, but mainly on the mundane world, and the reparation of this lower world is imagined as the ultimate purpose of all the exiles. This bridging of the gap between the lower and the higher is viewed as a mystical act, described by the term *devequt* or *hitdabbequt*.[120] As Tishby has correctly remarked, the eschatological function of the purification of the lower world is quite different from the collection of the sparks in Lurianic Kabbalah.[121] However, he did not attempt to address the question of the source of Luzzatto's model, which is indeed similar, as Tishby has mentioned, to Hasidism.

In my opinion, it is possible to see in the above passages a moderate form of the talismanic model. This proposal is corroborated by resorting to the term *hakhanah,* or preparation, and emphasizing the presupposition that there is a deep affinity between the deeds below and the influx descending upon these preparations.[122] There is an explicit statement in a manuscript identified by Tishby as having been penned by Luzzatto, which says that "power has been given to man so that he will be able to draw the power of the Shekhinah and her light downward by means of his soul; and He gave all the things of this world to his use, because by this [use] they also are repaired and the power of holiness drawn by him is spreading also over them."[123] This view recalls Moses de Leon's view of the rationales of the commandments and of the Cordoverian view of the soul as drawing down the divine influx.[124] So, for example, the Safedian Kabbalist indicates, in a manner quite reminiscent of Luzzatto's claims, that it is "well known that in accordance with the preparations [*hakhanot*] of the lower things, it is the desire of the higher ones to cleave to them."[125]

Under his influence, such a famous author as R. Moses Alsheikh in his widespread *Torat Moshe,* composed in Safed but printed also in Italy, resorted hundreds of times to the term *hakhanah.* The Italian Kabbalist R. Menaḥem 'Azariah of Fano wrote at the end of the sixteenth century that "there is a great preparation [*hakhanah*] inherent in the names of the righteous [which enables] the dwelling of the divine overflow on them, as it is written, "See I have called you by name," and only afterward [it is written], 'I shall fill him with the spirit of God' [Exodus 31:3]."[126] As we saw in the previous chapter, recourse to the verb *moshekh* in messianic contexts is found in an early-seventeenth-century Lurianic passage. In terms very similar to both Cordovero and Luzzatto, the Besht, the founder of Hasidism, was reported to have said, "Whoever wishes that the

Godhead [*'elohut*] should dwell upon him should consider himself to be 'Ayin [Nought], and the most important thing is to know and understand that within him there is [nothing] but Godhead, and this is a preparation [*hakhanah*] for the dwelling of the Godhead on him."[127]

However, the affinity between the model represented here, of the descent of the divine holiness and power on low, and the talismanic model is not only a phenomenological one, or one depending upon the similar usage of the term *hakhanah.* The talismanic model is closely related to astrology; this is obvious even in the Safedian Kabbalah, as represented by Cordovero.[128] Indeed, in *Da'at Tevunot* Luzzatto refers explicitly to astrological influences, describing them in such detail as to demonstrate not only that he was acquainted with astrology but also that he accepted the astrological model.[129] But he resorts again to the term *hakhanah* to explain the relation between man and the astral body that has an influence on him.[130] The astral sources of Luzzatto's thought were indeed quite influential on some forms of Jewish mysticism, particularly after the fourteenth century.[131] Unaware of the astral magical type of thought, Tishby envisaged Luzzatto as the source of similar positions in Hasidism, but this possibility has not been substantiated by a more detailed textual study.[132] In my opinion, Hasidism and Luzzatto were influenced by similar sources—Cordoverian ones, I assume. In order to clarify the greater diffusion of the talismanic mode of thinking, it would be sufficient to read the sources we have already adduced above, in chapters 3 and 5; but in any case, the common sources of Luzzatto and Hasidism will become more evident once the talismanic nature of Luzzatto's thought is better elucidated.

This more panoramic approach to the dissemination of the talismanic model, in particular its messianic version, will explain Tishby's quandary: the suppression in Luzzatto's writings of the Lurianic theory of extraction of the sparks, which Tishby deemed to be the most widespread and influential underpinning of messianic activity after the death of Luria.[133] In lieu of presupposing almost a reification of the relevant Kabbalah in Luria's thought and writings as being the single most influential and significant corpus of Kabbalistic thought, it would be much more reasonable to assume that the Cordoverian corpus has been, inter alia, influential to the same extent. Ironically enough, it was Tishby himself who quite correctly drew attention to the fact that in the seventeenth century, a struggle between Cordoverian and Lurianic types of Kabbalah was still going on. Tishby was much more concerned, however, with searching for the explicit mention of the name of Cordovero in the writings of some late-sixteenth- and early-seventeenth-century Kabbalists;[134] had he been aware of the astral magical aspects of Cordoverian Kabbalah and their reverberations in the subsequent phases of Jewish mysticism, he would have understood how influential such a model was on the overall development of Jewish mysticism, including the thought of Luzzatto.

The central role played by the Messiah in the transmission of divine power to Israel is dealt with again in one of the writings of Luzzatto, where the assumption is that the suffering of the Messiah alleviates the suffering of Israel during the exile, while his reception of power ensures the reception of power by the people of Israel.[135] Here the Messiah conspicuously plays an intermediary role even before the advent of the time of the end. The vicarious role of the Messiah's suffering is reminiscent of the Christian view of Jesus, which was already introduced in Jewish mysticism by R. Shlomo Molkho and, under his influence, by R. Isaac Luria and the Sabbatean authors.[136]

Thus, both Tzevi and Luzzatto were influenced by astrological terminology in their attempt to make sense of the traditional concept of Messiah. It is therefore quite evident that without integrating the astrological systems into the study of Kabbalah, it will be difficult to attain a better understanding of many issues in the development of Jewish mysticism.[137]

Messianism in R. Ya'aqov 'Emden

Our knowledge of Sabbateanism owes much to the writings of its most fiery opponent, R. Ya'aqov 'Emden. The author of numerous writings in the mid-eighteenth century criticizing Sabbateanism and its European branches, 'Emden contributed to the critical examination of Jewish mysticism. Moreover, as Liebes has pointed out, it seems that 'Emden also indulged in a form of messianic self-consciousness, which may explain his bitter opposition to Sabbatean messianism.[138] One passage, already examined by Liebes, deals with the different concepts of the Messiah: "In each and every generation God, blessed be He, sends a spark of the Messiah, either in order to redeem Israel when they repent, or to maintain the world during the wicked generation, like the generation of apostates, or to illumine the world during the exile by means of his Torah, so that the world will not be destroyed altogether, and Hezeqiah was a spark of the Messiah."[139]

I am interested here in the semantic field of the term. As in one of the quotations from Abulafia, where different meanings of this concept have been adduced together, here also the different functions are enumerated. In addition to the classical redemptive role, 'Emden mentions also the conservative role of the spark of the Messiah. In a manner reminiscent of the views of both Molkho and Tzemaḥ, he also conceives of the Messiah as sustaining the world either by fighting against the Serpent,[140] just as we learned from the text of Molkho, or by teaching his Torah. Again as in Molkho, the regular days, the "unredeemed" time, is the time when the Messiah also operates. As Liebes has suggested, the author saw himself as the spark of the Messiah fighting against the Sabbatean movement imagined as the Serpent. From the point of view of my concern here, it is important to notice the existence of the conservative vision of the Messiah in the eighteenth century.

Hasidism: Mystical Messianism and Mystical Redemption

It is known from the mouth of the Righteous:
"Let pray that man should not be in exile with[in] himself."
It seems to me that when the Messiah will come. . .
—REUVEN HA-LEVI HOROVITZ, *Diduim Basode,* I, fol. 44a

Modern Scholars on Hasidism and Messianism

EIGHTEENTH-century Hasidism combined extreme spiritual mystical elements with conspicuously messianic concepts and terminology, which were given to interpretations that moderated their apocalyptic aspects. Since Hasidism produced a huge literary output consisting of many hundreds of treatises written over a long period of time, it naturally displays a great variety of messianic views. Therefore I shall not attempt here to offer a unified view of messianism in Hasidism, nor a comprehensive survey of the various positions on this issue. Nonetheless, it is the most influential form of Jewish mysticism, a phenomenon whose messianic components have been widely disputed in modern research.

Modern scholarship is divided on the question of the status of messianism within the first two generations of Hasidic masters. We can discern three major approaches that attempted to explain the role of messianism in the Hasidic worldview. The first approach has been championed by Martin Buber and Simon Dubnov, who essentially considered acute messianism to be defunct within the framework of Hasidic ideals. Buber and Dubnow assumed that there had been a radical liquidation of messianic elements in classical Jewish sources.[1] In my opinion, this view is a more moderate continuation of the contemptuous attitude toward messianic phenomena found among some nineteenth-century scholars. Another approach, featured by Gershom Scholem and some of his students, posited the "neutralization" of the messianic idea in the writings of the first generations of Hasidic masters. In their formulation, Hasidism neither ignored nor totally eliminated messianic concepts, but rather "neutralized" them, in contrast to the Lurianic and Sabbatean effervescence. Actually, the term *neutralization* denotes the demythologizing of the apocalyptic elements found in messianic thought.[2] A third approach, espoused initially by Ben-Zion Dinur (Dinaburg) and more recently elaborated by Isaiah Tishby, Elliot Wolfson, and Mor Altshuler on the basis of important additional material,[3] argues for a significant messianic awareness in the founders of early Hasidism.[4] These three different approaches nevertheless agree upon one basic premise: that Hasidism espoused a spiritual interpretation of messianism, and that this interpretation was novel, though some of these scholars would emphasize more nationalistic forms of messianism as significant ingredients of Hasidism. These approaches differ in the emphasis placed on messianic elements of a national or historical nature. The different parties in this controversy accept without question the proposition that messianism is solely a national, apocalyptic type of redemption, but they debate the role of this view in the general economy of the Hasidic movement. In other words, the neutralizing attitude toward messianism has been considered a non-authentic interpretation of a well-established messianic phenomenon.

Let me engage two main passages from Hasidic sources adduced by the parties involved in this debate. A common theme of these passages has been neglected in the succinct treatments offered by previous scholars: the importance of what the magical component of the messianic mission in early Hasidism.

R. Yisrael Ba'al Shem Tov on Messianism

The Besht's Epistle to R. Gershon of Kutov

No single piece of Hasidic writing enjoyed more attention both from Hasidic masters and from modern critical scholars as the epistle sent by the founder of Hasidism, the Ba'al Shem-Tov, to his brother-in-law, R. Gershon of Kutov. This brief letter, rich in content and at the same time puzzling in its message, shows that the ascent to Paradise and the discussion with the Messiah are part of a messianic enterprise, a view that reinforces the claim of a profound relationship between mysticism and messianism. However, one of the main topics that has drawn the attention of those involved in the academic debate surrounding the Hasidic attitude toward messianism should be addressed in some detail, because the Messiah is mentioned explicitly. In the Besht's epistle, we read:

> On Rosh ha-Shanah of the year 5507[5] I performed an incantation [*hashba'ah*][6] for the ascent of the soul, known to you. And in that vision I saw wondrous things, which I had never seen until then from the day that I became spiritually aware. And

> it is impossible to relate and to tell what I saw and learned in that ascent thither, even in private. But when I returned to the lower Paradise,[7] I saw the souls of living and of dead persons, both of those with whom I was acquainted and those with whom I was not acquainted . . . numberless, in a to-and-fro movement, ascending from one world to the other through the column[8] known to adepts in esoteric matters[9] . . . And I asked my teacher and master[10] that he come with me, as it is a great danger to go and ascend to the supernal worlds, whence I had never ascended since I acquired awareness, and these were mighty ascents. So I ascended degree after degree, until I entered the palace of the Messiah, which is the place that the Messiah learns Torah, together with all the Tannaites and Amoraites and the seven shepherds. And there I have seen a very great joy . . . And I asked the Messiah: When do you come? And he answered: "You will know [the time], which is when your doctrine will be revealed in public and it will be disclosed to the world, and your fountains will well outside, what I have taught you and you apprehended, and also they [the people of Israel] will be able to perform the unifications[11] and the ascents [of the soul][12] as you do, and then the shells will be abolished and there will be a time of good will and redemption." And I was surprised by this [answer] and I was deeply sorrowful because of the length of the time when this will be possible: however, from what I have learned there, the three things which are remedies and three holy names, it is easy to learn and explain. Then my mind was calmed and I thought that it is possible for my contemporaries to attain this degree and aspect by these [practices] as I do, namely to be able to accomplish the ascents of souls and they will be able to study and become like me.[13]

This passage has provoked a small polemic between scholars of Hasidism.[14] The debate focuses on the divergences between a more acute messianic reading of the text, suggested by Benzion Dinur[15] and elaborated in a more critical way by Isaiah Tishby,[16] and a much less messianic one, found in Scholem's writings.[17] However, in spite of the interest expressed by the scholars in this small epistle, many of its details remain unexamined. The eagerness on the part of some scholars to demonstrate the importance of this text for the messianic nature of Hasidism, and the zeal on the part of the "neutralizers" to deny its importance, has undermined a detailed analysis of conceptual components of the text that are significant in themselves and may have an impact on the effort to settle the controversy. For example, Tishby, who broadly followed Dinur's strong messianic view of Hasidism, has somehow aligned himself on this point with Scholem's less messianic reading, when he writes that "as against the presupposition of Dubnov on one hand, and of Horodetzki and Dinur on the other, that the messianic goal attributed to the dissemination of the Besht's 'doctrine' and 'comprehension' consists in the Hasidic teaching, as laid down in the writings of his students and those of their students, I think that in the epistle solely the actions by means of unifications, ascents of the soul, the remedies and the [divine] names are dealt with [as messianic deeds], similar to the acts of other Kabbalists and masters of names in that period."[18]

By correctly comparing the content of the epistle to other forms of magical and mystical practices, Tishby intends to obliterate not the messianic cargo of the epistle but the messianic understanding of the "Hasidic teachings" considered as different from the magical topics, which were conceived as having some messianic valences. By creating an implicit either/or, Tishby assumes that the use of magical operations for messianic means is indeed found in the epistle, but they do not represent all the other Hasidic types of activities. However, this logic is fallacious for two reasons: it contradicts the content of the epistle, where it is said that the revelation of names and remedies are both means of messianic activity, as well as the teachings of the Besht.

Magic and messianism are not, either by definition or by historical antecedent, exclusive categories. On the contrary, an inspection of modern scholarship on the history of religion, such as the studies of Morton Smith,[19] or the history of Jewish messianism, including the corpus of *Sefer ha-Meshiv* as well as some discussions related to Joseph della Reina and Shlomo Molkho,[20] points in a rather different direction: magic is indeed one of the main avenues used to bring the Messiah. Moreover, the magical-messianic view of the divine names, ascents of the soul, and unifications should be understood as a magical concept of language which allows supernatural achievements, an issue that stands at the very heart of many important "Hasidic teachings." Unlike Tishby's view of the magical-redemptive operations mentioned in the epistle as the continuation of an older path—against Dinur's view that the epistle represents an innovation in the domain of messianism—while "Hasidic teachings" differ from the epistle on the point of magical activities, I would say that in Hasidism we have an application of the talismanic model to messianism. The model was old, indeed very old, but its appropriation for the sake of hastening the messianic era is novel. Though we have seen (chapter 3) a view, represented by R. Moses de Leon, of the king-Messiah's drawing down the divine forces, this view is less pregnant with immediate eschatological significance than the Hasidic one, and though having a magical value, it is still less talismanic. Unlike Joseph della Reina's magical messianism, which was intended to break the course of history, Hasidic messianism is much less interested in apocalyptic activity. In fact, aware as they sometimes were of della Reina's legend, the Hasidic masters attempted to distance themselves from his type of redemptive magic messianism. At least some details in the epistle, as I will show, describe the activity of the Besht as one concurring with the way medical magicians were conceived in his lifetime and magicians beforehand, but also with some eschatological topics found in the Middle Ages.

The medical aspect implicit in the term *segullot,* "remedies," which occurs together with the divine names, is fostered by a historical document that describes the Besht not only as a Kabbalist but also as *doktor* and *balsem* or *balszam.*[21] The two words which describe the Besht in a Polish document are to be found just after the designation of the Besht as a Kabbalist. Indeed, this pair of words seems to be part of a widespread way of describing similar persons. For example, we find in the magical book *Mif'alot 'Elohim,* attributed to Rabbi Yo'el ben Naftali Katz, a famous seventeenth-century magus described as Ba'al Shem, "master of a [magical] name," a quotation from the "writings of the Kabbalists" which deals with medical astrology. There it is written that the astrological details "are necessary both to the master of the name and to the doctor."[22] Therefore, the pair of words in the Besht's revelation is relevant to the various practices, mystical and magical, of the founder of Hasidism.

Yet despite the parallel between these phrases, the mention of the divine names together with *segullot* recalls the introduction to a much earlier magical book, *Shimmushei Torah.*[23] It is not only a question of linguistic similarity but also one of a similar context: in both cases the ascent on high is mentioned. Like Moses in the much earlier text, the Besht in the above passage had ascended on high and has received names and remedies.[24]

Moreover, it seems that this similarity is not the only one between the introduction to *Shimmushei Torah* and the Besht's epistle. The source of the phrase "your fountains will well outside" is a biblical verse, Proverbs 5:16, and may point to the dissemination of the Besht's teachings. But this metaphorical understanding does not exhaust the full meaning of the phrase. In a description of the Besht found in a writing of R. Yitzḥaq Aiziq Yehudah Safrin of Komarno, it is said that the wonders done by the Besht were not "heard from the days of the Tannaim . . . and a small word of his was a fountain of wisdom, a true principle for [the understanding of] all the writings of our master Yitzḥaq Luria . . . and he had comprehensions of the ascent of the soul, and ascent to the Pardes, the real comprehension of Rabbi Aqiva and his companions."[25] This comparison of the Besht with the Tannaim, either as wonder workers or as mystics, is relevant. The ascent to the Pardes is explicitly mentioned, and it seems that it was formative, at least as understood by the Rabbi of Komarno, for the understanding of the extraordinary figure of the Besht. Yet it also seems that the use of the phrase *ma'ayan ḥokhmah* is illuminating. This phrase, which is the title of several Kabbalistic books, is also the title of the introduction to *Sefer Shimmushei Torah,* where the divine names and the remedies are mentioned as revealed to Moses. Moreover, in a writing from the Heikhalot literature, the so-called Hebrew Enoch, this phrase also occurs, and there it stands for a mythical entity found in the supernal world.[26] Related phrases are found in a variety of rabbinic sources in the context of exceptional creativity.[27]

The occurrence of this phrase in the Besht's epistle, however, may point to an affinity with those texts in late antiquity where the ascent on high is important. What may be the significance of the Rabbi of Komarno's assumption that one "small word" of the Besht can become a clue to Lurianic Kabbalah? Again, this may be part of the exaggerated hagiography that surrounded the historical figure of the Besht. Yet the divine names may be a good candidate for a small word that is also a clue to Lurianic thought. The belief in the power of these remedies, apparently popular and sometimes more Kabbalistic magical recipes, and of the divine names thus constitutes nothing new in this period.

The Besht's recourse to these topics in his epistle can be seen from a double perspective. On the one hand, it is an unconscious attempt to enhance his reputation as a doctor, whose techniques were revealed to him from above, or at least recommended by the highest authority. On the other hand, the Besht resorted to an authoritative text, *Shimmushei Torah,* which mentions the techniques used by him as having been revealed to none other an authority than Moses. Therefore, the dissemination of the lore, or of the knowledge imparted to the Besht, will have an eschatological significance: people will be able to heal themselves and, according to another detail of the epistle, to perform ascents on high by means of the unifications, *yiḥudim,* as the Besht has done. It is the success in reproducing the attainment of the Besht that is tantamount to redemption. Thus, we should pay attention to the content of the eschaton as described here: it will consist in a change in nature, but this will be the human nature that will be healed, rather than a dramatic shift in history and objective nature. The healing of the body and the perfection of the soul by its ascent on high were presented here as the description of the eschaton. I would like to emphasize the personal aspects of the two forms of attainments: both the magical aspect and the mystical one are of such a nature that they should be better understood on the level of individual redemption rather than collective redemption. I am not aware of any mention of collective experiences triggered by the use of yiḥudim, nor of collective healings undertaken by the Besht. The eschaton as described here has an accumulative feature: the technologies for solving both corporeal and spiritual needs is available, and everyone is able to share them. Therefore, Dinur's emphasis on the historical, acute eschatology is not corroborated by this analysis. On the other hand, Scholem's attempt to get rid of the conspicuous eschatological content is also insufficient: the Messiah is indeed addressed by the Besht, and he actually offers a scheme for further developments, at long range. The above description of the Besht's message is important for another reason as well. Both the remedies and the divine names are anomian topics, namely forms of practices that are unrelated to the classical Jewish ritual. This tendency is reminiscent of Abulafia's mystical techniques, which are also anomian. This is the case even if we add to them the possibility that the yiḥudim may help someone to ascend on high.

There can be no doubt that the theme of the Besht's conversation with the Messiah returns to an ancient motif found in a text close to the Heikhalot literature and to a certain extent to the zoharic view of the Messiah.[28] Though this is a kind of nonhistorical, nonpolitical, and nongeographical eschatology, it is an eschatology nonetheless, which does not describe an abstract ideal program but is consonant with the main parameters of the Besht's religious activity. The spiritual experience of the ascension of the soul and the well-being of the body to be achieved, according to the epistle, by magical means could be attained by the very few already in the lifetime of the Besht. In general the messianic time is envisaged as a cumulative achievement of individuals, but hardly as the result of the advent or the activity of the redeemer. This view of messianism is reminiscent, at least phenomenologically, of that of Abraham Abulafia, who believed that the dissemination of his ecstatic Kabbalah, based on combinations of letters and divine names, would enable many others to reach a spiritual state tantamount to messianism. However, Abulafia's thought, deeply influenced by a more dualistic vision of man which marginalizes the ultimate role of the body in the redeemed state of being, does not present a program for redeeming the corporeal aspect of man. Moreover, the specific nature of the two topics found in this passage suggests that the ascent of the soul precedes the reception of the names and remedies. This sequence of topics is obvious in *Shimmushei Torah,* where Moses, after he ascended on high, was taught, in addition to the Torah, also divine names and remedies, *devar refu'ah.* Thus, spiritual attainment precedes the corporeal one.

Let us compare this analysis to a view quoted in the name of the Besht in the eighteenth century. R. Gedaliyah of Lunitz, a disciple of R. Jacob Joseph of Polonoy, wrote that "when mention of the exodus of Egypt provokes a certain impression in our soul,[29] in order to cause the spiritual redemption, then salvation will automatically follow, which is the corporeal redemption, as the Besht, may his memory be blessed, has said: that the quintessence of our prayer concerns the redemption that is incumbent to come, namely the individual redemption, which is the redemption of the soul, as it is written, 'Draw near to my soul and redeem it.' [Psalms 69:19]"[30] Thus, corporeal redemption is seen as an automatic consequence of the spiritual one, and it is the task of the Hasid to pray for the latter rather than the former. As in the passage from the epistle quoted above, mystical redemption is to be cultivated first. Since the two forms of redemption mentioned here parallel the two in the epistle, it appears that the very cultivation of the secrets revealed to the Besht constitutes a redemptive activity. Hasidism, namely the way to reach mystical experiences and the possibility of operating on the material level characteristic of the Besht and of later Hasidic masters, is immanently redemptive, and not imminently, as in what are conceived by scholars to be acute forms of messianism.

This conclusion should be compared to the mind-set in the passage from the Besht's epistle. When told by the Messiah that his advent depends on the dissemination of the Besht's thought, the Besht reacted with great sadness: "I was surprised by this [answer] and I was deeply sorrowful because of the length of the time when this will be possible." This reaction has been understood by Scholem as reflecting the Beshtian view of redemption: the Besht was in "great pain and sadness. For messianism has once more receded into the distant future."[31] So far Scholem seems to be right: this state of things could indeed create a "deeply melancholic" mood. However, this conclusion is based on one stage of the Besht's experience alone, and it should not be taken, as Scholem implies, as the final statement on messianism in the epistle. On the contrary, the "melancholy" was overcome quite easily, just a few sentences later, as the Besht tells his brother-in-law: "however, from what I have learned there, the three things which are remedies and three holy names, it is easy to learn and explain. Then my mind was calmed and I thought that it is possible for my contemporaries to attain this degree and aspect by these [practices] as I do, namely to be able to accomplish the ascents of souls and they will be able to study and become like me." I understand this statement, which seems to encapsulate the final message of the epistle, as reflecting a much more serene state of mind, even a certain self-confidence and optimism. By diffusing the relatively simple form of spiritual and magical activity, the Besht functions as a messianic figure. However, while the more accomplished masters operate on the two levels, spiritual and material, the regular Hasidim are supposed to do so only on the spiritual plane. In the terms I have proposed, the function and the message of the messianic figure are more important than his persona. The Besht can function messianically, even if he is not the ultimate personalization of the Messiah.

On the other hand, the fact that the Besht is describing his conversation with the Messiah cannot serve as a final proof of his not being the Messiah. After all, as we have seen in the case of Abulafia, this term may stand for the transpersonal and personal beings at the same time, and in fact a conversation between Abulafia and the transcendent redeemer, revealing himself as Yaho'el, was analyzed in chapter 2. Moreover, as in Abulafia's case, which will be discussed in appendix 1, so for the Besht, the Messiah is the teacher, who presumably imparted to the Besht the details of techniques to be disseminated. Thus, a certain continuum may be reconstructed between the transcendent Messiah who initiated the Besht in revelations, the Besht who is using them successfully, and the others who will become like the Besht. The Besht is therefore not only a disseminator of lore that will pave the way for the advent of the Messiah, but also the personal model that should inspire the behavior of others. From this point of view, the Beshtian story is much closer to Abulafian than to Lurianic or Sabbatean messianisms. If we remember that part of the techniques the Besht was expected to disseminate has to do with the linguistic devices concerning how to achieve ascents of the soul, then the affinity to Abulafia's teaching of mystical technique is even greater. In any case, my messianic reading of the epistle stands even if one does not accept an identification between the Besht and the Messiah. The Besht disseminates the crucial redemptive information, and thus his activity is to be understood, in his own terms, as messianic.

Finally, mention of the date, Rosh ha-Shanah, as well as of the technique of ascending on the pillar, may contribute to an eschatological understanding of the epistle. Abulafia's eagerness to meet with the pope on the eve of the Jewish New Year had to do with the idea that the Messiah would be revealed on that precise date. I do not claim that Abulafia's passage was known to the founder of Hasidism; neither is a plausible reason to assume that the Besht knew about Abraham Michael Cardoso's prophecy concerning the beginning of redemption at the New Year of 1674. However, the resemblance between the peculiar time of their enterprises is quite remarkable and may point to common sources. On the other hand, the resort to the motif of the ascent on the pillar to the Messiah is quite reminiscent of the famous zoharic description of the Messiah in the Garden of Eden, and of his occultation for a year in a pillar, as we learn from an important passage in Zohar (vol. 2, fol. 7b). Thus, two themes that define the time and location of the event described in the epistle recall sources dealing with messianic topics and thus strengthen a more eschatological significance of the epistle than that offered by Scholem.

A connection has been suggested between the Besht's epistle and the pogrom that took place shortly before the date of the "ascent." I see not problem in attempting to relate the social, economic, or political background to intellectual developments when such a approach is explicitly mentioned by the authors of the cultural creation, or when the content of the new writings cannot be explained on the ground of earlier traditions. Neither do I demand forensic proofs for such a nexus between cultural and paracultural processes.[32] However, in order to advance the plausibility of such a link, some affinity should be explicated beyond the mere statement that two phenomena are close in time. This form of what I have called proximism is a historicistic approach that I can hardly accept without additional facts to substantiate it.

The Besht and R. Menaḥem Naḥum of Chernobyl

The second important messianic passage ascribed to the Besht and discussed by scholars involved in the controversy is quoted by R. Menaḥem Naḥum of Chernobyl. One of the greatest masters of the second generation of Hasidism and a direct student of the Besht himself,[33] R. Menaḥem Naḥum offers an interesting vision of messianic activity:

> This unification [of speech and thought] is a secret of the construction of the stature of the Messiah as [explicated] in the dictum of the Besht, let his soul be in heavenly treasure: Each and every one of Israel has to repair and prepare the part of the stature of the Messiah which belongs to his soul, as known. Because 'ADaM is the acronym of Adam, David, Messiah. The stature of Adam has been from the beginning of the world to its end, as the souls of all the Israelites were comprised in him. Afterwards, his stature has been diminished by the sin. So also will the stature of the Messiah be complete, [formed] out of all the souls of Israel, which are seven hundred thousand, as before the sin of Adam. This is the reason why each and every one of Israel has to prepare that part which is the aspect of the Messiah that belongs to his soul until the entire stature is restored and rebuilt and a complete and everlasting unification[34] is achieved, may it be fast in our time.[35]

This passage has attracted the attention of both parties in the polemic surrounding the existence of messianic proclivities in early Hasidism. Tishby claimed that it is to be understood in rather acute messianic terms, while Scholem opted for a soft, utopian understanding. Another quotation from the same book affords a telling comparision and may help us to understand the Besht's passage by clarifying the background of that passage in a two ways. I assume that R. Menaḥem Naḥum would interpret the Besht's view against a spiritual background that informed the Besht but is not explicit in the short passage. However, even if someone were to argue the contrary, and there were no larger speculative background for the Besht's passage, still that passage was preserved solely in R. Menaḥem Naḥum's book and is available only embedded in his formulation of Hasidic eschatology. Therefore, even if the later Hasidic master, who was in direct contact with the Besht, did not offer a faithful understanding of the passage, still it is accessible only in the conceptual context as formulated, or as "created," by that author. At least it must be admitted that reception of the Besht's view has been mediated by the spiritual parameters that I shall discuss below.

Using a commonplace in Hasidic and some forms of Kabbalistic literature, the description of the righteous as a channel, pipe, or path for the transmission of the divine power on low,[36] R. Menaḥem Naḥum claims that without this mediation between the divine realm and the lower universe everything would return to primordial chaos.[37] This vitality or nourishing influx is the force that maintains the existence of the world, and when functioning as a conduit of supernal energy the righteous one serves as a cosmic factor. According to this passage, in the ancient times one righteous person alone sufficed to ensure the maintenance of the natural order, as the examples of Adam, Seth, Enoch, Noah, and the patriarchs demonstrate. With time, however, the paramount understanding and spiritual force of the righteous have diminished, and several righteous have to perform now, collectively, the same function, namely to draw down the vitality and influx. At the time of the Sinaitic revelation, the presence and activity of all the people of Israel were needed for the this purpose. They had to attain the status of Adam, the perfect creature of God, by their common enterprise. Capitalizing on a theme that has been already discussed above (chapters 5 and 6) concerning the comprehensive nature of the structure of the primordial man, R. Menaḥem Naḥum regards all the nation of Israel as one unit which corresponds to that of Adam's initial stature. This will be the case, according to the Hasidic master, with the advent of the Messiah: the primordial spiritual stature will be again complete, because the Messiah will possess the soul of Adam before the fall and at the same time the totality of the souls of the people of Israel.[38] Then, this master writes:

> the quintessence of our worship is to restore [*le-taqqen*] and finalize the part of the Messiah that corresponds to each and every one of us . . . and when the enterprise of the tiqqun of the complete stature is accomplished, he will be the righteous one, the foundation of the world, in a perfect manner, a great and unencumbered pipe [prepared to] receive the influx and vitality. This is the reason why the advent of our Messiah will cause the multiplication of goodness and knowledge in the world. This is because he will be the universal righteous one in a perfect manner, as he is called the "Messiah of our righteousness" [*mashiyaḥ tzideqenu*] who is [both] the great righteous one and the great pipe by means of which he transmits the influx for all the goodness. However, now, this is not the case, because of the sin of the [golden] calf, when the people of Israel have returned to their impurity . . . and there is no universal righteous one and hence each and every individual of Israel should be in the category of "righteous" in order to sustain the world in a perfect manner. Insofar as the number of the righteous will diminish, the influx in this world will diminish also . . . because when all [the people of Israel] are in the category of "righteous" and are a pipe for this world, namely serving as a path for the existence of the world, they will inherit the land.[39]

The entire discussion is based upon a decisive ambiguity: the universal or collective righteous, which is also the Messiah, can be conceived of both as an individual and as a corporate entity, the whole community of the souls of the people of Israel. As individuals, each member of the array of the righteous, starting with Adam, comprises in his stature the people of all the forthcoming individuals of the Israelite nation. Thus, these individual righteous ones are viewed as both individual and collective beings. In both cases, their task is identical: to constitute a median structure, designated explicitly by the Hebrew term *memutza'*,[40] between the divine supernal power and the lower world. The righteous' serving as a channel epitomizes their special status. In this case, it is obvious that the function is much more important than the individual persona, and perhaps even more than the collective edifice constituted by the different persona. The message, the maintenance of the world, is a nonverbal one, but it is part of the active description of sustaining existence. In fact, the messianic era is not a new, utopian state of being: it re-creates the paradisical moment, the Sinaitic situation, as well as the function fulfilled by several exceptional individuals in the "historical" interregnum. If the essence of this understanding of messianism is the role of a perfect mediation of the divine influx, there seems to be no difference between the great individuals, such as Noah, and the Messiah, both as an individual figure and as a collective, constructed structure. To resort to Scholem's view of messianism, utopian as this communal construction may be for the self-awareness of the specific individuals in the enterprise—as they actualized their eschatological potential for the first time—this is nevertheless quite a restorative project. As a collective figure, the Messiah does not redeem the Jewish people or community but rather represents a unified and spiritualized version of a collective of Jews, namely a situation where perfection has already been attained by a collective and cumulative effort. Unlike the Lurianic Kabbalah, which envisioned an other-worldly redemption as the collective achievement of the purified souls when returned to their source, Hasidic Kabbalah speaks much more about a present redemption that may be consummated here below.

In other words, individual perfection is the main avenue by which a person may contribute to the emergence of communal and cosmic forms of redemption. As such, it seems that the salvific role of the Messiah as a person, in the vein of the apocalyptic intervention of a persona in the course of history, is secondary, or at least derivative. It is interesting to note that in one case, the Messiah is presented straightforwardly as the reparation of primordial man: *tiqqun 'adam ha-rishon.*[41] This vision of the Messiah is quite reminiscent of the Christian and Sabbatean understandings of the aim of the Messiah as repairing the depravation, or *privatio,* of human nature that had been caused by Adam. Let me describe the above Hasidic passages from another point of view. In the case of the communal service that creates the stature of the Messiah, the ancient royal ideology surfaces unexpectedly as the perfect community, becoming the channel for the transmission of the divine power by its becoming the stature of the Messiah. Thus, the ritual and the myth are reunited.

What are the possible implications of this second text for understanding the quotation from R. Menaḥem Naḥum of Chernobyl attributed to the Besht? That text has been interpreted by Scholem as an attenuation of Lurianic messianism. Against Tishby's more acute reading of the views of R. Menaḥem Naḥum, Scholem sees a spiritualization of the Lurianic version of messianism.[42] However, his proposal to view this Hasidic author as preaching the perfection of the soul alone, because messianism is for the time being an utopian enterprise, is open to debate. Indeed, souls are mentioned explicitly in both texts; spiritual as these souls may be, however, they are supposed in both cases to become part of a construction, a stature, *qomah,* which according to the second passage mediates between heaven and earth and also transmits the supernal power. This is a much more active task than a mere aspiration, a preparation in passive expectation for the final eschatological revolution. By attaining one's own perfection, each person is able in the present to play the role he is destined to play in the final drama of redemption by becoming, according to R. Menaḥem Naḥum, a channel for the divine influx. Personal perfection as the main tool for the collective eschatological effort has some remarkable implications. Eschatology is not the unconditional self-negation of the individual for the sake of a larger goal, a self-denial of the revolutionary who is ready to deprive himself of the pleasure of well-being for the benefit of the next generations. On the contrary, the self-fulfillment of a particular individual is tantamount to his attaining the maximum in his personal life and playing the destined role in the "public" arena. Implied in this convergence of personal and collective eschatology is the correspondence between private time, the fulfillment of personal perfection and redemption, and historical and collective time, which emerges from the cumulative *cairos* of the personal times.[43]

Yet despite the supposition that it is the task of each and every Jew to participate in the gradually enfolding eschatological drama, there are persons who are particularly well suited for this role, namely the *tzaddiqim.* Naturally, they are the more cohesive part of the Jewish nature, because of their more adhesive mystical achievements, which bring them into the daily contact not only with their folk but also with God. Indeed, their cohesive, connective, and also universal nation, in comparison to that of the ordinary Jew, is reflected in the view of the righteous as symbolized by the word *kol,* "all," which also reflects the Kabbalistic symbolism of the righteous as the sefirah of Yesod, which unites the masculine and feminine within the divine infrastructure.[44]

The enactment in the present of the messianic role of the individual should be understood, however, as much more concrete. By one's personal perfection, one may not only serve as a passive pipe but be much more actively involved in the transmission of the influx. This author mentions, in the same context, those persons who cause the descent of the vitality, *moridei ha-ḥiyyut,* who are none other than the righteous.[45] This phrase reflects the influence of a very important sort of magic, prevalent in medieval Arabic and Jewish writings and in the writings of several fifteenth- and sixteenth-century Kabbalists, who envisioned the main magical activity as the drawing down of the astral or sefirotic and, ultimately, divine power—the vitality mentioned in the text—on the lower worlds. This view constitutes the core of what I propose to see as one of the most influential models of thought and action in Jewish mysticism, and is of crucial importance for Hasidic literature.[46]

Messianism, in its collective form is therefore envisaged as a cumulative project, which differs markedly from the possible attainment of the individual in terms of quantity, but hardly at all in terms of quality. There is, moreover, not merely a spiritual improvement involved here but also a more magical success conceived to be the quintessential aspect of worship.[47] In this enterprise both the spiritual and the corporeal aspects of personality are involved, as shown by the description of man, 'Adam, as composed of the letter *'aleph,* the soul which belongs to the supernal realm, and *DaM,* the animal soul embedded in the blood (*dam*).[48] Thus, the second passage promotes a less singularly spiritual, and also less totally utopian, view of the messianic activity. Indeed, in another text dealing with the achievement of perfection, this author explicitly speaks of joining the purified corporeal to the spiritual.[49] Everyone can become, by perfect worship, a partial Messiah or a Messiah of his part just now, and in the future his act will be integrated into the more universal activity.

Is such an activist reading of the Beshtian passage, which combines both spirit and body, accurate? Is Scholem's spiritual and utopian understanding more appropriate than that of R. Menaḥem Naḥum, a direct student of the Besht? In principle this may be the case; however, the way the first quotation is introduced points to the more integrative understanding: the unification mentioned by R. Menaḥem Naḥum is not that of the different parts of the stature, namely the souls of Israel, into an even greater, preexisting metaphysical unit or structure, the Lurianic *'adam qadmon* as Scholem assumes, but quite ostensibly the unification of human speech and thought. A cooperation between speech, representing the more corporeal aspect of man, and thought, which stands for his more spiritual part, therefore reflects a more integrative approach to personality and also points to a more inclusive understanding of the nature of redemption.

In any case, R. Menaḥem Naḥum probably gave expression to a view, stemming from the Besht himself, who was reported by his grandson, R. Moses Ḥayyim 'Efrayyim of Sudylkov, to have confessed that he did not possess enough "power of speech" to bring the Messiah. Although the succinct testimony of the grandson does not allow a definitive understanding of the Besht's intention, I nevertheless would take the risk of asserting that the Besht's admission bears the mark of talismanic magic, more specifically as mentioned by R. Ya'aqov Ḥayyim Tzemaḥ. According to some of the Hasidic talismanic views, the louder someone prays, the greater the spirituality he draws down.[50] However, the more magical reading of the Besht passage does not depend only on the way it has been introduced by R. Menaḥem Naḥum; it is corroborated by the way we have understood the other passage about the Besht and the Messiah as involving magical acts in the context of messianic activity. As Scholem has mentioned, the passage in the name of the Besht—and we may add the second quotation—"makes use of the traditional Lurianic formulation."[51] On this point he agrees with Tishby, though he relegates the fulfillment of the messianic aspiration to an indefinite future. There can be no doubt that both these scholars are to a certain extent correct: the Lurianic formulation indeed looms large in these Hasidic passages. However, what is the Hasidic view represented by the formulation here in a more specific manner? Both scholars presuppose a view similar, or perhaps even identical, to Lurianic views. But if our reading of the second text, penned by R. Menaḥem Naḥum, is accurate, and its implications for understanding the Beshtian text are well taken, then the Hasidic masters have offered a forced interpretation of the Lurianic formula.

The theurgical operation, namely unifying powers that constitute the perfect divine stature, is indeed implicit here. However, the emphasis is much less on what happens on high than on what is done below. The perfect unification stands first and foremost for a synthesis between two or more human acts, not between a plurality of divine powers. In Lurianic Kabbalah, the mystical repair affects the supernal anthropos, the divine man, who is essentially an emanation within the divine realm that has been affected both by a fault in the creative process and by human sins. *'Adam 'eliyon* is an entity that is part and parcel of the theogonic process, and in the Lurianic sources the theurgical effort is focused upon the attempt to restore the pristine completion of the divine structure. However, that is only rarely the case in the Hasidic texts quoted above. The Adam that is mentioned in those passages should not, in my opinion, be identified with the Lurianic anthropos but with the mythical primordial Adam of the midrashic and talmudic literatures. While the latter is part of the divine process of autogenesis, in those Hasidic sources under consideration here Adam stands for the corporate souls of the Israelites, an hypostatic entity that mediates between high and low, but it represents preeminently the lower rather than the higher realm. It is more a matter of a collective mystical or mythical anthropology, already well known from several rabbinic discussions, rather than an appropriation of Lurianic terminology. The manner in which this Adam functions, more than his origin, significantly distinguishes this idea from the concepts informing Lurianic Kabbalah and Sabbateanism. There the supernal anthropos is a divine entity, emerging from the infinity and involved in the drama of intradivine creation; consequently the break within his structure is the main impetus behind the whole religious outlook in Lurianic Kabbalah. The messianic enterprise, in this sort of Kabbalah, includes the extraction of the sparks from the coarse matter and their return to the higher structure; in other words, a dispersed divinity is reunified by the Kabbalistic tiqqun. This is a theocentric vision par excellence. In the Hasidic texts, however, the restoration of the pristine unity is followed by the act of mediation, which means turning to look to human needs, individual and communal, and providing for a perfect natural course. It is a more concrete outlook, not only because it is much more anthropocentric and much less theocentric than in Lurianism, but also because the discussions above are more concerned with an integrated vision of human personality. The human body, not the soul alone, is part of the collective *qomah* of Israel and is involved in the messianic enterprise. The concept of the pipe, or channel, should therefore be understood immanent in the above quotations: the stature is a pipeline for the divine power, and the righteous is supposed to pump the divine energy onto himself, or into the pipe, in order to distribute it here below. In other words, the Messiah is the collective community of righteous, a more comprehensive and superior version of the ordinary leader of the Hasidic group, the tzaddiq.

The Jewish masses commonly regard the Messiah in terms of power, which is instrumental in revenge over enemies. What is characteristic for Abulafia's Kabbalah is the view the Messiah reflects the embodiment of the spiritual axiology of the Neoaristotelian medieval philosophies, the individual and the separate intellects. For the Hasidic masters the Messiah is but the culmination of their ideal of leadership, which includes both the mystical attainment and the subsequent magical activity. Hence we read in a collection of teachings of the Great Maggid of Medziericz that "the faith of the tzaddiq is his ascent upwards and his causing the descent of the influx like a pipe."[52] The faith of the righteous, *'emunato,* has been understood in some Hasidic writings as a means for drawing down the influx. This is the case in one of R. Yitzḥaq of Radvil's quotations in the name of his father, R. Yeḥiel Mikhal of Zlotchov,[53] as well as in another text of R. Dov Baer of Medzierecz[54] and in R. Menaḥem Naḥum of Chernobyl's *Me'or 'Einayyim.*[55] The two moves presented here, the upward one in order to cleave to God and the descent in the context of bringing down the influx, are parallel to the integration of the righteous in the collective Messiah and subsequently to serve as conduits of the divine vitality. This double move is reminiscent of the Beshtian text analyzed above, where the founder of Hasidism ascended to the high world in order to bring down magical instructions. Hence one major component of the way the Besht has imagined messianism is as the active improvement of the plight of the people here below by means of magical activities which include, inter alia, the drawing down of the divine power for the benefit of the community. Far from being an eminently utopian concept, Beshtian messianism should be understood within the more general framework of his and some of the other masters' practical dedication to and care for the spiritual life and well-being of their communities. There were mystics who displayed genuine concern for their communities and as such were involved in the practice of magic for the benefit of their adherents. This is quite a different type of messianism than the Abulafian one, the Lurianic one, or the popular ones.

I do not doubt Scholem's and Tishby's tracing the sources of some of the formulations of the above Hasidic texts to Lurianic views. However, the Hasidic emphasis upon building or rebuilding the stature of the primordial Adam can be understood only to a certain extent—provided the precise and explicit Midrashic sources quoted by R. Menaḥem Naḥum—as a magical interpretation of the Lurianic divine anthropos. It is Lurianic insofar as the rabbinic views on the primordial terrestrial man have been reinterpreted as dealing with a multiplicity of parts, which have been dispersed as the result of his sin. It is magical insofar as it builds up a superconductive perfect structure that serves not only as a perfect pipe but also as a pump, as the phrases depicting the causing of the descent of the vitality show. I therefore propose to see in the differences between the Lurianic and the Hasidic understanding of Adam the result of two different moves: one backward, to the more rabbinic understanding of Adam, neutralizing the strong Lurianic theosophical understanding of this concept; the other, the other forward, toward a new meaning of the acts involved in restoring the lost unity. In fact, we find not only two different concepts of Adam in those kinds of Jewish mysticism but also two different conceptualizations of messianism, informed by two divergent models, a theosophical-theurgical one, in the case of Lurianic Kabbalah, and a magical one, in the case of Hasidism. The latter model serves as a powerful hermeneutical grid and was instrumental in the strong reshaping of the elements found in the first one. Thus Lurianism was significantly transformed by Hasidism.

The impetus for such a shift is not an unexplained innovative surge in Hasidism but the adoption of a magical model found in Cordoverian Kabbalah and in Kabbalistic ethical and exegetical literatures influenced by it, and in Luzzatto's Kabbalah, already active on the public scene for two centuries before the emergence of Hasidism.[56] Continuing, sometimes rhetorically, the terminology of Lurianic Kabbalah, the nascent Hasidism in many cases adopted non-Lurianic conceptual schemes that are the key to a proper understanding of the shifts that Lurianic concepts have undergone in Hasidic literature.[57] Thus, the controversy between Scholem and Tishby as to the impact of Lurianism in matters of messianism, dealing with the question of whether Hasidic eschatology should be understood in terms of Lurianic messianism, is beside the point. I would propose to discuss it rather along the lines of interactions between different models and not only in terms of the continuation or neutralization of one single model, the Lurianic one. One of the models involved in shaping the Hasidic spiritual physiognomy in general, and in our case some aspects of its eschatology as well, is the magical model. This model has escaped the attention of modern scholars, and its neglect is at least partially responsible for some scholarly misunderstandings of Hasidic texts.[58]

Let me return to the meaning of the unification as presented in the second passage of R. Menaḥem Naḥum. As mentioned above, the main significance of the term *yiḥud* is the union between speech and thought, rather than a unification of transcendental divine powers. To be sure, a theurgical unification of divine powers still recurs in the writings of this Hasidic author, but I am concerned here with the way he would like us to understand his messianic views. Thus, in the context of his discussion of messianism adduced above, *yiḥud* apparently stands for the healing of a break on the level of human personality, of a split between the various spiritual and corporeal functions, which should be healed by the concentrated effort of the Hasidic mystic. What could be the messianic value of such an anthropological union? The "perfect union" or unification, *yiḥud shalem,* is related by R. Menaḥem Naḥum to Torah and tefillah, whose counterparts are, respectively, thought and speech.[59]

In order to achieve this unification, which has messianic overtones, someone must have the urge to unify them. The Hasidic master calls this impetus Elijah, whose coming precedes the advent of the Messiah.[60] The intentionality that causes the consonance between speech and thought, between act and intention, is the messenger of the Messiah. His urging man to act simultaneously on these two levels is instrumental in the achievement of such a resonance, which is understood as a Messianic achievement, *beḥinat mashiyaḥ,* namely the personal aspect of Messiah. This messianic attainment can be reached daily, through prayer and study. However, while according to the Hasidic author this is nowadays a rather intermittent attainment, with the advent of the Messiah the unification of speech and thought will be permanent. We can easily perceive the integrative aspect of this conception; it is not only the divestment of corporeality which inspires the messianic attainment but also the synchronization between the spiritual and the corporeal. By acting in a harmonious manner, someone is preparing himself to integrate his attainment in the larger Adamic stature which is, at the same time, a collective of souls.[61] A conspicuous part of a move toward the eschaton, this integration is presented also as reconstructing the primordial unit destroyed by Adam's sin.

This reconstruction is a move in historical time, which seeks to recuperate the wholeness of the original completion. However, this completion is attainable not only at the end of time, with the purification of the last of the souls of the children of Israel, but also in moments of ritualistic reenactment of the situation of the paradisical perfection. To resort to a formulation of Agamben, the messianic moment is "a moment of authentic decision." In addition to the historical "progress," the linear accumulation of individual acts of perfection, there are also cyclical moments of collective restitution of the broken Adamic structure. For example, we read in R. Menaḥem Naḥum's book that every Sabbath, during the recitation of the collective response to the eighteen benedictions of the Mussaf, the prayer that starts with the word *keter,* "all the souls of Israel, even those found on a lower rank, ascend [on high] if they are linking themselves to the righteous and integrating themselves with them; then they ascend with the righteous upwards, because then the righteous, together with the holy parts in the souls of the Israelites, are approaching the high, just as in the [moment of the] act of creation, before the sin, when the souls were integrated on the highest rank, into Adam, as it is written,[62] 'Adam was extending from the beginning of the world to its end.' "[63] The integration of simpler Jews with the righteous seems to be but one version of the more comprehensive view of the soul of Adam as comprising all the souls. The tzaddiq was conceived as having his own statute, souls and sparks that belong to him and which he is destined to save.[64] Thus, we may assume that when all the righteous accomplish their task, this will mean the redemption of all the souls. Just as in the case of the messianic passage quoted above, so too in this context the descent of holiness and blessing on the lower world is mentioned as the result of the prior elevation of the souls.[65] What seems to be most interesting here, however, is the fact that the messianic ideal of total integration has been expressed outwardly in terms of ritual acts performed in public and attended by the whole community. The Mussaf is recited by the entire congregation, as a unison response to the cantor's recitation of the prayer of the eighteen benedictions, and is, in its initial forms, an attempt to imitate the angelic unison chorus on high.[66] This integration of the whole community in precisely this moment, and the assumption that a certain spiritual elevation is therefore supposed to take place, is warranted by much earlier sources. As part of this prayer, and in imitation of angelic acts, the person who prays is supposed to raise himself on his toes three times. The Hasidic interpretation of the collective aspect of this part of the prayer shows how an ordinary ritual can be understood as fraught with a messianic cargo. The righteous are described here as instrumental in the rebuilding of the presently fragmented existence and as re-creating the perfect Adam, together with all the people of Israel. Eschatology is not mentioned here explicitly; however, in a parallel to this passage, the reintegration of all the souls of Israel is strongly portrayed in messianic terms.[67]

Moreover, the affinity between this description and the other ones quoted above seems unmistakable. Another common denominator links the two discussions of re-creating the lost unity of Adam: both in the eschatological and in the retrieval scheme, it is the speech act, the prayer, that is instrumental, or at least constitutes the background, for the *restitutio ad integrum.* Let me therefore return to examine the way the Besht's quotation has been introduced by his disciple. Speech and thought are described as deeply related "semantically" to the term *mashiyaḥ.* In an impressive interpretive tour de force, R. Menaḥem Naḥum the term as pointing to *m[e]siaḥ,* a verb that can be understood intransitive, "to speak," as well as transitively, *masiaḥ,* "to cause to speak."[68] While the first meaning stands for the regular vocal activity, the second is very rare and is understood as the causative effect of thought: it affects man so that he speaks. Therefore, according to this master, "every time there is a unification of thought and speech, this is the restoration of the aspect of the Messiah, but it is not permanent."[69] Again, the search for harmony is extracted, now by means of a pseudo-semantic exploration: *mashiyaḥ* is the ideal state of a total consonance between the inner and the outer activity. Is this the meaning of righteousness? This is not explicated in the texts I am acquainted with. In another passage, however, this author mentions unification of speech and thought, again in the context of acts related to Torah and prayer: "the speech should be cleaving to thought, to the heart and to the brain, so that the unification will be with all the feeling of his limbs[70] and [moral] attributes, then a perfect union will be achieved in all the worlds, even on high."[71] The mentioning of the limbs, even though the reference is to the feeling related to them, emphasizes the corporeal component of the experience that is depicted as an "aspect of the Messiah." This more integrative approach, which does not suppress the corporeal in toto, is connected with the more magical aspect of the event, more precisely with the view of the mystic as a pipe for divine power. As seen above, there is a certain affinity between the way the individual messianic figure works and that of the Hasidic righteous: in both cases, some more physical elements should be added to the more spiritual aspects of messianism. This concreteness, which is also related to the immediateness of the personal experience, is phenomenologically reminiscent of Abulafia's claim that the feeling of the anointment is part of the messianic experience.

However, the main explanation for the great importance of the unification is a rather ecstatic one. According to Menaḥem Naḥum, Elijah, the urge that incites the desire to synchronize and unify speech and thought, does not merely coordinate two human acts but also invites an intense devotion related to the recitation of the prayer and the study of the Torah, so that the devotee will cleave to the divine in such a way that he may die.[72] If "Elijah" stands for the urge to enthusiastically undertake verbal activities, the intensity of the performance, which is believed to bring about the adherence of the soul to the words, a commonplace in Hasidic mysticism, is representative of the aspect of the messianic state. Thus, the messianic event implies a coordination of speech, thought, and emotion that may be so intense that it will work as a mystical technique to reach an extreme experience that may be lethal. In other words, complete devotion while uttering the words of prayer or while studying the Torah, synchronized with intellectual activity, bring about an experience that is messianic. This is an event which indeed resembles an ecstatic experience, unitive on the anthropological level, which may be conceived as preceding and inducing the universal messianic experience, which is unitive on the collective level. This event may take place on a daily base: "It is certain that in every appropriate prayer, which includes the unification of thought and speech, the restoration is made, which is 'an aspect of the Mashiyaḥ.' "[73]

This daily though ecstatic moment, which according to the above sources prepares the individual for the accumulative collective messianism, is to be combined with the magical accomplishment of becoming a pure channel for the divine power, which pours down for the benefit of the others. In a lengthy discussion in *Me'or 'Einayyim,* the author envisions the messianic era as a presence of the divine light, achieved by the perfect study of the Torah, which is able to remove the impurity and polish the soul. This intensive study, which brings about freedom from death because of the mystical union with the divine light, can also be attained in the here and now:

> whoever accepts the yoke of the Torah, the Torah will remove [from him] the impurity of the serpent because of his occupation with the Torah of the Lord and with the holy letters, which are the palace of the Lord.[74] And so he will be able to be united with Him, Blessed be He, and all the wrongdoers will be removed [from him] and no impurity and dirt will cling to him. This is why he is freed from the yokes of the [secular] dominion and of politeness, and of the subjugation to the [vicissitudes of] exile . . . and he will remove the serpent from himself and by them [namely by Torah and its letter] he merits [to witness] the advent of our Messiah.[75]

Just as in the case of prayer, so too the Torah can undo the exile, an impure condition, and liberate the mystic from the vicissitudes of this world, bringing him into direct contact with the divine which is found within the letters of the texts he studies. Those letters, considered to be the palace of the divine spirituality, constitute the locus of the encounter between the human and the divine. Though in this case the messianic experience is not expressed explicitly, I take this passage as pointing to the same stand as in the case of the prayer. It is in quotidian ritual, in everyday activities, that the devotion of the mystic can break the yoke of exile or impurity and actualize an experience of redemption. When the Jewish ritual is cultivated spiritually, the anticipation of the messianic time is available; as in the case of the interpretation of the Sabbath prayer, which has been understood as bringing the participants back to the paradisical situation, here too the snake's impurity is transcended by study, which will project the individual back to the paradisical moments.

The inducing of the messianic repair by means of ordinary ritual activity, when performed with great intensity, obviously calls into question Scholem's vision of the effect of messianism, that "in Judaism the messianic idea has compelled a life lived in deferment in which nothing can be done definitively."[76] His view that the intensity of religious life brought about by Hasidism was attained at the high price of abdicating "in the realm of messianism"[77] seems to be contradicted by our analyses of Hasidism, just as it is not supported by Abulafia's life and thought. Scholem would indeed be right if the only criterion for judging the studied texts were his own, quite modern one, namely a quasi-Zionist criterion which assumes that messianism should be understood as verifiable only in the historical realm and as involving political acts that will bring the Diaspora Jews back to the land of Israel. However, a proper understanding of the sources should allow them to present their ideals before they are submitted to criticism according to criteria different from their own. The manner in which I would propose to understand the above texts may suggest that as an individual, someone can complete his part in the messianic enterprise and enjoy an extreme experience, designated by the phrase "an aspect of the Messiah," without the need to defer the highest accomplishment to a utopian future. Their part in the messianic project can be accomplished and experienced on a daily basis, if the Hasidic reform of the religious life, the devotional and enthusiastic performance, is implemented. Or, to put it in terms of the Besht's epistle, if the teachings of the Besht are spread, the Messiah will come.

Is this a deferment of actual religious life for a distant utopian future, as Scholem would contend? Is this a less intense, less authentic and less vibrant messianic experience than the frantic adherence of Sabbateans to the belief in the messianic role of Sabbatai Tzevi? The answer may be positive, as Scholem would prefer, only if the apocalyptic and historical forms of messianism are thought to be the only genuine forms of messianism. Even if messianism is understood as a broader cluster of phenomena consisting of more than one model, as I have proposed, the question still remains: is this type of messianism an active, powerful, acute experience that informs the Hasidic masters and those who would adopt the Hasidic ideals of religious life, or is it a mere belief in a future attainment, from which individuals are virtually prevented before the advent of the Messiah? The implicit answer of the Scholemian school, including Tishby, would be negative: "real" messianism, and the acuteness of the belief in the apocalyptic type of redemption, is characteristic of those who subscribed to the Lurianic-Sabbatean faith alone, or of what I would designate as the theosophical-theurgical model. From this point of view there was no disagreement between Scholem and Tishby, because both of them believed in the the centrality of the apocalyptic mode in the Lurianic-Sabbatean forms of thought, though these scholars were divided on the presence of this kind of messianism in Hasidism. On the basis of the passages adduced above from just one Hasidic book, it seems that the concern with messianic topics in one of the major early Hasidic figures is quite impressive. It is not, however, the number of quotes that accounts for the intensity of the experience as envisioned and recommended by the Hasidic master, but the responsibility for furthering the messianic advent on the personal level, as well as its immediate availability. It is not faith or hope that is crucial here, but the mode of experiencing the quotidian religious behavior. While for a Sabbatean responsibility for the eschatological effort lies in the Messiah, while the believers are merely bystanders participating by their faith, in Hasidism it is mainly the religious act, in which all can participate, that counts. Messianic hopes do not hasten the messianic era if they do not actively transform the personal religious life.

Thus, I see in the Hasidic discussions of messianism a clear case of intensification of the religious praxis on the existential level, much more so than the faithful Sabbatean is required to perform in his passive participatory belief in Tzevi's messianism. By accepting the religious life within the parameters described by R. Menaḥem Naḥum, who espouses a view that is at least partially representative of the Besht's vision, one is required to intensify his religious efforts by taking personal responsibility for his actual rôle in the messianic drama. This is another model that is reminiscent of the ecstatic Kabbalah. At least insofar as phenomenological resemblances are involved, the nexus between ecstatic experience and messianism—as well as between manipulation of language and experience—is reminiscent of the ecstatic Kabbalah as analyzed above (chapter 2).[78] Unlike the Sabbatean approach, where the extraordinary, even enigmatic nature of the details related to the persona of the Messiah is to be reflected in the faith of the believer, in Hasidism it is more the intensification of the regular religious life of the tzaddiq, whether of a mystical or a magical character, that affected the search for perfection.

Spiritual Redemption in Hasidism

A composition written in the circle of the Great Maggid, R. Dov Baer of Medzierecz, gives a Hasidic interpretation of certain concepts fundamental to mystical thought: "Stripping away the corporeality is [tantamount to] the redemption [*ge'ullah*][79] of the soul of man, to his spirit, and his higher soul [*neshamah*],[80] who are all redeemed from the corporeality of the body . . . and they cling to the Creator, blessed be He, who is infinite."[81] This passage does not concern itself with a historical redemption or a geographical uprooting to the land of Israel. Rather, it discusses an inner process of suppressing and neutralizing the influence of the bodily instincts on human consciousness. This phenomenon reaches its climax with the communion, or union, with God or the 'Ein-Sof; therefore we can conclude that it represents to a pronounced spiritualization of the redemption. Numerous other examples can be found in the writings of R. Jacob Joseph of Polonoye, the other most important student of the Besht. Jacob Joseph often quotes traditions in the name of his master concerning the soul's redemption as an emphatically spiritual phenomenon.[82] The writings of Jacob Joseph several times sustain this mode of interpretation for Psalms 69:19: "Draw near to my soul and redeem it," a verse that illustrates, according to the Besht, the redemption of the soul.[83] He thus offers a spiritualistic reading: "The exile of the soul is the Evil Inclination, as I have heard from my master [the Besht] from the verse 'draw near to my soul and redeem it,' from its exile is the Evil Inclination."[84] Redemption is understood as the going forth from the inner exile, the exile that is in fact the Evil Inclination, in other words materiality or physicality. As Scholem has cogently remarked, this exodus or redemption is not *from* exile but *in* exile.[85] He is indeed correct if the sole plausible way of understanding exile were geographical and historical. This common understanding is, however, not the only possible one, nor is it the most plausible. The exile of the soul can be held to be as significant for a mystic as the historical exile is. If so, for the Hasidic master, exile may well mean the state of the soul while someone is an inhabitant of the land of Israel, as an ecstatic Kabbalist would contend.[86] It is only Scholem's preference for the objective significance over the mystical sense of a word that allows him to presuppose that when evading history and geography, one evades "authentic" messianism. Implicitly, his assumption is forged by the sources he has adopted as authentic: in order to be real, a phenomenon should be objectively verifiable. The Hasidic master indeed moves from one kind of understanding of the traditional terms to another, which should be conceived by scholars to be as concrete for the mystic as the plain sense of these terms. Is the Hasidic master's destruction of the exile by spiritualization, mentioned by

Scholem,[87] less concrete and less messianic than that of the Sabbatean Messiah? We can discern in the Hasidic texts the transfer of a concept of general redemption to the sphere of individual redemption, which is very similar to the spiritual understanding of messianism portrayed in ecstatic Kabbalah. Indeed, what is characteristic of Hasidic spirituality is the emphasis upon the redemption of the individual, which cumulatively means a more eschatological event.

Individual Redemption in Hasidism

The trend of spiritual messianism was no doubt central to the worldview of the Besht and his followers. Modern scholars have attempted to explain the emergence of what they believed to be a novel understanding of messianism. Gershom Scholem argued that due to the disastrous results of the historical messianism of the Sabbatian movement, which were already clear by the eighteenth century, the early teachers of Hasidism could not permit themselves to stress historical messianic elements, and certainly not any acute messianic elements that were integral to Lurianism and Sabbateanism. Scholem formulated his theory of a neutralization of the external modes of redemption, whereas in fact a perception that focused on the redemption of the individual was adopted by Hasidism.[88] This interpretation carries with it some difficulties. First and foremost, it arises from the belief that we are confronted in Hasidism with a completely novel conception within the history of the messianic idea, and that to fully understand and accept this new approach we need a distinctive explanation. Here is Scholem's opinion: "The question of private or individual redemption is a totally modern dilemma and does not exist in the Jewish tradition before 1750. If it does exist afterwards, it is still a debatable issue."[89] Apparently, the novelty of the notion of individual redemption was so compelling to scholars that they felt no need to check further for the existence of a possible previous mystical model of spiritual redemption. Just such a model, however, has been presented in chapter 2 on the basis of Abraham Abulafia's writings. Consequently, there is no need to resort to the extreme measure of positing a process of neutralization to account for the reaction to the Sabbatean upheaval created by the Lurianic mythical messianism. It would be more plausible to consider whether the appearance of a Hasidic spiritualistic interpretation of redemption is related to views that were already in existence within the Jewish mystical tradition. Such a tradition consisted of the works of Abulafia as well as other Jewish thinkers of the thirteenth and fourteenth centuries, some already in print by the sixteenth century. Hence it is not necessary to view a process of neutralization of messianism as playing a central role in the formation of the spiritualistic conception of redemption in Hasidism. It may even be possible to describe the special emphasis placed on the doctrine of individual redemption in Hasidic thought as a result of the resurgence of a peripheral trend, which had been relegated to the margins over a very long period of time and then, due to certain favorable historical or sociocultural circumstances, succeeded in returning to the forefront to leave its mark once again. Whether one of the reasons of this resurgence is a reaction to Sabbateanism is still an open question, which is secondary for the understanding of Hasidism as a religious phenomenon.

To illustrate the affinity between the philosophical-spiritualistic perceptions of the thirteenth century and those of Hasidism, I will give one short example. Hasidic texts as well as Abulafia's writings and philosophical works, which were inspired more by Aristotelian than by Neoplatonic sources, refer to the rescue from Egypt in terms of the soul's redemption from the "exile" of the material world.[90] This is one specific example of how two different strata of Jewish mystical thought completely transformed a historical event into a spiritual quest. To what extent can we pinpoint clear historical connections between the spiritualization of messianism and the influence of Jewish philosophy during the thirteenth century, on the one hand, and a similar spiritualization found in Hasidism of the eighteenth century? This question is yet to be resolved, in my opinion, by intense research of the sources that gave birth to Hasidic thought. Such scholarship will help us more successfully understand the ramifications of the great resemblance between these two Jewish mystical paradigms. For the spiritualistic metamorphosis is not limited to one topic alone, the transition from national redemption to individual redemption. Rather, Hasidism espouses spiritualizations, or to use Scholem's term "neutralizations," of the centrality of various topics which are only obliquely related to messianism or sometimes are totally unrelated to this issue: the Land of Israel, the Temple, the psychological interpretations of the sefirot, as well as the the theurgical act. The spiritualization of messianism is only one manifestation of a deeper shift in values within the Hasidic world.[91] This shift gave birth to a model of mystical thought extremely similar to ecstatic Kabbalah, which was after all one of the factors responsible for the doctrine of individual redemption. Ecstatic Kabbalah also has neutralized the centrality of the Land of Israel vis-à-vis the messianic process,[92] as it has neutralized the theosophical function of the ten sefirot.[93] In this case, the similarity between these two phenomena is more complex than just an isolated discussion of the notion of individual redemption.

Consequently, the second half of the eighteenth century was a time of awakening interest in and strengthening of a spiritualistic trend that had been located only at the margin of the map of Jewish mysticism during the seventeenth and the first half of the eighteenth centuries. Hasidism exhibits strong affinities to thirteenth-and fourteenth-century spiritualistic trends both in its terminology and in its concepts, a fact that allows for a most interesting study utilizing comparative and phenomenological approaches within the framework of the various stages of Jewish mysticism. In this context, the most important issue of all is the affinity between the coming to the fore of the concept of devequt in the ecstatic Kabbalah and its similar position within the spiritualistic value system of Hasidism.[94] In my opinion, it is not necessary to view the transfer from the highest value of tiqqun in the Lurianic-Sabbatian conception to that of devequt in the Hasidic literature as a total exchange but rather as a return of a certain value to a more central role, after it had been marginalized in some types of Kabbalistic literature. On this point there is no doubt that Hasidism is more similar to ecstatic Kabbalah and some forms of ethical-Kabbalistic literature written by Safedian Kabbalists than any other type of Kabbalistic thought. Thus, it seems curious that when attempting to characterize the peculiar Hasidic view of redemption, Scholem repeatedly mentions those forms of mystical literature which differ dramatically from Hasidism rather than those that are closer to it. Strangely enough, the name of Abraham Abulafia is totally absent from the essays on messianism in Scholem's book *The Messianic Idea.*[95] The argument for the neutralization of the active messianic element within Hasidism demands clarification from a perspective other than that of the existence of a preceding mystical model. The very recourse to the term *neutralization* assumes that "authentic" messianism is limited to the national-political variety of messianism, so that the spiritualistic conception of messianism can only be perceived as the neutralization of this ideal messianic element. In my opinion, this implicit assumption is based on the acceptance of the concept of individual messianism as a late and innovative development, emerging around 1750, in Jewish thought. Yet if we adopt another historical and phenomenological stand—namely that from the thirteenth century onward there were discussions of the Messiah allegorized as the Agent Intellect or Actualized Intellect, and that there are dozens of textual proofs to this effect—then we can legitimatize this phenomenon as an independent model and not view it in terms of a neutralization of another doctrine. In other words, Hasidic spiritualistic messianism may be but an expression of a broader phenomenon within Jewish tradition and should not be perceived solely as a reaction to or transformation of a previous doctrine. Since it is a complete system of thought possessing its own internal logic, it deserves to be studied on its own terms and not considered as a mere reaction to specific socioeconomic factors.

The first two generations of Hasidic writings emphasized the spiritualistic conception of messianism. During the third and fourth generations, however, more radical stands, closer to the apocalyptic model of messianism, became more conspicuous. By the nineteenth century there was evidence of a revival of several acute messianic phenomena, mainly in the messianic tendencies of R. Naḥman of Bratzlav and, later on, the messianic self-awareness of R. Yitzḥaq Aiziq Yehudah Yeḥiel Safrin, the founder of the dynasty of Komarno. The first rabbi of Komarno possessed an extremely heightened sense of messianic self-awareness and simultaneously had strong mystical experiences.[96] Here is a case of a distinctive integration of ecstatic mystical experiences with an acute messianic self-awareness which has yet to be studied in detail.

Let me explain the peculiar form of Hasidic messianism in the first generations of this movement in a slightly different manner. Lurianic Kabbalah, following the theosophical-theurgical Kabbalistic model, emphasized the need to perfect the divine as a prelude to the more mundane redemption. The theosophical model, so important in the main trend of Kabbalah, can be seen systemically as dealing with a period of time standing between the eon of historical imperfection and its completion ushered in by the advent of the Messiah. It is the supernal structure which must be repaired, saved from the imperfection caused by man, before man himself is redeemed here below. Even when spiritual improvement precedes the repair of the supernal anthropos, it is the latter that is the focus of the redemption. Numerous discussions in Hasidism, in a manner phenomenologically reminiscent of ecstatic Kabbalah, were, however, less concerned with supernal theosophical structures for their own sake or for theurgical purposes. It was the improvement of the terrestrial man, by imparting certain forms of salvific information—various concepts and practices related to divine names[97]—rather than the reparation of the supernal anthropos that was the main concern of both ecstatic Kabbalah and Hasidism. The two forms of Jewish mysticism, so different in many respects, have nevertheless focused their efforts either on the individual's spiritual perfection or the perfection of society.

Let me illustrate this move from the more Lurianic to the more anthropological understanding of a messianic topic. In a story attributed to the Besht by R. Yitzḥaq Aiziq Yeḥiel Yehudah Safrin of Komarno, the founder of Hasidism reported his intention to meet an important Kabbalist who came from Morocco and was dwelling for a while in Jerusalem, the famous R. Ḥayyim ben 'Attar. This meeting was supposed to unify the Besht's spirit, *ruaḥ,* deriving from the spirit of David found in the world of Emanation, with the soul, *nefesh,* of the Kabbalist, which stemmed from the lower ontological level designated as the soul of David in the world of Emanation. When such a conjunction between the soul and the spirit took place, two higher spiritual capacities would descend, the higher soul, *neshamah,* and an even higher capacity, *yeḥidah,* and the true redemption, *ha-ge'ullah ha-'amitit,* would emerge. Such an encounter was conditioned by the Besht's envisioning "his image [and] resemblance" in the supernal world in all its limbs.[98] The Besht did not, however, see his heels, *'aqevav,* and thus his attempt to meet the Moroccan sage failed. I understand this story as reinterpreting the Lurianic understanding of the heels of the Messiah and as dealing with the supernal anthropos in anthropological terms, namely by assuming that the messianic process does not depend on external theosophical processes but rather on the perfection of the individual. His being able to encounter his perfected nature opens the door for the messianic enterprise, which in this context was the joint effort of the Hasidic master and the Kabbalistic saint.[99]

Inner Redemption and Christian Redemption

Both the ecstatic and the Hasidic introversive versions of personal redemption are much more similar to the Christian spiritualistic versions that emphasize the inner transformation and marginalize the public event. Yet despite this crucial similarity, as well as other interesting parallels to Christianity pointed out above, I maintain that historically the two versions of personal redemption stem from different sources. At least insofar as the Jewish mystical sources are concerned, the formative factor was not direct Christian influence but Greek psychology, which provided the terminology for understanding inner processes, concepts that were missing in the Jewish tradition before the Middle Ages. I contend that the recourse to Greek psychological concepts and their appropriation has nothing to do with a sense of crisis in public Jewish life or even less with a reaction against an active apocalyptic messianism. It was, in my opinion, part of the enrichment of Jewish messianism by paradigms supplied by medieval theologies and psychologies new to medieval Jews. This remark, which has already be dealt with in the second chapter, has something to do with Jacob Taubes position that the interiorization of the messianic experience is part of the crisis of the outer messianism, or of the external eschatology. If we accept such a reading, then Taubes's criticism of Scholem has to be expanded not only to Scholem's vision of the Hasidic neutralization of messianism but also to Abraham Abulafia's brand of messianism, and I am inclined to doubt very much that this is appropriate. In general, Taubes's vision of the interiorization as belonging to the career of the "idea" assumes both a crucial role of history in the change of the nature of the messianic idea and the direction of the change, thereby establishing another type of link between the reaction against Sabbateanism and personal messianism in Hasidism. In principle, Taubes would like to legitimize the Hasidic concept of messianism, in contrast to Scholem's reluctance to recognize messianism in Hasidic thought. Though I agree with this part of Taubes's project, I am wary of his historical explanation, which is still deeply Scholemian. For Taubes, the Hasidic messianic idea can be understood "as the viable mythic response whereby Lurianic Kabbalah overcame the disastrous apocalyptic consequences manifested in the Sabbatean comedy."[100] Therefore Taubes, like Tishby, envisions Hasidic messianism rather as an inner development in Lurianic Kabbalah, which had to respond to the the Sabbatean debacle which it was itself responsible for. To a great extent, Taubes accepts a type of dynamics in the evolution of Jewish mysticism that is informed by Scholem's intellectual universe, even though he offers an explanation that was rejected explicitly by Scholem: he assumes that dialectical spiritual responses may solve quandaries created by earlier events. Like Tishby, he sees a continuation, though after a certain transformation, of the messianic drive in Hasidism.

On the other hand, Taubes mentions a resemblance to Christianity, and though the filiation of some of the Hasidic ideas discussed above seems to be independent of the Christian formulations, there is nevertheless in the restorative theory of the primordial man an affinity to the view, found in Christian thought, of the membership of the faithful ones in the body of Christ.[101] Recently, such an affinity has been proposed which presupposes the entrance of the Christian influences already in zoharic and Lurianic Kabbalah.[102] Whether this is true or not, the immediate sources of Hasidism are to be found in Jewish mystical texts. If the New Testament view, which turned into an influential concept in Christianity, is itself of Jewish extraction is an issue beyond the concerns of the present discussion.

Models of Messianism in Hasidism

The previous discussions suggest a new approach to the question of messianism in Hasidism. In lieu of embracing one "messianic idea," which is either present and vital, as Dinur and Tishby would assert, or neutralized and dormant, as Scholem has proposed, one should be more sensitive toward the material found in the numerous Hasidic sources that would allow for the existence of several different models that informed the various masters and their writings. The theosophical-theurgical model, which is better known as Lurianic, seems to be the less important one. From this point of view Scholem's claim as to the so-called neutralization is correct, since the influence of this specific model has been marginalized in Hasidic sources as part of a restructuring of Hasidism as mysticism in comparison to Lurianism. However, the two other models, the ecstatic and the talismanic, active in Jewish mystical literature for centuries, have produced other forms of messianism which become more evident in the Hasidic literature. In fact, the ecstatic and talismanic models are much more characteristic of Hasidic texts than the theosophical-theurgical model, a point that tells us much about the main spiritual concerns of the Hasidic masters.[103] Since

Hasidism is a late mystical phenomenon, it has combined many more modes of thought and experience than have most of the other Jewish mystical literatures, a fact that provokes new trends within these ways of thought and expression. Consequently, a less unified mode of thought should be surmised as informing this vast literature, which is diversified not only by the various idiosyncratic personalities but also by their panoramic approach.[104]

Diverse as those models are, however, in Hasidism they share a certain existential urgency which makes their respective understandings of messianism as acute as any other. More than the theosophical-theurgical model, as represented in the *Zohar* and in Lurianism, the Hasidic emphasis on experience should be understood as a move from hope to experience, to invert Mowinckel's formulation (see chapter 1),[105] where full-fledged messianism, as understood by him, emerges as a transition from present experience to hope. In the ecstatic and Hasidic treatments of messianism we may presuppose the availability of the messianic mode of existence which offers an immediate experience as much informed by hope as by real attempts to actualize the messianic potentiality of religious life. In a manner reminiscent of the ancient anointed kings who were portrayed, according to some scholars, as transmitting the divine power to their nation, now the whole community, by its spiritualization of ritual life, becomes the means of transmission of the divine power as part of the messianic state of being. Interestingly enough, the cycle of ritual and experience, which produced hope and expectations and which first appears in the biblical literature, reverberates in the latest form of Jewish mysticism. Hasidism, therefore, should be seen as a vital form of literature, praxes, and experiences that combine a great variety of models. More than a merely reaction to historical crises, the vitality of Hasidic mysticism draws from the creative appropriations of a full gamut of messianic ideas and models.

The Hasidic doctrine of individual redemption and spiritual messianism was very influential during the eighteenth and nineteenth centuries in circles where the various forms of Hasidism were prevalent. A messianic self-understanding is connected to a mystical vision of reality in the writings of R. Naḥman of Brazlav at the beginning of the nineteenth century and of R. Yitzḥaq Aiziq Yehudah Safrin of Komarno at mid-century.[106] In their writings, different as they are from from one another conceptually and aesthetically, different varieties of messianic consciousness are quite crucial.

Yet even in the Lubavitch Hasidism, seen as more cerebral than the other forms of Hasidism, there are messianic expectations. R. Aharon ha-Levi of Starosielce, one of the most important theologians of this movement, claims that the role of the Hasidic tradition he has inherited from R. Shneor Zalman of Liady was to disclose the real meaning of Kabbalistic texts. These texts, especially the Lurianic ones, have been sealed "by means of a thousand seals" and composed in a code that employs allegories and enigmatic language, which induced some of the later Kabbalists to favor some forms of anthropomorphism.[107] Tishby has correctly pointed out the messianic tone of such a claim,[108] though he could not support his reading by parallel sources. A contemporary of R. Aharon, however, offers an interesting parallel to the idea mentioned above, which also includes messianic phraseology. R. Pinḥas 'Eliyahu Hurwitz, the author of the famous *Sefer ha-Berit,* stemming from Lithuanian circles, claims that "those ancient days and generations of the fifth millennium are not similar to these days and generations. In those thousand years the gates of this lore were closed and sealed, and this is why there were but few Kabbalists . . . unlike this sixth millennium, that the gates of light and mercy have been opened, and it is close to the 'time of the end of the right hand' . . . especially because all the sacred writings of R. Yitzḥaq Luria, blessed be his memory, who had opened to us the gates of the Torah which were closed and sealed by a thousand seals[109] since ancient times, have been printed."[110]

It is interesting to see this Kabbalist's fine historical distinction between the state of Kabbalah at the middle of the thirteenth century, when Kabbalah took its first steps, and the diffusion of the lore at the end of the eighteenth century, a process that R. Pinḥas understood as an eschatological event. A similar view was expressed in another book by R. Pinḥas, were he pointed out that Lurianic writings are the gate for the exit from the exile and the joyful 'aliyah to the land of Israel. Thus, we may assume that the view of R. Aharon of Starosielce is but another version of an idea represented in his lifetime in other circles: that the disclosure of Lurianic Kabbalah indeed has some eschatological valences. R. Aharon could interpret Hasidism as one of those moves from the esoteric to exoteric treatment of secrets characteristic of messianic era.

Against the background of these Hasidic approaches to messianism, which are not only a matter of hope in a diffuse redemption and personal salvation but also in the messianic task of specific Hasidic leaders, it is easier to understand the recent messianic effervescence related to R. Menaḥem Mendel Schneersohn, the last rabbi of the Lubavitch school of Hasidism. Though continuing messianic hopes and speculations ushered in by his predecessor, R. Joseph Baer, which were formulated during and perhaps even triggered by the Holocaust, R. Menaḥem Mendel developed a rhetoric of more acute messianism, which inspired many of his followers to worship him as the Messiah, even after his death. The depth and breadth of messianic expectations and propaganda at the beginning of this decade stemming from Habad Hasidic circles had no precedence since Sabbateanism, though their effects on the actual religious behavior of the believers seem, at least for the time being, to be minor.[111] Even today messianic doctrines address the status of the Land of Israel and the ʿaliyah of Hasidim to reside in it. The contemporary Hasidic communities of the diaspora still maintain that individual redemption is attainable irrespective of time and place. Moreover, it is believed that mythical messianism, which is connected to time and place, is a dangerous idea and religiously troublesome because it depends on outside intervention in order to be realized.[112]

The main stand of Scholem and his school, namely the relegation of the early Hasidic attitude toward messianism to a neutralization, as well as the critiques of Tishby and Wolfson, admitting the greater influence of Lurianic messianic elements, implicitly restrict the relevant sources for examining the form of messianism. In accordance with the panoramic approach which postulates a much broader range of models available to and influential on Hasidism, the relative importance of messianic elements may be also addressed from the point of view of the early Hasidic masters' willingness to embrace a richer spectrum of extant views on messianism. Moreover, the present discussions should open the question of acute versus mild or neutralized messianism in a much more radical manner than statistical descriptions, as offered by Tishby, or quotations making the point of the existence of different models. The reduction of messianism to historical or external action, which unifies Scholem and Tishby, reduces the equal importance of the inner life as a significant criterion for determining the acuteness of a given phenomenon. The intensification of the spiritual life in Hasidism seems to be an unchallenged fact, and rightly so. Such an intensification might load even older commonplace messianic discussions with a cargo that is hardly suspected by a remote reader who relies too much on examining sources. In other words, the modernistic emphasis on external action and thus on verification might distort the understanding of impulses that flourished more on the hidden scene of the inner life.

R. Yitzḥaq Aiziq Yeḥiel Yehudah Safrin of Komarno

The survey of the Hasidic attitudes to messianism would be incomplete without mentioning the messianic expectations of one of the most mystical among the Hasidic masters, R. Yitzḥaq Aiziq Safrin of Komarno. His numerous writings in the mid-nineteenth century, as well as those of his uncle, R. Tzevi Hirsch Eichenstein of Zhidachov, who shaped his spiritual life, represent a dramatic return to a much more Lurianic and zoharic type of thought and expression. While the prior Hasidic literature constitutes a dilution of Lurianic thought, these two masters (and to a great extent also the writings of R. Yitzḥaq Aiziq of Zhidachov, another nephew of the first rabbi of Zhidachov, and R. Eliezer Tzevi, the rabbi's son) fill their works with zoharic and Lurianic terminology.

Indeed, zoharism and Lurianism are seen by R. Tzevi Hirsch as necessary for his times, which are considered to be near to messianic redemption. For example, he describes the background for one of his compositions, an introduction to Vital's *'Etz Ḥayyim:*

> The intelligent shall shine as the brightness[113] casting sparks on all sides, as the *Zohar,* our fortress in our exile and our soul's redemption. Let our King come, he is triumphant and victorious [Zechariah 9:9]. And what shall we say unto Thee, O Lord Our God, in this last generation in which for long seasons Israel has been without the true God, and without a teacher-priest and without Torah, every man doing that which is right in his own eyes,[114] and the power of heresy prevails. We have been left orphaned without a father. But Thou, O Lord our God, . . . hast sent us the teacher[115] of righteousness, the angel who descended in heavenly clouds, the celestial holy one from the high heavens, our holy teacher, the Ari, of blessed memory, and his holy disciples, chief of whom was our master, R. Ḥayyim Vital.[116]

Thus, the *Zohar* and its Lurianic interpretations are conceived of as helping the Jews to bear the hardness of the exile but at the same time to redeem their souls. Not only the spiritual redemption, however, concerned this master. Elsewhere in his book he mentions explicitly that his time is the heels of the Messiah,[117] while in another work, his commentary on the *Zohar,* he mentions specifically the year 1840,[118] a famous messianic date, as the beginning of the redemption and 1848 as the end of the messianic process.[119] Against these messianic expressions in his closest circle, it is much easier to understand the aspirations of R. Tzevi Hirsch's nephew, the first rabbi of Komarno, whose fascinating autobiographical testimony, entitled *Megillat Setarim,* is one of the most important examples of messianic spirituality in Judaism.[120]

Imitating Vital's *Sefer ha-Ḥezyonot,* the first part of *Megillat Setarim* deals with dreams, which have sometimes messianic significance. From the very beginning of the autobiography, we learn that Yitzạq Aiziq was born in the Jewish year 566 (1806 C.E.), which is the numerical value of the phrase *Mashiyaḥ ben Yosef.*[121] According to his testimony, he received "wonderful visions and holy spirit," "spoke words of prophecy," and "has seen from one extremity of the world to another"—an achievement attributed to the Besht—all this between the ages of two and five.[122] Later on, in 1823, he describes a vision of the light of the Shekhinah.[123] Elsewhere, he describes ascents of the soul and visions of souls of the departed righteous, most of them during sleep.[124] He refers to the adherence of his soul to the Shekhinah, and to his sins which caused the separation between them.[125] Therefore, to believe his testimony, some forms of revelations started quite early, and thus would be a prominent case where an intense mystical life produced messianic expectations from the individual himself. These expectations are contrived within a complex of affinities between his soul, that of his father, and classical figures such as R. 'Aqiva, Luria, Vital, and the Besht, all these under the strong influence of Vital's *Sefer ha-Ḥezyonot.*[126] Yet despite the megalomanic pedigree he created for himself, Yitzḥaq Aiziq's main path of redemption is classical and may be the most extreme example in Judaism of via passionis. His mysticism, and implicitly his messianic mission, involve unparalleled descriptions of self-abasement, declarations of extreme worthlessness, weeping, and a life of abstinence and poverty.[127] Apparently, this ascetic way was understood as the preparation of the "vessel," namely the body, to receive the divine light, and he confesses that he went to tzaddiqim in order that they might draw upon him the "light of God."[128]

Yitzḥaq Aiziq's messianic mission includes, according to his confession, abortive attempts to convince others to repent[129] and "operations" done on the eve of the Jewish New Year in 1845 for the sake of the nation of Israel in Russia.[130] These operations were intended to subdue the "angels" of Russia, and of Christianity in general, in order to obliterate deleterious decrees.[131] It seems that dreams during the days of the New Year were relatively more common.[132] In general, this master envisioned all of history as an ongoing contest between the redemptive figures, who return time and again as reincarnated persons, and the powers of evil, described as the "face of the dog" stemming from the time of the destruction of the Second Temple.[133] According to Yitzḥaq Aiziq, the time of the Besht was ripe for redemption, since "all the redemptions depended on the Besht and R. Ḥayyim ben 'Attar."[134] Elsewhere he claims that would the Besht continue to restore for two more years, redemption would come.[135] As to the more theoretical role of the Messiah, the rabbi of Komarno attributes to the Messiah, the son of David, the function of redeeming the Shekhinah from her exile, together with all the sparks that have fallen as part of the breaking of the vessels, while the Messiah ben Joseph was described as the redemer of the souls from their transmigrations.[136] Thus, the more national redemption seems to be marginalized. Elsewhere, in his commentary on the *Zohar,* he claims that redemption will be achieved by causing the ascent of Malkhut to Binah, a theurgical act that should be done by the people of Israel, especially through martyrdom, and by the Messiah ben David.[137] In any case, despite the messianic vision of his time (and that of his uncle) as already messianic, he might have been inhibited from more aggresive propaganda which could raise the spectre of Sabbateanism. Their propagandistic activity was more bookish and, from his point of view, less active on the popular level. Messianism can be interpreted in more than one manner; here the more passive one—writing introductions to already printed books, commenting on the *Zohar,* and undertaking extreme ascetic exercises—did not urge the audience to create a sociologically meaningful messianic phenomenon. The rabbi of Zhidachov and his nephew, immersed as they were in the belief that they were living in messianic times, concentrated their efforts on ascetic practices rather than emphasizing communal leadership. Indeed, extreme and fascinating forms of mysticism, or at least mystical expressions, are found in the writings of these masters, especially in those of the rabbi of Komarno, who apparently acted as a mystical Messiah who resorted to Lurianic theurgical techniques. From this point of view, R. Yitzḥaq Aiziq may well be the first Messiah who resorted to the model of Lurianic theurgy.

A small lesson in the history of religious developments should be learned from the avatars of the two Hasidic schools, in comparison to other more popular forms of Hasidism. The success of a certain form of spiritual teaching is only partially a matter of the "aggregate demand" of the market or an answer to a crisis; it is also, and perhaps more pertinently, the result of the decisions of individuals whose charismatic personalities create magnetic fields that change the course of what some scholars would think of as a historical development. The recent events related to another messianic understanding of Hasidism, in the Lubavitch school, easily demonstrate how activism is able to change the course of history.

Concluding Remarks

Objective Models and Spiritual Lives

ONE of the main purposes of this book has been to underline the importance of mystical models that inspired some forms of Jewish messianism and their place within the development of both Kabbalah and Hasidism. Only by presenting a more balanced view of the different and sometimes diverging manifestations of messianism, in their originality and their affinities with the antecedent phenomena, can a more accurate picture of the various Jewish messianic types of thought be attained.

Several models have informed Kabbalistic discussions on messianism. The Kabbalistic models I have discussed are stable enough to adopt messianic motifs from various Jewish traditions and adapt them without changing themselves dramatically. It is a remarkable fact that the discussions of messianic themes in the framework of these models do not appear at the initial stages of the absorption of the models in the Jewish speculative literature, but only in a relatively late period. The ecstatic model, with its individualistic penchant, occurs two generations after the adoption of Aristotelian psychology by Maimonides, whose thought informed this type of Jewish mysticism. The theosophical-theurgical understanding of messianism occurs two generations after the first testimonies of the theosophical-theurgical Kabbalah, when the term *mashiyaḥ* was discussed by R. Azriel of Gerona in the clear-cut context of the symbolism of sefirot. The talismanic interpretation of messianic themes appears well after the acceptance of the talismanic model in Kabbalah, and only rarely can we establish an uninterrupted transmission, in written form, of talismanic messianism. Thus, this model is quite independent of the messianic constellation of ideas. Consequently, I prefer to address the relations between messianism and Jewish mysticism as a variety of activations of different hermeneutical grids—the eschatological ones, on the one hand, and the various models, on the other—when they confronted each other as the result of historical events and spiritual physiognomies of eschatologically oriented Kabbalists and Hasidic masters. Historical events, such as the voluntary mobility of Kabbalists due to the flowering of some centers, or forced mobility, as exemplified by the expulsions from Spain, Portugal, and Sicily, were instrumental in facilitating encounters between models.[1] They might have electrified these encounters but they very rarely supplied speculative contents, which could shape the nature of the systems that entered these encounters. The rather hermeneutical question of whether in a certain mystical system specific Kabbalistic concepts are stronger, therefore more capable of transforming the meaning of messianic motifs, is to be addressed as part of the attempt to understand the changing affinities between these types of thought and experience. The various ideals—the theurgical activity aiming at the completion and perfection of the deity, known in a broader sense as tiqqun; the Aristotelian intellectual achievement of the individual, the eudaemonia; or the Neoplatonic search for union of the soul with its source, the ideal of henosis; or the magical efforts of drawing down the astral and divine powers—all had established themselves in strong positions before their encounters with the messianic elements took place or were expressed in writing. If this methodological presumption is correct, then a greater awareness to the phenomenological structure of the models that inform a given mystical system will be helpful not only for the better understanding of the system in general, but also for a more adequate description of the concepts, such as messianism, that were dealt with in that system. In broader terms, we may describe the characteristically Kabbalistic and Hasidic models of messianism as different from the political and apocalyptic views of salvation, for both these models indeed presuppose circumstances that were not mastered by the Jews. The emphasis found in some philosophically oriented formulations is on the political and national aspects of redemption, and upon the interplay of social and political forces that cannot be predicted, much less controlled, namely the ascent and decline of nations, as we have seen in chapter 2.

On the other hand, the bright light of apocalypticism was much more concerned with a violent break occurring in history because of the intervention of supernatural powers, either those of God or those of the Messiah conceived of as a warrior. According to most of the apocalyptic visions in Judaism, the Messiah is a scion of David, and the break in history is made by a person who was somehow related to the glorious past. So too is the case of God as a savior. Their extraordinary intervention, however, will be obvious only because their redemptive action is not visible in the ordinary sequence of events. Though possibly present throughout history, the apocalyptic Messiah and the apocalyptic God, both conceptualized as warrior figures, now refrain from acting salvifically by creating a crisis of the present order. But the transcendent, nonpersonalistic Messiahs of the ecstatic Kabbalah, namely Metatron and the Agent Intellect, or the sefirah of Malkhut in the case of the theosophical-theurgical model, are omnipresent salvific entities. It is not a crisis that will make manifest their miraculous intervention but rather the perfection of the present order, the human intellect in the ecstatic Kabbalah and the Kabbalistic performance of the commandments in the case of the other school. To a certain extent, this is also the case where the Messiah combats the evil powers in the present, as described in chapter 4 in a assertion by Shlomo Molkho. The crisical-apocalyptic approach deals fundamentally with horizontal fields, as it presupposes a dramatic change in the present order of reality but sees the next step in terms of a continuation, despite the crisis in this world. Some of the other Kabbalistic systems, by contrast, are better described as vertical, because the human Messiah will not descend into history; his perfection will not be achieved within the normal experiences of this world, but by adhering to another, higher spiritual world. It is a vertical move that allows to the mystic to experience redemption now, while the apocalyptics who attempt to transcend history do not intend to transcend horizontal geography. The hypostatic nature of the supernal Messiah, its incessant presence, therefore ensures an experience that is immediately available to the elite unrelated to the advent of a redemptive figure.

The Kabbalistic treatments analyzed above moved in three main directions, each one so powerful that it marginalized the crisical-apocalyptic and the political versions of messianism. One movement was more inward than the philosophers are capable of; one was more toward the divinity than the apocalyptic supernaturalists manage, as is the case in the theosophical-theurgical Kabbalah; and one was more activistic than politicians, resorting as the magical Kabbalists did to magical practices. In other words, analysis of the various versions of messianism may detect two major developments related to these themes, but also to Judaism in general. In addition to the more historically and nationally oriented forms of religion as represented in the Bible and rabbinic literature, some forms of Kabbalah offered a more inward version, influenced by Greek philosophy, and a more cosmic version, influenced by astrological views. By locating the ultimate flaw less in outward history and more in the various spiritual domains—the psychological or the noetic process, on the one hand, and the divine or the demonic, on the other—those realms became the main subject of discussion. When contemplated from a more modern skeptical point of view, however, the three realms may be viewed as more orderly or controllable than the political realm, where the play of powers is hardly predictable, as is the advent of the apocalyptic Messiah. Even the flaw in the divine system is still understood as part of the possibilities inherent in a certain system and can therefore be repaired. There is a rationale, an inner logic, in the theosophical-theurgical Kabbalah that transcends the irrationality of the totally mythical Messiah of the more popular apocalypse.

The soteriology of this brand of Kabbalah is built upon the double assumption that God's realm on high should be restored and that this restoration will be achieved with tools taken from ordinary religious life, such as the performance of the commandments. When God's absolute reign over the historical processes was envisaged as weakened or flawed, or at least problematic, man was conceived of as having been called to help consolidate it by devoting himself to the perfect system of behavior, the halakhic *dromena.* Thus, a certain "rationalizing" picture of the conjunction between God and man emerges. Man is responsible for, and in the case of the Kabbalists even deemed to know the reason for, the flaw in the divine, and he also has the tools to repair it. Most of the Kabbalists, unlike most of the apocalyptically oriented Jewish thinkers, took as their point of reference not the national and religious disaster, the destruction of the Temple,which is foremost a historical event, but rather the sin of Adam, a prehistorical or para-historical event that took place before the formation of a Jewish nation and kingdom. To a great extent, the regular, ordinary life has acquired in this literature a new sense, which is established in the awareness that the Jews, especially the Kabbalists, may and should perfect basic processes which shape reality in general, or human nature in particular, not only those which affect the Jews. This is most evident in the ecstatic-mystical model, where the study of philosophy and the practice of mystical techniques are available and recommended tools for generating messianic experiences. The flaw in this case is projected within the spiritual realm of the individual and thus becomes part of inner nature, which in principle, according to Abulafia, can be controlled. Such diverse approaches have been envisaged by scholars as escapist, because the mystics who formulated them have been described as refusing to engage in political activities, or as having neglected or being indifferent toward history. Scholem, for example, once formulated his vision of the Jewish mystics' attitude as follows: "But the cosmogonic and the eschatological trend[s] of Kabbalistic speculations . . . are in the last resort ways of escaping history rather then instruments of historical understanding; that is to say, they do not help us gauge the intrinsic meaning of history."[2] The various presuppositions that inform this grand statement reflect the whole question of the Scholemian scholarly attitude toward Jewish mysticism: this is a form of thought expected to reveal an "intrinsic meaning of history." When "failing" to do so, the Kabbalist is described as attempting to escape history. Quite revealing for the nature of Scholem's intellectual project is his admission that Kabbalistic speculations are worthless for someone in search for the significance within history, or as J. Dan has accurately put it, "the mystical dimension of history".[3] In other words, the absence of certain attitudes toward external reality or events, in the form of an indifference toward history, is seen by Scholem to be problematic.

It would be more reasonable not to establish overly strong modern taxonomies, shaped by the cultural preferences of the period in which a scholar is active, and then judge the medieval or premodern mystics by that standard. Would, for example, scholars of Christian and Muslim spirituality regret the absence of expressions that would manifest their respective attitudes toward history and then describe those mystics as escaping history? Why has the criterion of pondering history and offering insights into historical quandaries been imposed upon the Jewish mystics more than on Jewish poets, philosophers, scientists, or halakhists? Why overemphasize, as does Scholem, the deep involvement with history by those Kabbalists who allegedly coined some forms of Kabbalistic symbolism?

Both the positive and negative answers to these questions with regard to some or all of the Kabbalists presuppose a centrality of "history" in both the manifest and the hidden agenda of Kabbalists. This assumption, however, may emerge more from a modern academic preoccupation with the significance of history, influenced by Hegel, or a nationalistic proclivity, than from listening to the major concerns of a medieval Jewish mystic as he himself would explicate them. Though I am more inclined to discern in some forms of Kabbalah what I hope was the main concern of the Kabbalists, namely microchronic and macrochronic conceptualizations, the Kabbalists' concern with the present was more colored by a cyclical understanding of the religiously significant dimension of time.[4]

Let me explicate the differences between the way Scholem looked at the Kabbalists and the way I have attempted to do so. Both of us treat of a corpus of knowledge that may be defined as mythical, though I have taken into consideration Abulafia's thought, which is much less so. The mythical element is investigated by Scholem in order to discern the significance of the creation of the myth, the hidden core that is not expressed explicitly. Scholem's diagnosis of this core takes him in the direction of those Kabbalists who attempted to answer historical and national quandaries dealing with changing social, political, and perhaps even economical circumstances. This extraction of meaning, in fact a strong interpretation, invokes a new kind of interest in Kabbalah, as Scholem openly recognized, as this is one of the central themes of his historiography of sixteenth-century Kabbalah. By resorting to studies from the myth-and-ritual school, I have attempted to point out the nexus between the Kabbalistic myths and continuous or constant elements in Judaism, namely the rituals. My contention is that the models that informed the understanding of messianism were stable enough to appropriate the messianic elements, according to their own systemic forms of logic. In the case of the theosophical-theurgical Kabbalah, this was a strong nomian logic, which has been used in numerous basic writings of this type of Kabbalah in order to validate the significance of the ritual. Thus, the divergence between mine and Scholem's reading of Kabbalistic myths relates to how we understand the nature of myth, especially the myth that informed Lurianic Kabbalah. Since neither Scholem nor I have been told the intention of the author, both lines of argumentation are different forms of scholarly interpretation and no more. The proposed theory of models attempts to escape the imposition of one interpretation, and consequently a very rigid scholarly criterion, in order to allow for the emergence of a scholarly analysis that deals with a polychromatic gamut of affinities between messianism and other topics.

In my opinion, the Kabbalists and the Hasidic masters have conceptualized messianism by resorting to a conglomerate of attitudes that inform their understanding of their psyche, of nature, of God, of angels, and of demons. In other words, the Messiah is never alone in any system. The stronger the system, however, the more the concept of the Messiah will reflect the special physiognomy of that system. The angelic status of the Messiah in ancient and medieval sources represents quite a different type of discourse than the more prevalent popular assumption that the Messiah is a human scion of David. Historical events in the post-biblical era were conceived of as an issue less pregnant with intrinsic meaning, and that is why Kabbalists addressed them but rarely. It is not an historical escapism that informed the Kabbalistic and Hasidic forms of messianism, but an attempt to make the best sense of both their religious traditions and their particular spiritual concerns. This is one of the reasons I am reluctant to see the non-apocalyptic and spiritual understanding of messianism as a kind of life lived "in deferment."[5] Rather I would say that it is a much more intense type of expectation within messianism, or while messianism is being realized. The existential versions of messianism as expressed in the ecstatic Kabbalah and Hasidic literature, focused as they are on the immediate and relatively extreme experiences of the divine, are legitimate interpretations of the concept of the Messiah, because the mystics themselves explicitly expressed them in the context of the term *mashiyaḥ*, just as the apocalyptic interpretation did. They might well have been formulated by different layers in Jewish society, but in order to better understand both the messianic "idea" and Jewish mysticism, the value judgment implied in the preference for the apocalyptic mode seems to be at odds with the self-awareness of some important Kabbalists and Hasidic masters. In fact, Scholem's hypothesis about deferment, never demonstrated in detail, had become not only a main thesis but a hyperthesis that inspired many scholars who never inspected the material that could support such a claim. In my opinion, beyond the great concern of scholars with the involvement of the Jewish mystics with history, another factor has contributed to the bright career of the apocalyptic model in modern scholarship: its crisical nature.

Unlike the biblical "royal ideology" or "sacral kingship" discussed in the Introduction, which generated the messianic cluster of ideas by its later various avatars, namely the gamut of spiritual messianisms, apocalyptic messianism was fraught with a great potential of threat to the Jewish tradition, especially to its Halakhic component. This critical aspect has been duly emphasized by Scholem in a series of studies in *The Messianic Idea* and in his various studies of Sabbateanism and its metamorphoses. I contend that the emphasis on the historical crises generated a parallel emphasis on the phenomenology of the spiritual trends allegedly produced by the reverberations of these crises. The generic factors are conceived as having produced effects that essentially resemble them. This is the reason for Scholem's wariness of messianism as an actual phenomenon. I am confident that Scholem is correct in emphasizing the dangers inherent in a present actualization of messianic apocalypticism on the stage of history. These dangers for Jewish communities were amply exemplified by the debacles of Sabbateanism and Frankism in pre-modern times. Less visible, and perhaps less influential, are the quasi-apocalyptic approaches permeating some political factions in modern Israel and the Habad messianism in the more recent decades.

However, anyone aware of the multiple ways the messianic ideas may travel should also pay special attention to the role played by the variety of these ideas. A better understanding of how messianic ideas were cultivated without disrupting the normal religious way of life demands an awareness that the coexistence of different redemptive ideals could prevent the predominance of the apocalyptic model. The variety of the messianic ideas explains why messianism—despite its identification with apocalypticism, as asserted by Scholem—remained less dangerous historically. By fragmenting the "messianic idea"—understood by modern scholars as a rather unified concept which is basically apocalyptic—it loses not only its alleged solidity and homogeneity but also its strong impact on the historical plane. If different forms of messianism were acting on the religious scene, and were interacting among themselves, the influence of the apocalyptic is somewhat reduced, allowing a variety of religious persons to maintain different forms of messianic belief. This is, however, not only a matter of letting each person adopt a different model of conceptualizing the Messiah. In some cases, as we have seen, more than one messianic model informed the writings of a given Kabbalist, for example R. Yitzḥaq of Acre, or Hasidic master, such as R. Menaḥem Naḥum of Chernobyl.

Before turning to another topic, I would like to address a compositional problem, that emerges from the different methodological perspectives adopted throughout this book: the need to address the different ideas according to phenomenological models while keeping in mind the historical coordinates of the material under scrutiny. At issue is the organization of the academic presentation. One way of presenting the ideas I have discussed would have been to isolate one model and describe its literary manifestations in their historical sequence. Another alternative would have been to describe the various Kabbalists' systems separately and point out the different models operating within the same texts. Both approaches would have allowed me to explicate the theory of models insofar as the messianic material is concerned. I have chosen, however, a certain middle way between the two alternatives: whenever a certain group of texts display rather consistent emphases, I have described that group separately, as in the case of ecstatic Kabbalah in chapter 2 and the magical approach to messianism in most of chapter 4. But insofar as the more mixed types of corpora are concerned, such as the theosophical-theurgical, the Sabbatean, and the Hasidic, I have preferred to analyze in the same chapter the various trends, which only rarely would represent an elaborate and consistent worldview were they to be extracted from the larger corpus of literature and dealt with in themselves. This double approach is, in my opinion, dictated by the inner structure of the discourses of the various Kabbalistic systems, and I have preferred to have this complexity reflected by the very structure of the organization of the narrative in the chapters. I have attempted, insofar as possible, to keep the discussions focused around definite literary corpora. However, again in concord with the conceptual methodological assumptions of my approach, it is crucial to remember that models crossed history, just as history crosses models. That is the reason for the historical surveys, more in the vein of the history of ideas, that precede some of the discussions in the chapter on Sabbateanism, or for the attempt to point out the possible interaction between Abulafia's journey to see the pope and a passage in the *Zohar* in chapter three rather than chapter two, or for presenting the discussion of the talismanic model in four separate chapters. What guided my choice was the wish to present the topic of messianism in all its variety in mystical Jewish texts, rather than to demonstrate the importance of my theory of models. Ideas, concepts, and models evolve in the consciousness of persons whose relations to history vary greatly, and whose concerns are panoramic and rarely conditioned by the precise sequence of events or ideas in history. Thus, in addition to the national dimensions of the messianic themes, and the repercussions of some of those themes for the religious self-understanding of many Jews, a greater role should be allowed to their personal, idiosyncratic dimensions and interpretations.

In any case, there is a danger that the isolation of the different models from the larger systems within which they emerged and appeared, and their treatment in disparate chapters, would contributed to a mistaken perception of what the Kabbalistic literature is. In my opinion, what is characteristic of the various systems we have explored is not their conceptual purity, their concentrated expression of one sort of thinking, but the variety of models and the different balances struck by them. Only by an effort to describe the whole spectrum of components that contributed to each and every system, at least insofar as the messianic views are concerned, will a more appropriate understanding of the nature of the various schools that constitute Jewish mysticism be achieved.[6]

Individual Characters and Conceptual Continuities

There is no easy solution to the problems inherent in studying the inner life of the Messiahs. Recourse to the theory of models is only one component of a package of new methodologies that should be adopted for a more subtle analysis and for a better understanding of the conceptual fabric of medieval and later Jewish mystical texts. Abstract as these models are, they provide only the general molds of some of the building blocks that will constitute the complex systems. Models are but the skeletons of this worldview, while the process of building specific types of literature depends very much on the personal configuration of the mystic's psyche. This oftentimes-imponderable factor should not be underestimated, even when resorting to an analysis based on the abstract models. Even when detailed descriptions of the character of the mystical Messiahs are absent, attention to the sources that nourished their approach may contribute substantially to the understanding of their experiences, thoughts, and actions. After all, these Messiahs chose their models from a variety of approaches, and their choice may reflect not only the strength, relevance, or availability of these models but also the idiosyncracies in the character of each Messiah. Nevertheless, I do not propose to reconstruct a certain kind of personality who would automatically, or naturally, select a particular model. With the exception of the itinerant life that most of the figures led, it may be assumed that they shared some other, less important characteristics.

The strong emphasis, however, on historical factors, evident in some of the modern scholarship, should be transcended, and in some outstanding cases that has already happened. Yehuda Liebes, for example, in his essay "New Directions,"[7] favors a phenomenological methodology, which would allocate to history a rather more modest explanatory role and emphasize more the personal life and aspirations of the individual mystic. Messianic mystics should be seen more in the double prism of attempting to enrich their inner life, to describe it and find a particular meaning for their lifeion the historical arena, while such external factors as religious traditions, conceptual models, or historical events are also to be considered. The depersonalization of the Messiah by its identification with ontic entities or, as we shall see, with the descending influx, causes a more personalistic form of religiosity to emerge; and conversely, by a more personalized Messiah, emphasizing the enigmatic treats of his personal life, a more communal form of religious life may arise. The more personalized the Messiah, the less personal the religious life of his followers is likely to be.

The phenomenological approach, the model approach, and the psychological and sociological approaches should be as welcome as the historical-textological one. Together they yield a much richer understanding of the complex phenomenon of mystical messianism.[8] The historical approach, which immersed itself in the apocalyptic mode of messianism and in mass movements, should therefore be complemented by additional scholarly approaches.[9] Though manifesting ways of thought and types of experience at odds with apocalyptic trends, the more radical among the Jewish spiritualists would nonetheless rarely reject the apocalyptic mythologies explicitly; rather, they would attempt to interpret them spiritually or offer an additional eschatological discourse to the apocalyptic one. Thus, a greater continuity between the various phases of Jewish literature regarding messianism could be demonstrated while restricting the scholarly analysis mostly to apocalyptic elements. Consequently, the dominant scholarly surveys would find a rather uniform strand of apocalypticism weaving through millennia. In such a framework, Kabbalah was significant for only about two hundred years, between the sixteenth and eighteenth centuries, since only in this period were the apocalyptic elements combined with the Kabbalistic ones. In other words, though apocalypticism was continuously influential, Kabbalah was—according to Scholem—a conduit of this approach only for a short period. What were the conduits for the lasting influence of apocalyptic messianism? In popular sources, a variety of apocalyptic variations of messianic ideas either were propagated in a more active form or were dormant in several widespread types of texts. In lieu of this approach, which reduces the role of Kabbalah in the overall economy of Jewish messianism, I have proposed to attribute to the various Kabbalistic trends a greater concern with messianic themes, beliefs, and experiences, without restricting them to the apocalyptic type of messianism. This is the reason I have stressed, especially in chapter 6, the importance of *Sefer ha-Peliy'ah* as a decisive conduit for two different forms of Kabbalah, the ecstatic and the astrological, as well as Cordovero's, all of which have contributed to aspects of messianism in Sabbateanism. I have proposed resorting to a series of models which do not have to operate during the whole continuum of Jewish history but may surface from time to time, resuscitated by the peculiar spiritual concerns of individuals, by historical circumstances, or by combinations of factors. The variety of models described here, which may not exhaust all the acting models in Jewish mysticism but reflects my current position as to the state of the field, allows for much more flexible explanations of the relations between different systems, between different factors within one system, and the phenomenological resemblances between some historically distant messianic phenomena.

The above discussions strive to demonstrate that, in addition to Scholem's stratified history of Kabbalistic messianism, which seeks to detect innovations characteristic of a period because they are influenced by specific events, it is necessary to engage another approach, which will study the phenomena in accordance with their similarities and differences despite the huge temporal gaps that may separate them. The zoharic and Lurianic theurgical understandings of the messianic elements are much closer to each other than they are to the Abulafian Kabbalah, which was contemporary with the *Zohar.* Likewise, the Hasidic emphasis upon personal salvation is, phenomenologically speaking, distant from Lurianism and Sabbateanism, to which it is close in time; on the other hand, it is reminiscent of views found in the ecstatic Kabbalah regarding this issue. The continuity between the zoharic views and Luria's is evident because Luria was deeply immersed in the spiritual universe, or universes, of the *Zohar.* Whether the affinities between the ecstatic Kabbalah and eighteenth-century Hasidism are solely a matter of phenomenological resemblances, or they can be explained at least partially as the result of historical influences, is a matter for further investigation.[10]

The phenomenological analyses could and should, however, become an important tool for initiating a study of possible historical relations between phenomena that prima facie are historically unrelated. Mystical paradigms have traversed the historical continuum of the Jews, and they have been revived from time to time by historical situations and events. Nevertheless, history has very rarely been transformed by these models. By the same token, traditional models have traveled through the lives, works, and writings of various types of messianic characters. I assume that some of these characters have also been influenced by the models. It is quite difficult to assess the precise roles of models, history, and character in shaping the experiences and writings belonging to the Messiahs or those who had participated in messianic aspirations and movements. But the awareness of the potential contributions of the various models to a more complex presentation of the messianic material under discussion seems essential if we are to escape a more simplistic historicistic approach characteristic of many of the scholarly discussions of Jewish eschatology.

The survey of the types of personalities displayed by the messianic mystics may suggest another line of differentiation. The enigma of the Messiah's personality, so evident in Christianity and Sabbateanism, is much less apparent in Abulafia and the Besht, though perhaps it is somehow inherent in the image of Luria's persona as found in some of his students' perceptions.[11] I would resort to the concept of the messianic mystery rather than that of the secret, as the latter concept may imply an invitation to decode, while the former presupposes an enigma that is so idiosyncratic it cannot be solved. I would propose a typology of messianic personae; in the case where the Messiah proclaims that he has already accomplished his messianic mission, a more mysterious persona is required, while the Messiah who still strives to accomplish his mission is more prone to resort to secrets that will be revealed in the near future. The latter category is quite evident in Abulafia and the Besht. While messianic secrets must be revealed as part of the redemptive process, the mystery of the persona may become more accentuated the more this figure starts to play a role in the historical arena. His double alienation seems to be active: as a Messiah in the apocalyptic sense, his personality must be endowed with extraordinary power and wisdom; however, when he is unable to live up to the messianic criteria, elaborated theologies are articulated in order to emphasize the dissonance between the expectations and what seems to be historical reality. While waiting for Messiahs who will exercise their role in the public arena, the masses had to learn that the real nature of the Messiah is not the manifest but the hidden dimension. If the apocalyptic Messiah, ostensibly connected to a linear vision of time and history, excels in revealing the secrets of history, his personality has to become more mysterious and enigmatic while the redemptive drama is thought to be evolving. As Taubes has proposed, messianic movements are a matter of the interpretation that is offered concerning the life of the Messiah, and such cases are rare.[12]

The quintessence of some messianic movements is related at times to their reaction to the death of their Messiahs as much as to their lives. This is evidently the case with Christianity and Sabbateanism and, to a certain extent, with Bratslav Hasidism and, in more recent years, parts of Lubavitch Hasidism. The interpretation of the death of the redeemer is perhaps the most powerful form of acknowledging him in faith, as he apparently cannot provide the expected redemption in the short term but remains nevertheless the leader of the movement. The prolonged belief in the dead or departed Messiah, which may continue for centuries, is one of the most interesting examples of the efficacy of messianic models that transcend the specific circumstances that informed their emergence. Or, to put it in different terms, the historicistic attempts by Scholem's school to create strong nexuses between specific circumstances and forms of messianism that were derived from them or reacted to them must extend the relevant period of time to centuries, and by doing so the significance of a specific historical period becomes doubtful.

On Pitfalls of Periodization

The rather precise periodization of the relations between messianism and Jewish mysticism, as reconstructed in my exposition of Scholem's view (see Introduction), seems problematic for several reasons. One may admit that historical upheavals are sometimes formative factors in human creativity, and that they may have affected messianism and mysticism. Nevertheless, Scholem's implicit assumption is more inclined to a strong historicist understanding, for it implies that distinct historical phases produce new attitudes toward messianism, which are accepted almost unanimously by the Kabbalists living in a certain period. Thus, Scholem negates the existence of significant messianic elements in the first phase of the history of Kabbalah,[13] which includes Kabbalists active over a period of three hundred years on three continents and living under various social and political circumstances. Scholem's characterization of the early Kabbalists as having been indifferent toward messianism does not really address pertinent materials found in the two major forms of Kabbalah: the theosophical-theurgical and the ecstatic ones.[14]

As Yehuda Liebes has shown, the most influential type of Kabbalistic literature, the zoharic, which is the core of the theosophical-theurgical Kabbalah, has displayed important messianic concepts and overtones.[15] Yet whereas the theosophical-theurgical Kabbalah did not produce during its first phase a mystical Messiah, a historical figure who explicitly identified himself as the Messiah in public, the other main form of Kabbalah in the thirteenth century, the ecstatic, was instituted by an author who considered himself to be the Messiah and acted in accordance with that conviction. Moreover, Abraham Abulafia was not only a Kabbalist and a Messiah at the same time. He also proposed an interesting interpretation of messianism in terms of his particular form of Kabbalah. Thus, at least in his case, it is not that historical circumstances alone created the messianic awareness and the push to activism, but a confluence of several different factors. The attempt to attribute specific attitudes of Kabbalah toward messianism to definite historical periods is highly problematic because some of the phenomena so restricted by Scholem to one period either existed in earlier periods or misrepresent the facts as I understand them.[16] By the same token, in the time and place, Kabbalah and messianism may conceptualize tradition and history and express themselves differently, and I hardly see how a strictly historical approach, in fact a historicistic one, would account for the differences.

Messianic Kabbalists did not share one particular spiritual physiognomy. Some of them were more inclined toward active, theurgical contemplation; others were given to ecstatic experiences which could also induce political activity. Some of the Kabbalists were active in times of prosperity, and we can even attribute the ascent of messianic hopes to positive developments on the historical scene; others emerged during times of pressure and despair. Given the diversity of characters and situations that produced the various expressions of Jewish mystical messianisms, the affinities between some of these conceptualizations of messianism, which I refer to as models, is quite surprising from a historicistic point of view.

In principle, in this book I have worked from the assumption, already current in modern scholarship of apocalypticism but still absent in the study of Jewish messianism, that the effort to make sense of one's life by entering the web of messianic speculations and beliefs is important. In addition to the believing that history can sometimes create an apocalyptic mind-set, such scholars as Frank Kermode, Walter Schmithals, and Bernard McGinn have proposed to contemplate the idea that there are persons who are attracted by their character to states of crises, and therefore they are in search of that historical state. I assume that this may be also the case with some Kabbalists, such as R. Abraham ben Eliezer ha-Levi, who fervently inspected every significant historical event for symptoms of the advent of the Messiah. In the case of such a person, not only is history attractive and instructive, but its conceptualization is substantially shaped by his expectations, which are expressed by means of the Kabbalistic paradigms he is acquainted with. Those men in search of crisis have sometimes contributed to the formation of an atmosphere of crisis by their very resort to a kind of *imaginaire* that not only reflects history—if such a "faithful" type of imagination exists at all—but also re-creates it for those who did not experience the critical events at first hand. Expectations for the coming of the Messiah are especially prone to galvanize the spiritual ambiance beyond anything that has happened in external history. Being an obvious addition to the external events, these expectations are paradigms propelled onto external history not only as explanatory grids but also as "hard facts" which change the lives of those who are influenced by those expectations and their mystical formulations. Thus the role of "actual" events for the nature and emergence of messianic concepts and experiences is somewhat reduced, since the great influence is only rarely that of the external or objective events but, instead, is that of their reverberations in the memories of those who were eager to indulge in one type of Kabbalistic messianism or another.

The discussions in this book presuppose not only the existence of different models, which are important factors in determining the different forms of the messianic ideas, but also their influence, which in some cases traveled through history. The assumption has been that there is no one basic messianic idea but rather a stream of traditions. The persistence of some varieties of messianic ideas allows a view of availability that questions dramatically the importance of the historicistic descriptions of messianism in Jewish studies. The fact that a Messiah emerged in certain decades, and that he was determined by some historical, political, social, and religious circumstances, does not mean that the relevance of that messianic phenomenon is limited to that period. The perception that Lurianic messianism is the sole relevant form of messianism for Sabbateanism, because Luria was closest in time to Sabbatai Tzevi, is the result of the historicistic approach. However, the persistence of the ecstatic Kabbalah in Byzantium, and then in the Ottoman Empire via the quotations in *Sefer ha-Peliy'ah,* demonstrates the relevance of some forms of religiosity beyond the precise geographic confines of their formulation. In fact, periodization and geographical compartimentalization are extremely difficult in some cases. Abulafia roamed from country to country for three decades, was exposed to a variety of conceptual systems, and addressed different Jewish as well as non-Jewish communities. What, therefore, would be the most defining moment in his formulation of ideas on messianism: his former experiences, the traditions he was exposed to, or the immediate circumstances where his views were formulated? If his views had been known to Tzevi from the book he studied, while he rejected explicitly the views of Luria, what is the weight of the historicistic explanations? Availability of ideas, either by oral transmission or in print, reduce dramatically the scholarly attempts to restrict explanations to periods that are infused by a characteristic conceptual framework. The contextualization of a phenomenon, especially an elitist one such as those forms of messianism discussed above, should take into consideration elements stemming from different, even remote places and separated by large spans of time. These distances were easily bridged by written documents, and some of the most important ones were available and read. The centers of scholarly analysis of the historicist approach are the meaning and significance that the messianic phenomena might have both for those who first formulated them and for the later consumers, as well as the circumstances of these formulations. In the more panoramic and global approaches suggested above, more complex methodologies may do better justice to complex phenomena than the more historicistic ones. Reception theories may enable us to understand why much older ideas recur and even inspire intense religious lives.

The Proliferation of Messianic "Movements" in Scholarship

Modern scholarship overstates the popular-mythical aspects of messianism, since they are the most accessible type of phenomena for the historian to study and describe. Some such phenomena, modest though they may be, are referred to as "movements" and have inspired academic histories.[17] This scholarly tendency, often unconscious, to dramatically escalate the importance of apocalyptic messianism originates in specific ideological links and thus sometimes causes what I believe to be exaggerated descriptions of certain messianic phenomena. Here are just two examples.

In 1122, a convert to Judaism, apparently a former crusader, known as R. ʿOvadiyah the Proselyte, encountered in northern Israel a Karaite named Solomon, a Kohen,[18] who claimed that he was the Messiah and that he would reveal himself in two and a half months.[19] ʿOvadiyah did not believe this. The distinguished scholar Jacob Mann, who was preoccupied by the single document dealing with this Messiah, apparently conflated it with a more extensive messianic phenomenon related to David Alroy, which involved hopes, aspirations, prayers, and fasts. Nevertheless, the incident related to the Karaite was taken by Mann to be a messianic movement.[20] In another example, Abraham Abulafia's influence is sometimes depicted by scholars in terms that denote the creation of a movement. Yet all that we possess are those few statements discussed above, and it is a matter of speculation whether Abulafia managed in his lifetime to influence more than a few dozen people. Nevertheless, his views were depicted in a book that deals with messianic movements.[21]

This is also true, in my opinion, of other cases where the term *movement* is used indiscriminately and brings to mind the term *Zionist movement.* It is entirely possible that medieval and pre-modern events are described by scholars in an anachronistic manner as possessing sociohistorical proportions that are beyond what the documentation can prove. If we consider the numerous monographs written on the subject of messianism in the last two generations, we find that they clearly stress the historical and public phenomena of messianism, in fact mostly the apocalyptic aspects, while downplaying or relegating to the periphery the mystical and personal elements that were factors in determining certain messianic phenomena. Here we can detect a kind of relationship between the historical-ideological framework and the research materials and the way they were absorbed within the academy.

One stark example of this interest in the public type of messianism in the academic world is the unprecedented growth of research concerning the Sabbatean movement. In general, Sabbateanism is perceived as a movement that sought to change the general situation of the Jewish people. This is an overstatement. In recent studies by Yehuda Liebes, he presents a different model of certain Sabbatian phenomena, one that was more concerned with religious reform, internally linked to the change of the essence of Judaism, than with external issues, usually associated with Sabbatian messianism, such as ʿaliyah to the land of Israel.[22] My pointing out a relationship between Zionist ideology and the academic establishment when it addresses matters of messianism is not meant to denigrate those studies written under the existential pressure of Zionistic positions, nor is it an expression of an alleged non-Zionistic, anti-Zionism, or post-Zionist stand; rather it is a simple reflection of my consciousness of the influence of historical contexts upon the historian himself.[23]

The currently accepted approach to Hasidic messianism, which stresses the individual's redemption as a form of neutralization, in fact means the rejection of the messianic nature of that phenomenon. This rejection can be understood first and foremost to be a result of the tension between the ideological worldview of certain scholars, who themselves favored the "authenticity" of a certain type of messianism, and the anti-Zionistic Hasidic ideologies, which developed the alternative of individual redemption. In my opinion, this is the reason for the absence of more focused discussions on the subject, and of examination of the way in which mysticism provided its own explanation of messianism, one that transformed the ancient concepts, gravitating around the sudden arrival of an extraordinary redeeming individual, into ones that are directly relevant to the life of the individual. In fact, with the evolution of the messianic constellations of ideas, the more individualistic penchants came to the fore, so that we may speak about a gradual fragmentation of the uniqueness of the persona of the Messiah.

Two major forms of fragmentation may be discerned: one synchronic, the other diachronic. In the former, as represented by the Hasidic concept of the aspect of the Messiah found in every individual, those individuals coexist and constitute the Jewish community in a certain period. In the latter, we may mention the idea of the reincarnation of the Messiah in the various bodies, each of them possessing its own personality. The preponderance of function over persona is more evident in the later stages of the messianic complex of ideas, and this is one of the reasons for the turn to the many messianic figures who are collectively expected to accomplish a less dramatic effect than the one extraordinary mythical Messiah. Thus, from the ancient king-Messiah who represents in his personality the corporate community and saves its by his activity, it is possible to discern in the more recent developments a much more obvious role of that community, without the personality that once unified it. The more mundane and numerous Messiahs represent a development that started with the supernal one Messiah, God. The divine redeemer become less common, and instead the emergence of a semi-divine angel or personality that assumed the redemptive function is documented. Then, with the development of more articulated forms of individuality after the twelfth century, a concept of more mundane individuals who may perfect themselves and reach a salvific status emerges. Only the importance of the salvific function, central in the ancient form of sacral royalty, survived in different avatars until more recent forms of messianic thinking, which allow a plurality of human redeemers. In this development, which has nothing teleological about it, the angelic and median status of the Messiah in some forms of early Christianity and of Judaism is of a paramount significance. The incessant presence and activity of the hypostatic Messiah enabled its actualization on low in various individuals. This new development, which introduced in principle the multiple Messiahs, could create new situations that include tensions between personal and collective forms of redemption. The conflict between public messianism and private or individual messianism is more comprehensive and cultural, refracted by the attitude of scholars who reflect the sociocultural milieux active in the search of the "authentic" messianism. The public domain of the Zionist movement turned the attention of scholars informed by this ideology to the public aspects of Jewish messianism. In the course of research on Jewish messianism, interestingly, sociological methods were, nevertheless, only barely used.[24] In order to avoid misunderstandings, let me emphasize once again that despite my focusing on the inner aspects of messianism and my pointing out an overemphasis on the public, I do not assume that those public moments and movements are less important religious phenomena, but believe that a more balanced attitude should be adopted by scholars in order to mete justice to the complexity of the religious and historical events related to messianism.

Messianisms and Jewish Elites

Jewish messianism is a broad constellation of ideas that comprises both inner and outer aspects. The emphasis on the former should be more associated with elite figures, whose attempts to play a role on the public scene, what a modern person would describe on the historical arena, sometimes took the form of external activity which would rarely crystallize into movements. Thus, a certain stratification of the audience for the messianic phenomena may be offered: the classical messianic figures, who are quite few over Jewish history; those who took an active role in the transition between the self-awareness of the messianic figure and the masses, what may be called the prophets and the disseminators, who are more numerous than the messianic figures; and the believers, who were even more numerous than the propagators and who occasionally turned into significant groups of adherents to the claims of the messiahs and prophets.

By intention, the heavy reliance upon sophisticated systems of thought makes the Kabbalistic messianisms accessible only to a very small elite. Therefore, it would be prudent, when dealing with this complex combination of concepts, not to attribute to the esoteric lores concerning Kabbalistic eschatologies too great an influence, particularly on less learned audiences. The sociological aspect of the study of messianism is still in its incipient stages of research.[25]

The necessary distinction between mystical-messianic concepts—which may be more esoteric and thus have circulated solely in the elitist Kabbalah in small groups—and the more apocalyptic concepts, which contributed to the emergence of messianic mass-movements and were controlled by much simpler and cruder apocalyptic images, has not played its due role in modern scholarship. Not every attractive idea, radical innovation, or eccentric elaboration of a messianic figurewas meaningful or was widely disseminated among medieval or premodern Jews. Even if an elite figure in the periods under discussion here advanced some novel ideas, the breath of their diffusion is as crucial as the innovative aspects of those concepts. In other words, the question of the circulation of texts and ideas, messianic or not, at different levels of culture and in different strata of population is not conspicuously related to their alleged freshness or audacity.[26]

On the other hand, the question is whether the elitist groups of Kabbalists were open at all to the apocalyptic elements, or whether their messianism was of a radically different sort, shaped by more sophisticated types of thought. The tensions between the popular messianism and the elite is well known from the rabbinic attitude toward this issue, and it is exemplified by reactions of great Halakhists such as Maimonides or R. Shlomo ibn Adret. Leaders of mystical groups, such as R. Yehudah he-Ḥasid and ibn Adret, were much more reticent, if not openly hostile toward popular and sometimes even elite forms of messianism. As Vladimir Jankelevitch has audaciously formulated it, "The depersonalization of the Messiah who remains personal only in the popular beliefs is a phenomenon essential to the philosophical history of Judaism."[27] Thus, independent of their own visions of messianism—and I assume that all these figures professed one version or another of messianic traditions—it seems that the very approach of an elite in respect to new popular moves was often cautious and suspicious.

More open toward apocalyptic messianism were the book of the *Zohar* and the Kabbalists from the circle of *Sefer ha-Meshiv*. In these two cases, secondary elite figuresprotected their identity behind a cloak of anonymity. This secondary elite, eager to engage new ideas, played a greater role in the reinterpretation of traditional ideas was more mobile and energetic in disseminating their insights into larger masses. Abraham Abulafia, Shelomo Molkho, Sabbatai Tzevi, Abraham Michael Cardoso, Nathan of Gaza, Moshe Ḥayyim Luzzatto, and the Besht were all itinerants. Messianic ideas, as espoused by the secondary elite, should be understood as part of the cultivation of a broader range of topics that are characteristic of the creativity of this elite, including more complex forms of hermeneutics,[28] a propensity for exotericism,[29] or an interest in magic.[30] The most typical constellation of ideas, the messianic one, has been interpreted in many different manners, using a great variety of new imported concepts. This is just one of the most convincing examples of the more cosmopolitan nature of important segments of the Kabbalistic elite, who, like the Jewish philosophers, held significant dialogues with systems of thought formulated outside the pale of rabbinic Judaism. Kabbalah was sometimes a major factor in processes of acculturation, but it also influenced Jewish thought on general intellectual culture.

While the apocalyptic elements are more attactive to larger and popular segments of the Jewish society, the more sophisticated amalgams of ancient Jewish eschatological material and speculative approaches are more consonant with the secondary elites. The primary elites attempted to preserve the canonical eschatology as a theological and teleological dogma by moderating its apocalyptic cargo, but only rarely by featuring strong spiritualistic interpretations of the rabbinic material concerning the Messiah. In other words, each segment of Jewish society created its own sort of messianism or was attuned to a wavelength coming from the past that fitted its expectations. Thus, despite the shared stock of eschatological themes, the various parts of Jewish society over the ages have cultivated special forms of messianic tendencies. Moreover, the intensity of experiencing the messianic themes presumably differed from one sector to another—the Messiahs, the propagators of the ideas or self-consciousness of those Messiahs, and their believers. Thus, in lieu of speaking of messianism in general, a more nuanced system of distribution of experiences, concepts, and beliefs will help us to understand the manner in which the messianic themes and motives worked. I propose to drastically differentiate between the reverberations of the various facets of what is vaguely called messianism alongside much more stratified parts of the Jewish population involved in a messianic event. An inner development in the realm of the history of ideas and culture, the emphasis of the messianic elements in the Lurianic writings, sufficed, in Scholem's view, to provoke a mass movement. This approach has already been criticized by some scholars on both historical and sociological grounds.[31]

I would like to return to this issue from another angle, however. If indeed the ultraconservative Luria built up a mystical system that become a time bomb, then there is something in the tradition he was attempting to live up to that is inherently problematic. Yet such a crisical reading, as offered by some of the Sabbatean theologians, was not undertaken by other Lurianic Kabbalists, either before or after Sabbateanism. This is one of the reasons that I am inclined to reduce the potential explosive cargo of the Lurianic system. It was not this Kabbalistic system that created the crises, but independent crisical factors. We would do better to look more closely into the plausible impact of such factors as personalities and processes in Jewish forms of life that have impinged upon the reception of the messianic declarations of Tzevi, or Nathan's formulation of a certain ideology, than to concentrate on the shaky and changing circumstances encountered by the two. In other words, the messianic ideology was built in order to explicate the messianic declarations rather than create this reception. It would be sufficient to read the reaction of such a fine Lurianic Kabbalist as R. Moses Zacutto in order to see how unconvincing the arguments of Nathan were in his eyes.[32] Thus the crisis was less latent within the conceptual systems that nourished the elite of the Sabbatean movement, as in the wave of pressure created by the wide reception of the messianic claims from popular circles. The powers that pushed toward the Sabbatean explosion were created less by the Kabbalists' drawing of the ultimate implications of the concepts that structure the Lurianic system than by the pressures to explicate the messianic positions not only in terms of revelations from above, as at the beginning with Nathan, but to prove the messianism of Tzevi by resorting to Lurianic terminology.

The apocalyptic messianism of the masses had induced the theologians to strongly and often quite radically interpret Lurianicand other texts, in many cases distorting[33] or even inventing texts. It is less a matter of inner developments, as Scholem would put it, and more one of external factors that provoked the messianic hermeneutics. This is much more evident in the later phase of Tzevi's life, when the need to account for apostasy prompted some bizarre readings of texts, and even more so after the Tzevi's death. Sabbateanism as a movement is not so much a revolution from above as a series of pushes and pulls from above and below.. The messianic fermentation of the masses, incited by the declarations of Nathan and Tzevi, pushed them into a situation from which they had to explicate themselves, more emphatically in the paradoxical situations created by external events. Whereas Scholem and Tishby argued for the initial boldness and radicalness of Nathan's thought,[34] I see Nathan's early ideas as more as stemming from messianic traditions that Scholem and Tishby has failed to see in the context of the Sabbatean movement. I have attempted to point out the continuity between some themes in Sabbateanism related to the nature of the Messiah and previous Kabbalistic sources. Nevertheless, their actualization on the stage of history generated a dynamic that was intellectually creative, given more especially the outstanding literary and exegetical gifts of Nathan, though socially disruptive of the established religious orders competing in Judaism.

Most of the material discussed above deals with spiritual interpretations that could only rarely be understood by, let alone stir, the imagination of the masses. Nevertheless, it should be recognized that they sustained the vitality of eschatological traditions which might otherwise have become obsolete. Without the diverse readings of the messianic ideas in new manners earlier in the Middle Ages, those eschatological traditions would remain only the apanage of the vulgus and would not attract the attention of the later elitist figures, who were responsible for the actualization and personification of the abstract models. This seems to me to be the case regarding Sabbatai Tzevi's evolution. If my reading of the emergence of his self-consciousness is correct—and Tzevi was influenced by the nexus between Sabbatai and Messiah in *Sefer ha-Peliyah*—then we may extrapolate as to the importance of the enrichment of the constellation of messianic ideas by new vistas for a future exploitation of those vistas by aspirants to messianic roles.

Symbolism and Messianism

It would be reasonable not to relate all messianic concepts to all segments of the Jewish people. This observation, reflecting the importance I am inclined to attribute to the messianic pyramid, is especially pertinent to the more sophisticated forms of expressions found in Kabbalistic literature. These forms should be understood from at least two angles: on the one hand, the respective traditions that informed them, namely the Jewish theologoumena and the alien forms of thought that contributed to the formation of the above-mentioned models; on the other hand, literary and eidetic approaches of the imaginaire— namely, symbolism—as well as similar locutions in other forms of mysticism. The historical experiences of the Jewish people have been crystallized, according to Gershom Scholem, into powerful mystical symbols which, once disseminated among the masses, were able to affect the course of Jewish history.

Let us examine the Scholem's first claim, regarding "symbols of a very special kind, in which the spiritual experience of the mystics was almost inextricably intertwined with the historical experience of the Jewish people. It is this interweaving of two realms, which in most other religious mysticisms have remained separate, that gave Kabbalah its specific imprint."[35] Scholem proposed a correlation between the Kabbalistic symbols and the cumulative historical experiences of the people of Israel, which informed the mystic, who produced a fusion between the inner, personal experience and the collective experience. This is the reason for the mysterious affinity between some Kabbalistic symbols and Jewish national history. Moreover, Scholem explained the correlation between the two realms rather lucidly when he claimed, "The more sordid and cruel the fragment of historical reality allowed to the Jew amid the storms of exile, the deeper and more precise the symbolic hope which burst through it and transfigurated it."[36] Consequently, a deep continuity and consonance between the historical, especially the negative, experiences of the Jews and their Kabbalistic symbolism concerning messianism, or at least a part of of that symbolism, is taken to be crucial to the understanding of that branch of Jewish mysticism. The tears of a lachrymose "history" have reified into so many Kabbalistic symbols, which serve

see comments of Strauss in his letter!

as mirrors within which Jewish "traumatic" history receives its meaning. The mystic's consciousness becomes a test tube, a mysterious alembic, for this alchemical transformation, as well as the agent that symbolically transmits the meaning of the history of his generation. In short, Scholem invoked the theory of deprivation as the source of apocalypticism in order to make sense of some of the most decisive moments in the history of Jewish mysticism. The last passage, however, patently contradicts Scholem's own description of the Kabbalists' eschatology as escapist. Moreover, by emphasizing the connection between suffering and messianism, and by seeing symbolism as expressing the national experience, Scholem implicitly reduced the floruit of messianic-historical symbolism to the sixteenth century. Yet in this period Kabbalistic symbolism in the stricter sense of this word, even as used by Scholem, become less productive, and Kabbalists were more concerned with classifying them, or building larger nets, syntheses, and myths that bind them.[37]

In principle, I would not separate so sharply the process of the genesis and mystical significance of Kabbalistic symbols from those we encounter in other forms of mysticism. Scholem assumed that such a "historical" symbolism, allegedly characteristic of Jewish mysticism, would seem "strange to students of Christian mysticism, since it does not fit into the categories of 'mysticism' with which they are familiar."[38] But if our assumption as to the importance of preexisting theological and philosophical concepts and models for the formation of Kabbalistic symbolism is true, there is indeed no categorical difference between the manner in which Jewish and other mystical symbolisms have emerged. In all these cases, it would be reasonable to inspect the respective theologies and related types of literature in order to find out the literary sources of the mystics. Jewish theology was concerned with the problem of the history of the Jewish nation since the Bible, just as Christian theology was concerned with the story of Christ since the composition of the New Testament; the two respective types of mysticism have integrated in their symbolism theological concepts which may or may not be related to a "real" historical event or events.

Instead of two constitutive components of the emerging Kabbalistic symbols, the individual and the national experiences as proposed by Scholem, I would therefore propose three: the traditional concepts, for example galut, understood as a national event or situation; the Kabbalistic-symbolical significance of that concept, in this case the exile of the divine, often described as the Shekhinah, as the prototype or reflection of the national exile; and finally the mystical experience of the Kabbalists, a feeling or a state of personal alienation, an inner galut. This last element is an event which is rather imponderable in connection with the formative moment of the symbol, it is rather difficult to speculate on its relative importance. From some of the discussions above, however, we may conclude that an elite created its symbols from a rearrangement of the previous symbols and concepts in new nets. For Abulafia, the high priest becomes an allegory for the Messiah because the former was the person who recited the divine name. Tzevi appropriates the astrological view of Saturn as a messianic planet, while the Besht sees his magical-mystical practices as preparing the emergence of the Messiah. These rearrangements of prior material in messianic nets serve to validate one's claim in terms of values related to elitist types in the various earlier traditions. In other words, an eschatological reading of reality is accompanied by an eschatological reading of traditional texts and concepts, which regroups part of the material around the new forms of elite practices, described now as redemptive. Thus, mystical and magical practices, in addition to concepts related to the ancient first elites—such as kingship, prophet, teacher, and priesthood—were recharged with salvific valences as part of the secondary elite's efforts to move to the center of religious creativity and influence, on the one hand, and the search for meaning, on the other hand. More flexible and less secure spiritually, the secondary elite is much more open to new experiences and experiments than the first elite is.

Another issue related to the phenomenological aspect of the Kabbalistic symbols is the role of exile-redemption symbolism in the general economy of Kabbalistic symbolism. Scholem himself implies that this peculiar type of symbolism is relevant to a later stage of Kabbalistic thought, as the earlier Kabbalists did not pay attention to messianic issues in their systems. Moreover, even in the case of the Lurianic Kabbalah, the question of whether the exile-redemption problem is really the heart of the system is a question that can be debated. A highly complex type of literature, Lurianic Kabbalah can be read in different ways while allowing emphases on various key concepts, the exile-redemption polarity being only one of them. Other questions, which do not matter for our discussion here, also complicate Scholem's argument. Does he restrict the relationship between Kabbalistic symbols and historical-communal experience to the symbol of exile and redemption? Or does he assume that also in the case of nonredemptive symbolism there is a symbiosis between the two realms of experience, the private and the collective? Moreover, how is the private use of a symbol—the inner alienation as an interpretation of galut, for example, which allegedly encapsulates the historical experience—conveyed as an experience to other Kabbalists or to the masses?

Scholem would say that there is no special need for such transmission since, in a way reminiscent of Leibniz's monads, in the case of the Jewish Kabbalists "each individual was a totality."[39] His implicit assumption is that a certain generation of Jews shared, in its collective totality, a certain type of inner experience, which could open the members of that generation to the understanding of a certain symbol forged by another contemporary, in our case a Kabbalist. Such a far-reaching assumption, based on the corporate view of different Jewish communities and individuals as constituting one organic unit, still waits for an elaboration which I could not find in Scholem's printed studies. The resort to the idea of an organic totality seems to involve a metaphysics of the Jewish people, which is indeed well known in some Kabbalistic sources but quite difficult to substantiate on the historical level, by means of academic tools in use by scholars who would not automatically subscribe to a romantic vision of the Jewish nation. As I have pointed out, the three levels of involvement in messianic enterprises may display not only different intensities of belief but also different concerns toward various types of messianic themes.

Polychromatism and Messianism

Sociologically speaking, messianic themes are polychromatic by their hierarchical nature: total dedication and strong self-consciousness of the importance of one's persona and mission at the top of the pyramid, more dilute and confused awareness at its bottom. Messianic movements, like many other organizations and institutions, are pyramidal. Such a structure may explain better the vitality that messianic ideas enjoyed for so many centuries. Each layer of Jewish society, even each individual, could select a model, or a version of a certain model, that was more relevant to his personal aspirations or to his social or political circumstances. The polychromatic nature of messianism may help us trace the various appeals that the themes understood as messianic had for some many people in a variety of historical periods, geographical areas, and changing social circumstances.

The monolithic view of the people of Israel as an interpretive premise is quite problematic and even disturbing within the framework of a scholarly discourse. Indeed, it contradicts Scholem's otherwise much more pluralistic positions. Was it not Scholem who so emphatically proposed to accept as Judaism whatever belief was shared by the Jews of a certain period?[40] Would Scholem accept the idea that Sabbateanism was a liquidation of Halakhic Judaism or its neutralization and not just a certain type of spirituality, which should be judged in itself? If not, it would mean that, for Scholem, the Sabbatean movement is not a Jewish phenomenon. By his own methodology, we should confer the same status on the mystical and Hasidic interpretations of messianism that Scholem would allow the apocalyptic one. Thus, in the very spirit of his own emphasis on the need of a more open and pluralistic approach that would constitute an alternative to monochromatism, it should be appropriate to examine the mystical literature in order to pay more attention to the potential variety of its treatments of such a fascinating issue.

Therefore, it is plausible to view the constellation of ideas and beliefs designated as Jewish messianism as including various conceptual models, it would be advisable not to discriminate between them by preferring one over the other. The existence of those models within the religious vocabulary of Judaism is crucial for allowing alternative spiritual solutions that can be employed in different situations yet be considered to be legitimate and within the framework of the tradition. The importance of the model of personal redemption can be successfully interpreted particularly in a period of the rise of the earthly-mythical model.[41] The problem of absorbing models that are at odds with the prevalent ideology at the core of a certain culture is not limited to the discussion of messianism alone and is a well-known phenomenon among scholars. Even the present discussion exemplifies the relativity that exists in scientific research, for it is also influenced by the temporal circumstances and the interests of a certain group of scholars.

The discovery of the individual or self in the twelfth century is part of a more general development described by several historians of the medieval period as the shift from perceiving the tribe or nation as the source of the individual's self-definition to the granting of more substance to the individual, to his inner life and self-awareness. Consequently, it becomes possible to understand how a concept of community or national salvation underwent a dramatic transformation, and beginning in the twelfth century there are discussions about messianism concerned with the redemption of the individual. This trend gains strength in Renaissance thought, which emphasized the individual as a meaningful unit of being, his perfection and redemption granted an independent and meaningful status. Part of the greater interest in the persona of the Messiah in sixteenth-century mysticism should be connected to what I propose to call a turn toward the personality, which also is evident in Jewish sources.

Messianism versus Tradition

Readers of the preceding pages who are also acquainted with the Scholem's writings, in particulary his discussions of messianism, will not miss a sharp contrast between his form of treating the subject and mine. What seems come up quite often in Scholem is his sense of deep, persistent, inescapable tensions between the messianism and tradition.[42] Indeed, the sense of a latent crisis of tradition as part of the very nature of messianism—identical in Scholem's view with apocalypticism—is a leitmotif of Scholem's thought, as he assumed also a deep ambiguity and in some cases even great tensions between Jewish mysticism and Jewish tradition.[43] The absence of a significant reference to the crisical aspects of the relations between messianism and tradition in my discussions above is not to be seen as an implicit denial of existence of such tension. Indeed, the relations between Messiahs and rabbis have only rarely been simple, and they were never harmonious. The two major Messiahs whose thought has been discussed here, Abraham Abulafia and Sabbatai Tzevi, were fiercely attacked and banned by members of the rabbinic first elite. After the magisterial discussion of Tzevi's fascinating odyssey in Scholem's monograph, both the broad impact of Sabbateanism and the details of the negative reactions toward his adventure are more conspicuous than ever. Thus, I have refrained from repeating the findings of other scholars, in this case Scholem's view, when I do agree with them.

An even more essential reason for not addressing this tension, however, is my understanding of messianism, which presupposes a more diversified cluster of concepts and at the same time a view of the Jewish tradition as not only polychromatic in principle—a position characteristic of Scholem's worldview[44]—but also de facto. My impression, when perusing some of the analyses of the crises of tradition, is that "tradition" in the Scholemian nomenclature presupposes a rather rigid form of religious and cultural themes and experiences or, as he himself once formulated it, a "fixed tradition," just as his view of messianism is mainly focused on one major mode, the apocalyptic. Yet while the monochromatic vision of messianism that I have attempted to analyze is more conspicuous, Scholem's—and often also his followers'—monolithic view of tradition is much more difficult to locate and define. Moreover, the Scholemian school would assume a mythical locus for such a tradition, "in the very heart of Judaism."[45] In my opinion, following some of the more pluralistic vistas opened by Scholem himself, it would be reasonable to transfer the manner of treating the variety of mystical schools and models and their corresponding concepts of messianism to the investigation of more fluid Jewish traditions, which together constitute a larger and more vague spiritual entity named Judaism. It is not sufficient, I contend, to adopt Scholem's very liberal conception of Judaism as including Sabbateanism. It is indeed a positive landmark in liberal Jewish theology to rescue from oblivion and derision a repressed phenomenon and to include it as a "legitimate" Jewish form of expression. On some occasions, however, this acceptance has the nature of a mechanical addition of a formerly banned entity to an already existing but rather static body of practice and thought named "tradition." While effectively emancipating Sabbateanism from the suppression of traditional and sometimes too intellectually oriented nontraditional thinkers, Scholem has at the same time implicitly repressed the richer varieties of other Jewish traditions, including the non-apocalyptic messianic ones, which are all grouped together under the general rubric of tradition.[46] Are the Polish Jewish "traditions" of the middle seventeenth century identical to the contemporary Yemenite ones? Is the Amsterdam community of former conversos the same as the community of Italian Jews living for centuries in Rome? Take, for example, the religious outlook of R. Elijah Benamosegh, a rather conservative thinker at the end of the nineteenth century in Italy, and the sharp reaction to his more scientifically oriented commentary on the Pentateuch among Jews in Syria, where rabbis have burned it.[47] Both parties would argue persuasively that they are the authentic representatives of traditional Judaism. After having accepted the necessity of recognizing a greater variety of the models of Kabbalistic literature, we should be more open to the heterogenous character of non-Kabbalistic forms of traditional Judaism.

Martin Buber has attempted to unify "authentic" messianism around the concept of the prophetic, relegating the apocalyptic mode to the status of having been influenced by external sources. Scholem attempted, in the case of Sabbateanism, to construe a unified Jewish audience by proposing a strong Lurianic influence on the Jewish world. Yet even if one were to allow for a limited dissemination of this type of Kabbalah, the question is whether it absorbed in the same form in all the Jewish communities. Was its reception able to reduce the differences between a follower of the Maharal in Central Europe and a follower of Cordovero in Hebron or Jerusalem? The more dynamic vision of "traditional" Judaism, and of its various messianic concepts in the pre-Sabbatean period should be given greater emphasis, thus allowing a more complex explanation of the nature of Sabbateanism as both continuous in matters of the history of ideas, though also quite disruptive from the point of view of the religious praxis of the society. Rather, I would adopt an approach to history similar to that formulated by Marc Bloch: "there exists no train of privileged causal waves, no order of acts always and everywhere determinative, opposed to certain perpetual epiphenomena; . . . on the contrary, all society, like all spirit, issues from constant interaction. True realism in history is knowing that human reality is multiple."[48]

If human reality is indeed multiple, human imagination is much more variegated. And imagining a utopian topic seems to be even more multifaceted than imagining an entity which existed in a glorious past. An epiphenomenon such as Tzevi's study of *Sefer ha-Peliy'ah* had as much influence on the emergence of the messianic awareness of this figure as the privileged wave of causality represented by Scholem's claim of the dominant influence of Lurianism. Since I do not see in the diverse discussions on eschatology a monolithic messianic idea encountering an allegedly reified and static tradition defined in strong essentialistic terms, why not envision a wide spectrum of relations between messianism and tradition and rely less on crisis as the point of contact between them?[49]

Such an approach will inherently confine crisical explanations for the emergence of Jewish mystical and messianic phenomena to rare cases, an approach suggested in Gershon Cohen's important article "Messianic Postures." Instead of focusing on an explanation of Jewish messianism as shaped by a monolithic messianic idea, it may be prudent to take into account the more numerous instances when a less apocalyptic messianism was absorbed by mystical and other Jewish traditions. Though it may be a platitude that every religious system shapes its primary symbols in a way that is consonant to its main ethos,[50] I believe it would be wise to indicate that this is also the case with messianism. This situation may be understood as the emasculation of the subversive drives of messianism, but again such a formulation presupposes a reification of the "true" messianism as understood by the scholar. In other words, if authentic messianism is not defined in strong terms, and a broader variety of elements is regarded as messianic if accepted as such by the various traditions and mystical literatures, the very concepts of emasculation, neutralization, or crisis will lose some of their heuristic functions. Another approach, however, may do more justice both to the historical and the conceptual realities. Scholem had been looking more to explanations drawn from developments inherent in the conceptual process within the mystical system he viewed as informing both the emergence and the ideology of Sabbateanism: namely, Lurianism.

Nevertheless, the crises messianism created on the scene of history will certainly not disappear by an attempt at reducing the importance of the explanatory role of historical crises. These crises in Jewish history were severe and very often quite painful. The price paid for apocalyptic messianism was incomparably greater than for any other concept accepted and disseminated by Jews, an issue that may hardly be disputed. As individuals and as communities, Jews paid this price time and again, in disputes with Christians over whether the Messiah had already come or not, and in clashes between messianic Jewish movements and hard historical facts. There is no special reason to glorify either the prophetic or the apocalyptic forms of messianism, as done by Buber and Scholem respectively, as the one solely authentic form and to disregard the mystical interpretation of other, equally genuine and interesting versions of Jewish messianism. Scholem was more attracted to the apocalyptic and attempted to evaluate its impulses as the source of important stimuli for conceptual innovations and social dynamics. A proper analysis, however, should not only engage the new elements when they appear on the historical scene but also address the relative forces of all the elements that contribute to a given historical event or process. The "tradition," or what I prefer to call different traditions, is made up of inertial forces whose role in a particular development has to be carefully evaluated by means of "thick description" as proposed by Clifford Geertz, without favoring the new over the old or vice-versa. Otherwise, a historical analysis will be prone to become more similar to a journalistic description that highlights the scandalous or extraordinary, neglecting the average or normal. While a history of ideas is attracted much more to new vectors, a cultural history must engage also the older ones, in order to explain why in a given period a certain group or community embraced a messianic enterprise. Fascinated by the dynamics of religious ideas, Scholem and his school have been inclined to overlook, when dealing with messianic topics, the efficacy and spirituality of the stasis in traditional societies. A history of ideas has replaced the cultural history and dictated too strongly a logic of events guided by mystical concepts as formative of social events. I have attempted to point to some moments where messianic ideas should be seen in cultural context. This is the case with the assumption that the misunderstanding of the rumors related to the Mongolian invasion created messianic expectations in the second part of the thirteenth century, that the gloomy century between 1391 and 1492 was decisive for the emergence of the magical model of messianism in Spain in the circle of *Sefer ha-Meshiv*, that the apocalyptic atmosphere in Christianity during the sixteenth century may have contributed to a better understanding of the floruit of contemporary Kabbalistic messianism, and that Renaissance astrology underpinned some aspects of the reception of Sabbatai Tzevi as Messiah.

Messianic Ideas: Conduits, Conflicts, Syntheses

On the phenomenological plane, the few messianic ideas in the biblical literature point to interesting cases of primal or pre-axial approaches as they reflect the concerns of the group, tribe, or nation with their survival or their return to a lost autonomy. The individual, including the king-Messiah himself, was functioning within the frame of a communal enterprise, either by representing community or by being responsible for its welfare. This primal approach was accentuated much later than the sixth century B.C., when the axial age emerged, according to the exponents of this theory,[51] and to a certain extent it has been more pronounced in Judaism. The ongoing concerns with the preservation of the group, with its national continuation and physical existence, have strengthened the apocalyptic elements in popular circles. After the emergence of axial spiritual attitudes, however, with their emphases upon spiritual attainments rather than physical survival, upon individual achievements rather than group well-being, a variety of syntheses between the primal and axial values have taken place. These were described earlier (chapters 1 and 2) as hermeneutical moves which enabled the primal elements to survive while differentiating in new directions and assuming new meanings, consonant with the parameters of the axial period. Thus, as in other cases, the two sets of values, the group-oriented religion and the individualistic one, enriched each other. Moreover, due to the general acceptance of the primal, the medieval Jewish secondary elites also perpetuated these values, though in new forms palatable to their own more spiritual proclivities.

But even when reducing the apocalyptic elements of a certain system or period to the margin, these elements did not dissipate. This is the reason I assume that the speculative models reflecting the axial approaches have also been affected by their encounter with and absorption of the primal, pre-axial types of thought. This influence is quite evident in the case of the resurgence of magical elements in some of the theosophical, Sabbatean, and Hasidic forms of messianism, as well as in Abraham Abulafia's apocalyptic register. In any case, I see the oscillations between the different possibilities characteristic of the two approaches as a major factor that needs to be taken in account for a better understanding of the dynamics of Jewish messianism.[52]

In the more modern period, many of the primal elements of utopia have been de-nationalized in the form of socialism or communism, where the concern with social, economic, and political justice has been emphatically presented as intended for mankind in general. It is a conflict between the nineteenth-century ideologies and medieval and Renaissance doctrines of individuality that eventually developed, through many metamorphoses, into the Hasidism of the mid-eighteenth century. Hasidic doctrines did not remain static, however; one example is the dramatic shift of attitude toward to messianism in recent decades within Habad Hasidism. Originally, this Hasidic school sought to moderate acute messianism, following the lead of the Great Maggid, R. Dov Baer of Medzierecz. Ironically, this once nonmessianic Hasidic approach bears witness to a clear revival of the mythical element of messianism. Thus even within a specific intellectual system, there can be oscillations between different writings and various definitions of messianism, which fluctuate according to historical or personal circumstance, causing the rise of the importance of a notion that earlier had been rejected or marginalized.

It is possible to describe the variegated developments within Jewish messianism not only as the confrontations and syntheses between the primal and the axial modes of thought but also as conflicts between the mythical and the mystical or between myth and logos. Theosophical-theurgical Kabbalistic thought, which developed the more mythical messianism, following sometimes popular apocalyptic conceptions, was confronted by a different conception than that found in the ecstatic Kabbalah, which was based more on philosophical, namely axial, sources.[53] There is no question that this type of struggle between the two trends and the eventual preference for one trend or another was the result of specific historical or social circumstances. Sometimes the mythical elements—or the strong belief in a metahistorical personality who could enter history, invade the public scene, and solve the problems that the individual or even the nation could not—were preferred since this model could be explained to certain types of people. But in more clearly elitist systems, such as that of the ecstatic Kabbalah, the emphasis was placed on a more philosophical or intellectual basis, since the focus was less on external intervention in history as on gradual personal and spiritual progress that reaches its apex in the perfection of the connection between the soul or intellect with the divine. From this perspective I see the changes in emphasis within the history of messianism as representing conflicts between the mythical view and the logos. Despite the fact that the "logical" or natural approaches sometimes took on mystical form, we can still discern that the arena of salvation is the inner life and not external circumstances. In this context the ideal of devequt often played a great role.

Messianism and Devequt

Devequt is one of the most mystical of the religious values formulated in Jewish texts since the Bible. The question is whether, given its undeniably personal, axial quality in the philosophical and mystical literatures, it has been merged with eschatological concepts in Jewish literature. Scholem has repeatedly denied such a nexus. In *The Messianic Idea* he described devequt as "a value without eschatological connotations, i.e. it can be realized in this life, in a direct and personal way, by every individual, and has no messianic meaning. It is a state of personal bliss which can be attained without having recourse to the vast field of eschatology, utopianism, and Messianism."[54]

This view came under attack from Tishby, who has pointed out the connection between devequt and eschatology in Luzzatto and Hasidism.[55] Even after Tishby's critique, however, Scholem's view did not change. Scholem published a rejoinder to Tishby's article: "Devekut is clearly a contemplative value without Messianic implications and can be realized everywhere and at any time. None of the older Kabbalists who spoke of it with great emphasis as the goal of the mystic way dreamed of connecting it with Messianism."[56] Elsewhere in the same essay Scholem declares that "redemption of the soul without redemption of the social body, i.e. of the nation from its historical exile, of the outward world from its broken state, has never had a Messianic meaning in Judaism. It is a private affair of religious experience and is nowhere spoken of as a Messianic action."[57]

Indeed, Scholem is right in declaring that an experience of devequt can be realized outside the domain of eschatology, but this misses the point. The main question is whether this mystical value may nevertheless be part of the eschatological beliefs, practices, or enterprises. The answer is that starting with

Abulafia, in Kabbalah the mystical and the eschatological were often intertwined. As Yehuda Liebes has pointed out in some zoharic statements, mystical communion with God may be related to eschatological concepts,[58] as is the case with the passage from Moses de Leon discussed in chapter 3. Therefore, in addition to Luzzatto and Hasidism, where devequt has been blended with eschatological concepts, devequt is also found in some other crucial forms of Jewish mysticism. This statement should be understood as part of the communal aspects of Jewish mysticism in general, as I have attempted to show in my discussions of the mystico-magical model found in Kabbalah and Hasidism.[59] Apocalyptic traditions, being pre-axial and more concerned with the redemption of the community, have been conjoined since the Middle Ages with some axial values in order to actualize some of the hopes and promises of the messianic traditions: in order to be able to become a Messiah, one should first cultivate a rich spiritual life. Only persons who had have achieved mystical experiences may contribute to public life by assuming the role of the Messiah. The emergence of the different forms of mystical Messiahs is therefore the result of encounters between the private zone of mysticism and the more public sphere of eschatology. Only after feeling that they have redeemed themselves by becoming their own Messiahs were these mystical individuals able to proclaim themselves redeemers of others. Since we are dealing here more with the consciousness of the Messiahs than with popular beliefs, we should better understand the messianic occurrence as available in the present, or even actualized by the Messiahs and some of their followers.

But while in some cases these eschatological experiences are described by and generate extraordinary, eccentric anomian and antinomian forms of behavior, as in the cases of Abulafia and Tzevi, in other instances, as some forms of Hasidism, messianism is understood as a deepening of the nomian way of life, understood as permeating the traditional aspects of religion. In fact, messianism should be seen in a larger perspective within the modes of Jewish values. An active attitude in the elite, messianism was not embodied in a specific ritual. Though rituals having a messianic cargo are known in Judaism, such as the blessing of the new moon, the Passover seder, and the Havdalah, I am acquainted only with one messianic ritual introduced by Kabbalists: that related to the seventh day of Passover in Lurianic Kabbalah. Thus, we may assume that roughly speaking, neither rites nor myths have been created in the context of acute messianism, but prior elements have been combined and elaborated. Though dealing in most of the cases discussed above with relations between primordial beings and extraordinary personalities and man, the elitist thinkers and Messiahs only rarely developed a full-fledged myth of the Messiah. With the exception of Sabbateanism after Tzevi's conversion, it is hard to discern significant myths that would formulate very articulated forms of messianism. In other words, most of the material analyzed above was neither substantially related to a specific ritual nor systematized in messianic myths. Attempts, however, to ascribe the performance of the Jewish ritual to a messianic enterprise, and to insert the messianic figure into the larger scheme of the theosophical processes, represent the contribution of medieval, more systematic thinking to the constellation of messianic ideas.

Messianism: Restorative or Utopian?

The Scholem's well-known and helpful distinction between two main forms of conceptualizing the nature of the messianic times, the restorative and the utopian, has been highly influential in modern treatments of messianic topics,[60] and I have referred to it from time to time in this book.[61] As Scholem has pointed out, the different forms of messianism represent adaptations of both ways of understanding messianism. Moreover, Scholem often mentions that the dialectical tension between these two moments may be detected throughout the history of the messianic idea. It seems that only the importance given to the existence of one messianic idea serves as the starting point for the introduction of dialectics and tensions. If one resorts to the concept of the constellation of messianic ideas, the need to address different forms of messianism as part of one unit, and thus to create forms of dialectics and tensions, will be reduced. I emphasize *reduced* and not obliterated because of the eclectic and nonsystematic nature of mystical thought. The ecstatic Kabbalah is less concerned with the restorative elements as understood by Scholem, since the main national components of redemption have been marginalized. The absence of discussions of the reconstruction of the Temple or of the return of the Jewish people to the land of Israel is emblematic of the more spiritualistic bias of this system. Even the utopian aspect, however, has a rather peculiar character. If the main scene of the redemption is the human and the Agent Intellect, the salvific moment is indeed utopian par excellence, since it will not take place in any place (*topos*) but *in spiritu.* Moreover, the state of being designated as messianic is not relegated to the distant future but is conceptualized as attainable in the here and now.

Historical time, like geographical boundaries or sacred sites, may be conceived in certain models of thought as a secondary ingredient for the salvation of individuals, but its role has often been emphasized as crucial for the redemption of the nation or for mankind. The omnipresence, though not the omnipotence of the Messiah as an Agent Intellect, as found in ecstatic Kabbalah and in the writings of several Jewish medieval philosophers, opens the path to "messianic" experience during each and every moment, in what a mystic would take to be atemporal experiences. Such are Benjamin's, and to a certain extent also

Levinas's, views of messianism, where the more passive aspiration for the imminent advent of the Messiah has quite apocalyptic ingredients.[62] Thus, the utopian element, while present in the ecstatic Kabbalah, has its own contours that differ from the apocalyptic understanding of the distant era to be ushered in by the advent of the Messiah. In other words, the utopia is a matter more of the actualization of an ever-present potentiality than the of invasion of a deus-ex-machina persona. The talismanic model is in principle much more restorative, and the utopian element is present only insofar as the participants in the messianic enterprise are involved. By their common efforts, they believed it possible to re-create the broken unity of the primordial Adam. Thus, though the supernal anthropomorphic structure itself is not new and thus we may speak of a strong restorative mode of thought, for the individual souls, which are the particles involved in this restructuring, the situation may be novel and thus utopian. Much more restorative by its very nature is the theurgical-theosophical model. Envisioning a rebuilding of the Temple and a restoration of all Jewish rituals to their pristine form of performance as a essential for the messianic times, this model does not leave much room for the utopian aspects. Especially in the Lurianic version, the theosophical-theurgical Kabbalah strives toward the reconstruction of the shattered supernal anthropos.[63] Thus, insofar as the models found in the mystical literature, the utopian elements are marginal in comparison to the restorative ones.

It is evident, however, that even in the cases when an ideal past was believed to be reenacted in the utopian future, the imaginaire is as important as the "actual" historical past. The past was construed by using elements extracted from the medieval models, some of them stemming from an intellectual context that has nothing to do with any form of messianism and then projected into the future. Thus, the distinction between the two modes of imagining the future is rather attenuated. The core of both the ideal past and the ideal future is, at least in the mystical literature, less historical and more modeled on the type of mysticism adopted by one mystic or another. Adam, Moses, David, and Solomon have been described as ideal figures who personified the spiritual virtues accepted by the mystics. The distinction between what really happened in the past and what has been anachronistically attributed to those actors who shaped the past is quite tenacious in the Middle Ages.[64] If we do not presuppose such a strong bias for restructuring a "real" past, but allow a much more anachronistic understanding of the past given the strong grids of the powerful models available during the Middle Ages, the stark distinction between the restorative and the utopian will fade. Rather, the more popular utopian impulses are explications of present purposes, tensions, or crises, projected sometimes onto the historical scene in an indeterminate future and imagined as fulfilled, for the benefit of the masses, by the traditional apocalypse presided over by the omnipotent figure of the Messiah. In more general terms, mysticism, concerned as it often is with present experiences, projected its ideals both into the past and into the future, voiding the distinction between the restorative and the utopian modes of messianisms. Most useful in the analysis of the popular apocalyptic versions of messianism, this distinction becomes less effective when the main salvific events are imagined to take place in the realm of the spiritual, when the mystics would conceive their redemptive experience as atemporal. As we saw when analyzing Abulafia's two messianic registers, the spiritual allegory invites a form of discourse that is less concerned with verbs and less temporal.

On the Plenitude of Experiences in Some Forms of Mystical Messianism

The various forms of mysticism, which strove toward a fulfillment of what was believed to be the ideal spiritual life in the present and anticipated of the sublime forms of human existence, were not concerned with a systemic deferment of the highest forms of experience to an indefinite future related to national redemption and geographical relocation of all the Jews. Rather, they attempted to interpret the actualization of the mystical and mystical-magical ideals in more traditional eschatological terms. From this point of view Scholem's approach (as well as Kafka's and even Benjamin's to a certain degree) toward messianism as apocalyptic is much closer to some of the traditional apocalyptic conceptualizations, while some mystical forms of understanding eschatology are much closer to aspects of Benjamin's thought, as well as that of other modern Jewish thinkers, including Buber, Rosenzweig and Levinas.[65] In my opinion, the strong opposition between the circular-ritualistic and historical-messianic sorts of time, described by some scholars of the history of religions, is often an artificial dichotomy. Religious traditions such as those manifested in Judaism rarely prevent a messianic state of mind and redemptive experience by relying exclusively on the efficacy of the ritual; neither are the messianic hopes automatically divorced from the performance of religious rituals. Rather, it is assumption of the plenitude of ritual forms of time that gives linear time both direction and meaning; otherwise this "historical" time would invite a homogenous conception of instances, each of them void of any specific meaning. The various syntheses of circular and linear times created spiritual phenomena whose physiognomy still awaits complete analysis.

In the case of the ecstatic Kabbalah, where the role of circular time connected to the rhythm of the ritual dromena, the ecstatic moments that transcend time are understood as propelling the mystic into his own eschaton. Therefore, only very rarely should a delay connected to the deferred achievement of a religious perfection be imposed as a quintessential feature of main mystical forms of Judaism. Rather, the intensification of religious life by mystical performance is often an anticipation, on both the individual and the group level, of the more common experience of the many. As S. Talmon has appropriately formulated it, as concerns the biblical concept of redemption: "The concrete fabric of the expectation of redemption places upon the People of the Bible a responsibility for forming the future which grows out of their responsibility for forming their present . . . each person is called upon to help bring about the realization of the 'time of redemption' in history. Human obedience to divine command is expected to lead to a transformation of the world, not to bring about a world revolution."[66] The belief in the efficacy of the rabbinic ritual or of mystical anomian techniques provided, for some traditional Jews and for Kabbalists and Hasidic masters,[67] the possibility of attaining forms of religious experiences whose plenitude was conceived of as recalling or paralleling those of the future messianic age. For some Jewish mystics, the perfection attributed to the Messiah contributed to the emergence and sometimes the reinforcement of a paradigm to be imitated in the immediate present, not an experience to be deferred to an indefinite future, a fulfillment rather than solely a reminder of a deficient state of being. If for the larger masses expectations of the messianic age stirred hope in the perfection of a way of life that is hardly attainable in exile, for an elite Kabbalist the eschatological achievement, including the messianic attainment, is much more readily available.

Jewish mysticism gave to the Kabbalistic elites some paradigms of acting which offered them possibilities of messianic activities. Moreover, the hypostatical visions of the Messiah as the last sefirah—or as any of the other higher sefirot in the case of the theosophical-theurgical Kabbalah, or as identical with the Agent Intellect in the ecstatic Kabbalah, or as the praying community in Hasidism—presupposed a Messiah that is not only already in existence in potentia, but also present. At least in the forms of Kabbalah mentioned above, the Messiah is not only an eschatological event but also part of the protological—to use Levenson's term—events that remained active throughout history. The Messiah not only exists prior to the moment of redemption, as in many apocalyptic trends in Judaism, and waits, together with the Jewish nation in exile, for the destined date of his coming, all the while suffering. The hypostatical versions of the Messiah, which become part of the order of nature as much as they were part of the order of history earlier, are understood in the various types of Kabbalah as presently active and continuously available for meaningful contacts with individual mystics. The "present Messiahs" are the manner in which the higher divine power or powers have ruled this world throughout history. Thus, unlike those who haveneglected the importance of the mystical interpretations of messianism (even presupposing in some cases an antagonism between mysticism and messianism),[68] I suggest that some forms of Jewish mysticism served as triggers for new models of mystical messianism. If scholars will be more sensitive to the available material, in print and in manuscripts, where the very term *mashiyaḥ* occurs in quite mystical contexts, a more diversified picture of messianic ideas and models in Judaism will emerge. A neutralization of the scholarly neutralization of both the legitimacy and the importance of forms of the mystical messianisms will open the door for a much richer texture of a conglomerate of ideas, beliefs, and experiences.[69] In any case, the midrashic assertion that God is in exile together with the nation of Israel[70] opened the door for some Hasidic masters to claim that God may be more accessible while the Temple is destroyed than when it is built.[71] The destruction of the Temple, it should be said, only accelerated a process of transition from the religiosity gravitating around rituals performed in a sacred building, closer to the concept of *axis mundi,* to one that envisions the importance of the ideal human figure as the center of religious life, a move that took place in late antiquity and has been documented by Peter Brown.[72] Though socially and politically the situation of the Jews during the exilic period may invite the supposition that they lived in deference, as Scholem suggested, in the realm of religion this claim becomes a more complex and questionable statement that is rarely true in the case of the Jewish mystics.

Indeed, attempts to limit discussions of achieving mystical experiences to nonmessianic discourse, if those experiences do not fit the preconceived notion of "acute" messianism, unduly reduce the messianic dimensions of Jewish mysticism. Thus, for scholars working under the aegis of the Scholemian axiology, the sense of plenitude attained during messianic-mystical experiences could not be allowed to Jewish mystics. Let me inspect one such instance. In his short paper entitled "Mysticism and Messianism," R. J. Z. Werblowsky claimed, following Scholem, that R. Moses Ḥayyim 'Ephrayyim of Sudylkov neutralized messianism since he resorted to an allegorical interpretation of a biblical passage. It is he who chose the passage to analyze, believing that "statistical" considerations as to the occurrence of the term *Messiah* matter less than conceptual positions.[73] However, such an approach, which is useful after inspecting the relevant material in detail, becomes quite dangerous when the scholar suppresses the evidence to the contrary, as for example the claim of R. Moses Ḥayyim 'Ephrayyim of Sudylkov, the grandson of the Besht, that by means of the Besht's teachings the people of Israel will return from exile, a view already adduced by scholars in the famous debate on messianism and Hasidism.[74] The belief that someone practice the mystical path that will effectively liberate the people from exile is indubitably worthy of at least tangent consideration before relying on a single passage to validate the grand claim of neutralization already made by Scholem.

Even more worrisome, however, is the attempt in the same article to marginalize the messianic content of the thought of another Hasidic master, R. Menaḥem Naḥum of Chernobyl. Werblowsky mentions a few instances in order to argue, for example, that "[t]he spiritual state of communion known as *gadluth* is transient in the present dispensation; only in the messianic kingdom will it be permanent and general."[75] One has to carefully inspect the sources in order to discover that the picture in the texts may be somewhat different. No one would suspect, by reading the above quotation, that not only the term *gadlut* recurs in those discussions but also the phrase "days of Messiah" and the type of experience characteristic of the eschaton as available and attainable, to a certain extent at least, even today. Thus, in commenting on Song of Songs 8:5, Werblowsky wrote:

> She[76] is conjugated to her beloved in an union and integration[77] and so also at the time of the study of the Torah, because whoever merits to study the Torah out of fear and love, by *moḥin de-gadlut*,[78] by the means of this [practice] too exits the state of *qatnut* and diminution of the moon and attains the aspect of the *gadlut* of Knowledge and great Moḥin. And the coming close to God, blessed be He and His Name, that he feels the integration and the very great adherence to His love, blessed be He, within the world, and great union [*devequt gedolah*] similar to what happened in the moment of the promulgation of the Torah,[79] that consisted in an intercourse face to face, and the integration of the aspect of female into that of the male, the former liberated from all the diminutions . . . as we find in the case of some Tanna'im and 'Amora'im and the King David, blessed be his memory, who, because of their study of the Torah the angel of death could not affect them,[80] and all these for whoever studies the Torah in such a way[81] because he exits from all diminutions and it becomes for him as if he is in the aspect of the promulgation of the Torah in general, and similar to what will be at the time of the Messiah, soon in our days, in a permanent manner.[82]

Therefore, the messianic state of "greatness of the mind," *gadlut ha-moḥin,* is not postponed for the distant future but is attainable, though intermittently, even today, by means of studying the Torah with the enthusiasm and devotion recommended by Hasidism. The maximum experience of eupsychia can be achieved, and one may experience the days of the Messiah by becoming integrated and united with God. The existence of an ideal euchronia in the future does not deflect the Hasidic master from his conviction that this experience may be anticipated. The mystic, united with God, becomes a male and is called thus because of the divine function of the male in the erotic union of God and man.[83] Though Werblowsky is right in pointing out the intermittency of the nonmessianic experience, what concerns me here is the claim that it may nevertheless be attained in a rather everyday manner, at least by the elite.[84] Plenitude of the greatest possible degree is not a problem of constancy or temporal quantity, but one of quality. The Hasidic master believes that a Hasid can import the ideal into the present, and there is no reason to portray Hasidic messianism as less acute, because it is not "short-term," as Werblowsky claims.[85] We may describe acuteness in terms that are not indebted to the apocalyptic propensities of modern scholars. It should be emphasized that such a messianic-like inner state of consciousness is the result of the study of the Torah, a value that is considered worthy of constant cultivation, as is prayer.

Moreover, in the passage quoted above, particularly in its original context,[86] R. Menaḥem Naḥum mentions an additional rite that is able to induce the same experience of union with the divine: *qiddush levanah,* the sanctification of the moon, a rite that has some messianic implications. When sanctifying themselves for the sake of the sanctification of the moon, the Hasidic master claims that it is possible to transcend the ordinary life and diminution, and to reach the same state of intellectual and religious greatness. Indeed, this is quite an interesting example: a messianically and mythically oriented ritual, dealing with David as a living entity, was absorbed into a mystically oriented experience that enables someone to transcend ordinary time. It is also worth noting that in R. Menaḥem Naḥum's book Lurianic forms of nomian theurgy are explicitly understood messianically, a point that invalidates Scholem's and hence Werblowsky's denial of acute messianism as they defined it in Hasidism. For example, we learn:

> The [Messiah] son of David does not come but in a generation that is completely meritorious or completely wicked.[87] It is impossible to understand this dictum according to reason as dealing with the state when the generation is [utterly] wicked, but it is known that we, the people of Israel, by the dint of our prayers and worship, are stirring the supernal mercies by overcoming the evil by good, which is imprinted in our nature, and the left is integrated into the right, which is the good impulse and so it is also done above, in the supernal worlds, where the *gevurot* [stern powers] are comprised within the hasadim [the mercies].[88]

In fact, why not read here a position that is not only Lurianic, given its propensity for Lurianic terminology and concepts, but also even more acute than the standard Lurianic texts? Let me inspect in this context the view of an influential mid-nineteenth-century book, *Sefer Ma'or va-Shemesh.* R. Qalonimus Qalman claims the following:

> The coming of the Messiah will be when[89] the [sefirah of] Malkhut will ascend to [the configuration of] 'Attiqa' Qaddisha' and the Tzaddiqim will then draw the influx from the Supernal Constellation[90] from the "thirteen ammendations of the Supernal Beard"[91] to Malkhut, and therefrom to Knesset Israel.[92] Behold that every Sabbath there is a resemblance of this [process] that the Tzaddiqim are drawing down the influx from 'Attiqa' Qaddisha', from the Supernal Constellation . . . to

> Knesset Israel . . . each and every Sabbath it is done in this way that the Tzaddiqim cause the ascent of Malkhut to 'Attiqa' Qaddisha' and draw down the influx from there to Knesset Israel.[93]

We witness here a combination of theurgical activities, the elevation of Malkhut to the highest level of the sefirotic world and the drawing down of the influx upon the last sefirah. Then the influx is drawn to a lower entity described as Knesset Israel. If this term is understood in sefirotic terms, which is less plausible in a context where Malkhut is explicitly mentioned, then we have a third theurgical operation. If, however, the term is understood to point to the community of Israel here below, I would describe this phase as magical, for it addresses the material welfare of men in the mundane world. This process is depicted as the coming of the Messiah, in a manner that recalls a text by R. Ya'aqov Ḥayyim Tzemaḥ that was discussed earlier.[94] Whether the interpretation of this text be a combined theurgical operation or a theurgical-magical one, it is described as representing the descent of the Messiah. What concerns me here, however, is the fact that the descent of the Messiah is not conceived of as a mystery of the remote future but as an operation that occurs each and every Sabbath. This point is of paramount importance because it expresses the possibility that Hasidic masters, and also some of the Kabbalists, could experience what they though of as the sacred time of Sabbath as anticipating the messianic time, both from the point of view of the ascent to the highest divine level and from that of bringing down the influx that ensures material success.[95] The tzaddiqim are therefore the magicians that are able to bring about the descent of the supernal influx, which is conceived of in terms of the descent of the Messiah, just as the perfect performance of the liturgical ritual is a messianic experience according to R. Menaḥem Naḥum of Chernobyl, as discussed in the previous chapter. The Messiah is again depersonalized and envisioned as the influx drawn down, which by its descent will redeem the people of Israel, in a manner reminiscent of the way we have interpreted the Besht's magical-messianic self-perception. The two masters quoted above proposed the possibility of anticipating the messianic experience by means of the nomian performance. At least in the case of R. Qalonimus Qalman, cyclical time, represented in the passages referred to above by the reccurrence of the descent during the Sabbath, is the main framework for introducing perfection in the normal life. To what extent such a vision is less acutely messianic than Lurianic Kabbalah, which implied a remote reparation, is a matter of taste. I can easily imagine a claim that those Hasidic views openly discussing messianism are more acute than those of the Lurianic Kabbalists.

In summary, the perusal of two main Hasidic masters' writings reveals the coexistence of a variety of models—mystical, talismanic, and theosophical-theurgical—which allow a much greater concern with messianism than we might suspect from reading the conventional scholarship. Messianism is but one type of *ta'amei ha-mitzvot,* rationales for the commandments, which intensifies the religious awareness by emphasizing their eschatological dimensions. This vision of the commandments situates one hermeneutical grid, the eschatological, among many others and assumes that even the eschatological grid is deeply influenced by other sorts of logic, as represented by other models. Let me address the issue of plenitude from another point of view. While the Messiah has been separated from the common ritual in rabbinic sources, and the figure of the ancient king has often been replaced by God the Creator, as he was celebrated every New Year, in some Kabbalistic and Hasidic texts discussed above the nexus between the myth of the Messiah and the rite has been reconstructed. In other words, the pre-apocalyptic myth-and-ritual view of the ancient king dissolved in the moment the sacral royalty disappeared as a meaningful religious phenomenon, and was apocalypticized. With the mystical dis-apocalyptization of the messianic concepts, their actualization became for the mystics more plausible, and the ritual was again integrated into the messianic complex of ideas. The futuristic nature of the apocalyptic Messiah mades his myths incompatible with present rituals, conceived as obligatory and effective, and they reentered the eschatological schemes as a significant factor when the apocalyptic aspects of the salvific event were marginalized.[96] Moreover, the apocalyptic material in Jewish sources never attained the status of canonic writings, as the book of Revelation did in Christianity.[97] The graphic representations of the end are less substantial and thus less influential than they are in Christianity. To a great extent, the Jewish apocalyptic is often skeletal,[98] allowing a relatively fragmentary and, in my opinion, scant picture of the days of the Messiah, which would hardly satisfy the more systematic and demanding spiritual needs of an elite. Seen in the broader spectrum of the development of Judaism, Jewish mysticism and some aspects of Jewish magic were instrumental in attempts to re-create a sense of religious plenitude, sometimes more intense than in the ordinary instances of performing the Jewish ritual; the messianic ideas were understood as moments of supreme attainment of a plenitude in the present. Messianism could therefore serve not only to raise hopes for an expected though remote national and cultic renascence, as its apocalyptic mode did, but also as a conduit for the elitist experiences of religious perfection in the present.[99] Hence the complex nature of the relationship between tradition and messianism should be examined as a much more variegated affinity, one that is socially layered and historically variable.

Some Comparative Reflections

I hope that, by this survey, the existence of significant messianic and experiential dimensions in many of the Kabbalistic schools, and in Hasidism, has been proven. Indeed, not one form of messianism, but a variety of phenomena understood both explicitly and implicitly as messianic, informed many important discussions of the main forms of Jewish mysticism. This assertion asks for a more general assessment of the nature of Jewish mysticism as a spiritual phenomenon, to be characterized in the framework of mysticism in general. So, for example, when compared to Christian mysticism, Jewish mysticism's profound interest in the nature of the historical redeemer becomes obvious. Though many polemical treatises have been composed in order to debate the advent, or the misunderstanding of the advent, of the redeemer, there is a common denominator at the base of the pyramid of the messianic beliefs in the two religions: the redeemer enters history in order to save significant numbers of believers. Either a matter of the past or of the future, the redeemer must penetrate the order of the deteriorated historical and moral existence and reform it. If, however, the elite at the top of the pyramid believes in messianism, the historical event becomes much less important, while its reverberations in the experience of the mystic gradually becomes more decisive. The birth of Christ in the soul of the mystic is emphasized in the writings of such mystics as Meister Eckhart and Angelus Silesius. This corresponds to the more spiritualistic understanding of the messianic event in the ecstatic Kabbalah.

While the Christian mystic desires to imitate Christ, the redemptive function par excellence is already occupied by the ancient redeemer. In Jewish mysticism, however, the identification with the transcendent Messiah, Metatron, the sefirah Malkhut, or the Agent Intellect is not only a matter of imitation but is also the aspiration and, in some instances, the attempt to play the main role in history for the first time. This was the case insofar as Abraham Abulafia, Asher Lemlein, Shlomo Molkho, apparently Yitzḥaq Luria, Ḥayyim Vital, and Sabbatai Tzevi, are concerned. Yet even in the case of the Kabbalists who did not aspire to the role of the Messiah but treated this topic—R. Yitzḥaq of Acre, the anonymous author of *Sefer ha-Peliy'ah,* Menaḥem Naḥum of Chernobyl, and many others—the messianic function was conceived of as being open and in principle attainable in the future. While in Christianity such a claim would be considered heresy a priori, in Judaism it could become so only a posteriori, and solely in rare cases. The fullness of the messianic experience is viewed by the Jewish mystics as open in both the present and the future, representing the search for and awareness of the possibility of the plenitude. Thus, while in Christian mysticism redemption is ensured by faith and participation, in Jewish mysticism redemption is rarely related to faith—though this was the case in Sabbateanism—while the mystical enterprise is thought to be paramount for the salvation of both the individual and the nation. While in Christianity the theophany of a divine power in the past, the son of God conceived of as redeemer, is quintessential, in Jewish mysticism salvation has to do with the apotheosis of the mystic in the present or the future. The participation of the Christian in *corpus Christi,* his becoming part of the body of the redeemer, differs from the constituting moment of redemption by the theophany of Christ. The Christian mystic lives in the great religious space between the feeling of sinfulness and that of having been saved, and the tension between the two is part of the more emotional aspects of Christian mysticism. Jewish mysticism, less interested in the condition of sinfulness, is more confident in the possibility of initiated salvation, and thus discussions on humility, love, and devotion are less central; even when they do appear, they often become part of more detailed mystical techniques. In other words, the importance of salvation on the individual, national, cosmic, and even divine levels is greater in Judaism than in Christianity, and thus mysticism contributed to these issues more.

Another relevant case is the Buddhist concept of Bodhisattva. In Buddhism the personal salvific moment is conceived of as the moment of renunciation that will serve mankind by the return of the enlightened to illuminate others. The salvation of the other is a function of one's own renunciation of salvation, understood as extinction. Unlike Christianity, where the redeemer can be only one, in Buddhism the initial savior reverberates throughout the epochs and invites mystics both to attain the mystical peak and to renounce it. Nevertheless, the great paradigm has been already established in the past, as in Christianity, though in Buddhism it is a much more open form of experience. The personalizations of the savior figures is common to these two great religions.

In Jewish mysticism, the past personalizations that could serve as redemptive models are related only to the nonmystical attainments, such the royal functions, while their mystical achievements did not reach the maximum redemptive moment. The restorative aspects of messianism, I would claim, are less important in Jewish mysticism. It is less a matter of re-creation as one of creation that haunted the Jewish mystic in search of the peak experience that is conducive to messianism. In other words, while for a Christian mystic the main experience is salvific, in personal terms—since salvation of others is in any case available independent of his personal experience—and for the Buddhist personal salvation opens the way for the redemption of others, in Jewish mysticism the messianic experience, though somewhat closer to the Buddhist, never mentions, let alone emphasizes, the cardinal moment of renunciation. Even in Buddhist eschatology there is not only an ancient redeemer but also many other reverberations over the millennia.

It seems that of the three religions, only in Jewish mysticism may the eschatological achievement of the single mystic be so decisive. This is one of the reason why Jewish mysticism is more eschatological, and I wonder whether we should not include this characteristic among those which distinguish Jewish mysticism from others. Mysticism was conceived among the Jewish mystics as a way to make a decisive impact not only by one's salvation but also on other levels of reality. This attitude encouraged communal projects and self-perceptions whose grandiose expectations often induced deep disappointment and despair. The so-called price[100] for the messianic aspirations and claims might have been great, but the calculations are quite difficult and of less concern to my approach here. Indeed, the vision of one unified nation, which pays dearly or gains from messianic or other adventures, may invite such calculations. But this type of approach emphasizes the moments of deferment and ignores those of plenitude. It judges spiritual experiences by historical criteria and often also by theological assumptions. The profound experiences of the individual and those who believed in him are marginalized in the name of the national "achievements," verified against external experience. This is why even in the scholarly approaches more sympathetic with messianism, the Messiahs are sometimes pseudo-Messiahs, and their movements culminate in debacles. Would a scholar of Buddhism calculate the impact of the acceptance of Buddhism over Brahmanism or Christianity or Islam on the development of nations in south Asia? Would a scholar of Christian mysticism calculate the possible impoverishment of the intellectual life of common Christians because of the cultivation of mysticism in predominantly closed circles, such as monasteries?

Some Reflections at the End

These approaches to the questions related to the messianic constellation of ideas should be compared not only to the more dominant scholarly scheme, as represented by Martin Buber and the school of Gershon Scholem, but also to the different historical circumstances that hosted these interpretations. Buber and Scholem explicated their views against the background of a flowering national movement, Zionism, that emphasized historical and external actions as the sine qua non for a future national redemption. They were urged on by the possibility of demonstrating the emergence of an external change, immigration to the land of Israel, as the paramount criterion for entering history. This approach is still evident, though in a much more messianic manner, in some religious-nationalistic political fractions in modern Israel. The present treatment reflects, consciously or not, quite different historical circumstances. It is much more the struggle to secure and maintain the achievements of the earlier generation than an attempt to change them that characterizes the thrust of Israeli society. Is it the present moment that has inspired the emphasis on those more conservative elements in messianism that were marginalized earlier? Is the possibility of looking backward from a broader perspective related to a less tumultuous period that enables a scholar to adopt a less ideological definition, a more pluralistic and perhaps more centrifugal approach that is less concerned with the communal function of main ideas in Judaism? Is the attempt to emphasize the dialogue between the Jewish views and other, alien elements in a variety of domains, including messianic thought, part of a new historical situation? Is this novel, less apologetic situation also less dependent on the differences between Jewish thought and other systems, more open to seeing the common denominators, than the earlier emphases on the divergences? Or is the postmodern emphasis on variety and diversity having too great an impact on these inquiries, in comparison to the modern approach, which emphasized monochromatism? Is the retreat from the more communal narrative toward a more individualistic one, visible in Western culture in a decade that has seen the weakening and even the dissolution of ideologies, influencing my argument for a need to reevaluate the importance of the inner, personal experiences? Was the attempt to offer a substantially different overview of some the messianic phenomena—a reaction to what I see as a conceptual stagnation in many of the scholarly discussions of this topic in the Scholemian school[101]—sufficiently supported by new material and new analyses?

Being too close in time, too involved in the selection and inspection of the messianic material under consideration, I prefer to leave it to a careful reader to decide the answers to these questions. I have enumerated them in order to clarify for myself what forms of social and cultural circumstances may inform and eventually distort my discussions. The impact these circumstances may have on my work is an issue that readers and critics of this book may wish to engage. Meanwhile, the fact that new, neglected material extant in manuscripts, and different approaches to messianism, such as those proposed by Y. Liebes, corroborate views formulated independent of them may demonstrate that another look at the complex messianic constellation of ideas is worthwhile.

Ego, Ergo Sum Messiah: On Abraham Abulafia's *Sefer ha-Yashar*

The Return of Prophecy

At the end of 1278 or the beginning of 1279, Abraham Abulafia made his way from Patros in Greece to Capua, with a short forced stay in Trani, where he was imprisoned because he was denounced by the Jews.[1] In Capua he taught Maimonides' *Guide of the Perplexed* to four young students. He left for Rome on his abortive attempt to meet with the pope, an episode that has already been discussed in chapter 2. Sometime early in 1279, he composed in Patros a "prophetic book" called *Sefer ha-Yashar,* the first of a long series of prophetic books, all but one now lost, and most probably the first Kabbalistic writing composed in the Byzantine empire. Because of his own commentaries, however, short passages of the original prophetic books are still extant. In chapter 2 we dealt with passages regarding the nature of the Messiah, as expressed in some of the commentaries on the lost books. Here I would like to call attention to the implications of a passage that is more complex, written in a kind of code but highly relevant for the connections between mysticism, messianism, and Abulafia's Kabbalah. The beginning of the book deals with the recent return of prophecy:

> In the thirty-ninth year of the return of the word of 'Adonay YHWH to the mouth of His prophets, the angel of 'Elohim[2] came to me, Berakhiahu ben Shalviel, and announced a word to me. I have already mentioned to you that this is the first book that Raziel wrote in the form of prophecy,[3] namely that he mentioned in it [the formula] 'Thus has H [namely God] said,'[4] which is the form of the word of divine prophecy, which requires a mighty inquiry as to its matter and way. . . . You should know that Raziel is called in this book Berakhiahu ben Shalviel, in accordance with the first name, and this is because it is known that he received the blessing from the

> Name, and peace and serenity . . . and you should know that Raziel called this book by the title *Sefer ha-Yashar,* whose secret is *Shem ShYRaH, YeShaRaH.*[5]

The two divine names in the first sentence of this passage, 'Adonay YHWH, occur together in Ezekiel, in order to introduce the speech of God,[6] and they were chosen in this context deliberately. Their meaning may be better understood by comparing that statement to one found in a book written either by Abulafia or by his student, where the assumption is that the consonants which make up these divine names also constitute the words *'aHWY,* and *Ha-DYN.*[7] The ecstatic Kabbalist claims that whoever knows this secret will be the Master, who governs all mundane matters and will be called the angel of 'Elohiym. This hyperbolic description recalls the extraordinary powers of the Messiah, and indeed the Messiah is mentioned some lines before the above passage.[8] Moreover, according to Abulafia, the letters *'aHWY* are in fact the hidden divine name, which will be revealed to the Messiah.[9] Thus, the return of prophecy is reported in a statement that implies also the revelation of the unknown divine name.[10]

In *Sefer ha-Yashar,* Abulafia adopted for himself theophoric names, which are numerically equivalent to his original names. For example, the gematria of the name Berakhiyahu, which means, according to his own explanation, the person who has received the blessing of God, is 248, the same as Abulafia's first name, Abraham. Raziel, a more common name in his prophetic writings, is the name of an angel in ancient Jewish texts; it means "secrets of God" and amounts to 248 too. The name Shalviel means "serenity of God" and amounts to 377, as do the consonants of the name of Abulafia's father, Shmu'el. Therefore, the return of the word of God, or prophecy, means not only the reception of messages from the divine world but also a more ontological connection between the mystic and the deity, which transforms the recipient either by receiving a blessing or by receiving the secrets, so that his name should be changed,[11] all this in addition to the revelation of the new divine name. We may infer that the change in Abulafia's name points to revelatory experiences that happened prior to the composition of the original *Sefer ha-Yashar.* Indeed, the reception of the blessing, alluded to in the book elsewhere, is one of Abulafia's leitmotifs, and the blessing of the priests is one of the few commandments that he is eager to comment upon in several of his books. For him, blessing in general, and the priestly benediction in particular, is an allegory for the descent of the divine influx upon the prepared recipient.[12] Thus, the encounters with the divine powers induce certain changes in the mystic, apparently experiences of theosis that are expressed by the use of the theophoric names. It should also be mentioned that in the ancient sacral royalty ideology, the king's name has been given a theophoric prefix.[13]

Writing in 1279, Abulafia mentions the thirty-ninth year as the date for the renewal of prophecy, thus pointing to 1240, the year of his own birth. It is, of course, quite difficult to imagine that Abulafia believed he was a prophet already at the moment of his birth, a possibility that was never mentioned in any of his extant writings and would contradict his concept of prophecy as involving intellectual maturity. In fact, he speaks of 1279 as the ninth year of the beginning of his prophecy.[14] Moreover, his use of the term "prophets" in the plural shows that he thought there were other prophets who prophesied around the year 1240 C.E., which coincides with the Jewish year 5000, the beginning of the sixth millennium. In another statement, Abulafia claims that at the beginning of this millennium the Messiah will come, and he boasts[15] of his knowledge of the divine name.[16] Indeed, such an assumption is corroborated, at least in part, by a statement found in another of Abulafia's prophetic writings, where he describes himself as the last and best of the seven last prophets.[17] We may conclude, therefore, that the return of prophecy was envisioned by Abulafia as a historical phenomenon that is also connected to other figures, who presumably preceded him, though they apparently lived in his lifetime. This seems to be the significance of a passage in his commentary on the *Guide of the Perplexed,* composed in 1280 in Capua.[18] I have not come across a list of seven, or six, prophets believed to be active between 1240 and 1279, nor have I found indications as to their possible background. However, Abulafia described at least one of his contemporaries as a "prophet." In an autobiographical passage in *Sefer 'Otzar 'Eden Ganuz,* he mentions a certain R. Shmuel the prophet, unknown from other sources, as one of the few who received some forms of mystical traditions from him, in Castile, in the town of Medinat Celim, in the early 1270s.[19] A list of seven students described as close to him, which appears in the works Abulafia composed later on in Sicily, may point to a conscious effort to educate seven disciples to become prophets:

> Indeed, in this town that I am within now, called Senim,[20] which [actually is] Messina, I have found six persons, and with me I brought the seventh, from whom they [the six] have learned in my presence, for a very short while. Each of them has received something from me, more or less, and all of them have left me, except the one, who is the first and [he is also] the first reason for what each and every one of his friends had learned from my mouth. His name is R. Sa'adiah ben R. Yitzḥaq Sigilmasi, blessed be his memory. He was followed by R. Abraham ben R. Shalom, and was followed [in turn] by Rabbi Ya'aqov his son, and later was followed by R. Yitzḥaq his friend, and he was followed by the friend of his friend . . . and the name of the seventh was R. Natronay Tzarfati, blessed be his memory.[21]

Was Abulafia intending to create prophets by his intense literary and teaching activities in Messina during the 1280s? In any case, it may be worth mentioning that Enoch, treated in many texts as a prophet, was the seventh person counting from Adam, and his translation on high in the form of Metatron brought him closer to a messianic role, as we saw in chapter 2.

"The Knowledge of the Messiah and the Wisdom of the Redeemer"

Abulafia admits that he was less interested in discussing the issue of prophecy in *Sefer ha-Yashar,* since he planned to return to it in *Sefer ha-Haftarah.*[22] He hints his main topic, a great secret that has to do with the Tetragrammaton and the first six letters of the so-called name of forty-two letters, YHWH 'aBG YTTz, which are numerically equal to several phrases, all of them amounting to 532, one of them being Shem YHWH 'Elyon, which means "the Tetragrammaton is supernal." Then he writes: "Because of it, Raziel has sealed his book by four words, whose initials are YHWH, and whose final letters are TeḤiLaT,[23] and their secret is 'The Knowledge of the Messiah and the Wisdom of the Redeemer.' "[24] The four Hebrew words translated by the last line indeed start with the consonants of the Tetragrammaton and end with the term *teḥilat,* and each consists of five consonants. Therefore, it is quite certain that the secret of the book is to be found in the four Hebrew words *yediy'at ha-mashiyaḥ ve-ḥokhmat ha-go'el.* But Abulafia goes beyond decoding the initials and final letters of the four mysterious words. After alluding to the first and last letters, he points to the meaning of the middle letters of each of the four words. Thus, the first word, *yediy'at,* yields the noun *'ediy,* "my witness," which in Abulafia's writings sometimes means the celestial witness, referring to Enoch and, according to other sources, ShaHadiY, which is numerically identical to Metatron.[25] The second word, *ha-mashiyaḥ,* produces the combination of letters *shemy,* which means "my name." The middle consonants of the third word, *ve-ḥokhmat,* make *ḥakham,* which means "wise." The fourth word, however, *ha-go'el,* does not produce any word that has a significance in Hebrew. The three letters that remain after removing the first and last consonants are, according to the sequence in the word, *gimel, waw, 'aleph.* However, Abulafia changes the order of the three letters and writes *'alef, gimel, waw,* though this sequel also has no meaning in Hebrew. Thus, Abulafia offers the following sequence of six words generated by the four secret words: *TeḤiLaT, YHWH, 'EDiY, ShMiY, ḤaKhaM, 'GW.* The three "meaningless" letters have been placed by Abulafia, quite arbitrarily, at the middle of the six words and remain indecipherable in Hebrew. Resort to two other languages, however, may render them coherent, for these three consonants transliterate the Greek and Latin word *ego.* Such a reading is by no means exceptional in Abulafia, as he used both Greek and Latin words in his writings, including complex instances of gematria.[26] Moreover, it fits the occurrence of the first-person possessive in two words that follow *ego,* namely *shemiy* and *'ediy,* as well as the emphasis on the theophoric nature of the names Abulafia invented for himself in order to point to his mystical attainment. The egocentric discussion that precedes the above passage reinforces the importance of decoding the three letters in the manner I have suggested.

Let me return to the way I have translated the four nouns. Grammatically speaking, they constitute two phrases, each constructed of two nouns. The first phrase, *yediy'at ha-mashiyaḥ,* is quite ambiguous; I could not find any parallel to it in Hebrew, and there is more than one way to render its meaning. It could mean "knowledge of the Messiah," namely knowledge that is in the possession of the Messiah or information known by the Messiah. An alternative translation, which I have tentatively adopted above, would be "knowledge about the Messiah," and thus the intention would be that other persons have special knowledge about the Messiah. This is also the case insofar the second phrase, *ḥokhmat ha-go'el,* is concerned. I have never encountered this expression in a Hebrew text. One possible translation, corresponding to the first one proposed above in connection to the first phrase, would "wisdom of the redeemer," meaning that the redeemer possesses a certain type of wisdom. An alternative translation would be "wisdom regarding the redeemer." There can be no doubt that the two unusual phrases are the result of Abulafia's intention to construe four nouns that can be reconstructed so as to produce the six other words, an exercise which is in itself a tour de force. But which meaning would Abulafia would prefer? The passage that immediately follows the above lines may help us answer that question:

> This wisdom [*ḥokhmah,* the knowledge of reality] alone is the best instrument for [achieving] prophecy,[27] better than all the other [forms of] wisdom. And the essence of reality, when known by someone from what he learned from books dealing with it, should be called wise [*ḥakham].* But when he will know it by means of a tradition, transmitted to him by someone who knew it by means of the [divine] names, or [received it] from a Kabbalist, he should be called someone who understands [*mevin*]. But whoever will know it from [introspection into] his heart, by means of a negotiation in his mind[28] concerning what was available to him about mental reality [*ha-metziy'ut ha-neḥshav*], will be called knower [*da'atan*]. However, whoever will know reality by means of the three manners that gathered into his heart, namely wisdom [emerging] out of much learning, and understanding received from the mouth of true Kabbalists, and knowledge [emerging] out of much negotiation in [his] thought, I do not say that this person is called only a prophet, but as long as he was active, and he was not affected by the Separate Intellect, or he was affected but did not know by whom he was affected.[29] However, if he was affected, and he was aware that he was affected, it is incumbent upon me and upon any perfect person that he is called a teacher [*moreh*] "because his name is like the name of his Master,"[30] be it only by one, or by many, or by all of His names. For now he is no

> longer separated from his Master, and behold he is his Master, and his Master is he; for he is so intimately adhering to Him[31] that he cannot, by any means, be separated from Him, for he is He. And just as his Master, who is detached from all matter, is called the knowledge, the knower, and the known, all at the same time, since all three are one in Him, so shall he, the exalted man, the master of the exalted name, be called intellect, while he is actually knowing; then he is also the known, like his Master; and then there is no difference between them, except that his Master has His supreme rank by His own right and not derived from other creatures, while he is elevated to his rank by the mediation of creatures.[32]

Abulafia mentions three ways of knowing reality as preparatory stages for the even higher form of cognition, that of the prophet. One has to be wise, understanding, and knowledgeable, namely to comprehend reality by all possible ways starting with the mundane realm, before he is able to move to a higher way of receiving information from above. Only their combination will bring someone to receive the direct information that is not mediated by human teachers or books or by inner pondering. When one becomes aware that the Agent Intellect is illumining him, he reaches the rank of teacher. The relation between prophet and teacher is less than clear. One tentative proposal is that the prophet is lower than the teacher, the former being influenced by the Separate Intellect but unaware of the nature of the sources,[33] while the teacher definitively is aware of it. But according to another Abulafian source, whose other affinities to views expressed in *Sefer ha-Yashar* have been pointed out above, we may assume that the Messiah is indeed aware of the divine source of his revelation: "The Messiah confesses that his speech and conversation comes from the special name that is with him by nature, and it generates the speech, and actualizes it after it has been in potentia. And the simpletons do not feel from where their speech comes, and they are like an animal that produces a sound which is similar to speech, but does not understand the nature which is inherent in it."[34]

The teacher [*moreh*] and the redeemer possess some sort of wisdom and knowledge. Moreover, as Abulafia mentions elsewhere, the Messiah is a higher form of prophet, but a prophet nevertheless.[35] Thus, we may assume that the teacher, though higher than the prophet, nonetheless corresponds to the Messiah. Such a reading is corroborated by the emphasis on the complete cleaving of the human teacher to his spiritual supernal master or teacher, *rabbo,* which means the cleaving to the Agent Intellect.[36] As we have seen in chapter 2, however, the Agent Intellect was described in another prophetic writing as one of the meanings of the term *mashiyaḥ,* so that cleaving to it is tantamount to cleaving to the ontological and ever-present supernal Messiah and thus becoming united with it. Therefore, the teacher and the Messiah, even if they are not an identical entity, are still close enough to each other,[37] while the concept of *moreh tzedeq* in this literature has been connected to a prophetic and, according to some scholars, messianic figure.[38] The messianic nature of the teacher is also evident from another point of view: the teacher is described as attaining the mystical union which entitles him to possess the same name like that of his master. One of the major sources for such a view is found in *BT, Sanhedrin,* fol. 38a. Though a rare formula is rabbinic texts, the identity of the name of Metatron to that of his master appears in another relevant source. In one of the most important treatises of apocalyptic messianism, *Sefer Zerubbavel,* Metatron reveals himself in Rome to a messianic figure named Zerubbavel, and as part of their conversation Metatron describes himself thus: "I am he whose name is like the name of my Master, and His name is in me."[39] The discussion that follows this statement deals with the nature of the Messiah and the apocalyptic scheme. Thus, Abulafia's resort to this formula in the context of the teacher invites, for someone well acquainted with the apocalyptic literature, a messianic understanding of the nature of the teacher. Indeed, as I mentioned in the Introduction, the Messiah will be called by the name of God, more precisely the Tetragrammaton, an issue that suggests a deep affinity between the two entities. Just as in the way Abulafia uses the formula related to Metatron and God in order to point out the teacher's or the Messiah's identity with Metatron, so too the much earlier designation of the name of the Messiah as Tetragrammaton presupposes the preexistence, or the emergence, of a continuum between the perfected individual and the higher spiritual entities. In the text discussed above, the nominal identity is between the teacher and Metatron. But since elsewhere in his writings, in *Sefer Sitrei Torah,* a book composed in the same period as *Sefer ha-Yashar,* Abulafia describes the angel Metatron as someone whose name is identical with the divine name and thus with God's name, we may speak about the emergence of a linguistic continuum between God, Metatron, and the perfected human being that becomes the redeemer.

The Teacher and the Messiah

Abulafia's biography may illumine the quality of the teacher. In a short autobiographical note, Abulafia mentions that he studied Kabbalah from both written and oral traditions, and I assume that he understood these forms of knowledge as pointing to the nature of reality. Soon afterward, however, he started to teach Kabbalah in Spain, Greece, and Italy. When writing the above passage on the teacher, he was teaching Maimonides' *Guide of the Perplexed* to four students in the town of Capua near Rome and expressed his will to perfect his students, in the way he was perfected by his teachers: "I have also felt a very great joy, greater than that felt by my teachers when they taught me, and I have also looked to actualize the potential of the others, so that they will be perfected by my words and books."[40] Therefore, he saw himself not only a student of this lore but also as an intensive teacher. Abulafia conceived of himself as an actualizer who enables the intellect of the other to emerge, and by so doing he plays the role of the Agent Intellect or, according to his view, the Messiah as Agent Intellect. The nature of this intellect is its unrestrained and continuous emanation, and I assume that Abulafia saw this matter as messianic and attempted to imitate it. In fact, there is no other evidence for such an intense campaign to disseminate this lore beforehand, and there are only very rare examples afterward. From this point of view, Abulafia had good reason to see himself as a teacher at the very time when he resorted to the term *moreh* in order to describe the highest spiritual attainment. Since 1279–1280 was also the period when he attempted to meet the pope, we may assume that Abulafia could consider himself to be the teacher, a view that is connected with his messianism, namely the concept that disseminating his particular form of lore will open the gate to a general redemption of those who follow his teachings. Moreover, one of the conditions of becoming a teacher, being aware of the nature of the entity that reveals itself to him, is met in explicit terms by the very beginning of *Sefer ha-Yashar,* where he mentions his speaking in the name of God. And as mentioned in his *Sefer Sitrei Torah,* the Messiah, together with other prophets, will reveal the secrets of the Torah as part of the advent of the messianic days.[41]

If he conceived of himself as the teacher, someone who had an experience of union with God, and as possessing more qualities than mentioned in the context of the Messiah (knowledge and wisdom), is a teacher higher than the Messiah? In my opinion the answer is yes. The Messiah may stand, according to Abulafia, for the redeemed person, or more exactly his intellect, even if he does not act on the public arena.[42] However, the teacher, like the more advanced Messiah who plays a public role, is described as having additional qualities: recognition by men—after he was already recognized by God as a prophet—and the reception of power or strength, as the former redeemers had.[43] The teacher may, therefore, represent the peak of cognitive and mystical achievements when combined with external acts. I have proposed a reading of the phrases *yedi'at ha-mashiyaḥ ve-ḥokhmat ha-go'el* as dealing with the forms of cognition attributed to the redeemer. However, this interpretation is not self-evident from the grammatical structure of the phrases, though the above analysis corroborates it. I would like to suggest the possibility of an additional interpretation which was not expressed in my translation of the four words. The Hebrew phrases are, presumably, approximations of the Greek terms *soteriologia* and *christologia,* which stand for forms of theological discussion dealing with the nature of the redeemer.[44] Such a proposal corroborates the reading of the three Hebrew letters as a Greek or Latin word, *ego.*

R. Yitzḥaq of Acre on Messiah as Metatron

In *Sefer 'Otzar Ḥayyim* by R. Yitzḥaq of Acre, a Kabbalist discussed in chapter 3,[45] one cannot escape the feeling that a strong Metatronic tradition or traditions had inspired his concepts and experiences, since R. Yitzḥaq is often visited by Metatron. In fact, some of the most interesting accounts of his mystical experiences are explicitly related to that angel. In my opinion, the influence of some of the ideas discussed above may be discerned in the following passage:

> And indeed, MoSheH[46] "is a wheel in heaven"[47] and the secret of Sand[alfon][48] is "[a wheel] upon the earth" [Ezekiel 1:15], namely, in the [realm of] corporeality. And this is the reason why the double [final] letters, which are written only at the end of words, ş whose secret is PaR ["ox"],[49] are its secret, because it is the secret of the Prince of the Back, [which is] the Prince of the Wood.[50] The secret of Sand[alfon] is Par and Ya'ar. But the secret of MoSheH is "in heaven" namely, in spirituality,[51] "and the spirit will dwell upon them" [Num. 11:26], "and the Lord will put His spirit upon them" [Num. 11:29], "but by my spirit" [Haggai 2:5], " 'and the spirit of God hovers over the water' [Gen. 1:2] - this is the spirit of the Messiah" [Genesis Rabba 2:4], and it is MoSheH the High Priest, anointed by the oil, the supernal holy unction, the true Messiah, who will come today, if we listen to the voice of his Master,[52] whose name is found in him,[53] he will redeem us. And "In all our affliction he was afflited, and the angel of the face saved us,"[54] my intention concerns the verse "In all their affliction he was afflicted, and the angel of His face saved them" [Isa. 63:9][55] and "And the spirit of the Lord shall rest upon him" [Isa. 11:2], those and all similar to them hint at Metatron, the Prince of the Face."[56]

Here the term *mashiyaḥ* is mentioned explicitly as identical to the angel Metatron. Moreover, the quotation from Isaiah 11:2 was traditionally understood as pointing to the Messiah. What is the significance of both Metatron and *mashiyaḥ* in this passage? Both are identical to the spiritual realm, as against Sandalfon, which in R. Barukh Togarmi, Abulafia's master, in Abulafia himself, in the collectanaea of a certain R. Nathan, the teacher of R. Yitzḥaq of Acre, and in the anonymous *Sefer Sha'arei Tzedeq* is identical to corporeality and materiality, hinted at sometimes by the same terms used in the above passage: Ya'ar and Par.[57] The master mentioned here is apparently God, whose name is found within Metatron or the Messiah. By listening to His voice, the Kabbalists will be saved by the supernal Messiah. This listening means overcoming the corporeality for the sake of spirituality, or judgment for the sake of mercy, a theme that occurs often in R. Yitzḥaq.[58] By mastering corporeality, which is an individual project, one may attain redemption from the ongoing active Messiah qua Metatron.

The picture, however, is more complex and interesting. Immediately after this passage, the author again mentions Sandalfon as an ox, and "the Prince of the Back, the Prince of judgment, but the sheep, which is the innocent lamb [*Seh tamim*] is—in its entirety—good, and it is MoSheH, the Prince of Mercy."[59] The juxtaposition of the ox and the lamb, the latter standing for Metatron and Messiah, is reminiscent of the well-known motif of Jesus Christ as the lamb of God, *agnus Dei.*[60] Unlike Abulafia, who identified Jesus with matter and the Messiah ben David with the spirit, here the spiritual Messiah is described by using one of the most widespread Christian symbols.

Before presenting another example of the interface between messianic ideas and alien forms of thought, let me emphasize that R. Yitzḥaq, like Abulafia and other anonymous Kabbalists from his circle, does not simply recommend obedience to the divine imperatives but presupposes the need to resort to mystical techniques for achieving a mystical experience.[61] In any case, the many experiences of the angel Metatron, identified with the Messiah, allow a reading of some of his mystical experiences as redemptive.

To what extent the fact that the consonants of lamb, *SeH,* similar to the last two consonants of the acronym *MoSheH,* also contributed to the emergence of the above discussion is a difficult question. There are instances when R. Yitzḥaq uses the formula *Metatron SeH* instead of *Metatron SaR Ha-Panim.* This Kabbalist, like Abulafia, was very fond of playing with letters. Yet despite this observation, the identification of the lamb with a messianic figure, who is described as suffering or at least participating in the suffering of men, and the mention of mercy point to a Christian influence.

The resort to Christian symbolism in order to better understand R. Yitzḥaq's discussion may be fostered by another passage found in *Sefer 'Otzar Ḥayyim.* When dealing with a Hebrew version of the myth of Prometheus, R. Yitzḥaq indicates that he received the legend, already transferred to the figure of Solomon, from a Christian.[62] Despite the fact that he was aware of the alien extraction of the material, he offers Kabbalistic interpretations of its meaning:

> However, according to the way of the hidden [interpretation][63] Solomon hints at MoSheH[64] in relation to whom it is written, "In all their afflictions he was afflicted" [Isa. 63:9] and "I will be with him in distress" [Psalms 91:15]. And in accordance with the way of truth[65] Solomon is hinting at [the sefirah of] Ti[feret][66] and to [the sefirah of] 'A[tarah],[67] and the ravens mean, following the way of the sages of the Kabbalists of Sefarad,[68] the external ranks, which ascend and harass the divine powers. But in the days of the Messiah, may he come soon in our days, the external ranks will be lowered and return to the abyss of the earth, which is the place of their emanation, which is also identical to their annihilation [*'afisatan*],[69] and [then] the influxes of [the sefirah of] Pa[ḥad] will disappear, and efflux of [the sefirah of] ha-Ge[dulah] and Paḥad will come into the Ti[feret] and 'A[tarah].[70]

R. Yitzḥaq was much more eclectic than Abulafia and some of the other early Kabbalists, and he brought together in his writings different Kabbalistic systems of thought and symbols. In the above passage, a more Abulafian theme is represented by the first quotation in this paragraph, given the occurrence of Metatron, which parallels some of the features of this angel that we have already encountered. Given that Solomon, as presented in the legend, substituted Prometheus as sufferer, we have an excellent illustration of the via passionis in a manner reminiscent of the Christian savior. The second part of the passage, however, represents an example of symbolic interpretation in the vein of the Castilian Kabbalah. Prometheus' ravens become demonic powers, which harass the divine ones, a process that will cease only with the coming of the Messiah. Now it is the divine power that is suffering, not the angelic Metatron, a turn that brings the passage closer to the Greek discussion of the semidivine titan and to the Christian Christ. Despite the identification of Metatron with the Messiah, and its explicit spiritual nature, the *passio* is still quite distinct. Indeed, the participation of Metatron in the suffering of the lower human beings is quite exceptional, especially when it is compared to Abulafian views of the Agent Intellect, even when identified with the last sefirah, Malkhut. The founder of ecstatic Kabbalah emphasizes the via perfectionis, and I would like to compare his more philosophically oriented view to that of R. Yitzḥaq. Abulafia describes the last sefirah as one whose effects are all eternal, *kol 'aluleyah ṇitzḥiyyim,* and are included in its category because they are the individuals generated by a certain cause, designated as the "form of the intellect."[71] Eternity, union, and immortality are ensured by the intellectual nature of the Agent Intellect, namely the participation of the lower in the nature of the higher entity, while in the case of the more mythical Kabbalist, it is the participation of the higher in the suffering of the lower entities. The Metatronic nature of this Kabbalist's view of the Messiah, which is certainly not the single occurrence in his writings, nevertheless reflects the ontic-noetic understanding of ecstatic Kabbalah, which is integrated within the via passionis, influenced by theosophical Kabbalistic forms of thought, both Greek and Christian. This is but one more example for the complexities inherent in unfolding the constellation of messianic ideas.

By offering a variety of explanations of messianic concepts, R. Yitzḥaq shows that this was a significant issue, to be reflected by means of all the mystical systems at his disposition and to be integrated, experientially and not only conceptually, in his religious life. This does not mean that he had to become externally active as a Messiah, as Abulafia did, but it would be simplistic to exclude his interpretations of messianism from the descriptions of the "messianic idea," as indeed happened in the conventional scholarship. This Kabbalist, like

R. Menaḥem Naḥum of Chernobyl, is a fine illustration of the fascination of Jewish mystics with messianic ideas, which are interpreted time and again in the light of their diverse mystical concerns, producing divergent conceptualization of the meaning of the Messiah. These concepts of the Messiah represent not a mere inconsistency but the result of encounters with different types of Kabbalah, of a quest for new forms of knowledge, which together contributed to the multidimensional picture of messianic ideas in the writings of one Kabbalist. Abulafia contributed one aspect in R. Yitzḥaq's variegated interpretations of the nature of the Messiah.

Sefer ha-Yashar: A New Torah?

Referring to the title of his first prophetic book, *Sefer ha-Yashar,* Abulafia points out that the numerical value of *Ha-YaShaR* equals that of *ShYRaH,* "song," and *TeFiLLaH,* "prayer." Nonetheless, I could not detect anything poetical or liturgical in the sentences stemming from the book or in its commentary. Though he indeed used the poetic format in his single extant prophetic book, *Sefer ha-'Ot,* I see no reason to restrict the meaning of the title to this possible explanation. The first book's title is reminiscent of the lost *Sefer ha-Yashar* mentioned in the Bible.[72] This lost book was described in one of the apocalyptic discussions in Midrash as the book that God will reveal to the Messiah at the beginning of his apocalyptic deeds. It is described as so large that the entire Torah is but one line of it.[73] Is it possible to establish a connection between the two? As Abulafia indicated several times, each of his six prophetic books is to be considered as sealed by *Sefer ha-Haftarah,* another prophetic book of his, which he considered worthy to be read in synagogue after the reading of the Torah.[74] But while *Sefer ha-Haftarah* is the last of the first cycle of prophetic books, *Sefer ha-Yashar* is the first. Is the teacher, who has attained the union with God, the possible composer of an authoritative book that competes with the Torah? This idea may seem rather audacious, but it is less so if we remember that Abulafia took himself to be higher even than Moses[75] and called one of his other prophetic books in the same cycle *Sefer Berit Ḥadashah,* "Book of the New Covenant." Elsewhere in his prophetic books he asserts that a "new religion," *dat ḥadashah,* has been revealed, which is a religiosity based on the knowledge of the divine name.[76]

More straightforwardly he wrote in *Sefer ha-Haftarah,* in the name of God: "I innovate a new Torah within the holy nation, which is my people Israel. My honorable name is like a new Torah, and it has not been explicated to my people since the day I hid my face from them."[77] Did not the beginning of *Sefer ha-Yashar* also mention the return of the word of God? Is Abulafia, who built up many of his books on the divine name, as he explicitly indicates,[78] and proclaimed the importance of the study of the divine name,[79] not suggesting an attempt to reveal the new Torah? Is the loss of the original version of Abulafia's prophetic books a matter of accident, while almost all of his other books are extant in many manuscripts? It seems that Abulafia has come closer than any of the Jewish Messiahs to the concept of being the revealer of a new law, a more spiritual one, which is indeed a profound reform of religion able to take man to more radical religious experiences culminating in extreme mystical experiences conceived of as redemptive. His Kabbalah is therefore not only the exposure and disclosure of the esoteric sense of sacred Scripture but also, in his view, their radical fulfillment. The great wisdom of the redeemer, Abulafia claims, is to cause all three religions to "know the supreme name."[80] As we have seen in chapter 2, the nexus between the messianic experience and the recitation of the divine name was part and parcel of Abulafia's system and praxis. Hence the divine name is a basic ingredient of Abulafia's mystical technique, the goal of the more sublime mystical gnosis, and the name the Messiah is to call himself and by which he is to be called. The possession of such a powerful means and the belief that he may use it, as well as the resort to the term *ego,* which points to an awareness of a high personal attainment, illumine Abulafia's choice of a via perfectionis as the single manner of acting as a redeemer.

These discussions, together with the treatments of Abulafian thought in chapter 2, contribute to another picture of Jewish messianism in the Middle Ages and its reverberations in Christian Kabbalah, Sabbateanism, and Hasidism. They also, however, establish another perspective for understanding the transmission of ancient angelological traditions in the Middle Ages and their transformation in lived experiences, some of them fraught with salvific and messianic overtones. If in my earlier writings I sometimes emphasized the plausibility of continuity between some theosophical-theurgical traditions in antiquity and the Middle Age Kabbalah,[81] in this book I have attempted to put in relief the possible contributions of elements preserved in Abulafia toward another understanding of the history of Kabbalah.[82]

Tiqqun Ḥatzot: A Ritual between Myth, Messianism, and Mysticism

"Rites of Exile" or Ritualization of Religious Life in Safed

One of Scholem's main claims in support of his view that an acute messianism influenced sixteenth-century Kabbalah is that new rituals which were shaped in Safed expressed messianic beliefs: "The markedly ascetic note and apocalyptic mood which entered into Kabbalism after the expulsion from Spain were reflected in such rituals."[1] It is solely in this context that Scholem offers an extensive discussion of his view that the Kabbalists expressed in ritual the event undergone by the whole nation: "The historical experience of the Jewish people merged indistinguishably with the mystical vision of a world in which the holy was locked in desperate struggle with the satanic. Everywhere and at every hour the simple and yet so infinitely profound fact of exile provided ground for lamentation, atonement, and asceticism."[2] This entrance of the exilic consciousness into the rituals took place in Safed.[3] In order to illustrate his point Scholem analyzed two rituals, which he envisioned as "rites of exile": *tiqqun ḥatzot,* our subject of investigation here, and a ritual concerning Yom Kippur Qatan, which will not be discussed. As Scholem himself pointed out, however, "The strange[4] part of it is that these 'rites of exile' should have arisen in Palestine and not in countries of the Diaspora."[5] Scholem recognized that this problem threatened to undermine his theory, and he came up with an ingenious solution: "The Kabbalists who in the middle of the sixteenth century came to Safed from all over the world, in the intention of founding a 'community of holy men,' carried with them this acute consciousness of exile and gave it perfect ritual expression in the very place they expected the process of Messianic redemption to begin."[6] Scholem does not name the immigrant mystics who formulated the new rites out of a messianic mind-set, but the clear impression is that he is referring to R. Isaac Luria and R. Ḥayyim Vital.

Contrary to Scholem's implication that the Kabbalists came from abroad, Vital and Luria were born in the land of Israel. Although Luria lived for some years in Egypt, Vital left Israel only late in life, in a period not relevant to the emergence of the rituals. Thus, we remain with the quandary, not only that one of the rituals of exile was formulated in the land of Israel, but also that the main protagonists of this process were not born in exile. Another problem is the selective nature of Scholem's discussion. Safedian Kabbalah, in particular Lurianic Kabbalah, contributed to the formal institution of numerous rituals, most of them already in practice earlier and having nothing to do with messianism or with an exilic consciousness. Therefore, we may speak about a basic impulse for ritualization that is characteristic of the second half of the sixteenth century in Safed, which should be seen as the immediate framework for a comprehensive analysis of *all* the rituals. Indeed, the attempt to guide the masses in the form of the comprehensive Halakhic project of R. Joseph Karo's *Shulḥan 'Arukh,* the emergence of the rich literature dealing with *regimen vitae,*[7] the vast ethical Kabbalistic literature—all these should be added to the numerous rituals that were formulated in a more definitive manner in sixteenth-century Safed. Do these reflect the historical experience of the nation, or were they an attempt to shape the religious life so that it would become more vibrant? Are these forms of intensive religious life an attempt to express a collective experience or are they part of a project to impress?

Scholem argues—and here I totally agree with him—that the Safedian Kabbalists compiled most of the formulations of these rituals that become classical later on.[8] But as Scholem himself admitted, the rituals themselves were not new.[9] The Safedian innovation is more in the domain of contributing important details for the performance of the ritual, rather than for its very institution. Thus, the question again arises as to what extent the ritualization is connected with acute messianism or is to be explained against another form of religious activity, which strove to consolidate Jewish life rather than infuse an eschatological mind-set into larger masses.

Tiqqun Ḥatzot

The rite of *tiqqun ḥatzot,* namely the midnight reparation, is very complicated, and in his descriptions Scholem did not enter into details. Neither did some of the scholars who mentioned it after him, as they dealt with it only tangently.[10] The single exception is a very recent article by Shaul Maggid, who devoted a detailed analysis to this issue.[11] Given the basic differences between

Scholem's approach and my own, I shall engage again some of the main issues that are related to the nature of the messianic cargo as attributed by Scholem, and following him by Maggid, to this ritual.

All the scholars mention the fact that vigils related to midnight are not an innovation of Luria's. This has been made clear by Scholem and, more recently, by Maggid.[12] The extent of the Lurianic contribution, however, depends upon the nature of the pertinent elements already in existence in the Jewish tradition and in practice in Safed in Luria's time. For example, the very fact that R. Joseph Karo, hardly an innovative mystic and in fact a conservative Halakhic figure, mentions in his influential *Shulḥan 'Arukh* a prayer to be recited at midnight concerning the destruction of the Temple testifies to the existence of such a practice in the immediate vicinity of Luria, presumably before Luria's (or Vital's) formulation of his version of *tiqqun ḥatzot*.[13] In fact, a variety of vigils were practiced long before Luria, and some were maintained in the land of Israel in the sixteenth century, a fact that renders the question of Luria's contribution a rather thorny issue.[14] Moreover, even in Safed we may assume already in Luria's lifetime a rather widespread custom of praying and crying at midnight. Cordovero recommends the night vigil, which includes mourning and weeping over the destruction of the Temple,[15] and R. Abraham ha-Levi Berukhin mentions that "the majority of those who know Torah" practice a nocturnal vigil that consists in prayer, weeping, studying, and mourning.[16] These testimonies hardly fit a custom that was instituted quite recently by Luria.[17]

Scholem's quandary may appear less problematic if we inspect this ritual not only from the exilic but also from another point of view. Indeed, the Shekhinah and Her exile is mentioned in the ritual and is an integral part of it. Another set of symbols, however, is as crucial as the theme of the exile. The hope for rebuilding Jerusalem and Zion is mentioned several times, two terms which point to the two divine feminine powers, Leah and Rachel[18]—respectively, the *partzufim* of 'Imma' (corresponding to the third sefirah, Binah) and Nuqbba' (corresponding to Malkhut).[19] Resorting to a variety of biblical verses, especially from Psalms and Lamentations, the ritual deals concomitantly with the reparation within the intradivine structure and the rebuilding of the city on the mundane plane. The emphatic highlighting of the rebuilding of the city is, to my mind, quite remarkable in the general economy of the ritual. It is even more so if we remember that R. Isaac Luria, who apparently was instrumental in formulating the ritual, was born in Jerusalem and was perhaps active there for a period that was longer than we knew until recently.[20] Also R. Ḥayyim Vital, the other main protagonist in the formulation of the ritual, lived for some years in this city.[21] Thus, we may assume that some aspects of the ritual may reflect not so much the "acute messianism" imported by Kabbalists from abroad to Safed but the more intimate acquaintance of a Kabbalist coming to Safed from Jerusalem. As we know from several sources, vigils were instituted in Jerusalem for messianic purposes long before Luria and Vital.

In my opinion, some of the rituals instituted by Luria, like that of TW bi-Shevat, were prompted by the Kabbalists' more concrete experiences when living in the land of Israel: the encounters with the devastation of the city, in the case of the Tiqqun Ḥatzot, and with nature there, as in the case of the festival of TW bi-Shevat.[22] In fact, the encounter with the mythical geography of the Galilee, the real and imaginary tombs of the great figures of the glorious past, contributed new forms of mystical customs. In contrast, Scholem claimed that the center of the ritual was the identification of the Kabbalists, who represented the nation, with the plight of the Shekhinah in exile.[23] Let me address the issue of the "exile Shekhinah," which as Scholem remarked is Rachel. The main purpose of the ritual is to lament Rachel's suffering. There can be no doubt that Rachel, or the Shekhinah, is described as being in exile, and in one case even in exile amidst the impure powers.[24] However, the main thrust of the exile is the descent of Rachel not within the impure power but in the rather supernal realm of Beriy'ah, from the highest world of 'Atzilut.[25] This descent is indeed described as an exile, yet it has more to do with a certain constant, daily rhythm within the divine world, which is the main rationale for the ritual under scrutiny here. It is a momentary descent, during the middle of the night, which is overcome toward the dawn by the triumphant ascent. In fact, a cyclical event, whose deep structure does not parallel the nature of the historical linear exile, may thus reflect the historical exile only in some very limited forms. Let me explain this rationale as presented by R. Ḥayyim Vital himself.

Myth and Ritual: The Nightly *Hieros Gamos*

Three protagonists, all divine powers within the world of 'Atzilut, participate in the drama of the *hieros gamos,* or sacred marriage, pertinent for understanding the nightly ritual. During the first part of the night, Jacob, or Ze'ir 'Anppin, the male divine power, has sexual intercourse with Leah, the supernal feminine power, better known in Lurianic Kabbalah as the countenance of 'Imma', the great mother. This intercourse necessitates the growth of Leah to full size, which should consist of ten sefirot.[26] In order to attain this size, Leah takes some of the powers of Rachel, whose size is diminished during the first part of the night.[27] Moreover, the full size of Leah compels Rachel to descend from the world of 'Atzilut, the place of the hieros gamos, to that of Beriy'ah. This katabasis is basically the exile of the Shekhinah as understood in the explanations offered to the ritual. This diminution of Rachel, conceived as Nuqbba', Jacob's female counterpart par excellence, is the main reason for the first part of the *tiqqun ḥatzot* ritual: to enhance the size of Rachel's countenance and ensure that she will attain her full size, and thus to facilitate the hieros gamos between her and Jacob, the Ze'ir 'Anppin, during the second part of the night. The emendation of Rachel is therefore a restitution of her full size, a return to her position face to face with Jacob, and her return from the lower world of Beriy'ah to that of 'Atzilut. These are cyclic events, which are described from the systemic point of view as recurring night after night. During the second part of the night, however, it is Rachel's turn to keep Jacob's company, and Leah's stature is now diminished.[28] Whereas for the first part of the night Rachel lamented the destruction of the Temple and praised God, in the second part of the night she simply enjoys her connection to Ze'ir 'Anppin.[29]

The connection that Vital proposes between exile and the ritual is essentially related to the destruction of the Temple. Prior to the destruction, the supernal hieros gamos was quite independent of human "acts and prayers,"[30] apparently given the effect of the ongoing sacrifices in the Temple. The ritual is based therefore upon a cyclical rhythm, whose main logic is found in Lurianic theosophy, which deals with the divine countenances and their growth and diminution. These rhythms are the paramount and explicit explanation for the midnight vigil. Thus when dealing, for example, with the descent of Rachel into the world of Beriy'ah, Vital adduces not only the explanation that connects the descent with the sins of Israel, but also another one, which is based on a purely theosophical consideration. Vital claims that Rachel descends because the growth of Leah was so great that there was no room for her, as Leah's feet reached Rachel's head.[31] The image recalls the biblical story, for Leah is pushing Rachel out of the way. In other words, it is possible to find in the first Lurianic formulation of the ritual an explicit view for the descent of Rachel into the exilic realm, which is totally unrelated to history or human sins. Moreover, the descent or the exile of Rachel during the time of intercourse between Leah and Jacob creates an intimacy between her and the souls of the righteous.[32] I wonder whether the souls are those of the dead righteous in Paradise, or whether they are the righteous performing the ritual and serving as surrogates for Jacob. If the latter is the case, then the moment of lamenting involves not only desolation but also the establishment of an erotic or sexual intimacy, a point reminiscent of Maggid's argument.[33] In any case, those who perform the ritual were described as belonging to the entourage of the Matronita', namely Rachel, and ascending with her in the morning.

The exilic elements of the ritual, dealing with the mourning and lamenting over the destruction of the Temple and the exile of the Shekhinah, are not new but continue, as Scholem has pointed out, earlier pre-Kabbalistic and Kabbalistic (especially Zoharic) traditions. When one attempts to address the question of what is new in the Lurianic formulation of this ritual, the obvious answer is conveniently exposed in Vital's descriptions: the old motifs found in Kabbalah have been combined with the intricate theosophical visions of Luria. The connection with the sins of Israel and the impact they had is found in the ritual, but they belong to the earlier layers of the Kabbalistic tradition. A central proof of this argument is found in the exposition of the theosophical processes, which presupposes the importance of the study of the Torah, and sometimes also of prayer—namely the regular commandments—for the restitution of Rachel to her full size, without invoking the lamenting ritual at all.[34]

It is significant that Rachel does not lament the destruction of the Temple, nor is she described as being in exile; rather, she is described as descending within the world of "Beriy'ah, in the palace of the supernal Holy of Holies."[35] Therefore, the assumption is that Rachel, or the Shekhinah, is not in exile but os in her proper place, though at a lower state. In fact, the Kabbalists propelled the biblical sequence of relationship between Jacob and Leah and Rachel onto the theosophical level. In other words, the theosophical processes that serve as the background for the ritual of lamenting occur in Lurianic Kabbalah in much less exilic contexts as well, and they reflect the basic rhythm of the divine life. In this case, the reason for Rachel's diminishment in size or power is the "darkness of the night."[36] In some cases, however, these processes have been connected to exilic themes already represented in the zoharic literature. The emphasis on the destruction of the Temple, which is obvious in the ritual as formulated by Vital, explains why prayer and study of the Torah are the necessary antidotes—that is, why the ritualization process, which dominated the activity of Safedian Kabbalists, was so important. It should be mentioned that according to one version of the ritual, the destruction of the Temple symbolizes the deterioration of the countenance of the Female, *partzuf de-Nuqbba'*, and its descent to the realm of Beriy'ah.[37]

A pivotal moment in the sexual union with Jacob is his female partner's attainment of a full bodily size. Rachel and Leah are described as growing and diminishing during the night, in a rhythm that recalls the phases of the moon. The contraction and expansion of the body is described in some detail, and there can be no doubt as to the paramount importance of the "corporeal" processes within the more general emphasis on such processes in Lurianic Kabbalah, a landmark of this kind of theosophy. Nowhere in the texts belonging to the *tiqqun ḥatzot* ritual is it possible to detect a view that the female counterpart of Jacob becomes part of his body, more precisely his penis.[38] The feminine powers are independent manifestations which possess particular characteristics, some of them inspired by the biblical passages concerning Rachel and Leah, others by earlier Kabbalistic discussions.

The myth-and-ritual complex I have described proceeds in phases. In the first phase, the main protagonist of the complex, Rachel or the Shekhinah, is described as diminishing to her minimum size, namely that of point that stands for one of the ten sefirot. She is also excluded from the divine realm, wailing for her fate and in need of reparation (augmentation of her body) and a push from below in order to return her to the world of 'Atzilut. Her return is triumphal, as she comes with an entire retinue in order to consummate the *hieros gamos* with Jacob, the divine configuration of the male. This regular rhythm has been accompanied, according to the Lurianic Kabbalists, by the ordinary Jewish liturgy, and the rite we have described above is but an additional element in the myth-and-ritual complex. What is the deep structure of the above rhythm? The nightly katabasis and anabasis of the Shekhinah are reminiscent of the two basic moments in the sacral royal ideology, when the king has enacted the death of the God, or according to another view His imprisonment, and afterward His triumph. During the first stage of the myth-and-ritual drama, the people lamented and wailing, whereas during the second part they celebrated the victory of the king.[39] Moreover, in the ancient rite the king underwent a moment of humiliation.[40] Therefore, both the ancient royal myths and the Lurianic formulation of the ritual are perfect examples of via passionis. A more specific similarity between the two rites, however, is the manner in which the triumph was consummated: both the Babylonian rite and the Lurianic one deal with the sacred marriage, which takes place in the divine realm.[41] There are many important differences between the *tiqqun ḥatzot* and the Akitu ritual: most conspicuously, the former is a daily event, the latter an annual one; in the former, the protagonist is the Shekhinah, a goddess figure, while in latter it is a male god. Nevertheless, the similarities between them must to be addressed, since the affinity seems to be more on the level of the shared deep structure than a matter of historical influences. Yehuda Liebes has elucidated the basic struction of the Lurianic myth. It involves "the cyclical aspect, as expressed in *Sha'ar ha-Kavvanot* where it is maintained that the myth is not completed in the course of history but once in a year. More than the continuous historical development is described, it is the periodical myth that is dealt with, similar to Tammuz's or Adonis's death each year, in the pagan religions. The acute Messianic element emerged in Luria's Kabbalah only in its final stages."[42] Together with the annual cyclical rhythm, Lurianic Kabbalah as exemplified in the *tiqqun ḥatzot* ritual, as well as its more general vision of prayer, also cultivated the daily rhythm, which involved the nightly processes described above.

The Exile of the Torah

In most versions of *tiqqun ḥatzot* there is a historiosophical remark that is apparently unique to Lurianic Kabbalah. The Kabbalist bemoans not only the exile of Rachel and the destruction of the Temple but also another destruction and exile, that of the Torah. As part of the ritual, the Kabbalist is instructed to touch the dust of the ground with his face in order to direct his thought to "the burning of the Torah, which became ashes, and to what is written in my *Sha'ar Ruaḥ ha-Qodesh*[43] that from the day the House has been destroyed and the Torah was burned, Her secrets and arcana have been transmitted to the *ḥitztzonim,* and this is called the 'exile of the Torah'."[44] Therefore, in addition to the two disasters, that of the Shekhinah and that of the city and the Temple, the Torah has also been burned and exiled. Of utmost importance here is the emphasis that the "secrets and arcana" have been dispersed within the impure powers. This is reminiscent of the Lurianic view of the breaking of the vessels and the dispersing of the divine sparks in the realm of the qelippot or shells. However, unlike the ontological disaster, that of the secrets is an amazing statement when formulated in a school dominated by a particularistic attitude toward Kabbalah, as the Lurianic school is. It assumes that the secrets of the Torah, which are none other than the Kabbalah, are found in the realm of darkness, and the linkage to the destruction of the Temple makes plausible the view that the external powers, the *ḥitztzonim,* are the nations in general, and perhaps the Christians in particular.

Following the line found in the first Lurianic Kabbalists, R. Ya'aqov Ṭzemaḥ composed a poem to be recited, according to his siddur, as part of the ritual. The poem opens with these lines: "Let them cry over the beloved after midnight—as well as over the Torah and Her secrets, because they have been given over to the qelippot—In prison, and Her arcana have been obscured."[45] In other words, the secrets of the Torah, presumably identical with the lore of Kabbalah, is known by the gentiles, and this event coincides with the destruction of the Temple. Like the Torah and the divine configuration of the sefirot (before their breaking) as vessels, the Temple is in a state of total desolation since its content has been captured by the qelippot. What was the more historical picture as envisioned by Luria and Vital? According to *Sha'ar Ruaḥ ha-Qodesh,* the pride of Israel, which is the secrets, designated as *mistarim,* has been taken by the nations, which are viewed expressly as qelippot, and this is the reason for the weeping of God and of the Jews.[46] Even before the composition of the *Zohar* by R. Shimeon bar Yoḥai sometime in the second century, the gentiles already had access the secrets of the Torah. Are the Lurianic Kabbalists pointing to the emergence of Christianity as based upon the exile of the secrets of the Torah? Indeed, some Kabbalists before them had already mentioned such a possibility.[47] However, in addition to the possible repercussions of the medieval traditions on Christianity as a distortion of Kabbalah, I would suggest the possible impact of the emergence of the Christian Kabbalah as a formative element for some approaches of sixteeth-century Jewish Kabbalists in general and for some aspects of Lurianic Kabbalah in particular, especially its esotericism. That R. Moses Cordovero, Vital's and Luria's master, was aware of Christian Kabbalah is quite evident (see chapter 5). It seems, however, that Vital himself was preoccupied by the transmission of secrets to Christians. In one of his dreams (discussed in chapter 6) he mentions that the "Caesar of Rome," a phrase that Vital must have associated with the destruction of the Temple, was eager to learn the secrets of the Torah from him, and in the dream Vital indeed taught him some Kabbalistic secrets.

The rather surprising aspect of the "exile of the Torah" is the view, expressed powerfully in R. Ya'aqov Tzemaḥ's poem—who claims that he follows the view of the Rabbi, who is apparently Luria—that the secrets of the Torah are now obscure or sealed, *nistemu.* The captivity of the secrets within the realm of the qelippot is apparently the ontological correspondent of the epistemological obscuring of the secrets. Though consonant with some of Luria's main views dealing with the dispersion of the sparks, the obscuring of the secrets is interesting when advocated by the Lurianic Kabbalists. Formulated during one of the most creative periods of Kabbalah, when Luria was considered to the revealer of the secrets of Kabbalah,[48] the concept of the obscuring of secrets demands further treatment. As we have seen, the Kabbalists conceived the revelation of the secrets as part of the messianic scenario. In the ritual under consideration here, however, one does not get the impression that the secrets have been revealed, nor that such an imminent revelation is on the way. If acute messianism was one of the triggers of the ritual, it is not evident, at least insofar as the concept of the secrets of the Torah is concerned.

Weeping, Studying, and Revelation

An important part of tiqqun ḥatzot involves weeping. This is recommended in all the forms of the ritual I am acquainted with, and the recurrence of this issue in Safed in a variety of contexts is well established by several studies.[49] Indeed, the performance of the ritual is thought to be helpful in the reparation of the soul and in the "apprehension of wisdom,"[50] according to another version, in order to cause the indwelling of the divine spirit and purity.[51] Therefore, it is the individual's achievement of Kabbalistic knowledge and extraordinary experiences, rather than their revelation by the Messiah or an expansion of knowledge in the more diffused manner that was supposed to occur in the eschaton, that is important here.

Let me elaborate upon one of the mystical possibilities inherent in tiqqun ḥatzot. According to the version in *Siddur ha-'Ari,* the performance of the ritual will induce the divine and pure spirit. I wonder whether weeping during the ritual is not the main reason for such a mystical achievement. As I have attempted to show elsewhere, weeping has been a mystical technique in Jewish texts since antiquity,[52] and it was cultivated in the medieval period and in the circle of Luria, including by Vital.[53]

Like a Chariot

One interesting element of the ritual is found only later the version proposed by R. Nathan Neta' Hanover.[54] Vital mentioned that Luria recommended that he study after the performance of the rite in order to amend his soul.[55] This is just one more example of a recommendation of Luria's that is originally intended for the special need of an individual and apparently was never supposed to become part of the ritual as practiced by others. Nevertheless, after the conclusion of the second tiqqun, the tiqqun of Leah, some Kabbalists recommended a third part, which includes the following formulation: "After you have performed the *tiqqun ḥatzot,* prepare your soul and unify[56] the Holy One, Blessed be He, with His Shekhinah, onto each and every limb, and you should make your body a chariot for the Shekhinah."[57] Then a prayer is recommended wherein the performer expresses his desire that all the limbs of his body become the chariot of the Shekhinah. While the two main parts of the tiqqun deal, respectively, with the exile and the redemption of the Shekhinah, in the third phase as described by R. Nathan Hanover the Shekhinah is envisioned in rather differently, as dwelling upon the Kabbalist's body. This third part of the ritual may be understood as attempting to offer to the wandering Shekhinah a purified human body to serve as Her chariot, namely as a locus for Her stay in lieu of the destroyed Temple.[58]

The resort to the term *merkavah,* "chariot," in this context is reminiscent of the midrashic view of the perfect patriarchs as being the merkavah.[59] The templar implication of this stage is strengthened by the fact that during the first stage of the ritual the Kabbalist emphatically mourns the destruction of the Temple. Thus, the last phase may be understood as the reconstruction of the destroyed Temple by the purification of the body and the invitation of the divine couple to dwell upon the body. According to some traditions, the Temple served as the locus of procreation, and there is a widespread view in the Middle Ages that two divine powers coupling were symbolized by the two cherubim.[60] However, the concern for the plight of the Shekhinah, central as it is to the entire ritual and especially in the third part, should not prevent a more mystical reading of the last phase, which may be even more important than the messianic one. Indeed, the redemption of the Shekhinah by offering Her the human body as Temple is, at the same time, also a transformation of the human body itself, whose limbs become the locus wherein the divine *hieros gamos* takes place. The title given by the Kabbalists, *Tiqqun ha-Nefesh,* the "reparation of the soul," unmistakably points toward the new focus, the human being. Thus, the redemption of the Shekhinah in the first two stages is followed, in this version of the ritual, by a tiqqun of the individual, which has strong mystical implications, as his body is conceived of as becoming the new, albeit perhaps temporary, Temple.

Is the sequence of the three reparations, *tiqqun Raḥel,* dealing with the exile, *tiqqun Lea'h,* dealing with redemption, and *tiqqun ha-nefesh,* dealing with the body as Temple concept, arranged hierarchically? This is certainly the case insofar as the two first phases are concerned. Is the third phase the most important, the culmination of the two earlier phases? If this is the case, the more mystically oriented phase is to be regarded as higher than the eschatological ones. Or, to put it in other terms, the "historical" redemption is enacted in the first two phases, which serve as preparation for a third one. While in the first two phases the Shekhinah is treated as an ontological power that does not necessarily come in direct contact with the Kabbalist as part of the ritual, in the third case She, together with God, is expected to do it. While in the first two phases the Kabbalist is imitating the external, objective processes, namely exile and redemption, in the third phase the Kabbalist's experience is much more personal. If this analysis is correct, we may speak about a version of the rite that culminates in a personal experience of direct contact with God, a view that may be described as a mystical union. Unlike the first two phases, where the main concern is to induce a state of harmony between God and His female counterpart, in the third one the established harmony is encountered within the Kabbalist's body. As the title of the last phase indicates, however, this stage also involves a reparation of the soul. To put it differently, the Kabbalist not only imitates the exile of the Shekhinah and then Her redemptive ascent in the second phase of the ritual; he also strives to come into direct contact with the divine. This shows that the immediate experience of plenitude has been imagined as found within the pale of this ritual, despite the fact that it starts with lamentations over the destruction of the Temple.[61] Moreover, even in the more classical forms of the ritual, the Kabbalist is told to prepare himself, by means of the study of the Torah, to become part of the entourage of the Shekhinah—*benei heikhala' dida'* and *benei heikhala' de-Matronita'*—because in the morning, the triumphal Rachel will take him with her in the daily ascent on high.[62] The triumphant Rachel, as much as the lamenting Rachel, is the subject of the rite known as *tiqqun ḥatzot.* According to some latter versions, the ritual alwo involves an experience of contact with the divine couple, taking place on the purified body of the mystic.

Some Conclusions

The different explanations of the ritual of *tiqqun ḥatzot* show that one leading idea is rarely sufficient in order to explain the complex phenomena we encounter in mystical literature. In this case, resorting to one explanation of formative impact of the acute messianism allegedly imported by the Kabbalists from their prior exilic experiences is problematic, not only because it imposed a messianic ideology on entire groups of mystics without attempting to prove it in serious manner, but also because it is offered as the sole and sufficient explanation. More complex and multifaceted explanations are in order so that the variety of human experiences addressed by this ritual may be taken in account.[63] From a more conceptual point of view, for example, the ritual of lamenting the destruction of the Temple started with an historical fact, which in a short time became mythologized. God's lamenting every night over the destruction in the Talmud is an obvious proof. The historical event and the mythological participation of God in the ritual of lamenting do not leave room for a more mystical experience during the ritual. The emergence of other models, however, such as the theosophical-theurgical one as formulated by Lurianic Kabbalah and the talismanic one designated here as templar, earlier in the history of Kabbalah impregnated the older myth-and-ritual instances with new valences, which enabled the Kabbalist not only to mourn over the past but also to participate in theosophical-cyclical events of the present and to enjoy moments of plenitude absent in the pre-Safedian versions of the ritual. The additional valences did not enhance the exilic consciousness, nor were they intended to diminish it. But they did contribute new explanations, which reflected further facets of experience that are less historical and thus contributed to a certain marginalization of the exilic experiences. This analysis is based upon the Lurianic material as represented in the earliest and most authoritative sources. There, acute messianism is, in my reading, totally absent. This seems also to be the case in some of the later understandings of the ritual. In the Zhidichov-Komarno school, the most Lurianically oriented group in Hasidism and the most messianically inclined nineteenth-century Hasidic school, the emphasis is explicitly on the reparation of the soul, and the performance of the ritual depends of one's not been negatively affected by the hardness of the ritual by becoming melancholic.[64] There is nothing in the above treatment that attempts to eradicate messianic interpretations of this ritual when they are obvious, as some are.

However, a more nuanced understanding of the genesis of the ritual and its various interpretations may help us better understand the Safedian atmosphere and what Kabbalists were attempting to express.

For example, as in some other cases in theosophical Kabbalah, the ritual of *tiqqun ḥatzot* is performed for the sake of improving the plight of the female hypostasis. The Kabbalists performing the tiqqun do not mention the integration of the female into the male, nor to my best understanding is the female potency made part of the divine phallus. This Kabbalistic performance is a male ritual accomplished for the sake of two female powers on high. Their independence as full-fledged entities, rather than their absorption into the male configuration, is the underlying structure of the ritual. Even in the climax, the female powers do not lose their proper identity. Consequently, at least insofar as this ritual is concerned, it is difficult to corroborate Elliot Wolfson's view of Kabbalah as a phallocentric lore.[65] The ritual traveled through many of the Jewish communities and had a certain impact at the beginning of the seventeenth century. When formulated in a more accessible manner, however, in order to be performed, most of the theosophical aspects of the ritual have been marginalized. The thrust of the seventeenth-century descriptions was to encourage a certain type of behavior, much more than to teach a certain type of mystical lore. Indeed, as Elliot Horowitz has shown, the ritual was not accepted so easily, even in those circles of Jews who were ready to perform other, non-Lurianic vigils and studies at night.[66] Even the authority of Lurianism was not able to ensure a large-scale acceptance of this ritual, though it become better known than Luria's theosophy was in the first part of the seventeenth century. Indeed, its history exemplifies the distinction I proposed some years ago between the different impacts that various aspects of Lurianism had on Jewish knowledge and praxis: "The knowledge of Lurianic Kabbalah was, roughly speaking, limited to the elite; only a few Kabbalists could be considered to have really mastered this complicated type of theosophy. For example, when it was propagated in some limited circles or in confraternities in northern Italy, its influence was excerpted mainly in ritual and customs—*minhagim*—and only marginally in a *Weltanschauung*."[67]

Some Modern Reverberations of Jewish Messianism

Messianic ideas have played a multifaceted role in Jewish culture. Among elite and common people, those ideas have remained alive for generations. A succinct inspection of the biographies of three well-known figures active in the twentieth century, Theodor Herzl, Gershom Scholem, and Elie Wiesel, reveals the existence of messianic dreams and aspirations early in their life.[1] Apparently, such activist ideas, which eventually lost much of their eschatological cargo, had their effect on the later careers of these individuals.

Different forms of affinity between ancient and medieval mystical elements have constituted the messianic constellation of ideas. Jewish mysticism, however, has not remained a totally esoteric trend but was able to inform some of the more recent speculations concerning messianism, especially via Hasidic literature. Modern Jewish thinkers, philosophers, or writers, like some of their medieval predecessors, addressed various topics of messianism, and sometimes their formulations betray a dialogue with earlier views. Martin Buber, Franz Kafka, Walter Benjamin, or Emmanuel Levinas are good examples. Even more important, messianic ideas were instrumental in a variety of political and national movements, and again the impact of some mystical formulations can be discerned.[2] I would like to point out some of these affinities in order to show their role in the perpetuation of the move toward religious fragmentation.[3]

Messiah of All, or All as Messiahs

Martin Buber highly esteemed messianism, as he understood it. He asserted that messianism is "Judaism's most profoundly original idea."[4] What precisely messianism meant to him we may guess from a letter to Hugo Bergmann, dated December 4, 1917, where he addresses the insufficiency of personal experience (*Ichvorgang*) as a redemptive act:

> Never can the ascent of a man to God, the rebirth of man, be regarded as a messianic event, only the redemptive function of man can. Through the redemptive function, the redemptive deed of messianic individuals, the absolute future prepares itself in the present, in every present. The consummation of the future is beyond our consciousness—like God; its enactment is accessible to our consciousness—like man's experience of God. I believe in the fulfillment of the end of days, which may not be anticipated by anything transient. . . But precisely from this it follows that the consummation cannot be a past event, it is not localized in a precise place of the historical part; and it also follows that neither may it be transformed from an event within the world [*Weltvorgang*] into an event within the I [*Ichvorgang*]. The world-event must be experienced [*erlebt werden*] in the I [as self-redemption] . . . If the *Ichvorgang* is to mature to a redemptive task, every extra-temporal *Erlebnis* [must seek] temporal vindication and representation, and in this sense time is greater than eternity. The Messiah, the son of David, does not demand rule over the nations, but life—that is to say, not divine power, but human persistence [*Dauer*], time, and space for his deed. It seems to me [that the messianic idea] can mean nothing else.[5]

The emphasis on the importance of the deed as a criterion for a valid messianic experience is quintessential to Buber's thought. He believed that "[m]essianism prepared, as it were, the ground for the final and complete realization of Judaism's two other tendencies, the unity-idea and the deed-idea."[6] Therefore, unitive as the personal experience may be, it cannot exclude the deed-idea, which is oriented toward the other.[7] This emphasis, which illumines many forms of messianism, has to do with Buber's more general vision of the Jews as representatives of what he called the Oriental man, much more a motor type of person than Western man, who he saw as sensory.[8] The certainty that the inner experience alone cannot be messianic is a theological statement, which is not corroborated by many of the Kabbalistic discussions above. In this point of view Buber, one of the most important phenomenologists of Judaism, and Scholem, who adopted a much more historical approach, converge. But while Scholem was much more directed toward the mythical and preferred the view of one apocalyptic Messiah, Buber left room for what he called "messianic individuals," a series of redemptive figures who silently prepare for the end of days.

The opposition between the apocalyptic event and the mundane and gradual salvation is a major theme in Buber's novel *For the Sake of Heaven,* where the nineteenth-century Hasidic masters dramatically confront themselves when attempting to define the nature of messianism. The Yehudi, R. Yitzḥaq Ya'aqov of Pzysca, plays the role of the more patient waiters and preparer of the coming of the Messiah, while his master, R. Yitzḥaq Ya'aqov, the seer of Lublin, embodies the more apocalyptic—what Buber called magical, namely theurgical—view of messianic activity.[9] Buber obviously preferred the former, and from this point of view his thought inscribes itself in the distribution of the messianic function among many rather than its concentration in the hands of the mythical one, an attitude that attracted critical observations of Christian messianism. According to him, in early Christianity "a conflict flared up, the conflict between the messianic ideal and the transference of messianic concepts to the person of the leader and master."[10] I take this distribution to owe much to Hasidism, with its emphasis on the sparks of the Messiah found in every Jew.[11] Indeed, another emphasis in Buber seems to betray the impact of Hasidic treatments. In one of his earlier discussions of messianism, he emphasizes the importance of the community as the goal of the messianic event. Judaism's "longing for God is the longing to prepare a place for Him in the true community. . . . [Judaism's] wait for the Messiah is the wait for the true community. . . . Hence Judaism must not liken itself to other nations, for it knows that, being first-born, realization is incumbent upon it. . . . So long, therefore, as the kingdom of God has not come, Judaism will not recognize any man as the true Messiah, yet it will never cease to expect redemption to come from man, for it is man's task to establish God's power on earth."[12] Therefore, Buber does not renounce the ultimate deliverer, but apparently reduces this concept to the realm of what may be called on asymptotic hope. Given his vision of Christianity, we may infer that in the eschatological future Judaism would not embrace a powerful individual but rather a dissemination of the divine message within the community. Buber deals also with power, but this is what he calls "theopolitical power."[13] The "ultimate"—in my opinion the eternal asymptotic—Messiah would for Buber be more a proclamation than a theophany, or a manifestation of the divine. The more tangible version of messianism is the actual one, which may also involve the experience of the deed within the ego.

Like Buber, Emmanuel Levinas radically fragmented the one Messiah into everyone who is a consoler, resorting to a midrashic reflection on the significance of the messianic name Menaḥem.[14] A strong supporter of the approach I have described as via passionis, Levinas emphasized the importance of substitution, of the sympathetic identification with the suffering of the other, as a messianic function.

Franz Kafka and Walter Benjamin, or the Never- and the Ever-Coming Messiah

The cyclical time presiding over ritual, which may indeed be understood as continuously cairological,[15] has been absorbed by some forms of mystical understanding of eschatology, as Lurianism and Hasidism testify.[16] Thus, the Messiah or the messianic experience may come every moment if the person, or according to the other version the community, acts appropriately to achieve this goal. On the opposite pole stands Kafka's assertion that the Messiah will come only when he is no longer needed.[17] Like the death of the countryman before the gate destined to be entered only by him in Kafka's "Before the Law," the latecoming Messiah reflects, though in a different way, the crisis of the Westernized Jew, engulfed as he is in external history.[18] It is the pure expectation which apparently will not materialize, rather than action, that remains from the messianic constellation of ideas.

On the other hand, the ecstatic model, with its emphasis on instant redemptive experience, both in its initial form expressed by Abulafia's description of the Messiah as an inner event and in R. Menaḥem Naḥum of Chernobyl, is reminiscent of an even more recent attempt to define messianism by Walter Benjamin. In his famous *Theses on the Philosophy of History* he declared, "We know that the Jews were prohibited from investigating the future. The Torah and the prayers instruct them in remembrance, however. This stripped the future of its magic, to which all those succumb who turn to the soothsayers for enlightenment. This does not imply, however, that for the Jews the future turned into homogeneous, empty time. For every second of time was the strait gate through which the Messiah might enter."[19]

The imminence and acuteness of messianism, characteristic of an expectation that is stripped of its computation and calculation and involves also postponement, consists in a pure openness toward the invasion of the better future and is equidistant from both the apocalypse of popular messianism and the progressive reparation of the theosophical-theurgical Kabbalah. A concept of openness to the ever-expected inexplicable more closely resembles the vision of messianism as tantamount to individual salvation; the all-pregnant moments of time[20] are conceived of as possible gates to the messianic experience.

R. Abraham Yitzḥaq ha-Kohen Kook

Twentieth-century Hasidic thought is responsible for several anti-Zionist ideologies. Ironically, it also spawned another type of mystical thought, which has flourished particularly in the land of Israel and which compromised between mystical and national-mythical conceptions of messianism. This blend is apparent in the thought of Rabbi Abraham Yitzḥaq ha-Kohen Kook, the chief rabbi of the land of Israel during the 1920s and 1930s. Jewish mysticism is the overall conceptual framework that determines Rav Kook's thought. The theme of messianism is minor and understood as the future end of a process of divinely guided historical progression.[21] The mystical element is blatant in the approach of Rav Kook's preeminent student, R. David ha-Kohen, better known as ha-Nazir, the Nazirite. In his impressive work *Qol ha-Nevu'ah* (The Voice of Prophecy) he writes: "God willing we will merit a revival of the holy, a revival of the audible prophetic spirit, and a political revival in our Holy Land."[22] After this "revival" there will be a resurrection of the mystical element, termed the "prophetic spirit," predominantly an auditory experience, according to ha-Nazir's conception of "auditory logic." Redemption is seen through the prism of a return to a state of direct relationship with God, rather than a sanctification of an earthly political framework. Clearly this framework exists as well and is referred to as "a political revival in our Holy Land." The connection between prophecy and the subsequent political revival is reminiscent of the nexus between prophecy and messianism in Abulafia's thought. Indeed, as an autobiographical fragment printed recently shows, David ha-Kohen was acquainted with Abulafia's manuscripts.[23]

Despite the absence of conspicuous messianic motifs in the writings of R. Abraham Yitzḥaq ha-Kohen Kook, there was a sharp surge in the mythical-political interpretation of his teachings within the circle of R. Tzevi Yehudah ha-Kohen Kook and his followers, the repercussions of which are still recognizable today.[24] From these two interpretations of the teachings of R. Abraham Yitzḥaq ha-Kohen Kook, an important lesson about the conceptual framework that we have been studying can be learned: namely, there can be a varied selection of doctrinal elements, which will serve different needs within different systemic contexts, either historical circumstances or various religious concerns.

The modern trends mentioned here point to three major mystical interpretions of messianism. There is the existential or spiritual interpretation, as presented in some Hasidic positions, which affirms the possibility of realizing in the present a messianic moment, a certain plenitude which apparently was not allowed even by the thinkers closest to Hasidism in modern Jewish philosophy.[25] The second interpretation is found among twentieth-century Jewish philosophers, including Hermann Cohen, Martin Buber, Franz Rosenzweig, Isaiah Leibowitz, and Emmanuel Levinas, some of whom interiorized mystical views and conceived the hope for the advent in an asymptotic manner, where the ideal of expectation is preferred to that of realization.[26] In another form, the importance of the messianic ideal has been described as transforming everyday life even in the speech of a modern philosopher, who declared that the messianic tomorrow "is my to-day."[27] Third, the political activists such as the Kookian school, inspired by mythical-mystical concepts, emphasize the beginning of the realization of the messianic ideal in external reality.[28]

Political Messianism

It is possible to view the Zionist outlook of the late nineteenth and early twentieth centuries as a return to the definition of messianism that professes the centrality of the nation or tribe, more than in some preceding doctrines of Jewish mysticism. The Zionist view placed little emphasis on the individual's spiritual redemption and concentrated much more on the salvation of the group or the nation. It drew on general or public messianic concepts and phenomena that were crucial to Judaism in the periods preceding Zionism. Even at first glance, the recent studies of Zionism by scholars such as Israel Colat,[29] Shmuel Almog[30] or Anita Shapira,[31] to mention only a few, reveal an emerging consciousness of the relationship between classical Jewish messianic elements and its veiled expressions that were co-opted and become part and parcel of Zionist ideology. Even historians have started to describe messianic events in the past in Zionist terms. Cecil Roth, for example, designated the sixteenth-century adventurer David ha-Reuveni "a precursor of Jewish nationalist" in an article entitled, quite emblematically, "A Zionist Experiment in the Fifteenth Century."[32] As another historian once remarked, "There are cases in which the modalities of the imagination become the stuff of historical moments."[33]

Notes

Preface

1. See Idel, "Types of Redemptive Activities." On the three models see also my later and more detailed description in my *Hasidism: Between Ecstasy and Magic*, pp. 44–145.

2. Idel, "Shlomo Molkho as Magician."

3. Moshe Idel, *Meshiḥiyyut u-Mystiqah* (Misrad ha-Bitaḥon, Tel Aviv, 1989).

4. Most of Liebes's Hebrew original of the studies on Sabbatean views of messianism has been printed in his collection of articles entitled *On Sabbateaism and Its Kabbalah.*

5. See Gross, *Le messianisme juif;* Byron Sherwin, *Mystical Theology and Social Dissent* (London and Toronto, 1982), pp. 142–160.

6. Liebes, *Studies in Jewish Myth.*

7. Arieh Morgenstern, *Messianism and the Settlement of Eretz-Israel* (Yad Izḥak Ben-Zvi Publications, Jerusalem, 1985) (Hebrew), as well as his collection of articles *Ge'ulah be-Derekh ha-Teva' be-Kitvei ha-Gra ve-Talmidav* (Elkanah, 1989) and the critique of Israel Bartal, *Exile in the Homeland* (Jerusalem, 1994), pp. 236–295 (Hebrew).

Introduction: The Sources of Messianic Consciousness

1. See Lerner, *Powers of Prophecy*, p. 2.

2. See Plotinus, *Enneads*, 6.9.11. Insofar as Jewish mysticism is concerned, the term *contact* as reflecting the manner of relationship between the mystic and God has already been used, especially by Scholem, *On the Kabbalah*, p. 8, and *Major Trends*, p. 4. In other instances Scholem described the relations of the human and the divine as an "immediate experience" or "immediate awareness"; see, respectively, *On the Kabbalah*, p. 5, and *Major Trends*, p. 4. See also Idel, *Kabbalah: New Perspectives*, p. xviii. On the use of this term in discussions of mysticism in general see J. M. Rist, *The Road to Reality* (Cambridge University Press, Cambridge, 1967), p. 178; Phillip C. Almond, *Mystical Experience and Religious Doctrine* (Mouton, Berlin, 1982), pp. 158–159; and the important remarks of Merlan, *Monopsychism*, pp. 22–26, and more recently Bernard McGinn, "Mysticism," *Oxford Encyclopedia of the Reformation* (1996), 3:119.

3. On the relationship between apocalypticism and messianism see the bibliography adduced by Segal, "Paul and the Beginning of Jewish Mysticism," p. 120n24. On a very different view than that proposed here of the relation between the messianism and mysticism, inspired by G. Scholem, see Werblowsky, "The Safed Revival," in Green, ed., *Jewish Spirituality,* 2:11; for later Hasidism see his "Mysticism and Messianism," pp. 305–314. Werblowsky, in another context dealing with messianism, coined the phrase "experiential wave-length" to indicate the similarity between two different messianic views: the classical-apocalyptic and the modern Zionist. Indeed, it is possible to apply this term to the cases where the mystic and the Messiahs had inner, redemptive experiences. See his "Messianism in Jewish History," in Saperstein, ed., *Essential Papers,* p. 51, and compare to Scholem, *Studies and Texts,* p. 9, where he points out that in the "generation of national redemption" it is easier to understand the tragic manifestations of the Sabbatean search for redemption. On the emphasis on the need for a historiography based upon a national rather than an assimilation point of view, see Scholem, *Studies and Texts,* p. 15.

4. On the nexus between Jewish mysticism and the apocalyptic literature in ancient time see Scholem, *Messianic Idea in Judaism,* p. 7, and Collins, *Apocalyptic Imagination,* pp. 10–11.

5. "The Safed Revival," in Green, ed., *Jewish Spirituality,* 2:11. See also his "Mysticism and Messianism," pp. 305–306. I cannot resist adducing Solomon Zeitlin's explanation of the nexus between mysticism and messianism. After blaming Sabbateanism for its "calamitous" effects, he writes, rather candidly: "True, there were men who honestly believed themselves to be messiahs. They arrived at this belief because of their ascetic way of living and through their engrossment in the studies of mysticism and Kabbala. They fasted and prayed and thus their minds became deranged—they saw visions that God destined them to be messiahs to redeem His people and lead them to the Promised Land." See his essay "The Origin of the Idea of the Messiah" in Landman, *Messianism in the Talmudic Era,* p. 100.

6. See Scholem, *Messianic Idea in Judaism,* pp. 1–36. For a critical view of this position see Taubes, "Price of Messianism," pp. 595–600; Idel, "Introduction"; Liebes, *Studies in Jewish Myth,* p. 94.

7. Scholem, *Messianic Idea in Judaism,* pp. 15–17; *'Od Davar,* pp. 238–239.

8. See Liebes, *Studies in the Zohar,* pp. 52–55; Idel, *R. Abraham Abulafia,* pp. 395–399; idem, "Types of Redemptive Activities," pp. 259–262, 273. To a certain extent a nexus between *devequt* and messianism has been argued by Tishby, cf. his *Studies in Kabbalah,* 2:506–510, 3:981–987 in the case of Luzzatto's Kabbalah and some Hasidic instances. But Tishby's argument, correct in itself, deals only with the latest historical phases of Jewish mysticism, ignoring the relevance of the constitutive phases of Kabbalistic literature, the Zohar, and the ecstatic Kabbalah. On the other hand, he implicitly accepts Scholem's vision of messianism as apocalypticism (see below, chap. 7).

9. See Lord Raglan, *The Hero* (Vintage, New York, 1956). Raglan's book, very successful in itself, is a rather extreme expression of the myth-and-ritual school.

10. Walter Schmithals, *The Apocalyptic Movement; Introduction and Interpretation* (Abingdon, Nashville, 1975), p. 18; McGinn, *Visions of the End,* p. 31. See also McGinn's other discussion related to the concept of "validation from the future," which is part of the formation of the identity of a particular religious sect or order. Cf. his "Apocalyptic Traditions and Spiritual Identity in Thirteenth-Century Religious Life," in E. Rozanne Elder, ed., *The Roots of the Modern Christian Tradition* (Cistercian Publications, Kalamazoo, 1984), pp. 1–26, 293–300, reprinted in *Apocalypticism in the Western Tradition,* chap. 7. For a more extensive presentation of the deprivation theory and an elaborate critique of it see Cook, *Prophecy and Apocalypticism,* passim. See also, from a more theological point of view, Wolfhart Pannenberg, "Eschatology and the Experience of Meaning," in his *Basic Questions in Theology* (SCM Press, London, 1973), 3:192–210.

11. McGinn, *Apocalyptic Spirituality,* pp. 8–9; Barnes, *Prophecy and Gnosis,* p. 2. My analysis has been substantially influenced by McGinn's approach.

12. See Robert E. Lerner, "The Black Death and Western European Eschatological Mentalities," *American Historical Review* 86 (1981), pp. 533–552; idem, *Powers of Prophecy,* p. 193.

13. Frank Kermode, *The Sense of an Ending: Studies in the Theory of Fiction* (Oxford University Press, London, 1966), p. 22; also quoted by McGinn, *Power of Prophecy,* pp. 10, 13; Barnes, *Prophecy and Gnosis,* p. 2. See also John J. Collins, "Apocalyptic Eschatology as the Transcendence of Death," *Catholic Biblical Quarterly* 36 (1974), pp. 21–43. Most instructive is Hume's assertion that man is a "teleological animal"; cf. her *Fantasy and Mimesis,* pp. 168–197.

14. Joseph Dan, *The Hebrew Story in the Middle Ages* (Keter, Jerusalem, 1974), p. 45 (Hebrew); see also p. 44 and Dan's study mentioned in note 68 below. I fear that most of the discussions below dealing with a great variety of Kabbalists do not confirm Dan's sweeping statement. Moreover, many topics that will not be dealt with in this book in detail, such as the nexus between messianism, astronomy, and astrology, evident in R. Abraham bar Hiyya's influential *Sefer Megillat ha-Megalleh,* blatantly contradict Dan's statement.

15. For more on this issue see Idel, *Studies in Ecstatic Kabbalah,* pp. 1–20, and below, chap. 1.

16. Bernard McGinn, *The Foundations of Mysticism* (Crossroad, New York, 1991), pp. 5–6.

17. The single significant exception would be Philo of Alexandria's theology, but his spiritual legacy remained virtually extraneous to Jewish medieval forms of thought and mysticism until the Renaissance. On the impact of Philo on Christian spirituality see McGinn, *Foundations of Mysticism,* pp. 35–41. On Philo's spiritual understanding of eschatology see Richard D. Hecht, "Philo and Messiah," in J. Neusner et al., *Judaisms and Their Messiahs,* pp. 139–168; P. Borgen, " 'There Shall Come Forth a Man': Reflections on Messianic Ideas in Philo," in Charlesworth, ed., *Messiah,* pp. 341–361; Winston, *Logos,* pp. 55–58.

18. See, e.g., Jacques Le Goff, *L'Imaginaire medieval* (Gallimard, Paris, 1985); Jean-Claude Schmitt, "Introduccio a una historia de l'imaginari medieval," in *El mon imaginari i el mon meravellos a l'edat mitjana* (Fundacio caixa de Pensions, Barcelona, 1986), pp. 15–133; Claude Kappler, *Monstres, démons et merveilles à la fin du Moyen Age* (Payot, Paris, 1982); Durand, *Figures mythiques.* Another important avenue for the understanding of the building of messianic worldviews is the resort to literary theories concerning fictional worlds. See, e.g., Kermode's view cited above as well as Thomas G. Pavel, *Fictional Worlds* (Harvard University Press, Cambridge, 1986); Hume, *Fantasy and Mimesis.*

19. See Collins, *Apocalyptic Imagination,* pp. 14–17.

20. *Ha-Ra'ayon ha-Meshiḥi be-Yisrael,* published in English as *The Messianic Idea in Israel.* Klausner goes to great lengths to demonstrate the coexistence of different aspects as particularism and universalism within the category of the Jewish messianic idea; see ibid., pp. 11–12.

21. Klausner, *Messianic Idea in Israel.*

22. Ibid., pp. 237–252. Some other titles that presuppose a certain unity of the messianic theme are Joseph Sarachek, *The Doctrine of the Messiah in Medieval Jewish Literature,* esp. p. 3, and Silver, *History of Messianic Speculation.* Resort to the idiom of messianic idea is found in any number of discussions elsewhere in the Scholemian school; see, e.g., Werblowsky, "Messianism in Jewish History," in Saperstein, ed., *Essential Papers,* p. 44.

23. See Scholem, *Messianic Idea in Judaism,* pp. 4, 37.

24. Morton Smith, "What Is Implied by the Variety of Messianic Figures," *JBL* 78 (1959), pp. 66–72; idem, "Messiahs: Robbers, Jurists, Prophets, and Magicians," in Saperstein, ed., *Essential Papers,* pp. 73–82.

25. John J. Collins, "Patterns of Eschatology at Qumran," in B. Halpern and J. D. Levenson,

eds., *Traditions in Transformation: Turning Points in Biblical Faith* (Eisenbrauns, Winona Lake, Ind., 1981), pp. 351–375.

26. See Talmon, *King, Cult, and Calendar,* pp. 202–224; David Flusser, "The Reverberation of Jewish Messianic Beliefs in Ancient Christianity," in Baras, ed., *Messianism and Eschatology,* pp. 103–134 (Hebrew); Neusner, *Messiah in Context,* and "Mishnah and the Messiah," in *Judaisms and Their Messiahs,* Neusner et al., eds., pp. 278–282; B. M. Bokser, "Messianism, The Exodus Pattern, and Early Rabbinic Judaism," in Charlesworth, ed., *Messiah,* p. 240, and the references he adduced at n. 4.

27. Idel, "Types of Messianic Activities," pp. 253–279.

28. For a theory of models concerning Kabbalah and Hasidism see my *Hasidism: Between Ecstasy and Magic,* pp. 45–145. My resort to a distinction between the three models insofar as mystical language in Judaism is concerned can be found in "Reification of Language in Jewish Mysticism," in S. Katz, ed., *Mysticism and Language* (Oxford University Press, New York, 1992), pp. 42–79.

29. A similar situation is found also in Scholem's description of the idea of the Golem; see Idel, *Golem,* pp. xxii–xxiii. This unidimensional vision of history in general, as well as the history of ideas, is peculiarly problematic since it allows too great a role solely to the theoretical dimension of a quite complex situation.

30. See Scholem's interview with Muckie Tzur and Abraham Shapira, *Devarim be-Go,* pp. 35–38.

31. See Scholem, *Sabbatai Ṣevi,* pp. 125–138.

32. Harold Fisch, "The Messianic Politics of Menasseh ben Israel," in Y. Kaplan, H. Meshoulan, and R. Popkin, *Menasseh ben Israel and His World* (Brill, Leiden, 1989), pp. 232–233. See also Greenstone, *Messiah Idea,* pp. 206–207.

33. See especially Buber's novel *Gog and Magog,* which represents the clash between the magical attempt to bring the Messiah, as embodied in the Seer of Lublin, and the more hidden and preparatory form of activity represented by the Holy Jew. See, however, his response to Baruch Kurzweil, where he points out that one should not neglect the positive aspects of the Lublin traditions. Cf. Martin Buber, *Hope for the Present Hour* ('Am 'Oved, Tel Aviv, 1992), p. 138 (Hebrew).

34. See Avihu Zakai and Anya Mali, "Time, History and Eschatology: Ecclesiastical History from Eusebius to Augustine," *Journal of Religious History* 17 (1993), pp. 393–417; Barnes, *Prophecy and Gnosis,* pp. 19–20. On later Christian forms of apocalypticism, which do not fall short of the Jewish one and are even more colorful, see Paul J. Alexander, "Medieval Apocalypses as Historical Sources," *American Historical Review* 73 (1968), pp. 997–1018; Lerner, *Power of Prophecy;* Emmerson and Herzman, *Apocalyptic Imagination;* McGinn (n. 6 above); Norman Cohn, "Medieval Millenarism: Its Bearing on the Comparative Study of Millenarian Movements," in Thrupp, ed., *Millennial Dreams in Action,* pp. 31–43.

35. See *BT, Sanhedrin,* fol. 97a; *BT, 'Avodah Zarah,* fol. 9a; Urbach, *Sages,* pp. 677–678. Berger, "Three Typological Themes," pp. 149–150; Elliot R. Wolfson, "From Sealed Book to Open Text: Time, Memory, and Narrativity in Kabbalistic Hermeneutics," in Steven Kepnes, ed., *Interpreting Judaism in a Postmodern Age* (New York University Press, New York, 1996), p. 174n66.

36. Cf. the numerous discussions found in Richard Landes, "Lest the Millenium Will Be Fulfilled: Apocalyptic Expectations and the Pattern of Western Chronography, 100–800 C.E.," in W. Verbeke, D. Verhelst, and A. Welkenhuysen, *The Use and Abuse of Eschatology in the Middle Ages,* (Leuven University Press, Leuven, 1988), pp. 137–211; Firth, *Apocalyptic Tradition,* s.v. "Prophecy of Elijah"; Barnes, *Prophecy and Gnosis,* index, s.v. "Elijah, Prophecy of"; Yerushalmi, *From Spanish Court,* pp. 281–284.

37. *Golah ve-Nekhar,* 1:555. See also Berger, "Three Typological Themes," p. 162 and n. 82.

38. Ibid., pp. 552–555. Kaufman adduced two examples of fantastic messianism, Shelomo Molkho and Sabbatai Tzevi, and from the context it is obvious that he criticized Kabbalistic messianism.

39. Idel, "The Land of Israel"; Havivah Pedaya, "The Spiritual versus the Concrete Land of Israel in the Geronese School of Kabbalah," in M. Hallamish and A. Ravitzky, ed., *The Land of Israel in Medieval Jewish Thought* (Yad Itzhak Ben-Zvi, Jerusalem, 1991), pp. 233–289 (Hebrew)..

40. On the liberal attitude to messianism see Mendes-Flohr, "The Stronger and the Better Jews," p. 167. For another critique of the liberal attitude toward messianism see Schwarzschild, *Pursuit of the Ideal,* pp. 15–28.

41. Scholem's position has been followed by other scholars. See Joseph Dan, "The Legend of Messiah in the Middle Ages," *ha-'Ummah* 8 (1970), pp. 225–237 (Hebrew).

42. Though my subject matter is the elite conceptualizations and beliefs of messianism, the important role of the the average person who participated, passively and actively, in the messianic movement or a more modest enterprise should not be minimalized. The methodology and the significance of such research, however, belong to other domains of study than the history or phenomenology of Jewish mysticism. See Dinur, *Israel Ba-Golah,* vol. I, 1 p. 35; Ben Sasson, *Retzef u-Temurah,* p. 415.

43. See the more up-to-date summary of scholarship in Versnel, *Transition and Reversal,* pp. 41–48.

44. It is bizarre that the modern scholarship of Jewish mysticism has in fact neglected the various versions of the myth-and-ritual scholarship. See Idel, *Kabbalah: New Perspectives,* p. 197, and Green, *Keter,* pp. 1–7.

45. See "The Myth and Ritual Pattern," in Hooke, ed., *The Labyrinth,* p. 233; for the latter see his *He That Cometh,* p. 467 as well as below, chap. 1 note 13.

46. See J. C. VanderKam, *Enoch and the Growth of an Apocalyptic Tradition* (CBQMS, 16, Catholic Biblical Association of America, Washington, 1984); H. Kvanvig, *Roots of Apocalyptic: The Mesopotamian Background of the Enoch Figure and of the Son of Man* (Neukirchen-Vluyn, 1988); and John Collins's summary of this recent trend and some criticism in Collins and Charlesworth, *Mysteries and Revelations,* pp. 25–32, as well as his "Place of Apocalypticism," pp. 542–544, 549; Himmelfarb, *Ascent to Heaven,* pp. 123–124n76; Cohn, *Cosmos, Chaos,* pp. 166, 177; Schultz and Spatz, *Sinai and Olympus,* p. 628; and below, chap. 2, n. 36.

47. See his Cosmos, Chaos.

48. See Moshe Weinfeld, "Divine Intervention in War in Ancient Israel and the Ancient Near East," in H. Tadmor and M. Weinfeld, *History, Historiography and Interpretation: Studies in Biblical and Cuneiform Literatures* (Magnes Press, Jerusalem, 1983), pp. 142–143n119; Stephen Lieberman, "A Mesopotamian Background for the So-Called Aggadic 'Measures' of Biblical Hermeneutics?" *HUCA* 58 (1987), pp. 157–225; Jeffrey H. Tigay, "An Early Technique of Aggadic Exegesis," in Tadmor and Weinfeld, eds., *History, Historiography,* pp. 169–188; Simo Parpola, "The Assyrian Tree of Life: Tracing the Origins of Jewish Monotheism and Greek Philosophy," *Journal of Near Eastern Studies* 52 (1993), pp. 161–208; and Peter Kingsley, "Ezekiel by the Grand Canal: Between Jewish and Babylonian Tradition," *Journal of the Royal Asiatic Society,* 3rd ser., vol. 2 (1992), pp. 339–346; Adela Yarbro Collins, "The Seven Heavens in Jewish and Christian Apocalypses," in Collins and Fishbane, eds., *Death, Ecstasy,* pp. 59–93.

49. See Geo Widengren, *The Ascension of the Apostle and the Heavenly Book (King and Saviour III)* (Uppsala, Leipzig, 1950); idem, *Muhammad and his Sakrales Koenigtum.*

50. See below, chap. 1, n. 20; chap. 6, n. 86; and *Lamentation Rabba',* 1:51.

51. See the note of Solomon Buber in his edition to *Midrash Mishlei*, p. 87, adduced by Patai, *Messiah Texts*, p. 22.

52. See Idel, *Hasidism: Between Ecstasy and Magic.*

53. See esp. appendix 1.

54. Idel, *Kabbalah: New Perspectives*, pp. 51–58.

55. Scholem, *Messianic Idea in Judaism*, pp. 5–6; see also James Charlesworth, "Folk Traditions in the Jewish Apocalyptic Literature," in Collins and Charlesworth, eds., *Mysteries and Revelations*, p. 110.

56. Paul Ricoeur, *The Symbolism of Evil* (Beacon Press, Boston, 1969), p. 5. This view is consonant with the more anthropological project of Clifford Geertz in his *The Interpretation of Cultures*. On more recent treatments of early Jewish mythopoeic thought see Liebes, *Studies in Jewish Myth*, pp. 1–65, and Michael Fishbane, "Arm of the Lord: Biblical Myth, Rabbinic Midrash, and the Mystery of History," in S. E. Balentine and J. Barton, eds., *Language, Theology, and the Bible: Essays in Honour of James Barr* (Clarenton Press, Oxford, 1994), pp. 271–292.

57. See Claude Lévi-Strauss, *Anthropologie structurale* (Plon, Paris, 1974), pp. 233–234. For an interesting attempt to use the theory of Lévi-Strauss to explain the symbolic efficacy of the eschatological discourse see Jean-Claude Picard, "Observations sur l'Apocalypse Greque de Baruch," *Semitica* 20 (1970), pp. 77–103.

58. See Buber, *Kingship of God*, p. 14.

59. See Leach, *L'unité de l'homme*, pp. 223–224.

60. *Sabbatai Ṣevi*, p. 10.

61. See Geertz, *Interpretation of Cultures*, p. 26.

62. On their positive attitude to Kabbalah see Idel, *Kabbalah: New Perspectives*, pp. 7–9. See, more recently, the articles of Charles Mopsik, Paul Fenton, and Alessandro Gueta in *Pardes* 19–20 (1994), pp. 239–240, 216–238, 186–203, respectively.

63. Scholem, *Messianic Idea in Israel*, p. 255; idem, *Messianic Idea in Judaism*, pp. 8–9. This critique, correct in general, should not be exaggerated; see Ginzberg, *Legends of the Jews*, 4:233–235, who nevertheless discussed apocalyptic themes. On Graetz see below, note 17.

64. Leo Baeck, *Judaism and Christianity*, trans. Walter Kaufmann (Jewish Publication Society, Philadelphia, 1958), pp. 284–290. For another sustained comparison of Jewish and Christian messianism see Joseph Klausner, "The Jewish and the Christian Messiah," in Landman, ed., *Messianism in the Talmudic Era*, pp. 289–301, and *The Messianic Idea in Israel*, pp. 519–531, where the differences between the two concepts are explored in some detail. See also Schultz, *Judaism and the Gentile Faiths*, pp. 214–218. The present book is an attempt, in contradistinction to Baeck and Scholem, to present "Augustinian" aspects of Jewish mysticism.

65. *The Origin and Meaning of Hasidism*, trans. M. Friedman (New York, 1960), pp. 252–253; see Abraham Shapira, "Two Ways of Redemption in Hasidism from the Perspective of Martin Buber," in Oron and Goldreich, eds., *Massu'ot*, pp. 429–426, and Mendes-Flohr, "Stronger and the Better Jews," pp. 170–173. For more on Buber's concept of messsianism see Löwy, *Redemption et utopie*, pp. 63–75. For a critique of Buber's view concerning the history of eschatology in ancient Judaism see Paul D. Hanson, *The Dawn of Apocalyptic* (Fortress Press, Philadelphia, 1979), rev. ed., pp. 4–6. For more on his view of the Messiah see below, appendix 3. On apocalypticism and Rome see André Chastel, *The Sack of Rome*, trans. B. Archer (Princeton University Press, Princeton, 1983) and the articles printed in Reeves, ed., *Prophetic Rome.*

66. "Opening Address," in Werblowsky and Bleeker, eds., *Types of Redemption*, p. 12; see also below, the quotation from *'Od Davar*, p. 247, and Scholem's discussion of apocalypticism in *Messianic Idea in Judaism*, p. 323. See also Schultz and Spatz, *Sinai and Olympus*, pp. 643, 658n37;

Weiss, *Studies*, p. 240; Hurwitz, "Some Psychological Aspects," 131–133. On Scholem's view of Jewish and Christian messianism see *Messianic Idea in Judaism*, pp. 1–2, 15–16; Dan, "Gershom Scholem and Jewish Messianism," p. 80; Schwartz, "Neutralization of the Messianic Idea," p. 57. On Scholem and messianism see also Amos Funkenstein, "Gershom Scholem: Charisma, Kairos and the Messianic Dialectic," *History and Memory* 4 (1992), pp. 123–139. A point that seems to be relevant is the possible correlation between Scholem's overemphasis on apocalytpic messianism and the relegation of the more spiritualistic forms of messianism to the margin, as they were reminiscent of what he would conceive of as more characteristically Christian eschatology, and of the *unio mystica* types of experiences which were relegated to the periphery of Jewish mysticism. In the two cases, the attempt to distinguish too sharply between the Jewish and Christian forms of thought seems to be active in his phenomenonlogy.

67. *Messianic Idea in Judaism*, p. 4. It should be noted, however, that acute messianism can be understood also in individualistic terms, and in such a case strong soteriological aspirations, rather than apocalypticism, will emerge. See also ibid., p. 8. Another interesting point made by Scholem is that apocalypticism is secretive by nature and thereby differs from the more exoteric type of prophetic discourse. See ibid., pp. 6–7. In my opinion, in Scholem's definition of messianism the apocalyptic element, as he understood it, is already presupposed as evident, and therefore his definition is to a certain extent tautological. On the different meanings of *apocalypse, apocalypticism* and *apocalyptic* see Collins, *Apocalyptic Imagination*, pp. 1–17; idem, "Place of Apocalypticism," pp. 539–541; Hanson, *Dawn of Apocalyptic*; Gruenwald, "From Sunrise to Sunset"; Bloch, *On the Apocalyptic in Judaism;* and for the Middle Ages Bernard McGinn, *Apocalypticism in the Western Tradition* (Variorum, 1994), essays 1 and 2, and Barnes, *Prophecy and Gnosis*, pp. 2, 18; Tuveston, *Millennium and Utopia*, pp. 1–21. For the apocalyptic understanding of the concept of the Mahdi see Abdul Abdulhussein Sachedina, *Islamic Messianism: The Idea of the Mahdi in Twelver Shi'ism* (State University of New York Press, Albany, 1981). Scholem occasionally uses *apocalyptic* in its more classical sense as revelation in his *Kabbalah*, pp. 10–11.

68. Scholem, *Messianic Idea in Judaism*, pp. 7–8; See also ibid., p. 12; Löwy, *Redemption et utopie*, p. 27; and Biale, in Saperstein, *Essential Papers*, pp. 525–529. This is generally the case with other important modern approaches as well. See Idel, "Introduction," pp. 7–15. See also below, note 11. For a critique of Scholem's emphasis on the catastrophic in rabbinic literature see Urbach's note in *The Sages*, p. 990n3.

69. *'Od Davar*, pp. 234–235. Compare also *Messianic Idea in Judaism*, p. 4: "When the Messianic idea appears as a living force in the world of Judaism . . . it always occurs in the closest connection with apocalypticism." See also *Kabbalah*, pp. 68, 71–72. On this view of Scholem's see Goodman, *On Justice*, pp. 183–184. The different versions of the messianic idea, which competed for two millennia, were attributed by Scholem to the competition between the restorative and the utopian visions; see his *Devarim be-Go*, p. 578, and the description of Moses, *L'ange de l'histoire*, pp. 192–195; Joseph Dan, "The Utopia of the Future and the Utopia of the Past," in D. Kerem, ed., *Migvan De'ot ve-Hashqafot be-Tarbut Yisrael* (Rehovot, 1994), pp. 67–102; Talmon, *King, Cult, and Calendar*, p. 206; Ravitsky, "Maimonides on the Days of the Messiah," pp. 233–235; Löwy, *Redemption et utopie*, p. 24; Schultz and Spatz, *Sinai and Olympus*, pp. 646–647. For more on the famous distinction between the utopian and the restorative, introduced by Scholem in the analysis of messianism and realized by means of apocalyptic events, see below, Concluding Remarks.

70. Scholem, *Messianic Idea in Judaism*, p. 217. The use of the term *liquidation* here is to be compared to Scholem's description of what he called the liquidation of mythology by classical Judaism; see Scholem, *On the Kabbalah*, p. 88. Myths, understood sometimes as gnosticism or apocalyptic messianism, the two forces that according to Scholem have revived Judaism, were

therefore conceived of by him as having been liquidated by some forms of Judaism with which Scholem was not always very sympathetic. For more on this issue see Moshe Idel, "Subversive Catalysts," in David R. Myers and David Ruderman, eds., *The Jewish Past Revisited* (New Haven: Yale University Press, 1998). See also Schwartz, "Neutralization of the Messianic Idea."

71. See Löwy, *Redemption et utopie,* pp. 27–28, and the cogent critiques of Taubes, "Price of Messianism," pp. 595–600, and Goodman, *On Justice,* p. 184. For a view of eschatology that emphasizes the cosmological—namely the "perfection of creation"—see also Martin Buber, *Paths in Utopia,* trans. R. F. C. Hull (Beacon Press, Boston, 1950), p. 8. The formula "perfection of creation" is reminiscent of the Kabbalistic and Hasidic phrase *tiqqun ha-beriy'ah,* which has eschatological overtones. See, e.g., R. Nahman of Braslav, *Liqqutei Halakhot,* Hilekhot Hekhsher Kelim, chap. 4.

72. Cf. Bloom's essay "Scholem: Unhistorical or Jewish Gnosticism," in *Gershom Scholem,* ed. Harold Bloom (Chelsea House, New York, 1987), p. 217. See also Löwy's remark that the first decades of Scholem's research represent a profound concern with messianism: ibid., p. 82, as well as David Biale, *Gershom Scholem: Kabbalah and Counter-History* (Harvard University Press, Cambridge, 1979), pp. 154, 174.

73. Scholem, *Messianic Idea in Judaism,* p. 194; Hurwitz, "Some Psychological Aspects," pp. 131–133.

74. Concluding remarks printed at the end of *The Messianic Idea in Israel,* p. 254; Bloch, *On the Apocalyptic In Judaism,* p. 82. The phrase *the messianic idea* occurs also in ibid., p. 255, as well as in *Messianic Idea in Judaism,* pp. viii, and more interestingly on p. 2, where Scholem claims that "[t]he history of the Messianic idea in Judaism has run its course within the framework of this idea's never-relinquished demand for fulfillment of its original vision." The resort to the phrase *original vision* implied in the one "messianic idea" in this text is a good example of diachronic monochromatism (see below). For the resort to the locution *messianic idea* see also Salo Baron, "Reappearance of Pseudo-Messiah," in Saperstein, ed., *Essential Papers,* p. 242; see also Eliezer Schweid, "Jewish Messianism: The Metamorphoses of an Idea," ibid., pp. 53–70; Gross, *Le messianisme juif;* Manor, *Exile and Redemption,* p. 229. Hurwitz, "Some Psychological Aspects," pp. 134–135, while using the same phrase, attempts to detect tensions between different components of the idea. Immediately afterwards he applies the Jungian theory of a split within "the initially integral figure of the Messiah," emphasizing the spiritual nature of Messiah ben David versus the more mundane nature of Messiah ben Joseph. Then he describes the image of the Messiah as a "symbol of the internal unity and totality." For a succinct attempt to point out the variety of the ideas connected to messianism, mostly in non-Jewish sources, see Werblowsky, "Messianism and Jewish History," in Saperstein, ed., *Essential Papers,* pp. 37–39.

75. Scholem, *'Od Davar,* p. 240. See also his concluding remarks in *The Messianic Idea in Israel,* p. 256. For a more nuanced view of Second Temple messianism see the references below in chap. 1, note 30, where the assumption shared by many scholars in the field is that the apocalyptic version of messianism has been muted in most of the early rabbinic sources. For a different critique of Scholem's resort to the conception of one messianic idea see Neusner, *Messiah in Context,* p. 227.

76. Scholem, *'Od Davar,* p. 247. Interestingly enough, the preoccupation with the movement, more than with the individuals who compose it, is formulated by Scholem very early in his writings on messianism and Sabbateanism. See his *Studies and Texts,* p. 15. For a similar vision of messianism see also Klausner, *The Messianic Idea of Israel,* p. 10. Klausner's view, however, differs from Scholem's much more substantial emphasis on apocalypticism, as he attributes a much greater role to the ethical and universalistic aspects of the messianic phenomena. See ibid., p. 9. For the nationalistic background and consequences of Klausner's book see Myers, *Re-Inventing,* pp. 96–97. In any case, I wonder which texts underlie Scholem's somewhat socialistic proposal concerning the existence of a

future "just society" in the messianic age. In order to show that the emphasis on the oneness of the messianic idea was not so necessary it should be noted that many decades before the scholars mentioned above analyzed the constellation of messianic ideas, Maurice Vernes had already entitled his book *Histoire des idées messianiques* (Sandoz et Fischbacher, Paris, 1874) and used the phrase *idées messianiques* quite frequently.

77. On my theory of models see *Hasidism: Between Ecstasy and Magic,* pp. 45–145. For 'deep structures' in the study of the imaginary see Durand, *Figures mythiques,* p. 82.

78. Scholem, *'Od Davar,* p. 240. See also an open acknowledgement of the affinities between the national renascence and the concerns with history in Scholem's foreword to *Messianic Idea in Judaism,* p. viii. At least in an implicit manner the "historical consciousness" mentioned by Scholem in this context has to do with his own studies on messianism. On the other hand, a comparison of the two most comprehensive histories of the Jews, H. Graetz's and Salo Baron's, reveals a rather amazing situation. Graetz, who is the paragon of the rationalistic attitude towards Judaism, paid much more attention to the messianic phenomena than Baron did; see especially his essay "The Stages in the Evolution." Baron, who, historically speaking, could take great advantage of Scholem's comprehensive and inspiring treatments of his topic, nevertheless preferred to minimalize the possible contribution of the material adduced and analyzed by Scholem, including messianism, and thus some messianic phenomena are conspicuously absent in a work that claims to cover not only the social but also the religious history of the Jews. No doubt Scholem's approach was much more influential among the Israeli scholars of Jewish history. *Zion,* mentioned in the above quotation, is the name of a main journal of Jewish history, published by the Israeli Society of Historians, where many of the studies on messianism first appeared.

79. Scholem himself never explicitly divided his historical conception of Kabbalistic messianism into three well-defined periods. On Scholem's view of messianism in general see Biale (n. 7 above) and the essays of Robert Alter and W. D. Davies in Harold Bloom, ed., *Gershom Scholem* (Chelsea House, New York, 1987), pp. 21–28, 77–97, respectively, as well as Moses, *L'ange de l'histoire,* pp. 185–207. See Scholem, *Messianic Idea in Judaism,* p. 202. More recently, Scholem's views of messianism have been described, again, by Dan, "Gershom Scholem and Jewish Messianism," which also refers to the previous analyses of this issue.

80. See Scholem, *Major Trends,* pp. 244–245; *Messianic Idea in Judaism,* pp. 38–39, his "Concluding Remarks," in *Messianic Idea in Israel,* p. 259, and *Sabbatai Ṣevi,* pp. 15–17, where he writes that the Kabbalists' "own peculiar spiritual impulse had no specifically messianic quality."

81. Scholem wrote, for example: "This latter Kabbalah, as it developed in classical forms in Safed in Palestine in the sixteenth century, was in its whole design electric with Messianism and pressing for its release; it was impelling a Messianic outburst." See *Messianic Idea in Judaism,* p. 59. See also his remarks in *The Messianic Idea in Israel,* p. 260. However, in his *Kabbalah,* p. 68, Scholem claims that "messianism became part of the core of Kabbalah."

82. See, e.g., *Major Trends,* pp. 284, 287.

83. See *Messianic Idea in Judaism,* p. 13; *Major Trends,* p. 246. See also below, chap. 5, n. 84.

84. See *'Od Davar,* p. 271, and Scholem's postcript to *Messianic Idea in Israel,* pp. 259–260.

85. *Messianic Idea in Judaism,* pp. 186–187, 216–217. See also Winston, *Logos,* p. 55.

86. On this issue see below, chap. 7.

Chapter 1: Pre-Kabbalistic Jewish Forms of Messianism

1. Just as it would be a mistake to separate too easily some of the medieval concepts of the Messiah from some preceding concepts, so it would be simplistic to ignore repercussions of mystical

concepts of messianism on modern philosophical concepts. See e.g. Handelman, *Fragments of Redemption;* Löwy, *Redemption et utopie;* M. Idel, "Franz Rosenzweig and the Kabbalah," in *The Philosophy of Franz Rosenzweig,* ed. Paul Mendes-Flohr (University Press of New England, Hanover, N.H., 1988), p. 165. Both the ancient sources and the influences on modern thought will be treated here only tangentially, as my main approach is more concerned with the existential aspects of messianism for the mystical Messiahs and the Kabbalists, or eschatological beliefs of the Messiahs themselves.

2. The following presentations of the biblical and ancient Jewish and Christian views on the Messiah are deeply indebted to the studies of several biblical scholars, whose names will be mentioned below in the due places. I do not claim to make an original contribution in this field; rather, I shall attempt to stress those elements in the ancient texts which had an impact on the medieval and some later developments of the various concepts of Messiah. For an important discussion of the relationship between a biblical figure and later messianic speculations, especially in Kabbalah, see Liebes, "Jonas as Messiah ben Joseph," pp. 304–311.

3. See Talmon, *King, Cult, and Calendar,* pp. 140–164.

4. Following Talmon, ibid.

5. Leviticus 4:3, 6:15; Exodus 40:12–15.

6. This expression occurs in the two books of Samuel and only once elsewhere in the biblical literature, but it also appears in the apocalyptic literature; see e.g. *Sefer Zerubbavel,* in Even Shmuel, *Midreshei Ge'ullah,* p. 73.

7. See Talmon, *King, Cult, and Calendar,* pp. 35–36. For the absence of an expected savior in relation to all the occurrences of the term *mashiyaḥ* in the Bible see J. J. M. Roberts, "The Old Testament's Contribution to Messianic Expectations," in Charlesworth, ed., *Messiah,* pp. 39–51. On unctions in the Bible see, inter alia, Halpern, *Constitution,* pp. 125–127, and below, chap. 2, n. 21.

8. See Patai, *Man and Temple,* pp. 202–208, 222. For the medieval reverberations of this nexus see also Bloch, *Les rois thaumaturges,* pp. 216–224.

9. Mowinckel, *He That Cometh;* Bentzen, *King and Messiah;* J. Coppens, *Le Messianisme royal* (Le Cerf, Paris, 1968); Ricoeur, *Symbolism of Evil,* pp. 199, 264. For critiques of the myth-and-ritual approach see the bibliography mentioned by Talmon, *King, Cult, and Calendar,* p. 10n5, and Benjamin Uffenheimer, "Myth and Reality in Ancient Israel," in S. N. Eisenstadt, ed., *The Origin and Diversity of Axial Age Civilizations* (State University of New York Press, Albany, 1986), p. 135; Frankfort, *Kingship and the Gods,* pp. 337–344, and for a more philosophical and more mild formulation, Eric Voegelin, *Order and History,* vol. 1: *Israel and Revelation* (Louisiana State University Press, Baton Rouge, 1986), pp. 284–310.

10. See Mowinckel, *Psalms in Israel's Worship,* 1:51; *He That Cometh,* p. 41. To a great extent, the connection between ancient kingship and magic has been delineated already in J. C. Frazer's *Lectures on the Early History of the Kingship* and in his more famous *The Golden Bough: A Study in Magic and Religion,* abridged ed. (Macmillan, 1964), pp. 109–118. For an up-to-date survey of issues related to royal ideology see Versnel, *Transition and Reversal,* pp. 32–48.

11. Mowinckel, *Psalms in Israel's Worship,* 1:51; see also *He That Cometh,* pp. 80, 84, as well as his "Oriental and Israelite Elements in Israelite Sacral Kingdom," in *The Sacral Kingship,* p. 285. See also the earlier formulation of Aubrey R. Johnson, "The Role of the King in the Jerusalem Cultus," in Hooke, ed., *Labyrinth,* p. 77; Johnson writes in regards to the king: "the very rite of anointment, by which he is installed in office and in virtue of which he enjoys this title of 'Messiah,' not only indicates a particularly close connection with the national deity, but also suggests that as a result he has become a channel for the divine power." In this context Johnson refers to 1 Samuel 16:13. See also De Fraine, *L'aspect religieux,* pp. 374–375. For a more shamanic view of Saul see ibid., p. 376.

The more strongly magical functions of ancient kings, as assumed by some scholars (e.g. Frazer), were not attributed by Mowinckel to the Israelite kings. See F. M. Cornford, *From Religion to Philosophy: A Study in the Origins of Western Speculation* (Princeton University Press, Princeton, N.J., 1991), pp. 104–106, and the more extreme view of Engnell, *Divine Kingship,* passim.

12. Mowinckel, *Psalms in Israel's Worship,* 1:61; see also ibid., 1:49, 69, 74–75, 138, as well as Frankfort, *Kingship and the God,* pp. 259–261, who uses the very term *talisman* in order to describe the Mesopotamian, though not the Israelite, role of the king. See also the neglected study of Patai, *Man and Temple,* pp. 172–215, as well as the more famous treatment of Eliade, *Cosmos and History,* pp. 51–63. The extent of belief in the efficiency of the rituals for the very emergence of the power received and distributed by the king is a matter that has received scant attention in scholarship. See the succinct remark of Ringgren, *Messiah,* p. 24. Mowinckel's emphasis on the relation of the sacral kingship to vegetation myths has been criticized by Ch. Auffarth, *Die drohende Untergang: 'Schoefung' in Mythos und Ritual im Alten Orient und in Griechenland am Beispiel der Odysee und des Ezechielbuches* (Berlin, 1991), who, though accepting the myth-and-ritual theory, prefers a more politically oriented explanation. There is a certain similarity between Mowinckel's theory and G. van der Leeuw's explanation of the origin of the savior theme from natural, gradually personalized powers (*Religion,* pp. 101–114).

13. See Frost, "Eschatology and Myth," pp. 70–80, esp. p. 72; Mowinckel, *Psalms,* 1:191; Ricoeur, *Symbolism of Evil,* p. 202; Eliade, *Cosmos and History;.* Mowinckel has this formulation as to the type of experience involved in the cultic performance of the king in ancient Israel: "In the cultic drama the historical events are experienced anew; and victory over the political foes of contemporary history is promised, guaranteed, and experienced in anticipation." *He That Cometh,* p. 82. The idea of the experience built on anticipation seems to me extremely productive insofar as some of the mystical Messiahs analyzed above are concerned.

14. Bentzen, *King and Messiah,* p. 39, emphasis added.

15. Mowinckel, *Psalms in Israel's Worship,* 1:191; Bentzen, *King and Messiah,* p. 79. This stand is also typical of Mowinckel's important monograph on ancient messianism *He That Cometh.*

16. Bentzen, *King and Messiah,* pp. 73–80; this point has also been made by S. H. Hooke in his essay "The Myth and Ritual Pattern in Jewish and Christian Apocalyptic," in Hooke, ed., *Labyrinth,* pp. 213–233. See also Martin Buber, in the preface to his *Kingship of God,* trans. R. Sheimann (London, 1967). For a definition of messianism which combines the above elements in an interesting manner see J.-G. Heintz, "Royal Traits and Messianic Figures: A Thematic and Iconographical Approach," in Charlesworth, ed., *Messiah,* p. 52: "Situated at the intersection of a collective eschatology and a royal ideology, messianism depends upon both precisely at their point of contact." Indeed, I would like to inspect some forms of medieval messianism against the background of this definition, or that of De Fraine's phrase "royaulté messianique"; cf. *L'aspect religieux,* p. 5.

17. Frost, "Eschatology and Myth," p. 80. On the first sources of the apocalyptic attitude the views of scholars differ. Whereas some scholars see this attitude as an inner Jewish development, others, notably Buber, have envisioned it as an external influence. In fact, Buber considers eschatology the result of a "growing historical disillusionment." See his *Kingship of God,* p. 14; idem, *The Prophetic Faith* (Harper Torchbooks, New York, Evanston, 1960), pp. 153–154. For a recent return of the Iranian thesis see Cohn, *Cosmos, Chaos,* pp. 77–115, 220–228, who emphasizes the Zoroastrian impact on later forms of eschatology. See also Jon D. Levenson, *Creation and the Persistence of Evil* (Harper and Row, San Francisco, 1988), pp. 32–33, 161n19.

18. Again, this aspect of the Messiah's fate is to be seen in functionalistic terms, either national (cf. n. 38 below) or personal: cf. John J. Collins, "Apocalyptic Eschatology as the Transcendence of Death," *Catholic Biblical Quarterly* 36 (1974), pp. 21–43.

19. Mowinckel, *Psalms in Israel's Worship,* 1:53.

20. BT, *Babba' Batra',* fol. 75b according to Rashi's interpretation there and *Zohar,* vol. 1, fol. 93b. See also below, chap. 6, n. 86.

21. The bibliography on this issue is extensive; see e.g. Arthur J. Ferch, *The Son of Man in Daniel Seven* (Andrews University Press, Berrien Springs, Michigan, 1979); William O. Walker, "The Origin of the Son of Man Concept as Applied to Jesus," *JBL* 91 (1972), pp. 482–490; A. Yarbro Collins, "The Origin of the Designation of Jesus as 'Son of Man,'" *HTR* 80 (1987), pp. 391–408; idem, "The Apocalyptic Son of Man Sayings," in B. A. Pearson, ed., *The Future of Christianity* (Fortress Press, Minneapolis, 1991), pp. 220–228; Stone, *Fourth Ezra,* pp. 207–208, 211. The transcendence of the Son of Man as a messianic figure sometimes also implies its hiddenness. For the hypothesis, which I do not find convincing, that the hiddenness of the transcendent Messiah represents a Gnostic influence on Jewish messianism see Alexander Altmann, *The Meaning of Jewish Existence: Theological Essays 1930–1939,* ed. Alfred L. Ivry, trans. E. Ehrlich and L.H. Ehrlich (Brandeis University Press, Hanover, N.H., 1991), pp. 129–130. See Stone, *Fourth Ezra,* pp. 213–214, 405.

22. See Patai, *Man and Temple,* p. 208.

23. Talmon, "The Concept of the Mashiaḥ and Messianism in Early Judaism," in Charlesworth, ed., *Messiah,* p. 115.

24. Yehezkel Kaufman, *Toledot ha-'Emunah ha-Yisraelit,* vol. 6–7 (Mossad Bialik, Devir, Jerusalem, Tel Aviv, 1967), pp. 626–656 (Hebrew), for an important appendix on the place and nature of biblical eschatology.

25. Talmon, *King, Cult and Calendar,* pp. 140–164.

26. Levenson, "The Jerusalem Temple and Devotional and Visionary Experience," in Green, ed., *Jewish Spirituality,* 1:51. See also idem, *Sinai and Zion,* pp. 213–217, esp. pp. 216–217, where he sharply differentiates between Jewish and Christian messianism: the former links the ritualistic and the royal, or Sinaitic and Davidic covenants, while in the latter the Davidic, namely the messianic, marginalizes the Sinaitic. See also Neher, *Prophetic Existence,* pp. 243–244: "The Apocalypse takes us out of the time of the covenant."

27. See Mopsik, *Les grands textes,* pp. 35–37, and my preliminary observations in "The Contribution of Abraham Abulafia's Kabbalah to the Understanding of Jewish Mysticism," in P. Schaefer and J. Dan, eds., *Gershom Scholem's Major Trends in Jewish Mysticism, 50 Years After* (J.C.B. Mohr, Tuebingen, 1993), p. 141. On the two modes of sacral kingship see Frankfort, *Kingship and the Gods.* For the difference between the Egyptian and the Israelite attitudes toward kingship see the striking formulation in Neher, *Prophetic Existence,* p. 55: "In Egypt, the king was a god. In Israel, the God was a king." See also Buber, *Kingship of God,* p. 52. For a sensitive analysis of the similarities and differences between the Israelite and the Egyptian and Mesopotamian views of kingship see De Fraine, *L'aspect religieux,* pp. 392–396. For the first manifestations of the apotheotic impulse in Judaism see the interesting analyses of Himmelfarb, *Ascent to Heaven.* See also the important early material analyzed by Smith, *Map,* pp. 63–64 and Corbin, *Cyclical Time,* pp. 62–67.

28. The questions related to Qumranic messianism and the pertinent bibliography have multiplied in recent years. Since this corpus of writings did not influence the medieval Jewish material, I shall not engage in this question here. For important discussions of Qumranic messianism see Shemaryahu Talmon, "Waiting for the Messiah: The Spiritual Universe of the Qumran Covenanteers," in Neusner et al., eds., *Judaisms and Their Messiahs,* pp. 123–131; William M. Schniedewind, "King and Priest in the Book of Chronicles and the Duality of Qumran Messianism," *JJS* 45 (1994), pp. 71–78. On messianism and Qumran literature see John J. Collins, *The Scepter and the Star* (Doubleday, New York, 1995).

29. See e.g. Anthony Saldarini, "Apocalyptic and Rabbinic Literature," *Catholic Biblical Quar-*

terly 37 (1975), pp. 348–358; idem, "The Use of Apocalyptic in the Mishnah and Tosefta," *Catholic Biblical Quarterly* 39 (1977), pp. 396–409; Peter Schaefer, *Studien zur Geschichte und Theologie das Rabbinischen Judentums* (Brill, Leiden, 1978), pp. 37–43; B. M. Bokser, "Changing Views of Passover and the Meaning of Redemption According to the Palestinian Talmud," *AJSR* 10 (1985), pp. 1–18; idem, "Messianism, the Exodus Pattern, and Early Rabbinic Judaism," in Charlesworth, ed., *Messiah,* pp. 239–258; Lawrence Schiffman, "The Concept of the Messiah in Second Temple and Rabbinic Literature," *Review and Expositor* (1984), pp. 235–246, idem, *Law, Custom and Messianism in the Dead Sea Sect,* trans. Tal Ilan (Merkaz Shazar, Jerusalem, 1993) (Hebrew); Agus, *Binding of Isaac;* Manuel and Manuel, *Utopian Thought,* pp. 37–42, 44–46.

30. Neusner, *Messiah in Context,* p. 30; see also ibid., pp. 18–19.

31. See Jacob Neusner's description of the Mishnaic attitude toward eschatology, *Messiah in Context,* pp. 74–78, and Agus, *Binding of Isaac.*

32. I refer to the main concerns and literary genres of this literature without, however, defining the tannaitic masters as more inclined to legal studies than to mythical thought.

33. That a greater emphasis on the performance of the commandments may have an eschatological aspect has been duly recognized in a more explicit manner by Elisheva Carlebach, "Rabbinic Circles as Messianic Pathways in the Post-Expulsion Era," *Judaism* 41 (1992), pp. 208–216.

34. *BT, Pesaḥim,* fol. 54a; *BT, Nedarim,* fol. 39b; Even Shmuel, *Midreshei Ge'ullah,* pp. 15–16n1.

35. Compare this functionalistic approach in the case of the Messiah to the attitude toward the golem in Jewish sources. See Idel, *Golem,* p. 261.

36. See Bernard McGinn, *Anti-Christ: Two Thousand Years of the Fascination with Evil* (Harper, San Francisco, 1995).

37. Patai, *Man and the Temple,* pp. 202–208, 225, as well as his "Hebrew Installation Rites," p. 187.

38. Most of the collections of articles on messianism deal with the ancient and early medieval periods: see Charlesworth, ed., *Messiah;* Even Shmuel, *Midreshei Ge'ullah;* Neusner et al., *Judaisms and Their Messiahs,* as well as of the collection of Landman. It goes without saying that the anthologies of Aescoly, *Jewish Messianic Movements,* and Patai *The Messiah Texts,* also deal substantially with the ancient traditions.

39. See Neusner, *Messiah in Context;* Agus, *Binding of Isaac;* Even Shmuel, *Midreshei Ge'ullah;* Berger, "Three Typological Themes," pp. 141–142; Joseph Dan, *The Hebrew Story in the Middle Ages* (Keter, Jerusalem, 1974), pp. 33–45 (Hebrew). On the figure of the redeemer from the vantage point of literary strategies of building the messianic narrative in early literature, with a particular emphasis on *Sefer Zerubbavel,* see Yael Poias, *The Theme of the Redeemer in Hebrew Literature* (Ph.D. diss., University of Haifa, June 1995), pp. 21–76 (Hebrew). Poias also deals with later reverberations of the theme of the redeemer, including Kabbalah and especially modern Hebrew literature.

40. See Scholem, *Major Trends,* p. 72. See nevertheless Idel, *Kabbalah: New Perspectives,* p. 79, and Schaefer, *Synopse,* no. 218, and his *Hekhalot-Studien* (J. C. B. Mohr, Tübingen, 1988), p. 288. On the nexus between eschatology and ascent on high see Halperin, "Hekhalot and Miraj," and the traditions found in the Ashkenazi text printed by Marx, "Ma'amar," pp. 195, 197, and Steven M. Wasserstrom, "The 'Isawiyya Revisited," *Studia Islamica* 75 (1992), pp. 68–69. On the ascent of the Messiah on high, in a way reminiscent of Enoch's, see Stone, *Fourth Ezra,* p. 209n26.

41. *Heikhalot Rabbati,* chap. 39, in S. A. Wertheimer, ed., *Batei Midrashot* (Mossad ha-Rav Kook, Jerusalem, 1968), 1:130 (Hebrew); Liebes, *Ḥet'o shel 'Elisha',* pp. 35–37; Loewenthal, *Communicating the Infinite,* pp. 8–9. Scholem, *Messianic Idea,* p. 7. On an eschatological topic in this literature see Silver, *History of Messianic Speculation,* p. 48; Joseph Dan, *Ancient Jewish Mysticism* (Misrad ha-Bitahon, Tel Aviv, 1989), pp. 134–143 (Hebrew). The Heikhalot literature should be

seen as incorporating some aspects of the Enochic literature, and perhaps the eschatological elements inherent in some texts reflect its impact. On the apocalyptic elements in the Enochic literature and the possibility that this literature represents one of the earliest, if not the earliest, form of Jewish apocalypticism, see Collins, "Apocalypticism in the Religion of Israel," p. 544, and idem, "A Throne in the Heavens," pp. 45–46, where he points out the possible Babylonian underpinning of the Enochic literature, as well as Segal, "Paul and the Beginning of Jewish Mysticism," p. 117n19. On the possibility that Enochic literature, except the Hebrew Enoch and the different fragments from Qumran printed by J. T. Milik, could reach the Kabbalists living in the West in Syriac (in a manner reminiscent of the Syriac version of the *Wisdom of Solomon,* cf. Alexander Marx, "An Aramaic Fragment of the Wisdom of Solomon," *JBL* 40, (1921), pp. 57–69) see S. Brock, "A Fragment of Enoch in Syriac," *JTS* 19 (1968), pp. 626–631, and in a more general manner his "Jewish Traditions in Syriac Sources," *JJS* 30, (1979), p. 224, and Martha Himmelfarb, "R. Moses the Preacher and the Testaments of the Twelve Patriarchs," *AJSR* 9, no. 1 (1984), pp. 76–77.

Vestiges of the older Jewish literature from Enochic circles can be still detected in rabbinic literature; see Himmelfarb, "A Report on Enoch in Rabbinic Literature," *Society of Biblical Literature: 1978 Seminar Papers,* ed. P. J. Achtemeier (Missoula, Mont., 1978), vol. 1, pp. 259–269, and Levi, "Apocalypse," pp. 110–111. On the importance of Enoch's transformation into an angel for some developments in Shi'ite Islam see Halperin, "Hekhalot and Mi'raj." For the importance of the experience of transformation in ancient Jewish mysticism early Christianity see Segal, "Paul and the Beginning of Jewish Mysticism," pp. 95–122, esp. pp. 105–106; Elliot R. Wolfson, "Yeridah bemerkavah: Typology of Ecstasy and Enthronement in Ancient Jewish Mysticism," in R. A. Herrera, ed., *Mystics of the Book: Themes, Topics and Typologies* (Peter Lang, New York, 1993), pp. 13–44.

42. See S. Pines, "God, the Divine Glory, and the Angels according to a 2nd Century Theology," in ed. J. Dan, *The Beginnings of Jewish Mysticism in Medieval Europe* (Jerusalem, 1987), pp. 1–14 (Hebrew). For a similar view, concerning the sefirot as emerging and returning to God see his "Points of Similarity between the Exposition of the Doctrine of the Sefirot in Sefer Yezira and a Text of the Pseudo-Clementine Homilies," *Israel Academy of Sciences and Humanities, Proceedings,* vol. 7, no. 3 (Jerusalem, 1989), pp. 68–69. On the ancient Jewish texts that emphasized the divine action in instances when in other traditions there existed descriptions of angelic intervention, see Pines, " 'From Darkness to Light': Parallels to Haggada Texts in Hellenistic Literature," in Ezra Fleisher, ed., *Studies in Literature Presented to Simon Halkin* (Magnes Press, Jerusalem, 1973), pp. 173–179 (Hebrew). See also the texts adduced by Urbach, *Sages,* pp. 136–137, 741–742n5–6. Prof. Israel Ta-Shma has kindly drawn my attention to the unusual discussions of rescue by angels found in *Maḥzor Vitri,* ed. S. H. Horowitz (rpt. Jerusalem, 1963), p. 293, and in R. Yehudah ha-Levi's *Kuzari,* 3:73, where the angels implore God not to intervene by Himself in the drama of redemption from Egypt but to let them do it. See also *Haggadah Shelemah,* ed. M. Kasher and S. Ashkenazi (Jerusalem, 1967), pp. 186–187 (Hebrew). On Mopsik's view of Metatron see *Le Livre Hebrew d'Henoch ou Livre des Palais* (Verdier, Lagrasse, 1990), pp. 36–37. For an analysis of the type of emergence of the angel from God, as described by Pines, "God, the Divine Glory," and early Christology dealing with prolaxis see H. A. Wolfson, *The Philosophy of the Church Fathers,* 3rd ed. (Harvard University Press, Cambridge, 1976), pp. 295–300. Some of these issues are reminiscent of early Kabbalistic descriptions of emanation. See also the interesting observation of Smith, *Map,* p. 31, concerning the Prayer of Joseph, that "there is a remarkable consistency to the titles given Jacob-Israel in PJ. Indeed, it is strinking that many of Jacob-Israel's titles are applied by Philo to the Logos, by rabbinic literature to Michael, by mystical literature to Metatron and by Jewish Christianity to Jesus. This suggests, without arguing direct literary dependence, a community and continuity of tradition."

43. Idel, "Metatron." On Metatron as the divine face, a view that is reminiscent of the Son and

of Jesus as the divine face, see Deutsch, *Gnostic Imagination,* pp. 99–111. See also the nexus between face, angel, glory, and divine name in the biblical texts in James Barr, "Theophany and Anthropomorphism in the Old Testament," *Supplements to Vetus Testamentum* 7 (1960), pp. 33–34. An issue of extreme importance that can only be touched on here is the possible implication for the history of Christology of the existence of an angelic Messiah in Jewish apocalyptic sources or early medieval texts, and more in the later centuries on the one hand and the early Christian angelic views of the Christ on the other hand. This view, embraced only for a short time by Judeo-Christian writers and eliminated by Christian orthodoxy, recalls the angelic status of the Messiah in many of the sources to be discussed below. This affinity seems to be more than a phenomenological similarity, given the fact that several scholars have pointed out the resemblances between Metatron and Jesus. See Gedaliahu G. Stroumsa, "Form(s) of God: Some Notes on Metatron and Christ," *HTR* 76, (1983), pp. 269–288, esp. 287–288, where he suggests that the very name *Metatron* stems from *metron* "measure," much as *Mashiyaḥ* derives from the Aramaic verb *MShH* "to measure," (now in his *Savoir et Salut,* pp. 81–84), as well as Liebes, "Angels of the Shofar," p. 194n86. Liebes also suggests (p. 182) that the identification of Jesus as angel with Metatron is an ancient Judeo-Christian tradition that was known in the Middle Ages; see his *On Sabbateaism and Its Kabbalah,* p. 387n74. Liebes's innovative article "Angels of the Shofar" attracted some totally unfounded assaults which had to do with certain authors' problematic attitude toward Christianity. See also the view of Gilles Quispel as to the existence Judeo-Christian texts of an angelic Messiah invested with the name of God: "Qumran, John and Jewish Christianity," in *John and Qumran,* ed. J. H. Charlesworth (London, 1972), pp. 149–151. On Metatron and measurement see Wolfson, *Through a Speculum,* pp. 221–224, and Deutsch, *Gnostic Imagination,* pp. 89–90. For later instances of an identification of Metatron and Jesus see Abrams, "Boundaries", pp. 316–321. On Metatron in the talmudic literature see Liebes, *Ḥet'o shel 'Elisha,* pp. 29–41, and Alan F. Segal, *Two Powers in Heaven: Early Rabbinic Reports about Christianity and Gnosticism* (Brill, Leiden, 1977). On the angelic Christ see Danielou, *Theologie du Judeo-Christianisme,* pp. 203–207; Corbin, *Cyclical Time,* pp. 64–65, 69–71, 76–77. On ancient and medieval views of Jesus as angel see Couliano, *Tree of Gnosis,* pp. 79, 117, 218, 222–223.

44. See, on the one hand, J. N. Simḥoni, "The Ashkenazi Hasidism in the Middle Ages," printed serially in *ha-Tzefirah* (1917), par. 10 and 14; Scholem, *Major Trends,* pp. 87–90; Ivan Marcus, *Piety and Society* (Leiden, Brill, 1980), pp. 25, 29–35; Cohen, "Messianic Postures," pp. 207–212; Schultz, *Judaism and the Gentile Faiths,* pp. 223–225, as well as an unpublished lecture on Ashkenazi messianism delivered by Chaim Soloveitchik in 1977 at the International Congress for Jewish Studies in Jerusalem. On the other hand, see Joseph Dan's somewhat more messianically oriented understanding of the thought of Ḥasidei Ashkenaz in *Esoteric Theology,* pp. 241–245.

45. *She-yitgalleh le-'olam.* Scholem translates the phrase "tempt him to reveal his speculations." Apparently following him, Dan, *Esoteric Theology,* p. 241n1, proposes an emendation, which may be translated "in order to reveal to the world his prophecy." I believe that my translation reflects better the original intention.

46. *Sefer Ḥasidim,* ed. Reuven Margoliot (Mossad ha-Rav Kook, Jerusalem, 1970), p. 195, no. 206; ed. J. Wistinetzki and J. Friedmann (Frankfurt, 1934), no. 212; see also the translation in Scholem, *Major Trends,* p. 88, which differs on some points from the more literal one offered here; see also the important parallel material adduced by Dan, *Esoteric Theology,* pp. 241–242, as well as the discussions of Abraham Michael Cardoso in Scholem, *Studies and Texts,* pp. 319–320, and Jacob Sasportas, *Tzitzat Novel Tzevi,* p. 298.

47. See the analysis by Joseph Dan, *Esoteric Theology,* pp. 242–243.

48. Scholem, *Major Trends,* pp. 87–88.

49. Israel Kamehlar, *Rabbenu Eleazar me-Germaisa, ha-Roqeaḥ* (Risha, 1930), pp. 16–20 (Hebrew). For many more mentions of the Messiah than can be found in other writings of the same genres, see R. Eleazar, *Commentary on the Song of Songs,* ed. S. Y. Ch. Kanievsky, *Perush ha-Roqeah 'al Ḥamesh Megillot* (Benei Beraq, 1984), pp. 102, 113, 116, 118, 119, 123, 132, 136, 138.

50. Israel Yuval, "Vengeance and Damnation, Blood and Defamation: From Jewish Martyrdom to Blood Libel Accusations," *Zion* 58 (1993), pp. 33–90 (Hebrew).

51. *Sefer ha-Ḥesheq,* ed. Y. M. Epstein (Lemberg, 1865), fols. 7b–8a. This passage is found at the beginning of the two other, shorter versions, which differ slightly from each other, in R. Abraham Ḥamoi's edition, printed in *Sefer Beit Din* (Livorno, 1858), fol. 196b, and in Ms. Rome-Angelica 46, fol. 34a. On the various versions of this treatise see Dan, *Esoteric Theology,* pp. 220–221; idem, "The Seventy Names of Metatron," *Proceedings of the Eighth World Congress of Jewish Studies, Division C* (Jerusalem, 1982), pp. 19–23; Liebes, "Angels of the Shofar," pp. 171–196; Abrams, "Boundaries," pp. 301n33, 302–305. It is important to compare the above description of Metatron as both Son and high priest with a Philonic description of the Logos as conceived of in precisely these terms. See e.g. Winston, *Logos,* p. 16. Some of the more general characteristics of the Logos are reminiscent of those of Metatron, e.g. its basic function as an hypostatization of God; cf. ibid., pp. 49–50. On the other hand, the salvific nature of the union with the Logos (ibid., p. 42) is also found in a variety of Jewish traditions in connection with Metatron. Like this angel, the Logos is also described as the ruler of the world and the angel of the divine face. The Logos may also be identified with a messianic figure. See Harry A. Wolfson, *Philo,* Harvard University Press, Cambridge, Mass., 1982), 2: 415, and compare the analysis of the relevant passages by Winston (ibid., pp. 57–58), who accepts the messianic nature of Philo's discussions without mentioning the Logos in that context. On the great influence of Philo's view of the Logos on early Christology see e.g. Thomas H. Tobin, "The Prologue of John and Hellenistic Jewish Speculation," *Catholic Biblical Quarterly* 52, (1990), pp. 252–269. See also below, chap. 2, n. 75. Important remarks on Philo's Logos and Metatron are found in Joshua Abelson, *Jewish Mysticism* (London, 1913), p. 67; Abrams, *Book of Illumination,* p. 78.

52. The translation is based on a combined version of some corrupted texts: *Sefer Tosafot ha-Shalem,* ed. Jacob Gelis (Jerusalem, 1988), 7:134; R. 'Efrayyim, *Perush 'al ha-Torah,* 1:201, and Ms. Leningrad-Firkowitch, I, 324, fol. 12a. The gematria is 182 and 181 for the two Hebrew phrases. On the intervention of Metatron in saving the children of Israel by spliting the Red Sea see *Sefer ha-Ḥesheq,* fols. 4b, 6a. See also the shorter version of this treatise, printed in *Sefer Beit Din,* fols. 197b, 198a. To a great extant, the development of the hypostatical interpretations of these verses, as demonstrated by Fossum, *Name of God,* pp. 81–82, had served as major prooftexts for ancient Jewish and Judeo-Christian speculations. This is also the case in the reverberations of ancient views in medieval Judaism. For example, there are several instances in Ashkenazi literature where the anonymous angel mentioned in Exodus is expressly identified with Metatron; see e.g. the anonymous Ashkenazi *Commentary on the Pentateuch,* where in the context of mentioning the name of a certain R. Yehudah, in my opinion R. Yehudah he-Ḥasid, an interpretation of the term *angel* as Metatron is quoted. See Ms. Leningrad-Firkowitch I, 324, fols. 17b–18a, which adduces a view found in the *Commentary on the Pentateuch* by R. Yehudah he-Ḥasid, ed. Y. S. Lange (Jerusalem, 1975), p. 109; R. Eleazar of Worms, *Commentary on the Torah,* 2:129, and R. 'Efrayyim ben Shimshon, *Commentary on the Torah,* 1:270–271, as well as p. 57. See also Odeberg, *Hebrew Enoch,* p. 119.

For the antiquity of the concept of an important angel that has been attributed a great religious significance, whose vestiges are still evident in Ashkenazi texts, see Hurtado, *One God,* pp. 45, 85–92; John J. Collins, "Messianism, in the Maccabean Period," in Neusner et al., eds., *Judaisms and Their Messiahs,* pp. 98–103; H. A. Wolfson, "The Pre-Existent Angel of the Magharians and al-Nahawandi," *JQR,* n.s., 51 (1960–61), pp. 89–106; Fossum, *Name of God,* pp. 18, 329–332, 337;

idem, "The Magharians: A Pre-Christian Jewish Sect and Its Significance for the Study of Gnosticism and Christianity," *Henoch* 9 (1989), pp. 303–343; Couliano, *Expériences de l'extase,* pp. 70–71, idem, *Tree of Gnosis,* p. 54; Danielou, *Theologie du Judeo-Christianisme,* pp. 205–207. Also pertinent to our discussion is E. R. Wolfson's argument as to the possible impact of an ancient Judeo-Christian mythologumen on the book of Bahir. See his *Along the Path,* pp. 63–88. From the point of view of this study, it is less important whether the hypostatic angel is Jewish and pre-Christian, or indeed if there was a Jewish-Christian tradition that was adopted by later Kabbalistic sources. From the phenomenological point of view, both historical explanations may account for the origin of an hypostatic Messiah. In fact, some of the studies mentioned above allow the possibility that an ancient Jewish mythologoumenon had influenced both the later Jewish and the Jewish-Christian traditions. This assumption, which is consonant with some proposals made by Giles Quispel and Jarl Fossum, among others, as to the Jewish origins of some important Gnostic mythologoumena, explains more easily the emergence of the Ashkenazi and Abulafian discussions of the redemptive angel. On my thesis concerning the impact of older Jewish mythologoumena on early Kabbalah see *Kabbalah: New Perspectives,* pp. 30–34, 114–116, including the discussion of a text that deals with the Son of Man as a suffering and cosmic figure. See also Jung, *Aion,* pp. 218–219. On another case related to messianism, where a better explanation would be to see the early Christian material as reflecting preceding Jewish traditions, see Liebes, "Jonas as Messiah ben Joseph," pp. 271–272, and Jung, *Aion,* pp. 111, 117. On the existence of a cult of Metatron in the Middle Ages see M. Idel, "Kabbalistic Prayer in Provence," *Tarbiẓ* 122 (1993), pp. 269–277 (Hebrew); Abrams, "Boundaries," p. 301; idem, *Book of Illumination,* p. 346. For earlier sources see Odeberg, *Hebrew Enoch,* p. 116; Liebes, *Ḥet'o shel 'Elisha',* pp. 21–22n21.

53. See the studies collected and edited by S. N. Eisenstadt, *The Origin and Diversity of Axial Age Civilizations* (State University of New York Press, Albany, 1986).

54. See the Arabic source printed by Shlomo Pines, " 'Sefer 'Arugat ha-Bosem': The Fragments from Sefer Meqor Ḥayyim," *Tarbiẓ* 27 (1958), p. 221 (Hebrew). For the various Hebrew translations of this dictum see Idel, "Types of Redemptive Activities," pp. 257–258.

55. Cohen, "Messianic Postures," pp. 212–213. See also Raymond P. Scheindlin, "Redemption of the Soul in Golden Age Religious Poetry," *Prooftexts* 10 (1990), pp. 49–67. In general, it should be mentioned that though the Jewish Spanish authors are dealing with astrological and apocalyptic understandings of messianism, their quintessential contribution is to be found in the spiritual version of messianism. On astrology and messianism in twelfth-century Spain see Mann, "Messianic Movements," pp. 340–341. Though Cohen, "Messianic Postures," p. 215, is certainly correct when pointing out the more philosophical propensity of Sephardic Jews, both the Zoharic and Abulafian forms of messianism betray major deviations from this point of view, as they include apocalyptic elements in their messianic discussions.

56. See Sara Heller Wilensky, "Isaac ibn Latif—Philosopher or Kabbalist?" A. Altmann, ed. *Jewish Medieval and Renaissance Studies* (Cambridge, 1967), p. 206. It should be mentioned that cyclical eschatologies of astrological origins had become more and more influential since the twelfth century, basically by adopting more scientific views. This is the case of Abraham bar Ḥiyya, ibn Latif, and many other Kabbalists who subscribed to the theory of cosmic *shemittot* and *yovelim.* These developments problematize descriptions of "Judaic eschatologies" as solely historic. See Macey, *Patriarchs of Time,* p. 18.

57. See *Sha'ar ha-Razim,* ed. Michal Kushnir-Oron (Mossad Bialik, Jerusalem, 1989), pp. 105–106. On R. Todros ha-Levi Abulafia's view of redemption as the result of repentance see ibid., p. 15 and Goetschel, *Meir ibn Gabbay,* pp. 460–461.

58. On the great impact of this work on thirteenth-century Jewish thought see Paul B. Fenton

(Ynnon), "Shem Tov Ibn Falaquera and the Theology of Aristotle," *Daat* 29 (1992), pp. 27–40 (Hebrew).

59. Ms. Vatican-Neofiti A 43, fol. 101b. On this book see Marc Saperstein, "R. Isaac ben Yeda'ya: A Forgotten Commentator on the Aggada," *REJ* 158 (1979), pp. 17–45. The Hebrew original has been printed in Idel, "Types of Redemptive Activity," p. 258. On the repercussion of this passage in *Sefer Ḥesheq Shelomo* by R. Shelomo ben Yehudah of Lunel, an early fifteenth-century Provençal author, see Schwartz, "Neutralization of the Messianic Idea," p. 47. For Kabbalistic interpretations of the Yevamot passage see Goetschel, *Meir ibn Gabbay,* pp. 460–461.

60. This stand is shared also by Aristotelian thinkers such as R. Levi ben Abraham; see his *Livyat Ḥen,* Ms. Vatican 192, fols. 28a, 57b; cf. Idel, "Types of Redemptive Activities," p. 262 and n. 42.

61. *BT, Yevamot,* fol. 62a; see also Idel, "Types of Redemptive Activities," p. 258, n. 26.

62. Printed by David Kaufmann, *Meḥqarim be-Sifrut ha-'Ivrit* (Mossad Ha-Rav Kook, Jerusalem, 1965), p. 106 (Hebrew). Kaufmann did not distinguish between the pseudo-Empedoclian source and the addition of Alemanno. In fact, Kaufmann edited this text from Alemanno's anonymous treatise in Ms. Paris, Bibliothèque Nationale 849, while the same text, found in Alemanno's *Collectanaea* and extant also in Ms. Oxford 2234, fol. 151a, does not contain the messianic passage.

63. Kaufmann, *Meḥqarim,* p. 92.

64. See Havah Lazarus-Yafeh, "Is There a Concept of Redemption in Islam?" in Bleeker and Werblowsky, eds., *Types of Redemption,* pp. 170–171.

65. See Pines, *Between Jewish Thought,* pp. 292–294; Dinur, *Israel ba-Golah,* part 2, vol. 4, pp. 6–8; Yoel L. Kraemer, "On Maimonides' Messianic Posture," in I. Twersky, ed., *Studies in Medieval Jewish History and Literature* (Harvard University Press, Cambridge, 1984), 2:109–142; Ravitsky, "Maimonides on the Days of the Messiah"; idem, "The Prophet vis-à-vis His Society," *Forum* 32 (1978), pp. 89–103; Amos Funkenstein, "Maimonides: Political Theory and Realistic Messianism," in his *Perceptions of Jewish History* (University of California Press, Berkeley and Los Angeles, 1993), pp. 131–154; Goodman, *On Justice,* pp. 169–174, 177–183; Yeshayahu Leibowitz, "ha-Ge'ullah ha-Meshiḥit be-Mishnato shel ha-Rambam," in *'Emunah, Historiyah ve-'Arakhim* (Akademon, Jerusalem, 1982), pp. 89–101 (Hebrew); David Hartman, *Living Covenant,* pp. 249–254, 288–291; idem, "Maimonides' Approach to Messianism and Its Contemporary Implications," *Daat* 2–3 (1978/9), pp. 5–33; Liebes, "The Messiah of the Zohar," p. 173; idem, *Studies in Jewish Myth,* pp. 61–64; Heschel, *Prophetic Inspiration,* pp. 69–126. Schwartz, "The Neutralization of the Messianic Idea," David Berger, "On the Ironical Results of Maimonides' Rationalistic Approach to the Messianic Time," *Maimonidean Studies,* vol. 2 (1991), pp. 1–8 (Hebrew).

66. See Leo Strauss, "Quelques remarques sur la science politique de Maimonide et de Farabi," *REJ* 100 (1936), pp. 1–37.

67. See the quotation from R. Joseph Angelet's *Twenty-Four Kabbalistic Secrets* adduced in Idel, "Types of Redemptive Activity," p. 264n46.

68. *Sefer Liwiyat Ḥen,* Ms. Parma, de Rossi 2904, fol. 160b. On the context of this view see M. Idel, "On the History of the Interdiction against the Study of Kabbalah before the Age of Forty," *AJSR* 5 (1980), Hebrew Section, pp. 5–6; "Types of Redemptive Activities," p. 262. On this author and his book see Colette Sirat, "Les different versions du Liwyat Ḥen de Levi b. Abraham," *REJ* 122 (1963), pp. 167–177. See also Schwartz, "The Neutralization of the Messianic Idea," pp. 42–44.

69. *Sermon on Qohelet,* in Ch. D. Chavel, ed., *Kitvei ha-Ramban* (Mossad ha-Rav Kook, Jerusalem, 1963), 1:192. On the complex issue of nature and miracles in Nahmanides, including his antagonistic stand toward the much more naturalistic Maimonides, viewed as a paragon of the Greek notion of nature, see David Berger, "Miracles and the Natural Order in Nahmanides," in

I. Twersky, ed., *Rabbi Moses Nahmanides (Ramban): Explorations in His Religious and Literary Virtuosity* (Harvard University Press, Cambridge, 1983), pp. 113–116, 123, 128.

70. Pines, *Between Jewish Thought,* pp. 277–305.

71. There is a vast scholarly literature on Joachim's thought; see e.g. the various writings of Marjorie Reeves, especially her *Influence of Prophecy,* as well as B. McGinn, *The Calabrian Abbot* (Macmillan, New York, 1985), and Emmerson and Herzman, *Apocalyptic Imagination,* pp. 1–35; Manuel and Manuel, *Utopian Thought,* pp. 56–58.

72. On this difficult treatise see the analysis of Scholem, *Origins of the Kabbalah,* pp. 460–474; on Joachim's views, see pp. 464–465.

73. Gerona: ibid., pp. 460–461n233; Provence: ibid., pp. 461, 468.

74. I hope to devote a special study to this issue; see, for the time being, Moshe Idel, "The Meaning of 'Ta'amei ha-'Ofot Ha-Teme'im' of R. David ben Yehuda he-Ḥasid," in M. Ḥallamish, ed., *'Alei Shefer: Studies in the Literature of Jewish Thought Presented to Rabbi Dr. Alexandre Safran* (Bar-Ilan University Press, Ramat Gan, 1990), pp. 18–21 (Hebrew).

75. Yitzhak Baer, *Studies in the History of the Jewish People* (Historical Society of Israel, Jerusalem, 1985), 2:306–349 (Hebrew).

76. See Tishby, *Wisdom of the Zohar,* 3:1438–1439.

77. Reeves, *Influence of Prophecy,* pp. 175–290.

78. This statement, which may be qualified by further studies, does not imply that in other phases of Jewish Kabbalistic messianism Christian elements were not influential. See below, chap. 4; chap. 7, n. 102, and app. 1.

79. Compare the different stand of Scholem on this issue: *'Od Davar,* p. 240.

80. See the philosophical identity of most of the authors dealt with by Schwartz, "Neutralization of the Messianic Idea."

81. Idel, *Hasidism: Between Ecstasy and Magic,* pp. 9–15.

82. Moshe Idel, "Reification of Language in Jewish Mysticism," in S. Katz, ed., *Mysticism and Language* (Oxford University Press, New York, 1992), pp. 42–79; idem, "A la recherche de la langue originelle: Le teimognage du nourisson," *Revue d'histoires des religions* 213–214 (1996), pp. 417–420.

Chapter 2: Abraham Abulafia: Ecstatic Kabbalah and Spiritual Messianism

1. Most of the details of Abulafia's biography are from Jellinek, *Bet ha-Midrasch,* 3:xli–xlii. See also his *Auswahl kabbalistischer Mystik,* erstes Heft (Leipzig, 1853), German part, pp. 16–18. For mentioning of great wars in the vicinity of Acre in an eschatological context see the early medieval *Prayer of R. Shime'on bar Yoḥai,* in Even Shmuel, ed., *Midreshei Ge'ullah,* p. 278.

2. This journey to the Sambation River as an event fraught with eschatological expectations recalls the hopes of a later messianic figure, Sabbatai Tzevi. His prophet, Nathan of Gaza, foretold the visit of this Messiah to the legendary river, whence he was supposed to return with his new bride. See Nathan's text preserved in *Tzitzat Novel Tzevi,* p. 9. The scholarly attribution to Abulafia of the claim that he had already gone to the Sambation is a misrepresentation; Abulafia indeed broadcast his intention to go there, but he never claimed to have attained this goal. See, however, Friedlaender, "Shiitic Influences," in Saperstein, ed., *Essential Papers,* p. 156n172. On the utopia of Sambation see Shlomo Yaniv, "'The Utopian Society' beyond Sambatyon," *Karmeliyt* 21–22 (1977–1978), pp. 277–291 (Hebrew); Zvi Avni, "Sambation: Recurrence of Tradition," *Jewish Studies* 5 (1997), pp. 147–160 (Hebrew).

3. On the entire episode see Idel, *Chapters in Ecstatic Kabbalah,* pp. 45–61.

4. *Ve-Zot li-Yhudah,* p. 19. On some mistaken academic attempts to attribute to Abulafia a trinitarian penchant see Idel, *Chapters in Ecstatic Kabbalah,* p. 55n8. On Abulafia's view of *sefirot* see Idel, *Hasidism,* pp. 228–232, and Wolfson, "Doctrine of Sefirot," pp. 336–371.

5. On the ancient nexus between the two topics see J. Gilbert, "Prophetisme et attente d'un Messie prophete dans l'ancient Judaisme," in *L'Attente du Messie: Recherches Bibliques* (1954), pp. 85ff; Ferdinand Hahn, *The Titles of Jesus in Christology,* trans. H. Knight and G. Ogg (Lutterworth Press, London, 1969), pp. 352–406; Riesenfeld, *Jesus Transfiguré,* pp. 269–270; Oscar Cullmann, *The Christology of the New Testament,* trans. S. C. Guthrie and Ch. A. M. Hall (Philadelphia, Westminster Press, 1959), pp. 13–50; Benjamin Sommer, "Did Prophecy Cease? Evaluating a Reevaluation," *JBL* 115 (1996), pp. 31–47, which includes an up-to-date bibliography (Abulafia is mentioned on pp. 38–39). See also Heschel, *Prophetic Inspiration,* passim. Compare, however, Stephen Sharot's statement that Abulafia's and other Kabbalists' "mystical experience and prophetic announcements were closely related, their messianism was not a logical outgrowth of their cabbalistic doctrines." *Messianism, Mysticism and Magic,* p. 70.

It should be emphasized that Abulafia, having openly assumed the stance of prophet, at the same time mitigated the apocalyptic traditions. On the nexus between apocalypticism and pseudepigraphy see Scholem's insightful discussion in *Messianic Idea,* p. 7. The neglect of Abulafia's emphasis on the nexus between prophecy and messianism has produced simplistic statements such as Dan's, "Gershom Scholem and Jewish Messianism," p. 78: "His [Scholem's] findings made it impossible to regard mysticism and messianism as integrally related religious phenomena in Judaism." As to Abulafia's possible source for the nexus between prophecy and messianism see Maimonides, *Guide of the Perplexed,* 2:32, 36, and Isadore Twersky, *Introduction to the Code of Maimonides (Mishneh Torah)* (Yale University Press, New Haven, 1980), p. 68; Heschel, *Prophetic Inspiration,* pp. 112–126. In this context it is important to mention A. Neher's distinction between regular prophecy and what he proposed to call the "Christic prophecy," namely the prophetic phenomena that are believed to be contemporareous with the Messiah. See *Prophetic Experience,* pp. 61–62, 227. While Abulafia is a clear example of the fusion between the two concepts, Nathan of Gaza is a perfect example for Neher's second category.

6. Abulafia was thirty years of age in 1270, which corresponded to the thirtieth year in the sixth Jewish millennium (5030). See Abulafia's *Commentary* to his own *Sefer ha-'Edut,* Ms. Rome-Angelica 38, fol. 10a. See also Marc Saperstein, *Decoding the Rabbis* (Harvard University Press, Cambridge, 1980), pp. 103–105. According to Saperstein, the commentary to the *'Aggadot of the Talmud* was composed during the 1250s and had no bearing on Naḥmanides' words in the disputation. However, this supposition has yet to be proven. I would tend toward assigning a later date to this work, in the 1280s. See also the parallel contained in the words of R. Levi ben Gershom, better known as Gersonides, noted by Saperstein, *Decoding the Rabbis,* p. 247n112.

7. *ba'.* Naḥmanides discusses here a legend which was adduced by Paulus Christiani in the debate.

8. Exodus 7:26. For Moses as a type of Messiah see Berger, "Three Typological Themes," pp. 142–143.

9. See J. D. Eisenstein, *'Otzar ha-Wikkuḥim* (New York, 1928), p. 88; Levi, "Apocalypses," p. 112; Silver, *History of Messianic Speculation,* p. 146, note 145; Scholem, Major Trends, p. 128; idem, Origins of the Kabbalah, p. 459; Idel, *Studies in Ecstatic Kabbalah,* pp. 65–66; Chazan, *Barcelona and Beyond,* pp. 116–117; idem, *Daggers of Faith* (University of California Press, Berkeley and Los Angeles, 1989), pp. 91–92, as well as Mark Saperstein, "Jewish Typological Exegesis after Nahmanides," *Jewish Studies Quarterly* 1 (1993), pp. 167–168. The Messiah is placed in Rome according to both talmudic and apocalyptic sources. See esp. *JT, Ta'anit,* 64:1; *Sefer Zerubbavel,* in Even Shmuel,

ed., *Midreshei Ge'ullah,* p. 72, where not only Rome is mentioned but also *beit ha-toref,* understood to mean the place for prayer, though it stands for "house of obscenity." See Berger, "Captive at the Gate of Rome," pp. 4–5, 8–11. On Rome and messianism see Urbach, *Sages,* pp. 681–682; Levi, "Apocalypses," p. 112. For a targumic view of the Messiah as coming out of Rome see Wieder, *Judean Scrolls,* p. 46. Thus, Naḥmanides' discussion of the meeting of the Messiah with the pope has some earlier apocalyptic sources. For the assumption that the Messiah will come from Rome see also the statement found in the anonymous commentary on the Psalms written in the early sixteenth century, *Sefer Kaf ha-Qetoret,* Ms. Paris, Bibliothèque Nationale 846, fol. 125a, and in Yitzḥaq Abravanel's *Yeshu'ot Meshiḥo,* translated in Tishby, "Acute Apocalyptic Messianism," in Saperstein, ed., *Essential Papers,* p. 285n46.

10. Dan, *'Otzar ha-Vikkuḥim,* p. 88.

11. Ibid.

12. Cf. the phrase *marana tha',* which means "Our Lord, Come!"

13. On the various sources about the Messiah in Rome see Berger, "Captive at the Gate of Rome," pp. 1–17, as well as Scholem, *Researches in Sabbateanism,* p. 43n75, as well as idem, *Messianic Idea,* p. 12. Abulafia himself was imprisoned in Rome for two weeks after his abortive attempt to meet the pope in Soriano and then the pope's death; cf. Idel, *Chapters on Ecstatic Kabbalah,* p. 58. These traditions seem to be the background for Guillaume Postel's emphasis throughout his *Restitutio omnium rerum* that the Messiah will come out of Rome, just as Moses did from the desert. See the edition of this book printed at the end of his *Commentary on Sefer Yetzirah,* originally published in Paris in 1552, now reprinted (Frommann-Holzboog, Stuttgart-Bad, Cannstatt, 1994), ed. Wolf Peter Klein, pp. 152–153.

14. On Moses as a messianic figure see H. Teeple, *The Mosaic Eschatological Prophet* (Society of Biblical Literature, Philadelphia, 1957). On typology and messianism in general see Mowinckel, *He That Cometh,* p. 13n3; Bentzen, *King and Messiah,* p. 75; Saperstein, "Jewish Typological Exegesis," pp. 167–168; Berger, "Three Typological Themes."

15. On this issue see Idel, *Mystical Experience,* pp. 134–137. Abulafia's worldview can be described as "apocalyptic dualism" or "dualistic apocalypticism," to use Nickelsburg's phrases; see "The Apocalyptic Construction of Reality in 1 Enoch," in Collins and Charlesworth, eds., *Mysteries and Revelations,* p. 63. Abulafia emphasized the duality of intellect and body. Cf. Idel, *Mystical Experience,* pp. 141–143.

16. The original expression is *'adon ha-kol,* which stems from *Sefer Yetzirah,* a book that strongly influenced Abulafia's thought. On "All" in Jewish thought see Elliot Wolfson, "God, the Demiurge and the Intellect: On the Usage of the Word *Kol* in Abraham ibn Ezra," *REJ* 149 (1990), pp. 77–111, and Howard Kreisel, "On the Term 'All' in Abraham ibn Ezra: A Reappraisal," *REJ* 153 (1994), pp. 29–66, and their bibliographies.

17. See Abulafia's epistle *Ve-Zot Li-Yhudah,* pp. 18–19, corrected according to Ms. New York, JTS 1887. On the messianic awareness of Abulafia in general see also the useful study of Berger, "The Messianic Self-Consciousness of Abraham Abulafia," pp. 55–61. For more on the issues dealt with in this passage see my forthcoming " 'The Time of the End': Apocalypticism and Its Spiritualization in Abraham Abulafia's Kabbalah," in *Apocalyptic Time,* ed. Albert Baumgarten (Brill, Leiden, 1998).

18. In Hebrew *mashiyaḥ* initially meant the anointed one. See Naḥmanides' *Disputation,* p. 88, where the Messiah ought to be anointed by Elijah, as part of his advent. See also the texts related to anointment in context of kingship and messianism in Mowinckel, *He That Cometh,* s.v. "Anointing," and the discussions of Hahn, *Titles of Jesus,* s.v. "Anointing"; Johnson, *Sacral Kingship,* pp. 14–15; Zeev Weisman, "Anointing as a Motif in the Making of the Charismatic King," *Biblica* 57

(1976), pp. 378–398; Patai, "Hebrew Installation Rites," pp. 166–171. For a similar phenomenon in the Islamicate environment see Israel Friedlander, "Shiitic Influence in Jewish Sectarism," in Saperstein, ed., *Essential Papers,* pp. 135–136, 157–158, who collected also several examples, including Abulafia, of eschatological anointments. Regarding the connection between the apotheosis of Enoch and anointing with oil, see *The Ethiopic Book of Enoch* 22:8, quoted below. For the ancient Christian custom of anointing the infant before baptism as a type of second birth, see Gilles Quispel, *Gnostic Studies* (Nederlands Historische-Archeologisch Institute, Istanbul, 1974), 1:233–236. A similar stand to Abulafia's is found in an anonymous commentary on liturgy stemming from the circle of ecstatic Kabbalists in Spain, where it is said that "it is impossible that a [certain] act will be produced without the influx, and this is the reason why he is called Messiah, because he is anointed with the oil of holy unction." Cf. Ms. Paris, Bibliothèque Nationale 848, fol. 28b. On this treatise see Moshe Idel, "Ramon Lull and Ecstatic Kabbalah," *Journal of the Warburg and Courtauld Institutes* 51 (1988), pp. 170–174. On the redeemer as the influx descending onto the souls of the Jews see a passage from R. Yitzḥaq of Acre's *Sefer 'Otzar Ḥayyim,* discussed by Gottlieb, *Studies,* p. 241. On anointment as a state similar to angels see Greenfield, "Notes," p. 155.

19. Already in the Bible a prophet like Elisha has been anointed, though this is an exceptional case. On ointment as related to the reception of the divine spirit and extraordinary powers see already the king-ideology as represented in 1 Samuel 16:13. See Neher, *Prophetic Existence,* pp. 225–226, where he points out the nexus between the phenomenon of prophecy and anointment, namely messianism, in the case of David. This text presupposesa certain form of divine initiative, at least at the beginning of his career. If this approach is correct, Abulafia, like Nathan of Gaza, belongs to what Leach has called the "icon of subversion," namely a religious paradigm which assumes that millenarian revelations are direct and do not involve hierarchical mediation of priests and rituals. See *L'unité de l'homme,* p. 224. Abulafia's approach is much more anomian than that of other Kabbalists, whose millenarian approach fits what Leach called the "icon of orthodoxy." Ibid., p. 223.

20. Zach. 9:10. On this verse see in Naḥmanides' controversy with Paulo Christiani, cf. Chazan, *Barcelona and Beyond,* pp. 126–127. In general, the ancient concept of the ideal Israelite king was connected to universal recognition and dominion over all nations.

21. Compare this quite conspicuous messianic understanding of *devequt* to the various statements of Scholem, *Messianic Idea,* pp. 51, 185, 194, 204.

22. See Abulafia's *Sefer Mafteḥ ha-Tokheḥot,* a commentary on Deuteronomy, Ms. Oxford 1605, fol. 46b. On the miraculous powers of the prophet in Abulafia and the influence on R. Moses Narboni see Idel, *Studies in Ecstatic Kabbalah,* pp. 63–65. In this quotation, as in some others cited above, his Kabbalah and messianism, including some apocalyptic expressions, are linked. See, however, Scholem, *Sabbatai Ṣevi,* p. 15, one of the very few instances where he mentioned Abulafia in this important book on messianism: "Apocalyptic messianism and kabbalah remained distinct spheres of religious life."

23. *Sefer 'Otzar 'Eden Ganuz,* Ms. Oxford 1580, fol. 32b.

24. *Me-rov hidabbeqo.* Here there is a conspicuous case where intense cleaving has explicit messianic overtones. Or, to put it differently, the Messiah may be conceived of as the perfect philosopher and identical to the intellectual ruler of the Greek political tradition, especially the Platonic one. For another claim by a messianic figure, R. Shemariyah of Negroponti, that he had adhered to the separate intellects, see R. Moses de-Rocca Mibara's testimony printed in Aescoly, *Messianic Movements,* p. 243. Aescoly had already suggested that the Greek author might have been influenced by Abulafia. R. Shemariyah flourished during the first part of the fourteenth century, and his extant writings, which do not include messianic speculations, are philosophically oriented.

25. See Abulafia's *Commentary on Sefer ha-Melitz*, Ms. Rome-Angelica 38, fol. 9a; Ms. München 285, fol. 13a; Idel, *Studies in Ecstatic Kabbalah*, p. 66, and idem, *Mystical Experience*, pp. 127, 140. Abulafia and some views found in the circle of the Zohar presuppose both a transcendent and a human Messiah. Compare, however, Mowinckel's remark that there are no such Messiahs in later Judaism, *He That Cometh*, p. 467. I would say that when a supernal Messiah was included in the constellation of messianic ideas, the more popular concept of two human Messiahs was mitigated, marginalizing the figure of the Messiah ben Joseph.

26. On the various concepts of the Agent Intellect in the Middle Ages see the important survey of the philosophical understandings of this term by Davidson, *Alfarabi, Avicenna, and Averroes*. More recently Davidson has proposed a reading of Maimonides' *Guide of the Perplexed* that presupposes the possibility of the union between the Agent Intellect and the human one, offering thereby a vision of Maimonides that is closer to Abulafia's than to the more common perception of Maimonides as representing a much more agnostic approach, as it emerges from the studies of Shlomo Pines. See his "Maimonides on Metaphysical Knowledge," *Maimonidean Studies*, ed. A. Hyman, 3 (1992–1993), pp. 49–103, and, from other perspectives, Heschel, *Prophetic Inspiration*, pp. 69–126, and David Blumenthal, "Maimonides' Intellectualist Mysticism and the Superiority of the Prophecy of Moses," *Studies in Medieval Culture* 10 (1981), pp. 51–67. Mystical potentials of this concept in medieval philosophy have been explored in detail by Merlan, *Monopsychism*. For the mystical overtones of this concept in Islamic mysticism see the various studies of Corbin, especially his *Creative Imagination*, pp. 10–11, 17–18, 80; idem, *Cyclical Time*, p. 76; and, following him while stressing the more Averroistic understanding, Durand, *Figures mythiques*, pp. 78, 80.

27. The identification of Metatron with the Agent Intellect was quite widespread in the Middle Ages. See e.g. R. Moses ibn Tibbon, *Commentary on the Song of Songs;* R. Levi ben Abraham, *Livyat Ḥen*, Ms. Müenchen 58, fol. 11a; Yitzḥaq Albalag, *Sefer Tiqqun Ha-De'ot*, ed. Georges Vajda (Israel Academy of Sciences and Humanities, Jerusalem, 1973), p. 58, and Georges Vajda, *Isaac Albalag, Averroiste Juif, Traducteur et Annotateur d'Al-Ghazali*, (J. Vrin, Paris, 1960), pp. 201–203. On the Kabbalistic side, the two terms are related to each other in some texts already before Abulafia's floruit. See R. Yitzḥaq ben Jacob ha-Kohen, *Commentary on the Chariot of Ezekiel*, ed. Gershom Scholem, *Tarbiẓ* 2 (1931), p. 202, and the pertinent footnotes of the editor, or R. Barukh Togarmi, *Commentary on Sefer Yetzirah*, as analyzed in Idel, *Studies in Ecstatic Kabbalah*, p. 76. Compare, however, to J. Wach's assertion that forms of philosophies that include salvific elements have drawn them from some forms of religious systems, as the different forms of Platonism show. Cf. his introduction, pp. 194–195. It may easily be shown, however, that religious explanations of redemptive concepts also owe a lot to Platonic thinking. See, in the case of Judaism and Islam, chap. 1, pp. 51–53. For Halpern's thesis see *Constitution*, pp. 249–256.

28. Ms. Oxford 1582, fol. 67b; Idel, *Studies in Ecstatic Kabbalah*, p. 53. As I have attempted to show elsewhere, the term *na'ar*, when occurring in the context of Metatron, should be understood as pointing to a high-ranking official and not to a servant, as some modern scholars assume. See Idel, "Metatron," pp. 36. As to this meaning of *na'ar* in ancient texts, some which predate the Enochic literature, see Nahman Avigad, "The Contribution of Hebrew Seals to an Understanding of Israelite Religion and Society," in P. D. Miller, Jr., P. H. Hanson, and S. D. McBride, eds., *Ancient Israelite Religion: Essays in Honor of Frank Moore Cross* (Fortress Press, Philadelphia, 1987), p. 205, and see also Halpern, *Constitution*, pp. 126–130; Fossum, *Name of God*, pp. 312–313; Halperin, "Hekhalot and Mi'raj," pp. 281–282; and Corbin, *Creative Imagination*, pp. 275–276, 280–281. I would like to suggest here another possible nexus between Heikhalot literature and apocalypticism. In a lengthy description of Metatron, where the appellation *na'ar* occurs several times, the precious stone of this angel is designated *'amiel*. See Schaefer, *Synopse*, par. 487. On the other hand, one of

the names of the Messiah is Menahem ben 'Amiel. See Patai, *Messiah Texts,* pp. 24, 26–27, 122–123. For the time being there is no good explanation for the name 'Amiel, and I propose to see a nexus between the Menahem ben 'Amiel and the term *'amiel* in the Heikhalot text.

29. Idel, *Abraham Abulafia,* pp. 88–89, 92; idem, *Mystical Experience,* pp. 116–119. For another explicit identification of the Messiah with Metatron and *na'ar* see Abulafia's commentary on Exodus, entitled *Mafteaḥ ha-Shemot,* Ms. New York, JTS 1897, fol. 77a. For a possible talmudic nexus between a figure close to Metatron and the Messiah see Liebes, *Studies in Jewish Myth,* pp. 44–45. See also Elqayam, *Mystery of Faith,* pp. 325–326, who suggested that Abulafia's equation of Metatron and Messiah may be of Christian origin. Without denying the possible influence of Christian soteriology on Abulafia in principle, it seems that at least in this particular case a direct Christian impact on the ecstatic Kabbalist is rather implausible.

30. Ms. Paris, Bibliothèque Nationale 680, fol. 292a.

31. See the anonymous collectanaea, Ms. Paris, Bibliothèque Nationale 776, fol. 192b, and Oxford 1949, no pagination, summarizing a view expressed by Abulafia in his *Sefer 'Or ha-Sekhel,* Ms. Vatican 233, fols. 117b–118b, as well as the discussion in Idel, *Studies in Ecstatic Kabbalah,* pp. 12–13. The emanation of an emanation stands, apparently, for the human intellectual potential. On the hylic intellect in general see Davidson, *Alfarabi, Avicenna, Averroes,* pp. 61–68, 100–102, 258–262, 282–289. It seems that although in the last quotation a more Avicennian view of the material intellect is found, in some other discussions of Abulafia this term is closer to Averroes' views on the topic. See also Alexander Altmann, "Homo Imago Dei in Jewish and Christian Theology," *Journal of Religion* 48 (1948), p. 255.

32. *Sefer Ḥayyei ha-'Olam ha-Ba',* Ms. Paris, Bibliothèque Nationale 777, fol. 109. This passage has been printed by Jellinek as an addendum to *Sefer ha-'Ot,* p. 84. For an analysis of the context of this passage, see Idel, *Studies in Ecstatic Kabbalah,* pp. 15–16; idem, "Enoch Is Metatron," p. 236, and appendix 1 below, as well as my discussion of a passage from Nathan of Gaza, chap. 6. In R. Yehudah Albotini's *Sefer Sullam ha-'Aliyah,* p. 74, Abulafia's text has been appropriated in order to describe the exit of the mystic from the realm of the human and its entrance into that of the divine. On Metatron and the concept of Face see Idel, "Metatron," pp. 36–37. For another important example in Abulafia of the messianic understanding of Enoch qua Metatron see *Sefer Sitrei Torah,* Ms. Paris, Bibliothèque Nationale 774, fols. 129b–130a. The occurrence of the terms *anointed* and *messenger* demonstrates that the extreme mystic experience does not culminate in an escapist vision but is part of a preparation for a more active role to be played afterwards. Indeed, as we learn from another discussion in the same book, Ms. Oxford 1580, fol. 79b, the only pretext for returning "from God" is to instruct other people, which for Abulafia is a messianic enterprise.

33. See *The Slavonic Book of Enoch,* 22:8–10; *Le Livre des secrets d'Henoch,* ed. A. Vaillant (Paris, 1952), pp. 26, 18–27; Segal, "Paul and the Beginning of the Jewish Mysticism," p. 105; Matthew Black, "The Throne-Theophany Prophetic Commission and the 'Son of Man,'" in *Jews, Greeks and Christians: Religious Cultures in Late Antiquities: Essays in Honor of W. D. Davies* (Brill, Leiden, 1976), pp. 57–73; Himmelfarb, *Ascent to Heaven,* p. 40; Hurtado, *One God,* pp. 53–54.

34. On these two elements see Shemaryahu Talmon, "The Concept of *Mashiah* and Messianism in Early Judaism," in Charlesworth, ed., *Messiah,* p. 83.

35. Some discussions of Sabbatai Tzevi's anointment have been collected by Scholem, *Sabbatai Ṣevi,* pp. 140–142.

36. *'Al BaM* is a method of letter permutation which exchanges the first and last letters of the alphabet, the second and penultimate, and so on. Accordingly, *ShaDaY* is converted into *BQM.*

37. From this point on, until the word "Mohammed," the whole passage is omitted from the

Rome-Angelica manuscript, presumably out of fear of the censor. On Abulafia and blessing see below, appendix 1, where he derives one of his own theophoric names from the term "blessing."

38. Ms. Munich 285, fol. 22a; Ms. Rome-Angelica 38, fol. 22a. This section is based on a long line of numerological equivalences, only some of which will be deciphered below. On Abulafia as one of several prophets of his time see below, Appendix 1. On the formula "I am" used in the quoted passage see Widengren, *Muhammad,* pp. 48–54; T. W. Manson, "The Ego Eimi of the Messianic Presence in the New Testament," *Journal of Theological Studies* 48, (1947), pp. 137ff. The hint at the Messiah's building upon Jesus and Mohammed is perhaps related to the medieval supposition, found in such Jewish thinkers as R. Yehudah ha-Levi and Maimonides, as to the role of these religions is paving the way for the final messianic recognition of Judaism. On Jesus as Messiah in Sabbatean sources see Liebes, *On Sabbateaism and Its Kabbalah,* pp. 398nn18,19; 440n90.

39. See Ms. Oxford 1649, fol. 206a, discussed in more detail in Idel, *Studies in Ecstatic Kabbalah,* pp. 11–12. For the intellectual nature of redemption in this text see also Ms. Oxford 1649, fols. 201b–202a. In an important revelation Abulafia has the angel Yaho'el addressing him as "My son." On a scholarly interpretation of Psalm 2 in the context of the royal sonship see more recently Jon D. Levenson, "The Jerusalem Temple in the Devotional and Visionary Experience," in Green, ed., *Jewish Spirituality,* 1:47–49; idem, *The Death and Resurrection of the Beloved Son* (Yale University Press, New Haven, 1993), pp. 203–205; idem, *Sinai and Zion,* pp. 97–101; Patai, "Hebrew Installation Rites," pp. 169, 186. For scholarly discussions of the adoption and Sonship of the Israelite kings in general see e.g. Aubrey R. Johnson, in Hooke, ed., *Labyrinth,* pp. 79–81; idem, *Sacral Kingship,* pp. 28–30; Mowinckel, *He That Cometh,* pp. 96–98; Halpern, *Constitution,* pp. 128–130, 146; De Fraine, *L'aspect religieux,* pp. 236–249, 271–276; E. Huntress, " 'The Son of God' in Jewish Writings Prior to the Christian Era," *JBL* 54 (1935), pp. 117–123; Jan Assmann, "Die Zeugung des Sohnes," in J. Assmann et al., eds., *Funktionen und Leistungen des Mythos* (Vandenhoeck und Ruprercht, Göttingen, 1982), pp. 13–61.

40. See M. Idel, "On the History of the Interdiction against the Study of Kabbalah before the Age of Forty," *AJSR* 5 (1980), pp. 1–20 (Hebrew); idem, *Mystical Experience,* pp. 138–143, 195–203. For the anointment of the son of the king, alluded to by Abulafia in the above quotation, see 2 Kings 11:12. The occurrence of the name Shaday in this context may point to Metatron, which is numerically related to the name Shaday. See below, appendix 1.

41. See Ravitsky, "Maimonides on the Days of the Messiah," pp. 245–249.

42. Rosenberg, "The Return to the Garden of Eden," pp. 79–80.

43. Zach. 9:9. On the meaning of this verse in the biblical context see Yair Zakovitz, "Poor and Riding an Ass," in *Messianic Idea in Israel,* pp. 7–17 (Hebrew).

44. See Idel, "Types of Messianic Activities," pp. 255–256. Abulafia also addressed this verse in a manner reminiscent of the later Midrash, when he described Metatron, the Messiah, as riding on the angel Sandalphon, which designates (in Abulafian terminology) the material. See *Mafteaḥ ha-Shemot,* Ms. New York JTS, 1897, fol. 77a. See also Idel, *Studies in Ecstatic Kabbalah,* pp. 75–78. An interesting case of describing redemption as the salvation of intellectual soul from the exile of the evil drive, which is said to be a hindrance to intellection, is found in the work of a Kabbalist who was a student of Abraham Abulafia: R. Joseph Gikatilla's *Commentary on the Passover Haggadah,* in M. Kasher and S. Ashkenazi, eds., *Haggadah Shelemah* (Jerusalem, 1967), p. 114 (Hebrew).

45. See note 24 above and Berger, "The Messianic Self-Consciousness," in Saperstein, ed., *Essential Papers,* p. 253.

46. R. Moses ibn Tibbon, *Commentary on the Song of Songs* (Meqitzei Nirdamim, Lyck, 1874), preface, p. 12. Compare also ibid., p. 13, and in the commentary itself fols. 14a, 15a, 21a and the

allegorical interpretations of Go'el and Moshi'im, in another book by the same author, *Sefer Pe'ah,* Ms. Oxford 939, fol. 27ab. See also M. Idel, "Jerusalem in Thirteenth-Century Jewish Thought," in Joshua Prawer and Haggai Ben-Shammai, eds., *The History of Jerusalem, Crusaders and Ayyubids (1099–1250)* (Yad Izḥaq Ben-Zvi Publications, Jerusalem, 1991), pp. 284–286 (Hebrew). On the mystical sources of the above quotation see the review of the edition on the *Commentary on Song of Songs* printed in Bruell's *Jahrbuch für Judischen Geschichte und Literatur,* vol. 3 (1877), p. 175. On this commentary on the Song of Songs see Menachem Kellner, "Communication or the Lack Thereof among Thirteenth–Fourteenth Century Provençal Jewish Philosophers: Moses ibn Tibbon and Gersonides on Song of Songs," in Sophia Menache, ed., *Communication in the Jewish Diaspora: The Pre-Modern World* (Brill, Leiden, New York, Koeln, 1996), pp. 227–254. On the identification between Metatron and the Agent Intellect see Georges Vajda, "Pour le Dossier de Metatron," in R. Lowe and S. Stein, eds., *Ḥokhma Bina veDaat: Studies in Jewish History and Thought Presented to A. Altmann* (University of Alabama Press, University, Ala., 1979), pp. 345–354.

47. On this book and Abulafia's impact on it see Idel, *Mystical Experience,* pp. 200–201, 223–224. On the influence of Abulafia's eschatology on a fourteenth-century philosopher, R. Moses Narboni, see idem, *Studies in Ecstatic Kabbalah,* p. 66.

48. Or "messengers." According to the view that the name "ben David" refers to an angel, we may see it as an allegory for the Agent Intellect, which has already been identified with the Messiah in some of Abulafia's text.

49. *BT, Yevamot,* fol. 62a. For a spiritualization of Elijah in a Messianic context see also the philosophical texts adduced by Schwartz, "Neutralization of the Messianic Idea," p. 52, and below, the discussions of R. Menaḥem Naḥum of Chernobyl, ch. 7. On the eschatological function of Elijah see Robert Macina, "Le role eschatologique d'Elie le Prophete dans la conversion finale du peuple juif: Positions juives et chrétiennes à la lumiere des sources rabbiniques et patristiques," *Proche-Orient Chretien* 31 (1981), pp. 71–99; Klausner, *Messianic Idea in Israel,* pp. 451–457. For additional examples of spiritual interpretations of the Messiah in philosophical circles of the thirteenth and fourteenth centuries see Schwartz, "Neutralization," pp. 41–44. Interestingly enough, the more spiritual philosophical conceptualizations of the Messiah as an inner experience have been neglected by Sarachek, *Doctrine of the Messiah,* despite his emphasis on the philosophical literature.

50. *Sefer Toldot 'Adam,* Ms. Oxford 836, fol. 159a–159b. See also ibid., fol. 155b, where the intellectual influx is described as "the redeeming angel," which dwells in men, using the messianic verse from Isaiah 11:2. Compare to another passage, apparently also influenced by Abulafia, found in the work of a Spanish philosopher living in the second half of the fourteenth-century, R. Samuel ibn Tzartzah, *Sefer Mikhlol Yofi,* Ms. Los Angeles, UCLA X 779, fol. 102b: "Know and understand that Ben David is the king Messiah, by the influence of the Agent Intellect onto the human intellect when the latter is *in actu.* And he called the other material powers [by the name] 'souls in body' namely 'Ben David come,' namely the intellect is not able to cleave to the Agent Intellect, until the exhaustion of all the souls from the body, which are the material powers." Beyond the conceptual resemblance between this passage and Abulafia's eschatological allegory, in *Mikhlol Yofi* the gematria *yisra'el = sekhel ha-po'el* = 541 occurs. See ibid., fol. 62b. The Hebrew passage has been printed in Idel, *Abraham Abulafia,* p. 452. This and many other examples, including some adduced above, demonstrate that the history of the term *Agent Intellect* in Jewish philosophy should be studied in the light of the Greek and Arabic traditions, as has been done superbly by Davidson, *Alfarabi, Avicenna, and Averroes,* and in the light of the inner structure of Jewish thinking as represented by rabbinic and mystical concepts. See Davidson, *Alfarabi,* p. 209.

51. *'Od Davar,* p. 271. Though Scholem was indubitably aware of Abulafia's discussions, he nevertheless preferred to ignore them in his numerous discussions on messianism. For example,

Abulafia's name is totally absent in Scholem's most important collection of articles, *The Messianic Idea;* it is neglected in *Researches on Sabbateanism* and completely marginalized in his *Sabbatai Sevi,* a fact that is curious when the ignored figure is the first major Jewish mystic who proclaimed himself to be a Messiah and whose writings were extant, some fragments of them even having been studied by Sabbatai Tzevi.

52. On individualistic redemption in Judaism see Rosenberg, "Return to the Garden of Eden," pp. 84–86; Schwartz, "Neutralization of the Messianic Idea," pp. 41–44.

53. See Dan's ignoring—apparently following the later Scholem's marginalization—of Abulafia, in his "Gershom Scholem and Jewish Messianism," pp. 77–78. Dan's descriptive presentation reflects a fragmentary view of Kabbalah and ignorance of modern research on the subject that he attempts to present.

54. See Wach's essay, "The Savior in the History of Religion," in *Introduction,* p. 179, also pp. 191–193.

55. See ibid., pp. 179–180, 190–191.

56. *On the Kabbalah,* p. 2.

57. It is quite difficult to determine what exactly the term *memshalah* means in Abulafia's texts. Though it conspicuously reflects a certain form of sovereignty, its more precise contours are rather obscure. On the cycles of month and moon as metaphors for the alteration of exile and redemption see R. Jacob ha-Kohen, in Abrams, *Book of Illumination,* pp. 67–68 and later on, in a fascinating text by R. Moses Cordovero printed and analyzed by Sack, *Kabbalah of Rabbi Moshe Cordovero,* pp. 232–233, and the tradition adduced by R. Ya'aqov Tzemaḥ, in the name of R. Ḥayyim Vital, in a gloss of the latter's *Peri 'Etz Ḥayyim,* ed. Dubrovna, fol. 108c and in R. Menaḥem Naḥum of Chernobyl, *Me'or 'Einayyim,* pp. 7–9.

58. On this issue see Idel, *Abraham Abulafia,* pp. 399–400.

59. Ibid., p. 404.

60. See Sara O. Heller Wilensky, "Messianism, Eschatology and Utopia in the Philosophical-Mystical Trend of Kabbalah," in Baras, ed., *Messianism and Eschatology,* pp. 235–236 (Hebrew); S. M. Stern, *Aristotle on the World State* (Columbia University Press, New York, 1968), pp. 80–82. On the view that the course of time is causing the actualization of the potential, in a messianic context, see also R. Yehudah Loew of Prague (the Maharal), *Sefer Netzaḥ Yisrael* (Prague, 1599), fol. 38d, chap. 26; see also chaps. 35–36 of this treatise (Hebrew). On the Maharal's messianism in general see Byron L. Sherwin, *Mystical Theology and Social Dissent: The Life and Work of Judah Loew of Prague* (Littman Library, London, Toronto, 1982), pp. 142–160; Rivka Schatz, "Maharal's Doctrine: Between Existence and Eschatology," in Baras, ed., *Messianism and Eschatology,* pp. 301–324; Gross, *Le messianisme juif;* Scholem, *Sabbatai Ṣevi,* pp. 65–66. On the notion of actualization as part of the messianic process see also the later material discussed by Liebes, *On Sabbateaism and Its Kabbalah,* pp. 56, 307n62.

61. Ms. Paris, Bibliothèque Nationale 608, fol. 304a. For an interesting parallel to this view, found in R. Yehudah ibn Matka's *Sefer Midrash Ḥokhmah,* see Idel, "Some Concepts of Time and History," par. 3.

62. Pines, *Between Jewish Thought,* pp. 277–305. On this issue see also Y. H. Yerushalmi, "Spinoza on the Existence of the Jewish People," *Proceedings of the Israeli Academy of Science* 6, no. 10 (1983), and also Ravitsky, " 'To the Utmost of Human Capacity,' " p. 225n7; Scholem, *Sabbatai Ṣevi,* p. 544. The view of a limited messianic period is not new with Abulafia but is already found in ancient apocalyptic texts. See e.g. Stone, *Fourth Ezra,* pp. 215–216.

63. Cf. Idel, *Language, Torah and Hermeneutics,* pp. 176–177, 196n99.

64. See Ms. Rome-Angelica 38, fols. 14b–15a; Ms. Munich 285, fol. 39b. Compare also to

Scholem, *Major Trends*, pp. 140, 382 and Idel, *Mystical Experience*, pp. 126–127, where some other details of this passage have been analyzed. The reader is invited to complement the reading of our discussion here with the decodings of the gematria, found in these pages, which shall not be repeated in this context.

65. See Idel, *Chapters in Ecstatic Kabbalah*, pp. 58–59. Already in the BT, *Rosh ha-Shanah*, fol. 11ab, there is a dictum claiming that the world was created in the New Year, the people of Israel were redeemed on the New Year, and they will be redeemed again on the New Year. This view was adduced by Abulafia in his *Sefer Ḥayyei ha-Nefesh*, Ms. Munchen 408, fol. 18a. For redemption on New Year in a somewhat Lurianic vein of Kabbalah, which assumes that this day is the moment for repentance, after which Adam will restore creation to its pristine glory, described as the actualization of the potential, see R. Naḥman of Braslav, *Liqqutei Halakhot*, Hilekhot hekhsher Kelim, chap. 4. For the possibility that the month of Tishrei was the time when the coming of the Messiah was expected see Dodd, *Interpretation of the Fourth Gospel*, pp. 350–351.

66. See P. Volz, *Die Neujahrfest Jahwes* (Mohr, Tübingen, 1912); Mowinckel, *Psalms in Israel's Worship*, 1:106–107; idem, *He That Cometh*, pp. 139–143; *Zum israelitischen Neujahr und zur Deutung der Thronbesteinungspsalmen* (Oslo, 1953); Julian Morgenstern, "The New Year of Kings," in B. Schindler and A. Marmorstein, eds., *Occident and Orient: In Honour of Haham Dr. M. Gaster's 80th Birthday, Gaster Anniversary Volume* (Taylor's Foreign Press, London, 1936), pp. 439–456; idem, "The Mythological Background of Ps. 82," *HUCA* 14 (1939), pp. 44–70; idem, "The Cultic Setting of the 'Enthronement Psalms,'" *HUCA* 35 (1964), pp. 1–42; Widengren, *Sakrales Königtum*, pp. 62–79; Patai, "Hebrew Installation Rites," pp. 172, 188; Moshe Weinfeld, "Expectation of the Kingdom of God in the Bible," in Baras, ed., *Messianism and Eschatology*, pp. 73–96 (Hebrew); A. J. Wensinck, "The Semitic New Year and the Origin of Eschatology," *Acta Orientalia* 1 (1923), pp. 158–199; Frankfort, *Kingship and the Gods*, pp. 313–333; Engnell, *Divine Kingship*, pp. 33–36, 201; Halpern, *Constitution*, pp. 95–109; Eliade, *Cosmos and History*, pp. 51–73; Patai, *Man and Temple*, pp. 38–40. See also below, app. 2, n. 41. For a critique of the myth-and-ritual connection between the Jewish New Year and coronation of the king see Norman H. Snaith, *The Jewish New Year* (Society for Promoting Christian Knowledge, London, 1947), pp. 207–208. For other instances of redemption expected at the New Year, unrelated to Abulafia, see Abraham Michael Cardoso's prophecy concerning the beginning of redemption at the New Year of 1674; cf. *Tzitzat Novel Tzevi*, p. 361 as well as my discussion of the Besht, below, chap. 7. It should be mentioned that the phrase *beit ha-miqdash* is numerically equivalent to *rosh ha-shanah*, namely 861. The nexus between the two phrases was already pointed out by R. Eleazar of Worms, in two of this writings, *Sefer ha-Ḥokhmah* and *Commentary on the Torah;* see *Perush ha-Roqeaḥ 'al ha-Torah*, ed. S. Y. Kanievsky (Benei Beraq, vol. 1, pp. 17, 54 respectively. Once again the Hasidei Ashkenaz literature preserved an ancient view, which found a more elaborate expression in Abraham Abulafia's thought.

67. See Even Shmuel, *Midreshei Ge'ullah*, p. 70; translated in Patai, *Messiah Texts*, pp. 110–111. The double nature of the Messiah, as wounded and beautiful, perhaps influenced Abulafia's view of Metatron as both an old man, a *sheikh*, and a *na'ar*. See Idel, *Mystical Experience*, p. 117; idem, *Studies in Ecstatic Kabbalah*, p. 94, and Gedaliahu G. Stroumsa, "Polymorphie divine et transformations d'un mythologeme: 'L'Apocryphon de Jean' et ses sources," *Vigiliae Christianae* 34 (1981), pp. 422–424, now in his *Savoir et Salut*, pp. 56–59. On the importance of beauty in general in the Heikhalot literature and related ancient texts see Rachel Elior, "The Concept of God in Hekhalot Literature," *JSJT* 6, pp. 13–58 (Hebrew), and Deutsch, *Gnostic Imagination*, pp. 94–99. On the messianic overtones of R. Gadiel the infant, also described as *na'ar*, a figure that occurs in the pseudepigraphic *Seder Gan 'Eden*, and its similarity to Metatron see Scholem, *Devarim be-Go*, p.

280, and Liebes, "The Angels of the Shofar," p. 182. See also Liebes's discussion of revelations of young and old in the Zohar, "Myth vs. Symbol," pp. 219–223.

68. Idel, "Maimonides and Kabbalah," pp. 65–66.

69. On this expression as pointing to *unio mystica* see Idel, *Studies in Ecstatic Kabbalah,* pp. 10–12; idem, *Mystical Experience,* pp. 126–128. Here we have an important case which opens the way for a reading of the *mashiyaḥ* as a divine entity when functioning as a messianic figure according to Abulafia's understanding of the term *Messiah.* Compare, however, Scholem, *Kabbalah,* p. 334.

70. See especially *Sefer ha-'Ot* and the passage from this book translated by Patai, *Messiah Texts,* pp. 178–180. On the apocalyptic nature of *Sefer ha-'Ot* see Aescoly, *Jewish Messianic Movements,* p. 231. On the coexistence of two modes of approaching other topics related to messianism—the Temple and Jerusalem—see the interesting remarks of Levenson, *Sinai and Zion,* pp. 178–182; Idel, "Land of Israel," pp. 193–195. Compare, however, Taubes, "Price of Messianism," p. 496, who sees interiorization as the result of a "crisis within Jewish eschatology itself." This statement implies that there is one single messianic idea characteristic of Jewish eschatology which, when faltering, produces spiritualization, a view which is not far from the way Scholem portrayed the spiritualization of early sixteenth-century apocalypticism in Kabbalah of Safed. This attitude assumes the impossibility of coexistence of the different modes of redemption, an issue that seems to me to be simplistic. On allegorical interpretations of messianic issues in Abulafia see Idel, *Studies in Ecstatic Kabbalah,* p. 53.

71. Ms. Paris, Bibliothèque Nationale 774, fols. 129b-130b; Idel, *Mystical Experience,* p. 118. For a more explicit connection between Metatron, *mashiyaḥ,* and Son see Abulafia's succinct remark in his commentary on Exodus, *Mafteaḥ ha-Shemot,* Ms. New York, JTS 1897, fol. 77a.

72. *Medabber.* In the Middle Ages, this term can also be translated as "thinking." Nevertheless, the Agent Intellect is characterized by Abulafia in linguistic terms, several times in his writings, including its description as the primordial speech. See the material on speech and the Agent Intellect collected and discussed in Idel, *Abraham Abulafia,* pp. 92–93. A connection between the word and the Messiah is found already in the Gospel of John, which may have been influenced by Philo. See Dodd, *Interpretation of the Fourth Gospel,* pp. 68–73, 263–285, 318–332. For more on speech and messianism in Abulafia see below, app. 1, and in the discussions on speech and messianism in chap. 7. Both in ecstatic Kabbalah and in some Hasidic schools, the assumption of the existence of an ontological linguistic level, which plays a role in the messianic event, is determinative of the respective forms of messianism. The two forms of Jewish mysticism conspicuously emphasize the linguistic and audative aspects of human activity. Compare, however, Wolfson's assertion, *Through a Speculum,* as to the dominant visual aspect of Jewish mysticism.

73. This text is influenced by the Hebrew translation of Abu Nasr Al-Farabi's treatise, called *Hatḥalat ha-Nimtza'ot,* Filipowski, ed., printed in *He-'Asif* (London, 1847), p. 2. The same context has been quoted verbatim in another commentary on the *Guide of the Perplexed* by Abulafia, *Sefer Ḥayyei ha-Nefesh,* Ms. München 408, fol. 12b. See already the remarks of Moritz Steinschneider, *Al-Farabi* (St. Petersburg, 1869), p. 243.

74. 'Eliyahu, like *ben,* means "son" and is numerically equivalent to fifty-two.

75. In gematria, fifty-two equals twice the Tetragrammaton, as hinted at by "double name."

76. *Hu' ha-Go'el* in gematria equals fifty-two, as do the two following words. *Ba-kol* may point to an immanentistic theology. The description "ruler of the world" reflects both the talmudic concept of the prince of the world and the kingly perception of this figure in the Hebrew Enoch. For the same expression, *manhig ha-'olam,* in the context of Metatron see R. Eleazar of Worms, *Sefer ha-Ḥokhmah,* Ms. Oxford 1568, fol. 21a, quoted by Wolfson, *Through a Speculum,* pp. 259–260. On

the concept of the ruler of the world in ancient Jewish texts see Alan F. Segal, "Ruler of This World: Attitudes about Mediator Figures and the Importance of Sociology for Self-Definition," in E. P. Sanders and A. Mendelsohn, eds., *Jewish and Christian Self-Definition* (Fortress Press, Philadelphia, 1981), 2:245–268; Couliano, *Experiences de l'extase,* pp. 69–70. On Metatron as appointed over the world see also a text analyzed in Idel, "Kabbalistic Prayer," pp. 272–273, and idem, *Abraham Abulafia,* p. 92.

77. See esp. Abrams, "Boundaries," p. 301.

78. See Hurtado, *One God,* pp. 79–81. Fossum, *Name of God,* pp. 289, 318–321, has pointed out the significance of this angel within earlier Jewish traditions. See esp. p. 320, where he suggests a certain nexus between Yaho'el and the high priest, a motif that recurs in the case of Metatron later on. See also p. 307, where Fossum mentions the plausibility that Yao is a name of the Christ and has to do with a savior figure. The single instance when Yaho'el is mentioned together with Abraham in Jewish tradition, except in the Apocalypse of Abraham, is a passage in R. 'Ephrayyim ben Shimshon's *Commentary on the Torah,* 1:77, where the term *ba-kol* was interpreted, again by means of gematria, as pointing to Yaho'el, described as a magical name that belongs to the Prince of the Face. However, I doubt very much if Abraham Abulafia's encounter with Yaho'el stems from this passage.

79. G. H. Box, *Apocalypse of Abraham* (London, 1918) p. xxv; Odeberg, *Hebrew Enoch,* pp. 99, 144; Scholem, *Major Trends,* pp. 68–69; idem, *Origins of the Kabbalah,* p. 187; idem, *Jewish Gnosticism,* p. 51; idem, *Kabbalah,* p. 378; Smith, *Map,* pp. 51–53; Greenfield, *Prolegomenon,* p. xxxi; Wolfson, *Through a Speculum,* p. 224; Deutsch, *Gnostic Imagination,* pp. 52, 97–98; Schultz and Spatz, *Sinai and Olympus,* p. 652. For the occurrence of the two names in a text printed by Montgomery see Greenfield, *Prolegomenon,* p. xxxix; idem, "Notes," p. 156.

80. Scholem, *Major Trends,* pp. 68–69; idem, *Origins of the Kabbalah,* pp. 89, 186–187.

81. An issue that I cannot enter into here is whether Abulafia had access to a version of the Ashkenazi text where some additions have been inserted and was acquainted with less than the "original" Ashkenazi passage. On the Ashkenazi influence on Abulafia's Kabbalah see Idel, *Mystical Experience,* pp. 22–24.

82. See the version printed by Dan, *Esoteric Theology,* p. 221.

83. Exodus 23:20–21. On the theology of the divine name in ancient Judaeo-Christian tradition see the detailed treatment of Danielou, *Theologie du Judeo-Christianisme,* pp. 71, 75, 235–251, and Fossum, *Name of God,* passim, esp. pp. 81–82.

84. Scholem, *Major Trends,* p. 68.

85. See Stroumsa, *Savoir et Salut,* pp. 58–59, 62, 74, 79, 82–83; Deutsch, *Gnostic Imagination,* p. 98.

86. Liebes, "Angel of the Shofar."

87. See the version established by Liebes, "Angels of the Shofar," p. 176.

88. The scholarly literature on this issue is vast. Basic references include Flusser, *Judaism and the Origins of Christianity,* pp. 526–534; Mowinckel, *He That Cometh,* pp. 346–450; J. A. Emerton, "The Origin of the Son of Man Imagery," *Journal of Theological Studies* 9 (1958), pp. 225–242; T. W. Manson, "The Son of Man in Daniel, Enoch and the Gospels," *Bulletin of the John Ryland Library* 32, (1950), pp. 171–193; Dodd, *Interpretation of the Fourth Gospel,* pp. 241–249; Mueller, *Messias und Menschensohn,* passim; Black, "Throne-Theophany Prophetic Commission"; Paula Fredriksen, *From Jesus to Christ: The Origin of the New Testament Images of Jesus* (Yale University Press, New Haven, 1988), pp. 50–52, 84–85, 138–139; Pearson, *Gnosticism, Judaism,* pp. 64–65, 190–191; Cohn, *Cosmos, Chaos,* pp. 172–173.

89. Son of Man: see Mueller, *Messias und Menschensohn,* pp. 54–60; eschatological judge: see

Mowinckel, *He That Cometh,* pp. 393–399; in Ashkenazi text: see Liebes, "Angels of the Shofar," p. 175.

90. Patai, *Messiah Texts,* p. 167. On messianism in this book see Michael Stone, "The Question of the Messiah in 4 Ezra," in Neusner et al., eds., *Judaisms and Their Messiahs,* pp. 209–224, as well as his many discussions in his *Fourth Ezra;* J. H. Charlesworth, "From Messianology to Christology," in Neusner et al., eds., *Judaisms and Their Messiahs,* pp. 241–245.

91. See Idel, "Enoch Is Metatron"; idem, *Mystical Experience,* pp. 195–203.

92. See *Sefer Livyat Ḥen,* Ms. Vatican 192, fol. 76a, Ms. Munich 58, fol. 153a. On this treatise see Colette Sirat, "Les differentes versions du Liwyat Ḥen de Levi ben Abraham," *REJ* 122 (1963), pp. 167–177.

93. H. A. Wolfson, *The Philosophy of Spinoza: Unfolding the Latent Processes of His Reasoning* (New York, 1969), 1:243.

94. See the anonymous *Sefer ha-Tzeruf,* Ms. Paris, Bibliothèque Nationale 774, fol. 192b. See also Wolfson, "Doctrine of the Sefirot," p. 370n101.

95. See Wirszubski, *Pico della Mirandola,* pp. 231–233.

96. Collins, "Place of Apocalypticism," 541–542, 549; idem, *Apocalyptic Vision,* pp. 96–104. On the great importance of descriptions related to Enoch in ancient Jewish literature for the proper understanding of ancient Christianity see the outstanding remarks by Flusser, *Judaism and the Origins of Christianity,* pp. 531–534; Fossum, *Name of God,* pp. 295–298. For Enoch in magic bowls see Greenfield, "Notes," pp. 150–154.

97. See Mowinckel, *He That Cometh,* p. 357.

98. See Moshe Idel, "Hermeticism and Judaism," in I. Merkel and A. Debus, eds., *Hermeticism and the Renaissance* (Cranbury, N.J., Folger Library, 1988), pp. 59–76; Pearson, *Gnosticism, Judaism,* pp. 138–140.

99. This is the case with the references in the book of the Zohar to Books of Enoch which are dismissed as pseudepigraphy. For Abulafia's testimony that there is a "Kabbalah," about whose content he is not so happy, as it deals with corporeal survival—and apparently also their return in the eschaton—related to Enoch and 'Eliyahu which was accepted, as Abulafia explicitly indicates, even by the Christians—see *Sitrei Torah,* Ms. Paris, Bibliothèque Nationale 774, fol. 132b. On the corporeal ascent of these two martyrs in ancient Christianity see Danielou, *Theologie du Judeo-Christianisme,* p. 79. The whole question of the mention of books of Enoch in the *Zohar* and in Moses de Leon's Hebrew writings has not been examined closely by any scholar since Jellinek. See his *Bet ha-Midrasch,* 3:195–197 and Scholem's interesting remark in *Major Trends,* p. 200. For the impact of parts of Enochic literature on Manicheanism see John C. Reeves, *Jewish Lore in Manichaean Cosmogony* (Hebrew Union College Press, Cincinnati, 1992).

100. I hope to deal with the impact of Enochic traditions on Hasidism in a separate study. For the time being, see the mid-nineteenth-century view of R. Yehudah Leib of Yanov, *Sefer Qol Yehudah* (NP, 1906), reprinted in *Sefarim Qedoshim mi-Talmidei ha-Besht* (Brookline, Mass., 1984), vol. 14, fol. 21cd., where the theory of mystical union between the human and Agent Intellect is related to both the intellection of God and the transformation of Enoch into Metatron. Compare also ibid., fol. 3ab. On Mormonism see Hugh Nibley, *Enoch the Prophet* (Deseret Book Co., Salt Lake City, 1986); Harold Bloom, *The American Religion: The Emergence of the Post-Christian Nation* (Simon and Schuster, New York, 1992), pp. 99, 105.

101. In fact the concept of enthronement is obvious already in the Ethiopian Enoch; see the lengthy discussion of Mowinckel, *He That Cometh,* pp. 388–390.

102. See Widengren, *Muhammad,* pp. 199–213.

103. *Ha-pitronot.* Another possible translation would be the interpretation of enigmatic visions.

104. *Be-mare'h.* It is quite reasonable to assume that Abulafia is hinting at his first name, Abraham, an anagram of *be-Mar'eh.*

105. *Ho'il.* This is a pun on *Yaho'el.* On p. 85 the same verb is used in order to point to God's agreement to redeem.

106. In gematria 248 is the value of Abraham, Abulafia's name. This name recurs on p. 85.

107. This name is numerically equivalent to Shmu'el, the name of Abulafia's father.

108. *Meshiḥiy,* "my Messiah," is an anagram of *ḥamiyshiy.* This pun is found already in R. Eleazar of Worms' *Commentary on the Torah* (see n. 66, above), vol. 1, p. 77, and in R. Efrayyim ben Shimshon's *Perush 'al ha-Torah,* 1:11. See also R. Yitzḥaq of Acre's description of the ascending process of cleaving, which culminates with the fifth stage, the union with the Infinite; cf. Ms. Moscow-Guensburg 775, fol. 233b.

109. *Sefer ha-'Ot,* pp. 84–85.

110. See the translation of R. Rubinkiewicz, *The Old Testament Pseudepigrapha,* J. J. Charlesworth ed. (Doubleday, Garden City, N.Y., 1983) 1:697, par. 9. In *Sefer ha-'Ot* (as quoted above) and the Apocalypse of Abraham the same angel is causing Abraham to get to his feet after he fell on his face. As it has been pointed out, the Apocalypse, preserved only in ancient Russian, reflects a Hebrew original. See A. Rubinstein, "Hebraisms in Slavonic 'Apocalypse of Abraham,'" *JJS* 4 (1953), pp. 108–115; 5 (1954), pp. 132–135. Since since it seems improbable that the connection between Yaho'el and Abraham is mere coincidence, or that Abulafia's story about his encounter is derived from the Hebrew material I am acquainted with, I suggest that Abulafia may have known an inextant version of the Apocalypse of Abraham—perhaps a Greek version in Byzantium.

111. On this issue see Martha Himmelfarb, "R. Moses the Preacher and the Testaments of the Twelve Patriarchs," *AJSR* 9, no. 1 (1984), pp. 55–78.

112. See Exodus 24:18; 1 Kings 19:8.

113. *Liy hu',* an anagram of *'Eliyahu.*

114. *Sefer Ḥayyei ha-'Olam ha-Ba',* Ms. Paris, Bibliothèque Nationale 777, fol. 113a; Ms. Oxford 1582, fols. 22b-23a.

115. *Ḥanokh ben Yared.* The numerical value of this phrase is 350, which is precisely that of *mokhiaḥ dabbraniy.* In *Sitrei Torah,* Ms. Paris, Bibliothèque Nationale 774, fol. 130a, Abulafia quoted from a version of the Ashkenazi treatise mentioned above, and there it is written that Metatron is called Enoch.

116. *Mokhiaḥ dabbraniy.* This is an unusual expression, which was created in order to meet the numerical equivalence.

117. *Banu.* On this issue see Idel, *Mystical Experience,* pp. 83–86.

118. There is a venerable Christian tradition about the arrival of the two harbingers before the second coming of the Christ. However, one cannot exclude the possibility of an earlier Jewish tradition that influenced the Christian one and was marginalized in Jewish circles, to the extent that only Elijah remained the harbinger of the messianic message. Abulafia himself mentions this tradition in his *Sefer Sitrei Torah,* Ms. Paris, Bibliothèque Nationale 774, fol. 132b, and see Liebes, "Angels of the Shofar," pp. 178–179; Idel, "Enoch Is Metatron," p. 227.

119. Ms. New York, JTS 1801, fol. 13b.

120. *Commentary on Ma'arekhet ha-'Elohut,* fol. 96b. See also Werblowsky, *Joseph Karo,* pp. 220–221, and *Yalqut Re'uveni,* passim.

121. Idel, "Enoch Is Metatron," p. 229.

122. Liebes, "Angels of the Shofar," p. 175.

123. Liebes, ibid., interprets it as pointing to Jesus.

124. See Dan, *Esoteric Theology,* pp. 221–222.

125. *Sefer Sitrei Torah,* Ms. Paris, Bibliothèque Nationale 774, fol. 130a.

126. Ms. München 408, fol. 36b.

127. Job 19:26. On the medieval interpretations of this verse see Alexander Altmann, *Von der mittelalterichen zur modernen Aufklärung* (J. C. B. Mohr, Tübingen, 1987), pp. 1–33.

128. "My heart." On the heart as the locus of revelation see the above quotation from *Sefer ha-Ḥesheq.*

129. Ms. München 11, fol. 152b.

130. Compare the former's *Perush 'al ha-Torah,* 1:106, where he uses the numerical value of the unusual term *seter* to extract the value of *'elef ve-ra"tz.* Abulafia also uses this term for messianic computations. See e.g. *Sefer Gan Na'ul,* Ms. München 316, fol. 328b.

131. On the possible source of apocalypticism in priestly groups see Cook, *Prophecy and Apocalypticism,* pp. 71–74, 215–218. For the identification of the king with the high priest as part of the royal ideology see Widengren, *Sakrales Königtum,* pp. 17–33; E. O. James, "The Sacred Kingship and the Priesthood," in *The Sacral Kingship,* pp. 63–70; Flusser, *Judaism and the Origins of Christianity,* pp. 94n22, 97, 186, 284–287. For a medieval instance of a Messiah that was a Kohen, see Mann, "Messianic Movements," pp. 336, 338. Mann has already pointed out the similarity between this Messiah, who was a Karaite, and the Qumran view, found in *The Damascus Document,* 19:10–11, where the Messiah is also a descendant of Aharon. See also his "Obadya, Proselyte Normand Converti au Judaisme, et Sa Meguilla," *REJ* 89 (1930), pp. 255–256. The possible link between the priestly nature of the Messiah in Qumran and in the case of the Karaite, pointed out already by Mann, has passed unnoticed by Wieder, *Judean Scrolls,* pp. 54–55n2, whose important book is devoted to the affinities between Karaitism and the Qumran sect. See, however, the crucial remark of Baron, "Reappearance of Pseudo-Messiahs," in Saperstein, ed., *Essential Papers,* pp. 245–246. See also Liebes, *Studies in the Zohar,* pp. 65, 188 note 185. The existence of the Karaite Kohen who also claimed to be the Messiah in the early twelfth century may serve as an example for the possibility of a continuation of ancient messianic themes from antiquity until thirteenth-century Kabbalah. The nexus between the power of the Messiah to perform miracles by the spirit of his lips and Aharon's being the speaker for Moses is found in the collectanaea of Kabbalistic traditions stemming from Shlomo Molkho's entourage, Ms. Moscow-Guensburg 302. On a much later assumption that the Messiah is Moses, and thus a Kohen, see Manor, *Exile and Redemption,* p. 197. A contemporary of Abulafia, R. Levi ben Abraham, claims that "the [term] Mashiyaḥ will designate only the most noble and the greatest among the human rulers, [one who is] a Kohen, Mashiyaḥ and King." *Sefer Livyat Ḥen,* printed in *Ginzei Nistarot* (1875), p. 137.

132. Ms. New York, JTS 843, fol. 86a. See also Berger, "Abraham Abulafia," in Saperstein, ed., *Essential Papers,* p. 251, who claims that Abulafia was influenced by the Christian view of Melchizedek. Berger's view that in this passage Abulafia identifies with his wife following speculation related to the perfection of the androgynous state seems to me more than dubious.

133. On Melchizedek see Johnson, *Sacral Kingship,* pp. 47–48, 53, 131, 136; Paul J. Kobelski, *Melchizedek and Melchiresha'* (Catholic Biblical Association of America, Washington, 1981); Flusser, *Judaism and the Origins of Christianity,* pp. 186–192, 255–260, 265; Pearson, *Gnosticism, Judaism,* pp. 14–15, 23, 25–26, 108–123, 184–188; Ithamar Gruenwald, *Maḥanayyim,* vol. 124 (1970), pp. 93–94 (Hebrew); Greenfield, *Prolegomenon,* pp. xx–xxi; Hurtado, *One God,* pp. 78–79; Leach, *L'unité de l'homme,* pp. 240–259; Fossum, *Name of God,* pp. 183–187; Couliano, *Experiences de l'extase,* pp. 73–74. On medieval reverberations of this figure see Georges Vajda, "Melchisedec dans la mythologie ismaelienne," *Journal Asiatique* 234 (1943–45), pp. 173–183. For more on Mechizedek in Abulafia see Wolfson, "Doctrine of Sefirot," pp. 364–365. Extremely important in the context of the nexus between Abulafia and Melchizedek is a passage in *Leviticus Rabba* 25:6 where the

priesthood is described as taken away from Melchizedek and given to Abraham. See also BT, *Nedarim,* fol. 32b. Abulafia, unlike the Christian sources, was concerned not with the superiority of the priestly Melchizedek but with his rendering his priesthood to Abraham. André Feuillet, *The Priesthood of Christ and His Minister,* trans. M. J. O'Connell (Doubleday, Garden City, N.Y., 1975).

134. BT, *Qiddushin,* fol. 71a.

135. Here the term *qabbalah* may stand for either tradition in the broader sense of the word or, more plausibly, the Kabbalistic tradition, which was related in several early medieval texts, pre-Kabbalistic and Kabbalistic, to the divine name. See Moshe Idel, "Defining Kabbalah: The Kabbalah of the Divine Names," in R. A. Herrera, ed., *Mystics of the Book: Themes, Topics, and Typology* (Peter Lang, New York, 1993) pp. 97–122. See also Rachel Elior, "Between the Mundane Palace and the Celestial Palaces," *Tarbiẓ* 64 (1995), pp. 363–369 (Hebrew).

136. *Sefer Ḥayyei ha-'Olam ha-Ba',* Ms. Oxford 1582, fol. 13a. For more on the Messiah and names see above, n. 25, and *Sha'arei Tzedeq,* p. 16.

137. Abulafia is therefore reducing the function of the high priest to only one of his religious activities, the pronunciation of the divine name, ignoring the sacrificial duties.

138. For another instance of a nexus between the high priest and the Messiah see the seventeenth-century English thinker Anne Conway, who was acquainted with Lurianic Kabbalah: *The Principles of the Most Ancient and Modern Philosophy,* ed. Allison P. Coudert and Taylor Corse (Cambridge University Press, Galsgow, 1996), p. 24.

139. See Idel, *Mystical Experience,* pp. 105–108; idem, *Studies in Ecstatic Kabbalah,* pp. 125–126.

140. See *Sefer Ḥayyei ha-'Olam ha-Ba',* Ms. Paris, Bibliothèque Nationale 777, fol. 127b. See also *Mafteaḥ ha-Shemot,* Ms. New York, JTS 843, fol. 48a, and in a more detailed manner in app. 1 below.

141. *Sefer Ḥayyei ha-'Olam ha-Ba',* Ms. Oxford 1582, fol. 13a.

142. See Idel, "Defining Kabbalah," p. 109.

143. See the evidence brought by R. Jacob Sasportas, *Tzitzat Novel Tzevi,* p. 4, Scholem, *Kabbalah,* p. 247, and idem, Sabbatai Ṣevi, pp. 142–143, where Scholem attempts to weaken the messianic valence of the testimony by claiming that it is "a literary embellishment." Scholem's claim that there was no public messianic aspect of the pronunciation is not corroborated by Sasportas's passage, where he mentions some friends of the young Sabbatai, who encouraged him. See also the salient critique of Tishby on this point, *Paths of Faith and Heresy,* pp. 264–265. On the pronunciation of the divine name in the messianic era according to a late Hasidic author, see Weiss, *Studies,* pp. 241–242.

144. See Even Shmuel, *Midreshei Ge'ullah,* p. 103. Abulafia, who thought of himself as Messiah ben David, refers only rarely to Messiah ben Joseph, whom he identifies as Jesus. In general, his emphasis on *via perfectionis* did not leave room for a pivotal role for a figure that epitomizes *via passionis.* For the importance of this messianic figure in other forms of Kabbalah, see Liebes, "Jonas as Messiah ben Joseph," esp. p. 278.

145. Cf. *Numbers Rabba'* 12:12. See Himmelfarb, *Ascent to Heaven,* pp. 23–25, 45, 132 notes 73–74; Elior, "Between the Mundane Palace and the Celestial Palaces," pp. 349–351. On Metatron as high priest see also the magical text printed by Peter Schaefer und Shaul Shaked, *Magische Texte aus der Kairoer Geniza* (J. C. B. Mohr, Tübingen, 1994), 1:164, 173. Although I believe that Himmelfarb and Elior are right in pointing out the similarity between some of the details of the investiture of Enoch when he becomes Metatron and the anointment of the high priest, some of the other details of the description of the elevated Enoch are conspicuously reminiscent of a royal coronation, such as mention of a kingly crown. Thus, in addition to the figure of the high priest, the concept of the king is also essential for the new status of Enoch, who becomes a ruler or angelic governer, *sar.* Thus

again sacral royalty and messianism converge. The persistence of the priestly descriptions related to the ascent theme in the literature analyzed by Himmelfarb and Elior may have something to do with the nexus between the Messiah as a transcendent persona and his priestly extraction in some of the apocryphal writings. See Klausner, *Messianic Idea in Israel*, pp. 304–309. In *Sefer ha-Ḥesheq*, which deals with the seventy names of Metatron, the theme of the high priest is frequent. See Odeberg, *Hebrew Enoch*, p. 120.

146. *Yitboded*, a verb that may be translated also as "concentrate mentally": see Idel, *Studies in Ecstatic Kabbalah*, pp. 108–111.

147. Ms. Sasoon 56, fol. 34a.

148. On the Holy of the Holiest in Jewish mysticism see Scholem, *Major Trends*, p. 379n9; Wolfson, *Through a Speculum*, pp. 20–22. See also *Philo of Alexandria*, translation and introduction by David Winston (Paulist Press, New York, 1981), p. 254; Joshua Finkel, "The Guises and Vicissitudes of a Universal Folk-Belief in Jewish and Greek Tradition," *Harry Austryn Wolfson Jubilee Volume*, English section (Jerusalem, 1965), 1:236–240, 242–243, where the possible relationship between midrashic material and Philo on the ecstatic experience of the high priest was dealt with; see also Mareen R. Niehoff, "What Is a Name? Philo's Mystical Philosophy of Language," *Jewish Studies Quarterly* 2 (1995), pp. 232–233. Philo is conceived as being of priestly origin: see Daniel P. Schwartz, "Philo's Priestly Descent," F. E. Greenspahn, E. Hilgert, and B. L. Mack, eds., *Nourished with Peace: Studies in Hellenistic Judaism in Memory of Samuel Sandmel* (Scholars Press, Chico, Calif., 1984), pp. 155–171; Wolfson, *Along the Path*, pp. 55–56; M. Idel, "Conceptualizations of Music in Jewish Mysticism," in *Enchanting Powers: Music in the World's Religions*, ed. L. E. Sullivan (Harvard University Press, Cambridge, Mass., 1997), pp. 161–169. On the Temple as an allegory for the mystical experience see Corbin, *Creative Imagination*, pp. 235, 277, 281–282. On the Holy of the Holies as the place of a mystical initiation where also an act of anointment takes place before a mystical communion see the important Gnostic *Gospel of Philip*, whose affinities to Jewish material have been pointed out by several scholars, e.g. Fossum, *Name of God*, p. 307.

149. *Divrei Ymei Yisrael*, 5:185; Shimeon Bernfeld also bases his work on Graetz; cf. his *Da'at 'Elohim* (Warsaw, 1899), p. 386n1 (Hebrew). See also Israel Friedlander, "Jewish-Arabic Studies," in *JQR*, n.s., 3 (1912–1913), p. 287n428; L. I. Newman, *Jewish Influence on Christian Reform Movements* (New York, 1925), p. 179; W. J. Bouwsma, *Concordia Mundi: The Career and Thought of Guillaume Postel* (Harvard University Press, Cambridge, Mass., 1957), p. 141. In his *Major Trends*, p. 126, Scholem translates Abulafia's words as follows: "He went to Rome to present himself before the Pope and to confer with him in the name of Jewry," whereas later on, in his Hebrew lectures, printed as *Ha-Kabbalah shel Sefer ha-Temunah ve-shel Avraham Abulafia*, ed. J. ben Shelomo (Akademon, Jerusalem, 1969), p. 114, he says: "and to speak with him in the name of Jewry, i.e., to demand from him: 'Let my people go'—this indicates that Abulafia was on a Messianic mission" (Hebrew). Scholem was inclined to marginalize the messianic elements in Abulafia. See e.g. his very concise treatment of this topic in *Major Trends*, p. 128.

150. See Idel, *Chapters in Ecstatic Kabbalah*, p. 67; to the list of scholars mentioned there should be added Greenstone, *Messiah Idea*, p. 170, and Silver, *History of Messianic Speculation*, pp. 88, 146n145.

151. Material that confirms my suggestion to this effect is found in an anonymous treatise that was written, in my opinion, by Abulafia. I have dealt with this new passage in my " 'Time of the End."

152. See Abulafia's declaration that "despite the fact that I know that there are many Kabbalists who are not perfect, thinking as they are that their perfection consists in not revealing a secret issue, I shall care neither about their thought not about their blaming me because of the disclosure, since

my view on this is very different from and even opposite to theirs." *Sefer 'Otzar 'Eden Ganuz,* Ms. Oxford 1580, fol. 55a. For another passage from the same book pointing to the same issue see fols. 25b–26a.

153. The poetic epilogue to his book *Ḥayyei ha-'Olam ha-Ba',* printed by Jellinek as an appendix to Abulafia's *Sefer ha-'Ot,* p. 87. For the propagandistic activity of Abulafia see also his *Commentary on Sefer ha-Yashar,* Ms. Roma-Angelica 38, fol. 41a. On the linkage between messianism and "missionnisme" see Jankelevitch, "L'esperance et la fin des temps," p. 16, quoting the Russian philosopher Nicolai Losski.

154. See also chap. 3, p. 123. On the connection between the name of God and the Messiah see chap. 6, pp. 199–202.

155. On his activity while a resident of Sicily see M. Idel, "The Ecstatic Kabbalah of Abraham Abulafia in Sicily and Its Transmission during the Renaissance," *Italia Judaica* 5 (1995), pp. 330–340.

156. See Aescoly, *Jewish Messianic Movements,* pp. 231–233.

157. See e.g. ibid., p. 231, where Aescoly speculates that Abulafia's *Sefer ha-'Ot* might have influenced *Sefer ha-Peliy'ah,* but for the time being I am unable to corroborate this suggestion, though there can be no doubt as to Abulafia's influence on this book.

158. Aescoly's contribution to the modern scholarship of messianism suffered unjustly, both because of the marginalization of the collection of messianic texts and introductions printed only in 1956, years after his death, and the fact that his two other volumes containing collections of messianic texts, which he completed before his death, remained in manuscripts. See e.g. the absence to his views in Scholem's descriptions of messianism as well as the complete absence of his, as well as the marginalization of Klausner's, views in Saperstein's collection *Essential Papers.*

159. I have adduced in this chapter salient material in order to portray the profound messianic character of the ecstatic Kabbalah, but I have not exhausted the pertinent texts. For further discussion, see appendix 1 and Idel, *Studies in Ecstatic Kabbalah,* pp. 45–62.

160. See e.g. Scholem, *Messianic Idea,* p. 39; Werblowsky, "Mysticism and Messianism."

161. Ibid. and his "Safed Revival," in Green, ed., *Jewish Spirituality,* 2:11. See esp. Dan, "Gershom Scholem and Jewish Messianism," p. 78, who recently decided to exclude Abulafia's name from his own earlier account of thirteenth-century messianism. Compare his "The Emergence of Messianic Mythology," p. 58. This dogmatic approach may be one of the reasons for the absence of new vistas in the field of mysticism and messianism.

Chapter 3: Concepts of Messiah in the Thirteenth and Fourteenth Centuries: Theosophical Forms of Kabbalah

1. On the view that the period of time under consideration is to be seen as part of a Renaissance development see Ben Sasson, *Retzef u-Temurah,* pp. 384–385; Robert Chazan, *European Jewry and the First Crusade* (University of California Press, Berkeley and Los Angeles, 1987), p. 194; Ivan Marcus, "Une communauté pieuse et la doute," *Annales: Histoire, Sciences Sociales* 5 (September–October, 1994), pp. 1046–1047n48; Idel, "Maimonides and Kabbalah," pp. 71–72; idem, *Kabbalah: New Perspectives,* p. 251; Ḥaviva Pedaya, "Figure and Image in the Kabbalistic Interpretation of Naḥmanides," *Maḥanayyim,* vol. 6 (Jerusalem, 1994), p. 114 (Hebrew); Anna Sapir Abulafia, *Christians and Jews in the Twelfth-Century Renaissance* (Routledge, London, 1995).

2. Scholem, *Messianic Idea,* pp. 38–39; idem, *Sabbatai Ṣevi,* p. 15. This view has been reiterated oftentimes by Werblowsky; see e.g. his "The Safed Revival," in Green, ed., *Jewish Spirituality,* 2:11, where he mentions the alleged "lack of messianic tension in the teachings of the early Kabbalists."

3. See Scholem, *Major Trends,* p. 20; Idel, "Types of Redemptive Activity," p. 273n85; "Maimonides and Kabbalah," p. 40.

4. See Moshe Halbertal, "R. Menaḥem Meiri: Between Torah and Wisdom," *Tarbiẓ* 63 (1994), p. 97 and n. 65 (Hebrew).

5. See Pedaya, "'Flaw" and "Correction,'" passim, as well as the passages in R. Ezra of Gerona, *Le Commentaire d'Ezra de Gerone sur le cantique des cantiques,* trans. Georges Vajda (Aubier, Montaigne, Paris, 1969), pp. 108, 132, 135, 143.

6. See the text printed by Gershom Scholem, "New Remnants from the Writings of R. Azriel of Gerona," *Sefer Zikkaron le-A. Gullak ve-S. Klein* (Jerusalem, 1942), pp. 211–213 (Hebrew), to be compared with Reuchlin's remark in *De Arte Cabalistica* (Basel, 1557), p. 862: "est enim Messiha [*sic!*] Virtus Dei." See Liebes, *Studies in the Zohar,* p. 182n141, and his discussion on the similar stand of R. Joseph Angelet, *Sefer Livenat ha-Sappir,* fols. 2a, 8c. See also Elqayam, *Mystery of Faith,* pp. 133–134, 325–326n66. For the ancient Jewish-Christian view see Gilles Quispel, "Genius and Spirit," in *Essays on the Nag Hamadi Texts,* ed. M. Krause (Brill, Leiden, 1975), p. 158. For another discussion of R. Azriel about the Messiah as comprising six powers, and thus perfect, see the "Letter to Burgos," whose authorship has been established by Scholem; see *Mada'ei ha-Yahadut,* vol. 2 (1927), p. 75. R. Azriel mentions the sin of man as the reason for the loss of perfection, which will be restored by the advent of the perfect Messiah.

7. See Silver, *History of Messianic Speculation,* pp. 83–85; Sarachek, *Doctrine of the Messiah,* pp. 162–191; Chazan, *Barcelona and Beyond,* pp. 172–187; Hartman, *Living Covenant,* pp. 249–253; David Novak, *The Theology of Naḥmanides Systematically Presented* (Scholars Press, Atlanta, 1992), pp. 125–134; Yael Sagiv-Feldman, "Living in Deferment: Maimonides vs. Naḥmanides on the Messiah, Redemption and the World to Come," *Hebrew Studies* 20–21 (1979–1980), pp. 107–116. On the impact of Nahmanides' calculation of the date of the advent on the Messiah in 1358 in the circle of the *Zohar* see R. Yitzḥaq ibn Avi Sahulah's *Commentary on the Song of Songs,* ed. Arthur Green, *JSJT* 6 (1987), pp. 488–490.

8. Shlomo Pines, "Naḥmanides on Adam in the Garden of Eden in the Context of Other Interpretations of Genesis, Chapters 2 and 3," in A. Mirsky, A. Grossman, and Y. Kaplan, eds., *Exile and Diaspora: Studies in the History of the Jewish People Presented to Professor Haim Beinart* (Ben Tzvi Institute, Jerusalem, 1988), pp. 159–164 (Hebrew); idem, "Truth and Falsehood versus Good and Evil," in I. Twersky, ed., *Studies in Maimonides* (Harvard University Press, Cambridge, Mass., 1990), pp. 155–157.

9. See e.g. *Sefer Ma'arekhet ha-'Elohut,* fols. 91b, 95b, 101b, 104a, 105a: *zeman ha-ḥefetz* and *'olam ha-ḥefetz;* R. Menaḥem Recanati, *Commentary on the Torah* (Jerusalem, 1961), fol. 91d. See also R. W. Southern, *The Making of the Middle Ages* (Yale University Press, New Haven, 1963), pp. 107ff. The nexus between the fall and the messianic redemption is therefore a theme that is found among Kabbalists since the thirteenth century. Cf. Goetschel, *Meir ibn Gabbay,* p. 464.

10. See Dan, "Beginning of the Messianic Mythology," pp. 57–68. Dan, who was not acquainted with the material to be mentioned in the following notes (some of it in manuscript when he wrote his essay), overemphasized the uniqueness of R. Yitzḥaq ha-Kohen's interest in messianism.

11. See Idel, "Introduction," p. 15; idem, "Beginnings of the Kabbalah," pp. 8–12. Cf. Greenstone, *Messiah Idea,* p. 169, who claims that the Jews saw the "Tartar" as the eschatological Jewish "Antichrist," namely the mythical Armilus. For another proposal for the emergence of the interest in messianism among these thirteenth-century Kabbalists, namely attempts to counteract the Christian propaganda, see Chazan, *Barcelona and Beyond,* pp. 189–190. On fears and expectations provoked by the Mongolian invasion see esp. Aescoly, *Jewish Messianic Movements,* pp. 167, 212–215, and the long footnote of Yehudah Even Shmuel to Aescoly's book, ibid., pp. 268–269; Lerner,

Powers of Prophecy; McGinn, *Visions of the End,* pp. 149–157; and Yerushalmi, *Zakhor,* p. 37. I wonder whether the messianic computations of the late thirteenth-century homelist R. Jacob ben Ḥananel, marginally influenced by Kabbalistic motifs, were not also influenced by the expectations related to the Mongols. On his messianic typology see Marc Saperstein, "Jewish Typological Exegesis after Naḥmanides," *Jewish Studies Quarterly,* vol. 1 (1993), pp. 161–162.

The first scholar who pointed out the surge of messianic aspirations during one generation in the second half of the thirteenth century was Graetz, "Stages in the Evolution," p. 166, without however attempting to offer any explanation to this phenomenon. See also app. 7 to Graetz, *Divrei Yimei Israel,* 5:373–375, who attempts to describe some of the apocalyptic treatises attributed to R. Shimeon bar Yohai against the eschatological ambiance of the mid-thirteenth century. He does not, however, address the issue of the rumors about the Mongols and the development of Kabbalah.

In precisely this period at least three Jewish authors predicted the advent of the Messiah in the year 1260. See Ariel Toaff, "Hints at a Messianic Movement in Rome in the Year 1260," *Bar 'Ilan, Sefer ha-Shanah* 14/15 (1977), pp. 114–121 (Hebrew). The two others are R. Yehudah ben Nissim ibn Malkah, cf. Idel, "The Beginnings of Kabbala," pp. 4–15, and a certain R. Moses ben Yehudah, perhaps a relative of R. Yehuda, in a treatise widespread in manuscripts, entitled *Commentary on the Hebrew Alphabet;* see e.g. Ms. Paris, Bibliothèque Nationale 711, fol. 66b. R. Yehudah and R. Moses adduced astrological views on order to account for their prediction; R. Moses openly writes that "all [the data] amount to five thousand and twenty years [=1260] and [then] the rule of Saturn [Sabbatai] will commence and during it our redemption will be with the help of Shadday, blessed be His Name" (ibid., fol. 66b; see also there fol. 66a). See also the rather contemporary astrological view printed in Marx, "Ma'amar," p. 198, mentioning the *coniunctio maxima* between Saturn and Jupiter. See Eric Zafran, "Saturn and the Jews," *Journal of the Warburg and Courtauld Institutes* 42 (1979), pp. 16–27; Jung, *Aion,* pp. 74–77, 111. Since the astrological view is not, by definition, part of Kabbalah—though its influence on some forms of Kabbalah was great—I limit my discussion on this issue to those astrological elements that were influential in my opinion on Kabbalah. For the importance of the *coniunctia maxima* for the emergence of a seminal Jewish figure, a prophet or Messiah, see also Malachi Beit-Arieh and Moshe Idel, "An Essay on the End and Astrology by R. Abraham Zacut," *QS* 54 (1979), pp. 174–194, 825–826 (Hebrew).

12. Compare Dan, "Beginning of the Messianic Mythology," p. 57–68.

13. On a survey of the mystical thought of this corpus see e.g. Tishby, *Wisdom of the Zohar;* Liebes, *Studies in the Zohar;* Wolfson, *Through a Speculum,* pp. 326–392. On a vision of the *Zohar* as a messianic book see Graetz, "Stages in the Evolution," p. 168. See also the collection of messianic issues in the *Zohar,* compiled by Dinur, *Israel ba-Golah,* pt. 2, vol. 4, pp. 391–400.

14. See Idel, *Kabbalah: New Perspectives,* pp. 112–199.

15. On the subject of zoharic messianism see Liebes, "Messiah of the *Zohar,*" passim; Aescoly, *Jewish Messianic Movements,* p. 260; Idel, "Types of Redemptive Activities," p. 266. In the following I have chosen to discuss the eschatological understanding of prayer, a main ritual in Judaism. I do not intend to inspect all the rituals from the eschatological point of view. A topic that deserves separate analysis is the structure of messianic rituals in Judaism in general and in Kabbalah in particular. See e.g. Joseph Gutmann, "The Messiah at the Seder," *Studies in Jewish History Presented to Professor Raphael Mahler,* ed. Sh. Yeivin (Sifriat Po'alim, Tel Aviv, 1974), pp. 29–38.

16. See Liebes, *Studies in the Zohar,* pp. 86–90.

17. The prayer of eighteen benedictions. The symbolism of *ge'ullah* and *tefillah* as pointing respectively to the last (tenth) sefirah and perhaps the ninth is already found in the early thirteenth-century Geronese Kabbalist R. Ya'aqov ben Sheshet's *Sefer ha-'Emunah ve-ha-Bitaḥon,* chap. 5, ed. Ch. D. Chavel, in *Kitvei ha-Ramban* (Mossad ha-Rav Kook, Jerusalem, 1964), 2:368 (Hebrew). On

this passage see Micheline Chaze, "Le sens esoterique du voeu et du serment selon quelques auteurs des XIIIe et XIVe siècles en Espagne et en Italie," *REJ* 138 (1979), pp. 245–246. See also R. Menaḥem Mendel of Kossov, *'Ahavat Shalom,* pp. 212–213.

18. This phrase has erotic connotations. See Idel, "Types of Redemptive Activity," pp. 267–268.

19. *Ha-Kol,* literally "all." See chap. 2, n. 19.

20. Ms. New York, JTS, 1577, quoted in J. Wijnhoven, *Sefer Maskkiyyot Kesef: Text and Transmission* (M.A. thesis, Brandeis University, Waltham, Mass., 1961), pp. 30–31. See also the similar discussion in de Leon's *Sheqel ha-Qodesh,* p. 96; Mopsik, *Le sicle,* p. 225; and the sixteenth-century Kabbalist R. Joseph ibn Tzayyaḥ, *Tzeror ha-Ḥayyim,* Ms. London-Montefiore 318, fol. 81a–82a.

21. Cf. *The Commentary on the Talmudic Aggadot,* ed. Isaiah Tishby (Magnes Press, Jerusalem, 1983), p. 34n15; Idel, "Types of Redemptive Activity," p. 268n61.

22. See e.g. *The Book of the Pomegranate,* Moses De Leon's *Sefer ha-Rimmon,* ed. Elliot R. Wolfson (Scholars Press, Atlanta, 1988), pp. 27 (and note to line 3), 28, 112; *Sheqel ha-Qodesh,* p. 94, Mopsik, *Le sicle,* p. 225.

23. See *Zohar,* vol. 1, fol. 132b.

24. According to this formulation, the arrival of the sons of Israel to the land antedates the redemption, not being part of the process of redemption itself. On the land of Israel as a symbol for the last sefirah, see Idel, "Land of Israel," pp. 170–187. As I have shown in this article, the land of Israel has explicit erotic connotations in Kabbalah, some of them implicit in earlier sources.

25. In Aramaic *da'* means literally "this," and it stands for each of the two hypostases.

26. *Zohar Ḥadash: Midrash Ruth ha-Ne'elam,* ed. R. Margolioth, fol. 88b. For a French translation of this text see Charles Mopsik, *Le Livre de Ruth* (Verdier, Lagrasse, 1987), p. 179.

27. Compare a similar use in Moses de Leon's contemporary, and probably also his acquaintance, the famous Kabbalist R. Joseph Gikatilla, *Sefer Sha'arei Tzedeq* (Cracow, 1881), fol. 13b.

28. Idel, *Kabbalah: New Perspectives,* pp. 210–218.

29. At least in the first quotation there is also another set, stemming from a philosophical writing: the two lights. However, provided that they were already used in a Kabbalistic text written before the time of de Leon, we may ignore them as an independent set.

30. For significant eschatological elements implied in the theosophy and theurgy of R. Yitzḥaq Sagi Nahor, one of the main early Kabbalists, see Pedaya, " 'Flaw' and 'Correction.' "

31. See Idel, *Kabbalah: New Perspectives,* p. 57.

32. Liebes, "Messiah of the *Zohar,*" pp. 91, 99; ibid., *Studies in the Zohar,* pp. 1–12.

33. See Idel, *Kabbalah: New Perspectives,* pp. 210–218.

34. See the *Responsum of the* RASHBA, vol. 1, par. 548, printed in *Responsa of the* RASHBA, ed. C. Z. Dimitrovski (Mossad Ha-Rav Kook, Jerusalem, 1990), 1:100–107 (Hebrew).

35. See M. Idel, "On Symbolic Self-Interpretations in Thirteenth-Century Jewish Writings," *Hebrew University Studies in Literature and the Arts* 16 (1988), pp. 90–96.

36. This symbolism is widespread in the later phase of the zoharic literature called *Tiqqunei Zohar* and *Ra'ya' Meheymna';* See e.g. *Zohar,* vol. 3, fol. 243b.

37. Liebes, *Studies in the Zohar,* pp. 17–19; idem, *On Sabbateaism and Its Kabbalah,* pp. 62, 317n123; Wolfson, *Circle in the Square,* pp. 117–121, 231–232n198. See also R. Joseph Gikatilla's *Sefer Sha'arei 'Orah,* chap. 2, ed. Joseph ben Shlomo (Mossad Bialik, Jerusalem, 1970), 1:94, and the discussion of redemption of the late eighteenth-century Hasidic master strongly influenced by Lurianic symbolism R. Ḥayyim of Chernovitz, *Sefer Be'er Mayyim Ḥayyim* (n.d., n.p.), vol. 1, pt. 1, fol. 26cd.

38. See *Zohar,* vol. 1, fols. 84a, 238a; vol. 2, fol. 127a; see Scholem, *Studies and Texts,* p. 245n73.

Compare also the view of the horn of the Messiah in the anonymous *Sefer Ma'arekhet ha-'Elohut,* fol. 67b.

39. *Sefer Sheqel ha-Qodesh,* pp. 90–91, Mopsik, *Le sicle,* pp. 220–221. Compare also Scholem, *Kabbalah,* p. 334; idem, "Two Treatises by R. Moses de Leon," *Qovetz 'al Yad,* n.s., 8 (1976), p. 343 and n. 104 (Hebrew); idem, *Sabbatai Ṣevi,* pp. 870–871. See the discussion preserved in R. Alexander Axelrod's Keter Shem Tov, printed also under the name of a certain Kabbalist named R. Menaḥem, the student of R. Eleazar of Worms, in Jellinek, *Auswahl kabbalistischer Mystik* (Leipzig, 1853), p. 43. In some manuscripts of this widespread work, the passage on the Messiah as connected to the last sefirah is missing. See also Cordovero, *Tefillah le-Moshe,* fol. 59a. The nexus between the divine attribute of Malkhut and the Messiah may have something to do with the eschatological valence of the term *malkhut* in ancient Judaism, a valence that influenced early Christianity. See the material collected by Bloch, *On the Apocalyptic in Judaism,* pp. 62–65, and Dale C. Allison Jr., "A Plea for Throughgoing Eschatology," *JBL* 113 (1994), pp. 659–660. On the other hand, one should not exclude the possibility of the influence of medieval Christianity on Kabbalah, I see this possibility as less plausible. In general, neither the theosophical-theurgical nor the ecstatic Kabbalists used Malkhut to describe a salvific state of consciousness of the redemptive role of the Christ, as Christian mystics did (see J. A. Bizet, "La notion du royaume interieur chez les mystiques germaniques du XIVe siècle," *Sacral Kingship,* pp. 620–626), but regarded it as a divine hypostasis governing the events here below. Nevertheless, see R. Moses Cordovero, *Tefillah le-Moshe,* fol. 248a, where the eschatological indwelling of the last sefirah in the hearts of men is mentioned. On the identification of the Messiah with the last sefirah see the discussion of fourteenth-century R. Joseph Angelet in his commentary on the *Zohar* entitled *Livenat ha-Sappir,* fol. 79ac.

40. *Sheqel ha-Qodesh,* pp. 90–91, Mopsik, *Le sicle,* pp. 220–221.

41. The importance of the horn is emphasized already in a talmudic passage, BT, *Megillah,* fol. 14a.

42. This is a frequent symbol for the last sefirah. See also *Sheqel ha-Qodesh,* pp. 84–85, Mopsik, *Le sicle,* p. 213, as well as the important alchemical passage in *Zohar,* vol. 2, fol. 73ab, where the view of David as the first Messiah is adduced in the name of an "ancient" "book of the First Adam." On this passage see Patai, *Jewish Alchemists,* pp. 165–166. See also the more general presentation of zoharic eschatology, according to the treatise namee *Iddra' Zuta',* in Ariel Bension, *The Zohar in Moslem and Christian Spain* (Hermon Press, New York, 1974), pp. 180–182.

43. *Le-konen,* "to constitute." See *Sheqel ha-Qodesh,* pp. 84, 91, esp. p. 33, where this verb parallels the verb "create." See also ibid., p. 27, where another king, Shlomo, is described as wanting to constitute and cleave to the Shekhinah. See also *Zohar,* vol. 1, fols. 249–250a, discussed in Patai, *Jewish Alchemists,* pp. 161–162. Compare also Liebes, "Messiah of the *Zohar,*" p. 185n334. See also Idel, *Kabbalah: New Perspectives,* p. 197. The feminine nature of the Messiah, a theme that will take a much more personalistic turn in the mid-sixteenth-century Christian Kabbalist, is not, however necessarily important in de Leon or the *Zohar.* Though this implicitly feminine form of understanding the Messiah as identical to the Shekhinah could be compared to the feminine nature of Jesus in the twelfth- and thirteenth-centuries, I see no reason that would prevent Kabbalists from expressing such a stand more explicitly. See Caroline Walker Bynum, *Jesus as Mother: Studies in the Spirituality of the High Middle Ages* (University of California Press, Berkeley and Los Angeles, 1984), pp. 110–169. Moreover, according to some medieval texts Mary has assumed some of the redemptive roles of Jesus: see Kinsley, *Goddesses' Mirror,* pp. 236–239, thus offering another possible parallel to the feminine divine potency in Kabbalah as a redemptive attribute. So, while the more conservative stands in Christianity, mystical or not, were audacious enough to portray Jesus as a feminine power or Mary as the redeemer, one would expect theosophical Kabbalah, less inhibited by dog-

matic approaches, to be more explicit about a feminine nature of the Messiah as identical to the last sefirah.

44. This issue should be compared to the medieval view on the two bodies of the king analyzed by Kantorowicz, *King's Two Bodies.* As Kantorowicz proposed throughout his book, the affinities between the mystical-mythical conceptions and the views of the political king are quite evident in the Middle Ages. This thesis is crucial also in the Bible and in Near Eastern mythology, where the concept of "corporate personality" was pertinent for the royal ideology.

45. The adherence to the Shekhinah may be seen as a coronation, since the last sefirah was also symbolically called 'Atarah, "diadem." On the mysticism of cleaving and coronation see Idel, "Universalization and Integration," pp. 34–37; idem, *Kabbalah: New Pespectives,* p. 197; Wolfson, *Through a Speculum,* esp. p. 357n107. On the affinity between the ancient sacral royal ideology and some aspects of theosophical-theurgical Kabbalah see Idel, *Kabbalah: New Perspectives,* p. 197. On the crown and the oil as magical devices transmitting power to the king see C. J. Gadd, *Ideas of Divine Rule in the Ancient East* (Oxford University Press, London, 1948), pp. 48–49.

46. Mowinckel, *Psalms in Israel's Worship,* 1:50.

47. For a similar sequel of theurgy and *devequt* already at the beginning of Kabbalah see Idel, *Kabbalah: New Perspectives,* pp. 54–55.

48. This is the same verb as used in the aforecited passage about the Messiah's constitution of the Shekhinah. See n. 47 above.

49. *Litqon.* I take this verb to stand for the theurgical operation that has been designated in the earlier quotation by *le-konen.*

50. *Shekel ha-Qodesh,* p. 70; Mopsik, *Le sicle,* p. 193; Idel, *Kabbalah: New Perspectives,* pp. 168–169; Mopsik, *Les grands textes,* p. 194. See also below, chap. 6, our discussion of Luzzatto's similar views, and Frankfort, *Kingship and the Gods,* pp. 259–261.

51. *Sheqel ha-Qodesh,* pp. 94–95, Mopsik, *Le sicle,* p. 225.

52. *Sheqel ha-Qodesh,* p. 70. On the Messiah and the horn of oil see the anonymous Kabbalistic passage preserved in Ms. Paris, Bibliothèque Nationale 859, fol. 22a. On oil as a symbol for the descent of the divine influx in the messianic days see the important passage of Joseph Karo, describing the ointment of Molkho from above; cf. Aescoly, *Jewish Messianic Movements,* p. 436, and the text of a late seventeenth-century Lurianic Kabbalist R. Moses Graff Prager, quoted by Scholem, *Sabbatai Ṣevi,* p. 69.

53. See already in a text of R. Yitzḥaq Sagi Nahor's view, preserved by Moses de Leon, where *go'el,* "redeemer," is a symbol for the ninth sefirah. Cf. M. Idel, "On R. Isaac Sagi Nahor's Mystical Intention of the Eighteen Benedictions," Oron-Goldreich and Goldreich, eds., *Massu'ot,* p. 29 (Hebrew).

54. See Liebes, *Studies in Jewish Myth,* p. 46; Idel, *Kabbalah: New Perspectives,* pp. 161–162.

55. From the point of view of meaning, "strength" is the most convenient translation. Mention of this term together with the crown, however, would invite an understanding of the strength as related to the oil of unction. For the extraordinary powers of some medieval kings, see the fascinating analysis of Bloch, *Les roi thaumaturges;* interestingly enough, the first references to the special healing powers of the kings of France and England seems now to be dated after the middle of the thirteenth century, namely in the generation immediately preceding the composition of the *Zohar;* see esp. Jacques Le Goff's preface to Bloch's monograph, pp. xv–xvi, who implies that Bloch's earlier dating of the healing phenomena attributed to kings up to the twelfth century should be revised. The zoharic text mentions expressly not only the coronation but also the idea of kingship, in connection with the Messiah, as the expression "crown of kingship" shows.

56. On the Messiah's diadem see also *Zohar,* vol. 3, fols. 164b, 196b. Compare the God-king

complex described in Engnell, *Divine Kingship,* pp. 78–79, 180–181, and Patai, "Hebrew Installation Rites," p. 194. Green, *Keter,* p. 116.

57. *Zohar,* vol. 2, fol. 7b.

58. *Ma'arekhet ha-'Elohut,* fol. 72b. Similar explanations of the two versions of the name are found in R. Yitzḥaq of Acre, *Sefer Me'irat 'Einayyim,* and other texts quoted by Gershom Scholem, "Le-Ḥeqer Qabbalato shel Rabbi Yitzḥaq ben Ya'aqov ha-Kohen," *Tarbiz* 5 (1934), pp. 186–187n3; R. Yitzḥaq of Acre, *'Otzar Ḥayyim,* Ms. Oxford 1911, fol. 150b; Idel, *Mystical Experience,* p. 117; the anonymous collectanaea found in both Ms. Paris, Bibliothèque Nationale 859, fol. 29a, and Ms. Vatican 428, fol. 55a, and in the *Commentary on Sefer Sha'arei 'Orah,* Ms. Jerusalem, National and University Library, 80 144, fol. 2b; R. Hananel ben Abraham of Asqira, *Sefer Yesod 'Olam,* Ms. Moscow-Guensburg 607, fol. 130b; Wolfson, *Through a Speculum,* p. 261. For another combination of philosophical view of the Agent Intellect as *donator formarum* and some Kabbalistic views of Metatron see R. Reuven Tzarfati, *Commentary, Ma'arekhet ha-'Elohut,* fol. 97b, and the anonymous text in Ms. Oxford 1927, fol. 179b, and Idel, *Mystical Experience,* p. 128. For the nexus between Metatron and Malkhut see the fascinating Mandaic spell where the name of Metatron occurs together with Malkhut; cf. Greenfield, *Prolegomenon,* p. xl, and idem, "Notes," p. 154. For more on the identification of Metatron and Malkhut see Idel, *R. Abraham Abulafia,* pp. 91–92.

59. *Tzafnat Pa'aneaḥ,* Ms. Jerusalem, National and University Library, 40 154, fol. 113b. The term *Horadat ha-shefa',* "the descent of influx," points to a more magical understanding of Kabbalah and returns in Hasidism. The dew of blessing stands for the divine influx alone. However, it may also designate the power that brings the dead to life: see *BT, Ketubbot,* fol. 111b. If this additional meaning is introduced in this passage, then we have an echo of the zoharic view mentioned above, again in the context of the Messiah. On the observance of two days of Sabbaths see *BT, Sabbath,* fol. 118b, and the discussion of Goodman, *On Justice,* p. 183. I wonder whether the famous legend related to Luria's invitation of his companions to celebrate Sabbath in Jerusalem as crucial for the arrival of redemption is not an amplification of the talmudic view. See e.g. Benayahu, *Toledoth Ha-Ari,* pp. 168–169.

60. See Scholem, *Origins of the Kabbalah,* pp. 299–300; see also in Al-Ashqar's book, *Tzafnat Pa'anea,* fol. 70a, where again the return of all the things to their source is mentioned in a Messianic context, in connection with the acronym Adam, David, Messiah. See below, chap. 6. On the return of the things to their source as part of an eschatological event see Scholem, *Origins of the Kabbalah,* pp. 299–300, as well as Postel's use of the phrase *restitutio rerum omnium* to point to the eschatological situation which he thought was imminent; cf. Bouwsma, *Concordia Mundi,* pp. 281–282.

61. *'Otzar Ḥayyim,* Ms. Moscow-Guensburg 775, fol. 160a; Idel, *Mystical Experience,* p. 141. On this Kabbalist see Gottlieb, *Studies,* pp. 231–247.

62. See Idel, *Mystical Experience,* pp. 140, 176n334; idem, *Studies in Ecstatic Kabbalah,* pp. 50–51; idem, *R. Abraham Abulafia,* p. 412. The claim that the Messiah is higher than Moses is found already in the Midrash, and it is reverberated also in other messianic figures; see Israel Friedlaender, "Shiitic Influences," in Saperstein, ed., *Essential Papers,* pp. 130, 132; Flusser, *Judaism and the Origins of Christianity,* pp. 246–279.

63. See Liebes, "Messiah of the *Zohar,*" p. 172n297.

64. See *Ve-Zot Li-Yhudah,* p. 21; Idel, *Mystical Experience,* p. 132. For more on the meaning of this passage see idem, *Hasidism: Between Ecstasy and Magic,* p. 98.

65. Idel, *Hasidism: Between Ecstasy and Magic,* pp. 98–99. See also R. Yitzḥaq's *Me'irat 'Einayyim,* p. 70, where the same mystico-magical model is hinted at: Kabbalistic prayer is able to draw down the divine influx.

66. See Idel, *Mystical Experience,* p. 128, also pp. 33, 200; and below, app. 1.

67. Idel, *Mystical Experience,* p. 134; idem, *Studies in Ecstatic Kabbalah,* pp. 73–89.

68. Idel, *Mystical Experience,* p. 133; see also idem, *Golem,* pp. 106–107.

69. See Idel, *Hasidism: Between Ecstasy and Magic,* pp. 45–145.

70. Zachariah 3:8. The term *tzemaḥ,* "shoot, sprout," was interpreted in messianic terms. See Mowinckel, *He That Cometh,* pp. 160–164, 168.

71. Ms. London, Montefiore 332, fol. 8b. See also an anonymous remark in the margin of Abulafia's *Ḥayyei ha-'Olam ha-Ba',* Ms. Oxford 1582, fol. 13a: "The Messiah is the [High] Priest, greater than his brothers, and [he is] Metatron and he is the Messiah." In the two cases connected to Abulafia's book we witness a certain ontological reading of the Messiah as not only a perfect mystic, though still a man, but also an angelic power on high, like Abulafia himself. On the lower and higher Messiahs see Guillaume Postel, as discussed by Bouwsma, *Concordia Mundi,* pp. 162–163; in Postel's view, the higher Messiah is connected to the realm of intellect, while the lower is connected to the realm of the feminine.

72. According to de Leon's passage in *Sheqel ha-Qodesh,* pp. 90–91, Mopsik, *Le sicle,* pp. 220–221, the term *malkhut,* which is both a cognomen of the last sefirah and the word for dominion and kingship, recurs several times.

73. See Scholem, *Researches in Sabbateanism,* p. 117, and Liebes's remarks in ibid., p. 529n.

74. *Sefer ha-Peliy'ah,* I, fol. 57a, which is copied verbatim in Scholem, *Researches in Sabbateanism,* p. 175. The phrase *koaḥ keter 'eliyon* recurs in *Sefer ha-Peliy'ah,* part 1, fol. 57c, again under the influence of R. Joseph ben Shalom Ashkenazi's *Commentary on Sefer Yetzirah.*

75. Idel, *Hasidism: Between Ecstasy and Magic,* pp. 95–102.

76. See M. Idel, "Additional Remnants from the Writings of R. Joseph of Hamadan," *Daat* 21 (1988), pp. 47–53 (Hebrew). Compare the view of Cordovero, discussed in Sack, *Kabbalah of Rabbi Moshe Cordovero,* pp. 97–98; R. Moses Galante, adduced by Scholem, *Sabbatai Ṣevi,* pp. 57–58, who assumes that there must be some power of the demonic world in the Messiah for him to be able to succeed in his mission. Scholem, ibid., assumes that this view is part of Lurianic Kabbalah. For the assumption that incest is necessary for the birth of the Messiah see R. Qalonimus Qalman Epstein, *Ma'or va-Shemesh,* pp. 103–104, in a manner reminiscent of Cordoverian views; see Sack, ibid.

77. Tishby, *Wisdom of the Zohar,* vol. 3, pp. 1425–1426, 1457; Piekarz, *Beginning of Hasidism,* pp. 280–302.

78. Scholem, *Sabbatai Ṣevi,* pp. 806–807.

79. See Danielou, *Théologie du Judeo-Christianisme,* pp. 295–310; J. Kroll, *Gott und Holle: Der Mythos von Descensus-Kempfe* (rpt. Darmstadt, 1963); Charles H. Talbet, "The Myth of a Descending-Ascending Redeemer in Mediterranean Antiquity," *New Testament Studies* 22 (1976), pp. 418–439; Guy G. Stroumsa, "Mystic Descends," *Death, Ecstasy, and Other Wordly Journeys,* ed. John J. Collins and Michael Fishbane (State University of New York Press, Albany, 1995), pp. 137–152. This view has also been connected by some scholars to the ancient Near Eastern ideology of sacral kingship, especially the concept of the suffering Messiah; see e.g. Bentzen, *King and Messiah,* p. 47.

80. Ms. New York, JTS 1853, fol. 9a.

81. See Idel, *Hasidism: Between Ecstasy and Magic,* pp. 103–107.

82. *Tzaphnat Pa'aneaḥ,* Ms. Jerusalem 40 154, fol. 79a. The facsimile of this manuscript has been printed by Misgav Yerushalayim (Jerusalem, 1991), and in the introduction to this edition I have discussed some of the issues treated below; see pp. 51–53 (Hebrew).

83. See ibid., fols. 80b, 81b.

84. Ibid., fol. 82a.

85. Compare, however, the formulation of Sharot, *Mysticism, Messianism, and Magic,* pp. 152–

153. I hope to elaborate more on the katabatic redemptive model in Jewish mysticism in a separate study, dealing with the entrance into the "Pardes."

86. On the eschatology of this book see Scholem, *Sabbatai Ṣevi,* pp. 61–62. On the view of metempsychosis in this book, which involves a messianic understanding of history, see Rachel Elior, "The Doctrine of Transmigration in Sefer Galia Raza," *JSJT* 3 (1984), pp. 207–239, esp. pp. 217–220 (Hebrew), translated now in Fine, ed., *Essential Papers,* pp. 243–269.

87. See *Sefer Galia' Raza',* ed. Rachel Elior (Hebrew University, Jerusalem, 1981), pp. 172–175, and the part of the book printed in the edition of Mohilev, 1812, fol. 43b. On the messianic role of Seraiah and its possible connection to messianism see *Zohar,* vol. 3, fol. 194a–194b; Ginzberg, *Legends of the Jews,* 6:144; Berger, "Captive at the Gate of Rome," p. 9n27.

88. See Scholem, *Sabbatai Ṣevi* (Hebrew version), p. 745. This discussion is missing in the English, expanded version.

89. Scholem, *Messianic Idea,* p. 39; Liebes, *Studies in the Zohar,* pp. 84–134. See more recently Charles Mopsik's description of the *Zohar* as a Midrash on Midrash. *Le Zohar* (Verdier, Lagrasse, 1996), 4:16–23.

90. See M. Idel, "Midrash versus Other Forms of Jewish Hermeneutics: Some Comparative Remarks," in M. Fishbane, ed., *The Midrashic Imagination: Jewish Exegesis, Thought, History* (State University of New York Press, Albany, 1993), pp. 50–51. On the absence of midrashic influences in Abulafia's apocalypse see Aescoly, *Jewish Messianic Movements,* p. 232.

91. A pseudepigraphic Midrash, composed by R. Moses de Leon under the title of *Seder Gan 'Eden* and attributed to R. Eliezer ha-Gadol, is replete with mythical discussions on the nature and acts of the Messiah in the celestial paradise. I see a direct nexus between the Midrashic format and the content of this treatise. On the *Zohar* and messianism see also Scholem, *Messianic Idea,* pp. 39–40.

92. See *Zohar,* vol. 2, fols. 7b–8a, Patai, *Messiah Texts,* pp. 84–89. This text, which has attracted the interest of several scholars, has affinities to the zoharic passage that will be adduced immediately below. On zoharic apocalypticism see Bloch, *On the Apocalyptic in Judaism,* pp. 115–118, and Bension, *Zohar in Moslem and Christian Spain,* pp. 182–186. On a mythical bird (apparently related to the phoenix) who will be given dominion over the world as a forrunner of the Messiah see *Zohar,* vol. 3, fol. 212b.

93. A. Jellinek, *Moses ben Shem-Tov de Leon und sein Verhältnis zum Sohar* (Leipzig, 1851); see also Jellinek, *Auswahl kabbalistischer Mystik,* erstes Heft (Leipzig, 1853), German part, pp. 25–26.

94. Printed in his *Bet ha-Midrasch,* 3:xxxvii–xxxviii.

95. *Moses ben Shem Tov,* p. 8. Jellinek was inclined to think that there is a linkage between the *Zohar* and the youth of Avila, an illiterate who allegedly produced, in a wondrous manner, some eschatological writings. See ibid., pp. 39–40, 49–52.

96. This picture symbolizes the last sefirah, Malkhut, which is surrounded, at the time of the redemption by seventy stars, which stand for the seventy angels of the seventy nations. See *Zohar,* vol. 2, fol. 30b. On the idea of seventy angels surrounding the divine power see M. Idel, "The World of Angels in Human Form," in J. Dan and J. Hacker, eds., *Studies in Jewish Mysticism: Philosophy and Ethical Literature Presented to Isaiah Tishby* (Jerusalem, 1986), pp. 39–49 (Hebrew).

97. On the star of the Messiah see PT, *Ta'anit,* fol. 4:6, Even Shemuel, *Midreshei Ge'ullah,* p. 102. See also Paul J. Alexander, *The Byzantine Apocalyptic Tradition* (University of California Press, Berkeley and Los Angeles, 1985), p. 214, on the eschatological *stella mirabilis.* On messianic dreams about a star foretelling the advent of the Messiah in Sabbateanism see Scholem, *Studies and Texts,* pp. 321–322. On light symbolism in the context of the Messiah in general see Wieder, *Judean Scrolls,* pp. 26–27nn and Gruenwald, "From Sunrise to Sunset," pp. 21–25.

98. See also *Zohar,* vol. 2, fol. 8ab, where the destruction of some towers and palaces is described in an eschatological context, though not the death of the ruler of Rome.

99. *Zohar,* vol. 3, fol. 212b; Idel, *Studies in Ecstatic Kabbalah,* pp. 45–46; Greenstone, *Messiah Idea,* p. 178. Compare also the *Zohar,* vol. 2, fols. 7b–9a. Though there are some interesting affinities between these two passages, the mention of the twenty-fifth of Elul, crucial for Jellinek's argument, and of the sixth and seventh days, which are central to my argument, are not found in this passage. It may well be that the later pericope was composed later on and combined some apocalyptic themes found already in its earlier treatment with the rumors related to Abulafia or to the traditions that might have informed Abulafia's attempt. For the repeated zoharic treatments of the same topic see Liebes, "Messiah of the *Zohar,*" pp. 97–101.

100. It is worth noting the possible discrepancy of between the intended date of meeting, i.e. the eve of Rosh ha-Shanah, and the date of Abulafia's arrival in Soriano. There is no reason to assume that these two times are identical. It would be difficult to suggest that Abulafia would have arrived in Soriano on the very day designated for the meeting, which had been canceled by the pope—and for him to expect to achieve a meeting on that very day. If indeed he came a few days in advance, as implied in the formulation of the text, then the pope died during the evening that preceded his arrival, and there would be no lack of accord between Abulafia's report of the death of the pope and the intended meeting on Elul 29 (the eve of Rosh ha-Shanah). In his writings Abulafia does not note these dates as being identical. Regarding these questions see Hermann Vogelstein and Paul Rieger, *Geschichte der Juden in Rom* (Berlin, 1896), 1:248–249; Hermann Vogelstein, *The Jews of Rome* (Jewish Publication Society, Philadelphia, 1940), pp. 175–179.

101. Compare Scholem's view, expressed in his *Major Trends,* p. 194, as to the end of the composition of the *Zohar* by 1286. This view has been questioned by Tishby, *Wisdom of the Zohar,* 1:94, and more recently has been endorsed by Liebes, *Studies in the Zohar.*

102. Liebes, *Studies in the Zohar,* pp. 135–138.

103. See Idel, *Studies in Ecstatic Kabbalah,* p. 46. See also Liebes, "Messiah of the *Zohar,*" pp. 173–174 and n. 300, who pointed out some affinities between other topics related to spiritual messianism similar to or stemming from Abulafian sources and the circle of the Kabbalists related to the composition of the *Zohar.*

104. See *Sefer ha-'Ot,* p. 67; Idel, *Studies in Ecstatic Kabbalah,* p. 47.

105. On this name see also another quotation from the same book of Abulafia's adduced at the end of the previous chapter.

106. *Ḥayyei ha-'Olam ha-Ba',* Ms. Paris Bibliothèque Nationale 777, fol. 127a. For a fuller quotation and discussion of this text see Idel, *Studies in Ecstatic Kabbalah,* p. 51.

107. See the texts quoted in Idel, *Studies in Ecstatic Kabbalah,* pp. 51–52. On the relation between the Messiah and the Sabbath, which is presided over by the planet Sabbatai, namely Saturn, see chap. 6.

108. As far as I am acquainted with Christological analyses, this identification of Jesus with Tammuz in a conspicuously messianic context, which comprises the idea of a dead Messiah, is quite surprising; see especially the modern scholarly discussions on the so-called "Tammuz ideology," which presumably served as background for some features in the figure of the Christian savior. See e.g. Bentzen, *King and Messiah,* p. 51; Riesenfeld, *Jesus transfiguré,* pp. 23, 79, 92; Eliade, *Cosmos and History,* pp. 100–102; E. M. Yamauchi, "Tammuz and the Bible," *JBL* 84 (1965), pp. 283–290; Ringgren, *Messiah,* pp. 50–51, 54; Versnel, *Transition and Revival,* p. 44. For a suggestion for a connection between David and Tammuz see the literature discussed in De Fraine, *L'aspect religieux,* pp. 278–280.

109. See Idel, *Studies in Ecstatic Kabbalah,* pp. 51–52.

110. See Liebes, "Messiah of the *Zohar,*" pp. 171–172n297, and in a shorter form in *Studies in the Zohar,* p. 182n141. Later on, in Sabbateanism, we find the view that the redemption will start toward the fifth hour of the sixth day and materialize on the Sabbath. See the epistle of Nathan of Gaza printed in Scholem, *Studies and Texts,* p. 263 and notes.

111. See the quotation from an article of Marc Bloch, below, Concluding Remarks.

112. Compare Scholem, *Messianic Idea,* p. 41; *Sabbatai Ṣevi,* p. 18.

113. See Robert E. Lerner, "The Black Death and Western European Eschatological Mentalities," *American Historical Review* 86 (1981), pp. 533–552, who pointed out how medieval prophecies, existing for many decades, were appropriated and circulated in order to give comfort to the frightened Christian Europeans.

114. On the Messianic calculation of *Sefer ha-Temunah* see Silver, *History of Messianic Speculation,* pp. 93–94; Idel, "Types of Redemptive Activity," p. 265; Manuel and Manuel, *Utopian Thought,* pp. 55–56.131. See Liebes, *Studies in the Zohar,* pp. 1–84.

Chapter 4: Messianism and Kabbalah, 1470–1540

1. Tishby, *Messianism in the Time of the Expulsion,* pp. 143–144, 147, 149. On the messianic self-awareness of the anonymous Kabbalist who authored this layer of the *Zohar* see Amos Goldreich, "Clarifications on the Self-Consciousness of the Author of Tiqqunei Zohar," in Oron and Goldreich, eds., *Massu'ot,* pp. 459–495 (Hebrew).

2. On this literature see Scholem, *Kabbalah,* pp. 182–187. I would like to emphasize the difference between this magical model and the talismanic one: the former is much closer to the apocalyptic model, while the latter represents a much more stable vision of nature that may be restored to its completion by drawing down the divine power. See Moshe Idel, "Jewish Magic from the Renaissance Period to Early Hasidism," in Neusner et al., *Religion, Science, and Magic in Conflict and Concert* (Oxford University Press, New York, 1989), pp. 82–117. On magic and eschatology see Bryan R. Wilson, *Magic and the Millennium: A Sociological Study of Religious Movements of Protest among Tribal and Third-World Peoples* (Harper and Row, San Francisco, 1973).

3. Idel, "Types of Redemptive Activities," pp. 275–278. In the very same decades when the Kabbalistic literature that constitutes the corpus of *Sefer ha-Meshiv* was composed, the phenomena of apparitions were quite prevalent in Christian Spain. See William A. Christian, Jr., *Apparitions in Late Medieval and Renaissance Spain* (Princeton University Press, Princeton, N.J., 1981). This coincidence is quite remarkable, and it may point to an affinity that is the result of the acquaintance of the Jewish Kabbalists with outside mystical phenomena in their surroundings.

4. On the subject of the Kabbalistic literature composed in this school see Gershom Scholem, "The Maggid of Joseph Taitachek," pp. 69–112; Idel, "Inquiries"; idem, "The Attitude to Christianity in *Sefer ha-Meshiv,*" *Zion* 46 (1981), pp. 77–91 (Hebrew), English version, *Immanuel* 12 (1981), pp. 77–95; idem, "Neglected Writings." This literature is quite different from most of the preceding Kabbalistic literature, and there is no reason to accept Scholem's very general statement about an alleged "unmistakable flaccidity of religious thought and expression" in the fifteenth century. See *Major Trends,* p. 244. On the explicit influence of one of the texts belonging to this literature on Nathan of Gaza see Scholem, *Studies and Texts,* p. 244n72.

5. See Idel, "Attitude to Christianity," as well as the important article of Georges Vajda, "Passages anti-chrétiens dans *Kaf Ha-Qetoret,*" *Revue de l'histoire des religions* 117 (1980), pp. 45–58.

6. See Idel, "Inquiries," pp. 232–241; idem, "Magic and Kabbalah in the Book of the

Responding Entity," in M. I. Gruber, ed., *The Solomon Goldman Lectures* (Spertus College of Judaica Press, Chicago, 1993), pp. 125–138.

7. Idel, "Types of Redemptive Activities," p. 276. On the divine hand in ancient texts see Karl Gross, *Menschenhand und Gotteshand in Antike und Christentum* (Anton Hiersemann Verlag, Stuttgart, 1985), pp. 315ff, where no important aspect of magical use of the divine hand—unlike the human hand—is addressed. Compare Idel, "Types of Redemptive Activities," pp. 274ff. On the concept that Jewish masters knew how to destroy evil by their knowledge of practical Kabbalah, but did not do so in order not to interfere with the divine will, see Idel, "Shlomo Molkho as Magician," pp. 194–202.

8. See Idel, "Types of Redemptive Activities," pp. 275–278. In this corpus of writings, alchemical discussions occur from time to time. Compare the views expressed in an alchemical work attributed to Abraham Eleazar, which I propose to date to the end of the fifteenth or early sixteenth century, where a warning against resorting to anti-Christian, apparently messianic activities was issued. See Patai, *Jewish Alchemists,* pp. 251–252. Patai is inclined to date this writing much earlier, to the end of the fourteenth century.

9. See Idel, "Inquiries," pp. 244–250.

10. See G. Scholem, "On the Story of R. Joseph della Reina," in *Ḥokhma Bina veDaat: Studies in Jewish History and Thought Presented to A. Altmann* (Alabama University Press, University, Alabama, 1979), pp. 100–108 (Hebrew), reprinted in *'Od Davar,* pp. 249–262; Idel, "Inquiries." On the legend of Joseph della Reina see Meir Benayahu, "The Story of R. Joseph della Reina," *'Areset* 5 (Jerusalem, 1972), pp. 170–188 (Hebrew); Joseph Dan, "The Story of Joseph della Reina," *Sefunot* 6 (Makhon Ben Tzvi, Jerusalem, 1962), pp. 311–326 (Hebrew); Michal Oron, "The Expectation of Redemption, History and Literature in the Story of R. Joseph della Reina," in *Between History and Literature* (Tel Aviv, 1983), pp. 79–80 (Hebrew).

11. See Dan, "The Emergence of Messianic Mythology."

12. See J. Dan, "The Story of the Child's Prophecy," *Shalem* 1 (1974), pp. 229–231 (Hebrew).

13. See Scholem, *Major Trends,* p. 248, and *Messianic Idea,* pp. 32–33. On other writings by this anonymous author see Idel, "Neglected Writings," and R. Elior, ed., *Galia' Raza'* (Research Projects of the Institute of Judaic Studies, Jerusalem, 1981).

14. Ms. Jerusalem, Schocken, Kabbalah 10, fol. 42a. See Idel, "Introduction," and "Neglected Writings." On this passage see also Ravitzky, *Messianism, Zionism,* p. 240n48. On the issue of the three oaths see ibid., pp. 211–234. In his interpretation of the first verse of Psalm 118, the anonymous author of this text allegorizes the distress expressed by the author of the Psalm as "the vicissitudes of the exiles," punning on *meitzar/tzarot,* which is combined with *galuyyot,* while God's answer to him is described in the context of the expulsion from Spain. In other terms, the expulsion is tantamount to a certain liberty, *merḥav,* where God is responding to the mystic. See Ms. Paris, Bibliothèque Nationale 846, fol. 126b. These two fragments are important pieces of evidence as to the normal use made by scholars when attempting to describe the impact of the expulsion on the Kabbalist, and *Sefer Kaf ha-Qetoret* has often been enlisted as a major example for this argument. Thus Scholem, "Messianic Movements," p. 336, claims that "[a]n anonymous author in Italy wrote (ca. 1500) Kaf ha-Qetoret (Ms. Paris), a commentary on the Psalms, which finds in every word of the Psalms an allusion to the Messiah." In fact, according to the second text from this book, the expulsion created a certain feeling of freedom from exile and an experience of contact with God, ensured by the great confidence and faith of the author! A contemporary of the anonymous author, R. Yehudah Albotini, writing in Jerusalem at the beginning of the sixteenth century, likewise forbids resort to divine names in order to bring about the advent of the Messiah. See his *Sefer Sullam ha-'Aliyah,* pp.

70–71, in a manner reminiscent of the text referred to at the beginning of this note. Thus two expellees from the Iberian peninsula oppose resort to magical devices for messianic aims.

15. For an update on the works of R. Abraham ha-Levi, see G. Scholem's and M. Beit-Aryeh's introduction to *Meshareh Qitrin* (National University Library, Jerusalem, 1978) (Hebrew).

16. Scholem, *Major Trends,* p. 247. See also Scholem, *Messianic Idea,* p. 41: "the Kabbalists, like their fellows Jews in general, believed that complete redemption was around the corner. . . . There was no need for new religious concepts and principles; the end had already come. At any hour, any moment, the gates of redemption might swing open, and men's hearts must now be awakened to meet the future. For the span of one generation, during the forty years after the Spanish expulsion, we find a deep Messianic exitement and tension as before the eruption of the Sabbatian movement . . . the important thing now was propaganda, the dissemination of the apocalyptic message. The master propagandist of this acute Messianism in the generation after the expulsion was Abraham ben Eliezer ha-Levi, a rabbi from Spain who lived in Jerusalem and was one of the greatest Kabbalists of his day."

17. See Idel, "Inquiries," pp. 201–204.

18. See idem, "Introduction," p. 26.

19. See idem, "Inquiries," pp. 209–210.

20. Ibid., pp. 249–250. On the ten lost tribes in the literature of this period see Tamar, *Studies,* pp. 81–86; Avraham Gross, "The Ten Tribes and the Kingdom of Prester John: Rumors and Investigations Before and After the Expulsion from Spain," *Pe'amim* 48 (1991), pp. 5–41 (Hebrew), where the pertinent bibliography has been adduced. On the ten tribes see also Kirn, *Das Bild vom Juden,* p. 35, and below, chap. 6, n. 66, and in the text printed by Marx, "Ma'amar," p. 199.

21. See Idel, "On Mishmarot and Messianism," pp. 83–90. Compare to Ira Robinson, "Messianic Prayer Vigils in Jerusalem in the Early Sixteenth Century," *JQR* 72 (1981), pp. 32–42. Messianic implications of vigils are already visible in Karaite groups of mourner, called 'Avelei Tzion. See Wieder, *Judean Scrolls,* passim, as well as below, appendix 2. The fact that this Kabbalist was active for some of the years of his messianic propaganda in the Turkish empire may invite a comparison to the messianic perception of one of the sultans reigning during ha-Levi's life, Suleiman the Magnificient. See Cornell H. Fleisher, "The Lawgiver as Messiah: The Making of the Imperial Image in the Reign of Suleyman," in Gilles Veinstein, ed., *Soliman le Magnifique et son temps* (Ecole de Louvre, Ecole des Hautes Etudes en Sciences Sociales, Paris, 1992), pp. 159–177. Perhaps some of the sixteenth-century Jewish messianic impulses in the East should be seen against the background of Ottoman apocalypticism; this issue requires special investigation. See, for the time being, the important remark of Tishby, "Acute Apocalyptic Messianism," in Saperstein, ed., *Essential Papers,* pp. 281–283n34. See also the anonymous sixteenth-century text preserved in Ms. Leningrad-Firkowitch I, 322 [no page numbers], where an anonymous sultan was described as the first Koresh, to whom the biblical appelation *mashiyaḥ ha-Shem* is attributed explicitly in the text.

22. On this text see Scholem's introduction to *Meshareh Qitrin,* pp. 36–37, and the edition of Ira Robinson, "Two Letters of Abraham ben Eliezer Halevi," *Studies in Medieval Jewish History and Literature,* ed. I. Twersky, (Harvard University Press, Cambridge, 1984), 2:403–422.

23. Printed in Abraham David, "A Jerusalemite Epistle from the Beginning of the Ottoman Rule in the Land of Israel," *Chapters in the History of Jerusalem at the Beginning of the Ottoman Period* (Yad Ben Zvi, Jerusalem, 1979), p. 59 (Hebrew).

24. See Robinson, "Messianic Prayer Vigils," pp. 411–412. On this passage see Hayyim Hillel ben Sasson, "Ha-Yehudim mul ha-Reformatziah," *Proceedings of the Israeli Academy for Sciences and Humanities* (Jerusalem, 1970), 4:75–81 (Hebrew); Kirn, *Das Bild vom Juden,* p. 35 and n. 85. See also the epistle written by a contemporary of ha-Levi, R. Menaḥem Elijah Ḥalfan of Venice, where a

similar positive stand toward the emergence of Luther's reform may be discerned; cf. Idel, "Magical and Neoplatonic Interpretations," pp. 186–187. For Luther's own eschatology see Barnes, *Prophecy and Gnosis,* pp. 36–59. The awareness of the broadening of the study of the Hebrew language among the Christians was also interpreted eschatologically by ha-Levi; see Robinson, "Messianic Prayer Vigils," p. 411.

25. Cf. Idel, "Introduction," pp. 22–23. On messianism in ibn Gabbay see Goetschel, *Meir ibn Gabbay,* pp. 457–464, who has quite correctly pointed out the significance of ibn Gabbay's reliance on earlier Kabbalistic sources, a fact that undermines Scholem's attempt to relate this Kabbalist's short discussion of the Messiah to the impact of the expulsion from Spain. Though Scholem himself discovered ibn Gabbay's source in R. Joseph Al-Qastiel's responsa, written perhaps before the expulsion, he did not draw the due conclusion and still viewed ibn Gabbay's messianism as representing post-expulsion trends. See Scholem, *Sabbatai Ṣevi,* pp. 46–47.

26. These reactions are more evident in the version printed in the Ferrara edition, where the introduction is a little bit longer, revealing details that were not included in the Mantuan edition. Both of them were printed in the same year, 1558. On the various commentaries on *Ma'arekhet ha-'Elohut* see Gershom Scholem, "On the Questions Related to Sefer Ma'arekhet ha-'Elohut and Its Commentators," *QS* 21 (1944), pp. 284–295 (Hebrew).

27. Though not a full-fledged Kabbalist, Yavetz was sympathetic to this lore but very critical toward Jewish philosophy; this certainly created an affinity between the two expellees. Though I assume that Ḥayyat and Yavetz did not meet before their encounter in Mantua, their trajectory after the expulsion is similar. On Yavetz's thought see Isaac E. Barzilay, *Between Reason and Faith: Anti-Rationalism in Jewish Italian Thought, 1250–1650* (Mouton, The Hague, 1967), pp. 133–149; Gedaliah Nigal, "The Opinions of R. Joseph Yawetz on Philosophy and Philosophers, Torah and Commandments," *Eshel Beer-Sheva,* vol. 1 (1976), pp. 258–287 (Hebrew); Ira Robinson, "Halakha, Kabbala, and Philosophy in the Thought of Joseph Jabez," *Sciences religieuses/Studies in Religion* 11, no. 4 (1982), pp. 389–402.

28. Cf. Psalm 27:4. Barzilai, *Between Reason and Faith,* p. 143, is right when mentioning Yavetz's basic positive attitude toward Kabbalah. Scholem's assessment (*Sabbatai Ṣevi,* p. 21) that Yavetz's attitude toward Kabbalah, "like that toward the philosophy of Maimonides, is one of extreme reserve" is unfounded. In his *'Or ha-Ḥayyim,* quoted by Scholem, ibid., Yavetz criticizes only the study of Kabbalah by people who are not prepared for this esoteric lore. Even the reserve of Yavetz may, however, be understood in the context of the development of the study of Kabbalah in Italy, where relatively young persons, like Alemanno and David Messer Leon, were active.

29. As E. Gottlieb has shown, the author was an Italian Kabbalist named Reuven Tzarfati; see his *Studies,* pp. 357–369. On the thought of this Kabbalist see the master's thesis of Abraham Elkayam, *Issues in the Commentary of R. Reuben Zarfati on the book Ma'arekhet ha-'Elohut* (Hebrew University, Jerusalem, 1987) (Hebrew).

30. Despite the critiques of Ḥayyat as to the nature of this commentary, many parts of it were printed in the Mantuan edition of *Ma'arekhet ha-'Elohut,* beside those which were copied by Ḥayyat himself in his *Minḥat Yehudah.* As the printer of this edition, R. Immanuel of Bienivento has acknowledged he was not ready to leave out the views of the anonymous Kabbalist, though he had reservations about some of them.

31. Compare also the description of R. Yitzḥaq Mor Ḥayyim regarding the dispersion and fragmentation of the *Zohar.* This issue is worthy of a detailed discussion that cannot be done here. Other Kabbalists also testify that they were well acquainted with the *Zohar,* and I assume that this included *Tiqqunei Zohar,* already in Spain.

32. To be sure, Ḥayyat frequently cited long quotations from the latter layer of the zoharic

literature, *Tiqqunei Zohar;* nevertheless, for our purpose this fact does not matter, and I shall refer in the following to his quotations from the zoharic literature by the general term *Zohar.*

33. See also *Minḥat Yehudah,* fol. 165b.

34. On the basis of Yoḥanan Alemanno's extensive quotations from Ḥayyat's work, in his *Collectanaea* and in his untitled book extant in Ms. Paris, Bibliothèque Nationale, 849, which was written in 1498, I proposed to date the composition of *Minḥat Yehudah* between 1496 and 1498; See M. Idel, "The Study Program of R. Yoḥanan Alemanno," *Tarbiẓ* 48 (1979), p. 330 (Hebrew). Scholem dated the commentary between 1494 and 1500; see "On the Questions," p. 292. The earlier date, however, is impossible because in 1495 Ḥayyat was in Naples and he mentions the conquest of the city by the French during this year. The later date is improbable because Alemanno quoted the book already in 1498.

35. On this issue see Idel, "Neglected Writings," pp. 80–82.

36. This is also the case when we inspect the Kabbalistic writings of R. Joseph ibn Shraga, as I have shown in Idel, "Encounters between Spanish and Italian Kabbalists in the Generation of the Expulsion," in Benjamin R. Gampel, ed., *Crisis and Creativity in the Sephardic World* (Columbia University Press, 1997), pp. 189–222. Moreover, the existence of a messianic discussion does not impinge upon the general nature of his Kabbalistic writings. See, however, Elior, "Messianic Expectations," p. 36 and n. 4, where she refers to Ḥayyat in the context of her claim that he is the representative of those who expressed "various degrees of detachment from mundane life while striving to attain cultural segregation and a comprehensive spiritualization of all Jewish life." Since no specific page of a pertinent discussion was mentioned in Elior's article, my perusal of the two editions of *Minḥat Yehudah* was not helpful in detecting these discussions or the new formulations or even only particular emphases.

37. On this figure see Haim Beinart, *The Expulsion of the Jews from Spain* (Magnes Press, Jerusalem, 1994), pp. 467–480 (Hebrew). B. Netanyahu, *Don Isaac Abravanel: Statesman and Philosopher* (JPS, Philadelphia, 5732/1972), pp. 195–257, who emphasized the impact of Savonarola's eschatology on Abravanel; Tishby, *Messianism in the Generation of the Expulsion,* numerous remarks on the eschatological calculations of Abravanel; see index, sub voce Abravanel; Sarachek, *Doctrine of the Messiah,* pp. 225–299; Yshaiahu Leibovitz, *'Emunah, Historiah, 'Arakhim* (Akademon, Jerusalem, 1982), pp. 102–111 (Hebrew); Gross, "Ten Tribes," pp. 23–27, and more recently Eric Lawee, "'Israel Has No Messiah' in Late Medieval Spain," *Journal of Jewish Thought and Philosophy* 5, (1996), pp. 245–279. For more studies on Abravanel and messianism see Ravitzky, *Messianism, Zionism,* p. 238n34.

38. Tishby, *Messianism in the Time of the Expulsion.*

39. See Ephraim Kupfer, "The Visions of R. Asher ben R. Meir called Lemlein Ashkenazi Reutlingen," *Qovetz 'Al Yad* 8, no. 18 (Meqitzei Nirdamim, Jerusalem, 1976), pp. 387–423 (Hebrew). See also Silver, *History of Messianic Speculation,* pp. 143–145; Alexander Marx, "Le Faux Messie Ascher Lemlein," *REJ* 61 (1911), pp. 136–138; David Tamar, "On R. Asher Lemlein," *Zion* 52 (1987), pp. 309–401 (Hebrew). Tamar has correctly pointed out that Lemlein's messianic activity took place in 1500, not that the advent of the Messiah was predicted for this year. See ibid., pp. 400–401n13, versus Tishby, *Messianism in the Time of the Expulsion,* pp. 75–76nn236–237. See also Kirn, *Das Bild vom Juden,* pp. 30–33. Aescoly, though well aware that Lemlein was of Ashkenazi origin, nonetheless places him among those who were influenced by the expulsion; see *Jewish Messianic Movements,* p. 273.

40. Kupfer, "Visions of R. Asher," pp. 412, 417, 422.

41. See Idel, "Encounters"; Kupfer, "Visions of R. Asher," pp. 394–395.

42. Kupfer, "Visions of R. Asher," p. 412.

43. See, however, Sharot, *Messianism, Mysticism, and Magic,* p. 71.

44. Kupfer, "Visions of R. Asher," p. 398–399.

45. Compare Cohen, "Messianic Postures," pp. 219–223, and note 84 below.

46. Ruderman, "Hope against Hope," pp. 299–323; Malachi Beit-Arieh and Moshe Idel, "An Essay on the End and Astrology by R. Abraham Zacut," *QS* 54 (1979), pp. 174–194, (Hebrew); *QS* pp. 825–826. I have also found in a manuscript a Hebrew translation of one of the most famous apocalyptic documents in medieval Christianity, the so-called Prophecy of Tripoli, analyzed in detail in Lerner's *The Powers of Prophecy,* and I hope to discuss it elsewhere since it does not comprise mystical elements.

47. See Ms. Jerusalem-Mussaioff 24, fol. 34b; Ms. Jerusalem Mussayoff 5, fol. 120. See also in *Sefer ha-Meshiv,* Ms. Jerusalem, National and University Library 8° 147, fol. 102b, where the time of redemption is described as follows: "the verse (Isa. 62:5) said, 'For as a young man marries a virgin,' this is the mystery of the restoration of the Shekhinah to Her former state and first strength, as the verse suggests. That is the mystery of the descent of My Messiah from heaven before the eyes of all living creatures." For more on the whole issue see Idel, "Attitude to Christianity."

48. See the various versions of this dictum in Idel, "Attitude to Christianity," p. 94. Unlike the Abulafian and Sabbatean versions of the profound relation between the Messiah and the divinity, in this case we can speak more about a theophany than about a case of apotheosis.

49. See McGinn, *Apocalyptic Spirituality,* p. 198; Netanyahu, *Don Isaac Abravanel,* pp. 245–247, 251. In the same year, Marsilio Ficino wrote a famous letter proclaiming the beginning of the Golden Age; see Reeves, *Influence of Prophecy,* p. 429. On the background of Savonarola's eschatology see Donald Weinstein, "Millenarism in a Civic Setting: The Savonarola Movement in Florence," in Thrupp, ed., *Millennial Dreams in Action,* pp. 187–203.

50. See e.g. M. Reeves, "A Note on Prophecy and the Sack of Rome (1527)," in Reeves, ed., *Prophetic Rome,* p. 273: "The great eschatological myth of approaching catastrophe was shared by intellectuals and people alike. On the eve of the Sack Italy was rife with superstitions, calculations, and obsessions."

51. Cf. Elior, "Messianic Expectations."

52. See Werblowsky, *Joseph Karo,* pp. 127–128.

53. There is no comprehensive monograph on Shlomo Molkho. For material concerning him see Aescoly, *Jewish Messianic Movements,* pp. 389–391, 392–395, 400–405, 409–422; Idel, "Shlomo Molkho as Magician." More material concerning his views on messianism is extant in a manuscript, and I hope to make it available in the near future.

54. Werblowsky, *Joseph Karo,* pp. 72, 97–98, 100; Idel, "Shlomo Molkho as Magician"; see *Sefer ha-Mefo'ar,* pp. 40–44.

55. Silver, *History of Messianic Speculation,* pp. 134, 147–150; Rivka Shatz, "Lines for the Contour of the Messianic-Political Arousal after the Expulsion from Spain," *Daat* 11 (1983), pp. 53–66 (Hebrew); idem, "Gnostic Influences on the *Sefer ha-Mefo'ar* by Shlomo Molkho," in *Ancient Jewish Mysticism,* ed. J. Dan (Jerusalem, 1987), pp. 235–267 (Hebrew); Yoram Jacobson, "The Final Redemption in the Vision of Adam according to the Italian Rabbis during the Renaissance," *Daat* 11 (1983), pp. 67–90 (Hebrew). Molkho, in his *Sefer ha-Mefo'ar,* pp. 9–10, is introducing the motif of the savior as repairing Adam's sin quite explicitly, apparently under the influence of Christian thought. See also above, chap. 3, n. 10, and below, chap. 5, n. 71, and Rosenberg, "Exile and Redemption," p. 420.

56. See Idel, "Shlomo Molkho as Magician," p. 202.

57. See Scholem, "The Maggid," pp. 82–84, 89, Werblowsky, *Joseph Karo,* pp. 97–98, Idel, "Inquiries," p. 238n280; Bracha Sack, "R. Joseph Taitazak's Commentaries," in M. Idel, Z. Harvey,

and E. Schweid, eds., *Shlomo Pines Jubilee Volume* (Jerusalem, 1988), 1:341–356 (Hebrew). Aescoly pointed out the impact of *Sefer ha-Peliy'ah* on Molkho, an important and plausible point, though his proposal to see also an impact of Abulafia's messianic Kabbalah on the sixteenth-century figure via *Sefer ha-Peliy'ah* seems to me to be uncorroborated. See his *Jewish Messianic Movements,* pp. 232, 242n41, as well as his "Notes on the History of Messianic Movements," *Sinai* 12 (1943), pp. 84–89 (Hebrew). The affinity between Molkho and *Sefer ha-Peliy'ah* and Abulafia, on the one hand, and Sabbateanism, on the other, points to this book as an important conduit for messianic ideas, an issue that deserves more detailed analyses.

58. Werblowsky, *Joseph Karo,* pp. 97–98.

59. Idel, "Shlomo Molkho as Magician," p. 204n71. See also the view that Elijah will reveal himself suddenly in Rome; cf. *Sefer ha-Mefo'ar,* p. 43.

60. Idel, "Shlomo Molkho as Magician," p. 207.

61. Ibid., pp. 202–203.

62. On a messianic homily delivered in Mantua, see M. Idel, "An Unknown Drasha on R. Shlomo Molkho," *Studies in Jewish History Presented to Prof. Haim Beinart* (Ben Zvi Institute, Jerusalem, 1988), pp. 430–436 (Hebrew). Molkho's and David ha-Reuveni's stays in Venice and Molkho's messianic propaganda, which was joined by as important a figure as R. Menaḥem Elijah Ḥalfan, might have benefited from the messianic background of R. Asher Lemlein in the same region. Molkho mentions Venice in his most eschatological sermon, where he enumerates the cities that are conceived of as independent authorities, *serarot,* in the context of the Messiah's reception of the kingship from all the nations. See *Sefer ha-Mefo'ar,* p. 43. Their older contemporary, Egidio da Viterbo, and their younger contemporary, William Postel, had also been active in Venice for some years. An eschatological vision of Venice is central for the whole spiritual utopia of Postel, who lived and worked in the city in the middle of the sixteenth century. On Venice and Postel see the important studies of Marion Leathers Kuntz, "The Myth of Venice in the Thought of Guillaume Postel," in *Supplementum Festivum: Studies in Honor of Paul Oskar Kristeller,* Medieval and Renaissance Texts and Studies (Binghamton, 1987), pp. 505–523; idem, "Guilaume Postel e l'idea di Venezia come la magistratura perffeta," in M. L. Kuntz, *Postello, Venezia e il suo mondo* (Loschki, Firenze, 1988), pp. 163–178. On the myth of Venice among Jews see Abraham Melamed, "The Myth of Venice in Italian Renaissance Jewish Thought," *Italia Judaica* (Rome, 1983), 1:401–413. For messianic dreams that Abraham Michael Cardoso dreamed in Venice, according to his testimony, before Tzevi's public revelation as a Messiah, see the epistle printed by Scholem, *Studies and Texts,* p. 320. The nexus between sacred places and revelations in general, and messianic ones in particular, is reminiscent of the recently diagnosed "Jerusalem syndrome," a series of paranormal spiritual phenomena that recur in much greater intensity and more often when some persons come to Jerusalem, an issue that seems to be related to the more general situation of people believing that they approach a center of religious or other form of power.

63. This is the version published in my introduction to the new edition of Aescoly's book on David ha-Reuveni, pp. xxvii–xxx. "Salvation" translates *yesh'uah,* an overt allusion to Jesus. The nations will suffer indignities on account of their belief in Jesus and simultaneously because of the redemption of the Jewish people.

64. David Kaufmann, "Un poème messianique de Salomon Molkho," *REJ* 34 (1897), pp. 121–125.

65. See Scholem, *Sabbatai Ṣevi,* pp. 54, 309.

66. Idel, "Shlomo Molkho as Magician," pp. 194–202. Molkho refers several times to the eschatological revelation of Elijah in Rome; see e.g. *Sefer ha-Mefo'ar,* p. 43.

67. The terms *academy* here and *holy academy* below stand for the celestial academy, namely,

the collective of the souls of the righteous, the angels, the Messiah, and God Himself, who study Torah in the next world. The phrase *celestial academy,* in relation to revealing secrets from above, occurs several times in the introduction to *Sefer ha-Qanah,* which influenced Molkho's visions. See A. Z. Aescoly, "Notes on the History of Messianic Movements," *Sinai* 12 (1943), pp. 84–89 (Hebrew), as well as Idel, "Inquiries," p. 237, and compare Molkho's *Sefer ha-Mefo'ar,* p. 43. Both *Sefer ha-Qanah* and *Sefer ha-Peliy'ah* were written as partial revelations from above. For our discussion, the latter work is important for at least two reasons: it is a commentary on the first chapters of Genesis and therefore fits within the peculiar genre of interpretations dealt with here, such as pneumatic exegesis; and it has been profoundly influenced by Abulafian Kabbalah.

68. On instruction from heaven, see Isadore Twersky, *Rabad of Posquieres* (Harvard University Presss, Cambridge, 1962), pp. 296–297.

69. Printed from a manuscript in Idel, "Shlomo Molkho as Magician," pp. 204–206. See also idem, *Kabbalah: New Perspectives,* pp. 239–241. For complex exegesis in the messianic mode of biblical passages see the texts adduced and analyzed by Aescoly, *Jewish Messianic Movements,* pp. 383–395.

70. See Idel, "Introduction", pp. 24–26. See also the dates Postel brought in the name of the Venetian Virgin, who declared that it is incumbent on him to inform the entire world that either in 1539 or in 1541 the redemption started; cf. *Guillaume Postel et son interpretation du candelabre de Moyse,* ed. F. Secret (Nieuwkoop, B. de Graaf, 1966), p. 429n146, and also p. 394.

71. Cf. Ms. Moscow-Guensburg 302, n.p. The role of the Messiah here is reminiscent of that of the tzaddiq who sustains the world, especially of the hidden righteous, whose presence in the world is quintessential for its continuation. See Paul B. Fenton, "The Hierarchy of the Saints in Jewish and Islamic Mysticism" *Journal of the Muhyiddin Ibn 'Arabi Society* 10 (1991), pp. 12–34. Indeed, in R. Ḥayyim Vital's *Peri 'Etz Ḥayyim* (ed. Dubrovna), fol. 108c, there is a discussion similar to Molkho's but mentioning the tzaddiq in lieu of the Messiah. For the Messiah as a serpent in thirteenth-century Kabbalah see Liebes, *Studies in the Zohar,* p. 17; idem, *Sabbateaism and Its Kabbalah,* p. 205. On the transmigration of the soul of Adam through the prophets to the Christ see the view of William Postel, as adduced by J.-P. Brach, " 'Deux en une seule chair': Guillaume Postel et le Messie feminine," *Cahiers du groupe d'études spirituelles comparées* 3 [Feminité et spiritualité] (Arche, Edidit, 1995), p. 40n20.

72. See Werblowsky, *Joseph Karo,* pp. 97–100.

73. Ibid., pp. 2–7; Idel, "Shlomo Molkho as Magician," pp. 194–202. For more on the repercussions of the della Reina legend see Neḥemiah Ḥayyon's text translated in Carlebach, *Pursuit of Heresy,* p. 93, as well as below, chap. 7, n. 23.

74. Scholem, *Devarim be-Go,* p. 205; a shorter version of this passage is found in his *Messianic Idea,* p. 41. See also his more general formulation in an essay largely neglected by modern describers of Scholem's view of messianism, "Messianic Movements," pp. 335–336. See also Aescoly, *Jewish Messianic Movements,* pp. 260–264.

75. Compare to his *Kabbalah,* p. 68: "With the expulsion [from Spain] messianism become part of the very core of Kabbalah." See also ibid., p. 71, and Werblowsky, *Joseph Karo,* pp. 94–95. While sometimes Scholem emphasized the apocalyptic nature of the Kabbalah in the sixteenth century, at other times he underlined the symbolic nature of the Messiah. Cf. *Kabbalah,* p. 336. See also his *Messianic Idea,* pp. 42–43.

76. Scholem, *Major Trends,* p. 248, Idel, "Inquiries," pp. 195–201.

77. Namely, the lands of the Christians. This precise formulation may point to the fact that unlike the Jews of the lands of the crescent, where most of the Sephardi Jews found their refuge, the Ashkenazi and Italian ones were more open to messianic propaganda.

78. Cf. R. Jacob Ketzingon of Szrem, a student of R. Shlomo Luria, the Maharshal, in his *Ḥag Pesaḥ* (Cracow, 1597), fol. 27b, quoted and analyzed by Tamar, "On R. Asher Lemlein," p. 400. Tamar suggested that this passage was influenced by the description of R. Gedalyah ibn Yeḥiah's famous historical book *Shalshelet ha-Qabbalah.* Though the suggestion is reasonable, the description of the dissemination of Lemlein's propaganda seems to be much broader in Ketzingon's book than in *Shalshelet ha-Qabbalah,* where only "the whole Italian diaspora" is mentioned. See also the anonymous Prague chronicle from the beginning of the seventeenth century, where the tides from 1502, which are to be plausibly related to Lemlein, have produced a "great repentance" in all the Jewish diaspora. Cf. Abraham David, ed., *A Hebrew Chronicle from Prague (c. 1615)* (Dinur Center, Jerusalem, 1984), p. 5 (Hebrew). Thus, the amplitude of Lemlein's impact seems to be corroborated by several, and apparently independent, historical sources.

79. See M. Idel, "The Expulsion—Between Trauma and Creativity," in Aviva Doron, ed., *The Heritage of the Jews of Spain* (Lewinsky College of Education Publishing House, Tel Aviv, 1994), pp. 107–113 (Hebrew).

80. See Yosef Hayyim Yerushalmi, "Messianic Impulses in Joseph ha-Kohen," in Bernard D. Cooperman, ed., *Jewish Thought in the Sixteenth Century* (Harvard University Press, Cambridge, 1983), pp. 450–487, esp. pp. 483–484; idem, *Zakhor,* pp. 64–65.

81. Robert Bonfil, "How Golden Was the Age of the Renaissance in Jewish Historiography?" *History and Theory,* Beheft 27, *Essays in Jewish Historiography* (1988), pp. 78–102.

82. See Cohen, "Messianic Postures," esp. p. 206, where he attributes the messianic activism of Lemlein to Sephardi influences. There can be no doubt as to Abulafia's influence on Lemlein, and the formulations in the extant texts of this figure have much more to do with the more spiritual understanding of messianism than with the inauguration of an apocalyptic movement. Moreover, as mentioned above, Lemlein was one of the most articulate critics of the Sephardi Kabbalah. One may wonder if the distiction between Sephardi and Ashkenazi approaches should not be replaced by a more complex one, dealing with East and West, as I have proposed in my introduction; even in the West I see as an important desideratum to emphasis the importance of the Italian setting for the activity of both the Sephardi, in our case Abraham Abulafia, whose influence in Spain was minimal, and an Ashkenazi such as Lemlein.

Chapter 5: From Italy to Safed and Back, 1540–1640

1. Michel de Certeau, *La fable mystique,* vol. 1, *XVIe–XVIIe siècle* (Gallimard, Paris, 1982), pp. 211–212, reiterating the view of Henri Bremond, *Histoire littéraire du sentiment religieux en France,* vol. 2, L'invasion mystique, 1590–1620 (Paris 1916); Rufus M. Jones, *Spiritual Reformers in the Sixteenth and Seventeenth Centuries* (Beacon Press, Boston, 1959).

2. Reeves, *Influence of Prophecy,* pp. 235, 276–268, 365–366, 381, 429, 470, 503; and Genevive Javary, "A propos du thème de la Sekhina," in A. Faivre and F. Tristan, eds., *Kabbalistes Chretiens* (Albin Michel, Paris, 1979), pp. 300–302. On Egidio's relation to ha-Reuveni and his serving as an intermediary—and probably also as a translator—between ha-Reuveni and the pope see A. Z. Aescoly, *The Story of David Hareuveni* (Mossad Bialik, Jerusalem, 1993), pp. 34–35, 41, 152 (Hebrew). On the possible impact of the ha-Reuveni episode on Egidio's Kabbalistic writings see François Secret, *Les Kabbalistes chrétiens de la Renaissance* (Dunod, Paris, 1964), p. 117. A lost writing of this Augustinian cardinal was entitled *Opus contra Hebraeos de adventu Messiae et de divinis nominibus;* see Eugenio Massa, "Egidio da Viterbo e la metodologia del sapere nel cinquecento," in *Pensée humaniste et tradition chrétienne,* ed. H. Bedarida (CNRS, Paris, 1950), p. 185; Swietlicki, *Spanish Christian Cabala,* p. 85. On the special interest of Egidio in Abraham Abulafia's Kabbalistic

writings, Latin and Italian translations of which were prepared for his own use, see Moshe Idel, "Egidio da Viterbo and R. Abraham Abulafia's Writings," *Italia* 2 (1981), pp. 48–50 (Hebrew). It is obvious that the cardinal studied, inter alia, Abulafia's *Ḥayyei ha-'Olam ha-Ba'*. (On messianic stands in this book see above, chap. 2.) Compare François Secret, "Aegidiana Hebraica," *REJ* 121 (1962), pp. 409–416. On Egidio da Viterbo see more recently also Reeves, "Cardinal Egidio of Viterbo: A Prophetic Interpretation of History," in Reeves, ed., *Prophetic Rome*, pp. 91–109.

3. Reeves, *Influence of Prophesy*, p. 381; cf. Postel's French and Hebrew texts printed by François Secret, *Guillaume Postel, Apologies et Retractions* (Niewkoof, B. de Graaf, 1972), pp. 19–168. For an analysis of Postel's stands on the issues mentioned above see Bouwsma, *Concordia Mundi*, pp. 15, 45, 155, 162–164, 276–277; Popkin, "Conception of the Messiah," pp. 164–165. It seems that Johanna is the first lady to be attributed an understanding of the secrets of the *Zohar* or secrets of Kabbalah in general. According to one testimony, she encouraged Postel to translate the *Zohar* into Latin; see François Secret, *Le Zohar chez les Kabbalistes chrétiens de la Renaissance* (Mouton, Paris, 1964), p. 51. For more on the Venetian Virgin see the important studies of Marion Leathers Kuntz, *Guillaume Postel: The Prophet of the Restitution of All Things, His Life and Thought* (The Hague, 1981), pp. 69–142; idem, "Lodovico Domenichi, Guillaume Postel and the Biography of Giovanna Veronese," *Studi Veneziani*, n.s., 16 (1988), pp. 33–44; idem, "Guglielmo Postello e la 'Virgine Veneziana': Appunti storici sulla vita spirituale dell'Ospedatello nel Cinquecento," *Centro Tedesco di Studi Veneziani Quaderni* 21 (Venezia, 1981), pp. 3–24; Bernard McGinn, "Cabalists and Christians: Reflections on Cabala in Medieval and Renaissance Thought," in R. H. Popkin and G. M. Weiner, eds., *Jewish Christians and Christian Jews* (Kluwer, Dordrecht, 1994), pp. 23–24. See also J.-P. Brach, " 'Deux en une seule chair': Guillaume Postel et le Messie feminine," *Cahiers du groupe d'études spirituelles comparées* 3 [Feminité et spiritualité] (Arche, Edidit, 1995), pp. 40–42. In addition to Johanna's messianic role, see also the remark about Queen Christiana of Sweden's similar role, mentioned by Popkin, "Conception of the Messiah," p. 175n25. For the redemptive role of Mary, who, like Joanna, has been described as the second Eve, see Kingsley, *Goddesses' Mirror*, pp. 241–244, and Quirinus Kuhlmann's perception of Maria Anglicana.

4. See M. Idel, "Religion, Thought and Attitudes: The Impact of the Expulsion on the Jews," in Elie Kedourie, ed., *Spain and the Jews: The Sephardi Experience, 1492 and After* (Thames and Hudson, London, 1992), pp. 130–131.

5. E.g. Pico della Mirandola, Petrus Galatinus, or Guillaume Postel. See Yeshaiah Sonne, "The Place of the Kabbalah as a Means of Incitement of the Church in the 17th Century," *Bitzaron* 36 (1957), pp. 61–80 (Hebrew); W. J. Bouwsma, "Postel and the Significance of Renaissance Cabbalism," *Journal of the History of Ideas* 15 (1954), p. 230; Kenneth R. Stow, *Catholic Thought and Papal Jewry Policy, 1555–1593* (New York, 1977), pp. 204–208.

6. Yerushalmi, *Zakhor*, pp. 73–74; Ben-Sasson, *History of the Jewish People*, pp. 691–701.

7. It is sufficient to peruse Reeves, *Influence of Prophecy*, in order to see how important Italy was as the locus for the later reverberations of Joachimite eschatology. The impact of Italian Christian Kabbalistic thought related to eschatology is also evident in some cases in the Spanish sixteenth-century figures, see e.g. Swietlicki, *Spanish Christian Cabala*, pp. 7–8, 127, 144, 165; Karl A. Kottman, *Law and Apocalypse: The Moral Thought of Luis de Leon* (Martinus Nijhoff, The Hague, 1972), pp. 91–115. As to the more diffuse impact of Kabbalistic motifs on some Spanish mystics, a hypothesis advanced by Swietlicki, *Spanish Christian Cabala*, and by Deirdre Green, *Gold in the Crucible: Teresa of Avila and the Western Mystical Tradition* (Element Books, Longmead, 1989), I would adopt a much more cautious attitude. For the impact of Lutherianism on the numerous apocalyptic speculations and writings during the sixteenth century see Firth, *Apocalyptic Tradition*, and Barnes, *Prophecy and Gnosis*. See also the important contributions of John S. Mebane, *Renais-*

sance Magic and the Return of the Golden Age (University of Nebraska Press, Lincoln, 1989), and Harry Levin, *The Myth of the Golden Age in the Renaissance* (Indiana University Press, Bloomington, 1969); these two books deal with the more general turn toward utopian forms of thought in the sixteenth century, as does the chapter "Renovation mundi and Renaissance" in Reeves, *Influence of Prophesy,* pp. 429–452. I wonder whether the alchemical treatise attributed to the mysterious Abraham Eleazar, where messianic motifs are evident in the context of Kabbalistic views, was not written at the beginning of the sixteenth century and thus may be an additional example of the penetration of Jewish eschatology into Christian milieux together with Kabbalah. See Patai, *Jewish Alchemists,* pp. 238–257.

8. See e.g. *Zohar,* vol. 1, fol. 119a; vol. 2, fols. 7b, 9a, 120a; *Hanhagot ha-Ari,* printed in *The Toledoth Ha-Ari,* ed. Benayahu, p. 354; Scholem, *Sabbatai Ṣevi,* p. 53. For earlier traditions related to the arrival of the Messiah in Galilee see Wieder, *Judean Scrolls,* pp. 30–51. Wieder refers to this theme as part of a "Galilean tradition." For the Galilee as a place of revelation see George W. E. Nickelsburg, "Enoch, Levi, and Peter: Recipients of Revelation in Uper Galilee," *JBL* 100, no. 4 (1981), pp. 575–599. It is possible that the contact between the newcomers and the land of Israel, especially the place where the *Zohar* was composed, could in itself provoke messianic hopes. See Idel, "Land of Israel in Medieval Kabbalah," pp. 180–181, and also Pinchas Giller, "Recovering the Sanctity of the Galilee: The Veneration of Sacred Relics in Classical Kabbalah," *Journal of Jewish Thought and Philosophy* 4 (1994), pp. 147–169.

9. See Joseph Dan, *The Hebrew Story in the Middle Ages* (Keter, Jerusalem, 1974), p. 45 (Hebrew).

10. See the important monograph of A. Posnanski, *Schiloh* (Leipzig, 1904), and Berger, "Three Typological Themes," p. 164.

11. "The Year 1575 and the Messianic Excitement in Italy," in Tamar, *Studies,* pp. 11–38. On page 13 Tamar lists the various reasons for messianic irruptions in Italy, but he does not enumerate a reaction to the expulsion from Spain as one of them. For more on this computation see Berger, "Three Typological Themes," p. 164. On Dato's messianism in general see Jacobson, *Doctrine of Redemption,* esp. pp. 320–326, 335, 426, where the astrological approach to messianism is the most substantial source for his computations. On messianism in Italy see also the evidence adduced by Moshe Schulwas, *Roma vi-Yrushalayyim* (Jerusalem, 1944), pp. 41–88 (Hebrew); Joseph Hacker, "A New Letter on the Messianic Effervescence in Eretz Israel and in the Diaspora at the Beginning of the Sixteenth Century," *Shalem* 2 (1976), pp. 355–360 (Hebrew). More material related to Kabbalah and 1575 is found in manuscripts. See e.g. the tradition in the name of one of the important Italian Kabbalists, R. Moses Basola, who visited the land of Israel and was in contact with William Postel, that the Messiah will arrive in that year; cf. Ms. Oxford 2405, fol. 39b. Interestingly enough, in this manuscript the assumption is that the calculations concerning this year are "a tradition from the mouth of the ancient." What is more surprising, however, is to find a short passage adduced in the name of the famous Jewish Italian author "the maskkil R. 'Azariyah min ha-'Adumim," namely 'Azariyah de Rossi, as to the messianic valence of that year.

12. See Frank Kermode's expression "sense making paradigm," in *The Sense of an Ending: Studies in the Theory of Fiction* (Oxford University Press, London, 1966), p. 44.

13. On this figure see David Kaufmann, "Jacob Mantino: Une Page de l'Histoire de la Renaissance," *REJ* 27 (1893), pp. 30–60, 207–238.

14. I hope to develop this subject in another place. I would like to emphasize the fact that this author was an inhabitant of Venice, though he had good contacts with Rome. On Venice and messianism see above, chap. 4, n. 62.

15. *Sefer Ginnat Beitan,* chap. 52, Ms. Oxford 1578, fol. 63b. On this book see Gottlieb, *Studies,*

pp. 477–507, esp. p. 506, where part of the original Hebrew passage translated here has already been printed. Compare also to a similar messianic calculation, which adds the numerical value of the name Moshe, 345, to 1240 in order to suggest that the Messiah will come in the year 1585; see Bracha Sack, "The Commentaries of R. Abraham Galante and Their Affinities to the Writings of His Masters," *Meḥqrei Misgav Yerushalayyim be-Sifruyyiot 'Am Israel* (Jerusalem, 1987), pp. 85–86 (Hebrew). On cyclical time and history see G. W. Trompf, *The Idea of Recurrence in Western Thought: From Antiquity to the Renaissance* (University of California Press, Berkeley and Los Angeles, 1979), pp. 118–120; Mowinckel, *He That Comes,* pp. 151–152; as well as the many other references to scholarly views on the biblical linear theory collected by John Briggs Curtis, "A Suggested Interpretation of the Biblical Philosophy of History," *HUCA* 34 (1963), pp. 115–117; Cornelius Loew, *Myth, Sacred History and Philosophy* (Harcourt, Brace, New York, 1967), pp. 106, 146.

16. R. Joseph ben Shalom Ashkenazi, *Commentary on Sefer Yetzirah* (Jerusalem, 1965), fol. 3b.

17. See Rosenberg, "Return to the Garden of Eden," p. 57n54.

18. This understanding of the verb *ba'* occurs in *Sefer ha-Bahir* and the writings of Naḥmanides and his disciples.

19. On the issue of linear versus circular perceptions of history see Eliade, *Cosmos and History;* Paul Ricoeur, "The History of Religions and the Phenomenology of Time Consciousness," in J. M. Kitagawa, ed., *The History of Religions: Retrospect and Prospect* (Macmillan, New York, 1985), pp. 13–30; Macey, *Patriarchs of Time,* pp. 14–18; Tuveston, *Millennium and Utopia,* pp. 56–70. For an attempt to describe a more complex attitude toward time in Judaism, especially in some forms of Kabbalah which combined cyclical and linear time, see Moshe Idel, "Some Concepts of Time and History in Kabbalah."

20. As done e.g. by Tishby, *Messianism in the Generation of the Expulsions,* pp. 52–53; Elior, "Messianic Expectations," pp. 35–49.

21. See Idel, *Kabbalah: New Perspectives,* pp. 234–241.

22. See e.g. Devorah Dimant, "The Apocalyptic Interpretation of Ezekiel at Qumran," in *Messiah and Christos: Studies in the Jewish Origins of Christianity Presented to David Flusser,* ed. I. Gruenwald, S. Shaked, G. G. Stroumsa, (Mohr, Tübingen, 1992), pp. 31–51.

23. Ms. Leningrad-Firkowitch I, 325, fol. 4ab. The author quotes R. Yehudah he-Ḥasid, fol. 17b. Another mention of the Messiah, as the suffering servant, is found on fol. 16b.

24. Abraham Abulafia, introduction to *Commentary of the Torah,* Ms. Moscow-Guensburg 133, fol. 1a; Ms. Oxford 1956, fol. 76a.

25. Ms. Paris, Bibliothèque Nationale 774, fol. 119a. On the prophets that Abulafia assumes will proclaim the advent of the Messiah, a prophet himself, see below, appendix 1. See also the ecstatic treatise *Sha'arei Tzedeq,* p. 19.

26. Idel, "Neglected Writings."

27. Compare Scholem, *Major Trends,* p. 248; *Messianic Idea,* p. 42.

28. Idel, "Shlomo Molkho as Magician," p. 206.

29. On the Jerusalemite school of Kabbalists see the Gershom Scholem's introduction to R. Abraham ben Elieser ha-Levi, *Meshare Qitrin,* ed. M. Beit Arieh, (Jerusalem, 1978), pp. 9–42 (Hebrew).

30. Scholem, *Sabbatai Ṣevi,* p. 20. See also Solomon Schechter, *Studies in Judaism* (Atheneum, New York, 1970), pp. 231–297; Werblowsky, *Joseph Karo,* pp. 38–83; Mordechai Pachter, *From Safed's Hidden Treasures* (Merkaz Zalman Shazar, Jerusalem, 1994) (Hebrew).

31. Werblowsky, *Joseph Karo,* p. 128. If I am not mistaken, the author is prone to attribute a somewhat great importance to messianism in his later, "R. Joseph Karo."

32. See Bracha Sack, "Three Ages of Redemption in R. Moses Cordovero's 'Or Yaqar," in

Eschatology and Messianism, pp. 281–292 (Hebrew), as well as her numerous references to the Messiah in the thought of this Kabbalist in her *Kabbalah of Rabbi Moshe Cordovero.* For more on messianism in Safed see Gershom Scholem, "Sermon on Redemption by R. Shlomo de Turiel," *Sefunot,* vol. 1 (1957), 62–79 (Hebrew); R. Y. Z. Werblowsky, "A Collection of Prayers and Devotional Compositions by Solomon Alkabets," *Safed Volume,* ed. I. Ben-Zvi and M. Benayahu (Ben Zvi Institute, Jerusalem, 1962), 1:135–182 (Hebrew). It is appropriate to mention the possible relevance of a controversy that took place in the land of Israel between the more mystically oriented R. Jacob Berav, who was in favor of creating a rabbinic tribunal for authorizing the function of a rabbi, an act that was fraught with messianic meaning, and R. Levi ben *Ḥaviv of Jerusalem, who* opposed it. One of the reasons for the emergence of the controversy offered by Berav and accepted by scholars is the belief in an imminent advent of the Messiah, which should be preceded by the institution of *semikhah,* namely rabbinic ordination. On this issue see Katz, *Halakhah and Kabbalah,* pp. 5, 203, 217, 225–228, 231, 234–235. Katz relies on Berav, who adduces as the single testimony the view of Maimonides without resorting to any Kabbalistic argument. It is rather strange that an allegedly effervescent messianic-Kabbalistic center, as Safed was conceived to be by modern scholars, which hosted a sharp controvercy with the participation of R. Joseph Karo, a Kabbalist himself, did not contribute any Kabbalistic argument. Even the messianic explanation of the controversy, as presented by Katz, is a bit circular, as it relies on the messianic mood of the Safedian Kabbalists as solid fact. Moreover, as he himself correctly asserts, the stands of Berav and ben Haviv are not new but reflect more traditional positions on the subject. See Katz, *Halakhah and Kabbalah,* p. 228. The extent of the influence of Maimonides' view of messianism is visible long after the emergence of Lurianic Kabbalah; see the great effort of Abraham Michael Cardoso to counteract the arguments against the messianism of Tzevi on the basis of Maimonidean criteria in *Hilekhot Melakhim;* cf. Scholem, *Studies and Texts,* pp. 303, 319, 327–328.

33. See Mordechai Pachter, "Homiletical and Pietistic Literature of 16th Century Safed" (Ph.D. diss., Hebrew University of Jerusalem, 1976) (Hebrew); idem, "The Beginning of Kabbalistic Ethical Literature in 16th Century Safed," in J. Dan, ed., *Culture and History, Ino Sciaky Memorial Volume* (Misgav Yerushalayim, Jerusalem, 1987), pp. 77–94 (Hebrew). As to the origin of the messianic understanding of the activity of the Safedian Kabbalist before Luria see Scholem, *Major Trends,* 250; "This new Kabbalism stands and falls with its programme of bringing its doctrine home to the community, and preparing it for the coming of the Messiah." This view has been repeated oftentimes. See e.g. Werblowsky: "Schon im 16.Jhdt. war die (vorlurianische) kabbalistische Froemigkeits- und Devotionpraxis, inklusive Askese, durch and durch messianisch orientiert und motiviert." "Messianismus und Mystik," in P. Schaefer and J. Dan, eds., *Gershom Scholem's* Major Trends in Jewish Mysticism, *50 Years After* (J. C. B. Mohr, Tübingen, 1993), p. 21. Werblowsky's statement seems to me to overemphasize the modest role of those messianic elements, which indeed are present in this sort of literature. Historically and phenomenologically speaking, both Scholem's and Werblowsky's overemphasis on the messianic motivation and orientation of Kabbalistic literature and praxis is quite surprising for a skeptical reader of this literature like myself. Werblowsky's statement, apparently aimed at my skeptical stand toward the modern enthusiasm regarding the importance of messianism in Safed, remains unsubstantiated by any new example or even by a bibliographical reference, but relies on the conviction that Scholem's strong messianic reading of the sixteenth-century Kabbalah is obviously correct and thus does not require fresh reflection or additional textual proofs. Indeed, this characterization is proudly and explicitly embraced by Werblowsky himself, who wrote in this context that "[t]he author of this chapter will, for brevity's sake, be very dogmatic, well aware that this argument, which closely follows the late Gershom Scholem's theories, may

contradict the views of other authors in this collective volume." "R. Joseph Karo," p. 181. Indeed, he decided to ignore the scholarship on the topic he pretends to present, and this deliberate ignorance is evident also in his "Shabbetai Zevi." A capitulation to dogmatic recapitualation does not add weight to Scholem's argument, which should be examined against the proofs he brought in order to make his point, and not by assiduous repetition. I would suggest a comparison between the messianic reading of Safedian Kabbalah, and sometimes even of the whole literture of sixteenth- and seventeenth-century Jewish spirituality, nourished by Scholem's opinion, and the description of Safed by Solomon Schechter, whose more general account of the spiritual life in the city does not resort to the messianic element; see his *Studies in Judaism* (Jewish Publication Society, Philadelphia, 1908), pp. 202–306. The diferences between the two pictures of Safed reflect, in my opinion, two different intellectual ambiances that informed Jewish scholarship. Whereas a scholar expressing Scholem's views does assert that the "amazing achievement of the Safed Revival was its explosive (as subsequent developmemnts showed) combination of kabbalistic mysticism and messianism," thus anachronistically projecting the Sabbatean drama in Safed (cf. Werblowsky, "The Safed Revival," in Green, ed., *Jewish Spirituality,* 2:11), Schechter describes the Safedian masters much more as anticipating eighteenth-century Hasidic spirituality.

34. Gries, *Conduct Literature,* pp. 41–80. See also below, appendix 2.

35. Compare, however, the opposite claim found in Scholem's school, e.g. Werblowsky, "Messianism in Jewish History," in Saperstein, ed., *Essential Papers,* p. 48; Lawrence Fine, "The Contemplative Practive of Yiḥudim," in Green, ed., *Jewish Spirituality,* 2:94. For discussions of messianic topics in Safed see Sack, "Commentaries of R. Abraham Galante," pp. 62–86, and the pertinent bibliography adduced there. I do not deny the presence of messianic issues in the writings of the Safedian Kabbalist, but rather refute the formative role of these elements in the structure of the Kabbalistic literature, as claimed by modern scholars. See e.g. Katz, *Halakhah and Kabbalah,* pp. 225–228, 234–235.

36. See Idel, "R. Yehudah Ḥallewah," pp. 146–147; David B. Ruderman, *Kabbalah, Magic, and Science: The Cultural Universe of a Sixteenth-Century Jewish Physician* (Havard University Press, Cambridge, 1988), pp. 125–126.

37. Idel, "R. Yehudah Ḥallewah," pp. 146–148.

38. See R. Zakhariah Al-Tzahari's testimony adduced and discussed by Tamar, *Studies,* p. 117; On the presence in Safed of Jews interested in mysticism from all over the Jewish world see Scholem, *Kabbalah,* p. 72. On the spiritual atmosphere in Safed see also Solomon Schechter, "Safed in the Sixteenth Century," in his *Studies in Judaism* (JPS, Philadelphia, 1958), pp. 231–298; Tamar, *Studies,* pp. 69–106, 141–169; Idel, "R. Yehudah Ḥallewah," pp. 122–124.

39. On this literature see Gries, *Conduct Literature,* pp. 102–141; Ronit Meroz, "The *Ḥavurah* of R. Moses ben Makir and Its Regulations," *Pe'amim,* 31 (1987), pp. 40–61 (Hebrew). As Scholem has correctly put it, this literature "did more for the mass dissemination of Kabbalah than those books dealing with Kabbalah in the narrower sense whose mystical content was comprehensible only to a few." Cf. his *Kabbalah,* p. 73.

40. See the new material adduced by Abraham David, "Halakhah and Commerce in the Biography of Isaac Luria," in Elior and Liebes, eds., *Lurianic Kabbalah,* pp. 287–297 (Hebrew). Compare, however, to the claims of Tishby and Werblowsky—the latter reproducing Tishy's argument without mentioning him—that the Ashkenazi extraction of Luria is of no significance in order to disqualify his as a responder to the crisis of the expulsion. Without adducing any new material in order to substantiate their claim, and relying solely on a late and legendary, though not totally impossible, attribution of a Sephardi extraction of Luria's mother, the two scholars made

desperate efforts to save Scholem's hypothesis on the reaction to the expulsion in Luria's Kabbalistic system. See, respectively, "An Overthrow in Kabbalah Scholarship," *Zion* 54 (1989), pp. 222; "Imaginary Innovation in Kabbalah Research, *Zion* 54 (1989), pp. 490–491 (Hebrew); and "Messianismus und Mystik," p. 17. I hope to return to this issue in a separate study, where more material on the self-consciousness of Luria as an Ashkenazi will be adduced. Meanwhile, see Ronit Meroz, "Selections from Ephraim Penzieri: Luria's Sermon in Jerusalem and the Kavvanah in Taking Food," in Elior and Liebes, eds., *Lurianic Kabbalah,* p. 213 (Hebrew). Interestingly enough, Ariel Bension, an author strongly inclined to emphasize the Sephardi achievements in matters of mysticism, has built up a typology, too biased in my opinion, which compares Cordovero as the paragon of the Sephardi poetic mode of thought to Luria, who "represents" the "dry" Ashkenazi mode. See his *The Zohar in Moslem and Christian Spain* (Hermon Press, New York, 1974), pp. 229–233. The legend of the Sephardi mother of Luria is naturally absent in Bension's presentation. A study in itself may attempt to analyze the different appropriations of Luria's extraction to different academic and cultural goals, an issue that does not concern us here. See n. 60 below.

41. See Scholem, *Major Trends,* pp. 244–286.

42. See Idel, "Inquiries", pp. 239–243, and note 48 below.

43. Tamar, "The ARI and the RAHU as Messiah ben Yoseph," in *Studies,* p. 118. It should be noted that almost all the evidence related to Luria's messianism adduced by Tamar is either from writings of Vital or from those influenced by him.

44. Tamar, "ARI and the RAHU," pp. 115–120.

45. Tamar, "ARI and the RAHU," pp. 120–123; idem, "Messianic Dreams," pp. 211–229, and Michal Oron, "Dream, Vision and Reality in Ḥaim Vital's *Sefer ha-Ḥezyonot,*" in Elior and Liebes, eds., *Lurianic Kabbalah,* pp. 299–310 (Hebrew). Some of Vital's messianic dreams have been translated by Patai, *Messiah Texts,* pp. 267–270. A passage that has passed unnoted by modern scholarship of Kabbalah and whose authorship is not clear attributes to R. Ḥayyim Vital a revelation from Elijah concerning an enigmatic poem about the date of the advent of the Messiah. See Samuel Krauss, "Un texte cabbalistique sur Jesus," *REJ* 62 (1911), pp. 242–243.

46. Mordechai Pachter, *Milei Di-Shemaya' by Rabbi Elazar Azikri* (Tel Aviv, 1991) (Hebrew).

47. Compare the different view of Elior, "Messianic Expectations."

48. See Tamar, "Messianic Dreams," pp. 228–229.

49. See *Sefer ha-Ḥezyonot,* ed. Aharon Aescoly (Mossad ha-Rav Kook, Jerusalem, 1954), p. 137.

50. Idel, "Maimonides and Kabbalah," pp. 51–54.

51. The recurence of the theory of metempsychosis in the writings of Christian Kabbalists, either because of the influence of Pythagorean and Neoplatonic sources or because of Kabbalistic influences, could only strengthen the concern with this type of thought among the Jews. In any case, the possible phenomenological and historical similarities between the Jewish and pagan views of metempsychosis were pointed out both by opponents of Kabbalah and by Kabbalists: see Idel, "Differing Conceptions of Kabbalah," pp. 158–162. I hope to deal with this issue in a separate study. See also Ruderman, *Kabbalah, Magic, and Science,* and Liebes, *On Sabbateaism and Its Kabbalah,* p. 407n180.

52. Scholem, *Origins of the Kabbalah,* p. 459. I found this idea already expressed very clearly in a manuscript where Shlomo Molkho's Kabbalistic traditions were preserved; see above, chap. 4, n. 72. See also Scholem, *Sabbatai Ṣevi,* pp. 56–57. On the Lurianic use of metempsychosis for messianic aims see Liebes, "The Two Roes of a Doe," pp. 115–116.

53. See Idel, "Shlomo Molkho as Magician," pp. 216–217.

54. *Sefer ha-Ḥezyonot,* p. 68; Berger, "Captive at the Gate of Rome," pp. 16–17. For additional discussion of the identity of the Caesar see below, appendix 2.

55. Berger, "Captive at the Gate of Rome," 22; Tamar, "Messianic Dreams and Visions," pp. 214–215. On Vital's confrontations with R. Ya'aqov Abulafia see *Sefer ha-Ḥezyonot,* pp. 31–32.

56. Tamar, *Studies,* p. 16. Indeed, the most important messianic writing of sixteenth-century Italy, *Sefer Migdal David,* was composed after 1555, before Vital's visit to Safed. See Jacobson, *Doctrine of Redemption,* pp. 8, 13–26. Though Vital himself was a Kabbalist, it seems, as Jacobson suggests, that his Kabbalah did not substantially penetrate his messianic thinking. See *Doctrine of Redemption,* p. 99 and also p. 343n2.

57. See Ronit Meroz, "Faithful Transmission versus Innovation: Luria and His Disciples," in P. Schaefer and J. Dan, eds., *Gershom Scholem's* Major Trends in Jewish Mysticism, *50 Years After* (J. C. B. Mohr, Tübingen, 1993), pp. 257–275. On the possibility that Vital influenced the messianic image of his master because of his own strong messianic inclinations see Idel, "One in a Town," p. 104n88. See also Pachter, *From Safed's Hidden Treasures,* pp. 39–40n2, and Bension, *Zohar in Muslim and Christian Spain,* pp. 230–232, who attributes to Vital a great influence on the formulation and dissemination of Luria's thought and persona, insinuating even that Vital attributed his own views to his master.

58. "Is there a world that was expressed in human words that is more hidden and occult . . . than the Lurianic Kabbalah is?" From the second aphorism of Scholem's *Ten Unhistorical Aphorisms on Kabbalah* and the comments on this passage in David Biale, "Gershom Scholem's Ten Unhistorical Aphorisms," in Harold Bloom, ed., *Gershom Scholem* (Chelsea House, New York, New Haven, Philadelphia, 1987), pp. 105–106, and Joseph Dan, "Beyond the Kabbalistic Symbol," *JSJT* 5 (1986), pp. 369–370 (Hebrew).

59. The most detailed description of Lurianic theosophy available in print is by I. Tishby, *Doctrine of Evil and the Kelippah in Lurianic Kabbalism* (Magnes Press, Jerusalem, 1984) (Hebrew).

60. See Scholem, *Messianic Idea,* p. 59. See already the formulations in his *Major Trends,* pp. 244–286; this approach was to be adopted by many subsequent scholars, e.g. Yerushalmi, *From Spanish Court,* p. 43.

61. Ms. New York JTS 2122, fol. 1a copied, with some varia, at the end of Vital's preface to *'Etz Ḥayyim,* fol. 5c; see also R. Jacob Ḥayyim Tzemaḥ's version in his *Meqor Ḥayyim,* Ms. New York, JTS 2205, fol. 1a, and R. Moses Graff, *'Etz Ḥayyim,* fol. 6b. To be sure, this view of the task of Kabbalah is not new with Lurianic Kabbalah; it is explicitly found in Cordovero's writings and in those influenced by his thought. See Bracha Sack, "The Sources of R. Abraham Azulai's Book *Ḥesed Le-Avraham,*" *QS* 56 (1981), p. 168 (Hebrew). See also a Hasidic text attributed to R. Simḥah Bunem of Przyska, quoted in Louis Jacobs, *Hasidic Prayer* (Schocken, New York, 1978), p. 153. Compare also to *Tiqqunei ha-Zohar,* no. 69, fol. 109ab, where the assumption is that the destruction of the shells is part of the eschatological eon: "When the King Messiah will come, God will make the shells pass away, on high, on the middle and below." Unlike the later Kabbalistic formulations adduced above, in *Tiqqunei ha-Zohar* it is God who plays the main role in the fight with the demonic powers, while the use of Kabbalah itself is not involved with the cathartic process.

62. *Commentary on Tiqqunei ha-Zohar,* printed in *'Or Yaqar,* 1:24–25; quoted and discussed in Sack, "Three Dates of Redemption in R. Moses Cordovero's *Sefer 'Or Yaqar,*" in Baras, ed., *Messianism and Eschatology,* p. 292. See also another passage of Cordovero, printed in B. Sack's "The Attitude of R. Moses Cordovero to the Literature of the Zohar and to R. Shimon bar Yoḥai and His Circle," in *The Frank Talmage Memorial Volume,* ed. Barry Walfish (Haifa University Press, Haifa, and Brandeis University Press, 1993), 1:65 (Hebrew). Cordovero's discussions of the Messiah display a strong propensity toward the suffering role of the Messiah. See the interesting passages analyzed by Sack, *Kabbalah of Rabbi Moshe Cordovero,* pp. 232–234, where the zoharic views of the Messiah's *via passionis* have been amplified. See also Liebes, "Messiah of the Zohar," p. 206n406.

63. Liebes, "Two Young Roes of a Doe," p. 126. Compare, however, to Werblowsky's faithful presentation of Scholem's argument of the linear vision of history in Lurianic Kabbalah in "Shabbetai Zevi," pp. 207–208.

64. *'Adam 'eliyon.* On the ancient cosmic understandings of Adam, including his status as redeemer and redeemed, see Fossum, *Name of God,* pp. 266–291.

65. *Lehikallel bo.* On this term for entering the divine see Idel, "Universalization and Integration," pp. 38–39.

66. R. Ḥayyim Vital, *Sha'ar ha-Mitzwot* (Jerusalem, 1962), fol. 78; idem, *Sha'ar Ruaḥ ha-Qodesh* (Jerusalem, 1912), fol. 11a; Idel, *Kabbalah: New Perspectives,* p. 57. On tiqqun and redemption see Scholem, *Sabbatai Ṣevi,* p. 15; Rosenberg, "Exile and Redemption," pp. 417–418. On the identity between the Lurianic *'adam qadmon* and the Messiah in Knorr von Rosenroth, *Kabbala Denudata,* 2:2, see Wirszubski, *Pico della Mirandola,* p. 239–240. Under his influence there is an identification between the Lurianic *'adam qadmon*—and sometimes also the concept of the *tehiru,* namely the residue of divine light within the space of the *tzimtzum*—and the Messiah in several thinkers. See e.g. Anne Conway (cf. above chap. 2, n. 138), pp. 10–11, as well as p. 18; Carl G. Jung, *Mysterium Coniunctionis,* trans. R. F. C. Hull, Bollingen Series, 20 (Princeton University Press, Princeton, 1977), pp. 412–415. The same topic reverberates in Johann Georg Wachter, *Elucidarium Cabalisticus* (Rome, 1706), p. 16, and in Leibniz's *Remarques critiques de Leibniz après le manuscript original de la Bibliothèque de Hanovre,* printed by A. Foucher de Careil (Paris, 1854), p. 16–17.

67. *Tanḥuma',* pericope *ki tisa'.* See Idel, *Golem,* pp. 34–35, and also Bentzen, *King and Messiah,* pp. 39–47; Benjamin Murmelstein, "Adam, ein Beitrag zur Messiaslehre," *Wiener Zeitschrift für die Kunde des Morgenlandes* 35 (Vienna, 1928/29), pp. 242–275; 36, pp. 51–86; Ricoeur, *Symbolism of Evil,* pp. 232–278.

68. *Sha'ar ha-Pesuqim* (Tel Aviv, 1962), p. 12. See also ibid., p. 99.

69. See Liebes, "Messiah of the Zohar," pp. 109–110; Mopsik, *Les grands textes,* pp. 149–234.

70. See Pedaya " 'Flaw' and 'Correction,' " passim.

71. Meroz, *Redemption in Lurianic Teaching,* pp. 363–364.

72. See R. Ḥayyim Vital, *Sha'ar ha-Pesuqim* (Tel Aviv, 1962), pericope *Shemot,* fol. 2 col. 3; Vital, *Sefer ha-Liqqutim* (Jerusalem, 1913), fol. 89a.

73. *Sefer 'Emeq ha-Melekh,* fol. 1 cols. 1–3; Idel, "Land of Israel in Medieval Kabbalah," pp. 208–209.

74. *Sefer 'Emeq ha-Melekh,* intro., fol. 1 col. 3.

75. See Meroz, *Redemption in Lurianic Teaching,* pp. 31–32; 297–298; 360.

76. Ibid., pp. 287–291; 352–355.

77. I have borrowed the term *pre-eschatological* from R. J. Zwi Werblowsky, "Messianism in Jewish History," *Journal of the World History* 11 (1968–1969), p. 40, though Werblowsky himself would not apply it to Luria's Kabbalah.

78. The view that there is a spark of the Messiah in every generation was not originally formulated in connection with Luria; neither did he apply it to himself. See Scholem, *Sabbatai Ṣevi,* pp. 60–65.

79. See ibid., p. 44. See also pp. 67–68; Schultz, *Judaism and the Gentile Faith,* p. 230; Werblowsky, "Messianism in Jewish History," in Saperstein, ed., *Essential Papers,* p. 48, introduction, n. 22. In this passage Scholem is certainly right in acknowledging the absence of a clear formulation of a stand that he attributes to the Kabbalists. But his crucial assumption that despite its absence it is this allegedly Kabbalistic stand that is "clearly the view that underlies the whole Lurianic system" needs clarification in order to be accepted, even more so when it becomes what I propose to call a hyperthesis of Kabbalah scholarship.

80. Scholem, *Sabbatai Ṣevi,* pp. 33–66, 69–71, 75; *Major Trends,* pp. 285–286, 288–289; "Messianic Movements," p. 337. I find some of the scholars' formulations concerning the dissemination of Lurianic messianism quite dialectical and paradoxical. For example, Werblowsky says that the messianic valences of Lurianism are not to be found explicitly in this Kabbalistic literature (just as Scholem said above) while asserting that "[u]nderstandably enough, it was not so much the esoteric doctrine as its messianic high voltage that galvanized the public and crystalized its apocalyptic mood." Werblowsky, "The Safed Revival," p. 30. The same idea is faithfully repeated in his "Shabbetai Zevi," p. 209. How, though, could the "public" respond to the "high voltage" in an esoteric doctrine which only "implicitly" deals with messianism? Moreover, the whole claim of the dissemination depends upon the "popular preachers and moralists" who were instrumental in the propagandistic activity. For the time being, however, no study seems to support such a claim.

Werblowsky, "Shabbetai Zevi," p. 209, asks very pertinently, "Who were the 'missionaries' and authors whose zeal contributed to the phenomenal spread?" but gives no answer, since, as he writes immediately afterward, "If Scholem's thesis is correct, as no doubt it is, it would account for the messianic high-voltage in the atmosphere of the seventeenth century Jewry etc." He has not attempted to answer to his own important question; indeed, he believes that the answer is less important than his declaration of Scholem's correctness. In other words, the undeniable correctness of Scholem's thesis ensures the existence of mediators who spread Lurianic Kabbalah. It would be better to seek corroboration of the thesis in more recent scholarship. See e.g. Werblowsky's systematic ignorance of the material collected in the article mentioned in the next note.

81. Some of the issues discussed here are described in detail in Moshe Idel, "'One from a Town, Two from a Clan': The Diffusion of Lurianic Kabbala and Sabbateanism: A Re-Examination," *Pe'amim* 44 (1990), pp. 5–30 (Hebrew); English version, *Jewish History* 7 no. 2 (1993), pp. 79–104. To the evidence adduced in this study much more material can be added to the effect that Lurianic Kabbalah was less widespread than modern scholars assume. See e.g. Cardoso's testimony, in an epistle printed in Scholem, *Studies and Texts,* p. 330, as well as our discussion below in appendix 2.

82. Joseph Dan, "No Evil Descends from Heaven," in B. D. Cooperman, ed., *Jewish Thought in the Sixteenth Century* (Harvard University Press, Cambridge, 1983), pp. 102–103; Werblowsky, "R. Joseph Karo," p. 187.

83. *Major Trends,* pp. 257–258, where Scholem accurately observed that almost the whole dissemination of Lurianism in the last decade of the sixteenth century and the first decade of the seventeenth century is due to this Kabbalist and his followers.

84. See the discussion of Gries, *Conduct Literature,* p. 82.

85. See *Zohar,* vol. 3, fol. 124b (quoted also by Nathan of Gaza, cf. Scholem, *Sabbatai Ṣevi,* p. 126), and *Tiqqunei Zohar,* tiqqun no. 6 (Vilna, 1867), fol. 25a.

86. This is another work of Tzemaḥ's. The passage referred to here is from a manuscript of a student of Vital—who seems to have been the source of Tzemaḥ's discussion—and analyzed in Moshe Idel, "More on R. David ben Yehudah he-Ḥasid and R. Isaac Luria," *Daat* 7 (1981), pp. 69–70 (Hebrew).

87. On this text see also Meroz, *Redemption in Lurianic Teaching,* pp. 169–171.

88. This passage is a topos of Kabbalists, dealing with their awareness that the dissemination of Kabbalah and the disclosure of its secrets are signs for the last generation, namely that preceding the coming of the Messiah. Its source seems to be R. Yehudah Ḥayyat's preface to his commentary on *Sefer Ma'arekhet ha-'Elohut* named *Minḥat Yehudah,* fol. 1b, wherefrom it was copied time and again by numerous Kabbalists.

89. See Gershom Scholem, "On the History of the Kabbalist R. Jacob Ḥayyim Tzemaḥ and His Literary Activity," *QS* 26 (1950), p. 194 (Hebrew). Scholem, *Sabbatai Ṣevi,* p. 70n99, refers to

this text in a short remark without discussing the implications of Tzemaḥ's passage for his thesis. Scholem's note in *Sabbatai Ṣevi* was referred to also by Bernard D. Weinryb, *The Jews of Poland* (JPS, Philadelphia, 1973), p. 226, in the context of the status of Kabbalah in Poland; see also Idel, "One from a Town," pp. 85–86. My impression is that the model of drawing down the Messiah owes to Cordovero's attitude to Kabbalah.

90. I have found numerous uses of this way of describing the bringing about the advent of the Messiah in R. Naḥman of Braslav's *Liqqutei Halakhot,* Hilekhot Haksher Kelim, chap. 4, in the context of Elijah's drawing down the spirit of the Messiah. The verb used is *mamshikh.* See also my discussion of his contemporary, R. Qalonimus Qalman Epstein, below, Concluding Remarks.

91. Scholem's view, expressed in *Sabbatai Ṣevi,* pp. 69–70, to the effect that a statement quoted by R. Moses Prager Graff that the Messiah can be drawn down by Lurianic practices "was current in Kabbalistic circles even before Sabbatai's appearance" is not waranted, for the time being, by additional sources. Tzemaḥ's passage seems to be the single plausible Lurianic source for Scholem's phrase in *Sabbatai Ṣevi,* p. 70, "to draw down the Messiah." See also below, chap. 6.

92. Scholem, *Messianic Idea in Judaism,* p. 44.

93. Scholem, *Major Trends,* p. 261 (emphasis added). The rather qualified formulation at the beginning of the chapter on Luria turned more definitive at the end of the same chapter. See ibid., p. 286, where Scholem summarizes the views of the Lurianic Kabbalists: "For them, Exile and Redemption were in the strictest sense great mystical symbols which point to something in the Divine Being . . . the man of spiritual action who through the *Tikkun* breaks the exile, the historical exile of the Community of Israel and that inner exile in which all creation groans." On the existence of earlier Geronese, and perhaps even Provençal Kabbalistic traditions regarding theosophical interpretations of the concept of divine withdrawal, existent since the beginning of the Spanish Kabbalah, see Moshe Idel, "On the Concept of *Zimẓum* in Kabbalah and Its Research," in Elior and Liebes, eds., *Lurianic Kabbalah,* pp. 59–112 (Hebrew).

94. Sabbatai Ṣevi, p. 31.

95. Scholem, *Messianic Idea,* p. 45. For an important survey of concepts of exile in the sixteenth century see Rosenberg, "Exile and Redemption."

96. I consider to be a significant task of a creative scholar—as Scholem indeed was—to advance hypothetical and often speculative interpretations whenever there are no other better ways to understand and explain a religious phenomenon by resorting to more ordinary textual expressions that would describe the focus of a certain complex system of thought. Yet I fear that the uncritical repetitions of hypothetical interpretations, when adduced by other scholars who accept them as facts without introducing new material, might be a sign of academic epigonism. See also above, notes 35 and 42.

97. Scholem, *Messianic Idea,* p. 45.

98. Ibid., p. 46.

99. Cf. Scholem, *Major Trends,* p. 286. Scholem's view on withdrawal and exile reverberates in the most recent comprehensive book on Jewish history: Ben Sasson, ed., *A History of the Jewish People,* p. 697.

100. This stand does not easily concord with Scholem's different view as to the escapist nature of Kabbalistic eschatology. For this and more on symbols, messianism and history see below, Concluding Remarks.

101. See also below, appendix 2.

102. See Scholem, *Messianic Idea,* p. 39.

103. Ibid. See also *Sabbatai Ṣevi,* pp. 42, 48–49. See also the quotation from Werblowsky

above, Introduction, p. 2. On progress and redemption see Tuveston, *Millennium and Utopia,* pp. 153–203.

104. See Scholem, *Sabbatai Ṣevi,* p. 47. The single text adduced by Scholem to illustrate the concept of continuous progress stems from the son of R. Ḥayyim Vital, R. Shmuel Vital, who describes such a continuous refinement in the context of the exodus from Egypt. Though this may indeed reflect some earlier views, the absence of a clear-cut discussion of the the eschatological redemption in terms of a gradual tiqqun problematizes Scholem's emphasis on progress.

105. The religious life of the inhabitants of Safed has been described by scholars in quite rosy terms. See the ways it was presented by Schechter, Scholem, and Werblowsky. For a more complex description of some religiously problematic aspects of the life in Safed see Idel, "R. Yehudah Ḥallewah," pp. 122–124, and n. 38 above. See also Scholem, *Sabbatai Ṣevi,* p. 51.

106. See e.g. the Hasidic classic *Ma'or va-Shemesh,* by R. Qalonimus Qalman Epstein, p. 101.

107. Compare Scholem's claim that the masses alone subscribed to the apocalyptic vision of redemption, while the spiritual elite was concerned with the Lurianic theory of tiqqun. Cf. *Sabbatai Ṣevi,* p. 52. See, however, the quite apocalyptic description of the Messiah in the work of another Safedian Kabbalist, R. Moses Cordovero's text printed and analyzed by Sack, *Kabbalah of Rabbi Moshe Cordovero,* pp. 232–233.

Chapter 6: Sabbateanism and Mysticism

1. We will deal here only with some mystical aspects of the Sabbatean phenomena. This is not to say that mysticism is the only aspect of Sabbateanism worth discussing, for this mass movement obviously possessed other central features which should be addressed by different methodological tools from those adopted in this book. Gershom Scholem has already presented many of those elements in detail in his magisterial monograph on the movement, *Sabbatai Ṣevi, the Mystical Messiah,* while the mystical aspects of Sabbatai Tzevi's spiritual life have been discussed again more recently by Yehuda Liebes. For a variety of repetitions of Scholem's view of Sabbatai Tzevi which do not add any significant insight see the summaries of Werblowsky, e.g. "Shabbetai Zevi," where he offers in English a faithful version of Scholem's views ignoring all the scholarship written after the master's death. On the other hand, see the innovative approach to the subject by Liebes, *Studies in Jewish Myth,* pp. 93–114.

2. See Silver, *History of Messianic Speculation,* pp. 161–179; Yerushalmi, *From Spanish Court,* pp. 306–313; Sharot, *Messianism, Mysticism, and Magic,* pp. 103–104, 119–120; Yaakov Barnai, "Christian Messianism and the Portuguese Marranos: The Emergence of Sabbateanism in Smyrna," *Jewish History* 7 (1993), pp. 119–126; Yosef Kaplan, *The Western Sephardi Diaspora* (Misrad ha-Bitaḥon, Tel Aviv, 1995), pp. 119–126 (Hebrew).

3. Yaakov Barnai, "The Outbreak of Sabbateanism: The Eastern European Factor," *Journal for Jewish Thought and Philosophy* 4 (1994), pp. 171–183, who pointed out some remarks of Scholem as to the possible impact of the massacres on Sabbatai Tzevi, ibid., pp. 171–172. Compare, however, Dan, "Gershom Scholem and Jewish Messianism," p. 79, who claims that the absence of a connection between the massacres in Poland and Sabbatean messianism has been "reinforced by the intensive studies of other scholars over the past few decades." Unfortunately, he does not disclose the identity of those scholars or where may someone find these "intensive studies." See also J. Dan, "The Historical Conception of the late Prof. Gershom Scholem," *Zion* 47 (1982), p. 171 (Hebrew); Katz, *Halakhah and Kabbalah,* pp. 327–328n73.

4. Richard H. Popkin, "Three English Tellings of the Sabbatai Zevi Story," *Jewish History* 8

(1994), pp. 43–54; idem, "Jewish Messianism and Christian Millenarianism," *Culture and Politics from Puritanism to the Enlightenment,* ed. Perez Zagorin (Berkeley and Los Angeles, 1980), pp. 67–90; idem, "Conception of the Messiah," pp. 169–170; Matthew Goldish, "Sabbatean Enthusiasm" (forthcoming); Sharot, *Messianism, Mysticism, and Magic,* pp. 105–106.

5. Sharot, *Messianism, Mysticism, and Magic,* pp. 110–114.

6. In fact, the nexus between Sabbateanism and the dissemination of Lurianic messianism was already suggested as early as 1927 by Silver, *History of Messianic Speculation,* pp. 157–158.

7. See the first steps taken in this direction by Sharot, *Messianism, Mysticism, and Magic,* pp. 85–129.

8. Barnai, "Christian Messianism and the Portuguese Marranos."

9. See Tishby, *Studies in Kabbalah,* 2:335–336.

10. Scholem, *Sabbatai Ṣevi,* pp. 115–117; idem, *Kabbalah,* p. 246. On an earlier sixteenth-century combination of the study of these two Kabbalistic corpora in the Ottoman empire see Idel, "Neglected Writings," p. 78.

11. Scholem, *Sabbatai Ṣevi,* p. 115; Liebes, *Studies in Jewish Myth,* p. 110. For the Sabbatean view of the Messiah as stemming from the powers of impurity, and for earlier non-Lurianic Kabbalistic sources, see Liebes, *Studies in the Zohar,* pp. 169–170n53; M. Idel, "Additional Remnants from the Writings of R. Joseph of Hamadan," *Daat* 21 (1988), pp. 47–50 (Hebrew); Scholem, *Sabbatai Ṣevi,* p. 57.

12. On the details of Abraham Abulafia's significant influence upon the books of *ha-Qaneh* and *ha-Peliy'ah,* see Michal Kushnir-Oron, "The Kabbalistic books *ha-Peliah* and *ha-Qanneh:* Elements, Religious and Social Views, and Literary Design" (Ph.D. diss., Hebrew University of Jerusalem, 1980) pp. 75–76 (Hebrew). On the recurrence of manuscripts of *Sefer ha-Peliy'ah* in circles of Sabbateans see Meir Benayahu, *Sabbatean Movement in Greece* (Jerusalem, 1971–1977) pp. 350–354 (Hebrew).

13. For such an example see Idel, *Mystical Experience,* p. 174n310, where it should be read *Sefer ha-Peliy'ah* in lieu of *Sefer ha-Qanah; Studies in Ecstatic Kabbalah,* pp. 85–86n22. At least one of the most important Kabbalists who became a Sabbatean believer, R. Joseph Ḥamitz, was a great admirer of Abraham Abulafia's thought, and he collected his manuscripts and copied excerpts from his writings as well as writing an eulogious introduction to his compendium of Abulafia's *'Or ha-Sekhel.* See Tishby, *Paths of Faith and Heresy,* pp. 55–56; Idel, *R. Abraham Abulafia,* pp. 31–33.

14. *Sabbatai Ṣevi,* pp. 142–143, 154. This somehow forced explanation is based upon the argument that in the rabbinic tradition there is no connection between the pronunciation of the divine name and the Messiah. Though Scholem is correct insofar as the rabbinic literature is concerned, he did not express himself on the possibility of finding such a view in the Kabbalistic literature. For more on the issue of the Messiah and the divine name see below, appendix 1.

15. See Ms. Munchen 408, fol. 65a-65b; *Sefer ha-Peliy'ah,* I, fol. 35b. This text has already been printed by Jellinek as an appendix to *Sefer ha-'Ot,* pp. 85–86; See Idel, *Mystical Experience,* p. 21.

16. See Scholem, *Sabbatai Ṣevi,* p. 149.

17. See Idel, *Language, Torah and Hermeneutics,* pp. 51–52.

18. This expression is also found in Cordovero and Abulafia in the context of the combination of letters. See e.g. the text of Abulafia's *Ḥayyei ha-'Olam ha-Ba',* quoted in Idel, *Language, Torah, and Hermeneutics* p. 186n229, or the quotation from *Sefer Ḥayyei ha-'Olam ha-Ba'* printed in Jellinek as an appendix to *Sefer ha-'Ot,* p. 87, and in *Sefer ha-'Ot* itself, p. 79.

19. Scholem, *Researches in Sabbateanism,* p. 174.

20. See Cordovero, *Pardes Rimmonim,* Gate of the Colors, and M. Idel, "Kavvanah and Colors: A Neglected Kabbalistic Responsum," in M. Idel, D. Dimant, and S. Rosenberg, eds.,

Tribute to Sara: Studies in Jewish Philosophy and Kabbalah Presented to Professor Sara O. Heller Wilensky (Jerusalem, 1994), pp. 1–14 (Hebrew).

21. See Idel, *Mystical Experience,* pp. 22–24, and compare to p. 32.

22. This combination is found in manuscript material of the technique.

23. Idel, *Kabbalah: New Perspectives,* pp. 103–110.

24. See Ben Sasson, *History of the Jewish People,* p. 703. For a fresh and important analysis of the character and writings of Nathan of Gaza see Elqayam, *Mystery of Faith.*

25. Tishby, *Paths of Faith and Heresy,* pp. 204–226.

26. Liebes, *Studies in Jewish Myth,* pp. 93–114.

27. *Zohar,* vol. 1, fol. 261b. See also the text of Yonathan Eibeschuetz, adduced by Liebes, *On Sabbateaism and Its Kabbalah,* p. 131. For the nexus between Binah and redemption in general see Idel, "Types of Redemptive Activities," pp. 263–265. The false etymological connection between the words *binah* and *ben,* "son," was exploited in Christian Kabbalah for Christological speculations.

28. *Zohar,* vol. 2, fol. 46b. Similar views occur in Kabbalistic literature; see e.g. the late-fifteenth-century Italian Kabbalist R. Elijah ben Benjamin of Genazzano, *'Iggeret Ḥamudot,* ed. A. Greenup (London, 1912), p, 60, analyzed by Mopsik, *Les grands textes,* pp. 303–304. In general, the connection between the Messiah and an eighth entity is known already in *Baraiyta', 'Arakhin,* fol. 13b, and see also in Yoḥanan Alemanno's *Sha'ar ha-Ḥesheq* (Livorno, 1790), fol. 56a, and Patai, *Messiah Texts,* p. 245. Especially interesting is a discussion based on the *Baraiyta'* which occurs in an anonymous commentary on the Torah related to Abulafia's thought, Ms. Oxford 1920, fols. 2b, 34b, 54ab, where the eighth string of the violin of the Messiah is juxtaposed to the *yovel,* a symbol of the third sefirah, and the concept of *binah.* See also R. Joseph ibn Tzayyaḥ's early-sixteenth-century book *Tzeror ha-Ḥayyim,* a commentary on the thirteenth-century treatise *'Otzar ha-Kavod* by R. Todros ha-Levi Abulafia, Ms. London-Montefiore 318, fol. 81a–81b.

29. On R. Joseph Ashkenazi see the important study of Georges Vajda, "Un chapitre de l'histoire du conflit entre la Kabbale et la philosophie: La polemique anti-intellectualiste de Joseph b. Shalom Ashkenazi," *AHDLMA* 33 (1956), pp. 45–127.

30. R. David ben Yehudah he-Ḥasid, *Sefer Mar'ot ha-Tzove'ot,* ed. D. Ch. Matt (Scholars Press, Atlanta, 1982), pp. 100–101. Another example of a dense symbolic eschatological interpretation of intradivine processes is found in *Tiqqunei Zohar,* no. 50, fol. 22b, where the Shekhinah, the last sefirah, is redeemed by the third sefirah. Both R. David—under the influence of R. Joseph Ashkenazi—and the anonymous author of *Tiqqunei Zohar* resorted to explicit theosophical symbolism, while the bulk of zoharic literature is concerned more with implicit symbolism, on the one hand, and apocalyptic eschatology, on the other. Compare the discussion found in the printed edition of R. 'Efrayyim ben Shimshon, *Perush 'al ha-Torah,* vol. 1, p. 187, where the messianic notariqon of *'ADaM* is found. If indeed the Ashkenazi author had already adduced it, and it was part of the original commentary (which is far from being obvious because this passage is collected from later manuscripts), then the late-thirteenth-century Kabbalists only offered slight theosophical interpretation to a tradition already in existence long before them. See also Ms. Vatican 428, fol. 35b, where Adam is said to hint at the Messiah in a context related to metempsychosis.

31. Vatican 62, fol. 3a, printed in M. Idel, "The 'Zohar' Translation by R. David ben Yehudah he-Ḥasid," *'Alei Sefer,* vol. 8 (1980), p. 70 (Hebrew).

32. See Idel, "'Zohar' Translation." See also R. Meir ibn Gabbai, *Sefer 'Avodat ha-Qodesh* (Jerusalem, 1973), fol. 130c.

33. See Scholem, *On the Mystical Shape,* pp. 214–215; idem, *Kabbalah,* pp. 334–335. On the Messiah as reflecting the perfection of Adam as created in the image of God see the sources mentioned by Mopsik, *Les grands textes,* p. 304n31.

34. See Michal Oron, "The Doctrine of the Soul and Reincarnation in Thirteenth Century Kabbalah," in S. O. Heller Willensky and M. Idel, eds., *Studies in Jewish Thought* (Magnes Press, Jerusalem, 1989), pp. 287–288 (Hebrew). On the medieval view of the king see Kantorowitz, *King's Two Bodies,* pp. 314–316.

35. See Friedlaender, "Shiitic Influences," in ed., Saperstein, *Essential Essays,* pp. 128–130.

36. R. Isaac of Acre, *Me'irat 'Einayyim,* p. 224. On this passage see Georges Vajda, *Recherches sur la philosophie et la Kabbale dans la pensée juive du Moyen Age* (Mouton, Paris, 1962), p. 384. On the exalted status of the Messiah in comparison to that of Moses see above, chap. 3, n. 69.

37. See John Collins, "Patterns of Eschatology at Qumran," in B. Halpern and J. D. Levenson, eds., *Traditions in Transformation: Turning Points in Biblical Faith* (Eisenbrauns, Winona Lake, Ind., 1981), pp. 374–375.

38. *Sefer ha-Temunah* (Lemberg, 1892), fol. 44b.

39. See those sources in Idel, "Types of Redemptive Activity," pp. 264–265, 270–271. See also *Sefer ha-Temunah,* fol. 55ab.

40. See *Sefer ha-Mefo'ar,* p. 41. The astrological system that informs Molkho's sermon is different from that of R. Joseph Ashkenazi, but they nevertheless share the same view that redemption is connected to Binah.

41. *Sefer ha-Peli'yah,* from which the student of Nathan of Gaza has quoted, is attributed to a second-century Tannaitic figure, a revered mystic named R. Neḥuniah ben ha-Qanah, who is described as engaging in various mystical dialogues with Metatron, the highest of the angels. Both the occurence of the name of this mystic and the fact that this book is conceived of as being revealed from above were bound to add to the authority of the discussion on Sabbatai/Saturn.

42. This is the first group of letters that constitutes the forty-two-letter name, each group of six letters corresponding (according to Joseph Ashkenazi's *Commentary on Sefer Yetzirah*) to each of the seven planets.

43. *Commentary on Sefer Yetzirah,* fols. 51b–52a; *Sefer ha-Peli'yah,* part 1, fol. 57ac; quoted according to the version found in the Epistle of R. Abraham Peretz, named "Magen Abraham," printed in Scholem, *Researches in Sabbateanism,* pp. 175–176, which differs from the original in *Sefer ha-Peliy'ah* as printed later on only in insignificant details. The impact of this passage on pre-Sabbatean Kabbalists is an issue that needs separate investigation which may contibute to a better understanding of the reception of the views expressed in it as part of Sabbatean propaganda. For an important repercussion of this quotation see e.g. R. Moses of Kiev's *Commentary on Sefer Yetzirah,* called *'Otzar ha-Shem,* ibid., and especially R. Abraham Yagel's late-sixteenth-century *Gei Ḥizzayon;* cf. *A Valley of Vision: The Heavenly Journey of Abraham ben Ḥananiah Yagel,* trans. David B. Ruderman (University of Pennsylvania Press, Philadelphia, 1990), pp. 171–174, where the eschatological aspects of the quotation, drawn from R. Joseph Ashkenazi's commentary, have been conspicuously expanded. The version as preserved in R. Joseph Al-Ashqar's *Tzafnat Pa'aneaḥ,* fol. 71a, *Yom Rishon be-Shabbat,* does not really change the meaning; according to both *Sefer ha-Peliy'ah* and the Sabbatean sources, the first day is thought to have been formed in the year, namely in the dimension of time. Interestingly enough, despite the intrinsic significance of this recurrent passage for the history of the Saturn and melancholy complex and of Jewish messianism, it was passed over in the most important accounts of messianism as formulated by Aescoly and Scholem. On the passage of R. Joseph ben Shalom see the analysis of Havivah Pedayah, "Sabbath, Sabbatai, and the Diminutions of Moon: The Holy Conjunction, Sign and Image," in H. Pedayah, ed., *Myth in Judaism,* = *Eschel Beer-Sheva'* 4 (1996), pp. 150–153 (Hebrew). See also Moshe Idel, "Saturn and Sabbatai Tzevi: A New Approach to Sabbateanism," trans. Avriel Bar-Levav, *Jewish Studies* 37 (1997), pp. 161–183 (Hebrew), where additional materrial was adduced.

44. See the up-to-date French translation of R. Klibansky, E. Panovsky, and F. Saxl, *Saturne et Melancholie,* trans. L. Evrard (Gallimard, Paris, 1989); Macey, *Patriarchs of Time,* pp. 23–39; Versnel, *Transition and Reversal,* pp. 136–227; Manuel and Manuel, *Utopian Thought,* pp. 64–92. For the ancient psychology of melancholy, afterward connected to Saturn, see Jean Pigeaud, *Aristote, l'homme de génie et la melancholie* (Rivages, Paris, 1988); Jean Starobinski, *La melancolie au miroir* (Julliard, 1989); Vito Teti, *La melanconia del vampiro: Mito, storia, immaginario* (Manifestolibri, Roma, 1994), pp. 161–200. On the recurrence of the idea of melancholy in the period of Tzevi's life see Lawrence Babb, *The Elizabethan Malady: A Study of Melancholia in English Literature from 1580 to 1642* (Michigan State College Press, East Lansing, 1951), and John Owen King III, *The Iron of Melancholy: Structures of Spiritual Conversion in America from the Puritan Conscience to Victorian Neurosis* (Wesleyan University Press, Middletown, Conn., 1983), as well as the huge scholarly literature about Robert Burton's *Anatomy of Melancholy,* the most important discussion on melancholy printed shortly before the birth of Sabbatai Tzevi in Oxford in 1621. For an outstanding treatment of melancholy in the period of Tzevi see Michael Heyd, *"Be Sober and Reasonable": The Critique of Enthusiasm in the Seventeenth and Early Eighteenth Centuries* (E. J. Brill, Leiden, 1995), pp. 44–70. On the awareness of the nexus between Sabbatai and Saturn see the sixteenth-century Christian Kabbalist Francesco Giorgio of Venice, in his very influential book *De Harmonia Mundi,* I, 4,5. See Swietlicki, *Spanish Christian Cabala,* pp. 140–145, esp. p. 143, where the sefirah of Binah is also mentioned in this context. For Saturn in a sixteenth-century Jewish thinker, R. Abraham ibn Migash, see Rosenberg, "Exile and Redemption," pp. 406–407 and the pertinent footnotes. See the important study of Abraham Elqayam, "The Rebirth of the Messiah," *Kabbalah, Journal for the Study of Jewish Mystical Texts,* ed. D. Abrams and A. Elqayam, 1 (1996), pp. 104–111, 129, 136, 139–140, and notes 57, 162.

45. See Scholem, *Studies and Texts,* p. 267 and n. 288 and the text hinted at by Scholem, *Researches in Sabbateanism,* p. 44, and Liebes's remark, ibid., p. 175n143, as well as the quotation from *Sefer ha-Peliy'ah* adduced in R. Elijahu of Smyrna, *Midrash Talpiyyot* (ed. Smyrna, reprinted in Jerusalem, 1963), fol. 163a.

46. As Scholem has correctly indicated, both *Sefer ha-Temunah* and *Sefer ha-Qanah*—in fact he might have included even more appropriately *Sefer ha-Peliy'ah*—have "influenced the Sabbatians tremenduously." Cf. *Messianic Idea,* p. 111. The trend of Kabbalah represented by Joseph Ashkenazi, and adopted by many other important Kabbalists has been one of the most influential schools of Kabbalah. See M. Idel, "An Anonymous Kabbalistic Commentry on Shir ha-Yiḥud," in K. E. Groezinger and J. Dan, eds., *Mysticism, Magic and Kabbalah in Ashkenazi Judaism* (Walter de Gruyter, Berlin, New York, 1995), pp. 139–154. The planet Sabbatai is mentioned as appointed upon the land of Israel, in a very favorable context, in Abraham Abulafia's *Sefer Gan Na'ul,* Ms. München 58, fol. 327a, and this quotation has been copied in *Sefer ha-Peliy'ah,* I, fol. 76c, while elsewhere, Ms. München 58, fol. 323b, Sabbatai is expressly identified with Binah. See *Sefer ha-Peliy'ah,* I, fol. 75a. In the first passage the term *'eretz* is adduced in the context of a messianic computation which deals with the year 1290.

47. Scholem, *Researches in Sabbateanism,* pp. 214–215. For a Freudian interpretation of this passage, which emphasizes mention of "his mother," see Avner Falk, "The Messiah and the Qelippoth: On the Mental Illness of Sabbatai Ṣevi," *Journal of Psychology and Judaism* 7, no. 1 (1982), pp. 25–26. For another psychoanalytical interpretation of Sabbateanism see Siegmund Hurwitz, "Sabbatai Zwi, Zur Psychologie der haeretischen Kabbala," *Studien zur analytischen Psychologie C. G. Jungs, Festschrift zum 80. Geburtstag von C. G. Jung* (Rascher Verlag, Zurich, 1956), 2:239–263.

48. Scholem, *Sabbatai Ṣevi,* pp. 119–123, 146–147, 149; Liebes, *Studies in Jewish Myth,* 107–113.

49. This suggestion invites a more detailed investigation, which may find that the meaning of

the Sabbatean secret of the divinity changed over time as part of a belief in a development alongside the vector of time and of the ontic hierarchy of the sefirot. This means that the closer the messianic drama comes to the final stage, the higher the divine power that is appointed upon Sabbatai and consists of the "secret of divinity."

50. Scholem, *Researches in Sabbateanism*, p. 222.

51. See Tishby's remark in *Tzitzat Novel Tzevi*, p. 7n8.

52. *Tzitzat Novel Tzevi*, pp. 7–8; Scholem, *Sabbatai Ṣevi*, p. 270 and footnotes.

53. *Zohar*, vol. 3, fol. 136b. See Liebes, *Studies in the Zohar*, pp. 44–46, 60–62.

54. *Sabbatai Ṣevi*, pp. 275–276.

55. Tishby, *Tzitzat Novel Tzevi*, p. 11n9, mentions the parallel to *BT, Megillah*, fol. 17b.

56. On the nexus between Sabbath, the seventh day, and the Messiah see above, chap. 3.

57. *Tzitzat Novel Tzevi*, p. 11; Scholem, *Sabbatai Ṣevi*, pp. 273–274.

58. *Sabbatai Ṣevi*, pp. 125–138. Compare, however, the earlier marginalization of the mental illness of persons involved in a messianic movement in Scholem's famous essay "Mitzvah ha-Ba'ah ba-'Aveirah," reprinted in his *Studies and Texts*, p. 15: "What can we gain from all this? It is not that the question of the single individual is important, but the question how could he succeed in influencing and attracting. . . . The diagnosis of a nerve-physician does not count in this case." It is here that Scholem's emphasis on the collective, rather than the individual experience, even that of the Messiah himself, is expressed most eloquently. Later on, in his *Sabbatai Ṣevi*, this strong marginalization of the diagnosis of mental illness was mitigated.

59. On these figures, as well as many others, see Rudolf Witkover, *Born under Saturn* (London, 1963).

60. Simon Bernstein, "The Letters of Rabbi Mahalelujah of Ancona," *HUCA* 7 (1930), p. 515, and Scholem, in the Hebrew version of *Sabbatai Ṣevi*, p. 405 (not translated in the English version, p. 493). For another crucial nexus between Sabbatai the Messiah and the planet in a conspicuous astrological context see the epistle of R. Raphael Supino, printed in R. Ya'aqov Sasportas's *Tzitzat Novel Tzevi*, p. 93 (Hebrew); Scholem, *Sabbatai Ṣevi*, p. 647n155. Supino, like Mahaleluyah, was an Italian rabbi, and the importance of the Italian background is obvious in the astrological context. Moreover, according to another text preserved by Sasportas, Tzevi was described as transmitting the gift of prophecy to his close friend Abraham Yakhini: "The Master [Tzevi] put upon him his spirit of prophecy. Thereupon something resembling a brilliant star grew on his forehead—and it seems to me that it was the planet Saturn—and it is said that he [Yakhini] too then prophesied." Cf. Scholem, *Sabbatai Ṣevi*, p. 430; *Tzitzat Novel Tzevi*, pp. 165–166, also p. 186.

61. Liebes, "Sabbatai Tzevi's Attitude towards His Apostasy," *Sefunot*, n.s., 2 (1983), pp. 236–287 (Hebrew); idem, *Studies in Jewish Myth*, pp. 107–113.

62. G. Scholem, "Two Manuscript Fragments Belonging to the Adler Collection That Concern the History of Sabbatianism," *'Eretz Yisrael* 4 (1956), p. 192, reprinted in Scholem, *Researches in Sabbateanism*, p. 20. See also in a later epistle of Nathan, printed in Scholem, *Studies and Texts*, pp. 238–239, and the stand of Abraham Michael Cardoso, discussed in Yerushalmi, *From Spanish Court*, p. 318.

63. See also Nathan's epistle printed by Scholem, *Studies and Texts*, pp. 238, 240, quoting explicitly Maimonides' *Mishneh Torah, Hilkhot Yesodei Torah*, chap. 10.

64. Scholem, *Researches in Sabbateanism*, p. 20.

65. See Scholem, *Be-'Iqvot Mashiaḥ*, p. 6; Tishby, *Studies of Kabbalah*, 2:334.

66. See Scholem, *Researches in Sabbateanism*, p. 513n18; *Sabbatai Ṣevi*, pp. 337–354. On the lost tribes in the framework of sixteenth-century eschatology see above, chap. 4, n. 20; Popkin, "Conception of the Messiah," p. 169, and Yerushalmi, *From Spanish Court*, p. 306.

67. Scholem, *Researches in Sabbateanism,* p. 19. On the nexus between the two concepts in early-fourteenth-century ecstatic Kabbalah see Idel, *Studies in Ecstatic Kabbalah,* pp. 114, 150n49. For more on the practice of hitbodedut see a document of a later Sabbatean figure, Neḥemiah Ḥayyon, printed in *Researches in Sabbateanism,* pp. 481–482, where his communion with Metatron is reminiscent of the Abulafian Kabbalah.

68. Scholem, *Researches in Sabbateanism.*

69. On Nathan of Gaza's abrogation of Lurianic *Kavvanot* see Scholem, *Sabbatai Ṣevi,* pp. 272, 277–278; idem, *Messianic Idea,* pp. 102–103; idem, *On the Kabbalah,* pp. 150–151; Tishby, *Paths of Faith and Heresy,* pp. 224–225, Arthur Green, *Devotion and Commandment: The Faith of Abraham in the Hasidic Imagination* (Hebrew Union College Press, Cincinnati, 1989), pp. 81–82n43; Ada Rapoport-Albert, "God and the Zaddik as the Two Focal Points of Hasidic Worship," *History of Religions 18 (1979), pp. 315–325; Idel, Hasidism: Between Ecstasy and Magic,* pp. 149–150.

70. This is the position of Yehuda Liebes, "Sabbatean Messianism," pp. 4–20, pp. 93–106 in the English version.

71. See *The Hebrew Enoch,* chap. 48, ed. Odeberg, pp. 165–166.

72. For the use of this verse in earlier Kabbalistic descriptions of mystical union see Idel, "Universalization and Integration," pp. 27–58.

73. See the quotations from Abulafia's *Ḥayyei ha 'Olam ha-Ba'* and the commentaries on *Sefer ha-Ḥayyim* and *Sefer ha-'Edut,* above, chapter 2. Abulafia, like Nathan of Gaza, claimed that the Messiah will be called by the names of God; see Scholem, *Sabbatai Ṣevi,* p. 315, and Idel, *Abraham Abulafia,* pp. 407–408; Wirszubski, *Pico della Mirandola,* pp. 166, 218, 239, and, for earlier sources, above, chap. 1, n. 20. See also the epistle preserved in *Tzitzat Novel Tzevi,* p. 186, where it is said, in the context of Tzevi's allowing others to pronounce the divine name, that "his name is like that of his Master." The talmudic formula recurs several times in the context of Tzevi. See ibid., pp. 156, 188. This is quite a Metatronic understanding of the nature of the Messiah. Apparently, as we learn from ibid., pp. 129, 156, 189, this statement should be understood as pointing to the famous gematria Shabbatay Tzevy = 814 = Shin Dalet Yod. This plene calculation of Shaday has something to do with the gematria Metatron = Shaday, which comes up in messianic contexts in Abulafia, as we shall see below, appendix 1. The plene gematria of Shaday as 814 occurs already in Abulafia. On *shin dalet lamed* as the "seal of the Messiah" see Idel, *Mystical Experience,* p. 27. On an attribution of a magic name related to Metatron to the Turkish name of Tzevi, see Scholem, *Sabbatai Ṣevi,* p. 879n125.

74. Scholem, *Researches in Sabbateanism,* pp. 19–20; idem, *Sabbatai Ṣevi,* p. 168, where a shorter English version of the epistle is found. See also ibid., p. 871. For another discussion, among numerous other, on Adam and the Messiah in Sabbateanism see ibid., p. 222. For a critique of the stand that the Messiah is deified see the view of an important Sabbatean theologian, Abraham Michael Cardoso, in the text printed by Scholem, *Studies and Texts,* pp. 286–288. Already in *Sefer ha-Meshiv* one finds the view that the Messiah reflects the divinity of God. See ibid., n. 47.

75. Cf. Idel, "Enoch Is Metatron," passim. See also David H. Aaron, "Imagery of the Divine and the Human: On the Mythology of Genesis Rabba 8 #1," *Journal of Jewish Thought and Philosophy* 5 (1995), pp. 1–62.

76. Nathan might point here either to Tzevi's views or to 'principles' received as part of a revelation. See e.g. his epistle printed by Scholem, *Studies and Texts,* p. 252.

77. Scholem, *Researches in Sabbateanism,* p. 19n4, where he refers to R. Ḥayyim Vital's *Liqqut-tei Torah* (Vilna, 1880), fols. 13a–14d. See also R. Naftali Bakharakh, *'Emeq ha-Melekh,* fol. 20b. See also Scholem, *Sabbatai Ṣevi,* pp. 302–304.

78. See *Me'irat 'Einayyim,* ed. Goldreich, p. 112.

79. See also the important discussion of Elqayam, *Mystery of Faith,* pp. 134–135, 325. About the claim of a deep transformation of the Kabbalist, as exposed by the *Zohar,* see the view of Wolfson, *Through a Speculum,* pp. 333–392.

80. Later on, in an early-nineteenth-century Hasidic writing, there is a similar view of Enoch's becoming Metatron as a cleaving of the intellect to the supernal intellect: see R. Yehudah Leibush of Yanov, in *Qol Yehudah* (Pietrkov, 1906), fol. 21c.

81. On the mystical understandings of Enoch see Idel, "Enoch Is Metatron," pp. 235–236. Though the influence of ecstatic Kabbalah is plausible in some of the mystical expressions of Tzevi and Nathan, I was unable to find any trace of this form of Kabbalah in the writings of Abraham Michael Cardoso. Though he was also a mystically oriented author, in addition to being an important ideologist of Sabbateanism, the terminology used in his messianic dreams and revelations is reminiscent of R. Ḥayyim Vital's *Sha'arei Qedushah,* especially his recurent use of the term "lights," *'orot,* in order to describe the powers that were revealed to him. See e.g. the epistle printed in Scholem, *Studies and Text,* p. 320. According to Cardoso's claim, this more mystical type of revelation as the experience of lights was not induced by any techniques.

82. Namely the acronyms of the names of the seven planets in Hebrew. However, the gematria of these consonants amounts to 538, not 541, as the two other terms mentioned here do.

83. Scholem, *Researches in Sabbateanism,* p. 232.

84. *Language, Torah and Hermeneutics,* pp. 36, 40–41 passim.

85. Scholem, *Researches in Sabbateanism,* p. 204. Compare to the apotropaic role of the disclosure of Kabbalah in exile in one of the quotations above, chap. 5, p. 170.

86. See *Sefer Sitrei Torah,* Ms. Paris, Bibliothèque Nationale 774, fol. 134ab; *Sefer Ḥayyei ha-Nefesh,* Ms. München 408, fol. 6a, and our discussion in chap. 2 above. Part of this latter book has been quoted, anonymously, in *Sefer ha-Peliy'ah.*

87. Scholem, *Researches in Sabbateanism,* p. 20. On another view of the divine nature of the Messiah, one closer to the view that he shares the divine name, see the later Kabbalist discussed by Manor, *Exile and Redemption,* p. 194.

88. *'Otzar 'Eden Ganuz,* Ms. Oxford 1580, fol. 32b; Idel, *Mystical Experience,* p. 142. Note the occurence of the phrase "their God," which is reminiscent of Tzevi's leitmotif of "my God"; cf. n. 61 above. See also Abulafia's *Sefer ha-'Ot,* p. 81: *'Elohai ve-'Elohei 'avotai.*

89. So, too, did the sixteenth-century Jerusalemite Kabbalist R. Yehudah Albotini in his *Sefer Sullam ha-'Aliyah.* Idel, *Mystical Experience,* p. 182.

90. See Nathan's epistle printed in Scholem, *Studies and Texts,* p. 266.

91. See Idel, "Enoch Is Metatron," pp. 234, 236–237.

92. Cf. Liebes, "Religious Beliefs," pp. 192–286.

93. For a rather positive attitude toward Jesus in a Kabbalistic text written in the seventeenth century see Samuel Krauss, "Un texte cabbalistique sur Jesus," *REJ* 62 (1911), pp. 240–247.

94. Scholem, *Researches in Sabbateanism,* p. 20. See also Abraham Michael Cardoso's critique of the attribution of apotheosis to Tzevi, in an epistle printed by Scholem, *Studies and Texts,* p. 284.

95. See Morton Smith, *Jesus the Magician* (Harper and Row, San Francisco, 1978).

96. Scholem, *Research in Sabbateanism,* p. 20.

97. See also another text of Nathan's, the epistle printed by Scholem, *Studies and Texts,* p. 250.

98. Printed in Scholem, *Be-'Iqvot Mashiaḥ,* p. 104; see also Scholem, *Sabbatai Ṣevi,* pp. 809–810; Idel, *Kabbalah: New Perspectives,* p. 57.

99. See Idel, *Kabbalah: New Perspectives,* pp. 56–58, and iden, *Hasidism: Between Ecstasy and Magic,* pp. 95–145.

100. A question that cannot be answered in this context is the possible nexus between such a

view and the Hasidic comprehensive attitude toward mundane activity as potentially pregnant with mystical importance. See also our discussion, below, of Luzzatto's view.

101. Scholem, *Be-'Iqvot Mashiaḥ,* p. 84.

102. This view reverberates also in R. Moses Ḥayyim Luzzatto in a text to be dealt with later on in this chapter. See also R. Yonathan Eibeschuetz, in the text discussed by Liebes, *On Sabbateaism and Its Kabbalah,* p. 228.

103. Scholem, *Researches in Sabbateanism,* p. 20.

104. See Idel, "Enoch Is Metatron," pp. 232–233, and the pertinent footnotes.

105. I do not assume that by the very identification between the two figures the national elements will disappear; see e.g. a fifteenth-century text on a rather apocalyptic-national description of messianism, which starts with the assumption that the Messiah is Ben 'Adam. Cf. Patai, *Messiah Texts,* p. 328.

106. See Marcel Simon, "Adam et la rédemption," in Werblowsky and Bleeker, eds., *Types of Redemption,* pp. 62–71; Oscar Cullmann, *The Christology of the New Testament,* trans. S. C. Gutrie and H. A. M. Hall (Westminser Press, Philadelphia, 1959), pp. 146–164; James D. Tabor, *Things Unutterable: Paul's Ascent to Paradise* (University Press of America, Lanham, N.Y., 1986), pp. 14–18. See also another Sabbatean text, where again the Messiah is described as atoning for an intellectual sin of Adam's; cf. Scholem, *Researches in Sabbateanism,* p. 556. According to some scholars, there is an affinity between the Messiah figure and the Adam figure already in the biblical literature; see the discussion, not always convincing, of Bentzen, *King and Messiah,* pp. 39–47. See also Mowinckel's remarks, *He That Cometh,* pp. 422–429.

107. Scholem, *Sabbatai Ṣevi,* pp. 285–286. See, however, Scholem's other view, expressed in ibid., pp. 153–154, 796–797, and also Schulz, *Judaism and the Gentile Faiths,* pp. 234–236. This phenomenological attitude has been accepted even by an expert in Christian thought: see W. D. Dachies, "From Schweitzer to Scholem: Reflections on Sabbatai Ṣevi," in Saperstein, ed., *Essential Papers,* pp. 335–376, esp. p. 337, and Taubes's reaction in "The Price of Messianism,", ibid., p. 553.

108. M. Idel, "Differing Conceptions of Kabbalah in the Early 17th Century," in *Jewish Thought in the Seventeenth Century,* ed. Isadore Twersky and Bernard D. Septimus (Harvard University Press, Cambridge, Mass., 1987), pp. 198–200. On Cardoso see Scholem, *Researches in Sabbateanism,* p. 408 and Scholem's n. 37 and p. 409.

109. Liebes, "Religious Beliefs".

110. See Tishby, *Paths of Faith and Heresy,* p. 60, 78; Scholem, *Sabbatai Ṣevi,* pp. 772–774; Idel, "Shlomo Molkho as Magician," p. 197.

111. See the reprint of John Evelyn, *The History of Sabatai Ṣevi: The Suppos'd Messiah of the Jews* (1669; William Andrews Clark Memorial Library, University of California, Los Angeles, 1968), p. 60, and the Italian original, p. 28. Scholem was well aware of this source and used it several times in *Sabbatai Ṣevi.* I am not aware of any discussion of the passage quoted above. According to Evelyn, the epistle was originally written by Tzevi in Hebrew and translated to him into Italian, and he translated it into English. Scholem mentioned an Armenian parallel to the epistle. See ibid., pp. 615–616n35. On Jesus and Tzevi see Scholem, *Sabbatai Ṣevi,* p. 399.

112. On this issue see Werblowsky, *Joseph Karo,* pp. 257–286.

113. This important Kabbalist has been the subject of several studies, of which the best-known ones have been collected in volume 3 of Tishby's *Studies in Kabbalah.*

114. Tishby, *Paths of Faith and Heresy,* pp. 169–206.

115. See Zvia Rubin, "The Zoharic Works of R. Moses Ḥayyim Luzatto and His Messianic Attitude," in J. Dan, ed., *The Age of the Zohar* (Jerusalem, 1989), pp. 387–412 (Hebrew).

116. See I. Tishby, "Traces of R. Moshe Ḥaim Luzzatto in the Teachings of Hasidut," *Zion* 43

(1978), pp. 201–234; "The Dissemination of the Kabbalistic Writings of Luzzatto in Poland and Lithuania," *QS* 45 (1970), pp. 127–154 (Hebrew), translated into French as Isaiah Tishby, "Les traces de Rabbi Moïse Haïm Luzzato dans l'enseignement du Hassidism," *Hommage à George Vajda: Etudes d'histoire et de pensée juives,* ed. G. Nahon and Ch. Touati (Louvain, 1980), pp. 421–462.

117. See Ḥayyim Friedlander, ed., *Da'at Tevunot* (Benei Beraq, 1975), pp. 172–173. See also Tishby, *Studies in Kabbalah,* 3:977–981. Needless to say, the requirement of religious individual improvement, also designated as tiqqun, is found before Sabbateanism, in messianic contexts. See the text quoted by Scholem, *Sabbatai Ṣevi,* p. 69.

118. *Da'at Tevunot,* p. 111. See also Luzzatto's *Sefer Qine'at ha-Shem Tzeva'ot,* printed in *Ginzei Ramḥal,* pp. 130–131.

119. *Da'at Tevunot,* p. 172.

120. Ibid., p. 179.

121. Tishby, *Studies in Kabbalah,* 3:980.

122. See also the resort to hakhanah in *Ginzei Ramḥal,* pp. 24, 44–45, 58–59 passim. See also pp. 48–49, where the descent of the influxes is described as depending upon the change in the recipients, *shinnui ba-meqabbelim,* a view strikingly similar to the assumption, sometimes shared by Neoplatonic sources and talismanic magic, that the astral powers are received in accordance with the recipients. See also Idel, "The Magical and Neoplatonic Interpretations of Kabbalah," pp. 204, 206, 208, and idem, *Hasidism: Between Ecstasy and Magic,* p. 329n249. The concept of preparation below for the reception of the powers descending or attracted from above is important in Cordovero, as well as in his younger companion in Safed, the influential R. Moses Alshekh, the author of a widespread commentary on the Bible entitled *Torat Moshe.* On Cordovero and Luzzatto see Bracha Sack, "The Influence of R. Moshe Cordovero on R. Moshe Ḥayyim Luzzato," *Proceedings of the Tenth World Congress of Jewish Studies* (Jerusalem, 1990), pp. 1–5 (Hebrew).

123. Tishby, *Studies in Kabbalah,* 3:985 = "Les traces," pp. 451–452.

124. See Idel, *Hasidism: Between Ecstasy and Magic,* pp. 100–101.

125. *Pardes Rimmonim,* vol. 31, chap. 8; part II, fol. 75c. On the sources for this view see Idel, *Kabbalah: New Perspectives,* pp. 40–41, idem, "The Magical and Neoplatonic Interpretations of Kabbalah," pp. 127–129, 135.

126. *'Asarah Ma'amarot* (Frankfurt am Main, 1698), vol. 2, fol. 41b. On this Kabbalist see Robert Bonfil, "Halakhah, Kabbalah, and Society: Some Insights into Rabbi Menaḥem Azariah da Fano's Inner World," in *Jewish Thought in the Seventeenth Century,* ed. I. Twersky and B. Septimus (Cambridge, Mass., 1987), pp. 39–61; Joseph Avivi, "Rabbi Menaḥem Azariah of Fano's Writings in Matter of Kabbalah," *Sefunot* 4 (XIX) (1989), pp. 347–376 (Hebrew).

127. Cf. *Doresh Tov,* a compilation of teachings of the Besht by R. Shimeon Ze'ev Zelig (Warsau, N.D.), fol. 32c, quoting a book entitled *'Or ha-Ganuz,* apparently the work of R. Aharon Kohen of Apta.

128. Cf. Idel, *Hasidism: Between Ecstasy and Magic,* pp. 66–68. See also the "negative talismanics" related to eschatology found in Ḥayyim Vital's *Sefer ha-Ḥezyonot,* pp. 72–73, and some earlier related traditions adduced and discussed in my introduction to ha-Reuveni's diary, ed. A. Z. Aescoly, pp. xxxvi–xxxviii. In Safed and Jerusalem a tradition was circulated which become a dream of Vital's as to the existence of a magical stone in the Weeping Wall, which should be removed in order to bring redemption to Israel. I propose to read this tradition as related to talismanic qualities.

129. *Da'at Tevunot,* pp. 198–200.

130. ibid., p. 200. The verb *hakhen,* to prepare, recurs in many cases in Luzzatto's writings in cosmogonic contexts. See e.g. *Ginzei Ramḥal,* pp. 23, 36–37. In general, see the extensive discussions of the macrocosmos-microcosmos relationship in the context of the lower anthropos corre-

sponding to the higher anthropos and receiving the influxes from him in *Sefer ha-Kelalim,* printed together with *Da'at Tevunot,* pp. 322–323.

131. See Idel, *Hasidism: Between Ecstasy and Magic,* pp. 66–68, 73.

132. Tishby, *Studies in Kabbalah,* 3:980–981.

133. Tishby, *Studies in Kabbalah,* 3:980.

134. Ibid., 1:177–203.

135. *Sefer Qine'at ha-Shem Tzeva'ot,* in *Ginzei Ramḥal,* p. 132.

136. Scholem, *Sabbatai Ṣevi,* pp. 54, 309.

137. For the importance of astrological-magical terminology for the better understanding of Kabbalah and Hasidism see Idel, *Hasidism: Between Ecstasy and Magic,* index, s.v. "astrology." On Kabbalah and astrology in general see Jacques Halbronn, *Le Monde Juif et l'Astrologie* (Arche, Milano, 1985), pp. 289–334; Ronald Kiener, "Astrology in Jewish Mysticism from the *Sefer Yeṣira* to the *Zohar,*" *JSJT* 6 (1987), pp. 1–42; Georges Vajda, *Juda ben Nissim ibn Malka: Philosophe Juif Marocain* (Collection Hesperis, Paris, 1954), pp. 45–46, 136–141, 143; M. Idel, "The Beginning of Kabbalah in Northern Africa? A Forgotten Document by R. Yehuda ben Nissim ibn Malka," *Pe'amim* 43 (1990), pp. 4–15 (Hebrew). See also Eugenio Garin, *Astrology in the Renaissance* (Arkana, London, 1983).

138. Liebes, *On Sabbateaism and Its Kabbalah,* pp. 198–211.

139. *Sefer Tzitzim u-Ferahim,* as corrected and analyzed in Liebes, *On Sabbateaism and Its Kabbalah,* pp. 203–205. For the motif of the spark of the Messiah see above, chap. 5, n. 78.

140. See Liebes, *On Sabbateaism and Its Kabbalah,* pp. 204–206.

Chapter 7: Hasidism: Mystical Messianism and Mystical Redemption

1. On Dubnov's stand see his *Toledot ha-Ḥasidut* (Tel Aviv, 1931), pp. 7, 60–62, 205 (Hebrew); On Buber's stand see Abraham Shapira, "Two Ways of Redemption in Hasidism from the Perspective of Martin Buber," in Oron-Goldreich and Goldreich, eds., *Massu'ot,* pp. 429–426 (Hebrew).

2. Scholem, *Major Trends,* p. 329; *Messianic Idea,* pp. 176–202; Rivka Schatz, "The Messianic Element in Hasidic Thought," *Molad,* n.s., 1 (1967), pp. 105–111 (Hebrew); idem, *Hasidism as Mysticism,* pp. 326–339; Werblowsky, "Mysticism and Messianism"; Mendel Piekarz, "The Messianic Idea in the Early Days of Hasidism through the Lens of Ethical and Homiletic Literature," *The Messianic Idea in Israel,* pp. 250–253 (Hebrew); Shapira, ibid., pp. 445–446; Winston, *Logos,* p. 55. Scholem has posited a neutralization of messianism despite his recognition that other religious elements have been interpreted spiritually, in Hasidism. See his *Messianic Idea,* p. 200, where he attributed the process of spiritualization to Kabbalistic preachers apparently writing in the sixteenth and seventeenth centuries. However, he does not explain what precisely is novel with the Hasidic spiritualization of these terms and why messianism was spiritualized in reaction to heretical messianism if such a trend was already in existence in other circles. See Idel, *Studies in Ecstatic Kabbalah,* pp. 100–101; idem, "Land of Israel," pp. 178–180. On the spiritualization of the sefirotic ontology of the theosophical Kabbalah, which is evident already in the thirteenth-century ecstatic Kabbalah, and its early Hasidic manifestations see Idel, *Kabbalah: New Perspectives,* pp. 146–153; idem, *Hasidism,* pp. 228–232.

3. Tishby, *Studies in Kabbalah,* 2:475–519; almost all the articles mentioned in the preceding note are responses to Tishby's study. Tishby's work is characterized by rich documentation, while Scholem's discussion of Hasidic messianism, in his previous studies as well as in his response to Tishby, only rarely engaged detailed analyses of texts. Scholem's rather synthetic views on messia-

nism are uncharacteristically based more on his general impression of of the vast amount of material he has perused, while Tishby, a more textually oriented mind, was more interested in engaging Scholem's view by adducing material that remained beyond the scope of scholarship in order to undermine Scholem's understanding of early Hasidism. On a view of Hasidism closer to Tishby's, see Wolfson, *Along the Path,* pp. 88–109, and Altshuler, *Rabbi Meshulam Feibush Heller,* pp. 285–291. Both scholars focused their discussions on the existence of Lurianic messianic elements in Hasidism. Here I shall attempt to point out the contributions of non-Lurianic messianic elements, or new understandings of Lurianic elements inspired by different models, on Hasidic view of messianism.

4. A similar view has been propounded more recently by J. Taubes, "The Price of Messianism," and will be discussed in more detail toward the end of this chapter.

5. The Jewish New Year that falls in the autumn of 1746 C.E.. In the same document, another ascent of the soul is described as taking place on Rosh ha-Shanah of 5510 (1749). See also Rosman, *Founder of Hasidism,* p. 109. On the Jewish New Year and messianism see above, chap. 2, as well as the nexus between the New Year and messianic plans in R. Naḥman of Braslav; see Arthur Green, "Naḥman of Bratslav's Messianic Strivings," in Saperstein, ed. *Essential Papers,* p. 422. On the expectation of the advent of the Messiah during the New Year see the Hasidic text translated in Patai, *Messiah Texts,* pp. 78–79.

6. The Hebrew word is strongly magical and uncommon in similar contexts dealing with the ascent of the soul. See Idel, *Kabbalah: New Perspectives,* p. 321n137 and the special version of a parable of the Great Maggid as adduced by his student, R. Elimelekh of Lisansk, *Sefer No'am 'Elimelekh* (Jerusalem, 1960), fol. 21a, where the attainment of prophecy in ancient times was attributed to *hashba'ot* and *hitbodedut.*

7. The theory of a double Paradise is found in many places in Kabbalistic eschatology, e.g. in Naḥmanides' eschatology as well as in the *Zohar;* see e.g. *Zohar,* vol. 2, fol. 8ab, and it was accepted by the Besht; see the legend related to him and adduced by Martin Buber, *Tales of the Hasidim, Early Masters,* trans. Olga Marx (Schocken Books, New York, 1964), p. 84.

8. The column linking the lower Paradise to other levels of reality is well known from earlier apocalyptic and Kabbalistic sources. See e.g. *Sefer Zerubbavel,* in Even Shmuel, ed., *Midreshei Ge'ullah,* p. 323, and ibid., pp. 140, 282, and in *Seder Gan 'Eden,* a pseudepigraphic midrash attributed to R. Eliezer the Great (but in fact written by R. Moses de Leon, as pointed out by Scholem, *Devarim be-Go,* pp. 270–283) and printed in J. D. Eisenstein, *'Otzar ha-Midrashim* (New York, 1969), pp. 85–86; see also the passage from the *Zohar,* vol. 2, fol. 7b, succinctly discussed in chapter 3 above. For the earlier eschatological valence of the pillar of fire in ancient Jewish and Christian sources see Wieder, *Judean Scrolls,* pp. 39–43. See also the reverberation of this theme in R. Aharon Berakhiah of Modena, *Sefer Ma'avar Yabboq* (Wilna, 1896), fols. 118b–119a. The motif of the pillar climbed by shamans or by dead souls recurs in various traditions; see e.g. the Judaeo-Arabic tradition on the ladder of the souls discussed by Alexander Altmann, "The Ladder of Ascension," *Studies in Mysticism and Religion Presented to Gershom G. Scholem* (Magnes Press, Jerusalem, 1967), pp. 1–32, and Idel, "Types of Messianic Activities," pp. 259, 265. According to a Hasidic legend, the last subject discussed by the Besht before his death was the pillar of the souls; see Buber, *Tales of the Hasidim, Early Masters,* p. 84. For earlier traditions on the eschatological column of light see Stroumsa, *Savoir et salut,* pp. 267–268; Couliano, *Tree of Gnosis,* pp. 172–173.

9. Again, the impression is that the Besht does not deal with a new theme but elaborates upon a topic already known to the addressee.

10. Apparently the biblical figure Ahijah the Shilonite; on this prophet as a mystical mentor see Liebes, "Messiah of the Zohar," p. 113n114.

11. This term will be elaborated upon later in this chapter. There is a testimony by Menaḥem

Naḥum of Chernobyl as to the Besht's use of the unification, *yiḥud,* for the sake of curing, a distinctly magic act, which will be addressed in some detail in the following. Cf. Rosman, *Founder of Hasidism,* pp. 134–135.

12. On the connection between unifications and ascents of the soul see a "wondrous legend" attributed to the Besht in a later source, R. Israel Berger's book *'Ateret Ya'aqov ve-Yisra'el* (Lvov, 1881), n.p., where it is written, "beha'alot nafsho be-Yiḥudim," namely by the ascent of his soul by means of *yiḥudim.*

13. See the version printed in *Shivḥei ha-Baal Shem Tov,* ed. J. Mondshine (Jerusalem, 1982), pp. 233–235, Koretz version; idem, *Migdal 'Oz* (Kefar Habad, 1980), p. 124; Benzion Dinur, "The Messianic-Prophetic Role of the Baal Shem Tov," in Saperstein, ed., *Essential Papers,* p. 378; Tishby, *Studies in Kabbalah,* 2:505–506; Patai, *Messiah Texts,* pp. 270–272; Idel, *Kabbalah: New Perspectives,* p. 94; I. P. Coulianu, *Out of this World* (Shambhala, Boston and London, 1991), p. 186; Sharot, *Messianism, Mysticism, and Magic,* pp. 149–150; and the detailed analysis of Rosman, *Founder of Hasidism,* pp. 97–113; Rosman's translation of the passage under discussion here is found on p. 106. See also Altshuler, *Rabbi Meshulam Feibush Heller,* pp. 127–134.

14. See Dan ben Amos and J. R. Mintz, *In the Praise of Baal Shem Tov* (London, 1979), p. 57; Mendel Piekarz, *Studies in Braslav Hasidism* (Mossad Bialik, Jerusalem, 1972), p. 66 (Hebrew); Liebes, "Messiah of the Zohar," pp. 113–114; Emanuel Etkes, "Hasidism as a Movement: The First Stage," in B. Safran, ed., *Hasidism: Continuity or Innovation?* (Harvard University Press, Cambridge, Mass., 1988), pp. 16–17; Steven T. Katz, "Models, Modeling and Mystical Training," *Religion,* vol. 12 (1982), p. 259; Abraham Rubinstein, "The Mentor of the Besht and the Writings from Which He Studied," *Tarbiẓ* 48 (1978–1979), pp. 146–158 (Hebrew); Gedaliah Nigal, *Magic, Mysticism and Hasidism* (Tel Aviv, 1992), p. 30 (Hebrew); Shmuel Ettinger, in Ben-Sasson, ed., *History of the Jewish People,* p. 769, as well as his "Hasidism and the Kahal in Eastern Europe," in Rapoport-Albert, ed., *Hasidism Reappraised,* p. 70; and the Hasidic text of the twentieth century and analysis in Schweid, *From Ruin to Salvation,* pp. 117–118; Loewenthal, *Communicating the Infinite,* pp. 6, 13.

15. See note 37 below and the more expanded Hebrew version in Dinur's *Be-Mifneh ha-Dorot* (Jerusalem, 1955), pp. 181–184 (Hebrew).

16. Tishby, *Studies in Kabbalah,* 2:503–507. A messianic reading of the significance of the epistle is already found in Hasidic sources: see e.g. R. Shalom of Kaidanov, a late-nineteenth-century Hasidic author, in his *Divrei Shalom* (Vilnius, 1882), fol. 6b, where he claims, in the context of a quotation from the epistle, that with the Besht, the sparkling of the Messiah, *hitnotzetzut,* namely the beginning of the messianic era, has started. For more material, representing a somewhat later period (the end of the eighteenth and the beginning of the nineteenth century) that supports a more messianic understanding of some traditions related to the disclosure of Kabbalah, see below, p. 243.

17. Scholem, *Messianic Idea,* pp. 182–184.

18. Tishby, *Studies in Kabbalah,* 2:506. See also ibid., p. 519, where again he emphatically distinguishes the magico-messianic meaning of the epistle from the Hasidic teachings, convinced as he was of the less magical or nonmagical nature of Hasidic teachings. However, such a distinction is artificial (see next paragraph). See also Scholem, who pointed out the artificial nature of Tishby's too-strong distinction between the two elements of the epistle; *Messianic Idea,* p. 183.

19. Morton Smith, *Jesus the Magician* (Harper and Row, San Francisco, 1978).

20. Sharot, *Messianism, Magic, and Magic,* passim. One of the most important Hasidic masters, R. Jacob Joseph of Polonoy, was acquainted with the story on R. Joseph della Reina and in his *Toledot Ya'aqov Yosef,* fol. 134b, mentions his name, though he rejected his approach.

21. See the document printed and analyzed by Moshe Rosman, "Medziebuz and R. Israel Ba'al Shem Tov," *Zion* 52 (1987), p. 185 (Hebrew).

22. *Mif'alot 'Elohim* (Zolkiew, 1865), n.p., under the rubric "Kokhavim."

23. See M. Idel, "The Concept of Torah in the Heikhalot Literature and Its Reverberations in Kabbalah," *JSJT* I (1981), pp. 27–29 (Hebrew).

24. Ibid., pp. 25ff. As to the nature of the 'three names' mentioned in the epistle, I would suggest that they are three Tetragrammata. Compare the three *hawayyiot* which are related to the drawing down from the "supernal constellation," namely the sefirah of Keter, in R. Qalonimus Qalman Epstein, *Ma'or va-Shemesh,* pp. 132, 134, 358.

25. *Notzer Ḥesed* (Jerusalem, 1982), p. 131. See also Idel, *Kabbalah: New Perspectives,* p. 95.

26. See Michael Fishbane, "The Well of Living Water: A Biblical Motif and Its Ancient Transformations," *Sha'arei Talmon: Studies in the Bible, Qumran and the Ancient Near East Presented to Shemaryahu Talmon,* ed. M. Fishbane and E. Tov (Eisenbrauns, Winona Lake, Ind., 1992), pp. 3–16.

27. See Alon Goshen-Gottstein, "Rabbi Eleazar ben 'Arakh: Symbol and Reality," *Jews and Judaism during the Period of the Second Temple, of the Mishnah and of the Talmud,* ed. A. Offenheimer, I. Gafni, M. Stern (Jerusalem, 1993), pp. 173–197 (Hebrew).

28. See Even Shemuel, *Midreshei Ge'ullah,* p. 73, and *Zohar,* vol. 2, fols. 7b–8a.

29. The term here is *hitpa'el,* a verb that is used similarly in some medieval texts and which will become in the Habad literature one of the most common terms for various mystical experiences. See e.g. the text of Abraham Abulafia quoted and translated in Scholem, *Major Trends,* pp. 140, 382.

30. *Teshu'ot Ḥen* (Brooklyn, 1982), fol. 52b. See also Scholem, *Messianic Idea,* pp. 210–211. See also the view of the same Hasidic author, ibid., fol. 91b, where he adduces the view of the Besht that by means of prayer, the pain of the Shekhinah is alleviated and the salvation of the person who prays will immediately come.

31. Scholem, *Messianic Idea,* p. 198.

32. On proximism see Idel, *Hasidism: Between Ecstasy and Magic,* pp. 6–9.

33. See Dinur, "The Messianic-Prophetic Role of the Baal Shem Tov," in Saperstein, ed., *Essential Papers,* pp. 379, 381–382; Tishby, *Studies in Kabbalah,* 2:509–510, on the one side, and Scholem, *Messianic Idea,* p. 199, on the other. On this figure see Green's introduction to Menaḥem Naḥum, *Upright Practices,* pp. 20–24. To Menaḥem is attributed the story that the Messiah told the Besht that he could bring redemption by opening the gate of the palace of the Nest. See Amos and Mintz, *In the Praise,* p. 58.

34. Scholem understood this phrase in a Lurianic vein: his translation reads "permanent and universal unity.".

35. *Me'or 'Einayyim,* pp. 166–167. Compare also to R. Yehudah Tzevi Streitner's formulation: "Each Jew has within himself an element of the Messiah, which he is required to purify and mature. The Messiah will come when Israel has brought him to the perfection of growth and purity within themselves." In I. Berger, ed., *'Eser Tzaḥtzaḥot* (Piotrkov, 1910), p. 138; cf. Schultz, *Judaism and the Gentile Faiths,* p. 242.

36. On the tzaddiq as a channel see Idel, *Hasidism: Between Ecstasy and Magic,* pp. 114, 198–203, 233. On the similarity between the role of the righteous in the ancient Jewish texts and that of the Messiah as maintaining the world see Patai, *Man and Temple,* pp. 198, 225–226. On the tzaddiq compared to the heels of the Messiah, who maintains the world, see the mid-nineteenth-century text of R. Shlomo of Radomsk, translated and analyzed in Louis Jacobs, *Hasidic Prayer* (Schocken Books, New York, 1978), p. 135.

37. *Me'or 'Einayyim,* p. 109.

38. *Me'or 'Einayyim,* pp. 109–110. On this acronym see above, chap. 6, pp. 189–190. See also chap. 4, n. 72.

39. *Me'or 'Einayyim,* p. 110. See also Tishby, *Studies in Kabbalah,* 2:509–510. For a parallel passage, see *Me'or 'Einayyim,* p. 86. A similar position to that presented by this passage is found some few decades later in the teachings of R. Naḥman of Braslav. There also the construction of the stature is mentioned, in the context of the prayers of the people of Israel. Nevertheless, in R. Naḥman's discussions, the prayers are to be brought to the tzaddiq, and he alone is able to build the divine stature. Here we witness the ascent of the importance of the communal tzaddiq, whose role is much more marginal in the discussion of R. Menaḥem Naḥum. See *Liqqutei Moharan* (Benei Beraq, 1972), I, no. 2:6 fol. 2ab; I, no. 9, fol. 12b. On R. Naḥman's eschatology see Liebes, *Studies in Jewish Myth,* pp. 115–128.

40. *Me'or 'Einayyim,* p. 109. The importance of the corporate identity as part of the messianic event presupposes a continuity between the spiritualistic salvation of the individual and the communal redemption, which is much more messianic. Compare, however, Schatz Uffenheimer, *Hasidism as Mysticism,* p. 336.

41. *Me'or 'Einayyim,* p. 244.

42. Tishby, *Studies in Kabbalah,* pp. 509–510, Scholem, *Messianic Idea,* p. 199.

43. Compare to the vision of the relationship between the ancient Israelite king and his people as a matter of a "corporate personality" or a "psychic whole." Cf. Aubrey R. Johnson, "The Role of the King in the Jerusalem Cultus," in Hooke, ed., *Labyrinth,* pp. 74–76; Johnson, *Sacral Kingship,* pp. 2–3; H. Wheeler Robinson, *Corporate Personality in Ancient Israel* (Fortress Press, Philadelphia, 1964), and a critique of this concept in J. W. Rogerson, "The Hebrew Conception of Corporate Personality: A Re-Examination," *JTS,* n.s., 21 (1970), pp. 1–16; Himmelfarb, *Ascent to Heaven,* p. 97. See also above, chap. 3, n. 48.

44. See Scholem, *On the Mystical Shape,* pp. 92–109.

45. *Me'or 'Einayyim,* p. 110. See also ibid., p. 143: *moridim ḥiyyut ha-bore',* "the persons who cause the descent of the vitality of the Creator," as well as p. 109, where the causing of the descent of the influx and vitality is mentioned twice, again in an activistic mode: *horadat ha-shefa' ve-ha-ḥiyyut.* This form of activity is reminiscent of the somewhat later attempt of the Seer of Lublin to bring the Messiah by magical means. Though the talismanic technique was not mentioned in this peculiar context, there can be no doubt that the Seer was well acquainted with this model: see Idel, *Hasidism: Between Ecstasy and Magic,* p. 77; compare to Shapira, "Two Ways of Redemption." The supreme mystical attainment in the school of the Great Maggid is to purify oneself and annihilate one's personality to the extent that one may become a channel for divine speech and thought. See the texts discussed by Daniel Matt, "Ayin: The Concept of Nothingness in Jewish Mysticism," in Robert K. C. Forman, ed., *The Problem of Pure Consciousness, Mysticism and Philosophy* (Oxford University Press, New York, 1990), p. 142.

46. See Idel, *Hasidism: Between Ecstasy and Magic,* pp. 45–145. For the vision of the ancient king as a talisman see Frankfort, *Kingship and the Gods,* pp. 259–261. For the implicit messianic significance of the act of charity that is described as drawing down the divine influx and vitality see R. Shneor Zalman of Lyady in his influential *Sefer ha-Tanya,* 'Iggeret ha-Qodesh, chap. 10.

47. See *Me'or 'Einayyim,* p. 109, where the path and the trajectory, *mesillah,* built by pure worship and communion with the divine, are mentioned.

48. Ibid. On this theme see Idel, *Kabbalah: New Perspectives,* pp. 62–67.

49. Green, *Upright Practices,* pp. 222–223.

50. See Gershom Scholem, "The Historical Image of Israel Baal Shem Tov," *Molad* 18 (1960),

p. 348 (Hebrew); Rosman, *Founder of Hasidism,* pp. 132, 258n36; On the view of R. Ya'aqov Ḥayyim Tzemaḥ see above, chap. 5, pp. 178–179. On praying loudly see Idel, *Hasidism: Between Ecstasy and Magic,* pp. 160–168, esp. 168. Recently, a description of R. Yeḥiel Michal of Zlotchov, as a messianic figure and as someone who received the speech of the Shekhinah, has been proposed by Altshuler, *Rabbi Meshulam Feibush Heller,* pp. 114–126, 134–140, 285–292. Some of the phenomena of the speech should be seen against the background of the views found already in the thought of the Besht and represented explicitly by R. Menaḥem Naḥum's view of messianism and speech, as well as against the background of the impact of the ecstatic and talismanic types of Kabbalah, which were influential on the Maggid of Zlotchov. See Idel, *Kabbalah: New Perspectives,* p. 68; idem, *Hasidism: Between Ecstasy and Magic,* pp. 56, 77–78. On the influence of the talismanic Kabbalah stemming from Cordovero's *Pardes Rimmonim* dealing with prayer, on the student of the Maggid of Zlotchov, R. Meshullam Feibush of Zbarazh, see Idel, *Hasidism,* p. 166. On the importance of the speech of God within the mouth of man see the text printed in R. Barukh of Medzibuz, the Besht's son, in *Botzina' Qadisha',* 'Amarot tehorot (Jerusalem, 1985), pp. 112–113, which is very reminiscent of the style of his nephew, R. Moses Ḥayyim Ephrayyim.

51. Scholem, *Messianic Idea,* p. 199.

52. *'Or Torah,* p. 28. On the idea of the pipe see Scholem, *Messianic Idea,* p. 179 and Idel, *Hasidism: Between Ecstasy and Magic.* In this collection of teachings of the Great Maggid, the verb *horid,* "caused the descent," which is reminiscent of the terms mentioned above (n. 55), occurs several times.

53. *Sefer 'Or Yitzḥaq,* p. 104.

54. *Maggid Devarav le-Ya'aqov,* pp. 244–246.

55. *Me'or 'Einayyim,* p. 198. Compare also to R. Shemuel Shmelke of Nikolsburg, *Divrei Shemuel,* p. 96, on awe as maintaining the pipe, which safeguards the drawing down of the influx. According to this master, ibid., p. 97, the awe is tantamount to faith. On faith in some forms of Jewish mysticism see R. J. Z. Werblowsky, "Faith, Hope and Trust: A Study in the Concept of Bittaḥon," *Papers of the Institute of Jewish Studies* (Jerusalem, 1964), 1:95–139. See also Idel, *Hasidism: Between Ecstasy and Magic,* p. 237, where faith is described as the ability to draw down the influx from on high.

56. On this issue see Idel, *Hasidism: Between Ecstasy and Magic,* pp. 65–81.

57. See ibid., pp. 86–95. For another example of the understanding the advent of the Messiah as the completion of the process of tiqqun, which implies also the descent of the divine power on the lower world, see R. Menaḥem Mendel of Kossov, *'Ahavat Shalom,* p. 1; ibid., pp. 210–211, 214, where the drawing down of the 'Aleph, a recurrent symbol for God, into the *golah,* the diaspora, is conceived as inducing redemption, *ge'ullah.* This understanding of the midrashic pun recurs in numerous sermons of R. Menaḥem Mendel of Lubavitch. See also Gross, *Le messianisme juif,* p. 222.

58. For the more recent overemphasis of the importance of the Lurianic form of Kabbalah for understanding the specific spiritual physiognomy of Hasidism see Rachel Elior, "Historical Continuity and Spiritual Change," in P. Schaefer and J. Dan, eds., *Gershom Scholem's Major Trends in Jewish Mysticism, 50 Years After* (J. C. B. Mohr, Tübingen, 1993), pp. 303–322, esp. 317, where she emphasizes the continuity between Lurianism and Hasidism on both the terminological and the conceptual level. Though no one had ever denied the substantial resort of Hasidic masters to Lurianic terminology, the strong conceptual transformations of these terms under the formative impact of Kabbalistic models different from the Lurianic one should be viewed as a major factor in Hasidic spirituality. See Moshe Ḥallamish's reaction to Elior's lecture, "Response," ibid., p. 325; Idel, *Hasidism: Between Ecstasy and Magic,* pp. 86–95.

59. *Me'or 'Einayyim,* p. 166. On the eschatological value of the unification of speech and thought see also R. Moses Ḥayyim Ephrayyim of Sudylkov, *Degel Maḥaneh 'Efrayyim* (Jerusalem, 1963), p. 100. On the history of the term *yiḥud* in Kabbalah and Hasidism see Mark Verman, "The Development of *Yiḥudim* in Spanish Kabbalah," in J. Dan, ed., *The Age of the Zohar* (Jerusalem, 1989), pp. 25–42; Lawrence Fine, "The Practice of *Yiḥudim* in Lurianic Kabbalah," in A. Green, ed., *Jewish Spirituality* (Crossroad, New York, 1987), 2:64–78; Tishby, *Studies in Kabbalah,* 3:657–658; Scholem, *Messianic Idea,* pp. 213–217, 246–247; Idel, *Hasidism: Between Ecstasy and Magic,* pp. 185–186, 275–276n53. Scholem's strong denial of Buber's view of Hasidic yiḥud ("none other than the normal life of man, only concentrated and directed toward the goal of unification," *Messianic Idea,* p. 247) is therefore a mistake, as the unification of thought and speech should indeed be envisioned as part of the normal life of man. See also below, note 79. Compare a similar view in a discussion of Luzzatto, where the tiqqun is concerned with the union of speech and voice. See his *Qovetz Ketavim* (Jerusalem, 1984), fol. 274b. On causing the entrance of the thought into the speeches of Torah and prayer as drawing down the divine power see R. Moshe 'Eliaqim Beri'ah, the son of the Maggid of Kuznitz, *Binat Moshe* (Cracow, 1888), fol. 11a. On speech and thought in Hasidic thought in general see Schatz Uffenheiemer, *Hasidism as Mysticism,* pp. 204–214, and Weiss, *Studies,* pp. 69–83, who nevertheless deal with the more passive moments, ignoring the above treatments, which betray a more activistic attitude.

60. *Me'or 'Einayyim,* p. 116. The continuous arrival of Elijah is treated elsewhere by this master, see p. 69, though the eschatological significance there is less explicit. See also Green, *Upright Practices,* pp. 227–229, and Shatz Uffenheimer, *Hasidism as Mysticism,* pp. 333–334. In this context, an earlier discussion of the relationship between Elijah and the Messiah should be mentioned. In *Commentary on Ruth,* written at the end of the sixteenth century in Safed, R. Moses Alsheikh describes Elijah as causing the ascent of the acts of commandments to three spiritual worlds, while the Messiah takes them to the fourth and highest one. What seems interesting here is the involvement of the two figures in the common ritual. See *Be'ur Ḥamesh Megillot* (Jerusalem, 1990), 1:142 (Hebrew). The nexus between the Messiah and the Jewish ritual appears to be quite ancient; see Riesenfeld, *Jesus transfiguré,* pp. 58–61. See also the view of R. Dov Baer of Lubavitch, as described in Loewenthal, *Communicating the Infinite,* p. 186.

61. An issue that cannot be elaborated upon here is the affinity between the collective stature of souls, to which everyone is to be attached, and the Neoplatonic idea of the cosmic or universal soul, an idea hinted at in *Me'or 'Einayyim,* p. 143, where Israel is described as the "soul of the world." For other traces of Neoplatonic terminology in the writing of this master see Idel, *Kabbalah: New Perspectives,* pp. 66–67. For the recommendation for integration of the variety of human qualities, which stems from Neoplatonic sources, see Idel, "*Hitbodedut* as Mental Concentration in Jewish Philosophy," *JSJT* 7 (1988), pp. 39–40 (Hebrew). Compare the communal aspect of the prayer here, which has messianic aspects, with the messianic role of the group, *havurah,* of R. Yehiel Mikhal of Zlotchov, as analyzed by Altshuler, *Rabbi Meshulam Feibush Heller,* pp. 285–291.

62. *BT, Ḥagigah,* fol. 12a.

63. *Me'or 'Einayyim,* p. 149. The same ideas are repeated on the same page again.

64. On this concept see Idel, *Hasidism: Between Ecstasy and Magic,* pp. 206–207.

65. *Me'or 'Einayyim,* p. 149.

66. This view of prayer is quite ancient in Jewish mysticism and is already found in the Heikhalot literature.

67. *Me'or 'Einayyim,* p. 330, and see also the text translated by Green, *Upright Practices,* p. 232.

68. This view recurs *Me'or 'Einayyim,* p. 120. The single parallel of "mystical philology," which derives the term *mashiyaḥ* from speech, is found in writings of Abulafia; see his treatment of this

issue in *Sefer ha-Melammed,* Ms. Paris, Bibliothèque Nationale 680, fol. 297b, where the assumption is that the Messiah receives the speech and the conversation, *siḥo,* from God, or from the divine name (see below, appendix 1), as well as in *'Otzar 'Eden Ganuz,* Ms. Oxford 1580, fol. 158b: *meshiḥo: mah siḥo.* See the view of George Steiner, as presented by Finkelstein, *The Ritual of New Creation,* pp. 101, 105. On speech and redemption see Handelman, *Fragments of Redemption,* pp. 15–50.

69. *Me'or 'Einayyim,* p. 167. For another discussion of a redemptive effect of the unification of speech and thought see also ibid., p. 282, where the thought is described as riding the speech, which brings them to the state of the next world, *'olam ha-ba'* and *yeshu'ah.* See also ibid., p. 180.

70. *Hargashat 'eivarav.* For similar sensations see in Abulafia's writings, cf. Idel, *Mystical Experience,* pp. 74–76. For the importance of the feeling of the limbs as part of a revelatory experience in Hasidism see the sources mentioned in R. Hayyim Meir Yeḥiel of Magalnitza, *Sefer Tif'eret Ḥayyim* (Warsau, 1905), fols. 4d–5a.

71. *Me'or 'Einayyim,* p. 278. At the end of this quotation, as in some other cases, e.g. ibid., p. 283, the union points to a theurgical act which affects the higher worlds, as in the theosophical-theurgical Kabbalah.

72. Ibid.

73. Ibid., p. 166. See also p. 167. On the concept of the "aspect of the Messiah," expressed in terms that are apparently not historical but much more personal, see the R. Abraham David Wahrman of Buczacz, *Ḥozeh David* (printed as the second part of *Maḥazeh David*) (N.p., 1876), fol. 18cd. The phrase *beḥinat mashiyaḥ* recurs in the writings of R. Naḥman of Braslav.

74. On the letters as palaces for the divine powers see Idel, *Hasidism: Between Ecstasy and Magic,* pp. 158–164. R. Menaḥem Naḥum is, to the best of my knowledge, the Hasidic master who emphasizes this issue more than any other author in the Hasidic movement.

75. *Me'or 'Einayyim,* p. 113.

76. Scholem, *Messianic Idea,* p. 35. See also ibid., pp. 7, 202. For more on my view of Scholem's evaluation of historical linear time, which informs his view of deferment, implicitly minimizing the circular and daily experiences, see my "Some Concepts of Time and History in Kabbalah." For other critiques of this view of Scholem's see Hartman, *Living Covenant,* pp. 225–226; Taubes, "Price of Messianism," pp. 556–557, William Scot Green, "Introduction: Messiah in Judaism: Rethinking the Question," in Neusner et al. eds., *Judaisms and Their Messiahs,* p. 9. For various discussions of "deferment" see Handelman, *Fragments of Redemption,* pp. 44–46; Hans Blumenberg, *Work on Myth,* trans. Robert M. Wallace (MIT Press, Cambridge, Mass., 1990), pp. 227–228; Finkelstein, *Ritual of New Creation,* pp. 7, 120–121; Myers, *Re-Inventing,* p. 167. Compare also below, Concluding Remarks, as well as Talmon, *King, Cult and Calendar,* pp. 161–162.

77. Scholem, *Messianic Idea,* p. 202. Compare the view expressed in a story from the Sadigora dynasty, to the effect that the light of redemption is gradually descending and is found, in the author's time, "at the level of our head. We do not notice it because our heads are bowed beneath the burden of exile. Oh, that God might lift up our heads!" Cf. Martin Buber, *Tales of Hasidim: Later Masters* (Schocken Books, New York, 1948), p. 72. The imminence of messianic experience is quite explicit.

78. The intensification of the feeling of a messianic mission does not automatically provoke an apocalyptic attitude. Compare to Scholem's view adduced above, Introduction, n. 72. On the contrary, it is not a destruction but a construction that will initiate the messianic era, on both the personal and the national level. See also the view of R. Levi Yitzḥaq of Berditchev, who argues that the course of history is directed toward the messianic redemption, and all the events should be interpreted in such a way; though this interpretation is unknown to men, it is clear to God. From his discussion we may conclude that the advent of the Messiah is not a rupture but part of a

premeditated development. See *Qedushat Levi* (Jerusalem, 1993), p. 243 (Hebrew). Compare also ibid., p. 95, where the assumption is that the good deeds of the children of Israel will induce a sort of redemption that does not involve the dramatic intervention of God. The apocalyptic redemption will occur, according to the Berditchever rabbi, only if the Jews will not obey the divine commandments. Another Hasidic master, a contemporary of R. Levi Yitzḥaq, presupposes a continuous process of redemption starting with the exodus from Egypt and culminating in the final redemption. See R. Zeev Wolf of Zhitomir, *Sefer 'Or ha-Me'ir* (Perizek, 1815), fol. 104ab.

79. For interesting discussions of personal redemption in early Hasidism see Gedalya Nigal, *Tzafnat Pa'aneaḥ* (Koretz, 1782), introduction, pp. 39–50 (Hebrew), and for the later period see Morris M. Faierstein, "Personal Redemption in Hasidism," in Rapoport-Albert, ed., *Hasidism Reappraised,* pp. 214–224.

80. For a similar view of spiritual redemption as the unification of the spiritual powers of man see R. Yitzḥaq Aizik Yehudah Safrin of Komarno's attribution of this view to the Besht himself in *Netiv Mitzvotekha* (Jerusalem, 1983), p. 7 (Hebrew). The recommendation to unify the spiritual powers of man occurs in several Kabbalistic sources from the thirteenth century on.

81. *Sefer Shemu'ah Tovah* (Warsaw, 1938), fols. 79b–80a; See also Rivka Schatz-Uffenheimer, *Hasidism as Mysticism* (Magnes Press, Jerusalem, 1968), pp. 170–172; Piekarz, "Messianic Idea," pp. 250–253. Compare also to the nexus between total devotion to God, which is described as the transformation of the I, *'ani,* into the divine name, and redemption, in R. Menaḥem Mendel of Viznitz's *Sefer Tzemaḥ Tzadiq* (Haifa, 1988), fol. 263b. On the coming of the Messiah as related to the conquest of corporeality see also in the late eighteenth century R. Reuven ha-Levi Horovitz, *Sefer Diduim Basode* (Lemberg, 1859), vol. 1, fols. 44a, 59a.

82. *Sefer Toledot Ya'aqov Yoseph* (Koretz, 1780), fols. 79b, 198a.

83. See also above, in the quotation from R. Gedalyah of Lunitz, as well as R. Menaḥem Mendel of Kosov, *'Ahavat Shalom,* pp. 64, 210, and R. Moses Hayyim Ephrayyim of Sudylkov, *Degel Maḥaneh 'Efrayyim,* p. 42.

84. *Toledot Ya'aqov Yoseph,* fol. 27b.

85. Scholem, *Messianic Idea,* p. 195.

86. Compare Idel, *Studies in Ecstatic Kabbalah,* p. 100n40. For the concept of inner exile see Bernard Dov Hercenberg, *L'Exil et la Puissance d'Israel et du Monde* (Actes Sud, 1990).

87. Scholem, *Messianic Idea,* p. 195.

88. Ibid., pp. 195–196; Schatz Uffenheimer, *Hasidism as Mysticism,* pp. 326–339.

89. *'Od Davar,* p. 271. Scholem repeated his view much later in his life, in his concluding remarks to *Messianic Idea,* pp. 259–260. This statement of Scholem's does not contradict his description of early Kabbalah as dealing with the return of the soul to the origin. See above, chap. 3, pp. 000ff. The Kabbalists are described by Scholem—but not explicitly by the Kabbalists themselves—as searching for salvation by returning to the primordial source of being, while the Hasidic masters were explicitly using soteriological terminology, which points to their understanding of the eschaton.

90. See Idel, *Language, Torah, and Hermeneutics,* pp. 67–70, 72–72, 181– 182, and above, the quotation from R. Jacob Joseph of Polonoy's book, as well as chap. 1, pp. 51–52.

91. See Scholem, *Messianic Idea,* p. 200; Idel, *Hasidism: Between Ecstasy and Magic,* pp. 16–17.

92. See Idel, "The Land of Israel in Medieval Mystical Jewish Thought," pp. 207–208, 209–214.

93. Idel, *Kabbalah: New Perspectives,* pp. 146–153.

94. Compare Scholem, *Devarim be-Go,* p. 339.

95. This is also the case in some of the numerous articles on the subject by R. J. Zwi Werblowsky.

96. See Arthur Green, "Naḥman of Bratslav's Messianic Strivings," in Saperstein, ed. *Essential Papers,* pp. 389–432, reprinted from Arthur Green, *Tormented Master: A Life of Rabbi Naḥman of Bratslav* (University of Alabama Press, University, Ala., 1979), pp. 182–220; Ada Rapoport-Albert, "Hasidism after 1772," in Rapoport-Albert, ed., *Hasidism Reappraised,* pp. 113–114. On latter messianic phenomena in Bratslav Hasidism see Mendel Piecarz, "The Turning Point in the History of the Bratslav Hasidic Messianism," in Baras, ed., *Messianism and Eschatology,* pp. 325–342 (Hebrew).

97. See the passage from Abulafia's *Sitrei Torah* quoted above, chap. 5, pp. 161.

98. *Netiv Mitzwotekha* (Jerusalem, 1983), pp. 6–7. I am inclined to understand this story against the background of the ecstatic meeting of the mystic with his double, or with his perfect nature, during a mystical experience rather than in terms of Lurianic Kabbalah, as dealing with the contemplation of a supernal anthropos or supernal Messiah. On the meeting with the double see Scholem, *On the Mystical Shape,* pp. 251–260; Idel, *Mystical Experience,* pp. 88–95. See especially the view of R. Moses Isserles adduced by Scholem, *On the Mystical Shape,* pp. 258–259, and found in a text that was available to the Hasidic masters as to the reflection of the form of the prophet into the supernal glory. On the different legends relating the Besht with R. Ḥayyim ben 'Attar see Dan Manor, "R. Ḥayyim ben Attar in Hasidic Tradition," *Pe'amim* 20 (1984), pp. 88–110 (Hebrew); Rosman, *Founder of Hasidism,* pp. 129–130. In one of these traditions, which apparently served as an important source for the rabbi of Komarno's discussion above, the Besht describes ben 'Attar as possessing a spark of the Messiah. See Rosman, *Founder of Hasidism.*

99. For a Lurianic understanding of this story see Wolfson, *Along the Path,* p. 100, who assumes, on grounds of the occurrence of the expression *'aqevav,* "his heels," interpreted by him as the heels of the Messiah, that the whole passage "refers to the divine image and form of the Messiah in the celestial realm." I see no plausible reason for such a reading, which would corroborate the content of Hasidic discussions on different messianic issues influenced by Lurianic Kabbalah. However, I consider it implausible to impose on this specific passage from the Rabbi of Komarno views stemming from Lurianism. The term *mashiyaḥ* was not mentioned even once in the whole context, so that the possessive form *'aqevav* must refer to the Besht. If my interpretation is correct, we may see a more anthropological turn which views the utmost human perfection as the sine qua non for messianic activity, represented in this context by the attempt to join efforts with the Kabbalist living in Jerusalem in order to bring about a messianic event, described here in psychological terms, namely the descent of the higher soul and of *yeḥidah.* En passant, the Hasidic master portrays the Besht as spiritually higher than ben 'Attar, but compare the different description found in Wolfson, *Along the Path.*

100. Taubes, "Price of Messianism," p. 556. I am inclined not to accept Taubes's solution because he assumes, even more than Scholem did, the centrality of Lurianism in Hasidic messianism without being aware of the diversity of the "messianic idea." See also Werblowsky, "Mysticism and Messianism," p. 307.

101. Byron L. Sherwin, "Corpus Domini: Traces of the New Testament in East European Hasidism?" *Heythrop Journal* 35 (1994), pp. 267–280.

102. Liebes, *Studies in the Zohar,* pp. 139–161.

103. Compare, however, Elior's view, quoted above, n. 68.

104. On the panoramic approach see Idel, *Hasidism: Between Ecstasy and Magic,* pp. 9–15.

105. This suggested linkage between the vision of some scholars of the ancient Israelite sacral kingship and the Hasidic tzaddiqim should be compared to Martin Buber's suggestion as to the continuity of the typology of another messianic topic: the suffering and dying Messiah, namely Messiah ben Joseph, and the stories told about the fate of various tzaddiqim. Cf. Martin Buber, *The Prophetic Faith* (Harper Torchbooks, New York, 1960), p. 234. On the Messiah and the concept of

tzaddiq in Kabbalah see Bracha Sack, "The Commentaries of R. Abraham Galante: Some Observations to the Writings of His Masters," in E. Ḥazan, ed., *Misgav Yerushalayim Studies in Jewish Literature* (Misgav Yerushalayim, Jerusalem, 1987), p. 75 (Hebrew). For the messianic role of the tzaddiq in Hasidism see also the interesting remark of Jacob B. Agus, "Bringing Clarity into the Mystical," a critical review of Scholem's *Messianic Idea,* printed in *Judaism* 21, no. 3 (1972), p. 380.

106. This stand is more evident in his autobiography, *Megillat Setarim,* ed. Naftali ben Menaḥem (Mossad Ha-Rav Kook, Jerusalem, 1944) (Hebrew). See also Idel, *Kabbalah: New Perspectives,* pp. 308–309.

107. See Idel, *Hasidism: Between Ecstasy and Magic,* pp. 34–43.

108. Tishby, "Messianic Idea," pp. 39–41; the text of R. Aharon ha-Levi has eschatological overtones, since in this context it is said, inter alia, "through his merit the Messiah shall come." Tishby's eschatological interpretation has been questioned by Rachel Elior, *The Theory of Divinity of Hasidut Ḥabad, the Second Generation* (Magnes Press, Jerusalem, 1982), pp. 374–375n9, (Hebrew) who suggests that R. Aharon merely used a commonplace formula.

109. This is precisely the phrase used by R. Aharon.

110. *Sefer ha-Berit,* p. 291. See the whole context on pp. 290–291. On this author in general, and on his peculiar Kabbalistic background, see Monford Harris, "The Book of the Covenant: An Eighteenth Century Quest for the Holy Spirit," *The Solomon Goldman Lectures,* vol. 6, ed. Nathaniel Stampfer, (Spertus College, Chicago, 1982), pp. 39–53.

111. On these issues see the forthcoming study of Naftali Loewenthal, "The Neutralization of Messianism and the Apocalypse." I gratefully acknowledge the author for kindly sharing with me his study before publication. On messianism in this school see Ravitzky, *Messianism, Zionism,* pp. 263–276.

112. See Idel, "Land of Israel," pp. 193–194, 210–214.

113. Cf. Daniel 12:3, and the remark of Louis Jacobs ad locum.

114. Cf. 2 Chronicles 15:3. On the history of the interpretation of this verse in Jewish mysticism see Elqayam, *Mystery of Faith,* pp. 49–63.

115. On the teacher as a messianic figure see below, appendix 1.

116. See Zevi Hirsch Eichenstein, *Turn Aside from Evil and Do Good: An Introduction and a Way to the Tree of Life,* English translation with an introduction by Louis Jacobs (Littman Library of Jewish Civilization, London, Washington, 1995), p. 6.

117. Ibid., p. 32.

118. On this year as a messianic date see Arieh Morgenstern, "Messianic Concepts and Settlement in the Land of Israel," in Saperstein, ed., *Essential Papers,* pp. 433–455.

119. Cf. *Sefer 'Ateret Tzevi* (Lvov, 1871), part 2, fol. 3d.

120. Considering the vast extent of the rabbi of Komarno's writings and the poor scholarly analysis of his thought, a more profound understanding of his messianism is still a desideratum. On his extreme mysticism see the remarks in Idel, *Kabbalah: New Perspectives,* index, p. 410, sub voce "Isaac Yehudah Safrin of Komarno," and idem, "Universalization and Integration," pp. 48–49, 55.

121. *Megillat Setarim,* ed. Naftali ben Menaḥem (Mossad ha-Rav Kook, Jerusalem, 1944), p. 7.

122. Ibid., p. 9.

123. Ibid., p. 14.

124. Ibid., pp. 15–16, 18–19, 20–21. For examples of revelations during a state of wakefulness see p. 26.

125. Ibid., pp. 16–17.

126. Ibid., pp. 9–11.

127. Ibid., pp. 12, 13, 19, 23.

128. Ibid., p. 14. More on this formulation of the talismanic mystical model see his *Zohar Ḥai* (Israel, 1973), vol. 2, fols. 267a–268a. This discussion, like many others in his writings, are inspired by Ḥayyim Vital's *Sha'arei Qedushah.*

129. *Megillat Setarim,* pp. 16–17.

130. Ibid., pp. 19–20.

131. Ibid.

132. Ibid., p. 20, and see also pp. 17–18, 22, 27. More on the New Near and messianism see note 7 above.

133. Ibid., pp. 7, 33–34.

134. Ibid., pp. 33–34. See also above, note 108, the text from *Netiv Mitzvotekha.*

135. Ibid., p. 37. The traditions about the Besht, found in this book as well as in many others of the Rabbi of Komarno, cannot be corroborated from other, earlier Hasidic sources, and may reflect the creativity of the vivid imagination of this mystic. That does not mean that he invented all the traditions related to the Besht. From our point of view see his discussion of the issue of the dialogue between the Besht and the Messiah, dealt with in detail above, in his *Zohar Ḥai,* vol. 3, fol. 76b. See also note 90 above.

136. Ibid., pp. 26–27.

137. See *Zohar Ḥai,* vol. 4, fol. 139ad.

Chapter 8: Concluding Remarks

1. See Moshe Idel, "On Mobility, Individuals, and Groups: Prologomenon for a Sociological Approach to Sixteenth-Century Kabbalah," *Kabbalah: Journal for the Study of Jewish Mystical Texts* 3 (1998), pp. 141–169.

2. Scholem, *Major Trends,* p. 20. See also idem, *Messianic Idea,* pp. 1–2, and J. Taubes, "The Price of Messianism," in Saperstein, ed., *Essential Papers,* pp. 552–553.

3. Cf. the subtitle of Dan's book about Gershom Scholem. For a reified vision of Jewish history and of its attitude toward Kabbalah see Dan's interesting statement, "It seems as if Jewish history kept the Kabbalah in reserve for many generations until the right time came for it to appear and assume its role." Cf. his introduction to J. Dan and F. Talmage, eds., *Studies in Jewish Mysticism* (Association for Jewish Studies, Cambridge, Mass., 1982), p. 13. A similar reification of history is also evident in Werblowsky, "Shabbetai Zevi," p. 214: "Jews had to recognize . . . that history had given its verdict." The use of the term *history* as the key to understanding religious phenomena become a leitmotif in the scholarship of Kabbalah. I would say, following Reinhold Niebuhr, that "the dominant note in modern culture is not so much confidence in reason as faith in history. The conception of a redemptive history informs most diverse forms of modern culture." See Niebuhr, *Faith and History: A Comparison of Christian and Modern Views of History* (Scribner, New York, 1949), p. 6, quoted in Tuvesone, *Millennium and Utopia,* p. xi. See also ibid., p. 203. As Henry Corbin has pointed out, "L'eschatologie laicisée ne dispose plus que d'une mythologie du sens de l'histoire." Cf. his *En Islam iranien* (Gallimard, Paris, 1971), 1:23. I would say that the Jewish version corresponding to Corbin's observation, as embodied by the expression "mystical dimension of Jewish history," is much more teleological, as it envisions history as moving toward the modern Zionist version of the solution of the plight of the Jews in exile.

4. See the different stand of Neher, *Prophetic Existence,* pp. 243–244, where he claims that the mode of apocalyptic time is cyclical while the covenantal one is linear.

5. See above, chap. 7, n. 77.

6. On this argument in general see Idel, *Hasidism: Between Ecstasy and Magic,* pp. 45–145.

On the importance of inconsistencies in religion see Versnel, *Transition and Reversal.* Versnel's claim, formulated in the context of ancient religions, is even more salient in the case of the latter forms of Judaism, which absorbed many earlier and diverging layers of literature and modes of thought.

7. See his "New Directions."

8. Too often, the unfounded and sometimes absurd allegation that I propose to neglect textological studies has been ventilated. See, more recently, Peter Schaefer, "The Magic of the Golem: The Early Development of the Golem Legend," *JJS* 46 (1995), p. 258. This claim, never substantiated by the writers who made it, blatantly contrasts explicit statements in my writings to the effect that a phenomenological, sociological, or psychological approach, or any other new method, should be coupled by philological-historical treatments of the relevant material. I hope that the content of my studies reflects this programmatic view. See e.g. Idel, *Kabbalah: New Perspectives,* p. 23. Why some few scholars claim the opposite is less a matter of facts than of psychology.

9. McGinn, *Visions of the End,* p. 31, and Collins, *Apocalyptic Imagination,* p. 11.

10. See Liebes, "Messiah of the Zohar," pp. 109–110, and Idel, *Hasidism: Between Ecstasy and Magic,* pp. 53–65.

11. On the issue of the messianic secret in late antiquity see Jonathan Z. Smith, "No News Is Good News: Secrecy in Late Antiquity' " in Kees W. Bolle, ed., *Secrecy in Religions* (Brill, Leiden, 1987), pp. 76–77. Compare also to the interesting remark of Jankelevitch, "L'espérance et la fin des temps," p. 16, and Scholem, *Messianic Idea,* pp. 6–8.

12. Taubes, "Price of Messianism," pp. 554–555.

13. See Scholem, *Major Trends,* pp. 20, 244–245. On periodization in Scholem and Dinur see Myers, *Re-Inventing,* p. 167.

14. On these two main forms of Kabbalah see Scholem, *Major Trends,* p. 124; Idel, *Kabbalah: New Perspectives,* pp. xi–xvii; idem, "Contributions," pp. 124–127.

15. Liebes, "Messiah of the Zohar."

16. See also Liebes, "New Directions," pp. 154–156.

17. See Scholem, *Devarim be-Go,* p. 205, where "the resuscitation of the movement of Shelomo Molkho and ha-Reuveni and several other movements" is mentioned; or Aescoly, *Messianic Movements,* p. 273, and Tishby, *Messianism in the Time of the Expulsion,* p. 52, where Tishby describes the "messianic amok" of the Molkho and Reuveni movement as well as that of "other" movements. See also the salient observations of Yonina Talmon, "Social Movements," *International Encyclopedia of Social Sciences* 14 (1968), pp. 438–439 and her important article "Millenarian Movements," *Archives Européenes de Sociologie* 7 (1966), pp. 159–200.

18. On the problem of the Messiah as a Kohen, see above, chapter 2.

19. Mann, "Messianic Movements," p. 336; idem, "Obadia le Proselyte," *REJ* 71 (1921), pp. 89–93; 89 (1930), pp. 252–253. See especially p. 253n3, where Mann mentions that the widespread messianic phenomenon is related to David Alroy. See also Aescoly, *Messianic Movements,* pp. 181–183, who included this incident in his monograph on movements.

20. Mann, "Messianic Movements," p. 336.

21. Aescoly, *Messianic Movements,* pp. 216–235.

22. See Liebes, *Studies in Jewish Myth,* pp. 93–106.

23. See, for example, the studies mentioned in notes 28–31 of appendix 3. In fact, the affinity between the Zionist experience and the messianic one has been adumbrated already by Scholem at the very beginning of his studies on Sabbateanism; see *Studies and Texts,* p. 9.

24. See, however, Sharot, *Messianism, Mysticism, and Magic,* passim, and the recent analysis of Cook, *Prophecy and Apocalypticism.*

25. See Sharot, *Messianism, Mysticism, and Magic;* Idel, "Introduction," pp. 10–11; "One in a Town," pp. 96–97.

26. In general, the problem of the circulation of texts and ideas is a difficult one: see Dominick Lacapra, "Rethinking Intellectual History and Reading Texts," *History and Theory* 19 (1980), pp. 263–264; See also Zeev Gries, *The Book in Early Hasidism* (Hakibbutz Hameuchad, Tel Aviv, 1992) (Hebrew).

27. "L'espérance et la fin des temps," p. 17.

28. See M. Idel, "PaRDeS: Some Reflections on Kabbalistic Hermeneutics," in John J. Collins and M. Fishbane, eds., *Death, Ecstasy, and Other Worldly Journeys* (State University of New York Press, Albany, 1995), pp. 251–256.

29. M. Idel, "Kabbalah and Elites in Thirteenth-Century Spain," *Mediterranean Historical Review* 9 (1994), pp. 5–19.

30. See Moshe Idel, "On Judaism, Jewish Mysticism, and Magic," in P. Schäfer and H. Kippenberg, eds., *Envisioning Magic* (Brill, Leiden, 1997), pp. 207–214.

31. Sharot, *Messianism, Mysticism, and Magic;* Michael Löwy, "Pour une sociologie de la mystique juive; a propos et autour du Sabbatai Sevi," *Archives de Sciences Sociales de Religions* 57 (1984), pp. 8–10.

32. Scholem, *Researches in Sabbateanism,* pp. 510–529.

33. See e.g. Tishby, *Studies of Kabbalah,* 2:337.

34. See ibidem, 2:334–335.

35. Scholem, *On the Kabbalah,* p. 2. On Scholem's emphasis on the power of Kabbalah to transmute things into symbols see his *On Jews and Judaism in Crisis,* ed. W. J. Dannhauser (Schocken Books, New York, 1976), p. 48. I wonder if the source of Scholem's view of the new "historical symbols," conceived of as unique to Jewish mystics when compared to Christian mysticism, is not to be found in Yehezkel Kaufmann's claim that the Israel kingship is unique, seeking out "symbols of election, new historical symbols, symbols of grace of YHWH which was disclosed to Israel." Cf. *Toledot ha-'Emunah ha-Israelit* (Mossad Bialik, Jerusalem, 1959), 2:181, as translated and discussed by Levenson, *Sinai and Zion,* pp. 107–108. As Levenson has shown, Kaufmann's attempt to distinguish between the pagan and the Israelite symbols did not work out. For more on symbol and historical experience in Lurianic Kabbalah, see below, appendix 2.

36. Scholem, *On the Kabbalah,* p. 2. See also idem, *Messianic Idea,* p. 7, as well as chap. 7, n. 86, and Moses, *L'ange de l'histoire,* pp. 190–191. See, nevertheless, the denial by Dan, "Gershom Scholem and Jewish Messianism," p. 79, that Scholem ever made a connection between persecutions and the floruit of messianism. Scholem himself, however, wrote quite explicitly that "the magnitude of the messianic idea corresponds to the endless powerlessness in Jewish history during all the centuries of exile." *Messianic Idea,* p. 35, as well as his *Major Trends,* pp. 287–288. See also Taubes, "Price of Messianism," p. 556. A more recent attempt to connect messianism with persecutions or crises is found in Stephen Sharot, "Crises et mouvements messianiques," in Shmuel Trigano, ed., *La societé juive a travers l'histoire* (Fayard, Paris, 1992), 1:263–308, esp. 1:266–268. See also Sarachek, *Doctrine of the Messiah,* p. 2. For a more recent adherence of an anthropologist to the theory of deprivation without resorting to this term, though following the lead of the essays edited by Thrupp, see Leach, *L'unité de l'homme,* p. 230. These explanations, which may sometimes be pertinent for mass movements, are far from sufficient insofar as the emergence of the messianic self-consciousness of the Messiah himself. The deprivation theory, backed by more sociological approaches, such as in many of the contributions to Thrupp, ed., *Millennial Dreams in Action* (cf. the editor's summary, p. 26), can only rarely be successfully applied to the case of elite individuals. Despite the resort to the deprivation theory in some of Scholem's discussions above, he also denied

its importance in the case of Sabbateanism. See e.g. his *Sabbatai Ṣevi,* pp. 392, 461. Let me adduce just one major example from a Sabbatean text printed by Scholem himself. Abraham Michael Cardoso, one of the most impressive Sabbatean thinkers, describes at length his good life in North Africa, as part of an argument for the sincerity of his belief in the messianism of Tzevi. He says, inter alia, *li - 'ein galut,* "I have no [experience of] exile." Cf. Scholem, *Studies and Texts,* p. 319. Compare, however, the strong nexus between exile and messianism in Werblowsky, "Shabettai Zevi," p. 210. In this case, as in many others, there is no doubt that Werblowsky offers a much more faithful account of Scholem's stand.

37. On the decline of creative symbolism after the expulsion from Spain see Idel, *Kabbalah: New Perspectives,* pp. 217–218. Liebes even assumed that it is hard to speak about symbols in Lurianic Kabbalah at all; see his "Myth vs. Symbol," in Fine, ed., *Essential Papers,* pp. 212–242.

38. Scholem, *On the Kabbalah,* p. 2.

39. Ibid., p. 2. A similar strong characterization is found in Aescoly, *Jewish Messianic Movements,* p. 298, where he refers to ha-Reuveni has telling the story of his generation.

40. See Scholem, *Messianic Idea,* p. 84.

41. See Taubes, "Price of Messianism," p. 600.

42. Scholem, *Messianic Idea,* pp. 49–77. See also ibid., pp. 21–22, and more recently Kochan, *Jews, Idols, and Messiahs: The Challenge from History* (Basil Blackwell, Oxford, 1990).

43. The inherent tension between medieval Jewish mysticism and tradition is found, according to Scholem, in the very nature of the Gnostic myth, considered sometimes as a historical influence on Kabbalah, sometimes only as a phenomenological parallel that informs Kabbalah. See M. Idel, "Rabbinism versus Kabbalism: On G. Scholem's Phenomenology of Judaism," *Modern Judaism* 11 (1991), pp. 281–296.

44. Scholem, *Sabbatai Ṣevi,* pp. x–xi, 283.

45. Scholem, *Messianic Idea,* pp. 2, 77, 106, 276; idem, *On the Kabbalah,* p. 3; idem, *Studies and Texts,* p. 9, or Tishby's reference to the "heart of Judaism" where the "abyss of heresy" has emerged; cf. *Studies of Kabbalah,* 2:336. For a critique of Scholem's view of Judaism as a unified concept see Neusner, *Messiah in Context,* p. 227.

46. On a much more spiritual vision of traditional Judaism see the various presentations of rabbinic literature by R. Joseph Baer Soloveitchik, Abraham J. Heschel, Emmanuel Levinas, and David Hartman.

47. See Zvi Zohar, "Militant Conservatism: On the Socio-Religious Policy of Rabbis in Aleppo in Modern Times," *Pe'amim* 55 (1993), pp. 57–78 (Hebrew).

48. Marc Bloch, *Mèlanges historiques* (Ecoles des Hautes Etudes en Sciences Sociales, Paris, 1963), 2:838.

49. For a more diversified vision of the notion of tradition, insofar as the material concerning Jewish magic and mysticism, see Idel, *Golem,* pp. xxii–xxv. See also Elisheva Carlebach, "Rabbinic Circles as Messianic Pathways in the Post-Expulsion Era," *Judaism* 41 (1992), pp. 208–216.

50. On primary symbols see Peter Slater, *The Dynamics of Religion* (Harper and Row, New York, 1978), pp. 29–30.

51. See the collection of articles edited by S. N. Eisenstadt, *The Origins and Diversity of Axial Age Civilizations* (State University of New York Press, Albany, 1986). When addressing here the issue of pre-axial and axial modes of thought, I do not identify them with the old and the new elements, or with the traditional and the Kabbalistic views which were discussed above. Axial concepts, such as Maimonides' theology and psychology, may become traditional, while pre-axial, mainly mythical themes may become "new" and rebellious elements in a given situation, as is the case with Sabbateanism and Frankism.

52. To a certain extent, the tensions between two modes so crucial for the understanding of the history of messianism is found also in Scholem's important distinction, already adumbrated by Ernst Bloch, between utopian and restorative, though his categories differ from what I propose here. See Anson Rabinbach, "Between Enlightenment and Apocalypse: Benjamin, Bloch and Modern German Jewish Messianism," *New German Critique* 34 (1985), pp. 81–124, and Benjamin Uffenheimer, "From Prophetic to Apocalyptic Eschatology," in Baras, ed., *Messianism and Eschatology,* p. 29 (Hebrew).

53. On the synthesis in religion between the axial and pre-axial aspects see Ewert H. Cousins, *Christ of the 21th Century* (Element, Rockport, Mass., 1992), and Idel, *Hasidism: Between Ecstasy and Magic,* p. 225. On the move from mythos to logos, as opposed to the move from the logos, as the Word, to the flesh in early Christianity, see Ringgren, *Messiah in the Old Testament,* pp. 66–67.

54. Scholem, *Messianic Idea,* p. 204.

55. See Tishby, *Studies in Kabbalah,* 2:475–519.

56. Scholem, *Messianic Idea,* p. 185. The emphases are mine. See also the quotation from Scholem's *'Od Davar,* above, chap. 7, pp. 239–240, and n. 99 there.

57. Ibid., p. 194. The emphases are mine.

58. Tishby, *Studies in the Zohar,* pp. 52–55, 67–74.

59. Idel, *Hasidism: Between Ecstasy and Magic,* pp. 203–207.

60. Scholem, *Messianic Idea,* pp. 1–36.

61. See above, Introduction, n. 8, as well as n. 55 in this chapter.

62. See Handelman, *Fragments of Redemption,* pp. 170, 328; Richard Wolin, *Walter Benjamin: An Aestetic of Redemption* (University of California Press, Berkeley, 1994), p. 117.

63. See, however, Scholem, *Messianic Idea,* p. 13, who opts for a much more utopian feature of Lurianic Kabbalah.

64. James S. Preus, "Theological Legitimation for Innovation in the Middle Ages," *Viator* 3 (1972), p. 20. On Abulafia's adducing the antecedents of Moses, Joshua, David, and Solomon as messianic figures who received divine power see above, chap. 2.

65. Moses, *L'ange d'histoire;* Handelman, *Fragments of Redemption,* passim; Mendes-Flohr, " 'The Stronger and the Better Jews,' " p. 167; Finkelstein, *Ritual of New Creation,* pp. 120–121. See also below, appendix 3.

66. Talmon, *King, Cult and Calendar,* p. 162. See also Hartman, *Living Covenant,* pp. 285–286; Goodman, *On Justice,* p. 185; Jankelevitch, "L'espérance et la fin des temps," p. 17.

67. The difference between my approach above and some neo-Orthodox visions of rabbinic spirituality, as well as some more secular modern Jewish approaches to messianism, is the emphasis I put on the relevance and importance of a variety of ways to reach an experience, conceived by the mystic as one of redemptive plenitude, either halakhic—that is, nomian—or anomian and even antinomian. While the neo-Orthodoxy will glorify the nomian way alone, and the seculars the antinomian one, I prefer to regard them, as well as the anomian techniques, as different and equally valid paths, both from the historical and from the phenomenological point of view.

68. Werblowsky, "Mysticism and messianism."

69. Compare Scholem, *Messianic Idea,* p. 4. See also above, Introduction.

70. See e.g. *Baraita'* in *BT, Megillah,* fol. 29a; *Berakhot,* fol. 9b; Klausner, *Messianic Idea in Israel,* p. 471; Rosenberg, "Exile and Redemption," pp. 418, 420–421, and app. 1 and 2 below.

71. This is the case in some passages of the Great Maggid, as discussed in Idel, "Land of Israel," pp. 209–210.

72. See Peter Brown, *The World of Late Antiquity* (London, 1971), pp. 102–103; idem, "The Rise and the Function of the Holy Man in Late Antiquity," *Journal of Roman Studies* 61 (1971), pp.

80–101; Smith, *Map,* pp. 186–187, and the interesting remarks of Patai, *Man and Temple,* pp. 224–225. On the temple as the human body see also Arthur Green, "The Zaddiq as Axis Mundi in Later Judaism," in Fine, ed., *Essential Papers,* pp. 291–314; Idel, *Hasidism: Between Ecstasy and Magic,* pp. 16, 46–47, 197.

73. See Werblowsky, "Mysticism and messianism," pp. 309, 314. Nevertheless, let me emphasize that there are dozens of discussions on the Messiah in the not-so-voluminous works of R. Menaḥem Naḥum of Chernobyl, and only a few of them will be discussed below, in addition to those discussed in the previous chapter.

74. Cf. Dinur, "The Messianic-Prophetic Role of the Besht," in Saperstein, ed., *Essential Papers,* p. 379.

75. Werblowsky, "Mysticism and messianism," p. 311.

76. Namely, the people of Israel, designated as *knesset yisrael,* cf. *Me'or 'Einayyim,* p. 8, or the soul of the student of the Torah. The view of the mystic as a female that becomes a male is already found in ecstatic Kabbalah. See Idel, *Mystical Experience,* pp. 179–180, 184–190.

77. *'Aḥdut ve-hitkalelut.* On these two terms as referring to mystical union see Idel, "Universalization and Integration."

78. For the Lurianic source of this term and its history in both Kabbalah and Hasidism see the literature mentioned in Liebes, "'Two Young Roes of a Doe,'" and Mordekhai Pachter, "*Katnut* ('Smallness') and *Gadlut* ('Greatness') in Lurianic Kabbalah," in Elior and Liebes, eds., *Lurianic Kabbalah,* pp. 113–170 and 171–210, respectively (Hebrew).

79. For the Sinaitic revelation as a mystical experience of union with the divine see *Me'or 'Einayyim,* p. 8.

80. *BT, Sabbath,* fol. 30a.

81. For the experiential study of the Torah in Hasidism, which involves union with God, see Idel, *Hasidism: Between Ecstasy and Magic,* pp. 171–188.

82. *Me'or 'Einayyim,* p. 9. A similar view, again mentioning the time of the advent of the redeemer, is found on p. 8. In general, according to this master, Moses, unlike the people of Israel, retained his experience even after the sin of the calf.

83. Ibid., p. 9.

84. See especially the important passage in *Me'or 'Einayyim,* p. 202. There the author insists that in the messianic times everyone will enjoy the union between the divine powers and between man and God, while in the exile only the few do.

85. Werblowsky, "Mysticism and Messianism," p. 311.

86. *Me'or 'Einayyim,* pp. 8–9. See also chapter 2 above and appendix 2 below.

87. *BT, Sanhedrin,* fol. 98b.

88. See *Yismaḥ Moshe,* p. 375 (printed at the end of *Me'or 'Einayyim*). See also above, chap. 7, n. 52. For a strong theurgical view of religious life see *Yismaḥ Moshe,* p. 301.

89. The Hebrew formulation is not so clear: *yehieh zeh she-ta'aleh.*

90. *Mazzal 'elyon.* This is a classical symbol for the sefirah of Keter.

91. This is another symbol for the first sefirah, both in the *Zohar* and in R. Joseph Gikatilla. This Hasidic master resorts numerous times to these two terms for designating the source of the influx to be drawn down.

92. In theosophical Kabbalah this term stands for the last sefirah, but here it seems that such a reading would be implausible. Compare to a similar passage, *Ma'or va-Shemesh,* pp. 120, 132–133, 360, and esp. pp. 121, 134, 136, 143, where the drawing down of the influxes and the blessing upon the four worlds, thus including the mundane world, is mentioned. See, however, ibid., p. 483, where a more theosophical reading is plausible. On the basis of a discussion on p. 122, it is possible

that he refers to both the supernal and the lower Knesset Israel. I suspect, on the basis of a discussion found in this book, p. 139, that there was an affinity between two different words, *mashiyaḥ* and *meshikhah*, the drawing down, which was due to their similar pronunciation.

93. *Ma'or va-Shemesh*, p. 103.

94. See above, chap. 5, n. 87.

95. See e.g. the view of R. Moses Cordovero, who claims that because of the tiqqun that is accomplished during the Sabbath, which affects the sefirot of Tiferet and Malkhut, redemption occurs, and there is no more galut. Cf. his *Tefillah le-Moshe*, fol. 217b. This Kabbalist also uses the term *tiqqun ha-shekhinah* in similar contexts; cf. ibid., fol. 241a. Sabbath as an anticipation of the next world is a commonplace in rabbinic Judaism.

96. See also above, the formulations I adduced from Levenson and Neher in chap. 1, n. 27.

97. See, more recently, the collection of articles entitled *The Apocalypse in the Middle Ages*, ed. Richard K. Emmerson and Bernard McGinn (Cornell University Press, Ithaca, N.Y., 1992).

98. See, in another context, Robert Alter, "The Apocalyptic Temper," *Commentary* 41 (June, 1966), pp. 62–63.

99. On the idea of plenitude see also the interesting observations of Durand, *Figures mythiques*, pp. 78, 337.

100. See Scholem, *Messianic Idea*, p. 35.

101. See above, chap. 5, n. 33.

Appendix 1: Ego, Ergo Sum Messiah: On Abraham Abulafia's *Sefer ha-Yashar*

1. See *Sefer ha-'Edut*, Ms. München 285, fol. 36ab.

2. The biblical phrase "angel of 'Elohim" occurs several times in Abulafia's discussion of messianism. On its significance as pointing to both a prophet and an angelic messenger see William M. Schniedewind, *The Word of God in Transition: From Prophet to Exegete in the Second Temple* (Sheffield Academic Press, JSOT, 1995), pp. 82–84.

3. This view is also expressed in the commentary on *Sefer ha-'Edut*, Ms. München 285, fol. 36a.

4. Compare the formula used by Nathan of Gaza when he introduced his most important vision: "Thus speaks the Lord." Cf. Scholem, *Sabbatai Ṣevi*, pp. 204–205; Idel, *Kabbalah: New Perspectives*, pp. 81–82.

5. Ms. München 285, fol. 24a.

6. Cf. Ezekiel, 39:20, 29. On this formula see Cook, *Prophecy and Apocalypticism*, p. 117.

7. See Ms. Paris, Bibliothèque Nationale 680, fol. 298a. These two names are referred to in the theosophical-theurgical Kabbalah as representative of the male and female divine potencies, 'Adonay standing for the Malkhut and YHWH for Tiferet, and they are conjoined in order to induce and symbolize a state of union between these potencies. See Mark Verman, *The History and Variety of Jewish Meditation* (Jason Aronson, Northvale, N.J., 1996), pp. 191–210, esp. 199, and Abulafia, *Sefer ha-'Ot*, p. 69.

8. Ibid., fol. 297b.

9. On this divine name see Idel, *Mystical Experience*, pp. 18, 22, 31; Wolfson, "Doctrine of Sefirot," pp. 353–354n54.

10. See also the eighth-century Muslim author who claimed prophethood and the revelation of the divine name mentioned in Widengren, *Muhammad*, p. 30. See also ibid., pp. 141–142, where Enoch is described, in a rather ancient text, the *Book of John the Evangelist*, as both a teacher and a

revealer of the divine name. On prophecy and the divine name in early-thirteenth-century sources see also Wolfson, *Through a Speculum,* pp. 181–187.

11. For more on this issue see Idel, *Studies in Ecstatic Kabbalah,* p. 47. For an interesting parallel in Islamic mysticism, see Corbin, *Creative Imagination,* p. 256.

12. See Idel, *Hasidism: Between Ecstasy and Magic,* p. 98. See also below, my discussion of the Messiah as high priest.

13. See De Fraine, *L'aspect religieux,* pp. 207–208, 223–230; Frankfort, *Kingship and the Gods,* pp. 224–226.

14. Cf. *Commentary to Sefer ha-'Edut,* Ms. München 285, fol. 36a.

15. *Yitpa'er.* This verb is used by Abulafia in the context of his own claim to have received a revelation of the date of the end. See the passage from his epistle *Ve-Zot li-Yhudah,* p. 18.

16. See his *Mafteaḥ ha-Shemot,* Ms. New York JTS 843, fol. 45b.

17. See the passage from commentary on *Sefer ha-Ḥayyim,* translated above, chap. 2, pp. 73–74. The number seven may point to a vision of sealing a cycle or sealing the whole series of prophets. The concept of sealing is implied in the very title of the last of the first series of Abulafia's prophetic writings, *Sefer Ḥotam ha-Haftarah.* On sealing of prophecy see Gedaliahu G. Stroumsa, " 'Seal of Prophets': The Nature of a Manichaean Metaphor," *Jerusalem Studies in Arabic and Islam* 7 (1986), pp. 61–74; Yohanan Friedmann, *Prophecy Continuous* (University of California Press, Berkeley and Los Angeles, 1989), pp. 49–82. On seven figures who were apparently also seen as prophets who precede the Messiah, already in the Judeo-Christian tradition preserved in the Pseudo-Clementine Homilies, 17:4, see Hans-Joachim Schoeps, *Jewish Christianity: Factional Disputes in Early Church,* trans. D. R. A. Hare, (Fortress Press, Philadelphia, 1969), pp. 70–73. On the relation between the seventh benediction and redemption see Urbach, *The Sages,* pp. 654–655, 676–677.

18. See above, chap. 5, p. 161.

19. Ms. Oxford 1580, fol. 164b, printed in Jellinek, *Beit ha-Midrasch,* 3:xli.

20. This is a play on the Hebrew consonants of Messina.

21. *Sefer 'Otzar 'Eden Ganuz,* Ms. Oxford 1580, fol. 165b, printed in Jellinek, *Beit ha-Midrasch.*

22. Ms. München 285, fol. 24a.

23. It is ironic that the last letters constitute the noun *teḥilat,* which means "beginning."

24. Ms. München 285, fol. 25a. The four words are therefore not the title of a book, as Scholem suggested, *Major Trends,* p. 382.

25. See Idel, *Mystical Experience,* p. 89. The double gematria, 'Ediy = Ḥanokh = 84 and Sa-hadiy = Metatron = 314 is already found among Ḥasidei Ashkenaz. See e.g. Rokeach [R. Eleazar of Worms], *A Commentary on the Bible,* ed. Chaim Konyevsky (Benei Beraq, 1986), 1:95.

26. See e.g. Idel, *Mystical Experience,* p. 102; *Language, Torah, and Hermeneutics,* p. 21.

27. The Hebrew form is *keli qarov la-nevu'ah.* Compare the similar formulation found in *Sefer 'Otzar 'Eden Ganuz,* Ms. Oxford 1580, fol. 149b: *derekh . . . qerovah.*

28. This view of knowledge is closer to the Aristotelian or Platonic view, while Abulafia is concerned more with the higher experience of knowledge as a sudden revelation. For the two types of knowledge see Neher, *Prophetic Experience,* pp. 103–104.

29. The Hebrew formulations are unclear here.

30. *BT, Sanhedrin,* fol. 38a. See also above, chap. 2, n. 32, where the same formula serves for conveying the sense of a mystical union between the human intellect and the Agent Intellect. Apparently the term *rav,* pointing to God in the talmudic literature, with which the angelic Metatron was related by having the same name, has been transposed onto Metatron itself, and the mystic is described as sharing with it the same name, in our case *moreh.* See also *Major Trends,*

p. 140, where Scholem compares this term with the Indian *guru.* In some texts found in Ashkenazi Hasidism, Metatron is described as a teacher of infants who died before studying the Torah. See e.g the text inserted in a manuscript of Heikhalot literature printed in A. M. Haberman, *Ḥadashim Gam Yeshanim* (Mass Printing House, Jerusalem, 1972), p. 99 (Hebrew).

31. Here the term *devequt* is used.

32. Ms. Rome—Angelica 38, fols. 31b–32a; Ms. München 285, fol. 26b, printed in Scholem, *Major Trends,* pp. 140- 141, 382. See also Schultz, *Judaism and the Gentile Faiths,* p. 325n5, who suggests, on the basis of the quotation adduced by Scholem, that Abulafia's view of *ḥokhmah, binah va-da'at* had perhaps influenced Lubavitch Hasidism, which highlighted these terms.

33. This criterion is mentioned also in the ecstatic *Sefer Sha'arei Tzedeq,* pp. 22–24.

34. Ms. Paris, Bibliothèque Nationale 680, fol. 297b.

35. See above, chap. 2, pp. 00–00, in the quotation from Sefer *Mafteaḥ ha-Tokheḥot.*

36. On the Agent Intellect as Metatron and Messiah see above, chap. 2, esp. n. 30.

37. If the two titles describe different spiritual moments, they should be compared to the double Messiah in some Qumranic texts, while in others they are paralleled by a Messiah and Doresh ha-Torah. See 4Q Florilegium, discussed by Lawrence H. Schiffman, "Messianic Figures and Ideas in the Qumranic Scrolls," in Charlesworth, ed., *The Messiah,* p. 125.

38. See Wieder, *Judean Scrolls,* pp. 86–87 and the bibliography mentioned there, as well as the more recent discussions of M. A. Knibb, "The Teacher of Righteousness—A Messianic Title?" in P. R. Davies and R. T. White, ed., *A Tribute to Geza Vermes* (Sheffield, 1990), pp. 51–66, and Collins, "A Throne in the Heavens," pp. 54–55. Collins proposed to interpret a description of enthronement found in the Qumran literature as reminiscent of Moses and the teacher of righteousness, though not of the Messiah, and thus distinguishes between a somewhat eschatological figure and the Messiah. His only piece of evidence for a parallel to the Qumran text is Moses' enthronement, as found in Ezekiel's *Exagoge;* see ibid., p. 51. What seems to be interesting is that a view similar to the ancient description of Moses as seeing the past, present, and future is found in ecstatic Kabbalah. See Idel, *Studies in Ecstatic Kabbalah,* pp. 74, 84n7. For more on the Messiah as an educator see Klausner, *Messianic Idea in Israel,* p. 324, referring to the Psalms of Solomon. For a contemporary of Abulafia, R. Moshe of Burgos, who mentions the excellence of the esoteric studies of the Messiah, and the book of the *Zohar* itself, see Liebes, *Studies in the Zohar,* p. 18.

39. See Even Shmuel, *Midreshei Ge'ullah,* p. 74, translated in Patai, *The Messiah Texts,* p. 125. See also the parallel text translated by Patai, ibid., pp. 26–27. See also above, chap. 6, n. 73, for the use of this talmudic formula in the context of Sabbatai Tzevi.

40. See *Sefer Sitrei Torah,* Ms. Paris, Bibliothèque Nationale 774, fol. 129b. He refers to Capua in his commentary to *Sefer ha-Yashar* several times, implying that this book was already in existence and had been criticized before he left the place. See Ms. München 285, fol. 24b.

41. See Ms. Paris, Bibliothèque Nationale 774, fol. 119a.

42. In *Sefer ha-'Edut,* quoted in chapter 2.

43. See the passage from *Sefer Mafteaḥ ha-Tokheḥot,* quoted in chapter 2.

44. The history of the term "soteriology" is not clear, and on its availability depends the possibility of an influence on Abulafia's phrases.

45. On this Kabbalist see the discussions of Gottlieb, *Studies,* pp. 231–247.

46. In R. Yitzḥaq of Acre's writings, this is an common acronym for *Metatron, Sar Ha-panim.*

47. There is no verse to this effect; R. Yitzḥaq created a dichotomy between a wheel on earth, mentioned in continuation, and one on high.

48. In many sources from ecstatic Kabbalah, this angel is related to the lower elements in creation and in man.

49. The gematria of the consonants is 280, like the five final characters. Compare also to a similar discussion found in another collection of fragments from *'Otzar Ḥayyim,* Ms. Oxford 1911, fols. 158b–159a.

50. *Ya'ar* means "wood," and its gematria is again 280. Since in other cases Sandalfon is identified with matter, I wonder whether the term *hyle* does not underlie the resort to the term "wood." See Idel, *Studies in Ecstatic Kabbalah,* p. 77. The connection between hyle and Sandalfon is evident also in R. Shmuel ibn Motot, *Sefer Tehillot ha-Shem,* Ms. Vatican 225, fol. 54a.

51. *Ruḥaniyut.* This term has several meanings in Hebrew. See Idel, *Hasidism: Between Ecstasy and Magic,* index, sub voce *ruḥaniyut.*

52. Namely the voice of God, the master of Metatron.

53. See *BT, Sanhedrin,* fol. 38b.

54. A reformulation of Isaiah 63:9.

55. This verse is also quoted below, in another passage from the same book and an anonymous discussion dealing with a variety of forms of Metatron. The book was written,in my opinion, by R. Yitzḥaq of Acre; it has been preserved solely in R. Moses of Kiev's *Sefer Shoshan Sodot* (Koretz, 1784), fols. 71a–72a. There he mentions the "emanated Metatron," the "created Metatron," the "sensible Metatron," and even a "compounded Metatron." Another unknown passage by R. Yitzḥaq has been identified by scholars some lines before the passage on Metatron, ibid., fol. 69b. See Gottlieb, *Studies,* p. 247. I suspect that another short discussion concerning the two angels, which includes a view of Metatron as participating in the grief of Israel, is preserved in *Sefer ha-Peliy'ah,* vol. 1, fol. 23d. Metatron could even be part of the human soul, in which case it may be possible to have the Messiah within own's soul. See *'Otzar Ḥayyim,* Ms. Sassoon 919, p. 32, where Metatron and Sandalfon stand, respectively, for the divine and the acquired intellects dwelling in the rational soul. This view is well represented both in ecstatic Kabbalah and in some late-thirteenth-century philosophers. The assumption that the perfect inner spiritual experience may have a messianic overtone may be corroborated by a detailed analysis of the context of the important passage of R. Yitzḥaq of Acre discussed above, in chapter 3.

56. *Sefer 'Otzar Ḥayyim,* Ms. Moscow-Guensburg 775, fol. 93ab.

57. See Idel, *Studies in Ecstatic Kabbalah,* pp. 76–79. Sometimes Sandalfon even is identified with Sammael. See Abulafia's *Sefer ha-Melammed,* Ms. Paris, Bibliothèque Nationale 680, fol. 307a.

58. Cf. Idel, *Studies in Ecstatic Kabbalah,* pp. 78, 86n28. See also *Sefer Sha'arei Tzedeq,* written by a student of Abulafia, pp. 17–18. I would like, however, to draw attention to an interesting passage that deals with the hastening of the coming of the Messiah by means of a corporeal device. In a collection of passages from *'Otzar Ḥayyim,* found in Ms. Oxford 1911, fol. 158b, the Kabbalist describes positively the seclusion of someone for the sake of mystical life after fulfilling the commandment to procreate. But despite his approval of this behavior, he mentions another alternative: to continue to procreate in order to augment the supernal image by dint of the dictum in *BT, Yevamot,* fol. 62a, which deals with the advent of Ben David, namely the Messiah, when all the souls will be exhausted from the apparently supernal body. Intensive procreation is described as "hastening the time of the coming of our Messiah." I assume that as intense spiritual life ensures a messianic experience by the encounter with the spiritual Metatron qua transcendent Messiah, intense procreation brings about the descent of the Messiah in the more public arena, probably in a manner more consonant with the apocalyptic traditions.

59. See *Sefer 'Otzar Ḥayyim,* Ms. Moscow-Guensburg 775, fol. 94a. The relation between sheep and the Messiah is also found elsewhere in Abulafia's circle. In the anonymous *Sefer Ner 'Elohim,* Ms. München 11, fol. 148b: "Kavshi'el is *ha-mashiyaḥ, kovesh be-koaḥ.*" All these words in gematria amount to 363. Two different interpretations of the consonantal roots KBS and KBSh

display two different understandings of the messiah. The former root, related to sheep, implies suffering, while the latter implies the conquest of the Messiah, namely the idea of power.

60. Cf. e.g. John 1:29. See Dodd, *Interpretation of the Fourth Gospel,* 230–236; Jon D. Levenson, *The Death and Resurrection of the Beloved Son: The Transformation of Child Sacrifice in Judaism and Christianity* (Yale University Press, New Haven, 1993), pp. 200–219.

61. See Idel, *Studies in Ecstatic Kabbalah,* pp. 112–119.

62. M. Idel, "Prometheus in a Hebrew Garb," *Eshkolot,* n.s., 5–6 (1980–1981), pp. 119–120 (Hebrew). Meanwhile I have identified a new manuscript, Ms. Budapest A 240, p. 215.

63. *Ha-derekh ha-nistar.* This is the lowest of the four ways of Kabbalistic interpretations in this Kabbalist's hermeneutics.

64. When I first published the Hebrew original of this text in *Eshkolot,* I decoded these consonants as MoSheH, namely Moses. But as Dr. Boaz Huss, in an unpublished article entitled "NiSaN, The Wife of the Infinite: The Mystical Hermeneutics of Rabbi Isaac of Acre," has correctly proposed, it is much more plausible to decode the same consonants as an acronym of *Metatron, Sar Ha-panim.*

65. *Derekh ha-'emmet* is one of the lower symbolic ways of interpretation in R. Yitzḥaq's hermeneutics.

66. This is the sixth sefirah, which is the center of the last seven divine powers and is situated on the median line of the entire sefirotic realm. On the median line in early Kabbalah see Alexander Altmann, "The Ladder of Ascension," in *Studies in Mysticism and Religion Presented to Gershom G. Scholem* (Magnes Press, Jerusalem, 1967), pp. 27–29; Idel, "Types of Redemptive Activities," pp. 259, 265.

67. This is an appellation for the last sefirah, Malkhut, which is also situated on the median line.

68. In many cases this term stands not for Spain in general but for Castile. See Idel, "Maimonides and Kabbalah," p. 72.

69. Compare the view of R. Yitzḥaq of Ya'aqov ha-Kohen, a Castilian Kabbalist who describes the disappearance of evil using the very same words. See his "Ma'amar ha-'Atzilut ha-Semalit," printed by Gershom Scholem, *Madda'ei ha-Yahadut* (Jerusalem, 1927), p. 250: *me-'eyin 'atzilutam haytah 'afisatam.*

70. *Sefer 'Otzar Ḥayyim,* Ms. Moscow-Guensburg 775, fol. 85b.

71. See *Sefer ha-Ḥesheq,* Ms. New York, JTS 1801, fol. 17a. Compare also Abulafia's *Sefer 'Or ha-Sekhel,* Ms. Vatican 233, fols. 117b–118a.

72. Josh. 10:12; 2 Sam. 1:17–19.

73. See *Shir ha-Shirim Zuta'* 5:2; translated in Patai, *Messiah Texts,* pp. 136–137.

74. Cf. Idel, *Mystical Experience,* p. 140.

75. Ibid.; Idel, *Studies in Ecstatic Kabbalah,* pp. 50–51.

76. See *Sefer ha-'Edut,* Ms. München 285, fols. 37b, 40b. See also the text adduced in Idel, *Mystical Experience,* pp. 140–141. Abulafia was apparently well aware of the messianic significance of such a phrase, for he describes Jesus as someone who founded "a new religion" and assumed the title of the Anointed One. See his *Sefer Sitrei Torah,* Ms. Munichen, 341, fol. 160b. See also Idel, *Studies in Ecstatic Kabbalah,* pp. 53–54.

77. Ms. Roma-Angelica 38, fol. 37a.

78. *Commentary on Sefer ha-'Edut,* Ms. München 285, fol. 37b.

79. See *Commentary on Sefer ha-Yashar,* Ms. Roma-Angelica 38, fol. 41a.

80. *Sefer Mafteaḥ ha-Shemot,* Ms. New York, JTS 843, fol. 68b. For a possible source of this view see R. Abraham bar Ḥiyya's *Sefer Megillat ha-Megalleh* (Berlin, 1924), p. 43: "and the supreme

order of them all [of all the types of prophecy] is that He will tell him the meaning of the name, as He told it to Moses."

81. See Idel, *Kabbalah: New Perspectives,* passim.

82. See also Moshe Idel, "Defining Kabbalah: The Kabbalah of the Divine Names," in *Mystics of the Book: Themes, Topics, and Typology,* ed. R. A. Herrera (Peter Lang, New York, 1993), pp. 97–122.

Appendix 2: *Tiqqun Ḥatzot:* A Ritual between Myth, Messianism, and Mysticism

1. Scholem, *On the Kabbalah,* p. 146; see also ibid., p. 152.

2. Ibid., p. 146.

3. Ibid., p. 149.

4. In the German original the word is *merkwürdig;* cf. *Zur Kabbala und Ihrer Symbolik* (Rhein-Verlag, Zurich, 1960), p. 196. In the Hebrew version of the article, the translator has chosen a more dramatic rendering, *mufla',* "wonderful."

5. Scholem, *On the Kabbalah,* p. 149.

6. Ibid.

7. See Gries, *Conduct Literature.*

8. In fact, Kabbalists, mostly Lurianic ones such as R. Moses Alsheikh, R. Ḥayyim ha-Kohen in Aleppo, and R. Ya'aqov Ḥayyim Tzemaḥ in Jerusalem, had composed poems connected to the ritual, and some of them have become an integral part of it. In this context it is important to mention the occurrence of an anonymous poem described as having been brought from Jerusalem: cf. *Siddur ha-'Ari,* fol. 37a.

9. Scholem, *On the Kabbalah,* pp. 146–148. In fact, Scholem contradicts himself, since on the same page (146) he claims that from the experience of the exile of the nation "there sprang a great wealth of rites." See also ibid., p. 149.

10. Peter Kuhn, *Gottes Trauer und Klage in der Rabbinischen Überlieferung (Talmud und Midrasch)* (Brill, Leiden, 1978), pp. 426–427; Israel Ta-Shma, "Halakhic Allusions in ibn Zabara's Sefer ha-Sha'ashu'im," *Sinai* 67 (1970), p. 282 (Hebrew); Moshe Hallamish, in an appendix to Daniel Sperber, *Minhagei Israel* (Mossad ha-Rav Kook, Jerusalem, 1994), 2:219–220 (Hebrew); Liebes, *Studies in the Zohar,* p. 196n19; *Toledoth Ha-Ari,* ed. Benayahu, pp. 227–228.

11. Magid, "Conjugal Union."

12. See especially Magid, "Conjugal Union," pp. xix–xxv. More material that predates the sixteenth-century vigils is extant, but I would like not to enter the historical question in this context. See, for non-Kabbalistic sources, Moshe Zucker, "Reactions to the Movement of 'Avelei Tzion in the Rabbinic Literature," in *Jubilee Volume for Prof. Hanoch Albeck* (Jerusalem, 1963), pp. 378–401 (Hebrew); Bernard Bamberger, "A Messianic Document of the Seventh Century," *HUCA* 15 (1940), pp. 425–431. The religious importance of this group for a Safedian Kabbalist is quite evident in a text by Cordovero: see Sack, *The Kabbalah of Rabbi Moshe Cordovero,* p. 232, who follows the lead of the *Zohar.*

13. See *'Oraḥ Ḥayyim,* 1:2. Compare, however, Maggid, "Conjugal Union," p. xix, n. 7, who considers Karo's statement to have been written under the impact of the Lurianic ritual. If Karo's statement preceded Luria, which seems likely since his book was already in print (Venice, 1565) for four or five years before Luria arrived in Safed. Maggid's claim that "it is only with Luria that this nocturnal ritual become a formalized prayer service" (ibid., pp. xix, xxiv) is called into question.

14. See Ira Robinson, "Messianic Prayer Vigils in Jerusalem in the Early Sixteenth Century," *JQR* 52 (1981), pp. 38–42; Idel, "On Mishmarot and Messianism." As I have argued, I prefer not to deduce the mourning customs in Safed from their Jerusalemite antecedents. On the other side,

however, the Jerusalemite practices have earier sources, predating the expulsion, and they betray a special eschatological atmosphere characteristic of Jerusalem.

15. See Cordovero, *Hanhagot,* no. 26, printed by Solomon Schechter, *Studies in Judaism* (Jewish Publication Society, Philadelphia, 1908), p. 293.

16. See Idel, "On Mishmarot and Messianism," p. 89n30.

17. The complexity of the ritual of the midnight vigil, which occurs in different versions in the vast Lurianic literature, prevents an in-depth analysis here. The basic discussion of the ritual, giving its theosophical-theurgical premises and some details of its practice, is found in two lengthy treatments in Vital's *Peri 'Etz Ḥayyim,* pp. 18–22, 344–352. More elaborate descriptions of the ritual, including numerous details of the mystical intentions, and various poems, are found in the Kabbalistic *siddurim.*

18. Ibid., pp. 349–351; *Siddur ha-'Ari,* fols. 37b, 39b. See Maggid, "Conjugal Union," p. xl, n. 77.

19. On the more precise Lurianic treatment of the feminine elements in the divine sphere, in comparison with earlier Kabbalah, see Liebes, "Myth vs. Symbol," pp. 225, 229–233; Lawrence Fine, "The Contemplative Practice of Yihudim in Lurianic Kabbalah," in Green, ed., *Jewish Spirituality,* 2:65–70; Wolfson, *Circle in the Square,* pp. 110–119.

20. Ronit Meroz, "Selections from Ephraim Penzieri: Luria's Sermon in Jerusalem and the Kavanah in Taking Food," in Elior and Liebes, eds., *Lurianic Kabbalah,* pp. 211–214.

21. See Meir Benayahu, "Rabbi Ḥayyim Vital in Jerusalem," *Sinai* 31 (1942), pp. 65–75 (Hebrew).

22. See *Peri 'Etz Ḥayyim,* p. 542–544.

23. Scholem, *On the Kabbalah,* p. 149: "The memory of a half-forgotten observance combined with the Zoharic conceptions of midnight and of the exiled Shekhinah to create a new rite symbolizing the experience of the Jews of that generation."

24. *Peri 'Etz Ḥayyim,* p. 348.

25. See Maggid, "Conjugal Union," p. xxviii.

26. *Peri 'Etz Ḥayyim, p. 21.*

27. Ibid., pp. 21, 349–350.

28. Ibid., p. 21. Scholem's description of Leah's "perpetually repeated reunion with her Lord," *On the Kabbalah,* p. 149, is inaccurate.

29. Ibid., pp. 345, 348.

30. Ibid., pp. 18, 345; Maggid, "Conjugal Union," pp. xxii–xxiii.

31. See *Peri 'Etz Ḥayyim,* pp. 346–347.

32. Ibid., p. 347.

33. See "Conjugal Union," pp. xxxii–xliv. To what extant his suggestion (p. xliv) as to the reparation of the female configurations through study of the Torah, which replaces the male effluence, contributes to an understanding of the ritual remains a matter for future research.

34. See *Peri 'Etz Ḥayyim,* p. 21, and also in Tzemaḥ, *Naggid u-Metzavveh,* p. 13, where the study of the Torah, not the lamenting, is described as theurgically efficacious.

35. *Peri 'Etz Ḥayyim,* p. 21.

36. Ibid.

37. *Siddur ha-'Ari,* fol. 35a. See also ibid., fol. 37a, the phrase *horban ha-shekhinah.*

38. Compare Wolfson, *Circle in the Square,* pp. 98–121.

39. See Frankfort, *Kingship and Gods,* pp. 315–330; Mowinckel, *He That Cometh,* pp. 457–459.

40. Johnson, *Sacral Kingship,* pp. 25–26, 111–112, 115, 126, 135; Ringgren, *Messiah,* pp. 51–52.

41. See Frankfort, *Kingship and Gods,* pp. 330–331; Patai, "Hebrew Installation Rites," pp. 165–166; E. Douglas Van Buren, "The Sacred Marriage," *Orientalia* 13 (1944), pp. 1–73, esp. pp. 35–63;

De Fraine, *L'aspect religieux,* pp. 249–263; Kingsley, *Goddesses' Mirror,* pp. 121–124. See more recently the description of the *hieros gamos* in a document written in Aramaic, which is described as reminiscent of the akitu rite, in Richard Steiner, "The Aramaic Text in Demotic Script: The Liturgy of a New Year's Festival Imported from Bethel to Syene by Exiles from Rash," *Journal of the American Oriental Society* 125 (1995), pp. 362–363. For more on this interesting document see C. F. Nims and Richard Steiner, "A Paganized Version of Psalm 20:2–6 from the Aramaic Text in Demotic Script," *Journal of the American Oriental Society* 103 (1983), pp. 261–274. the existence of a hierogamic ritual performed in the Rosh ha-Shanah of Tishrei, according to these scholars in Bethel (Samaria), may indicate that Babylonian rites found their way to the immediate vicinity of the ancient Jerusalem.

42. Liebes, "Two Young Roes of a Doe," p. 126. This attitude may be found in a quite messianic text of Cordovero, where Raḥel, the moon, and cyclical time are treated together. See the important text printed by Sack, *Kabbalah of Rabbi Moshe Cordovero,* pp. 232–233.

43. Cf. Jerusalem, 1912, fol. 17ab.

44. Vital, *Peri 'Etz Ḥayyim,* p. 348; See also R. Ya'aqov Tzemaḥ, *Siddur Kavvanot ha-Tefillot bi-Qetzarah* (Jerusalem, 1986), p. 78; idem, *Naggid u-Metzavveh,* p. 23. Compare to Maggid, "Conjugal Union," pp. xxxix–xl.

45. *Siddur Kavvanot,* p. 79.

46. See Kuhn, *Gottes Trauer,* pp. 254–257. On the myth of mistarim see *BT, Berakhot,* fol. 3a, which has been exploited but interpreted in a quite different manner than the original myth.

47. For the view that Christianity includes misunderstandings of Kabbalistic principles see Gershom Scholem, "Considerations sur l'histoire des debuts de la Kabbale chrétienne," in A. Faivre and F. Tristan, eds., *Kabbalistes Chrétiens* (Albin Michel, Paris, 1979), p. 30.

48. See e.g. Tzemaḥ's own description of Luria as the revealer of the secrets in a poem printed by Meir Benayahu, "Ha-'Ari in the Poetry of the Kabbalists and the Tiqqun of the Fifth of Av," in Israel Weinstock, ed., *Temirin* (Mossad ha-Rav Kook, Jerusalem, 1981), 2:188.

49. See Idel, *Kabbalah: New Perspectives,* pp. 75–79; Elliot R. Wolfson's important study "Weeping, Death, and Spiritual Ascent in Sixteenth-Century Jewish Mysticism," in Collins and Fishbane, eds., *Ecstasy, Death,* pp. 209–247.

50. See e.g. Tzemaḥ, *Siddur Kavvanot,* p. 82.

51. See *Siddur ha-'Ari,* fol. 32a.

52. See Idel, *Kabbalah: New Perspectives,* pp. 75–79; Daniel Merkur, "The Visionary Practices of Jewish Apocalypticism," *Psychoanalytic Study of Society* 14 (1989), pp. 119–148. More recently, Himmelfarb, *Ascent to Heaven,* p. 107, has adduced even more material from apocalyptic literature on weeping, concluding that "the association of weeping or at least mourning with visionary experience and ascent is even more widespread in the apocalypses" than I thought. Nevertheless, she concluded that it is an "unwarranted leap" to conclude that in the ancient texts weeping is indeed a technique, as in the medieval texts, and she surmises that it may be a later development that accounts for the technical use of weeping. There is, however, no need to reread the concepts found in medieval material into the ancient one, neither have I proposed to do so. The midrashic material that I have adduced in that context (op. cit., pp. 77–79), not taken into account by Himmelfarb, may reasonably point to traditions contemporary for the apocalyptic authors. But I assume that we may even go earlier than the midrashic literature. Additional material, related to ancient Jews, which escaped my attention when dealing with the above topic and was not adduced in the texts collected by Himmelfarb, is found in Origen. See A. Marmorstein, "Deux réseignements d'Origene concernant les juifs," *REJ* 61, (1920), p. 196n2.

53. Idel, *Kabbalah: New Perspectives,* pp. 80–88. Ms. Oxford 1706, fol. 494b: Compare to

Hanhagot ha-'Ari; cf. Benayahu, ed., *Sefer Toldoth ha-'Ari,* p. 319; R. Jacob Ḥayyim Tzemaḥ, *Naggid u-Metzavveh,* fol. 22a, (quoted in the name of Vital's *Collectanaea*).

54. *Sefer Sha'arei Tziyon* (Amsterdam, 1735), col. 3, fol. 3b–4a.

55. *Peri 'Etz Ḥayyim,* p. 351.

56. The Hebrew verb is *tityaḥed,* which presupposes a reflexive mode.

57. See R. Nathan Neta' Hanover, *Sha'arei Tzion* (Prague, 1662), col. 4, fol. 2b.

58. For the human body as a temple see Idel, *Kabbalah: New Perspectives,* pp. 306–307nn69,71; idem, *Hasidism: Between Ecstasy and Magic,* p. 194. See also the Kabbalistic texts adduced by Dinur, *Israel ba-Golah,* 2 (4):410–411, 434–435n114.

59. Cf. *Genesis Rabba,* 82:7, etc. On the mystical interpretations of this dictum see the learned study of Micheline Chaze, "De l'identification des patriarches au char divin: recherche du sens d'un enseignement rabbinique dans le midrash et dans la Kabbale prezoharique et ses sources," *REJ* 149 (1990), pp. 5–75.

60. Idel, *Kabbalah: New Perspectives,* pp. 130, 132–133.

61. In fact, the assumption that the Kabbalist should become a chariot for the Shekhinah is implied in R. Joseph ibn Tabbul's *Commentary on 'Iddra' Rabba',* in Israel Weinstock, ed., *Temirin* (Mossad ha-Rav Kook, Jerusalem, 1981), 2:129–130.

62. R. Ḥayyim Vital, *Peri 'Etz Ḥayyim,* p. 348; R. Ya'aqov Ḥayyim Tzemaḥ, *Naggid u-Metzavveh,* p. 13. See also *Siddur ha-'Ari,* fol. 38a. On the integration of the souls of the righteous within the Shekhinah see *Zohar,* vol. 1, fol. 60b; R. Moses Cordovero, *Tefillah le-Moshe,* fol. 248a. See also the proposal of Wolfson, *Circle in the Square,* pp. 111–112, who claims that in this context the male becomes female.

63. The need for multiple interpretations of rituals is recurrent in modern anthropology. See e.g. Victor Turner, "Symbols in Ndembu Ritual," in Max Gluckman, ed., *Closed Systems and Open Minds* (Aldine, Chicago, 1964), pp. 20–51; Geertz, *Interpretation of Cultures,* pp. 402–453; for multiple interpretations of Jewish rituals see the forthcoming article by Harvey Goldberg, "Shevirat ha-Kos be-Ḥatunah bi-Reiy'ah Anthropologit-Rabbanit," in O. Abuhav, E. Herzog, H. Goldberg, and I. Marks, eds., *Yisrael: Anthropologiah Meqomit* (Cherikover, Tel Aviv, 1998) (Hebrew). Thanks are due to Prof. H. Goldberg for references dealing with multiple interpretations in anthropology.

64. See Zevi Hirsch Eichenstein, *Turn Aside from Evil and Do Good: An Introduction and a Way to the Tree of Life,* trans. Louis Jacobs (Littman Library of Jewish Civilization, London, Washington, 1995), pp. 28–31; R. Eliezer Tzevi Safrin of Komarno, Introduction to his commentary on the *Zohar, Dameseq 'Eliezer* (Jerusalem, 1972), vol. 2, fol. 5bc.

65. See esp. Wolfson, *Through a Speculum,* pp. 274–275n14.

66. Elliott Horowitz, "Coffee, Coffeehouses, and the Nocturnal Rituals of Early Modern Jewry," *AJS Review* 14, no. 1 (1989), pp. 17–46. Compare, however, Scholem, *Sabbatai Ṣevi,* p. 67.

67. *Kabbalah: New Perspectives,* p. 258. This seems also to be the gist of Maggid's approach, "Conjugal Union," esp. p. xvii, n. 1, though he fails to refer to the above statement but instead quotes some discussions of mine which are irrelevant to this point.

Appendix 3: Some Modern Reverberations of Jewish Messianism

1. See some texts on Hertzl collected by Patai, *Messiah Texts,* pp. 266, 272–273. On messianism and activism see Ravitzky, *Messianism, Zionism,* pp. 122–131.

2. On collective messianism among early-twentieth-century intellectuals in Germany, some of them of Jewish extraction, see Paul Honigsheim, "Soziologie der Mystik," *Versuche zu einer*

Soziologie des Wissens, ed. Max Scheler, (Leipzig, 1924), p. 343; Michael Löwy, "Jewish Messianism and Libertarian Utopia in Central Europe (1900–1933)," *New German Critique* 20 (1980), p. 105; Löwy, *Redemption et Utopie.*

3. For another significance of a process of modern fragmentation see Jay M. Harris, *How Do We Know This? Midrash and the Fragmentation of Modern Judaism* (SUNY Press, Albany, 1995). The topic of fragmentation recurs time and again in recent studies. In addition to Handelman, *Fragments of Redemption,* see Caroline Walker Bynum, *Fragmentation and Redemption* (Zone Books, New York, 1992).

4. Buber, "Renewal of Judaism," in *On Judaism,* p. 50. The importance of the "messianic idea" has been duly recognized not only by scholars of mysticism and messianism but also by some Jewish historians. Ben Zion Dinur, for example, envisioned two major factors in the constitution of Judaism: a sociopolitical one, described as statical, represented by the structure of family and the ritual, and a psychological factor, described as dynamic, consisting in the messianic belief and the striving for redemption. See Dinur, *Israel ba-Golah,* 1 (1):30–31. See also Ben Sasson, *Retzef u-Temurah,* p. 487.

5. Translated by Paul Mendes-Flohr, *From Mysticism to Dialogue: Martin Buber's Transformation of German Social Thought* (Wayne State University Press, Detroit, 1989), p. 107.

6. Buber, "Renewal of Judaism," in *On Judaism,* p. 51.

7. See also Buber's "Jewish Religiosity" in *On Judaism,* p. 86, where he emphasizes the absolute value of man's deed.

8. Buber, "The Spirit of Orient and Judaism," in *On Judaism,* pp. 57–60.

9. There were various interpretations of Buber's novel, some of them emphasizing its affinities to Christianity, though Buber flatly denied such a connection.

10. Buber, "Renewal of Judaism," in *On Judaism,* p. 51.

11. See above, chap. 7, p. 222.

12. Buber, "The Holy Way," in *On Judaism,* pp. 110–111. See also Mendes-Flohr, *From Mysticism to Dialogue,* p. 115.

13. See *The Prophetic Faith* (Harper and Row, New York, 1960), p. 140. See also his *Kingship of God,* trans. R. Sheiman (London, 1967), pp. 14–15.

14. See Emmanuel Levinas, *Difficile Liberté* (Albin Michel, Paris, 1976), p. 98. On Menaḥem as a name of the Messiah see the various texts printed by Even Shmuel in *Midreshei Ge'ullah.*

15. I have adopted this term from Giorgio Agamben's description of Benjamin's and Heidegger's positions on history and time in *Infancy and History: Essays on the Destruction of Experience,* trans. L. Heron (Verso, London, New York, 1993), pp. 104–105.

16. See above, chaps. 5, 7.

17. See Franz Kafka, *Parables and Paradoxes* (Schocken Books, New York, 1966), pp. 80–81. On Kafka's view of messianism see Löwy, *Redemption et utopie,* pp. 92–120.

18. See Giuliano Baioni, *Kafka: Letteratura ed Ebraismo* (Einaudi, 1984), p. 293, Idel, *Kabbalah: New Perspectives,* p. 271.

19. Walter Benjamin, *Illuminations,* ed. Hannah Arendt, trans. H. Zohn (New York, Schocken Books, 1969), p. 264; Scholem, *Devarim Be-Go,* p. 580; Agamben, *Infancy and History,* pp. 102–103, in general on Benjamin's messianic thought, see Irving Wolfhart, "On the Messianic Structure of Walter Benjamin's Last Reflections," *Glyph* 3 (1978), pp. 148–212.

20. See the similar view of time and messianism in Franz Rosenzweig as discussed in Robert Gibbs, *Correlations in Rosenzweig and Levinas* (Princeton University Press, Princeton, 1993), pp. 108–110; Mendes-Flohr, " 'The Stronger and the Better Jews,' " pp. 165–169; Schwarzschild, *Pursuit of the Ideal,* pp. 211–212.

21. See Benjamin Ish-Shalom, *Ha-Rav Kook: Between Rationalism and Mysticism* ('Am 'Oved, Tel Aviv, 1990), pp. 254, 262.

22. *Qol ha-Nevu'ah* (Mossad ha-Rav Kook, Jerusalem, 1970), p. 11 (Hebrew).

23. See Dov Schwartz, "The Personality and Characteristics of a Contemporary Jewish Mystic," *Tarbiẓ* 61 (1991), pp. 145–146 (Hebrew).

24. Aviezer Ravittky, "Providence in the Divided: Messianism, Zionism and the Future of Israel Religious Outlooks within Israel," in A. Har-Even, ed., *Israel Towards the 21st Century* (Mossad Van Leer, Jerusalem, 1984), pp. 107–146 (Hebrew); idem, *Messianism, Zionism,* pp. 56–59.

25. See *The Writings of Martin Buber,* ed. Will Herzberg (Meridian Books, New York, 1956), p. 311.

26. See Mendes-Flohr, " 'The Stronger and the Better Jews,' " p. 168.

27. See Jankelevitch, "L'esperance et la fin des temps," p. 21.

28. For the status of messianism in modern Israel, see, in addition to the studies mentioned in the following notes, also the important essays of Jacob Katz, Uriel Tal, and Menachem Kellner in Saperstein, ed., *Essential Papers,* pp. 475–518, as well as Ravitzky's comprehensive monograph, *Messianism, Zionism.*

29. Israel Colat, "Zionism and Messianism," in Baras, ed., *Messianism and Eschatology,* pp. 419–431. See the view of Greenstone, *Messiah Idea,* pp. 266–279, as well as that of Lionel Kochan, *Jews, Idols, and Messiahs: The Chalenge from History* (Basil Blackwell, Oxford, 1990), pp. 180–191.

30. Shmuel Almog, "Messianism as a Challenge for Zionism," in Baras, ed., *Messianism and Eschatology,* pp. 433–438."

31. Anita Shapira, *To Walk on the Horizon* ('Am 'Oved, Tel Aviv, 1988), pp. 11–22 (Hebrew); Werblowsky, "Messianism in Jewish History," in Saperstein, ed. *Essential Papers,* pp. 51–52; Ravitzky, *Messianism, Zionism,* pp. 53–54.

32. *Midstream* 9, (1963), pp. 76–81, at 81. See also the Zionist understanding of the Sabbatean immigration of R. Yehudah he-Ḥasid and his group in Ben-Zion Dinur, *Be-Mifneh ha-Dorot* (Mossad Bialik, Jerusalem, 1971), p. 27 (Hebrew); cf. Myers, *Re-Inventing,* pp. 146–147.

33. André Chastel, *The Sack of Rome,* trans. B. Archer (Princeton University Press, Princeton, 1983), pp. 16–17.

References

Abbreviations

AJSR	*Association of Jewish Studies Review*
BT	*Babylonian Talmud*
HTR	*Harvard Theological Review*
HUCA	*Hebrew Union College Annual*
JBL	*Journal for Biblical Literature*
JJS	*Journal of Jewish Studies*
JQR	*Jewish Quarterly Review*
JTS	*Journal for Theological Studies*
JSJT	*Jerusalem Studies in Jewish Thought*
PAAJR	*Proceedings of the American Academy of Jewish Research*
QS	*Qiriat Sefer*
REJ	*Revue des Etudes Juives*

Primary Sources in Hebrew

'Ahavat Shalom, by R. Menaḥem Mendel of Kosov (Jerusalem, 1984).

Commentary on Sefer ha-Yashar, by Abraham Abulafia, Ms. Roma-Angelica 38.

Commentary on Sefer ha-Melitz, by Abraham Abulafia, Ms. Rome-Angelica 38.

Commentary on Sefer Yetzirah, by R. Joseph ben Shalom Ashkenazi (Jerusalem, 1961).

'Emeq ha-Melekh, by R. Naftali Bakharakh (Amsterdam, 1648).

Ginzei Ramḥal—Sefer Ginzei Ramḥal, ed. Ḥayyim Friedlander (Benei Beraq, 1980).

Ḥayyei ha-Nefesh, R. Abraham Abulafia's *Commentary on the Guide of the Perplexed,* Ms. München 408.

Ḥayyei ha-'Olam ha-Ba', by R. Abraham Abulafia, Ms. Oxford 1582.

Livenat ha-Sappir, by R. Joseph Angelet, ed. S. Mussaiof (Jerusalem, 1913), mistakenly attributed in print to R. David ben Yehudah he-Ḥasid.

Mafteaḥ ha-Tokheḥot, Abraham Abulafia's Commentary on Deuteronomy, Ms. Oxford 1605.

Ma'or va-Shemesh, by R. Qalonimus Qalman ha-Levi Epstein (Jerusalem, 1992).

Me'irat 'Einayyim, by R. Yitzḥaq of Acre, ed. Amos Goldreich (Hebrew University, Jerusalem, 1984).

Me'or 'Einayyim, by R. Menaḥem Naḥum of Chernobyl (Jerusalem, 1975).

Midreshei Ge'ullah, ed. Yehudah Even Shmuel, *Midreshei Ge'ullah: Pirqei ha-'Apocalypsah ha-Yehudit,* 2nd ed. (Mossad Bialik, Jerusalem, Tel Aviv, 1954).

Naggid u-Metzavveh, by R. Ya'aqov Tzemaḥ, *Sefer Naggid u-Metzavveh* (Jerusalem, 1975).

'Otzar 'Eden Ganuz, by Abraham Abulafia, Ms. Oxford 1580.

'Otzar Ḥayyim, by R. Yitzḥaq of Acre, Ms. Moscow-Guensburg 775.

Pardes Rimmonim, by R. Moses Cordovero, 2 parts (ed. Muncasz, repr. Jerusalem, 1962).

Peri 'Etz Ḥayyim, by R. Ḥayyim Vital, ed. Abraham Brandvein (Jerusalem, 1980).

Perush Rabeinu 'Efrayyim 'Al ha-Torah, ed. Yoel Klugmann (Jerusalem, 1992).

Sefer ha-Ḥezyonot, ed. Aaron Z. Aescoly (Mossad ha-Rav Kook, Jerusalem, 1954).

Sefer Ma'arekhet ha-'Elohut (Mantua, 1558).

Sefer ha-Mefo'ar—R. Shelomo Molkho, *Sefer ha-Mefo'ar* (Jerusalem, 1962).

Sefer ha-'Ot, ed. A. Jellinek, "'Sefer Ha-Ot': Apokalypse des Pseudo-Propheten und Pseudo-Messias Abraham Abulafia," in *Jubelschrift zum siebzigsten Geburtstage des Prof. Dr. H. Graetz* (Breslau 1887) pp. 65–85.

Sefer ha-Peliy'ah, attributed to R. Neḥunyah ben ha-Qanah, in 2 parts (Premislany, 1883). A late fourteenth-century Kabbalistic classic.

Sefer ha-Zohar, ed. R. Margolioth, 5 vols. (Jerusalem, 1978).

Sha'arei Tzedeq, from Abulafia's school, ed. J. E. Porush (Makhon Sha'arei Ziv, Jerusalem, 1989).

Siddur ha-'Ari (Zolkwo, 1781).

Sitrei Torah, by R. Abraham Abulafia, Ms. Paris, Biblioteque Nationale 774.

Sheqel ha-Qodesh, by R. Moses de Leon, ed. A. W. Greenup (London, 1911).

Sullam ha-'Aliyah, by R. Yehudah Albotini, ed. J. E. Porush (Jerusalem, Makhon Sha'arei Ziv, 1989).

Synopse zur Hekhalot-Literatur, ed. Peter Schaefer (J. C. B. Mohr, Tübingen, 1981).

Tefillah le-Moshe, by R. Moses Cordovero (Premizsla, 1892).

The Toledoth Ha-Ari, ed. Meir Benayahu (Makhon ben Tzvi, Jerusalem, 1967).

Tzafnat Pa'aneaḥ, by R. Joseph Al-Ashqar, Ms. Jerusalem 40 154, facsimile ed. (Jerusalem, 1989).

Tzitzat Novel Tzevi, by Ya'aqov Sasportas, eds. Z. Schwartz and I. Tishby (Mossad Bialik, Jerusalem, 1954).

Ve-Zot li-Yhudah, Abraham Abulafia's epistle, printed by A. Jellinek in his *Auswahl kabbalistscher Mystik,* erstes Heft (Leipzig, 1853), pp. 13–28.

Secondary Sources

Abrams, Daniel, *"The Book of Illumination" of R. Jacob ben Jacob Ha-Kohen* (Ph.D. diss., New York University, New York, 1993).

——, "The Boundaries of Divine Ontology: The Inclusion and Exclusion of Metatron in the Godhead," *HTR* 87 (1994), pp. 316–321.

Aescoly, Aaron Zeev, *Jewish Messianic Movements,* 2nd ed. (Mossad Bialik, Jerusalem, 1987) (Hebrew).

Agus, Aharon, *The Binding of Isaac and Messiah: Law, Martyrdom, and Deliverance in Early Rabbinic Religiosity* (State University of New York Press, Albany, 1988).

Altshuler, Mor, *Rabbi Meshulam Feibush Heller and His Place in Early Hasidism* (Ph.D. diss., Hebrew University, Jerusalem, 1994) (Hebrew).

Beinart, Haim, ed., *The Sephardi Legacy,* 2 vols. (Magnes Press, Jerusalem, 1992).

Baras, Zvi, ed., *Messianism and Eschatology: A Collection of Essays* (Zalman Shazar Center, Jerusalem, 1983) (Hebrew).

Barnes, Robin Bruce, *Prophecy and Gnosis: Apocalypticism in the Wake of the Lutheran Reformation* (Stanford University Press, Stanford, Calif., 1988).

Barr, James, "Theophany and Anthropomorphism in the Old Testament," *Supplement to Vetus Testamentum* 7 (Oxford, 1959), pp. 31–38.

Ben Sasson, Ḥayyim H., *Retzef u-Temurah,* ed. J. Hacker ('Am 'Oved, Tel Aviv, 1984) (Hebrew).

Ben Sasson, Ḥayyim H., ed., *A History of the Jewish People* (Harvard University Press, Cambridge, Mass., 1976).

Bentzen, Aage, *King and Messiah* (Lutterworth Press, London, 1955).

Berger, Abraham, "The Messianic Self-Consciouness of Abraham Abulafia: A Tentative Evaluation," in *Essays on Jewish Life and Thought Presented in Honor of Salo Wittmayer Baron* (New York, 1959), pp. 55–61.

Berger, Abraham, "Captive at the Gate of Rome: The Story of a Messianic Motif," *PAAJR* 44 (1977), pp. 1–17.

Berger, David, "Three Typological Themes in Early Jewish Messianism: Messiah Son of Joseph, Rabbinic Calculations, and the Figure of Armilus," *AJSR* 10 (1980), pp. 141–164.

Bloch, Joshua, *On the Apocalyptic in Judaism* (Dropsie College, Philadelphia, 1952).

Bloch, Marc, *Les rois thaumaturges* (Gallimard, Paris, 1983).

Bouwsma, William J., *Concordia Mundi: The Career and Thought of Guillaume Postel, 1510–1581* (Harvard University Press, Cambridge, Mass., 1957).

Buber, Martin, *On Judaism,* ed. Nahum N. Glazer (Schocken Books, New York, 1972).

——, *The Kingship of God,* 3rd ed., trans. Richard Scheiman (Harper Torchbooks, New York, 1973).

Carlebach, Elisheva, *The Pursuit of Heresy: Rabbi Moses Hagis and the Sabbatian Controversy* (Columbia University Press, New York, 1990).

Charlesworth, James H., ed., *The Messiah, Developments in Earliest Judaism and Christianity* (Fortress Press, Minneapolis, 1992).

Cohen, Gershon D., "Messianic Postures of Ashkenazim and Sepharadim," in Saperstein, ed., *Essential Papers,* pp. 202–233.

Cohn, Norman, *Cosmos, Chaos, and the World to Come* (New Haven, Yale University Press, 1933).

Collins, John J., *The Apocalyptic Imagination* (Crossroad, New York, 1984).

——, "The Place of Apocalypticism in the Religion of Israel," in P. D. Miller, Jr., P. D. Hanson, and S. D. McBride, *Ancient Israelite Religion: Essays in Honor of Frank Moore Cross* (Fortress Press, Philadelphia, 1987), pp. 539–558.

——, "A Throne in the Heavens, Apotheosis in Pre-Christian Judaism," in Collins and Fishbane, eds., *Death, Ecstasy,* pp. 43–58.

Collins, John J., and Michael Fishbane, *Death, Ecstasy, and Other Wordly Journeys* (State University of New York Press, Albany, 1995), pp. 43–58.

Collins, John J., and Charlesworth, James H., eds., *Mysteries and Revelations: Apocalyptic Studies since the Uppsala Colloquium, Journal for the Study of the Pseudepygrapha,* Supplement Series, 9 (Shefield Academic Press, Shefield, 1991).

Cook, Stephen L., *Prophecy and Apocalypticism: The Post-Exilic Social Setting* (Fortress Press, Minneapolis, 1995).

Corbin, Henry, *Creative Imagination in the Sufism of Ibn 'Arabi,* trans. Ralph Manheim, Bollingen Series 91 (Princeton University Press, Princeton, N.J., 1969).

——, *Cyclical Time and Ismaili Gnosis* (Kegan Paul, London, 1983).

Couliano, Ioan P., *Experiences de l'extase: Extase, Ascension et recit visionaire de l'Hellenisme au Moyen Age* (Payot, Paris, 1984).

——, *The Tree of Gnosis,* trans. Hillary Wiener and Ioan P. Couliano (Harper, San Francisco, 1992).

Dan, Joseph, "The Emergence of Messianic Mythology in 13th Century Kabbalah in Spain," in *Occident and Orient: A Tribute to the Memory of A. Schreiber* (Budapest/Brill, Leiden, 1988). pp. 57–68.

——, "Gershom Scholem and Jewish Messianism," in Paul Mendes-Flohr, ed., *Gershom Scholem, The Man and His Work* (State University of New York Press, Albany, 1994).

——, *The Esoteric Theology of Ashkenazi Hasidism* (Mossad Bialik, Jerusalem, 1968) (Hebrew).

Danielou, Jean, *Theologies du Judeo-Christianisme* (Desclee/Cerf, Paris, 1991).

Davidson, Herbert, *Alfarabi, Avicenna, and Averroes, on Intellect, Their Cosmologies, Theories of the Active Intellect, and Theories of Human Intellect* (Oxford University Press, New York, Oxford, 1992).

De Fraine, J., *L'aspect religieux de la royauté israelite: L'institution monarchique dans l'ancient testament et dans les textes mesopotamiens* (Potificio Istituto Biblico, Rome, 1954).

Deutsch, Nathaniel, *The Gnostic Imagination: Gnosticism, Mandaeism, and Merkabah Mysticism* (Brill, Leiden, 1995).

Dinur, Ben Zion, *Israel ba-Golah,* 2nd ed. (Devir, Tel Aviv, Mossad Bialik, Jerusalem, 1960).

Durand, Gilbert, *Figures mythiques et visages de l'oeuvre, de la mythocritique à la mythanalyse* (Dunod, Paris, 1992).

Dodd, C. H., *The Interpretation of the Fourth Gospel* (Cambridge University Press, Cambridge, 1972).

Eliade, Mircea, *Cosmos and History: The Myth of the Eternal Return* (Harper Torchbooks, New York, 1959).

Elior, R., and Y. Liebes, eds., *Lurianic Kabbalah: Proceedings of the Fourth International Conference on the History of Jewish Mysticism = Jerusalem Studies in Jewish Thought,* vol. 10 (Jerusalem, 1992) (Hebrew).

Elior, Rachel, "Messianic Expectations and Spiritualization of Religious Life in the Sixteenth Century," *REJ* 155 (1986), pp. 35–49.

Elqayam, Abraham, *The Mystery of Faith in the Writings of Nathan of Gaza* (Ph. D. diss., Hebrew University, Jerusalem, 1993) (Hebrew).

Emmerson, Richard K., and Ronald B. Hertzman, *The Apocalyptic Imagination in Medieval Literature* (University of Pennsylvania Press, Philadelphia, 1992).

Engnell, Ivan, *Studies in Divine Kingship in the Ancient Near East* (Almquist & Wiksells, Uppsala, 1943).

Fine, Lawrence, ed., *Essential Papers on Kabbalah* (New York University Press, New York, 1995).

Finkelstein, Norman, *The Ritual of New Creation: Jewish Tradition and Contemporary Literature* (State University of New York Press, Albany, 1992).

Firth, Katharine R., *The Apocalyptic Tradition in Reformation Britain 1530–1645* (Oxford University Press, Oxford, 1979).

Flusser, David, *Judaism and the Origins of Christianity* (Magnes Press, Jerusalem, 1988).

Fossum, Jarl E., *The Name of God and the Angel of the Lord* (J. C. B. Mohr, Tübingen, 1985).

Frankfort, Henri, *Kingship and the Gods: A Study of Ancient Near Eastern Religion as the Integration of Society and Nature* (University of Chicago Press, Chicago, 1965).

Frost, S. B., "Eschatology and Myth," *Vetus Testamentum* 2 (1952), pp. 70–80.

Ginzberg, Louis, *Legends of the Jews,* 7 vols. (Jewish Publication Society, Philadelphia, 1947).

Goetschel, Roland, *Meir ibn Gabbay: Le Discours de la Kabbale Espagnole* (Peeters, Leuven, 1981).

Goodman, Lenn E., *On Justice: An Essay in Jewish Philosophy* (Yale University Press, New Haven, 1991).

Gottlieb, Efraim, *Studies in the Kabbalah Literature,* ed. J. Hacker (Tel Aviv University, Tel Aviv, 1976) (Hebrew).

Graetz, Zvi, *Divrei Ymei Yisrael* (Hebrew translation of Graetz) (Warsau, 1897), vol. 5.

Graetz, Heinrich, "The Stages in the Evolution of the Messianic Belief," in Ismar Schorsch, trans. and ed., *Heinrich Graetz: The Structure of Jewish History and Other Essays* (Jewish Theological Seminary of America, New York, 1975), pp. 151–171.

Green, Arthur, *Keter* (Princeton University Press, Princeton, N.J., 1997).

Green, Arthur, ed. *Jewish Spirituality,* 2 vols. (Crossroad, New York, 1986–1987).

Green, Arthur, trans. *Upright Practices, The Light of the Eyes,* by Menahem Nahum of Chernobyl (Paulist Press, New York, 1982).

Greenfield, Jonas C., "Notes on Some Aramaic and Mandaic Magic Bowls," *Gaster Festschrift, Journal of the Ancient Near Eastern Society of Columbia* 5 (1973), pp. 149–156.

——, *Prolegomenon to a reprint of 3 Enoch* (Ktav, New York, 1973).

Greenstone, Julius H., *The Messiah Idea in Jewish History* (Jewish Publication Society, Philadelphia, 1906).

Gries, Ze'ev, *Conduct Literature, Regimen Vitae, Its History and Place in the Life of Beshtian Hasidism* (Mossad Bialik, Jerusalem, 1989) (Hebrew).

Gross, Benjamin, *Le messianisme juif: "L'Eternité d'Israel" du Maharal de Prague, 1512–1609* (C. Klincksieck, Paris, 1969).

Gruenwald, Ithamar, "From Sunrise to Sunset: The Image of the Eschatology and Messianism in Judaism," in *The Messianic Idea in Jewish Thought* (Israeli Academy, Jerusalem, 1982), pp. 18–36 (Hebrew).
Halperin, David J., "Hekhalot and Mi'raj: Observations on the Heavenly Journey in Judaism and Islam," in Collins and Fishbane, *Death, Ecstasy,* pp. 269–288.
Halpern, Baruch, *The Constitution of the Monarchy in Israel* (Scholars Press, Ann Arbor, Michigan, 1981).
Handelman, Susan A., *Fragments of Redemption: Jewish Thought and Literary Theory in Benjamin, Scholem, and Levinas* (Indiana University Press, Bloomington, 1991).
Hartman, David, *A Living Covenant: The Innovative Spirit in Traditional Judaism* (Free Press, New York, 1985).
Himmelfarb, Martha, *Ascent to Heaven in Jewish and Christian Apocalypse* (Oxford University Press, New York, Oxford, 1993).
Heschel, Abrahama J., *Prophetic Inspiration after the Prophets: Maimonides and Other Medieval Authorities,* ed. Morris M. Faierstein (Ktav, Hoboken, N.J., 1996).
Hooke, S. H., *The Labyrinth: Further Studies in the Relation between Myth and Ritual in the Ancient World* (Macmillan, New York, 1932).
Hume, Katryn, *Fantasy and Mimesis: Responses to Reality in Western Literature* (Methuen, New York, 1984).
Hurtado, Larry W., *One God One Lord: Early Christian Devotion and Ancient Jewish Monotheism* (Fortress Press, Philadelphia, 1988).
Hurwitz, S., "Some Psychological Aspects of the Messianic Idea in Judaism," in ed. H. Kirsh, *The Well-Tended Tree: Essays into the Spirit of Our Time* (Putnam, New York, 1971), pp. 130–142.
Idel, Moshe, *Abraham Abulafia's Works and Doctrine* (Ph. D. diss., Hebrew University, Jerusalem, 1976) (Hebrew).
——, "The Beginnings of the Kabbalah in North Africa? The Forgotten Document of R. Yehudah ben Nissim ibn Malka," *Pe'amim* 43 (1990), pp. 8–12 (Hebrew).
——, *Chapters in Ecstatic Kabbalah* (Akademon, Jerusalem, 1992) (Hebrew).
——, "The Contribution of Abraham Abulafia's Kabbalah to the Understanding of Jewish Mysticism," in P. Schaefer and J. Dan, eds., *Gersom Scholem's Major Trends in Jewish Mysticism, 50 Years After* (J. C. B. Mohr, Tübingen, 1993), pp. 117–143.
——, "Enoch Is Metatron," *Immanuel* 24/25 (1990), pp. 220–240.
——, *Hasidism: Between Ecstasy and Magic* (State University of New York Press, Albany, 1995).
——, "Inquiries in the Doctrine of Sefer Ha-Meshiv," *Sefunot* 17, ed. J. Hacker (Jerusalem, 1983), pp. 185–266 (Hebrew).
——, Introduction to Aaron Z. Aeshkoly, *Jewish Messianic Movements* (Mossad Bialik, Jerusalem, 1987), pp. 9–29 (Hebrew).
——, *Kabbalah: New Perspectives* (Yale University Press, New Haven, 1988).
——, "The Land of Israel in Medieval Jewish Mystical Thought," in M. Hallamish and A. Ravitsky, eds., *The Land of Israel in Medieval Jewish Thought* (Ben-Zvi Press, Jerusalem, 1991), pp. 193–214 (Hebrew).
——, "The Land of Israel in Medieval Kabbalah," in L. Hoffman, ed., *The Land of Israel:*

Jewish Perspectives (University of Notre Dame Press, Notre Dame, Ind., 1986), pp. 170–187.

——, *Language, Torah, and Hermeneutics in Abraham Abulafia,* trans. M. Kallus (State University of New York Press, Albany, 1989).

——, "The Magical and Neoplatonic Interpretations of Kabbalah in the Renaissance," in Bernard D. Cooperman, ed., *Jewish Thought in the Sixteenth Century* (Harvard University Press, Cambridge, Mass., 1983), pp. 186–242.

——, "Metatron: Observations on the Development of Myth in Judaism," in Ḥaviva Pedaya, ed., *Myth in Judaism* (Beer Sheva', 1996), pp. 29–44 (Hebrew).

——, *The Mystical Experience in Abraham Abulafia,* trans. J. Chipman (State University of New York Press, Albany, 1987).

——, "Neglected Writings by the Author of Sefer Kaf ha-Qetoret," *Pe'amim* 53 (1993), pp. 75–89 (Hebrew).

——, " 'One from a Town, Two from a Clan'—The Diffusion of Lurianic Kabbala and Sabbateanism: A Re-Examination," *Jewish History* 7, no. 2 (1993), pp. 79–104.

——, "On Mishmarot and Messianism in Jerusalem in the 16th–17th Centuries," *Shalem* 5 (1987), pp. 83–94 (Hebrew).

——, "R. Yehudah Ḥallewah and His Composition *Tzafenat Pa'aneaḥ,*" *Shalem* 4 (1984), pp. 119–148 (Hebrew).

——, "Shlomo Molkho as Magician," *Sefunot* 3 (1985), pp. 193–219 (Hebrew).

——, "Some Concepts of Time and History in Kabbalah," in E. Carlebach, J. Efron, and D. Myers, eds., *Between Jewish History and Jewish Memory* (University Press of New England, Hanover, 1998).

——, *Studies in Ecstatic Kabbalah* (State University of New York Press, Albany, 1988).

——, "Types of Redemptive Activities in the Middle Ages," in Baras, ed., *Messianism and Eschatology,* pp. 253–279 (Hebrew).

——, "Universalization and Integration: Two Conceptions of Mystical Union in Jewish Mysticism," in M. Idel and B. McGinn, eds., *Mystical Union and Monotheistic Faith: An Ecumenical Dialogue* (Macmillan, New York, 1989), pp. 27–58.

Jacobson, Yoram, *The Doctrine of Redemption of Rabbi Mordecai Dato* (Ph.D. diss., Hebrew University, Jerusalem, 1982) (Hebrew).

Jankelevitch, Vladimir, "L'esperance et la fin des temps," in Eliane Amado Levy-Valensi and Jean Halperin, *La conscience juive: Face à l'histoire: Le Pardon* (Presses Universitaires de France, Paris, 1965), pp. 7–21.

Jellinek, Adolf, *Bet ha-Midrasch,* 6 vols. (Wahrman, Jerusalem, 1938).

Johnson, Aubrey R., *Sacral Kingship in Ancient Israel* (University of Wales Press, Cardiff, 1967).

Jung, Carl G., *Aion: Researches into the Phenomenology of the Self,* trans. R. F. C. Hull, Bollingen Series 20 (Princeton University Press, Princeton, N.J., 1979).

Kantorowicz, Ernst H., *The King's Two Bodies: A Study in Medieval Political Theology* (Princeton University Press, Princeton, N.J., 1957).

Katz, Jacob, *Halakhah and Kabbalah: Studies in the History of Jewish Religion, Its Various Faces and Social Relevance* (Magnes Press, Jerusalem, 1984) (Hebrew).

Kaufman, Yezekel, *Golah ve-Neikhar,* 2 volumes (Devir, Tel Aviv, 1928–1929) (Hebrew).
Kingsley, David, *The Goddesses' Mirror* (State University of New York Press, Albany, 1989).
Kirn, Hans-Martin, *Das Bild vom Juden im Deutschland des fruehen 16.Jahrhunderts* (J. C. B. Mohr, Tübingen, 1989).
Klausner, Joseph, *The Messianic Idea in Israel from Its Beginning to the Completion of the Mishnah,* trans. W. F. Stinespring (Macmillan, New York, 1955).
Leach, Edmund, *L'unité de l'homme et autre essays* (Gallimard, Paris, 1980).
Lerner, Robert E., *The Power of Prophecy: The Cedar of Lebanon Vision from the Mongol Onslaught to the Dawn of the Enlightenment* (University of California Press, Berkeley and Los Angeles, 1983).
Levenson, Jon D., *Sinai and Zion: An Entry into the Jewish Bible* (Winston Press, Minneapolis, Chicago, New York, 1985).
Levi, Israel, "Apocalypses dans le Talmud," *REJ* 48 (1880), pp. 108–114.
Liebes, Yehuda, "The Angels of the Shofar and Yeshua Sar ha-Panim," in J. Dan, ed., *Early Jewish Mysticism* (Jerusalem, 1987), pp. 171–196 (Hebrew).
——, *Het'o shel Elisha,* 2nd ed. (Akademon, Jerusalem, 1990) (Hebrew).
——, "Jonas as Messiah ben Joseph," in J. Dan and J. Hacker, eds., *Studies in Jewish Mysticism, Philosophy and Ethical Literature Presented to Isaiah Tishby* (Magnes Press, Jerusalem, 1986), pp. 269–311 (Hebrew).
——, "The Messiah of the Zohar," in *The Messianic Idea in Jewish Thought* (Israeli Academy, Jerusalem, 1982), pp. 87–234 (Hebrew).
——, "Myth vs. Symbol in the Zohar and Lurianic Kabbalah," in Fine, ed., *Essential Papers,* pp. 212–242.
——, "New Directions in Kabbala Research," *Pe'anim* 50 (1992), pp. 150–170 (Hebrew).
——, *On Sabbateaism and Its Kabbalah: Collected Essays* (Mossad Bialik, Jerusalem, 1995) (Hebrew).
——, *Studies in Jewish Myth and Jewish Messianism,* trans. Batya Stein (State University of New York Press, Albany, New York, 1993).
——, *Studies in the Zohar,* trans. A. Schwartz, S. Nakache, and P. Peli (State University of New York Press, Albany, New York, 1993).
——, " 'Two Young Roes of a Doe': The Secret Sermon of Isaac Luria before His Death," in Elior and Liebes, eds., *Lurianic Kabbalah,* pp. 113–169 (Hebrew).
Loewenthal, Naftali, *Communicating the Infinite: The Emergence of the Ḥabad School* (University of Chicago Press, Chicago, 1990).
Löwy, Michael, *Redemption et utopie: Le judaisme libertine en Europe centrale* (Presse Universitaire de France, Paris, 1988).
Macey, Samuel L., *Patriarchs of Time: Dualism in Saturn-Cronus* (University of Georgia Press, Athens, 1987).
Maggid, Shaul, "Conjugal Union, Mourning and Talmud Torah in R. Isaac Luria's Tikkun Ḥazot," *Daat* 36, (1996), pp. xvii–xlv.
Mann, Jacob, "The Messianic Movements in the Period of the First Crusades," *Ha-Teqqufah* 23 (1925), pp. 243–261; 24 (1926), pp. 335–358.
Manor, Dan, *Exile and Redemption in Moroccan Jewish Philosphy* (Habermann Institute for Literary Research, Lod, 1988) (Hebrew).

Manuel, Frank E., and Fritzie P. Manuel, *Utopian Thought in the Western World* (Belknap Press, Harvard University Press, Cambridge, Mass., 1980)

Marx, Alexander, "Ma'amar 'al Shenat ha-Ge'ullah," *Ha-Tzofeh le-Ḥokhmat Yisrael* 5 (1921), pp. 194–202 (Hebrew).

McGinn, Bernard, *Apocalyptic Spirituality* (Paulist Press, New York, 1979).

——, *Visions of the End* (Columbia University Press, New York, 1979).

Mendes-Flohr, Paul, " 'The Stronger and the Better Jews': Jewish Theological Responses to Political Messianism in the Weimar Republic," in Jonathan Frankel, ed., *Jews and Messianism in the Modern Era: Metaphor and Meaning = Studies in Contemporary Jewry* 7 (1991), pp. 159–185.

Merlan, Phillip, *Monopsychism, Mysticism, Metaconsciouness: Problems of the Soul in the Neoaristotelian and Neoplatonic Tradition* (Martin Nijhoff, The Hague, 1963).

Meroz, Ronit, *Redemption in Lurianic Teaching* (Ph.D. diss., Hebrew University, Jerusalem, 1988) (Hebrew).

The Messianic Idea in Jewish Thought: A Study Conference in Honour of the Eightieth Birthday of Gershom Scholem (Israeli Academy for Science, Jerusalem, 1990) (Hebrew).

Mopsik, Charles, *Les grands textes de la Cabale, les rites qui font Dieu* (Verdier, Lagrasse, 1993).

——, *Le sicle du sanctuaire* (Verdier, Lagrasse, 1996).

Moses, Stephane, *L'ange de l'histoire: Rosenzweig, Benjamin, Scholem* (Le Seuil, Paris, 1992).

Mowinckel, Sigmund, *He That Cometh* (Oxford, Blackwell, 1959).

——, *The Psalms in Israel's Worship*, 2 vols., trans. D. R. Ap-Thomas (Jsot Press, 1922).

Mueller, Ulrich B., *Messias und Menschensohn in jüdischen Apocalypsen und in der Offenbarung des Johannes* (Guetersloher Verlagshaus, Gerd Mohn, 1972).

Myers, David, *Re-Inventing the Jewish Past* (Oxford University Press, New York, 1995).

Neher, André, *The Prophetic Existence*, trans. William Wolf (A. S. Barnes, South Brunswick, London, 1960).

Neusner, J., *Messiah in Context* (University Press of America, Lanham, Md., 1988).

Neusner, J., W. S. Green, and E. S. Frerichs, eds., *Judaisms and Their Messiahs at the Turn of the Christian Era* (Cambridge University Press, Cambridge, 1987).

Odeberg, Hugo, ed., *The Hebrew Enoch* (Cambridge, Cambridge University Press, 1928).

Oron-Goldreich, Michal, and Amos Goldreich, eds., *Massu'ot: Studies in Kabbalistic Literature and Jewish Philosophy in Memory of Prof. Ephraim Gottlieb* (Mossad Bialik, Jerusalem, 1994) (Hebrew).

Patai, Rapahel, "Hebrew Installation Rites," *HUCA* 20 (1947), pp. 143–225.

——, *The Jewish Alchemists* (Princeton University Press, Princeton, N.J., 1994).

——, *The Messiah Texts* (Wayne State University Press, Detroit, 1979).

——, *Man and Temple in Ancient Jewish Myth and Ritual*, 2nd ed. (Ktav, New York, 1967).

Pearson, Birger A., *Gnosticism, Judaism, and Egyptian Christianity* (Fortress Press, Minneapolis, 1990).

Pedaya, Haviva, " 'Flaw' and 'Correction' in the Concept of the Godhead in the Teachings of Rabbi Isaac the Blind," *JSJT* 6 (1987), pp. 157–285 (Hebrew).

Pines, Shlomo, *Between Jewish Thought and the Thought of the Nations* (Mossad Bialik, Jerusalem, 1977) (Hebrew).

Popkin, Richard, "Jewish Christian Relations in the Sixteenth and Seventeenth Centuries: The Conception of the Messiah," in Barry Walfish, ed., *The Frank Talmage Memorial Volume* (Haifa University Press, Haifa, and Brandeis University, 1993), 2:163–177.

Rapoport-Albert, Ada, ed., *Hasidism Reappraised* (Littman Library of Jewish Civilization, London, Portland, 1996).

Ravitsky, Aviezer, *Messianism, Zionism and Jewish Religious Radicalism,* trans. Michael Swirsky and Jonathan Chipman (University of Chicago Press, Chicago, 1996).

——, " 'To the Utmost of Human Capacity': Maimonides on the Days of the Messiah," in Joel L. Kraemer, ed., *Perspectives on Maimonides: Philosophical and Historical Studies* (Oxford University Press, Oxford, 1991), pp. 221–256.

Reeves, Marjorie, *The Influence of Prophecy in the Late Middle Ages: A Study in Joachimism* (University of Notre Dame Press, Notre Dame, Ind., 1993).

Reeves, Marjorie, ed., *Prophetic Rome in the High Renaissance Period* (Clarendon Press, Oxford, 1992).

Ricoeur, Paul, *The Symbolism of Evil* (Beacon Press, Boston, 1969).

Riesenfeld, Harald, *Jesus Transfiguré* (Ejnar Munksgaard, Kobenhaven, 1947).

Ringgren, Helmer, *The Messiah in the Old Testament* (SCM Press, London, 1967).

Rosenberg, Shalom, "Exile and Redemption in Jewish Thought in the Sixteenth Century: Contending Conceptions," in Bernard D. Cooperman, ed., *Jewish Thought in the Sixteenth Century* (Harvard University Press, Cambridge, Mass., 1983), pp. 399–430.

——, "The Return to the Garden of Eden: Remarks for the History of the Idea of the Restorative Redemption in the Medieval Jewish Philosophy," in *The Messianic Idea in Israel,* pp. 37–86 (Hebrew).

Rosman, Moshe, *The Founder of Hasidism: A Quest for the Historical Ba'al Shem Tov* (University of California Press, Berkeley and Los Angekes, 1996).

Ruderman, David, "Hope against Hope: Jewish and Christian Messianic Expectations in the Late Middle Ages," in *Exile and Diaspora Studies in the History of the Jewish People Presented to Prof. Haim Beinart* (Makhon ben Tzvi, Jerusalem, 1991), pp. 185–202.

Sack, Bracha, *The Kabbalah of Rabbi Moshe Cordovero* (Ben Gurion University Press, Beer Sheva, 1995) (Hebrew).

The Sacral Kingship: Contributions to the Central Theme of the VIIth International Congress for the History of Religions, Rome, April 1955 (Brill, Leiden, 1959).

Saperstein, Marc, ed., *Essential Papers on Messianic Movements and Personalities in Jewish History* (New York University Press, New York, 1992).

Sarachek, Joseph, *The Doctrine of the Messiah in Medieval Jewish Literature,* 2nd ed. (Hermon Press, New York, 1968).

Schatz Uffenheimer, Rivka, *Hasidism as Mysticism: Quietistic Elements in Eighteenth Century Hasidic Thought,* trans. Jonathan Chipman (Princeton University Press, Princeton, N.J., Magnes Press, Jerusalem, 1993).

Scholem, Gershom, *Be-'Iqvot Mashiaḥ* (Sifrei Tarshish, Jerusalem, 1944) (Hebrew).

——, *Devarim be-Go* ('Am 'Oved, Tel Aviv, 1976) (Hebrew).

——, *Jewish Gnosticism, Merkavah Mysticism, and Talmudic Tradition* (Jewish Theological Seminary of America, New York, 1970).

——, *Kabbalah* (Dorset Press, New York, 1987).
——, *Major Trends in Jewish Mysticism* (Schocken Books, New York, 1967).
——, *The Messianic Idea in Judaism* (Schocken Books, New York, 1972).
——, "Messianic Movements after the Expulsion from Spain," in *The Jewish People: Past and Present* (Jewish Encyclopedic Handbooks, New York, 1946), pp. 335–347.
——, *'Od Davar: Explications and Implications* ('Am 'Oved, Tel Aviv, 1989).
——, *On the Kabbalah and Its Symbolism*, trans. Ralph Manheim (Schocken Books, New York, 1969).
——, *Origins of the Kabbalah*, trans. A. Arkush, ed. R. J. Z. Werblowsky (Jewish Publication Society and Princeton University Press, Princeton, N.J., 1987).
——, *Researches in Sabbateanism*, ed. Yehuda Liebes ('Am 'Oved, Tel Aviv, 1991) (Hebrew).
——, *Sabbatai Ṣevi, the Mystical Messiah*, trans. R. J. Z. Werblowsky (Princeton University Press, Princeton, N.J., 1973).
——, *Studies and Texts Concerning the History of Sabbetianism and Its Metamorphoses* (Mossad Bialik, Jerusalem, 1974) (Hebrew).
Schultz, Joseph P., *Judaism and the Gentile Faiths* (Fairleigh Dickinson University Press and Associated University Presses, Ruthford, Madison, Teaneck, 1981).
Schultz, Joseph P., and Lois Spatz, *Sinai and Olympus: A Comparative Study* (University Press of America, Lanham, Md., 1995).
Schwartz, Dov, "The Neutralization of the Messianic Idea in Medieval Jewish Rationalism," *HUCA* 64 (1993), pp. 37–58 (Hebrew).
Schwarzschild, Steven, *The Pursuit of the Ideal: Jewish Writings*, ed. M. Kelnner (State University of New York Press, Albany, 1990).
Schweid, Eliezer, *From Ruin to Salvation* (Hakibbutz Hameuchad Publishing House, Tel Aviv, 1994) (Hebrew).
Segal, Allan, "Paul and the Beginning of Jewish Mysticism," in Collins and Fishbane, eds., *Death, Ecstasy*, pp. 95–122.
Sharot, Stephen, *Messianism, Mysticism, and Magic: A Sociological Analysis of Jewish Religious Movements* (University of North Carolina Press, Chapel Hill, 1982).
Silver, Abba Hillel, *A History of Messianic Speculation in Israel from the First through the Seventeenth Centuries* (Peter Smith, Gloucester, Mass., 1978).
Smith, Jonathan Z., *Map Is Not Territory* (University of Chicago Press, Chicago, 1993).
Stone, Michael E., *Fourth Ezra: A Commentary on the Book of Fourth Ezra* (Fortress Press, Minneapolis, 1990).
Stroumsa, Gedaliahu Guy, *Savoir et Salut* (Editions du Cerf, Paris, 1992).
Swietlicki, Catherine, *Spanish Christian Cabala* (University of Missouri Press, Columbia, 1986).
Talmon, Shemaryahu, *King, Cult and Calendar in Ancient Israel* (Magnes Press, Jerusalem, 1986).
Tamar, David, *Studies in Jewish History in Israel and Italy* (Reuven Mass, Jerusalem 1973) (Hebrew).
——, "The Messianic Dreams and Visions of R. Ḥayyim Vital," *Shalem* 4 (1984), pp. 211–229 (Hebrew).
Taubes, Jacob, "The Price of Messianism," in Saperstein, ed., *Essential Papers*, pp. 551–557.

Thrupp, Sylvia, ed., *Millennial Dreams in Action: Essays in Comparative Study* (Mouton, The Hague, 1962).

Tishby, Isaiah, *Paths of Faith and Heresy* (Massada, Ramat Gan, 1964) (Hebrew).

——, *Studies in Kabbalah and Its Branches*, 3 vols. (Jerusalem, 1982–1992) (Hebrew).

——, *Messianism in the Time of the Expulsion from Spain and Portugal* (Merkaz Zalman Shazar, Jerusalem, 1985) (Hebrew).

——, *The Wisdom of the Zohar*, 3 vols., trans. David Goldstein (Oxford University Press, Oxford, 1989).

Tuveston, Ernest Lee, *Millennium and Utopia: A Study in the Background of the Idea of Progress* (Harper Torchbooks, New York, Evanston, London, 1964).

Urbach, E. E., *The Sages, Their Concepts and Beliefs*, trans. I. Abrams (Magnes Press, Jerusalem, 1979).

Versnel, H. S., *Transition and Reversal in Myth and Ritual* (Brill, Leiden, 1993).

Van der Leeuw, G., *Religion in Essence and Manifestation*, trans. J. E. Turner (Princeton University Press, Princeton, N.J., 1986).

Wach, Joachim, Joseph M. Kitagawa, and Gregory D. Alles, eds., *Introduction to the History of Religions* (Macmillan, New York, 1988).

Weiss, Joseph, *Studies in Eastern European Jewish Mysticism*, ed. David Goldstein (Littman Library, Oxford University Press, 1985).

Werblowsky, R. J. Zwi, *Joseph Karo: Lawyer and Mystic* (Jewish Publication Society, Philadelphia, 1977).

——, "Mysticism and Messianism, the Case of Hasidism," in *Man and His Salvation: Essays in Memory of S. G. F. Brandon* (Manchester, 1973), pp. 305–314.

——, "R. Joseph Karo, R. Solomon Molkho, Don Joseph Nasi," in Beinart, ed., *Sephardi Legacy*, 2:179–191.

——, "Shabbetai Zevi," in Beinart, ed., *Sephardi Legacy*, 2:207–216.

Werblowsky, R. J. Zwi, and Bleeker, C. Jouco, eds., *Types of Redemption* (Leiden, Brill, 1970).

Widengren, Geo, *Muhammad, the Apostle of God, and His Ascension* (Uppsala, Wiesbaden, 1955).

——, *Sakrales Koenigtum im Alten Testament und im Judentum* (Verlag W. Kohhammer, GMBH, Stuttgart, 1955).

Wieder, Naphtali, *The Judean Scrolls and Karaism* (East and West Library, London, 1962).

Winston, David, *Logos and Mystical Theology in Philo of Alexandria* (Hebrew Union College Press, Cincinnati, 1985).

Wirszubski, Chaim, *Pico della Mirandola's Encounter with Jewish Mysticism* (Harvard University Press, Cambridge, 1989).

Wolfson, Elliot R., *Along the Path: Studies in Kabbalistic Myth, Symbolism, and Hermeneutics* (State University of New York Press, Albany, 1995).

——, *Circle in the Square: Studies in the Use of Gender in Kabbalistic Symbolism* (State University of New York Press, Albany, 1995).

——, *Through a Speculum That Shines: Vision and Imagination in Medieval Jewish Mysticism* (Princeton University Press, Princeton, N.J., 1994).

——, "The Doctrine of Sefirot in the Prophetic Kabbalah of Abraham Abulafia," *Jewish Studies Quarterly* 2 (1995), pp. 336–371.

Yerushalmi, Yoseph Hayyim, *Zakhor: Jewish History and Jewish Memory* (2nd ed., Schocken Books, New York, 1989).

——, *From Spanish Court to Italian Ghetto: Isaac Cardoso, a Study in Seventeenth-Century Marranism and Jewish Apologetics* (University of Washington Press, Seattle, 1981).

Index

Subjects

Adam, 87, 107, 155, 172, 189, 354n65, 366n42, 379n71, 388n64, 393nn30, 33, 397n74, 399n106
ADaM, 189–90, 205, 221, 225, 393n30
Adam qadmon, 171, 388n66
Adonis, 314
Agnus Dei, 304
Akitu, 314
Angel, 420n48; angelogy, 24, 46, 48, 50, 116; angelophany, 24, 72, 85, 109, 198; *Maggid,* 144, 206; power, 85, 94. *See also* Metatron, Sandalfon, Yaho'el
Apocalyptic: idea, 32; literature, 41, 46; messianism, 20–21, 97, 101, 259; phenomenon, 7; prophecies, 8; vision, 42
Apotheosis, 42, 48, 64, 89, 91, 170, 200, 203, 338n27, 348n18, 397n74, 398n94
Aristotelian concepts, 10, 51, 53, 65–66, 75, 101, 419n28
Ascent of the soul, 213–17, 220, 227
Astrology, 193, 195, 216, 225, 250, 277, 343n55, 364n12, 382n41, 396n60, 398n82, 401n137, 404n24
Attika' Qaddisha', 194, 287–88
Axis mundi, 113, 416n72
'Azah, 93
'Azriel, 93

Ben 'adam, 91, 92. *See also* Son of Man
Ben David, 74, 77–78, 83, 194, 334n74, 349n25, 352n48, 421n58
Ben Joseph, 96, 114, 123, 334n 74, 349n25
Bible, 91, 95, 161, 191, 198
Bodhisattva, 291
Brahmanism, 291
Buddhism, 13, 291–92

Channel, 222–24, 226–27, 232, 405n45
Chariot, divine, 47, 202, 317, 426n61
Christ, 3, 62, 85, 86, 87, 95, 119, 124, 151, 155, 202, 290, 304–5, 340n42, 341n43, 351n38, 358n118, 366n43, 371n108, 378n63, 379n71, 398n93, 399n111
Christianity, 10, 13, 43, 24, 134, 146–47, 154, 202, 205, 240–41, 259, 265, 270, 276, 289, 290–91, 315, 323, 329n17; Christian mysticism, 10, 270, 290, 291
Christian Kabbalah, 89, 134, 307, 316, 381n7, 386n51, 425n47
Crises, 6, 9, 181, 414n36

Deus revelatus, 67
Devequt, 37, 204, 207, 208, 279–81, 328n8, 367n47. *See also* Union

'Ehyeh 'asher 'ehyeh, 96
Elijah, 78, 87, 88, 90–91, 93, 155, 161, 165, 174, 182, 231–32, 352n49, 357n96, 358n118, 378n66, 386n45, 390n90, 407n60
Enoch, 22, 48, 50, 68, 72, 85, 88, 94, 200, 339nn40, 41, 398nn80, 81

Names

Sources